BUSINESS
communication
in person, in print, online

10*e*

Tap into **engagement**

MindTap empowers you to produce your best work—consistently.

MindTap is designed to help you master the material. Interactive videos, animations, and activities create a learning path designed by your instructor to guide you through the course and focus on what's important.

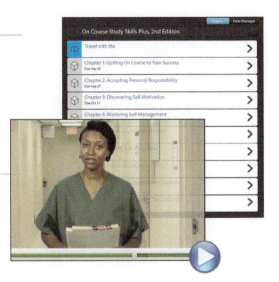

MindTap delivers real-world activities and assignments

that will help you in your academic life as well as your career.

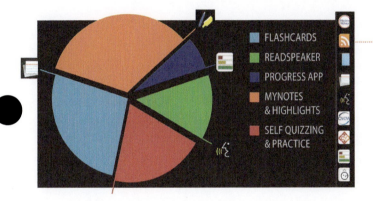

MindTap helps you stay organized and efficient

by giving you the study tools to master the material.

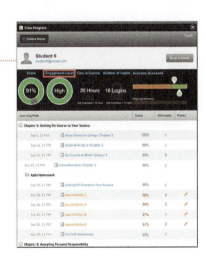

MindTap empowers and motivates

with information that shows where you stand at all times—both individually and compared to the highest performers in class.

"MindTap was very useful – it was easy to follow and everything was right there."
— Student, San Jose State University

"I'm definitely more engaged because of MindTap."
— Student, University of Central Florida

"MindTap puts practice questions in a format that works well for me."
— Student, Franciscan University of Steubenville

Tap into more info at: **www.cengage.com/mindtap**

Source Code: 14M-AA0105

BUSINESS
communication
in person, in print, online

10*e*

NEWMAN

Business Communication: In Person, In Print, Online, Tenth Edition
Amy Newman

Senior Vice President, General Manager: Social Sciences, Humanities and Business: Erin Joyner

Product Director: Jason Fremder

Product Manager: Heather Mooney

Senior Content Developer: John Rich

Product Assistant: Brian Pierce

Marketing Manager: Jeffrey Tousignant

Content Project Managers: Megan Guiliani and Nadia Saloom

Manufacturing Planner: Ron Montgomery

Production Service: MPS Limited

Senior Art Director: Linda May

Internal Designer: Studio Montage

Cover Designer: Studio Montage

Cover Image: istockphoto.com/ Rawpixel Ltd

Intellectual Property

    Analyst: Diane Garrity

    Project Manager: Sarah Shainwald

For product information and technology assistance, contact us at
Cengage Customer & Sales Support, 1-800-354-9706

For permission to use material from this text or product, submit all requests online at **www.cengage.com/permissions**
Further permissions questions can be emailed to
permissionrequest@cengage.com

Unless otherwise noted all items © Cengage.

Library of Congress Control Number: 20159442869

Student Edition ISBN: 978-1-305-50064-8

Cengage
200 Pier 4 Boulevard
Boston, MA 02210
USA

Cengage is a leading provider of customized learning solutions with employees residing in nearly 40 different countries and sales in more than 125 countries around the world. Find your local representative at **www.cengage.com**.

To learn more about Cengage platforms and services, register or access your online learning solution, or purchase materials for your course, visit **www.cengage.com**.

Printed at CLDPC, USA, 10-20

Brief Contents

Contents

PART 2 DEVELOPING YOUR BUSINESS WRITING SKILLS 102

REFERENCE MANUAL   439

About Amy Newman

Amy Newman specializes in business communication at the Cornell University School of Hotel Administration. As a senior lecturer, she teaches two required undergraduate communication courses: a freshman business writing and oral communication class and an upper-level persuasive communication class. Newman also teaches a graduate-level management communication course and an elective, Corporate Communication, which focuses on communication strategy, crisis communication, and social media.

Newman was an adjunct instructor at Ithaca College; Milano, The New School for Management and Urban Policy in New York City; and eCornell, where she taught classes online. She has won several awards for excellence in teaching and student advising and grants to develop technology-based learning solutions.

Prior to joining Cornell, Newman spent 20 years working for large companies, such as Canon, Reuters, Scholastic, and MCI. Internally, she held senior-level management positions in human resources and leadership development. As an external consultant, Newman worked to improve communication and employee performance in hospitality, technology, education, publishing, financial services, and entertainment companies.

A graduate of Cornell University and Milano, Newman is author of the eighth, ninth, and tenth editions of *Business Communication: In Person, In Print, Online*. Newman has developed several multimedia company scenarios to accompany the book, has created an interactive tool for managing speech anxiety, and maintains a blog, BizCom in the News.

Acknowledgments

Business Communication: In Person, In Print, Online was inspired by my teaching and learning from students at Cornell, and I am grateful for how they have shaped my thinking about business communication and who I am as an instructor.

Throughout the tenth edition revision process, I have consulted many colleagues, friends, and family for their valuable feedback on book content and, when needed, a sympathetic ear: Kathy Berggren, Joshua Bronstein, Eric Clay, Curtis Ferguson, Daphne Jameson, Kim Kenyon, David Lennox, Daniel Meyerson, Laura Newman, Peggy Odom-Reed, Andrew Quagliata, Crystal Thomas, and Maria Loukianenko Wolfe.

The following instructors participated in the editorial review board for the tenth edition. Throughout each stage of the revision process, they offered creative input that influenced the chapter content and dynamic design. I thank each of them for their valuable feedback and suggestions:

Kate Archard, *University of Massachusetts, Boston*

Fiona Barnes, *University of Florida*

Christina Bergenholtz, *Quinsigamond Community College*

David Bolton, *University of Maryland*

Dominic Bruni, *University of Wisconsin, Oshkosh*

Melisa Bryant, *Forsyth Technical Community College*

Marilyn Chalupa, *Ball State University*

Sara Cochran, *Drury University*

Cindi Costa, *Mohave Community College*

Melissa Diegnau, *Riverland Community College*

Pat Farrell, *Roosevelt University*

Peggy Fisher, *Ball State University*

Jorge Gaytan, *North Carolina A&T State University*

Beverly George, *University of Texas at Arlington*

Bill Graham, *Seton Hall University*

Valerie Gray, *Harrisburg Area Community College*

Mary Groves, *University of Nevada, Reno*

Teresa Horton, *Baker College*

Gloria Lessman, *Bellevue University*

Andrew Lutz II, *Avila University*

Molly Mayer, *University of Cincinnati*

Karen Messina, *SUNY Orange*

Bill McPherson, *Indiana University-Purdue*

Zachary Owens, *University of Cincinnati*

Hem Paudel, *University of Louisville*

Jessica Rack, *University of Cincinnati*

Renee Rogers, *Forsyth Technical Community College*

Jean Anna Sellers, *Fort Hays State University*

Stacey Short, *Northern Illinois University*

Lynn Staley, *University of Missouri, St. Louis*

Kathleen Taylor, *SUNY Utica*

Sanci C. Teague, *Western Kentucky Community and Technical College*

I would also like to acknowledge the following reviewers for their thoughtful contributions on previous editions:

Lisa Barley, *Eastern Michigan University*

Lia Barone, *Norwalk Community College*

Carl Bridges, *Arthur Andersen Consulting*

Annette Briscoe, *Indiana University Southeast*

Mitchel T. Burchfield, *Southwest Texas Junior College*

Janice Burke, *South Suburban College*

Leila Chambers, *Cuesta College*

G. Jay Christensen, *California State University, Northridge*

Cheryl Christiansen, *California State University, Stanislaus*

Connie Clark, *Lane Community College*

Miriam Coleman, *Western Michigan University*

Anne Hutta Colvin, *Montgomery County Community College*

Doris L. Cost, *Metropolitan State College of Denver*

L. Ben Crane, *Temple University*

Ava Cross, *Ryerson Polytechnic University*

Nancy J. Daugherty, *Indiana University-Purdue University, Indianapolis*

Rosemarie Dittmer, *Northeastern University*

Gary Donnelly, *Casper College*

Graham N. Drake, *SUNY Geneseo*

Kay Durden, *The University of Tennessee at Martin*

Laura Eurich, *University of Colorado at Colorado Springs*

Mary Groves, *University of Nevada, Reno*

Phillip A. Holcomb, *Angelo State University*

Larry R. Honl, *University of Wisconsin, Eau Claire*

Kristi Kelly, *Florida Gulf Coast University*

Margaret Kilcoyne, *Northwestern State University*

Michelle Kirtley Johnston, *Loyola University*

Alice Kinder, *Virginia Polytechnic Institute and State University*

Emogene King, *Tyler Junior College*

Richard N. Kleeberg, *Solano Community College*

Patricia Laidler, *Massasoit Community College*

Lowell Lamberton, *Central Oregon Community College*

E. Jay Larson, *Lewis–Clark State College*

Kimberly Laux, *Saginaw Valley State University*

Michael Liberman, *East Stroudsburg University*

Julie MacDonald, *Northwestern State University*

Marsha C. Markman, *California Lutheran University*

Beryl McEwen, *North Carolina A&T State University*

Diana McKowen, *Indiana University, Bloomington*

Maureen McLaughlin, *Highline Community College*

Sylvia A. Miller, *Cameron University*

Billie Miller-Cooper, *Cosumnes River College*

Russell Moore, *Western Kentucky University*

Wayne Moore, *Indiana University of Pennsylvania*

Gerald W. Morton, *Auburn University of Montgomery*

Danell Moses, *Western Carolina University, Cullowhee, NC*

Jaunett Neighbors, *Central Virginia Community College*

Judy Nixon, *University of Tennessee at Chattanooga*

Rosemary Olds, *Des Moines Area Community College*

Richard O. Pompian, *Boise State University*

Rebecca Pope-Ruark, *Elon University*

Karen Sterkel Powell, *Colorado State University*

Seamus Reilly, *University of Illinois*

Carla Rineer, *Millersville University*

Jeanette Ritzenthaler, *New Hampshire College*

Betty Robbins, *University of Oklahoma*

Joan C. Roderick, *Southwest Texas State University*

Mary Jane Ryals, *Florida State University*

Lacye Prewitt Schmidt, *State Technical Institute of Memphis*

Jean Anna Sellers, *Fort Hays State University*

Sue Seymour, *Cameron University*

Sherry Sherrill, *Forsyth Technical Community College*

John R. Sinton, *Finger Lakes Community College*

Curtis J. Smith, *Finger Lakes Community College*

Craig E. Stanley, *California State University, Sacramento*

Ted O. Stoddard, *Brigham Young University*

Vincent C. Trofi, *Providence College*

Deborah A. Valentine, *Emory University*

Randall L. Waller, *Baylor University*

Maria W. Warren, *University of West Florida*

Michael R. Wunsch, *Northern Arizona University*

Annette Wyandotte, *Indiana University, Southeast*

Betty Rogers Youngkin, *University of Dayton*

Several business communication instructors devoted time and energy to making this edition a success. Because of their professionalism and creativity, the tenth edition will provide an enhanced teaching and learning experience for adopters. Elizabeth Christensen of Sinclair Community College and David Lennox of Cornell University wrote a comprehensive test bank to reinforce students' learning. In addition, I value the excellent contributions of Karen Howie, Northwestern Michigan College, who developed digital content for the CourseMate website.

Finally, I am grateful to the inspiring team at Cengage Learning. It is a true pleasure to work with this team and their staff, who nurtured the book from a list of ideas to printed copy and every step along the way:

Erin Joyner, Vice President, General Manager,
   Social Science & Qualitative Business
Jason Fremder, Product Director
Heather Mooney, Product Manager
Jeffrey Tousignant, Marketing Manager
John Rich, Senior Content Developer
Megan Guiliani, Content Project Manager
Linda May, Senior Art Director

BUSINESS
communication
in person, in print, online

10*e*

PART 1

CHAPTER

1

Understanding Business Communication

" *We're sorry we even started down this path. And we do hope you'll accept our apology.* "[1]

—Kirstie Foster, Director of Corporate and Brand Communications for General Mills

CHAPTER INTRODUCTION

General Mills Reverts Back to Its Former Legal Terms

Business communication is more complex and more highly criticized than ever. General Mills discovered this when the company changed its legal terms to ward off lawsuits.

The company's new legal terms restricted customers' right to sue if they subscribe to an email, download a coupon, "like" a brand on Facebook, or enter an online contest. As you can imagine, General Mills' popular brands—Cheerios, Progresso, Pillsbury, and others—inspire consumers to interact online, and people didn't respond well. One attorney summed up the problem: "It's essentially trying to protect the company from all accountability, even when it lies, or say, an employee deliberately adds broken glass to a product."[2]

In what *The New York Times* called "a stunning about-face," the company reverted its legal terms back to what they were.[3] In the statement, you can almost hear the discussion between the corporate communication staff, who protect the company's brand, and the lawyers, who protect the company financially. Most of the statement has a conversational tone ("So we've listened"), but one part has legal jargon and this disclaimer: "That last bit is from our lawyers."[4]

Like most companies, General Mills clearly is struggling with how to balance the incredible opportunities of social media with the inevitable challenges.

> **General Mills** @GeneralMills · Apr 17
> Explaining the changes to our website privacy policy and legal terms
> bit.ly/1eOVKOB
> Details   ↩ Reply   ⇄ Retweet   ★ Favorite   ••• More

> **Francisco Hernandez** ⚙ ⁺👤 Follow
> @invalidchars
>
> @GeneralMills HA. I'm sure clicking that link will cost me my legal right to sue you. #nothanks

1-1 Communicating in Organizations

Walk through the halls of any organization—a start-up company, a *Fortune* 500 giant, a state government office, or a not-for-profit organization—and what do you see? Managers and other employees drafting emails, attending meetings, writing reports, conducting interviews, talking on the phone, and making presentations. In short, you see people *communicating.*

Communication is the process of sending and receiving messages—sometimes through spoken or written words, and sometimes nonverbally through facial expressions, gestures, and voice qualities. If someone sends a message to you, and you receive it, communication will have taken place. However, when Jamie Dimon, Chairman and CEO of JPMorgan Chase, testified before the U.S. Senate Banking Committee about billions of dollars in trading losses, he used a common U.S. business expression. But was his communication universally understood?[5]

"We generally are open kimono with the regulators and tell them what they want to know."

Jamie Dimon uses a common but potentially misunderstood business expression, which means revealing information to outside parties. Some consider the term sexist and racist.[6]

1-1a Employers' Perspective

People in organizations must communicate to share information, coordinate activities, and make better decisions. In most jobs, people communicate more than they do any other activity. Employers know the value of good communication:

- Communication skills—oral, listening, written, and presentation—are the top four most important skills in new graduate business school hires. According to a Graduate Management Admission Council survey of corporate recruiters, "[E]mployers ranked communications skills twice as important as managerial skills."[7]
- Written and oral communication skills are among the top skills and qualities employers look for on college students' resumes, according to the National Association of Colleges and Employers' Job Outlook Survey, shown in Figure 1.[8]
- "People who cannot write and communicate clearly will not be hired and are unlikely to last long enough to be considered for promotion," according to The College Board, based on a survey of human resource directors.[9]

But many employees lack essential communication skills:

- The College Board also reports that one-third of employees in U.S. blue-chip companies write poorly, and companies spend as much as $3.1 billion each year on remedial writing training.[10]
- Eighty percent of employers say colleges should put more emphasis on written and oral communication, according to a survey by the Association of American Colleges and Universities.[11]

- A *Wall Street Journal* article reports that, although "M.B.A. students' quantitative skills are prized by employers, their writing and presentation skills have been a perennial complaint. Employers and writing coaches say business-school graduates tend to ramble, use pretentious vocabulary, or pen too-casual emails."[12]

1-1b Personal Perspective

Clearly, good communication skills are crucial to your success in an organization. Competence in writing and speaking will help you get hired, perform well, and earn promotions. If you decide to go into business for yourself, writing and speaking skills will help you find investors, promote your product, and manage your employees. These same skills will also help you in your personal life with family, friends, and partners.

Knowing yourself is critical to your development as a skilled business communicator. How do others perceive you, and how do you react to others? A recent study showed that jerks don't know they're jerks. People who were overly aggressive during negotiations had no clue how they were perceived. Equally troublesome, people who were viewed as appropriately assertive thought they came across too strongly.[13]

Having an accurate view of yourself is part of emotional intelligence. People with high emotional intelligence (or EQ, for emotional quotient) share four competencies (Figure 2).[14]

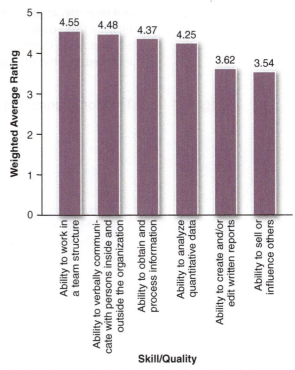

Employers Rate Importance of Candidates' Skills/Qualities | **Figure 1**

1 = Not at all important; 2 = Not very important; 3 = Somewhat important; 4 = Very important; 5 = Extremely important

Emotional Intelligence Competencies | **Figure 2**

- **Self-Awareness:** Understanding one's own emotions and how they affect others, recognizing one's strengths and limitations, and demonstrating self-confidence.
- **Self-Management:** Keeping emotions in check, acting with integrity, being adaptable, striving for excellence, taking initiative, and demonstrating optimism.
- **Social Awareness:** Demonstrating empathy by recognizing others' perspectives and taking them into consideration, understanding group dynamics, and considering customers' needs.
- **Relationship Management:** Developing others, inspiring people, initiating or managing change, influencing, managing conflict, and working with others toward shared goals.

Emotional **INTELLIGENCE**

How do you feel about your own communication skills? What messages and feedback about your writing and oral presentations have you received from your family and teachers that may affect how you approach this course?

In each book chapter, look for questions with the "Emotional Intelligence" icon in the margin. Responding honestly will improve how well you understand yourself and how your communication affects your relationships with others.

1-2 The Components of Communication

LO1 Identify the components of communication.

How does communication happen among people and throughout an organization? In this section, we'll discuss the communication model (or process) and the directions of communication within a company.

1-2a The Communication Model

The communication model consists of the communication need, sender, message, audience, and response, as shown in Figure 3. Consider the example of one company acquiring another. Imagine that you are the VP, business development, and need to announce this decision to all employees. Other stakeholders—for example, customers and investors—will have to be informed, too, but let's use the example of internal communication here.

Figure 3 | The Communication Model

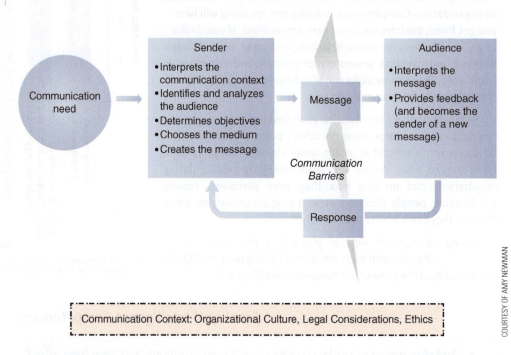

Communication Context: Organizational Culture, Legal Considerations, Ethics

COURTESY OF AMY NEWMAN

Communication Need

A communication need—either from the sender's mind or from an organizational situation—starts the process of communication in organizations. After you and the rest of the executive management team decide to acquire a company, you agree that you'll announce the decision to employees.

Sender

As the message sender, you have a lot of work to do to ensure that the message is received as you intend:

- **Interpret the communication context**: You'll consider the organizational culture (e.g., how formal the language should be), legal constraints (e.g., whether you should avoid making certain statements in writing), and the ethical circumstances (e.g., whether employees will be worried about losing their jobs).
- **Identify and analyze the audience**: You'll think about the wide range of employees who will receive the message. What is important to them, and how are they likely to react?
- **Determine objectives**: You'll specify what you want employees to think, do, or feel about your message.
- **Choose the medium**: You'll choose a way to convey your message, for example, by email.
- **Create the message**: Finally, you'll write the email and get it ready for distribution.

Message

Whether a communication achieves the sender's objectives depends on how well you construct the message (the information to be communicated). Oral messages might be transmitted through a staff meeting, individual meeting, telephone conversation, voice mail, podcast, conference call, videoconference, or even less formally, through the company grapevine. Written messages might be transmitted through an email, a report, a blog, a web page, a brochure, a tweet, a post, or a company newsletter. Nonverbal messages might be transmitted through facial expressions, gestures, or body movement. As we'll discuss later in this chapter, choosing the right medium for your audience, message, and objectives is critical to the success of your communication.

The purpose and content of your message may be clear, but messages often are obstructed by verbal and nonverbal barriers. Employees may misinterpret your email or not read it at all.

Audience

As the receiver of your message, the audience filters the communication and reacts by doing the following:

- **Interprets the message:** Each audience member (in this situation of acquiring a new company, each employee) will filter the message according to his or her knowledge, experience, background, and so on. When communication is successful, the message is interpreted as originally intended.
- **Provides feedback:** Employees may be happy about the news and apply for a job to work in the new company, or they may believe the company is expanding too rapidly and will gossip about it during lunch.

At this point, the audience becomes the sender of a new message—the response.

Response

As a new message, the audience's response to your communication begins the cycle again—and is subjected to the same complexities of the original process.

The Dynamic Nature of Communication

You probably know from your own experience that communication rarely flows neatly from one stage to the next, with the sender and audience clearly identified at any given point. Two or more people often send and receive messages simultaneously. For example, the look on your face when you receive a message may tell the sender that you understand, agree with, or are baffled by the message being sent. And your feedback may prompt the sender to modify what he or she says. The model helps us understand each step of the process—but communication is far more complicated than presented in the graphic.

1-2b Directions of Communication

For an organization to be successful, communication must flow freely through formal and informal channels.

The Formal Communication Network

Three types of communication make up an organization's formal communication network: downward, upward, and lateral. Information may be transmitted in these directions, which we'll illustrate with Starbucks' organization chart, shown in Figure 4.[15]

Downward Communication. Downward communication is the flow of information from managers to their employees (people who report to them). From the Starbucks organization chart, we could assume that Howard Schultz, as CEO and president, communicates downward to his

Figure 4 | Starbucks' Organization Chart

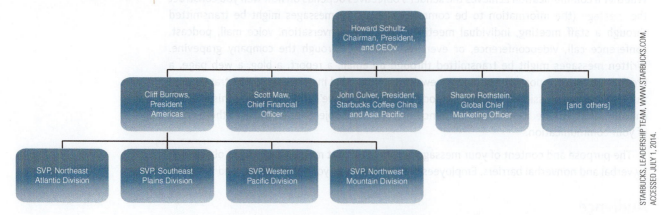

STARBUCKS, LEADERSHIP TEAM, WWW.STARBUCKS.COM, ACCESSED JULY 1, 2014.

direct reports. When Starbucks decides to close stores, for example, he would likely communicate this message to Cliff Burrows (president, Americas), who would then communicate the bad news to his direct reports, the divisional senior vice presidents. This is called cascading communication, which directs information from one level in an organization down to another.

Employees have many justifiable complaints about their managers' communication. A study of more than 60,000 employee satisfaction surveys led the authors to conclude, ". . . many firms rely on a 'cascade' mechanism. . . . Our results suggest that this faith in cascades may be misplaced. Employees need to hear from senior managers themselves—through straight talk, and ideally in reciprocal exchanges, so that workers feel their own views are heard."[16]

Upward Communication. Upward communication is the flow of information from lower-level employees to upper-level employees or managers. Upward communication provides management with feedback about their communication, suggestions for improving the business, and information needed for decision making.

In the example of Starbucks closing stores, Scott Maw, as chief financial officer, probably gave oral and written financial reports to Howard Schultz to tell him which stores were underperforming. Lower-level employees may have expressed their frustration about the closings through formal upward communication channels, for example, during team meetings.

Lateral (or Horizontal) Communication. Lateral communication (also called horizontal communication) is the flow of information among peers within an organization. Through lateral communication, employees coordinate work, share plans, negotiate differences, and support each other. At Starbucks, managers responsible for closing a store probably communicate with each other to coordinate messages and timing—and perhaps to console each other during the process.

Lateral communication can be challenging in an organization because you're trying to influence people but have no management authority over them. This is particularly difficult when the lateral communication is cross-functional—across different departments, divisions, or branches. In these situations, you'll need to rely on your relationship-building and persuasive communication skills to rally support and accomplish your goals.

The Informal Communication Network

Employees share information through the informal communication network (or grapevine). Without good formal communication, the grapevine will take over. People need information, particularly when they fear change that may affect them: layoffs, benefit cuts, or organizational restructurings. Although the grapevine is surprisingly accurate,[17] managers who let the grapevine function as employees' main source of information miss out on the chance to convey their own messages.

Websites such as Glassdoor.com provide a public forum for current and former employees to voice their opinions about companies. As you can imagine, employees posted negative comments when Starbucks closed stores. This is potentially embarrassing for a company, but there's little management can do about the site—or any informal communication network.

Rather than trying to eliminate the grapevine (a futile effort), competent managers pay attention to it and act promptly to counteract false rumors. They use the formal communication network (meetings, email, the intranet, and newsletters) to ensure that all news—positive and negative—gets out to employees as quickly and as completely as possible. Savvy managers also identify key influencers in an organization to get accurate messages infused into the grapevine.

The free flow of information within the organization allows managers to stop rumors and communicate their own messages to employees. However, managers face additional challenges at work: verbal and nonverbal barriers to communication.

1-3 Communication Barriers

LO2 Identify the major verbal and nonverbal barriers to communication.

Considering the complexity of the communication process and the many communication channels, your messages may not always be received exactly as you intend. As mentioned earlier, verbal and nonverbal barriers can interfere with the communication process (see Figure 5).

Verbal and Nonverbal Barriers to Communication | Figure 5

Verbal

- Inadequate Knowledge or Vocabulary
- Differences in Interpretation
- Language Differences
- Inappropriate Use of Expressions
- Overabstraction and Ambiguity
- Polarization

Nonverbal

- Inappropriate or Conflicting Signals
- Differences in Perception
- Inappropriate Emotions
- Distractions

1-3a Verbal Barriers

Verbal barriers are related to what you write or say. They include inadequate knowledge or vocabulary, differences in interpretation, language differences, inappropriate use of expressions, overabstraction and ambiguity, and polarization.

Inadequate Knowledge or Vocabulary

Assume that you're Sharon Rothstein, global chief marketing officer for Starbucks. In your role, you'll need to inform international employees that several U.S. stores will be closed. The decision may not affect stores in Europe, the Middle East, and Africa directly, but employees should be aware of the move and should hear the rationale from you—not public news organizations. You know all of the background information and are ready to announce the change to staff. Or are you?

Have you analyzed your audience? Do you know whether international employees already know about the closings, so you can decide how much background information to include? Do you know how much detail about the decision to provide? Employees should know why certain

Emotional **INTELLIGENCE**

Which of the verbal and nonverbal barriers do you find most challenging? What can you do to overcome these barriers at work and in your personal life?

stores were selected, but do they need to see the financial performance of each? How personal should your communication be? Are international employees worried about their own jobs? Should you reassure them about the company's plans in other countries, or would that just worry them more? Determining the answers to these questions will be important for you to achieve your communication objectives.

Differences in Interpretation

Sometimes senders and receivers attribute different meanings to the same word or attribute the same meaning to different words. When this happens, miscommunication can occur.

Every word has both a denotative and a connotative meaning. Denotation refers to the literal, dictionary meaning of a word. Connotation refers to the subjective, emotional meaning that you attach to a word. For example, the denotative meaning of the word *plastic* is "a synthetic material that can be easily molded into different forms." For some people, the word also has a negative connotative meaning—"cheap or artificial substitute"—or they associate the term with its environmental impact. For other people, the word means a credit card, as in, "He used plastic to pay the bill."

Most interpretation problems occur because people ascribe different connotative meanings to a word. Do you have a positive, neutral, or negative reaction to the terms *broad, bad, aggressive, workaholic, corporate raider, head-hunter, golden parachute,* or *wasted*? Are your reactions likely to be the same as everyone else's? Some terms cause an emotional reaction that turns off the receiver and could harm your relationship.

International COMMUNICATION

Language Differences

International businesspeople say that you can buy in your native language anywhere in the world, but you can sell only in the local language. Most communication between U.S. or Canadian firms and international firms is in English; in other cases, an interpreter (for oral communication) or translator (for written communication) may be used. But even with such services, problems can occur.

To ensure that the intended meaning is not lost in translation, important documents should first be translated into the second language and then retranslated into English. Of course, communication difficulties arise even among native English speakers. If your British coworker told you he was going to put your lunch date in his diary, would you picture a flowery journal entry about your time together? He probably just means he'll schedule it: *diary* in the United Kingdom typically refers to a calendar or planner.

JOHN HENSHALL / ALAMY

Poor translations can be funny or confusing.

Inappropriate Use of Expressions

The intended meaning of an expression differs from its literal interpretation. Examples of expressions include slang, jargon, and euphemisms.

- Slang is an expression, often short-lived, identified with a specific group of people. Business has its own slang, such as *24/7, bandwidth, bottom line, strategic fit,* or *window of opportunity.* Using slang that your audience understands serves as a communication shortcut. But issues arise when the sender uses slang that receivers don't understand, either because they're excluded from a group or because of language differences.

- Jargon is the technical terminology used within specialized groups—sometimes called "the pros' prose." Technology, for example, has spawned a whole new vocabulary. Do you know the meaning of these common computer terms?

OS	FAQ	JPEG	retweet
POS	Trojan horse	VoIP	AI
SEO	hacker	followers	spam
thumbnail	HTML	patch	CAD

As with slang, problems arise not when simply using jargon—jargon provides a very precise and efficient way of communicating with those familiar with it. Problems arise when we use jargon just to impress others, which can alienate people.

- Euphemisms are expressions used instead of words that may be offensive or inappropriate. Sensitive communicators use euphemisms when appropriate; for example, some consider "passed away" more pleasant than "died."

Euphemisms, like slang and jargon, shouldn't be overused. Euphemisms for firing people have become a corporate joke; now companies downsize, rightsize, smartsize, rationalize, amortize, reduce, redeploy, reorganize, restructure, offshore, outsource, and outplace. In a Merck layoff memo, the president avoided "jobs" or "layoffs." Instead, a journalist identified twelve euphemisms and accused the writer of "swallow[ing] a thesaurus of business-writing clichés before he began his email."[18] On a website, employees posted memorable expressions that managers used to tell them they were fired (see Figure 6).[19]

Euphemisms Used to Fire Employees | **Figure 6**

RAGAN COMMUNICATIONS FORUM. "HAVE YOU BEEN FIRED?" WWW.MYRAGAN.COM. ACCESSED JULY 10, 2010.

Overabstraction and Ambiguity

An abstract word identifies an idea or a feeling instead of a concrete object. For example, *communication* is an abstract word, but *newspaper* is a concrete word, a word that identifies something that can be seen or touched. Abstract words are necessary to describe things you cannot see or touch, but we run into difficulty when we use too many abstract words or when we use too high a level of abstraction. The higher the level of abstraction, the more difficult it is for the receiver to visualize exactly what the sender has in mind. For example, which sentence communicates more information: "I acquired an asset at the store" or "I bought a printer at Staples"?

Ambiguous terms such as *a few, some, several,* and *far away* may be too broad for business communication. What does ASAP (as soon as possible) mean to you? Does it mean within the hour, by the end of the day, or something else? A more specific deadline, for example, January 20 at 3:00 p.m., will improve your chances of getting what you need when you need it.

Polarization

Not every situation has two opposite and distinct poles—usually we can see gray areas. Is a speaker telling the truth or lying? What the speaker says may be true, but she may selectively omit information and give an inaccurate impression. Most likely, the answer is somewhere in between. Competent communicators avoid inappropriate either/or logic and instead make the effort to search for middle-ground words to best describe a situation.

Although we're discussing verbal barriers to communication, what you do *not* say can also cause issues in communication. What if you congratulated only one of the three people after a company presentation? How would the other two presenters feel—even though you said nothing negative about their performance?

1-3b Nonverbal Barriers

Not all communication difficulties are related to what you write or say. Some are related to how you act. Nonverbal barriers to communication include inappropriate or conflicting signals, differences in perception, inappropriate emotions, and distractions.

Inappropriate or Conflicting Signals

Suppose a well-qualified applicant for an auditing position submits a résumé with a typographical error or shows up to an interview in jeans. When verbal and nonverbal signals conflict, we tend to believe the nonverbal messages because they are more difficult to manipulate than verbal messages.

Many nonverbal signals vary from culture to culture—both within the United States and internationally. What is appropriate in one context might not be appropriate in another. We'll explore this further when we discuss intercultural communication in the next chapter.

Differences in Perception

Even when they hear the same presentation or read the same report, people will form different perceptions because of their filters. When employees receive an email from the company president, they'll probably react differently based on their experience, knowledge, and points of view. One employee may be so intimidated by the president that he accepts everything the president says, whereas another employee may have such negative feelings about the president that she believes nothing the president says.

© ICON DESIGN/SHUTTERSTOCK.COM

In her TED Talk, "On Being Wrong," journalist Kathryn Schulz describes how she mistook this sign for picnic area as Chinese characters.

Emotional INTELLIGENCE

Can you think of a time when your emotions got in the way of communication? How do you keep your emotions in check?

Inappropriate Emotions

Although a moderate level of emotional involvement intensifies communication and makes it more personal, too much emotional involvement can hinder communication. For example, excessive anger, prejudice (automatically rejecting certain people or ideas), stereotyping (placing individuals into categories), and boredom can create obstacles to effective communication. These emotions tend to close your mind to new ideas and cause you to reject or ignore information that is contrary to your prevailing belief. Keeping an objective, open mind is important for effective communication—and for you to develop as a person.

Distractions

Noise, or environmental or competing elements, can hinder your ability to concentrate and can affect communication. Examples of *environmental* noise are extreme temperature, uncomfortable seating, or even your coworker's body odor. Examples of *competing* noise are too many projects, meetings, or emails.

Communication technologies themselves can cause distractions. Can you watch TV, listen to music, and text at the same time? You may think you're good at multitasking, but a Stanford University study concludes the opposite: "Heavy multitaskers are lousy at multitasking."[20]

More accurately, multitasking means switching, or "rapid toggling" between activities—the interruption of one task to perform another. In a Carnegie Mellon University study, people who were interrupted while reading scored less well on test questions than people who weren't interrupted, making people "20% dumber," according to the study sponsors.[21]

Competent communicators try to avoid verbal and nonverbal barriers that might cause misunderstandings. They also choose the best communication media for their messages.

1-4 Communication Media Choices

LO3 Describe criteria for choosing communication media.

As a business communicator, you have many options (channels or media) through which you can communicate a message. The real challenge is deciding which medium to choose.

1-4a Traditional Communication Channels

Traditional forms of oral and written communication still exist in all organizations today.

Traditional Written Communication

Organizations still print slick, colorful brochures; internal newsletters for employees without computer access; financial statements for customers who don't choose the online option; solicitation letters; and periodicals such as magazines, journals, and newspapers. Complex reports also may be printed because they're difficult to read on a computer screen.

How much longer will some of these print communications exist? It's hard to say. In an office environment today, you'll likely receive few interoffice memos and postal letters. These communications are considered more official and formal, so you may receive important information about your pay or benefits but not much else. You may receive a report that you'll print, but it will probably come as an email attachment.

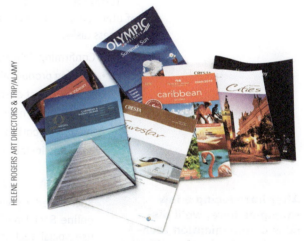

Travel brochures, a traditional form of written communication, use photos of exotic destinations to lure customers.

HELENE ROGERS ART DIRECTORS & TRIP/ALAMY

Traditional Oral Communication

Fortunately, people do still meet in person. Face-to-face meetings are the most personal form of business communication and the best choice for building relationships. Traditional meetings include one-on-one (individual), small group (team), or large group gatherings.

At many organizations, flip charts and handouts are still used during meetings and training programs. Some companies don't have technology available in all meeting rooms, and some believe smartphones during meetings hinder communication. At times, low-tech options may be best to stay within organizational norms and to achieve your communication goals.

Communication
TECHNOLOGIES

1-4b Technology-Based Communication Media

Technology has changed workplace communication, providing many options for sending a message. Depending on the type of message, you may choose from a variety of communication technologies, including portable, mobile technologies.

Email, Phone, Voice Mail

Although they are technology based, email, the phone, and voice mail are considered more conventional channels of communication. Email is so pervasive in organizations that it has become the default choice for communication.[22] Landline office phones persist, but who knows for how long, considering that smartphones have replaced so many home phones. People still call each other at work, but sending an email to someone in the next cubicle is common. It's no surprise that so many people believe email is used too often instead of face-to-face communication.[23]

Emotional
INTELLIGENCE

What is your preference for communicating with others? Do you sometimes avoid talking with someone on the phone and send a text, IM, or email instead?

Instant and Text Messaging

Instant messaging (IM) and texting are becoming increasingly popular at work. For short messages and quick questions, these channels are ideal.[24] Of course, with smartphones, email also may elicit an instant response, but this varies by organization and people. The real value of IMing is "presence awareness"—you know when someone is available to respond immediately. Although some people consider IM an annoying interruption at work, people who use IM at the office report fewer disruptions[25] and believe that IM saves time and provides timely, relevant information. One large, global study found that 73% of respondents use IM daily to communicate with coworkers and external contacts, spending an average of 41 minutes per day on IM.[26,27]

Texting is still considered quite informal for communicating at work. And texting in front of other people—particularly during class!—may be considered rude. But it's useful for these business tasks:

- Confirming deliveries
- Sending product alerts
- Providing fast client contact
- Advertising a new product or service
- Sending important information in a meeting
- Providing instant reminders[28]

Social Media

Social media gives companies tremendous opportunities to connect with people online. Social media is about having a *conversation*. To promote interaction, companies use social technologies, for example, blogs, wikis, video, and social networking sites. These tools are used on the Internet (for the public), on a company's intranet (for employee access only), and on extranets (private networks for people outside the company, e.g., customers or franchisees). Examples of social media are shown in Figure 7.

For many companies, social media focuses on user-generated content (UGC), also called consumer-generated media (CGM). This content can be blog entries, product reviews, videos, or other messages posted about a company. As we discussed earlier in the Glassdoor.com example, content isn't always positive and is one of the more difficult communication challenges for companies. Next, we'll look at five types of social media and how businesses use each.

After introducing a few examples here, we'll discuss communication technologies where relevant throughout the book. For example, we'll explore wikis for team communication; social networking for interpersonal communication; email, blogs, and instant messaging for written communication; user-generated content for customer communication; and video for oral presentations.

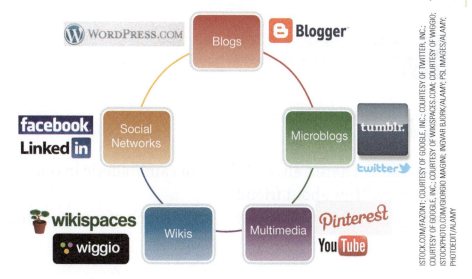

ISTOCK.COM/FAZON1; COURTESY OF TWITTER, INC.; COURTESY OF GOOGLE, INC.; COURTESY OF WIKISPACES.COM; COURTESY OF WIGGIO; ISTOCKPHOTO.COM/GIORGIO MAGINI; INGVAR BJORK/ALAMY; PSL IMAGES/ALAMY; PHOTOEDIT/ALAMY

Blogs. Companies use blogs to connect with employees and customers. Successful blogs are updated regularly with news or commentary, and many encourage interactivity through comments, email subscriptions, and RSS (Really Simple Syndication) feeds to share news and other content. Of the *Fortune* 500 companies, 34% have corporate blogs, with the highest percentage (44%) coming from specialty retailers.[29]

Wegmans, a regional supermarket, has an active blog called "Fresh Stories" to educate and engage customers—and keep them coming back. The blog includes videos, photos, and posts by CEO Danny Wegman. In one recent post, the CEO wrote,

> With the spring season upon us (*we hope*! It's been a cold April in the Rochester area), I wanted to kick off the season with a fresh story from the farm. I'm hoping you'll start sharing your growing stories and questions as we experience this new season together![30]

With a blog, a CEO can build direct relationships with customers and personalize the company, particularly with a conversational style such as Danny Wegman's.

Microblogs. Microblogs are used for short messages with timely information. Twitter, a popular microblogging site, allows for only 140 characters per message. Although Twitter feels like a social network, relationships with "followers" are weak and primarily one-way (for updates only).[31,32] As a college student, you may not be excited about Twitter: only 35% of 18- to 29-year-olds are on Twitter,[33] and about 23% are on Tumblr,[34] although these numbers are increasing.

As a business tool, Twitter is useful for reporting news and connecting with customers. With a well-established online presence, Southwest Airlines and JetBlue, for example, quickly respond to customers' concerns. The tweet in Figure 8 shows us the type of informal conversation that can happen online. Representatives from the companies are bantering with each other and catching attention.

Multimedia. Multimedia may incorporate several forms of media. Corporate videos, for example, promote products and services, illustrate product functionality, address crisis situations, and excite prospective employees. Deloitte Consulting held a contest—the Deloitte Film Festival—for employees to create videos showing what it's like to work at the company. The

Visit the author's blog at www.bizcominthenews.com for current communication examples.

Figure 8 | JetBlue's Tweet About Southwest Airlines

Alexa Rae @aiexa08   01 Feb
You guys like friends or something? @JetBlue @SouthwestAir

JetBlue Airways ✔   🐦 Follow
jetBlue @JetBlue

@aiexa08 There's always a level of camaraderie in our industry. How about friendly competitors? (& @SouthwestAir is a heck of a competitor)

videos were fun for employees to create and watch, and examples posted on YouTube became an effective recruiting tool.

With less tolerance for text, customers are migrating toward visual communication. Companies are increasingly using Pinterest, Instagram, Vine, and other sites to reach their audiences. Podcasts are also useful for companies to provide portable audio or video content about their products and services.

Wikis. Wikis are online spaces where people collaborate. Wikipedia, for example, allows people to edit a web page to co-create content. Within a company, wikis allow workgroups to share documents and track revisions, schedule team meetings, communicate online, and manage deadlines. More web content and small group work are moving to "the cloud" (stored centrally on the Internet), as we'll see in Chapter 2.

Social Networking. Under the social media umbrella, social networking sites are for communities of people who share common interests or activities. Facebook has certainly evolved from its collegiate roots, with the average user now 40.5 years old and strong growth among middle-aged and older users.[35] Now that mom and dad (and grandma) are on Facebook, it's less intriguing for young teens, who are frequenting Twitter and Instagram instead.[36,37] As a business student, you'll find it useful to be on LinkedIn, the popular professional networking site: 97% of *Fortune* 500 companies have a page on the site, while 83% manage a Twitter feed, and 80% have a Facebook page.[38]

Social networking tools often are integrated into other social media platforms. For example, companies install social networking software on their intranets to connect employees within the organization. Google⁺, a relatively new entrant into the social media world, is, according to Google, a "social layer" rather than a social network. Although some analysts don't see the distinction, Google⁺ may be more of a social destination—and the evolution of Google itself.[39] In Chapter 3, we'll explore how companies use social networking to connect with customers and employees.

1-4c Choosing Communication Media

Given all of these media choices, which is best for your message? You should always consider your audience and communication objectives first. What do you want your audience to do, think, or feel differently as a result of your message, and what's the best medium to achieve this?

Although perceptions of communication media vary, we can think of our choices along the continuum shown in Figure 9. Do you agree with this sequence? From your own experience and perspective, which would you move, and why? For example, is a text message more personal than an email because it's sent immediately to someone's phone? Or is an IM richer than a brochure because it starts a conversation, even though graphics are rare? As you plan your messages, you also might find the considerations in Figure 10 useful.

Continuum of Communication Media | Figure 9

The richest medium is a face-to-face (in-person) conversation or meeting, where you are physically present and have the most communication cues, such as body language.

Rich media are more interactive than lean media. You have the opportunity for two-way communication: the receiver can ask questions and express opinions easily in person. Rich media also include more visual elements.

Rich media are best for difficult, complex, or emotional messages, such as decisions that people won't agree with or changes that negatively affect people.

You might find media _roughly_ in this order along the continuum.

Face-to-Face Meeting	Videoconferencing	Teleconferencing Phone Call Voice Message	Blog Microblog	Brochure Newsletter Flier

Rich ←————————————————————————→ **Lean**

In-Person Oral Presentation	Online Meeting	Video	Report	Email IM Text Message

Lean media do not allow for many cues, for example, facial expressions, to complement your message. Written communication typically is leaner than oral communication, yet more visual elements can enrich text-based messages.

With little opportunity for two-way communication, lean media are one-way and static.

Lean media are best for routine, neutral, simple messages, such as a regular meeting request, a weekly report, or a product update.

Companies often will use multiple communication channels as part of a large communication strategy. Sending multiple messages through a variety of communication media helps the company reach different audiences. To announce a company acquisition, for example, executives may hold a conference call with analysts, meet with the management team in person, send an email to all employees, and post a video on the company intranet. This coordination is part of a strategic communication plan, typically created at senior levels in an organization.

1-4d Convergence of Communication Media

Technology is blurring many forms of communication—oral and written, face-to-face, and online. Imagine that you're meeting with a customer In person and send a text to someone back at the office to ask a quick product question. Or, you're on a phone call and respond to an IM. These examples could be considered multicommunicating, or synchronous (at the same time), overlapping conversations.[40]

Multicommunicating can be effective—up to a point. As you can imagine, with too many conversations going at the same time, it's easy to get confused. And you can be effective at

Figure 10 | Considerations for Choosing Communication Media

RELATIONSHIP CONSIDERATIONS	LOGISTICAL CONSIDERATIONS
• What is your relationship with the audience? Do you have a strong, existing relationship, or are you building a new one?	• How long is the message? How complex is the information?
• Is the communication neutral, positive, or potentially bad news? How is the audience likely to react?	• How many people will receive the message?
• To what extent do you want immediate feedback? Will this communication be one-way or two-way?	• How urgent is the message? Do the receivers need it immediately?
• What would your audience prefer? What are the organizational norms for this type of communication? If you're responding to a message, in what form did you receive it?	• Where are the receivers located?
	• What is most practical and efficient?
• At what level of the organization is the receiver? Is this person senior, junior, or at your level?	• How easily will the receivers understand your message? What's their primary language and reading proficiency?
• Is this message confidential or private in some way?	• What access to technology does your audience have?
• Do you need the message or conversation documented?	

multicommunicating only if people around you tolerate this. In some work situations, texting during a meeting may be acceptable, but not in others. Pay attention to what your respected peers do, and adjust your behavior to match theirs.

Communication technologies themselves are also connecting and converging. Mashups, for example, are web applications or pages that combine content from different sources. Geolocation services such as Foursquare display mashups based on where you are. Some programs allow you to open an email and listen to an attached voice message or open a text and watch a video. What will distinguish email, IM, and texting in the future if communication becomes more and more immediate? This remains to be seen.

LO4 Avoid potential legal consequences of communication.

1-5 Potential Legal Consequences of Communication

In a business environment, we need to consider legal consequences—and other repercussions—of our communication. When you work for a company, anything you write and say may become public if your company is sued or is part of a government investigation. During legal discovery, the company must produce evidence related to an inquiry, including emails, IMs, recorded phone conversations, voice mail messages, and other communications the attorneys believe are relevant.

General Motors (GM) was accused of covering up an ignition defect that caused 13 deaths. An internal investigation revealed, according to CEO Mary Barra, "GM personnel's inability to address the ignition switch problem, which persisted for more than 11 years."[41]

What evidence was used to discover the "history of failures"?[42] Email, jokingly called "evidence mail." Emails showed that several executives knew a Chevy Cobalt issue could have been fixed nine years prior for 57 cents. GM faced further embarrassment when, with kitschy fonts, an internal PowerPoint instructing staff to manage their word choice became public (Figure 11).[43]

GM PowerPoint Instructs Staff to Avoid Certain Words | **Figure 11**

COURTESY OF NATIONAL HIGHWAY TRAFFIC SAFETY ADMINISTRATION

When you join a company, you will probably sign several policies about communicating at work. These are designed to protect the company against lawsuits, public relations nightmares, and breaches of confidentiality, privacy, and security. Your company may provide guidelines, such as the following examples from Time Warner Cable's (TWC) social media policy:

- Follow copyright, fair use, and financial disclosure laws.
- Don't publish confidential or other proprietary information.
- Don't cite or reference clients, partners, or suppliers without their prior approval. When a reference is made, where possible, link back to the source.
- When communicating online, behave professionally and with the utmost respect for those individuals involved in the discussion. Ethnic slurs, personal insults, foul language, or conduct that would not be acceptable in TWC's workplace should not be used.
- On social networks where you identify yourself as an employee of TWC, be mindful that the content posted will be visible to coworkers, customers, and partners. Make sure the information posted is the most professional reflection of your opinions and beliefs.
- Do not insult or disparage TWC, its products and services, or any fellow employees, even if specific names are not mentioned.[44]

Apple's social media policy—which was leaked (a violation of the policy itself)—concludes with this sound advice for all employees:

> In sum, use your best judgment. Remember there may be consequences to what you post or publish online, including discipline. . . .[45]

You can protect yourself and your company by paying careful attention to what you put in writing and what you say. A law firm suggests asking yourself, "Would I be comfortable two years from now being cross-examined in federal court in front of a jury about the content of this email I am about to send?"[46] If you wouldn't, then don't send the email. You might ask yourself the same question for all communications related to your company.

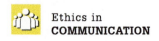

LO5 Communicate ethically.

Ethics in **COMMUNICATION**

1-6 Ethics and Communication

Beyond the legal requirements, companies will expect you to communicate ethically. As a senior director of corporate communications boarded a plane for South Africa, she fired off a tweet from her personal account (Figure 12).[47]

Figure 12 | Offensive Tweet

Going to Africa. Hope I don't get AIDS. Just kidding. I'm white!

◀ Reply ⟲ Retweet ★ Favorite ••• More

289 RETWEETS   **106** FAVORITES

COURTESY OF TWITTER, INC.

The situation is further complicated because she worked for a communications company. Although a friend says she was experimenting with tweets that were "just a little bit risqué or outrageous," perhaps she should have known better than to cross this line. She was terminated from her company.

But was the reaction to her tweet ethical? During the flight, her tweet went viral, and a hashtag asking whether she landed from the plane became popular. On Twitter, people threatened rape and murder. Bad behavior doesn't justify more of it, but her failing teaches us to avoid offensive comments, particularly for a laugh at others' expense.

Each of us has a personal code of ethics, or system of moral principles, that go beyond legal rules to tell us how to act. Our ethics represent our personal belief about whether something is right or wrong. As children, we begin forming our ethical standards based on how we perceive the behavior of our parents, other adults, and our peer group.

Let's consider three types of ethics:

- Professional ethics are defined by an organization. Employees and members are expected to follow these guidelines, which define what is right or wrong in the workplace—often beyond established laws. For example, 97% of *Fortune* 500 companies protect their employees from discrimination in the workplace based on sexual orientation. This goes beyond the U.S. federal legal requirement.[48]

- Social ethics are defined by society. For example, although accepting gifts from suppliers is strictly frowned upon in North American societies, this practice may be common place and accepted in other societies.
- Individual ethics are defined by the person and are based on family values, heritage, personal experience, and other factors. For example, most universities have guidelines to deter plagiarism. In addition to the guidelines that represent professional ethics, you probably have your own beliefs about cheating.

1-6a What Affects Ethical Behavior

According to ethicists, when people make unethical decisions, they do so for one of three reasons:

- We do what's most convenient. In other words, we take the easy route.
- We do what we must to win. Some people think that embracing ethics would limit their ability to succeed—that "good guys finish last."
- We rationalize our choices. We decide that the decision we make depends on the particular circumstances (this is called situational ethics).

The corporate culture affects ethics. If everyone spends time during the workday on Facebook, you are likely to do the same (the "everybody-does-it" defense). If managers are aware of unethical practices and don't stop them, they are condoning these actions.

When a strict code of ethics is in effect and enforced, employees have fewer opportunities to be unethical. Employees know what is expected of them and what happens if they fail to live up to these expectations.

1-6b Ethics Pays

Companies that are considered the most ethical outperform the S&P 500 and FTSE 100. The Ethisphere Institute publishes an annual list of ethical companies based on their corporate citizenship and responsibility, innovation that contributes to public well-being, executive leadership and tone from the top, and other criteria. Pharmaceutical company Bristol-Myers Squibb won an Ethisphere award and leads the list of "100 Best Corporate Citizens," published by *Corporate Responsibility Magazine*.[49,50]

Many companies include corporate social responsibility (CSR) into their business model. CSR (or being socially responsible) means that companies consider the public's interest in their business practices. CSR extends beyond a solely numbers-driven measurement of success and instead focuses on a "triple bottom line" of people, planet, and profit. Progressive companies communicate their CSR practices in annual responsibility reports, as Bristol-Myers Squibb does on its website (Figure 13).[51]

Bristol-Myers Squibb Communicates Its Corporate Social Responsibility | **Figure 13**

Reducing Health Disparities
The Bristol-Myers Squibb Foundation helps build bridges to health for underserved populations.

Sustaining Our World
We foster sustainability through environmental, social and economic progress.

Paying for Your Medication
We assist eligible patients who have financial hardships and who need our medicines.

Building Our Communities
We are a good neighbor, supporting the communities where we live and do business.

COURTESY OF BRISTOL MYERS SQUIBB

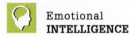
Emotional INTELLIGENCE

1-6c Framework for Ethical Decision Making

When faced with an ethical decision, consider the factors shown in Figure 14. Using these criteria, we can assess the ethics of the corporate communication director's tweet. Sure, her tweet was legal, but did it comply with her company's guidelines? You could say that what she does with a personal Twitter account is her choice, but senior managers represent their company online—particularly a communications company that sets the standard for good online behavior. Who was affected by her tweet? Clearly, many people who suffer from AIDS and those who might be offended by her implying that White people are somehow protected from the disease. According to her employer, her tweet didn't comply with company values: "The offensive comment does not reflect the views and values . . . We take this issue very seriously, and we have parted ways with the employee in question."[52] Finally, how did the director feel after the tweet became public? Not very good, according to her apology statement:

> Words cannot express how sorry I am, and how necessary it is for me to apologize to the people of South Africa, who I have offended due to a needless and careless tweet.
>
> For being insensitive to this crisis—which does not discriminate by race, gender or sexual orientation, but which terrifies us all uniformly—and to the millions of people living with the virus, I am ashamed.
>
> This is my father's country, and I was born here. I cherish my ties to South Africa and my frequent visits, but I am in anguish knowing that my remarks have caused pain to so many people here: my family, friends and fellow South Africans. I am very sorry for the pain I caused.[53]

Figure 14 | Framework for Ethical Decision Making

1. Is the action legal? If the decision does not comply with workplace laws, such as workplace safety, equal opportunity, privacy, and sexual harassment, then don't do it.

2. Does the action comply with your company's policies and guidelines? This may be the time to re-read documentation or ask your manager or human resources representative.

3. Who will be affected by your decision and how? Determine who has an important stake in the outcome of your decision. Stakeholders might include employees, customers, suppliers, and the wider community. What is at stake for each?

4. Does the action comply with the company values? Even without a formal code of conduct policy, is the decision consistent with general business practices?

5. How will you feel after the decision is known? What if your actions were published on the company intranet or in the local paper? Could you face yourself in the mirror?

In business, ethics are almost always a consideration in how we communicate. We constantly make decisions about what information to include and what information to exclude from our messages. For the information that is included, we decide how to phrase the message, how much to emphasize each point, and how to organize the message. Business communicators must consider the impact of their messages to ensure that receivers are not deceived.

1-7 Introducing the 3Ps (Purpose, Process, Product) Model

Every chapter in this text concludes with a 3Ps model to illustrate important communication concepts covered in the chapter. These short case studies, which relate to each chapter introduction, include the *purpose*, the *process*, and the *product* (the 3Ps). The *purpose* defines the situation and discusses the need for a particular communication task. The *process* is a series of questions that provides step-by-step guidance for accomplishing the communication. Finally, the *product* is the result—the final communication.

The 3Ps model demonstrates examples of communication so that you can see the *process* of communicating, not just the results. This approach helps you focus on one aspect of your communication at a time. Using the 3Ps in your own communication will help you produce messages more easily and deliver a better result. Pay particular attention to the questions in the *process* section, and ask yourself similar questions as you prepare your own messages.

3Ps
> IN ACTION

An Ethical Decision at General Mills

>>> PURPOSE

Consider the chapter introduction: General Mills changing its legal terms to try to reduce lawsuits. Imagine that you are the company's corporate ethics officer and are asked—before the decision was made—whether the changes are ethical.

>>> PROCESS

To help you decide whether the changes are ethical, you use the Framework for Ethical Decision Making. You choose the following questions because they are most relevant to the situation:

1. **Is the action legal?**
   This is a tricky one. The company lawyers think so, but other legal experts find potential problems: could merely—even accidentally—clicking on a website force someone to give up her right to sue? What if the company did something harmful and intentional?

2. **Who will be affected by the decision and how?**
   Consumers and other Internet users may limit their access with the company, which could be an unintentional negative effect of these new terms. Also, can we reasonably expect consumers to read our long legal agreement before downloading a coupon? And how we will prove that someone visited the website? Confiscate his computer hard drive? That doesn't seem ethical or practical.

3. **Is this action in line with the company's guidelines and values?**
   Our mission is "to make lives healthier, easier, and richer." This change doesn't support the mission, particularly making lives easier. One of our values is "Do the right thing, all the time." Restricting consumers' rights doesn't feel right.

>>> PRODUCT

Based on the answers to these questions, you advise the attorneys not to change the legal terms. You'll warn them about potential consumer backlash, which may outweigh the savings from fighting lawsuits.

Using the Communication Model to Plan a Message

>>> PURPOSE

After General Mills experienced such backlash about its new legal terms, the company issued a statement reverting back to the original policy. Imagine that you're the head of corporate communications for the company.

>>> PROCESS

To plan your message about the reversal, use the following questions from the Communication Model in Figure 3:

1. What is the communication need? State it clearly and simply.

2. What is the communication context? Consider the organizational culture, potential legal consequences, and ethics.

3. Who are the primary and secondary audiences for your message? What is important to know about them?

4. What are the company's objectives? What, specifically, do you want to accomplish with your message?

5. What is the best medium for your message?

6. What are the potential communication barriers? What may get in the way of meeting your objectives?

>>> PRODUCT

Prepare the message for the company. When you're finished, compare your message to the company's, which you'll find here: www.bizcominthenews.com/files/general-mills2.pdf.

LO1 Identify the components of communication.

The components of communication explain how communication happens. The communication process begins with a need, which is conveyed by the sender through a message to the audience, who responds, therefore creating a new message. The organizational context and communication barriers complicate this process. These components of communication are used in both formal and informal communication networks. The formal communication network consists of downward, upward, and lateral (horizontal) communication, while the informal communication network (the grapevine) consists of information transmitted through unofficial channels.

LO2 Identify the major verbal and nonverbal barriers to communication.

Barriers may interfere with effective communication. Examples of verbal barriers are inadequate knowledge or vocabulary, differences in interpretation, language differences, inappropriate use of expressions, overabstraction and ambiguity, and polarization. Examples of nonverbal barriers are inappropriate or conflicting signals, differences in perception, inappropriate emotions, and distractions.

LO3 Describe criteria for choosing communication media.

Verbal communication includes oral and written communication. Traditional communication channels, such as face-to-face meetings and letters, still exist, but technology-based communication, such as social media, are increasingly popular for business communication. When deciding which channel (medium) to use for your message, first identify your audience and communication objectives. Consider lean channels for routine and neutral messages and rich channels for complex messages and bad news.

LO4 Avoid potential legal consequences of communication.

Although communication is essential to all organizations, oral and written communication may have negative consequences as well. Email and other messages may be part of a legal discovery process, and inappropriate communication may be the impetus for litigation. To avoid these damaging situations, follow your company's guidelines and policies regarding email and other communication.

LO5 Communicate ethically.

Beyond the legal requirements, we all have our own system of moral practices that guide our behavior. At the company level, corporate social responsibility (CSR) has become part of progressive organizations' communication strategy. At the personal level, you're responsible for behaving ethically, which includes how you communicate at work. The Framework for Ethical Decision Making will help guide your behavior and ensure that you communicate ethically.

LO1 Identify the components of communication.

> EXERCISES

1. **Examine your own feelings about communication.**

   In an email to your instructor, respond to the following questions:

   - What are your strengths in business writing? What would you like to improve?

   - How confident would you feel about writing an email that would be distributed to the entire school?

- What are your strengths in oral presentations? What would you like to improve?
- How confident would you feel about delivering a presentation to the entire school?

2. **Identify communication components in a current news story.**

   Use a current news item to identify the components of the communication process. You may use examples from the author's blog at www.bizcominthenews.com. After reading background information about the story, choose one aspect of communication and identify the need, sender, message, audience, and response. You may add your own assumptions if you don't have enough details from the story.

3. **Examine your own communication filters.**

   Looking at the same news story, list at least ten ways you personally are filtering the information you receive. Consider such factors as your individual experiences, culture, emotions at the moment, personality, knowledge, socioeconomic status, and demographic variables.

4. **Create an organization chart to identify a company's formal communication network.**

   Think of an organization where you've recently worked. Create an organization chart for two or three levels of employees. Then add arrows to identify the three directions of the formal communication network.

5. **Describe a company's grapevine.**

   For the same organization you explored in the previous question, consider the informal communication network. With a partner, discuss how you heard about unofficial information about the company. How accurate do you think this information was? Was senior management plugged into the grapevine? Do you have examples of how management responded to information spread through the grapevine? If management ignored the grapevine, what do you think should have been done instead?

6. **Identify communication barriers between a manager and an employee.**

   In the movie *Office Space*, watch Scene 13, "Flair." This communication does not go very well. Identify the verbal and nonverbal barriers of communication in this scene.

   LO2 Identify the major verbal and nonverbal barriers to communication.

Scene from the movie *Office Space*

7. **Identify communication barriers between a retail sales representative and a customer.**

   Watch the video clip from the fictitious retail store, Aggresshop. Identify the verbal and nonverbal barriers of communication in this scene. Think about the interaction from both perspectives: that of the sales associate and that of the shopper.

   Scene from the Aggresshop video

8. **Identify communication barriers in an episode of *Mad Men*.**

   Watch an episode of *Mad Men*, the television series on AMC about an advertising agency in the 1960s. What verbal and nonverbal barriers do you notice? What could the characters do to avoid these barriers in future interactions?

9. **Discuss communication barriers.**

   Consider a time when you were responsible for creating a communication barrier—we have all done so either intentionally or unintentionally. Discuss the situation with students in class. Identify your role and what you could have done differently.

10. **Adapt jargon for your audience.**

    Think of a topic you know well (e.g., a sport, a hobby, or an academic subject). Write an email to a colleague who is also an expert on the subject. Include at least six jargon terms that flow easily into the context of your email.

    Now assume that you are sending the same email to someone who is not at all familiar with the topic. Revise your original message to make it appropriate for this reader. Which email is longer? Which is more effective? Why?

LO3 Describe criteria for choosing communication media.

11. **Analyze print communication.**

    Find an example of print communication, for example, a flier on campus, a newsletter, or a magazine ad. With a partner, discuss why the creator of the message may have chosen a print medium. In your opinion, was this the best choice? What technology-based media may have worked instead or could supplement the printed message?

12. **Explore how a company uses social media.**

    What's your favorite company? Spend some time exploring how the company uses social media. Does it have a customer blog, Facebook page, Twitter account, and other online places to connect with audiences? Now compare this company's online presence to one of its close competitors' online presence. Which has more online activity, for example, more followers on Twitter, more people who "like" it on Facebook, or more blogs targeted to different audiences? In small groups, discuss findings about each of your favorite companies.

13. **Choose communication media for different audiences.**

    Imagine that you're the CEO of a retail store such as Aggresshop (described at the end of this chapter and at www.cengagebrain.com). Let's say you're planning to redesign each of the 16 stores in the United States. As part of this effort, you'll need to close stores for two weeks at a time. Working in teams, identify in the communication plan template below which medium you would use to communicate with each audience. You may have multiple communications for some audiences. Include the rationale for your decisions.

Audience	Communication Medium (or Media)	Rationale for Choosing the Communication Medium
Store managers		
Store sales representatives		
Corporate office employees		
VIP customers		
Other customers		
Suppliers		

14. Choose how to reject a job offer.

We'll discuss employment communication in Chapter 12; for now, consider a situation in which you're offered a summer internship but decide not to accept it. With a partner, discuss the most appropriate communication channel to use for your message. Would you use a different channel if you received the offer by email or by phone?

15. Give your manager advice about communication media.

For this exercise, you'll help your manager be a better communicator. Let's say you're lucky enough to have a good working relationship with your manager, and he or she tells you—before the rest of the team—that your department will be moving from downtown Chicago to a suburb. This is a major change and will be bad news for most people.

In response to this email from your manager, write a reply to suggest that he also hold a face-to-face meeting for employees. Explain why you think this is important.

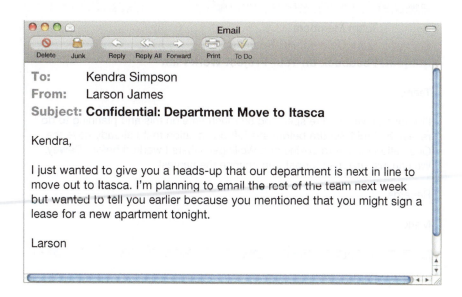

To: Kendra Simpson
From: Larson James
Subject: **Confidential: Department Move to Itasca**

Kendra,

I just wanted to give you a heads-up that our department is next in line to move out to Itasca. I'm planning to email the rest of the team next week but wanted to tell you earlier because you mentioned that you might sign a lease for a new apartment tonight.

Larson

16. **Research a lawsuit about communication.**

Find an example of a company that was sued because of its communication. Research the situation with a particular focus on the communication that was called into question (e.g., email messages, unclear reports, or discriminatory language).

Imagine that you're a consultant who was hired by one of the company's competitors. The competitor would like to avoid a similar situation and wants to hear what you learned about the case. Prepare and deliver a short presentation to your class, summarizing the main points. Focus on how the company can avoid a similar lawsuit.

17. **Write a policy about email use.**

Draft a policy about employees' email use. Consider what would be important for a company to communicate to employees about their email communication. Next, search the Internet to find a sample policy about appropriate use of email. You may find one on your school's website (perhaps you had to read and sign a policy when you first enrolled). Compare your draft to the sample. Did you miss any important points? Revise your policy if necessary.

Then, in small groups, discuss your policy and be honest about how your use of email may violate the policy. Now that you know what is expected, would you handle email differently? Why or why not?

18. **Discuss a questionable restaurant sales strategy.**

A diner at a steakhouse in Atlantic City was charged $3,750 for a bottle of wine he thought was $37.50. Read about the situation at bit.ly/1w89oTB. In groups, discuss who is responsible for the discrepancy. Have some members of your group argue that the customer is responsible, and have other members argue that the restaurant (or perhaps the server) is responsible. Try to come to some agreement or compromise. Then decide what should be done to resolve the issue.

19. **Respond to an email that suggests an unethical practice.**

Imagine that you're an intern for the law firm Dewey, Wright, and Howe. As part of a team, you're developing an Orientation Plan for future interns. Your team receives an email from the HR recruiter at the firm.

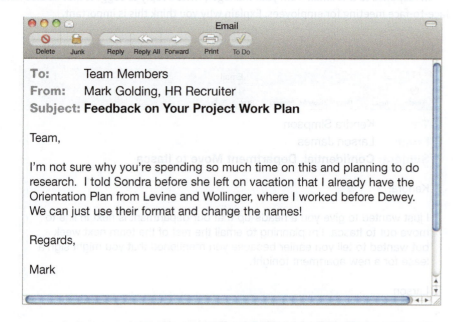

In response to this email from your manager, write a reply to suggest that he also hold a face-to-face meeting for employees. Explain why you think this is important.

To: Team Members
From: Mark Golding, HR Recruiter
Subject: Feedback on Your Project Work Plan

Team,

I'm not sure why you're spending so much time on this and planning to do research. I told Sondra before she left on vacation that I already have the Orientation Plan from Levine and Wollinger, where I worked before Dewey. We can just use their format and change the names!

Regards,

Mark

In small groups, first discuss the situation and why this is an ethical dilemma. Then, on your own, write an email to respond to Mark's suggestion. You will want to balance ethics with tone to avoid accusing Mark of anything inappropriate and potentially making him feel defensive. When you're finished, share your draft with your group members and compare emails. Which works best and why?

20. **Discuss ethical dilemmas.**

Working in small groups, identify at least one ethical dilemma one of you has experienced in each of the following categories. Using the Framework for Ethical Decision Making discussed in this chapter, analyze how you handled the situation and what, if anything you could have done differently.

a) Copyright issues or academic integrity, for example, discovering that a friend plagiarized a paper or responding to a request for test or homework answers.

b) Confidentiality, for example, deciding whether to share information that would be useful to your friend although you were asked not to.

c) Employment, for example, receiving a better job offer after you already accepted one.

d) Customer service, for example, giving a customer information you know isn't true.

COMPANY SCENARIO

Aggresshop

Each chapter ends with a company scenario available at www .cengagebrain.com. This first scenario, Aggresshop, is also used at the end of Chapter 8, "Bad-News Messages."

Imagine that you work for Aggresshop, an upscale women's clothing boutique with 16 stores throughout the United States. At www .bizcominthenews.com/aggresshop, you'll find Aggresshop's company blog for customers and employees.

As you'll read in the scenario, Aggresshop is experiencing many customer complaints about its sales associates' overtly aggressive techniques (two posts are shown below). The CEO decides to change the sales compensation structure to address this issue.

On the blog, you'll see examples of several communication concepts discussed in Chapter 1: directions of communication, communication media, barriers to

CATEGORIES

Complaints
Compliments

COMPANY INFORMATION

Welcome, Aggresshop Customers!
About Aggresshop
Employees' Entrance
Management's Entrance

No fighting in front of the customer, please!

I was at the register waiting to check out, and two of the sales associates had an argument in front of me about who gets the sale. I guess one of them suggested the dress, but the other one got me a different size. Whatever! Why don't they just split it?

Check out this video

My boyfriend filmed me in an Aggresshop in San Diego, and this is what happened! All of the customer complaints are true!

Aggresshop video on YouTube

communication, and ethics in communication. This scenario will also help you learn to do the following:

- Respond to customer complaints on a company blog.
- Communicate a change internally.
- Tailor message content and tone for different audiences and communication channels.

To help you practice your business communication, your instructor may assign the following activities now or later in the semester:

- Write customer service standards for Aggresshop sales associates.
- Respond to customer comments on the blog.
- Write an article for customers on the blog.

Endnotes

1. Kirstie Foster, "We've listened – and we're changing our legal terms," *General Mills Blog*, April 19, 2014. www.blog.generalmills.com/2014/04/weve-listened-and-were-changing-our-legal-terms-back-to-what-they-were/, accessed April 26, 2015.

2. Stephanie Strom, "When 'Liking' a Brand Online Voids the Right to Sue," *The New York Times*, April 16, 2014, www.nytimes.com/2014/04/17/business/when-liking-a-brand-online-voids-the-right-to-sue.html, accessed April 26, 2015.

3. Stephanie Strom, "General Mills Reverses Itself on Consumers' Right to Sue," *The New York Times*, April 20, 2014, www.nytimes.com/2014/04/20/business/general-mills-reverses-itself-on-consumers-right-to-sue.html, accessed April 26, 2015.

4. Kirstie Foster.

5. "Jamie Dimon Testifies," *Erin Burnett OutFront*, CNN, June 13, 2012, transcripts.cnn.com/TRANSCRIPTS/1206/13/ebo.01.html, accessed April 26, 2015.

6. Bruce Watson, "Buzzword of the Week: Open Kimono," *Daily Finance*, www.dailyfinance.com/2010/12/17/buzzword-of-the-week-open-kimono/, April 26, 2015.

7. Graduate Management Admission Council, "2014 Corporate Recruiters Survey Report," GMAC Website, www.gmac.com/market-intelligence-and-research/research-library/employment-outlook/2014-corporate-recruiters.aspx, accessed April 28, 2015.

8. National Association of Colleges and Employers, "The Job Outlook for the Class of 2014," NACE Website, www.naceweb.org/uploadedFiles/Pages/MyNACE/grab_and_go/students/job-outlook-2014-student-version.pdf, accessed June 9, 2014.

9. "Writing: A Ticket to Work . . . Or a Ticket Out?" The College Board, The National Commission on Writing, September 2004, www.collegeboard.com/prod_downloads/writingcom/writing-ticket-to-work.pdf, accessed April 28, 2015.

10. Sam Dillon, "What Corporate America Can't Build: A Sentence," *The New York Times*, December 7, 2004, www.nytimes.com/2004/12/07/business/07write.html, accessed April 28, 2015.

11. Association of American Colleges and Universities, "It Takes More than a Major: Employer Priorities for College Learning and Student Success," AACU Website, www.aacu.org/leap/documents/2013_EmployerSurvey.pdf, accessed June 9, 2014.

12. Diana Middleton, "Students Struggle for Words," *The Wall Street Journal*, March 3, 2011, online.wsj.com/article/SB10001424052748703409904576174651780110970.html, accessed April 28, 2015.

13. Daniel R. Ames and Abbie S. Wazlawek, "Pushing in the Dark: Causes and Consequences of Limited Self-Awareness for Interpersonal Assertiveness," *Personality and Social Psychology Bulletin*, Vol. 1 (2014), pp. 1–16, www.columbia.edu/~da358/publications/Pushing_in_the_dark.pdf, accessed April 28, 2015.

14. Steven B. Wolff, "Emotional Competence Inventory (ECI)," Hay Group, McClelland Center for Research and Innovation, 2005, Technical Manual, www.eiconsortium.org/pdf/ECI_2_0_Technical_Manual_v2.pdf, accessed April 28, 2015.

15. Starbucks, Leadership Team, www.starbucks.com, April 28, 2015.

16. Charles Galunic and Immanuel Hermreck, "How to Help Employees 'Get' Strategy," *Harvard Business Review*, December 2012, https://hbr.org/2012/12/how-to-help-employees-get-strategy, accessed April 28, 2015.

17. Bruce Fortado, "A Field Exploration of Informal Workplace Communication," *Sociology Mind*, Vol. 1, No. 2 (2011), pp. 212–220, file.scirp.org/Html/7877.html, accessed April 28, 2015.

18. Jim Edwards, "A Layoff By Any Other Name: Merck Memo Uses 12 Euphemisms for Job Cuts," CBS News, September 19, 2011, www.cbsnews.com/news/a-layoff-by-any-other-name-merck-memo-uses-12-euphemisms-for-job-cuts/, accessed April 28, 2015.

19. Ragan Communications Forum, "Have you been fired?" www.myragan.com, accessed July 10, 2010.

20. Clare Baldwin, "Media Multitasking Doesn't Work, Say Researchers," Reuters, August 24, 2009, www.reuters.com/article/2009/08/24/us-multitasking-stanford-idUSTRE57N55D20090824, accessed April 28, 2015.

21. Bob Sullivan and Hugh Thompson, "Brain, Interrupted," *The New York Times*, May 3, 2013, www.nytimes.com/2013/05/05/opinion/sunday/a-focus-on-distraction.html, accessed June 9, 2014.

22. David Lennox, Amy Newman, and Maria Loukianenko Wolfe, "How Business Leaders Communicate in 2012: Classroom Strategies for Teaching Current Practices," Association for Business Communication 11th European Conference, Nijmegen, Netherlands, May 2012.

23. Thomas W. Jackson, Anthony Burgess, and Janet Edwards, "A Simple Approach to Improving Email Communication," Communications of the ACM 49 (June 2006): 107–109.

24. Judi Brownell and Amy Newman, "Hospitality Managers and Communication Technologies: Challenges and Solutions," *Cornell Hospitality Research* 9 (December 2009).

25. R. Kelly Garrett and James N. Danziger, "IM = Interruption Management? Instant Messaging and Disruption in the Workplace," *Journal of Computer-Mediated Communication* 13 (2007): article 2.

26. Sara Radicati, "*Corporate IT and Business User Survey, 2012–2013*," The Radicati Group, Inc., www.radicati.com/wp/wp-content/uploads/2012/08/Corporate-IT-and-Business-User-Survey-2012-2013-Executive-Summary.pdf, accessed April 28, 2015.

27. Business User Survey 2013, The Radicati Group, www.radicati.com/wp/wp-content/uploads/2013/08/Business

-User-Survey-2013-Executive-Summary.pdf, accessed April 28, 2015.

28. "Ten Ways to Use Texting for Business," *Inc.com*, www.inc.com /ss/ten-ways-use-texting-business, accessed July 1, 2014.

29. Nora Ganim Barnes and Ava M. Lescault, "The 2014 *Fortune* 500 and Social Media: LinkedIn Dominates As Use of Newer Tools Explodes," Charlton College of Business Center for Marketing Research, University of Massachusetts Dartmouth, 2014, www.umassd.edu/cmr/socialmediaresearch /2014fortune500andsocialmedia/, accessed April 28, 2015.

30. Danny Wegman, "Down on the Farm: Watching Our Tomatoes Grow," *Wegmans Blog*, May 3, 2011, www.wegmans.com/blog/, accessed April 28, 2015.

31. Dan Zarrella. "Is Twitter a Social Network?" *HubSpot* (blog), June 22, 2009, blog.hubspot.com/blog/tabid/6307/bid/4859 /Is-Twitter-a-Social-Network.aspx, accessed April 28, 2015.

32. Mary Madden, et al., "Teens, Social Media, and Privacy: Part 1: Teens and Social Media Use," PewResearch Internet Project, www.pewinternet.org/2013/05/21/part-1-teens-and -social-media-use/, accessed April 28, 2015.

33. PewResearch Internet Project, "Social Networking Fact Sheet," January 2014, www.pewinternet.org/fact-sheets /social-networking-fact-sheet/, accessed April 28, 2015.

34. Brian Chappell, "2012 Social Network Analysis Report— Demographic—Geographic and Search Data Revealed," *Ignite Social Media*, July 31, 2012, www.ignitesocialmedia.com /social-media-stats/2012-social-network-analysis-report/, accessed April 28, 2015.

35. James Brumley, "Facebook Users Are Getting Older . . . and That's a Good Thing," *InvestorPlace*, February 4, 2014, investorplace.com/2014/02/facebook-users-demographics/#. VIsVzyvF-So, accessed April 28, 2015.

36. Jennifer Van Grove, "Facebook fesses up: Young teens are getting bored," *CNet*, October 30, 2013, www.cnet.com/news /facebook-fesses-up-young-teens-are-getting-bored/, accessed April 28, 2015.

37. Mary Madden, et al.

38. Nora Ganim Barnes and Ava M. Lescault.

39. Ray Hiltz, "The Google⁺ Social Layer Explained," Google⁺, Blog Post, February 2013, https://plus.google.com /107624559327351970888/posts/XbBiN1d1VUH, accessed April 28, 2015.

40. N. Lamar Reinsch, Jr., et al., "Multicommunicating: A Practice Whose Time Has Come?" *Academy of Management Review* 33 (2008): 391–408.

41. Chris Isidore and Poppy Harlow, "Botched recall: 'Fundamental failure,'" *CNN Money*, June 5, 2014, money.cnn.com/

2014/06/05/news/companies/gm-recall-probe/, accessed April 28, 2015.

42. Chris Isidore and Poppy Harlow.

43. Jacob Fischler, "69 Words General Motors Didn't Want Its Employees To Use When Describing GM Cars," *BuzzFeedNews*, May 17, 2014, www.buzzfeed.com/jacobfischler/ways -general-motors-really-didnt-want-its-employees-to-de, accessed April 28, 2015.

44. Lydia Dishman, "Social Media Policies: The Good, The Mediocre, and the Ugly," *Fast Company*, June 9, 2010, www .fastcompany.com/1668368/corporate-social-media-policies -good-mediocre-and-ugly, accessed April 28, 2015.

45. Jon Hyman, "Apple's social media policy: A lot to like . . . and one huge thing to hate," *Ohio Employer's Law Blog*, December 6, 2011, www.ohioemployerlawblog.com/2011/12/apples-social -media-policy-lot-to-like.html#.U7LRShAvm8A, accessed April 28, 2015.

46. Douglas C. Northup and Ronald J. Stolkin, "Legal Issues Affecting Business E-mails." *Fennemore Craig*, June 13, 2007, www.fclaw.com /newsletter/materials/Business EmailsUpdate6-13-07.pdf, accessed April 28, 2015.

47. Nick Bilton, "Is the Internet a Mob Without Consequence?" *The New York Times*, December 24, 2014, bits.blogs.nytimes .com/2013/12/24/is-the-internet-a-mob-without-consequence/, accessed April 28, 2015.

48. Equality Forum, "*Fortune* 500 Project," August 2012, www .equalityforum.com/fortune500, accessed April 28, 2015.

49. Ethisphere, "Bristol-Myers Squibb Earns Compliance Leader Verification from Ethisphere Institute," June 17, 2013, ethisphere.com/bristol-myers-squibb-earns-compliance -leader-verification-from-ethisphere-institute/, accessed April 28, 2015.

50. Corporate Responsibility Magazine, "CR's 100 Best Corporate Citizens 2014," www.thecro.com/files/100BestList.pdf, accessed April 28, 2015.

51. Bristol-Myers Squibb Website, www.bms.com/responsibility /Pages/home.aspx, accessed April 28, 2015.

52. Natalie DiBlasio, "PR director no longer with company after racist tweet," *USA Today*, December 21, 2013, www .usatoday.com/story/news/nation/2013/12/21/justine-sacco -tweet/4156011/, accessed April 28, 2015.

53. Agence France-Presse, "Fired public relations executive Justine Sacco apologizes for racist AIDS tweet," *The Raw Story*, December 22, 2013, www.rawstory.com/rs/2013/12/22 /fired-public-relations-executive-justine-sacco-apologizes-for -racist-aids-tweet/, accessed April 28, 2015.

CHAPTER 2

Team and Intercultural Communication

LEARNING OBJECTIVES

After you have finished this chapter, you should be able to

LO1 Communicate effectively and ethically in small groups.

LO2 Collaborate to improve team writing.

LO3 Communicate with intercultural audiences.

LO4 Communicate with diverse populations.

> *"Gap's Response to Racist Graffiti on a Subway Ad Was Perfect."* [1]
>
> – Richard Feloni, *Business Insider*

CHAPTER INTRODUCTION

Gap Responds Swiftly to Racist Comments

To represent the diversity of its customers, Gap created an ad featuring Waris Ahluwalia, an Indian-American designer and actor, and Quentin Jones, a model and filmmaker. Much of the reaction was positive, but not everyone was happy with the portrayal.[2] A graffitied version of the ad in a New York City subway included stereotypes of people wearing turbans as bombers and taxi drivers.

When Gap learned of the offensive comments, the company said nothing directly about the controversy but published this statement:

> Gap is a brand that celebrates inclusion and diversity. Our customers and employees are of many different ethnicities, faiths, and lifestyles, and we support them all.[3]

In addition, Gap changed its Twitter banner to the original image. Support for the company's response traveled throughout Twitter, with people thanking Gap and promising to shop the store for the holidays.

Companies must embrace the increasing diversity of their employees and consumer base. Gap took a risk, and the outcome seemed to outweigh the temporary backlash.

2-1 Work Team Communication

By definition, people who work in organizations communicate with other people. Working in small groups and with diverse groups of people is one of the most enriching—and sometimes one of the most challenging—aspects of a business environment. In this chapter, we'll explore ways that you can get the most out of your experience working with and learning from others.

A team is a group of individuals who depend on each other to accomplish a common objective. Teams are often more creative and accomplish more work than individuals working alone; a group's total output exceeds the sum of each individual's contribution. As a manager, if you work well as part of a team and can resolve conflicts, you will likely be seen as an effective leader with potential for promotion.[4]

On the other hand, teams can waste time and create a toxic environment. If you have worked as part of a team, you know all too well that people don't always contribute equally. Someone you might call a "slacker" is practicing social loafing, the psychological term for avoiding individual responsibility in a group setting.

Two to seven members—with five often as an ideal—seem to work best for effective work teams.[5] Smaller teams often lack diversity of skills and interests to function well, and larger teams struggle with managing their interactions because two or three people may dominate discussions and make key decisions.

2-1a The Variables of Group Communication

Three factors—conflict, conformity, and consensus—greatly affect a team's performance and how much team members enjoy working together. Let's consider a situation when these variables would come into play. Imagine that you worked for Disney when a young boy was killed by a bus at the Florida theme park.[6] To address this tragedy, you are working on a crisis management team with managers from several departments: transportation, public relations, human resources, and legal. To be successful, this crisis team needs to navigate the variables that shape group communication, explained in Figure 1.

2-1b Initial Group Goals

Teams work more effectively when the members know each other well—their strengths and weaknesses, work styles, experiences, attitudes, and so on. Starting off by getting to know each other improves the social dimension of your work, which may make tasks go more smoothly and help you enjoy the team experience more.

Small talk about friends, family, and social activities before and after meetings is natural and helps establish a supportive and open environment. Even in online meeting environments, you can post a profile to introduce yourself or spend time IMing to learn about each other.

Too often, decisions just happen on a team; members may go along with what they think everyone else wants. Instead, teams should agree on how they'll operate and make decisions; for example, consider discussing the following early on with your team:

- What if someone misses a deliverable or team meeting? How should he or she notify the team? What are the consequences?
- What if someone needs help completing a task? How should he or she handle this situation?
- What if two team members are having a conflict? How should it be resolved?
- Which decisions will be most important for the team? How should the team make those decisions?

Conflict: Should teams avoid conflict?	Many group leaders work hard to avoid **conflict**, but conflict is what group meetings are all about. On the Disney crisis team, you would want people to voice different opinions. The head of transportation might be confident about bus safety, while the attorney is more cautious and suggests stopping all bus routes until the cause of the accident is properly understood. Without conflict, teams miss out on productive discussion and debate.
	However, healthy conflict is about *issues*, not about *personalities*. Interpersonal conflict, such as personal attacks, can doom a team. If the head of transportation took the attorney's advice personally ("You don't know anything about transportation, and I've been doing this for 15 years"), the situation could get ugly.
Conformity: Should team members try to conform?	**Conformity** is agreement to ideas, rules, or principles. Crisis team members can disagree about whether the buses should be suspended, but certain fundamental issues, such as when the group meets, should be agreed to by everyone.
	However, too much conformity can result in **groupthink**, when people think similarly without independent thought. Groupthink stifles opposing ideas and the free flow of information.
	If the pressure to conform is too great, negative information and contrary opinions are never even brought out into the open and discussed. What if the attorney never raises the question of suspending buses? The team could make a bad decision, which might be apparent if another accident happened at the park.
Consensus: Should teams always strive for consensus?	**Consensus** means reaching a decision that best reflects the thinking of all team members. Consensus is not necessarily a unanimous vote or even a majority vote. With a majority vote, only the members of the majority are happy with the end result; people in the minority may have to accept something they don't like at all. But with a consensus decision, people who have reservations can still support the idea. For example, the Disney team might agree to suspend the bus routes for only two days.
	Not every decision needs to have the support of every member. This would be too difficult and take too long. The team should decide which decisions are important enough to get everyone on board.

2-1c Constructive Feedback

Giving and receiving constructive feedback is critical to working through team problems. These proven methods for giving and receiving criticism work equally well for giving and receiving praise.

Acknowledge the Need for Feedback

Imagine a work environment—or a class—in which you never receive feedback on your performance. How would you know what you do well and what skills you need to develop? Feedback is the only way to find out what needs to be improved. Your team must agree that giving and receiving feedback is part of your team's culture—how you'll work together. This way, no one will be surprised when he or she receives feedback.

Give Both Positive and Negative Feedback

Many people take good work for granted and give feedback only when they notice problems. In one study, 67% of employees said they received too little positive feedback.[7] Hearing only complaints can be demoralizing and might discourage people from making any changes at all. Always try to balance positive and constructive feedback. Figure 2 suggests ways to give both positive and constructive feedback.

Use "I" statements to describe how someone's behavior affects you. This approach focuses on your reaction and helps avoid attacking or blaming the other person. Use the guidelines in Figure 3, but adapt the model to your own language, so you're authentic and sound natural.[8]

 Emotional **INTELLIGENCE**

How easily do you accept feedback? How comfortable are you giving feedback? Do you tend to invite or avoid conflict?

Figure 2 | How to Give Positive and Negative Feedback

Be descriptive. State objectively what you saw or heard. Give specific, recent examples from your own observations, if possible.	**Avoid labels.** Words like *unprofessional*, *irresponsible*, and *lazy* are labels that we attach to behaviors. Instead, describe the behaviors and drop the labels.	**Don't exaggerate.** Be exact. To say, "You never finish work on time" is probably untrue and unfair.	**Speak for yourself.** Don't refer to absent, anonymous people ("A lot of people here don't like it when you . . .").	**Use "I" statements.** Instead of saying "You often submit work late," say, "I get annoyed when you submit work late because it holds up the rest of the team." "I" statements create an adult/peer relationship.

Figure 3 | Using "I" Statements When Giving Feedback

SEQUENCE	EXPLANATION
"When you . . ."	Start with a "When you . . ." statement that describes the behavior without judgment, exaggeration, labeling, attribution, or motives. Just state the facts as specifically as possible.
"I feel . . ."	Tell how the behavior affects you. If you need more than a word or two to describe the feeling, it's probably just some variation of joy, sorrow, anger, or fear.
"Because I . . ."	Now say why you are affected that way. Describe the connection between the facts you observed and the feelings they provoke in you.
(Pause for discussion.)	Let the other person respond.
"I would like . . ."	Describe the change you want the other person to consider . . .
"Because . . ."	. . . and why you think the change will help alleviate the problem.
"What do you think?"	Listen to the other person's response. Be prepared to discuss options and compromise on a solution.

How the feedback will work: "When you [do this], I feel [this way], because [of such and such]." (Pause for discussion.) "What I would like you to consider is [doing X], because I think it will accomplish [Y]. What do you think?"

Example: "When you submit work late, I get angry because it delays the rest of the project. We needed your research today in order to start the report outline." (Pause for discussion.) "I'd like you to consider finding some way to finish work on time, so we can be more productive and meet our tight deadlines. What do you think?"

2-1d Conflict Resolution

As discussed earlier, conflicts are a natural and effective part of the team process—until they become personal or disruptive. Most conflicts in groups can be prevented if a group spends time developing itself into a team, getting to know each other, establishing ground rules, and discussing norms for group behavior. However, no matter how much planning is done or how conscientiously team members work, conflicts occasionally show up. Consider using these strategies to manage team conflicts:

- **Ignore fleeting issues.** Try not to overact to minor annoyances. If someone introduces an irrelevant topic once during a meeting, you can probably let it go.
- **Think of each problem as a group problem.** It's tempting to defuse conflicts by making one member a scapegoat—for example, "We'd be finished with this report now if Sam had done his part; you can never depend on him." Rarely is one person solely responsible for the success or failure of a group effort. Were expectations clear to Sam? Was he waiting for data from someone else? Did he need help but couldn't get it from the rest of the team? What is the team's role in encouraging or allowing behavior, and what can each of you do differently to encourage more constructive behavior?
- **Be realistic about team performance.** Don't assume responsibility for others' happiness. You're responsible for being a fully contributing member of the team, behaving ethically, and treating others with respect. But the purpose of the group is not to develop lifelong friendships or to solve other people's time-management or personal problems. If someone is sick, you may decide to extend a deadline, but you do not need to spend 20 minutes of a meeting talking about the illness.
- **Encourage all contributions, even if people disagree.** You may not like what someone has to say, but differences contribute to productive conflict. Try to respond in a nonthreatening, constructive way. If the atmosphere temporarily becomes tense, you can make a light comment, laugh, or offer a compliment to restore harmony and move the group forward.
- **Address persistent conflicts directly.** If interpersonal conflict develops into a permanent part of group interactions, it's best to address the conflict directly. Working through the conflict as a team may not be fun, but it will bring you to greater understanding and a higher level of productivity. It takes a brave manager to say, "I'd like to talk about how we interact with each other at these meetings. It seems like we often end up fighting—it's not productive, and someone usually gets hurt. Does anyone else feel that way? What can we do differently?"

2-1e The Ethical Dimension of Team Communication

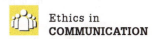
Ethics in
COMMUNICATION

When you agree to participate on a team, you accept certain standards of ethical behavior. One of these standards is to put the good of the team ahead of personal gain. In baseball, team ethics are clear. If a runner is on base, the batter may bunt the ball, knowing he'll probably be thrown out (i.e., the pitcher will get the ball to first base before he gets there). The batter makes the sacrifice for the good of the team, so that the teammate can advance a base.

Team members also have an ethical responsibility to respect each other's integrity and emotional needs. Everyone's ideas should be treated with respect, and no one should feel a loss of self-esteem. Team members should be encouraged to produce their best work, rather than feel criticized for not performing up to standard. When a baseball player hits a home run, the entire team celebrates. When a player strikes out, you'll never see team members criticizing him.

Finally, each member has an ethical responsibility to promote the team's well-being—refraining from destructive gossip, dominating meetings, and sabotaging work. When New York Yankee Alex Rodriguez admitted using performance-enhancing steroids, for example, his behavior created controversy and bruised the reputation of the entire team. One team member's behavior can undermine the team's ability to reach its goals.

2-2 Collaboration on Team Writing Projects

LO2 Collaborate to improve team writing.

The increasing complexity of the workplace makes it difficult for any person to have the time or expertise to write long or complex documents on his or her own. Team writing is common in organizations for sales proposals, recommendation reports, websites, financial analyses, and other projects that require input from people in different functions or departments.

2-2a Applying Strategies for Team Writing

Let's take an example of a start-up business. If you and two friends want to open an ice cream store and need funding—from either a bank or private investors—you would write a business plan. You would probably all do extensive research to make sure the business is feasible. Then, you might have one person write the financial projections, another write the marketing plan, and so on, until you complete the business plan. No one person will have expertise in all areas of planning your new business. When you present your idea to investors, each of you will create slides for your part of the presentation. And later, when you create a website, you may divide up the writing for that too. Consider the steps in Figure 4 when writing as part of a team.

Figure 4 | Steps for Team Writing

Identify Project Requirements	Determine project goals: who is the audience, and what result do you want? Identify project components: what research do you need, what topics will you cover, and what deliverables will you produce? Decide how you'll share information: how will you collaborate online, and when will you meet in person?
Create a Project Plan	Divide work fairly: which tasks suit each team member's strengths and interests? Create a project plan: who will complete which task by when? (See Figure 5 for a sample.)
Draft the Writing	Begin with an outline: what major sections in what order will be included in the final product? Agree on a writing style: if different people write different sections, what style will you use (e.g., how formal)? Share information: if one person will create the entire first draft for consistency, how will each team member provide his or her expertise?
Revise the Writing	Allow enough time for editing the draft: finishing a first draft the day before a project is due does not leave enough time. Provide feedback: see the tips for commenting on peers' writing (Figure 6). Make sure you have a single "voice" in the project: the final report should be coherent and cohesive. Have each team member review the entire draft: look for errors in content (gaps or repetition) and effective writing style.
Finalize the Project	Have everyone proofread the final document: you are all responsible for the final version. Be clear about delivery: who will submit the final version, in what format, and by when?

Figure 5 shows the start of a simple project plan. You can create something much more detailed, or keep it simple and build on these steps.

2-2b Commenting on Peers' Writing

Commenting on a peer's writing is useful for both of you. Your peer receives feedback to improve his or her writing, and you practice techniques to objectively evaluate others'—and eventually your own—writing. When done effectively, giving each other feedback can build a sense of community within the team. Follow the tips in Figure 6 for commenting on peer writing.

WRITING A BUSINESS PLAN		
WHO	**TASK**	**BY WHEN**
Madeline	Create wiki.	April 20
Madeline	Draft an outline for the business plan.	April 22
Griffin	Draft company overview section (mission, vision, etc.).	April 24
Beata	Draft management profiles.	April 24
Madeline	Research local ice cream shops and other businesses for competitive analysis section.	April 30
To be continued . . .		

Tips for Commenting on Peer Writing | **Figure 6**

- Read first for meaning; comment on the large issues first—the information, organization, relevance for the audience, and overall clarity.
- Assume the role of reader—not instructor. Your job is to help the writer, not to grade the assignment.
- Point out sections that you liked, as well as those you disliked, explaining specifically why you thought they were effective or ineffective (not "I liked this part," but "You did a good job of explaining this difficult concept").
- Use "I" language (not "You need to make this clearer," but "I was confused here").
- Comment helpfully—but sparingly. You don't need to point out the same misspelling a dozen times.
- Emphasize the *writer* when giving positive feedback, and emphasize the *text* (rather than the writer) when giving negative feedback: "I'm glad *you* used the most current data from the annual report." "*This argument* would be more persuasive for me if it contained the most current data."
- Avoid taking over the text. Accept that you are reading someone else's writing—not your own. Make constructive suggestions, but avoid making decisions or demands.

Communication
TECHNOLOGIES

2-2c **Using Technology for Work in Teams**

Although working in teams can be a challenge, online collaborative tools can help you manage documents and deadlines—and may improve your team communication. More businesses are using online tools and are finding these useful results: improved work processes and outcomes, better collaboration, more contributions, improved knowledge management, less email, and fewer meetings.[9,10]

Wikis are websites where groups of people collaborate on projects and edit each other's content. At LeapFrog, the toy maker, a team of researchers, product designers, and engineers uses a wiki to "log new product ideas, track concepts over the course of their development, and spark better collaboration between team members."[11] Wiggio and Wikispaces are free and offer enough functionality for small team projects, whereas enterprise wikis offer more functionality and control for large companies and major projects.

A happy customer with one of LeapFrog's interactive toys. Product teams at the toy maker use wikis to collaborate on new product designs.

Google products offer much of a wiki's functionality. On Google Drive, you can share documents (Google Docs) and revise and comment on others' work (Figure 7). If you're using Microsoft applications rather than Google Docs, you can still show revisions using the "Track Changes" and "Comment" features. Although this type of sharing doesn't offer the functionality—or the benefits—of using a wiki, these tools may be just enough for simple projects.

Figure 7 | Google Drive for Online Collaboration

COURTESY OF GOOGLE, INC

International
COMMUNICATION

2-3 Intercultural Communication

Intercultural communication (or cross-cultural communication) takes place between people from different cultures when a message is created by someone from one culture to be understood by someone from another culture. More broadly, multiculturalism refers to appreciating diversity among people, typically beyond differences in countries of origin.

To be successful in today's global, multicultural business environment, managers need to appreciate differences among people. Although English may be the standard language for business, by no means do we have one standard for all business communication. If you want to do business abroad, you need to understand different cultures and adapt to the local language of business.

With a dozen hotel brands in 91 countries, Hilton Worldwide knows the challenges of employees working and traveling internationally. The company's online resource "Culture Wise" prepares employees to navigate cultural differences. For several countries, employees learn about travel tips, business practices, employee development, negotiations, and so on.[12]

When we talk about culture, we mean the customary traits, attitudes, and behaviors of a group of people. Ethnocentrism is the belief that an individual's own cultural group is superior. This attitude hinders communication, understanding, and goodwill between business partners.

Diversity has a profound effect on our lives and poses opportunities and challenges for managers: opportunities to expand our own thinking and learn about other cultures—and challenges in communication. Although you'll learn in this chapter about communicating with people from different cultures, keep in mind that each member of a culture is an individual. We generalize here to teach broad principles for communication, but you should always adapt to individuals, who may think, feel, and act quite differently from the cultural norm or stereotype.

2-3a Cultural Differences

Cultures differ widely in the traits they value. For example, Figure 8 shows that international cultures vary in how much they emphasize individualism, time orientation, power distance, uncertainty avoidance, formality, materialism, and context sensitivity.[13]

We can look at communication differences even more deeply through a lens of "high-context" and "low-context" cultures, the last value listed in Figure 8. According to anthropologist Edward T. Hall, high-context cultures rely less on words used and more on subtle actions and reactions of communicators. Communication for these cultures is more implicit and emphasizes relationships among people. Silence is not unusual in these cultures, as it could have great meaning. Low-context cultures, on the other hand, rely on more explicit communication—the words people use. In low-context cultures, tasks are more important than relationships, so people use a direct style of communication, which we'll explore more when we discuss how to organize a message.[15] See examples of high- and low-context cultures along a continuum in Figure 9.

Emotional INTELLIGENCE

To help you understand differences, compare your own culture with another via the Hofstede Centre (geert-hofstede.com /countries.html).[14]

Cultural Values | **Figure 8**

VALUE	HIGH	LOW
Individualism: Cultures in which people see themselves first as individuals and believe that their own interests take priority.	United States Canada Great Britain Australia Netherlands	Japan China Mexico Greece Hong Kong
Time Orientation: Cultures that perceive time as a scarce resource and that tend to be impatient.	United States Switzerland	Pacific Rim and Middle Eastern countries
Power Distance: Cultures in which management decisions are made by the boss simply because he or she is the boss.	France Spain Japan Mexico Brazil	United States Israel Germany Ireland Sweden
Uncertainty Avoidance: Cultures in which people want predictable and certain futures.	Israel Japan Italy Argentina	United States Canada Australia Singapore
Formality: Cultures that attach considerable importance to tradition, ceremony, social rules, and rank.	China India Latin American countries	United States Canada Scandinavian countries
Materialism: Cultures that emphasize assertiveness and the acquisition of money and material objects.	Japan Austria Italy	Scandinavian countries
Context Sensitivity: Cultures that emphasize the surrounding circumstances (or context), make extensive use of body language, and take the time to build relationships and establish trust.	Asian and African countries	Northern European countries
To learn more about cultural differences, read Geert Hofstede, *Culture's Consequences: Comparing Values, Behaviors, Institutions and Organizations Across Nations*, 2nd ed. (Thousand Oaks, CA: Sage Publications)		

Figure 9

High- and Low-Context Cultures

High-Context Cultures

Japan
Arab Countries
Greece
Spain
Italy
England
France
North America
Scandinavian Countries
German-Speaking Countries

Low-Context Cultures

With restaurants in 119 countries, McDonald's adapts its marketing to local markets. For example, in Latin America, a collectivist society, McDonald's "Glad You Came" (#quebuenoqueviniste) campaign profiled people rather than products, which it showcases for individualist societies (Figure 10).[16]

Companies customize their websites for different cultures too. Site navigation for high-context cultures, for example, might include subtle guidance and new pages opening in several new browser windows. This strategy allows the user to select new entry points for further exploration. But for low-context cultures, which tend to have more linear thought patterns, navigational cues may be more explicit, and new pages will open within the current window, to allow the user to go back and forth easily.[17]

We all interpret events through our own mental filter, and that filter is based on our unique knowledge, experiences, and perspectives. For example, the language of time is as different among cultures as the language of words. Americans, Canadians, Germans, and Japanese are very time conscious and precise about appointments; Latin American and Middle Eastern cultures tend to be more casual about time. For example, if your Mexican host tells you that he or she will meet with you at 3:00, it's most likely *más o menos* (Spanish for "more or less") 3:00.

Businesspeople in both Asian and Latin American countries tend to favor long negotiations and slow deliberations. They exchange pleasantries for a while before getting down to business. Similarly, many non-Western cultures use silence during meetings to contemplate a decision, whereas businesspeople from the United States and Canada tend to have little tolerance for silence in business negotiations. As a result, Americans and Canadians may rush in and offer compromises and counterproposals that would have been unnecessary if they were more comfortable with the silence—and more patient.

Figure 10 | McDonald's Tailors Advertising in Colombia

McDonald's Colombia ✔
@McDonaldsCol

⚙ ＋👤 Follow

"Nunca vamos a dejar de ir a McDonald's ¡Nos encanta!" #QuéBuenoQueViniste
pic.twitter.com/cZ3GV9zG7q

🌐 View translation

↩ Reply ⇄ Retweet ★ Favorite ••• More

Daniella, Valeria, Margarita y Natalia / Colombia

Comparte tu momento con
#québuenoqueviniste
Nosotros lo compartimos
con el mundo.

qué **bueno** que **viniste**

COURTESY OF TWITTER, INC

Body language, especially gestures and eye contact, also varies among cultures. For example, our sign for "okay"—forming a circle with our forefinger and thumb—means "zero" in France, "money" in Japan, and a vulgarity in Brazil (Figure 11).[18] Americans and Canadians consider eye contact important. In Asian and many Latin American countries, however, looking a colleague full in the eye is considered an irritating sign of poor upbringing.

Same Sign, Different Meanings | **Figure 11**

OK sign
France: you're a zero;
Japan: please give me coins;
Brazil: an obscene gesture;
Mediterranean countries: an obscene gesture

Thumb and forefinger
Most countries: money;
France: something is perfect;
Mediterranean: a vulgar gesture

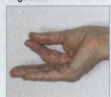

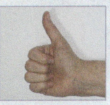

Thumbs-up
Australia: up yours;
Germany: the number one;
Japan: the number five;
Saudi Arabia: I'm winning;
Ghana: an insult;
Malaysia: the thumb is used to point rather than the finger

Thumbs-down
Most countries: something is wrong or bad

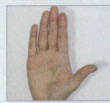

Open palm
Greece: an insult dating to ancient times;
West Africa: You have five fathers, an insult akin to calling someone a bastard

COURTESY OF CRYSTAL BULLEN. USED BY PERMISSION.

The use of physical touch is very culture specific. Many Asians do not like to be touched except for a brief handshake in greeting. However, handshakes in much of Europe tend to last much longer than in the United States and Canada, and Europeans tend to shake hands every time they see each other, perhaps several times a day. In much of Europe, men often kiss each other upon greeting; if you don't know this custom, you might react inappropriately and embarrass yourself.

Our feelings about space are partly an outgrowth of our culture and partly a result of geography and economics. For example, Americans and Canadians are used to wide-open spaces and tend to move about expansively, using hand and arm motions for emphasis. But in Japan, which has much smaller living and working spaces, such abrupt and extensive body movements are not typical. Likewise, Americans and Canadians tend to sit face-to-face so that they can maintain eye contact, whereas the Chinese and Japanese (to whom eye contact is not so important) tend to sit side-by-side during negotiations.

Also, the sense of personal space differs among cultures. In the United States and Canada, most business exchanges occur at about five feet, within the "social zone," which is closer than the "public zone," but farther than the "intimate zone" (see Figure 12). However, both in Middle Eastern and Latin American countries, this distance is too far. Businesspeople there tend to stand close enough to feel your breath as you speak. Most Americans and Canadians will unconsciously back away from such close contact.

Finally, social behavior is very culture dependent. For example, in the Japanese culture, who bows first upon meeting, how deeply the person bows, and how long the bow is held depend on one's status.

Before you travel or interact with people from other countries, become familiar with these and other customs, for example, giving (and accepting) gifts, exchanging business cards, the degree of formality expected, and how people entertain.

Figure 12 | Personal Spaces for Social Interaction

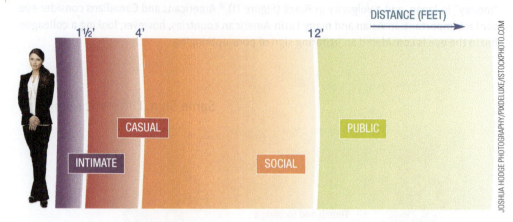

DISTANCE (FEET)

1½' 4' 12'

CASUAL

PUBLIC

INTIMATE

SOCIAL

JOSHUA HODGE PHOTOGRAPHY/PIXDELUXE/ISTOCKPHOTO.COM

2-3b Group-Oriented Behavior

As shown earlier, the business environment in capitalistic societies, such as the United States and Canada, places great value on how individuals contribute to an organization. Individual effort is often stressed more than group effort, and a competitive atmosphere prevails. But in other cultures, originality and independence of judgment are not valued as highly as teamwork. The Japanese say, "A nail standing out will be hammered down." The Japanese go to great lengths to reach decisions through group consensus.

The Toyoda family changed the company name to Toyota in 1937 for its clearer sound and more favorable number of strokes for writing the name.[19]

Closely related to the concept of group-oriented behavior is the notion of "saving face." People save face when they avoid embarrassment. When Akio Toyoda, the Japanese president of Toyota Motor Corporation, apologized for many vehicle recalls, he demonstrated emotion and great humility—far more than might have been expected of an American business leader.

AP IMAGES/KOJI SASAHARA

Akio Toyoda apologizes at a recall press conference for Toyota Motor Company.

Human relationships are highly valued in Japanese cultures and are embodied in the concept of *wa*, the Japanese pursuit of harmony. This concept makes it difficult for the Japanese to say "no" to a request because it would be impolite. They are very reluctant to offend others—even if they unintentionally mislead them instead. A "yes" to a Japanese person might mean "Yes, I understand you" rather than "Yes, I agree." To an American, the Japanese style of communication may seem too indirect and verbose. At one point during Toyota's testimony before Congress, the committee chair said, "What I'm trying to find out . . . is that a yes or a no?" To Japanese viewers, this sounded rude and disrespectful.[20]

Latin Americans also tend to avoid an outright "no" in their business dealings, preferring instead a milder, less explicit response. For successful intercultural communications, you have to read between the lines because what is left unsaid or unwritten may be just as important as what is said or written.

2-3c Strategies for Communicating Across Cultures

When communicating with people from different cultures, whether abroad or at home, use the following strategies.

Maintain Formality

Compared to U.S. and Canadian cultures, most other cultures value and respect a much more formal approach to business dealings. Call others by their titles and family names unless specifically asked to do otherwise. By both verbal and nonverbal clues, convey an attitude of propriety and decorum. Although you may think these strategies sound cold, most other cultures consider these appropriate.

Show Respect

Learn about your host country—its geography, form of government, largest cities, culture, current events, and so on. Delta Air Lines missed a step when congratulating the United States on a victory against Ghana during the World Cup. In a tweet, the company showed the United States represented by the Statue of Liberty and Ghana represented by a giraffe (Figure 13). Jokes ensued: the only giraffes in Ghana are at a zoo and a showing of *The Lion King.*[21]

Delta Air Lines Misrepresents Ghana | **Figure 13**

 Delta ✓
@Delta

 Follow

Congrats team #USA🇺🇸! Nice goal @clint_dempsey @soundersfc! #USAvGHA #USMNT #DeltaSEA
pic.twitter.com/7C8iRzPzoa

↩ Reply ⇄ Retweet ★ Favorite ••• More

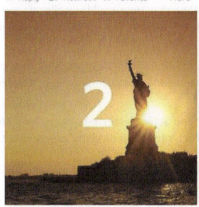 

COURTESY OF TWITTER, INC.

When interacting with people from other cultures, withhold judgment. Although different from your own, attitudes held by an entire culture are probably based on sound reasoning. Listen carefully to what is being communicated, trying to understand the other person's perspective.

Expect to adapt to different cultures. For Japanese business practices, it is not uncommon for the evening's entertainment to extend beyond dinner. You can expect a second round of drinks or an invitation to a coffee shop. Refusing a drink during social business engagements may even be considered rude or impolite. If you're not a drinker, think about how you would handle the situation in advance.

Communicate Clearly

To make your oral and written messages understood, follow these guidelines:

- Avoid slang, jargon, and other figures of speech. Expressions such as "They'll eat that up" or "out in left field" can confuse even a fluent English speaker.

- Be specific and illustrate your points with concrete examples.
- Provide and solicit feedback, summarize frequently, write a summary of points covered in a meeting, ask your counterpart for his or her understanding, and encourage questions.
- Use a variety of media: handouts (distributed before the meeting to allow time for reading), visuals, models, and so on.
- Speak plainly and slowly (but not so slowly as to be condescending); choose your words carefully.
- Use humor sparingly; humor is risky—it may be lost on your counterpart, or worse, it may offend someone.

People who know more about, and are more comfortable with, different cultures are more effective managers because they reap the benefits of international business and avoid misunderstandings.

<table>
<tr><td>LO4 Communicate with diverse populations.</td></tr>
</table>

2-4 Diversity and Inclusion Within the United States

Of course, we have much diversity within the United States. Each year, the United States becomes even more diverse, which creates tremendous opportunities for companies—and a few challenges for business communicators.

2-4a The Value of Diversity

Imagine a company in which everyone is exactly the same. How would you allocate work when everyone has the same skills? How would you generate new ideas when everyone thinks the same way?

Diversity among employees provides richness and strength for an organization. People from varied backgrounds and perspectives help companies solve problems, make better decisions, and create a much more interesting place to work.

Companies recognize the need for diversity and actively seek employees from different backgrounds. Clothing retailer Abercrombie & Fitch's focus on diversity is prominent on the career pages of its website (Figure 14).

Figure 14 | Abercrombie & Fitch's Careers Website

Many companies today go beyond thinking simply about diversity—which tends to focus on numbers of people—and strive for inclusion. Do all employees feel included and welcomed at work? Are they able to contribute fully to an organization, or do invisible barriers prevent people from participating in relevant meetings, making significant decisions, getting their ideas implemented, and getting promoted? Focusing on an inclusive work environment ensures that all employees can reach their full potential with a company.

As you look at companies' websites, you'll see that many of them, like Abercrombie & Fitch's, refer to both diversity and inclusion. State Farm, the insurance company, defines diversity and inclusion as follows:

> **Diversity** is the collective strength of experiences, skills, talents, perspectives, and cultures that each agent and employee brings to State Farm. It's how we create a dynamic business environment to serve our customers.

> **Inclusion** is about respecting and valuing the unique dimension each agent and employee adds to the organization. We recognize that agents and employees are at their creative and productive best when they work in an inclusive work environment.[22]

PepsiCo Chairman and CEO Indra Nooyi promotes bringing our whole selves to work.

PepsiCo Chairman and CEO Indra K. Nooyi believes bringing our whole selves to work is the key to inclusion:

> The only way we will hold on to the best and brightest is to grasp them emotionally. No one may feel excluded. It's our job to draw the best out of everyone. That means employees must be able to immerse their whole selves in a work environment in which they can develop their careers, families and philanthropy, and truly believe they are cared for.[23]

Nooyi wants people to be who they are at home and at work—not playing a role on the job. One of her eight leadership lessons is "Put your whole self into the job: head, heart and hands."[24]

We work (and live) best together when we know each other. This requires us to be vulnerable sometimes and awkward other times. It can be difficult to share we who are and ask for what's important to us. But this kind of openness—both revealing ourselves and accepting what we learn about others—is essential to an inclusive work environment.[25]

2-4b Diversity of Thought

When people think of diversity or inclusion, they often jump to differences in race and sex, but the concept of diversity is far more complex and interesting. When you're working with a team, you notice how differently everyone approaches a project. Karen sees only problems, Kai jumps right to a solution, and Stephanie wants to put together a schedule.

What causes these differences in thought and approach? We all come from different places and bring with us what has shaped us. Growing up in a large family, practicing Judaism, living in an urban area, struggling financially, being diagnosed with Asperger's, being gay—these qualities and experiences make us who we are. The Chancellor's Committee on Diversity at The University of California, San Francisco, defines diversity as "The variety of experiences and perspective which arise from differences in race, culture, religion, mental or physical abilities, heritage, age, gender, sexual orientation, gender identity, and other characteristics."[26]

Diversity of thought challenges our notion that people within a group all think and act alike. We are far more diverse than our skin color, age, or sex reveal. You may hear people in underrepresented minority groups referred to as "diverse," but they are no more diverse than White males (who are likely members of a minority group as well).[27]

Deloitte calls diversity of thought "the new frontier. . . . a more powerful and nuanced kind of diversity." The consulting firm offers ways managers can manage thought diversity, for example, by hiring for skill gaps and considering candidates who don't always get the "right" answers and by encouraging debate and facilitating tension, rather than avoiding it.[28] This thinking about tension is consistent with team communication, discussed earlier in this chapter: a certain degree of conflict is healthy and necessary for organizations.

2-4c Strategies for Communicating Across Differences

Communication, particularly language, is an important part of helping people feel comfortable to express alternative ideas. How we interact with people affects how they feel about themselves and ultimately how they contribute to the organization. Following are tips for communicating across differences.

Emotional INTELLIGENCE

What about your background affects how you communicate with others? What biases may get in the way of your relationships with others?

Race and Ethnicity

Race, ethnicity, and heritage are complex in the United States. Just because someone looks like a particular race doesn't mean that person identifies with it. He could be adopted, from a mixed-race home, or a third-generation American. Repeatedly hearing "Where are you from?" can get tiresome for someone who has lived in the States his entire life.

Even our definition of "minority" is becoming unclear. By 2050, although the non-Hispanic White population will remain the largest group, no one group will represent a majority of the United States.[29] Will we all be "minorities"?

Terminology used to refer to groups is constantly evolving. The U.S. Census Form allowed people to select from several categories to identify their origin and race (Figures 15 and 16).[30] But

Figure 15 Question 8 on the U.S. Census Form

8. Is Person 1 of Hispanic, Latino, or Spanish origin?

- ☐ No, not of Hispanic, Latino, or Spanish origin
- ☐ Yes, Mexican, Mexican Am., Chicano
- ☐ Yes, Puerto Rican
- ☐ Yes, Cuban
- ☐ Yes, another Hispanic, Latino, or Spanish origin — *Print origin, for example, Argentinean, Colombian, Dominican, Nicaraguan, Salvadoran, Spaniard, and so on.*

UNITED STATES CENSUS, "EXPLORE THE FORM," HTTP://2010.CENSUS.GOV/2010CENSUS/ABOUT/INTERACTIVE-FORM.PHP

Figure 16 Question 9 on the U.S. Census Form

9. What is Person 1's race? *Mark* ☒ *one or more boxes.*

- ☐ White
- ☐ Black, African Am., or Negro
- ☐ American Indian or Alaska Native — *Print name of enrolled or principal tribe.*
- ☐ Asian Indian
- ☐ Chinese
- ☐ Filipino
- ☐ Other Asian — *Print race, for example, Hmong, Laotian, Thai, Pakistani, Cambodian, and so on.*
- ☐ Japanese
- ☐ Korean
- ☐ Vietnamese
- ☐ Native Hawaiian
- ☐ Guamanian or Chamorro
- ☐ Samoan
- ☐ Other Pacific Islander — *Print race, for example, Fijian, Tongan, and so on.*
- ☐ Some other race — *Print race.*

UNITED STATES CENSUS, "EXPLORE THE FORM," HTTP://2010.CENSUS.GOV/2010CENSUS/ABOUT/INTERACTIVE-FORM.PHP

even these categories may not apply to how each person prefers to be identified. Some White Americans prefer the term *European American* or *Caucasian*, and some Asian Americans prefer to be identified by their country of origin—for example, *Chinese American* or *Indonesian American*. Others prefer different designations. What we call ourselves is not a trivial matter. The terms used to refer to other groups are not ours to establish, and it's easy enough to use terms that others prefer.

Sex and Gender Identity

Of course, more differences exist within each gender group than between groups. We should be careful not to stereotype and wrongly assume that *all* women or *all* men communicate or behave in one way. And yet, recognizing that common differences do exist may help us understand each other better and improve communication overall (see Figure 17).[31]

Differences in Male and Female Communication Patterns | **Figure 17**

MALE	FEMALE
Communicate primarily to preserve independence and status by displaying knowledge and skill	Communicate largely to build rapport
Prefer to work out their problems by themselves	Prefer to talk out solutions with another person
Are more likely to be critical	Are more likely to compliment the work of a coworker
Tend to interrupt to dominate a conversation or to change the subject	Tend to interrupt to agree with or to support what another person is saying
Tend to be more directive in their conversation	Emphasize politeness
Tend to internalize successes and to externalize failures: "That's one of my strengths." "We should have been given more time."	Tend to externalize successes and to internalize failures: "I was lucky." "I'm just not good at that."
Speak differently to other men than they do to women	Speak differently to other women than they do to men

Again, these differences are best thought of along a continuum, with plenty of overlap between men and women. Also, for most of us, whether we're male or female is an easy question, but for some, it's not so straightforward. What a culture defines as male or female may not fit how an individual self-identifies. For example, a transgender person may not identify with his or her biological sex or socially defined gender. An individual's biological sex may be different from what we can see. Therefore, male or female pronouns (he or she, him or her) may not work for everyone, and we should be open to other labels to describe one's gender identity. Recognizing these issues, Facebook offers more than 50 gender options for user profiles.[32]

In addition to accepting potential differences, we can improve working relationships by avoiding gender-specific language. Follow the strategies in Figure 18 for using inclusive, gender-neutral language.

Age

Because people are living and working longer, more generations are represented in the workforce. Much has been written about differences among the generations, but according to recent research, some of these differences—particularly the negative effects—may be overstated. According to one study of approximately 100,000 people in 34 countries within North America, Europe, and Asia Pacific, 42% of employees say they have experienced intergenerational conflict at work, but the same percentage say that generational differences *improve* productivity. These numbers are very consistent by generation and geographic region. Between 68% and 75% of employees do adapt their communication style for colleagues from different generations; however, the method people prefer for communicating (e.g., face-to-face or email) is similar across generations and countries.[33,34]

Figure 18 | Strategies for Inclusive, Gender-Neutral Language

1. Use neutral job titles to avoid implying that a job is held by only men or only women.

INSTEAD OF	USE
salesman	sales representative, sales associate
male nurse	nurse
waitress	server
stewardess	flight attendant
businessmen	employees, managers

2. Avoid words and phrases that unnecessarily imply gender.

INSTEAD OF	USE
best man for the job	best person for the job
executives and their wives	executives and their partners
you guys	everyone
housewife	homemaker
manmade	artificial, manufactured
mankind	people, human beings
manpower	human resources, employees

3. Use appropriate personal titles and salutations.

- If a woman has a professional title, use it (Dr. Martha Ralston, the Rev. Deborah Connell).
- Follow a woman's preference in being addressed as *Miss*, *Mrs.*, or *Ms.*
- If a woman's marital status or her preference is unknown, use *Ms.*
- If you don't know the reader's sex or gender, use a gender-neutral salutation (Dear Investor, Dear Neighbor, Dear Customer, Dear Policyholder). Or, you may use the full name in the salutation (Dear Chris Andrews, Dear Terry Brooks).

4. Avoid *he* or *his* as generic pronouns (e.g., "Each manager must evaluate *his* employees annually"). This is debatable, but is easy enough to work around with these alternatives:

- Use plural nouns and pronouns. "All managers must evaluate their employees annually." (But not: "Each manager must evaluate *their* employees annually," which uses a plural pronoun to refer to a singular noun.)
- Use second-person pronouns (*you, your*). "You must evaluate your employees annually."
- Omit the pronoun. "Each manager must evaluate employees annually."
- Use *his or her* (sparingly). "Each manager must evaluate his or her employees annually."
- Avoid using "one" as a singular pronoun, which is considered too formal for business communication in the United States.

It's best to be aware of potential differences but—as discussed throughout this section—not to judge people based only on their age. Assuming that an older worker doesn't understand technology or that a younger worker doesn't understand the business is unfair to individuals and may lead to bad business decisions. Also, avoid age-biased language, such as referring to people as "old," "senior citizens," or worse.

Sexual Orientation

Although same-sex marriage is now legal and has become more accepted in the United States, can gays and lesbians bring their whole selves to work? Can they speak about their social and family lives, just as straight people talk about theirs? To pave the way for others, Apple CEO Tim Cook wrote "I'm proud to be gay" in an open letter in *BloombergBusinessweek.*[35] In his chapter in *Passion and Purpose,* Josh Bronstein talks about his decision to "come out"—to be openly gay at work:

On *The Tonight Show*, actor Jonah Hill apologized for a homophobic remark.

> The energy required to hide my identity from those who I assumed wouldn't like it distracted me from the work I was being paid to do. Since then, being openly gay has only helped me professionally—I've benefited from a stronger sense of community and a professional network that spans functional silos, more confidence when speaking with senior leaders, and the comfort of always being able to use accurate pronouns.[36]

Homophobic and heterosexist language is still far too common and should never be used in the workplace. Jonah Hill, actor and outspoken supporter of gay rights, insulted an aggressive paparazzo with a homophobic slur. He apologized on *The Tonight Show*:

> I wanted to hurt him back, and I said the most hurtful word that I could think of at that moment. I didn't mean it in the sense of the word. . . . [but] that doesn't matter. . . . The word I chose was grotesque, and no one deserves to say or hear words like that. . . . I've been a supporter of the LGBTQ [lesbian, gay, bisexual, transgender, queer/questioning] community my entire life, and I completely let the members of that community and everybody else down . . .[37]

Ability

Managers who want to hire the best employees for their companies go beyond the legal requirements and accommodate people with disabilities. One way to think about people is that we're all "differently abled"—each with strengths as well as areas that need development or accommodation. You may have a great eye for design but need help with construction. No one is perfect.

Always, everywhere, avoid using language like, "Are you deaf?" "He's a little slow," or "What are you, blind?" Jokes about people with disabilities don't go over well.

Instead of using potentially disparaging language, use "people-first language," which respects people's dignity and avoids labels.[38] With people-first language, you identify the person before his or her disability; for example, say, "Alejandro is a sophomore who has epilepsy," rather than referring to "the epileptic"—there's much more to Alejandro than his disability. Also avoid referring to someone as "handicapped." We still have "handicapped" parking spaces—an outdated term—but, when referring to people, a handicap may imply a limitation and a disadvantage. A high school in Texas printed yearbooks that referred to some students with special needs as "mentally retarded." Understandably, parents and students were "shocked" and "appalled."[39]

The best approach for communicating with people with disabilities is to use your natural way of speaking and natural eye contact. Try to be yourself.

Religion

Whether we were raised in a certain tradition or adopted it later in life, religion helps people create meaning in their lives. At many companies, discussing religious beliefs, like political beliefs, is discouraged. But some companies allow people to practice what is most important to them during the day. Technology companies, for example, are beginning to use prayer rooms as a recruiting tool. In-flight Internet service provider Gogo is building dedicated spaces for Muslims and others to use for prayer or meditation.[40]

At the same time, people who don't practice religion should not be forced to do so. Unless the organization is identified with a particular religion, and new hires know this before accepting a job, employees may not want to, for example, pray before business meals.

Be mindful about religious differences. Not everyone wants to hear "Merry Christmas" when it's not their holiday. Try to avoid assumptions based on appearance, names, or the majority.

Income Level or Socioeconomic Status

Wealth has become a polarizing issue around the world. In the United States, for example, the Occupy Movement has inspired protests about—and backlash from—the so-called "one-percent" of earners, and McDonald's and other companies are under fire for paying low wages.

Workers protest for higher wages at McDonald's.

In the office, family background and income level may give people an advantage. Someone raised in a family of business executives may understand important work behaviors, for example, what to wear and how to interact with senior-level managers. What if someone can't afford to wear tailored clothes or go out to lunch with the team? Try to be sensitive to financial pressures and how they can affect relationships and perception.

Other Characteristics

What else do we bring to work? Veteran status, political views, whether we have children, and many other qualities make each of us unique and full contributors to an organization. We are all members of different groups with different customs, values, and attitudes.

2-4d Offending and Taking Offense

In a truly inclusive working environment, we encourage differences rather than squelch them. This kind of management inspires diversity of thought and ultimately leads to better decisions.

But this isn't necessarily an easy way to work, and sometimes, we mess up. We make assumptions that aren't accurate and use terms that unintentionally offend. In her book *35 Dumb Things Well-Intended People Say,* Maura Cullen tells about using the word *blackmail* during a meeting, which someone found to have racial connotations.[41] Was the woman being overly sensitive? Who's to judge? Cullen didn't; she simply replaced the word with *coerced* and then spoke with her colleague after the meeting so they could understand each other better.

We have to be our own advocates. When we bring our whole selves to work, we take risks— and we have responsibilities. You may have to educate coworkers who don't know you and what you need.

When something offends you at work, you have every right to say so, but try to address issues rationally. Calling someone a racist likely won't improve your working relationship or change the person's behavior. Use the tips for team communication at the beginning of the chapter for giving constructive feedback and resolving conflicts. With this approach, you'll contribute to the type of place where everyone feels valued and wants to work.

A Diversity Statement for Gap

3Ps
‹ IN ACTION

⟩⟩⟩ PURPOSE

As the new diversity manager for Gap, you have been asked to write a statement on the company's career web pages.

⟩⟩⟩ PROCESS

You consider the following questions as you craft your statement:

1. **Who are the primary and secondary audiences for the message?**
   The primary audience includes prospective employees. Customers also may visit the site.

2. **What do you want to convey to these audiences?**
   I want to portray Gap as a place that welcomes everyone to work and shop. I need to include our commitment as an equal opportunity employer, but I want to go beyond that generic statement.

3. **What else is important to include?**
   Particularly for the primary audience of prospective employees, the message should include employees' responsibilities for maintaining a discrimination- and harassment-free working and shopping environment.

⟩⟩⟩ PRODUCT

You produce the following statement, which you'll find at www.gapinc.com/content/gapinc /html/careers/lifeatgap/diversity.html.

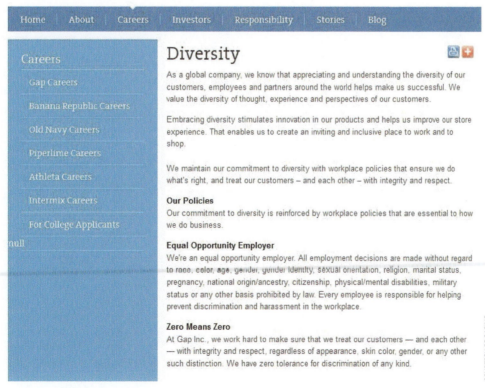

COURTESY OF GAPINC

3Ps IN PRACTICE

Learning About Bangladesh

>>> PURPOSE

As an employee at Gap, you're going to visit Bangladesh to conduct a brand standards training session to ensure consistency in all stores. Your manager asks you to prepare for your trip by researching the country using the categories in Hilton Worldwide's "Culture Wise" resource discussed earlier in the chapter.

>>> PROCESS

1. How would you describe Bangladesh? What's important to know about its history, people, location, and culture?

2. What common phrases and names will be important for you to know?

3. What do's and don'ts would help you be successful in your interactions with people?

4. What do you need to prepare for the travel: flights, hotels, getting around, and so on?

5. What business practices will you be sure to follow?

>>> PRODUCT

Write an email to your manager summarizing your research.

> SUMMARY

LO1 Communicate effectively and ethically in small groups.

Teams can accomplish more and better quality work in less time than individuals can if the teams function properly. Otherwise, teams can waste time and cause interpersonal conflicts. Conflict about ideas is a helpful part of the group process, but interpersonal conflicts are detrimental. Consensus and conformity can lead to productivity, but too much focus on either can lead to groupthink.

When a team first forms, group members should get to know each other and decide how they'll operate. They should acknowledge the need for positive and negative feedback and know how to give productive feedback, particularly on team writing. When problems arise, group members should react to them appropriately, consider them as group problems, and be realistic about what to expect from the group.

LO2 Collaborate to improve team writing.

For group writing projects, team members should identify project requirements, create a project plan, draft the writing, revise the writing, and finalize the project. Teams find it useful to collaborative online for writing projects. Wikis can lead to improved work processes, more contributions, better work outcomes, and fewer meetings.

LO3 Communicate with intercultural audiences.

Understanding cultural differences is essential to success in a global business environment. Although individuals often defy stereotypes, consider differences in context sensitivity, feelings about space, group-oriented behavior, and other factors. When communicating with people from other cultures, maintain formality, show respect, and write and speak clearly.

LO4 Communicate with diverse populations.

In the United States, the population is becoming increasingly diverse. This diversity brings great value to companies and encourages us to appreciate differences and create an inclusive workplace. You can demonstrate respect through your language choices about race and ethnicity, sex and gender identity, age, sexual orientation, ability, and other variables among employees.

> EXERCISES

1. **Analyze a team's communication.**

   Think about a recent situation when you worked as part of a team. In retrospect, what worked well about the communication, and what could have been improved? Call or meet with one of your former team members to talk through your assessment and find out how he or she viewed the experience. What can you learn from this experience that may help you work with teams in the future?

   > **LO1** Communicate effectively and ethically in small groups.

2. **Explain a team's communication.**

   After analyzing a team's communication, briefly describe for the class (in two or three minutes) the purpose of the team and how well you functioned. Describe how the variables of group communication—conflict, conformity, and consensus—were or were not incorporated. Was groupthink an issue? How did the other team member view the experience? In what ways was this similar or different from your own, and why do you think this might be?

3. **Provide feedback.**

   Imagine that you're working as part of a team to create a five-year marketing plan. Everyone had agreed to have his or her part drafted by the time your team met today. What would be an appropriate response to each of the following situations at today's meeting? Discuss your responses in small groups.

   a. Fred did not have his part ready (although this is the first time he is late).

   b. Thales did not have his part ready (the third time this year he has missed a deadline).

   c. Anita not only had her part completed but also had drafted an attractive design for the final document.

   d. Sunggong was 45 minutes late for the meeting because his car had skidded into a ditch as a result of last night's snowstorm.

   e. Elvira left a message that she would have to miss the meeting because she was working on another report, which is due tomorrow.

4. **Identify poor team behavior in a business movie.**

   Watch a movie about business: *The Social Network, The Company Men, Office Space, Thank You for Smoking, Up in the Air, Boiler Room,* or something else. See how many flaws in their interactions you can identify. For example, what incidents of disruptive, interpersonal conflict do you observe? How do individuals demonstrate a lack of respect for each other? How do they provide feedback to each other?

LO2 Collaborate to improve team writing.

5. **Comment on a peer's writing.**

   Use the "Tips for Commenting on Peer Writing" to provide feedback on another student's writing. Exchange draft documents with another student and use "Track Changes" in Microsoft Word to make comments. After you have commented on each other's work, review each other's suggestions. Then, discuss your reactions to the other's feedback. To what extent do you feel that your partner followed the tips presented in this chapter? How could your partner have given you better feedback?

6. **Create a project plan.**

   Working in groups of four or five, imagine that you are creating a new website for a local business. First, choose a business that all of you know well. Next, complete the first two steps for team writing: identify project requirements and create a project plan.

7. **Contribute to Wikipedia.**

   To experience a wiki, contribute to an article on Wikipedia. Find a topic on which you consider yourself an expert, for example, your college, your neighborhood, a sport, or a game. Make one or two changes to a relevant article on Wikipedia. In one week, track your contribution: did it hold, or was it changed by someone else?

8. **Set up a wiki.**

   Set up a wiki for a class project or campus organization. Take the lead to structure the site, post initial content, and encourage everyone to participate. If you have already used wikis with teams, try a different site (e.g., Wiggio or Google Drive) to experience a new approach and to see whether you prefer one to another.

LO3 Communicate with intercultural audiences.

9. **Interpret two messages from international offices.**

   Imagine that you work for the law firm Dewey, Wright, and Howe as an intern. With a team of employees, you are working on an orientation program for new interns. Part of your plan is to have interns do research online about the firm before their date of hire. You believe this research, which will take about two hours, will give new interns a jump-start before they start working.

In response to your draft Orientation Plan, you receive two emails from partners in the firm—the first from the German office and the second from the Japanese office. From these messages, you realize that Mr. Yamashita misunderstood your intent: he thought your plan was for interns to come to the office before their start date, but you meant only for them to do research online.

Working in small groups, discuss how you interpret these messages. What feedback are the partners giving you? Consider cultural differences discussed in this chapter.

These email messages are part of the company scenario Dewey, Wright, and Howe, available at www.cengagebrain.com.

Email

To: Team Members
From: Karla Zimmermann, Managing Partner, Berlin Office
Cc: Akira Yamashita, Managing Partner, Tokyo Office
Sondra Simmons, HR Manager, Corporate Office
Subject: **Feedback on Your Proposed Orientation Plan for Interns**

I do not like having interns spend time on Dewey business before their start date. We would need to pay them for work before they are officially employed.

The rest of your plan is acceptable to me.

KZ

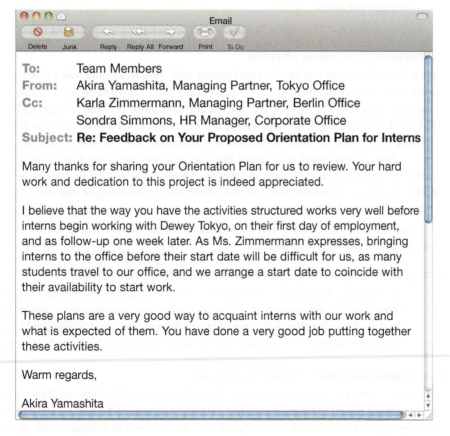

Email

To: Team Members
From: Akira Yamashita, Managing Partner, Tokyo Office
Cc: Karla Zimmermann, Managing Partner, Berlin Office
Sondra Simmons, HR Manager, Corporate Office
Subject: **Re: Feedback on Your Proposed Orientation Plan for Interns**

Many thanks for sharing your Orientation Plan for us to review. Your hard work and dedication to this project is indeed appreciated.

I believe that the way you have the activities structured works very well before interns begin working with Dewey Tokyo, on their first day of employment, and as follow-up one week later. As Ms. Zimmermann expresses, bringing interns to the office before their start date will be difficult for us, as many students travel to our office, and we arrange a start date to coincide with their availability to start work.

These plans are a very good way to acquaint interns with our work and what is expected of them. You have done a very good job putting together these activities.

Warm regards,

Akira Yamashita

10. **Adapt to cultural differences in email responses.**

   After you discuss your interpretation of the emails in the previous exercise, individually write separate email responses to Ms. Zimmermann and Mr. Yamashita. How can you address their concerns about the Orientation Plan, while adapting your communication style for cultural differences?

11. **Research international communication and write an advice memo.**

   Working with a teammate, select a country for your research. Using three or more websites, outline cultural differences of the country that might impact international business dealings. Look for differences regarding customs, use of space, hand gestures, time orientation, social behavior, how business is conducted, and other business-related issues. Write a memo with your advice to someone planning to travel to this country for business.

12. **Present cultural differences to the class.**

   Choose one or two students from your class to discuss their experience traveling internationally. The students may use the following questions to guide their ten-minute presentation:

   - Which country did you visit, and what was the reason for your trip?
   - What surprised you most about the people? What were the most obvious differences you noticed from your own culture?
   - How do you interpret the cultural values of the region? Review the following dimensions discussed in this chapter: individualism, time orientation, power distance, uncertainty avoidance, formality, materialism, and context sensitivity.
   - What observations did you make about the people's feelings about space and group-oriented behavior?
   - What advice would you give to someone planning to do business in the region?

13. **Analyze an intercultural situation.**

   Joe arrived 15 minutes late for his appointment with Itaru Nakamura, sales manager for a small manufacturer to which Joe's firm hoped to sell parts. "Sorry to be late," he apologized, "but you know how the local drivers are. At any rate, since I'm late, let's get right down to brass tacks." Joe began to pace back and forth in the small office. "The way I see it, if you and I can come to some agreement this afternoon, we'll be able to get the rest to agree. After all, who knows more about this than you and I do?" Joe sat down opposite his colleague and looked him straight in the eye. "So what do you say? Can we agree on the basics and let our assistants hammer out the details?" His colleague was silent for a few moments, then said, "Yes."

   Discuss Joe's intercultural skills. Specifically, what mistakes did he make? What did Nakamura's response probably mean?

14. **Analyze how well a company adapts to international audiences.**

   Choose a large, global company and explore their website. Do you find multiple versions of the company's site for different countries? In what ways does the company adapt its writing style, use of graphics, and other features to adapt to different cultures? Write a brief report on your findings, and include screenshots of the company's website(s) to illustrate your points.

LO4 Communicate with diverse populations.

15. **Learn about someone's cultural background.**

   Interview a partner about one aspect of his or her cultural background. First, ask your partner which aspect of his or her cultural identity (e.g., race and ethnicity, sex and gender identity, age, sexual orientation, ability, religion, income level or socioeconomic status) he or she feels comfortable discussing.

You might ask questions such as the following:

- In what ways do you identify with this characteristic?
- How, if at all, do you think this characteristic distinguishes you from other people?
- How do you feel similar to others who share this characteristic? Within your group, what differences do you observe?
- In what ways does your background influence how you communicate with others?
- In a work environment, in what ways have you seen this characteristic contribute to your performance and business relationships?

Next, switch roles so you can share information about one aspect of your own background.

16. Share your background with your peers.

In groups of three, share some of your background that people may not know about you. You might talk with your peers first to determine what you're comfortable sharing with each other and how you would like each other to react. Then, if you feel comfortable, take some risks in telling your peers something about yourself.

17. Respond to domestic intercultural issues.

As a manager, how would you respond to each of the following situations? What kind of helpful advice can you give to each party?

a. Alton gets angry when several of the people he works with talk among themselves in their native language. He suspects they are talking and laughing about him. As a result, he tends to avoid them and to complain about them to others.

b. Jason, a slightly built office worker, feels intimidated when talking to his supervisor, a much larger man who is of a different racial background. As a result, he often is unable to negotiate effectively.

c. Raisa is embarrassed when she must talk to Roger, a subordinate who has a major facial disfigurement. She doesn't know how to look at him. As a result, she tends to avoid meeting with him face-to-face.

d. Sheila, the only female manager on staff, gets incensed whenever her colleague Alex apologizes to her after using profanity during a meeting.

e. When Jim arrived as the only male real estate agent in a small office, it was made clear to him that he would have to get his own coffee and clean up after himself—just like everyone else. Yet whenever the FedEx truck delivers a heavy carton, the women always ask him to lift the package.

18. Use inclusive language.

Revise the following sentences to eliminate biased language.

a. The mayor opened contract talks with the union representing local policemen.

b. While the salesmen are at the convention, their wives will be treated to a tour of the city's landmarks.

c. Our company gives each foreman the day off on his birthday.

d. Our public relations director, Heather Marshall, will ask her young secretary, Bonita Carwell, to take notes during the president's speech.

e. Neither Mr. Batista nor his secretary, Doris, had met the new family.

19. Discuss your views of using inclusive language.

In small groups, discuss your views about the previous sentences. If you worked for a company and read or overheard each of these statements, would you be offended? Do you believe others might be offended? Discuss the value—and potential downsides—of using inclusive language.

20. **Improve diversity training.**

On the television show *The Office*, the company holds "Diversity Day," a misguided attempt at diversity training for the staff. Watch Season 1, Episode 2, and see all that goes wrong. Then, be prepared to talk in class about how a diversity training program could be successful. (Watch an excerpt of the episode on YouTube: http://bit.ly/uayAf3.)

21. **Use gender-neutral language.**

Identify at least one gender-neutral word for each of the following words:

   a. Policeman

   b. Clergyman

   c. Fireman

   d. Salesman

   e. Mailman

   f. Bellman

   g. Handyman

   h. Repairman

   i. Manhole cover

   j. Waitress

22. **Discuss your views about Apple CEO Tim Cook's announcement.**

In small groups, discuss your thoughts about Tim Cook's article in *BloombergBusinessweek*. Read his statement (buswk.co/1DBoBfo) and pay attention to the organization, word choice, and tone. Why do you think Cook chose an open article to confirm that he's gay? Was this the best choice? What reaction do you think he expected from shareholders, customers, and employees, and other stakeholders?

COMPANY SCENARIO

Dewey, Wright, and Howe

Dewey, Wright, and Howe LLP

Dewey, Wright, and Howe is an international law firm that hires college interns. This company scenario, described at www.cengagebrain.com, challenges you to face many of the issues discussed in Chapter 2. Working through the activities for Dewey, Wright, and Howe, you'll have the opportunity to do the following:

- Collaborate in a wiki to produce team results.
- Practice participating in meetings and giving and receiving feedback.
- Manage conflict in a multicultural environment.

Your team of interns at Dewey is asked to create an Orientation Plan for new hires—and you'll run into a few obstacles along the way: conflicting messages, different communication styles, and a questionable ethical situation. But don't worry—you'll have plenty of direction with a detailed work plan, and you'll rely on your team members for good, sound advice throughout the process.

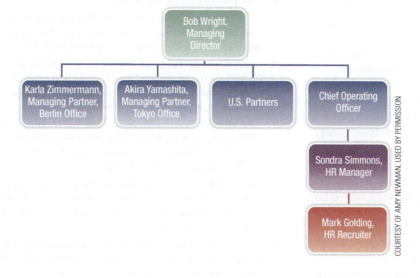

Endnotes

1. Richard Feloni, "Gap's Response to Racist Graffiti on a Subway Ad Was Perfect," *Business Insider*, November 27, 2013, www.businessinsider.com/gap-responds-to-defacement-of-sikh-ad-2013-11#ixzz3688udMde, accessed April 28, 2015.

2. Richard Feloni.

3. Christine Hauser, "A Defaced Gap Ad Goes from the Subway to the Web to Its Demise," *The Lede,* November 27, 2013, November 27, *2013*, http://thelede.blogs.nytimes.com/2013/11/27/a-defaced-gap-ad-goes-from-the-subway-to-the-web-to-its-demise, accessed April 28, 2015.

4. "Conflict Resolution: Don't Get Mad, Get Promoted," *Training* (June 2002): 20.

5. John R. Pierce, "Communication," *Scientific American* 227 (September 1972): 36.

6. Michael Schneider, "Boy Killed by Bus on Disney Property Identified," Associated Press, April 2, 2010, www.msnbc.msn.com/id/36137020 /ns/travel-news/t/boy-killed-bus-disney-property-identified/, accessed April 28, 2015.

7. "Managers Are Ignoring Their Employees," Leadership IQ, December 2, 2009, www.leadershipiq.com, accessed December 30, 2012.

8. Adapted from Peter R. Scholtes, *The Team Handbook*, 2nd ed. (Madison, WI: Joiner Associates, 1996), p. 6–27. Reprinted with permission.

9. A. Majchrzak, C. Wagner, and D. Yates, "Corporate Wiki Users: Results of a Survey," *Proceedings of the 2006 International Symposium on Wikis,* Odense, Denmark, 2006.

10. Collaborative Writing, http://en.wikipedia.org/wiki/Collaborative_writing, accessed on July 14, 2010.

11. Stewart Mader, *Wikipatterns* (Indianapolis, Ind.: Wiley, 2008).

12. Hilton Worldwide University, "Welcome to Our World," Culture Wise, http://culture-wise.global-dynamics.com/, accessed April 28, 2015.

13. A. J. DuBrin, *Human Relations* (Upper Saddle River, NJ: Prentice-Hall, 1997). Adapted with permission.

14. Geert Hofstede, *Culture's Consequences: Comparing Values, Behaviors, Institutions and Organizations Across Nations*, 2nd ed. (Thousand Oaks, CA: SAGE Publications, 2001).

15. Elizabeth A. Tuleja, "Intercultural Communication for Business," *Managerial Communication Series*, James S. O'Rourke IV, ed. (South-Western, Canada, 2005).

16. IMS, "For Marketers, 'One-Size-Fits-All' Doesn't Fit in Latin America," *Mashable,* May 13, 2014, http://mashable.com/2014/05/13/brand-marketing-latam/, accessed April 28, 2015.

17. Elizabeth Würtz, "A Cross-Cultural Analysis of Websites from High-Context Cultures and Low-Context Cultures," *Journal of Computer-Mediated Communication,* 11(1), 2005.

18. Atlanta Committee for Olympic Games, by Sam Ward, *USA Today*. Taken from Ben Brown, "Atlanta Out to Mind Its Manners," *USA Today*, March 14, 1996, p. 7c.

19. "Toyota Motor Company," The Yamasa Institute, http://yamasa.org/japan/english/destinations/aichi/toyota.html, accessed April 28, 2015.

20. Roland Kelts, "Toyota and Trust: Was the Akio Toyoda Apology Lost in Translation?" *CS Monitor*, February 25, 2011, www.csmonitor.com/Commentary/Opinion/2010/0225/Toyota-and-trust-Was-the-Akio-Toyoda-apology-lost-in-translation, accessed April 28, 2015.

21. Miles Kohrman, "Delta Air Lines Loses the World Cup: What Do Giraffes Have To Do With Ghana?" *Fast Company,* June 16, 2014, www.fastcompany.com/3032004/fast-feed/delta-airlines-loses-the-world-cup-what-do-giraffes-have-to-do-with-ghana, accessed April 28, 2015.

22. State Farm Insurance Website, Diversity and Inclusion, Workplace Diversity Definition, www.statefarm.com/about-us/diversity-inclusion/workplace/employee-resource-groups, accessed April 28, 2015.

23. "Indra Nooyi's Leadership Lessons: Head, Heart & Hands," *Enactus Career Connections,* January 2, 2014, www.enactuscareerconnections.com/indra-nooyis-leadership-lessons-head-heart-hands/, accessed April 28, 2015.

24. "Indra Nooyi's Leadership Lessons."

25. Eric Clay, "The Made of Clay Report," WRFI Radio, Interview with Aloja Airewele, June 15, 2014, http://madeofclay.org/aloja-airewele-and-eric-clay/, accessed April 28, 2015.

26. University of California, San Francisco, "Chapter 12: Managing Diversity in the Workplace," http://ucsfhr.ucsf.edu/index.php/pubs/hrguidearticle/chapter-12-managing-diversity-in-the-workplace/, accessed June 12, 2014.

27. Luke Visconti, "Ask the White Guy: Can You Measure Diversity of Thought and Innovation?" *DiversityInc,* www.diversityinc.com/ask-the-white-guy/can-you-measure-diversity-thought-innovation/, accessed June 12, 2014.

28. Anesa "Nes" Diaz-Uda, Carmen Medina, and Beth Schill, "Diversity's New Frontier," Deloitte University Press, July 23, 2013, http://dupress.com/articles/diversitys-new-frontier/, accessed April 28, 2015.

29. "U.S. Census Bureau Projections Show a Slower Growing, Older, More Diverse Nation a Half Century from Now," U.S. Census Bureau Newsroom, December 12, 2012, www.census.gov/newsroom/releases/archives/population/cb12-243.html, accessed April 28, 2015.

30. United States Census 2010, "Explore the Form," www.census.gov/schools/pdf/2010form_info.pdf, accessed April 28, 2015.

31. Jennifer Coates, *Women, Men, and Language* (New York: Longman, 1986); Deborah Tannen, *You Just Don't Understand* (New York: Ballantine, 1990); John Gray, *Men Are from Mars, Women Are from Venus* (New York: HarperCollins, 1992); Patti Hathaway, *Giving and Receiving Feedback*, rev. ed. (Menlo Park, CA: Crisp Publications, 1998); and Deborah Tannen, *Talking from 9 to 5* (New York: William Morrow, 1994).

32. Nathan Olivarez-Giles, "Facebook Adds New Options for Gender Beyond Male, Female," *Wall Street Journal Digits,* February 13, 2013, http://blogs.wsj.com/digits/2014/02/13/facebook-adds-new-options-for-gender-beyond-male-female/ accessed April 28, 2015.

33. Kelly Services, "Kelly Global Workforce Index," www.kellyservices.com/web/training/refresh_training_site/en/pages/zmag_kgwi_testpage.html, accessed July 19, 2010.

34. "CareerBuilder Survey Identifies Generational Differences in Work Styles, Communication, and Changing Jobs," CareerBuilder.com, September 13, 2012, www.careerbuilder.com/share/aboutus/pressreleasesdetail.aspx?sd=9/13/2012&id=pr715&ed=9/13/2099, accessed April 28, 2015.

35. Tim Cook, "Tim Cook Speaks Up," *BloombergBusinessweek,* October 30, 2013, www.businessweek.com/articles/2014-10-30/tim-cook-im-proud-to-be-gay, accessed April 28, 2015.

36. John Coleman, Daniel Gulati, and W. Oliver Segovia, *Passion & Purpose* (Boston: Harvard Business Review Press, 2012).

37. "Jonah Hill Addresses His Controversial Remarks," *The Tonight Show Starring Jimmy Fallon,* June 3, 2014, www.youtube.com/watch?v=PMz80FKusUA#t=127, accessed April 28, 2015.

38. Washington State Developmental Disabilities Council, "The Missing Page in Your Stylebook," www.ddc.wa.gov/Publications/090720_RespectfulLanguage.pdf, accessed April 28, 2015.

39. James Rose, "Mesquite ISD apologizes for 'retarded' in yearbook," KDFW Fox 4, May 18, 2012, www.myfoxdfw.com/story/18560196/mesquite-isd-apologizes-for-retarded-in-yearbook, April 28, 2015.

40. John Pletz, "The Next Thing in Tech: Workplace Prayer Rooms," *Crain's Chicago Business,* May 19, 2014, www.chicagobusiness.com/article/20140517/ISSUE01/305179985/the-next-thing-in-tech-workplace-prayer-rooms, accessed April 28, 2015.

41. Maura Cullen, *35 Dumb Things Well-Intended People Say* (Garden City, NJ: Morgan James Publishing, 2008).

3 | Interpersonal Communication Skills

LEARNING OBJECTIVES

After you have finished this chapter, you should be able to

LO1   Explain the meaning and importance of nonverbal messages.

LO2   Listen and show empathy in business situations.

LO3   Use social media to build business relationships.

LO4   Use voice technologies and texting effectively in business situations.

LO5   Plan, facilitate, and participate in business meetings.

> *I would never call someone I worked with. It would always be a video call.*
>
> – Justin Forman, Google, Account Executive

CHAPTER INTRODUCTION

Video Conferencing at Google

As you might expect, Google employees use Google tools. For meetings, video-conferencing is most popular because employees can see each other.

Justin Forman, an account executive, participates in video meetings in Hangouts as often as he meets with people in person. He prefers video to phone calls: "I would never call someone I worked with. It would always be a video call. You pick up a lot of cues seeing someone rather than just listening to them." With Forman's back-to-back meeting schedule, video is the easiest way to meet with people in other locations. His office is in New York City, but Google headquarters is in Mountain View, CA, and his manager works in Chicago. In one day, Forman had an in-person meeting at his office, called a client in Boston, participated on a video call with two colleagues at his office, visited a client about a half-hour away, and participated on another video call with the San Francisco office.

Justin Forman on a video call at Google in New York City.

COURTESY OF AMY NEWMAN

Unlike more formal videoconferencing, Google video calls can be quick and spontaneous. At some point during an email conversation, an employee may suggest getting on a "VC" to resolve an issue more quickly.

Google executives also hold weekly all-hands meetings that employees can watch from anywhere in the world via Livestream. Employees submit questions for other employees to rate. The most highly rated questions are answered by an executive on the call.

According to Forman, video calls save Google travel time and money—and may improve relationships and decision making.

3-1 Nonverbal Communication

Not all communication at work is spoken, heard, written, or read—in other words, verbal. According to management expert Peter Drucker, "The most important thing in communication is to hear what isn't being said."[1] A nonverbal message is any message that is not written or spoken. You may use a nonverbal message with a verbal message (smiling as you greet a colleague) or alone (sitting in the back of the classroom). Nonverbal messages are typically more spontaneous than verbal messages, but they're not necessarily less important. The six most common types of nonverbal communication in business are discussed in this section.

3-1a Body Movement

International **COMMUNICATION**

By far, the most expressive part of your body is your face—particularly your eyes. Pamela Meyer, author of *Liespotting,* says "The real smile is in the eyes."[2] Research shows that receivers read facial expressions quite consistently. Paul Ekman, known as the lie detector, claims that facial expressions are universal—not cultural. He has isolated 43 facial muscles that, among other variables, tell us whether a smile is genuine.[3] Eye contact and eye movements tell you a lot about a person, although—as we discussed earlier—maintaining eye contact is not perceived as important (or even polite) in some cultures.

Can you tell which smile is real in Figure 1? If you guessed the one on the left, you are correct. One clue is how the woman contracts the many muscles in the corners of her eyes, which is hard to fake unless the smile is genuine.[4]

Figure 1 | Which Smile is Genuine?

AMY SNYDER, © EXPLORATORIUM, WWW.EXPLORATORIUM.EDU

Gestures are hand and upper-body movements that add important information to face-to-face interactions. As the game of charades proves, you can communicate quite a bit without using oral or written signals. More typically, gestures are used to help illustrate and reinforce your verbal message. A Chicago psychiatrist studied former President Bill Clinton's grand jury testimony about his relationship with intern Monica Lewinsky. Dr. Alan Hirsch found that the president touched his nose once every four minutes when he gave answers that later were shown to be false. By contrast, he did not touch his nose at all when he gave truthful answers.[5]

Body stance (e.g., your posture, where you place your arms and legs, and how you distribute your weight) is another form of nonverbal communication. For example, leaning slightly toward someone would probably convey interest and involvement in the interaction. On the other hand, leaning back with arms folded across the chest might be taken (and intended) as a sign of boredom or defiance.

3-1b Physical Appearance

Our culture places great value on physical appearance. Television, magazines, and the Internet are filled with advertisements for personal-care products, and the ads typically feature attractive product users. Attractive people tend to be seen as more intelligent, more likable, and more persuasive than unattractive people. In addition, people perceived as attractive earn more money.[6]

What does the body language convey in this *Mad Men* scene?

Your appearance is particularly important for making a good first impression. Although you can't change all of your physical features, make choices that enhance your professional image in the business environment, such as using clothing, jewelry, and hairstyle to emphasize your strong points.

3-1c Voice Qualities

No one speaks in a monotone. To illustrate, read the following sentence aloud, each time emphasizing the italicized word. Note how the meaning changes with each reading.

- *Allison* missed the donor meeting. (Answers the question, "Who missed the meeting?")
- Allison *missed* the donor meeting. (Emphasizes that Allison wasn't at the meeting.)
- Allison missed the *donor* meeting. (Clarifies which meeting Allison missed.)

Voice qualities such as volume, speed, pitch, tone, and accent carry both intentional and unintentional messages. For example, when you are nervous, you tend to speak faster and at a higher pitch. People who speak too softly risk being interrupted or ignored, whereas people who speak too loudly are often seen as being pushy or insecure.

A significant number of voice qualities are universal across all human cultures. One study showed that "vocalizations communicating the so-called 'basic emotions' (anger, disgust, fear, joy, sadness, and surprise)" were recognized across two very different cultures.[7] Around the world, adults use higher-pitched voices when speaking to children, when greeting others, and during courtship.[8]

International **COMMUNICATION**

3-1d Time

How do you feel when you're late for an appointment? When others are late? The meaning given to time varies greatly by culture, with Americans and Canadians being much more time-conscious than members of South American or Middle Eastern cultures.

International **COMMUNICATION**

Time is related not only to culture but also to status within the organization. You would be much less likely to keep your manager waiting for an appointment than you would someone who reports to you.

Time is also situation-specific. Although you normally might not worry about being five minutes late for a staff meeting, you would probably arrive early if you were the first presenter or meeting with a prospective client for the first time. Are you more likely to be late if you can text message your lunch date? Some people feel justified in being five minutes late so long as they send a text—but not everyone will be forgiving.

3-1e Touch

Touch is the first sense we develop, acquired even before birth. Some touches, such as those made by a physician during an examination, are purely physical; others, such as a handshake, are a friendly sign of willingness to communicate; and still others indicate intimacy.

The importance of touching behavior varies widely by culture. One international study found that in typical social exchanges, people from San Juan, Puerto Rico, touched an average of 180 times an hour; those in Paris touched 110 times per hour; those in Gainesville, Florida, touched 2 times per hour; and those in London touched not at all.[9]

Microsoft founder Bill Gates was criticized when he kept one hand in his pocket while meeting South Korean President Park Geun-hye.

LEE JIN-MAN/AFP/GETTY IMAGES

Because of litigation in the United States, touching in the office has become an issue for many companies. Although handshakes are certainly appropriate, in most companies—depending on the organizational culture—any other touching is frowned upon.

3-1f Space and Territory

When you are on a crowded elevator, you probably look down, up, or straight ahead—anything to avoid looking at the other people. Most people in the U.S. culture are uncomfortable in such close proximity to strangers. In Chapter 2, we discussed cultural differences regarding space; now let's look more closely at how Americans use space to interact with others (Figure 2).

Figure 2 | Personal Spaces for Social Interaction

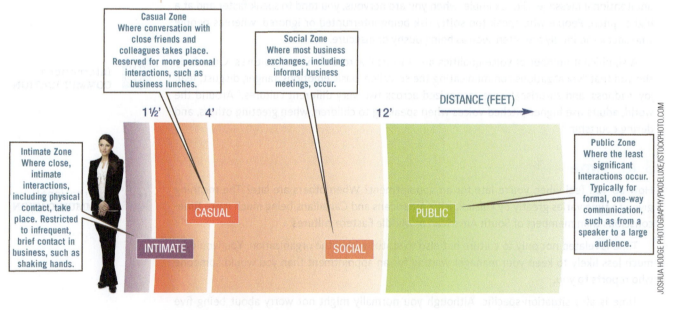

Intimate Zone
Where close, intimate interactions, including physical contact, take place. Restricted to infrequent, brief contact in business, such as shaking hands.

Casual Zone
Where conversation with close friends and colleagues takes place. Reserved for more personal interactions, such as business lunches.

Social Zone
Where most business exchanges, including informal business meetings, occur.

Public Zone
Where the least significant interactions occur. Typically for formal, one-way communication, such as from a speaker to a large audience.

DISTANCE (FEET)

1½'   4'   12'

INTIMATE   CASUAL   SOCIAL   PUBLIC

JOSHUA HODGE PHOTOGRAPHY/PIXDELUXE/ISTOCKPHOTO.COM

Competent communicators recognize their own personal space needs and the needs of others. Look for cues from others, such as people backing away or moving their chairs, to determine whether they prefer more or less space. Try to accommodate differences to make people feel comfortable.

3-2 Listening and Empathy

LO2 Listen and show empathy in business situations.

Across continents or across a conference table, effective communication requires both sending and receiving messages. Whether you are making a formal presentation to 500 people or speaking with one person over lunch, listening is essential to understanding.

Listening involves much more than just hearing. You can hear and not listen (just as you can listen and not understand). Hearing is a passive process, whereas listening is an active process. When you *perceive* a sound, you're merely aware of it; you don't necessarily comprehend it. When you *listen*, you interpret and assign meaning to the sound.

When your car is operating normally, even though you *hear* the sound of the engine as you're driving, you're barely aware of it; you tune it out. But the minute the engine begins to make a strange sound—not necessarily louder or harsher, but just *different*—you tune back in, listening intently to determine the problem. You *heard* the normal hum of the engine but *listened* to the strange noise.

Beyond listening is showing empathy, understanding and sharing another's feelings. You can listen to an employee's stress about workload, but can you really see the situation from his or her perspective—feel what he or she feels? Does the interaction bring up your own stress? With this level of communication, you'll more fully help the employee without judging him or her.

Empathy is different from sympathy, which is simply understanding and providing comfort. Dr. Brené Brown, who researches shame, describes empathy as "feeling with people." Brown says that "empathy is a vulnerable choice because, in order to connect with you, I have to connect with something in myself that knows that feeling."[10] When we take risks to be more vulnerable with others, we allow them to be more open with us.

Emotional INTELLIGENCE

When you have felt truly understood? How did someone show empathy towards you, and how did it make you feel?

3-2a The Value of Listening and Empathy

Listening is essential to business. Imagine trying to tell your manager about a potential new client, an idea to save money, or a product safety issue—and being ignored.

A recent study found that being ignored is more harmful to employees and causes more turnover than harassment.[11] Fully 91% of employees surveyed had experienced "being ignored, avoided, shut out of conversations, or treated as invisible over the past year, whereas 45% reported being harassed, such as by being teased, belittled, or embarrassed."[12] Ostracism can be insidious—a pervasive process with painful results.

Effective managers know that good listening improves tasks and relationships (Figure 3).[13] Listening contributes to employee engagement, creating a culture where employees feel passionate about their company and are enthusiastic about their jobs.

Emotional INTELLIGENCE

Have you felt ignored at work or in an organization? How did you handle the situation?

How Listening Improves Business | **Figure 3**

TASKS	RELATIONSHIPS
Improves problem solving	Increases interpersonal trust
Improves product and service design	Improves customer service and loyalty
Improves accuracy of communication	Increases employee commitment and morale
Reduces misunderstandings about new tasks	Encourages timely feedback
Increases frequency of sharing information	Increases perceptions of integrity

3-2b The Problem of Poor Listening Skills

Although listening is the communication skill we use the most, it is probably the least developed of the four verbal communication skills (writing, reading, speaking, and listening). Why are we such poor listeners? First, most people have simply not been taught how to listen well. When you think back to your early years in school, chances are you spent time on reading, writing, and perhaps speaking, but few students receive formal training in listening. Second, we can think about four times faster than we can speak. When listening to others, our minds begin to wander, and we lose our ability to concentrate on what is being said.

Still, poor listening skills are not as readily apparent as poor speaking or writing skills. It's easy to spot a poor speaker or writer but much more difficult to spot a poor listener because a poor listener can fake attention—and may not even know this is a weakness.

3-2c Keys to Better Listening

The good news is that you can improve your listening skills. To listen more effectively, give the speaker your undivided attention, stay open-minded, avoid interrupting, and involve yourself in the communication.

Give the Speaker Your Undivided Attention

It's easy to get distracted. During a business presentation, the audience may tune the speaker out and let their minds wander. During a job interview, the recruiter may take phone calls. Or, during class, you may doodle or think about an upcoming exam.

This Zappos employee may have trouble listening because of all of the distractions in her work space.

In a work environment, some distractions are easier than others to eliminate. A messy office, with lots of toys to play with, can diffuse your focus when you're listening on the phone. This is within your control. But in a cubicle or open environment, you can't control all of the noise and diversions around you. Your coworker may be typing loudly, talking on the phone, or clipping his toenails (true story!). Your best bet is to use your proficient communication skills to explain how the behavior is affecting your work and politely request a change.

Mental distractions are even more difficult to eliminate. But with practice and effort, you can discipline yourself to postpone thinking about how tired you are or how much you're looking forward to a social event. Temporarily banishing competing thoughts will allow you to give the speaker your undivided attention.

Try to focus on the content of the message. Although a speaker's nonverbal communication, such as dress and body language, can be distracting, don't let unimportant factors prevent you from listening openly. Delivery skills can steal our attention—sometimes more than they should. If someone is nervous or speaks too softly, challenge yourself to listen beyond these surface issues. Almost always, *what* is said is more important than *how* it is said.

Also, avoid dismissing a topic simply because it's uninteresting or not presented in an exciting way. "Boring" does not mean unimportant. Information that's boring or difficult to follow may prove to be useful and well worth your effort to give it your full attention.

Stay Open-Minded

Regardless of whom you're listening to or what the topic is, keep your emotions in check. Listen objectively and empathetically. Be willing to accept new information and new points of view, regardless of whether they mesh with your existing beliefs. Concentrate on the content of the message rather than on its source.

Consider the conversations in Figure 4. In the first conversation, the manager believes she knows the right answer. She doesn't allow the employee to explain his situation.

In the second conversation, the manager refrains from jumping to conclusions too quickly and solving the problem for the employee. Listening openly gives the manager more information from which to evaluate the situation. Sure, it takes a little longer, but in the future, the employee may walk through this type of thinking on his own—and ultimately solve problems more independently.

Two Conversations: Listening with an Open Mind | Figure 4

Conversation 1: Not Listening with an Open Mind

Employee: I haven't heard back from Janet about the proposal.

Employee: No, but . . .

Manager: Did you email her?

Manager: Well, send her a quick email. She's always responsive. You should do a better job of following up.

Conversation 2: Listening with an Open Mind

Employee: I haven't heard back from Janet about the proposal.

Employee: Well, I was hoping by Friday because I sent the proposal on Wednesday, so I expected to hear by the end of the week.

Employee: She's always so responsive.

Employee: I don't know. Maybe she needs more time to look at the budget. It is higher than we originally talked about.

Employee: I could wait a couple more days, or maybe I'll send her a quick email to check in.

Employee: She might feel like I'm forcing a decision, which I don't want to do. It's only been two days . . .

Manager: That's too bad. When did you expect to hear from her?

Manager: I see . . . two days isn't that long . . .

Manager: True, she usually responds to emails the same day, but this is a bigger decision. What do you think is going on?

Manager: It could be.

Manager: How do you think she would react to an email now?

Don't Interrupt

Perhaps because of time pressures, we sometimes get impatient. As soon as we've figured out what a person is going to say, we tend to interrupt to finish the speaker's sentence, particularly when he or she speaks slowly. Or, as soon as we can think of a counterargument, we tend to rush right in—regardless of whether the speaker has finished or even paused for a breath.

Interruptions have many negative consequences. First, they are rude. Second, instead of speeding up the exchange, interruptions may drag it out because they interfere with the speaker's train of thought, causing backtracking. But the most serious negative consequence is the message an interruption sends: "I have the right to interrupt you because what I have to say is more important than what you have to say." Of course, this hinders effective communication.

Don't confuse listening with simply waiting to speak. Even if you're too polite to interrupt, if you're constantly planning what you'll say next, you can hardly listen attentively to what the other person is saying.

Americans tend to have low tolerance for silence. But waiting a moment or two after someone has finished before you respond has several positive effects—especially in an emotional exchange. It gives the person speaking a chance to elaborate, which could draw out further insights. It also helps create a quieter, calmer, more respectful atmosphere, one that is more conducive to solving the problem.

Involve Yourself

As we have said, hearing is passive, whereas listening is active. You should be *doing* something while the other person is speaking. Follow these suggestions to be a more active listener:

- Jot down notes, translating what you hear into writing. Keep your notes brief and focus on the main ideas; don't become so busy writing that you miss the message.
- Listen for what you need. Constantly ask yourself, "How does this point affect *me*? How can I use this information to perform my job more effectively?" Personalizing the information will help you concentrate more easily—even if the topic is difficult to follow or if the speaker has annoying mannerisms.
- Maintain eye contact, nod in agreement, lean forward, and use encouraging phrases such as, "Uh huh" or "I see."

Respond by Paraphrasing or Reflecting

Consider three levels of responding, each with increasing involvement (Figure 5). To repeat what someone says feels like parroting; it demonstrates that you are hearing but not necessarily listening. Paraphrasing is better: this approach shows that you are interpreting the message and restating it in your own words. Often, reflecting is best: you are telling the person that you hear, understand, and care about the underlying message.

Reflecting is particularly appropriate if you see someone visibly upset (and may be inappropriate for other interactions). Conveying your understanding of the content and the emotions without judgment may open up the discussion and encourage the person to talk more about what's happening and how you can help solve the issue. You may find it easier to empathize with someone once you identify emotions in this way.

Notice how true empathy sounds in a conversation between a manager and employee (Figure 6). This is a difficult interaction because the manager thinks the work can be done, but she can still see the situation from the employee's point of view. What's important is to reserve judgment and genuinely, physically feel

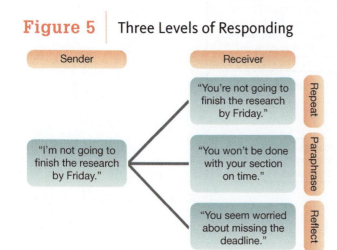

Figure 5 | Three Levels of Responding

Sender

"I'm not going to finish the research by Friday."

Receiver

"You're not going to finish the research by Friday." — Repeat

"You won't be done with your section on time." — Paraphrase

"You seem worried about missing the deadline." — Reflect

Employee: I'm not going to finish the research by Friday.

Manager: What's going on? You look really stressed.

Employee: Chi just asked me for the budget projections by tomorrow.

Manager: Oh, my. I thought he didn't need them until next week.

Employee: Me too. I'm not going to be able to do it all!

Manager: No wonder you're stressed. It's a lot to take on.

Employee: Right. Can I get Robby to help me?

Manager: Robby is working on the North Face proposal and will need the research by Friday to complete it.

Employee: Ugh. I don't know how I'll get it done!

Manager: Let's figure out what's doable. Why don't we meet for a few minutes now to map out what has to be done.

Employee: OK, I guess that will help.

Manager: Good. Let's just take it one step at a time.

Emotional INTELLIGENCE

When have you had a difficult time showing empathy towards another person? What got in the way of understanding and sharing his or her feelings?

what the employee feels. Telling people to "relax" or "calm down" usually has the opposite effect. At the same time, empathy doesn't always mean agreement. During this interaction, the manager uses empathy to defuse the situation and help the employee solve the problem.

Many of the principles for effective listening apply to online interactions, which we'll discuss next.

LO3 Use social media to build business relationships.

Communication TECHNOLOGIES

3-3 Social Media for Building Business Relationships

Ask anyone responsible for social media for a company, and he or she will likely say the same thing: it's all about the "conversation." Building meaningful relationships with customers and employees online requires good interpersonal communication, particularly listening.

3-3a Engaging Customers Online

Listening is the first objective described in *Groundswell*, a book about capitalizing on social technologies. According to Forrester Research, which provided the foundation for the book, listening is "learning from what your customers are saying. It's tapping into that conversation. They're talking about your company. If you can listen, the information flows back in the other direction."[14,15]

A Gallup study found that few people are influenced by companies' social media presence alone. Instead of chasing fans and followers, companies should focus on building relationships with existing customers to convert them to brand advocates. To do this, Gallup suggests that companies be authentic and responsive.[16]

American Airlines understands this and prides itself on responding to every tweet in a conversational way. When the company's social media teams brainstormed words for their Twitter responses, they came up with "genuine," "authentic," "transparent," "savvy," "clear," "professional," and "warm"—never "scripted."[17]

Individuals and small businesses owners who hire ghostwriters miss the point of authenticity in social media relationships. George Takei, 1960s *Star Trek* cast member, learned this lesson when one of his writers admitted that he was paid $10 per joke posted on Takei's Facebook page. With 4.1 million likes, Takei's page is a mix of cartoons, memes, and other lighthearted commentary. Takei called the controversy "hoo-ha," and the writer apologized and seemed to regret the exposure. But at least some fans felt deceived, thinking that the posts were all written by Takei himself.[18]

When customers have a complaint, they want a response. In a recent study of 1,300 consumers who tweeted a complaint about a product, service, or brand, only 29% heard back from the company.[19] This is consistent with another study, which found that only 46% of the biggest brands sent one or more @replies each day, although they were all active on Twitter.[20] Both studies point to bad news for companies wanting to increase sales: in response to another survey, 64% of Twitter users said they would be more likely to purchase from a company that responded to their question.[21]

When companies do respond, they got high marks from consumers, as shown in Figure 7. When asked, "How did you feel when the company contacted you as a result of your tweet?" 83% said, "I loved it" or "I liked it," and 74% were "very satisfied" or "somewhat satisfied" with the response. This is good news for companies that do take the time to respond to complaining tweeters.[22]

Figure 7 | Consumers Appreciate When Companies Respond

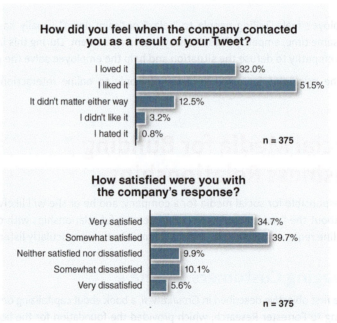

Source: www.maritzresearch.com/~/media/Files/MaritzResearch/e24/ExecutiveSummaryTwitterPoll.ashx

Several companies have tried using social media to inspire conversations about their brands, but many have backfired. McDonald's Twitter campaign, #McDStories, intended to provoke heartfelt stories about the burgers and fries, but people wrote negative comments about the food and working conditions.[23]

How companies handle these unexpected responses is critical to restoring brand image. When U.K. upscale supermarket Waitrose asked people to tweet reasons they shop at the store, snarky comments included "because I hate poor people" and "So people know I'm filthy rich and therefore automatically better than they are." This wasn't exactly what Waitrose had in mind, but the company's response was gracious, good natured—and authentic (Figure 8).[24]

Another way companies engage customers online is to offer online chat, a nice service for customers browsing a website. But consider the following entertaining exchange with a telephone system company. If companies don't handle online chat well, they may be better off sticking with a toll-free number.

> **Customer** All I want to be able to do is call in and out of the building.
>
> **Customer** Hello?
>
> **Customer** Is anybody there?
>
> **Nicole** *You're local provider will be able to assist you.*
>
> **Customer** So you can't answer my question?
>
> **Customer** (You spelled "you're" incorrectly, by the way. It's "your." Just so you know, for the future.)

3-3b Engaging Employees Online

Smart companies find ways to engage employees online as well as in face-to-face communication. Considered "internal customers," employees also have valuable feedback that companies should hear.

An intranet site is a good way to encourage employees to participate in the conversation about the company—and to keep their comments internal. Rather than posting embarrassing information about a company on public websites, employees can give feedback about products, organizational changes, and management on an employee-only intranet site.

With a young employee population, Best Buy has implemented the following avenues to engage employees online:

- The Watercooler, where employees post comments and executives hold "virtual town halls." Unlike a previous version of this forum, employee comments are not moderated or screened.
- Employee Newsletter, a daily online publication. Employees comment on articles and rate each other's comments.
- Executive Blogs, which provide a way for senior-level management to communicate directly with employees.[25]

One popular social networking tool for employees is Yammer (owned by Microsoft). Similar to Facebook's interface and functionality, Yammer allows employees to connect online—behind a firewall, so conversations are kept within the company (Figure 9).

Figure 9 | Yammer Internal Social Network

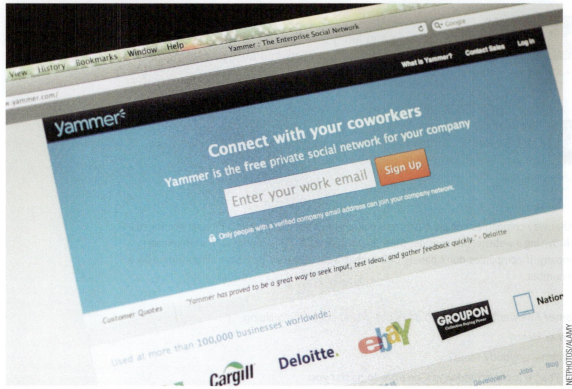

Source: www.yammer.com/product/features/accessing-yammer/

LO4 Use voice technologies and texting effectively in business situations.

 Communication **TECHNOLOGIES**

3-4 Voice and Text Messaging

Voice technologies and text messaging are good choices for interpersonal communication at work. A richer medium than email, the telephone allows you to convey and hear tone of voice, one of the cues for interpreting messages. But the telephone—and certainly text messaging—is not nearly as rich as face-to-face communication, which includes nonverbal cues such as gestures and body language. Without these cues, voice tone and etiquette are critical to ensure understanding and demonstrate professionalism.

Being comfortable with voice and text technologies are important signals of your credibility. Voice mail is falling out of favor and was discontinued at Coca-Cola's headquarters because of declining use.[26] And many companies have replaced office phones with cell phones. Still, you may find the phone and texting the best way to reach someone, particularly for a quick answer. Follow the suggestions in Figures 10 and 11 to present yourself well using these technologies.

LO5 Plan, facilitate, and participate in business meetings.

3-5 Business Meetings

Meetings in organizations take many forms and serve many purposes. Whether in person or through technology, people meet to share information about the business, provide team progress updates, solicit and provide input, solve problems, make decisions—and start, maintain, and sometimes end relationships.

(1) Making Outgoing Calls
- Be respectful of timing; don't call at 4:55 p.m. when the office closes at 5 p.m., and don't call late at night to leave a voice mail.
- Plan what you will say for important calls; prepare your first couple of sentences.
- Prepare to speak with the person directly and to leave a voice mail message—you never know which.
- Leave a complete, but brief voice mail message: your name, the reason for your call, and your phone number.

(2) Conveying a Positive, Professional Image
- Use your natural voice, but make sure you don't sound bored; try smiling when you answer the phone.
- Give the caller your full attention; people can hear if you're typing, eating, or moving papers.
- Avoid saying anything that you might regret; conversations can be recorded.
- Schedule a time for important calls so you can arrange for a private, quiet place to talk.
- Avoid taking calls during meetings; unless this is the norm in your company, it's likely considered rude.
- Be mindful of people around you; don't block traffic—or get hit by it!

HEMERA TECHNOLOGIES/PHOTOOBJECTS.NET/JUPITER IMAGES

Unfortunately, many meetings are unnecessary and poorly run. Seventy-five percent of employees who attend meetings say they could be more effective.[27] The cartoon in Figure 12 shows what a joke meetings have become in many organizations.

Meetings can work well. After choosing an appropriate meeting format, an effective communicator plans, facilitates and participates in, and follows up a meeting.

3-5a Determining the Meeting Format

Choosing an appropriate format for your meeting is an important part of good meeting planning. In some cases, logistics, such as people working in different locations and time zones, will drive how you meet. In other cases, your meeting purpose, for example, trying to close a deal, will determine how you meet. Your company also will have standard practices, and people within the company will have personal preferences. All of these factors—and research about effective meetings—will help you decide on a structure for your meeting.

The Case for Face-to-Face

With all of the technology available, most people prefer face-to-face meetings. A global Kelly Services study found that between 74%

- Send texts to people at or below your level in the organization—or to your manager if you know this is acceptable to him or her.
- Reserve texts for quick messages that require an immediate response, usually for logistical information; don't send texts for heavy content or important business decisions.
- Avoid texting during meetings unless this is acceptable at your company.
- Use informal language, but know that anything you write may become public.
- Never text while driving; this is dangerous and not worth the risk.

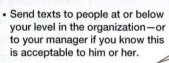
"Board mtg. starts in 2 hrs. Please send John the PPT."

SIMON DENSON/ALAMY

Figure 12 | Meeting Humor

and 82% of employees prefer face-to-face communication with their colleagues and coworkers.[28] A Harvard Business Review group study of 2,300 managers from North America, Asia, and Europe found that more than 50% of managers preferred face-to-face communication—even if it means traveling—for the following purposes:[29]

- Meeting new (94%) or existing clients (69%) to sell business
- Negotiating contracts (82%)
- Interviewing senior staff for key appointments (81%)
- Understanding and listening to important customers (69%)
- Identifying growth opportunities (55%)
- Building relationships/managing geographically dispersed teams (55%)
- Initiating discussions with merger and acquisition targets (52%)

Only 20% of managers in this study agreed with the statement, "You can achieve the same results with virtual meetings as you can with in-person meetings."[30]

Clearly, some of the most important business dealings are handled in person. This makes sense, considering what we discussed in Chapter 1: face-to-face is the richest medium and the best choice for interpersonal communication. Plus, face-to-face communication is strongly preferred over other forms of communication by three generations of workers and employees in Asia Pacific, Europe, and North America (Figure 13).

And yet, managers are using new technologies for meetings and expect to do so more in the future. The Harvard Business Review group study also found that most managers anticipate participating in more or the same number of teleconferences or audio conferences and videoconferences, but in-person meetings that require travel will decrease or stay the same.[31] Budget restrictions on travel are expected to push meeting technologies as a more popular choice in the future.[32]

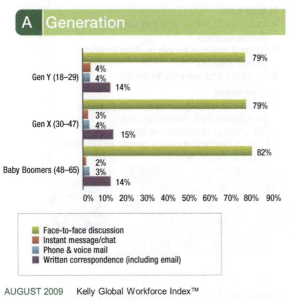

In communicating with your colleagues and coworkers, which method do you prefer?

A Generation

Gen Y (18–29): 79% / 4% / 4% / 14%

Gen X (30–47): 79% / 3% / 4% / 15%

Baby Boomers (48–65): 82% / 2% / 3% / 14%

0% 10% 20% 30% 40% 50% 60% 70% 80% 90%

- Face-to-face discussion
- Instant message/chat
- Phone & voice mail
- Written correspondence (including email)

AUGUST 2009   Kelly Global Workforce Index™

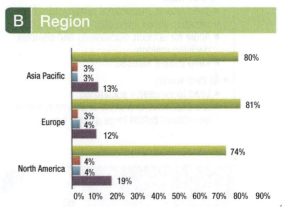

B Region

Asia Pacific: 80% / 3% / 3% / 13%

Europe: 81% / 3% / 4% / 12%

North America: 74% / 4% / 4% / 19%

0% 10% 20% 30% 40% 50% 60% 70% 80% 90%

KELLY. COURTESY OF KELLY SERVICES

Considering Alternatives

Although the best choice for many situations, face-to-face meetings are not always practical or ideal for all business purposes. Figure 14 compares the best and worst of face-to-face and virtual meetings (conference calls, online meetings, and videoconferences).

Some companies use virtual, three-dimensional environments, such as Second Life, for meetings. Although broad adoption has been slow, Second Life is far less expensive than in-person meetings and provides a simulated environment for companies to test new ideas. IBM, for example, held one conference that saved the company $320,000 in travel expenses and lost productivity. Other companies, such as CIGNA and Children's Memorial Hospital in Chicago, have used Second Life for training and disaster planning.[33] The technology isn't for everyone, but with proper planning and for the right purpose, Second Life presents a viable alternative to the traditional meeting.

3-5b Planning the Meeting

Even without technology and travel expenses, meetings are expensive. You can download the Meeting Cost Counter to see the total expense of a meeting measured by salary and time (www .effectivemeetings.com/diversions/meetingclock.asp).[34] Managers must make sure they get their money's worth from a meeting, and that requires careful planning: identifying the purpose and determining whether a meeting is necessary, deciding who should attend, preparing an agenda, and planning the logistics.

Identify Your Purpose

The first step is always to identify your purpose. The more specific you can be, the better results you will get. A purpose such as "to discuss how to make our marketing staff more effective" is

Figure 14 | Comparison of Four Meeting Formats

- **Description:** In-person meetings for any number of people
- **At their best:**
  - Build strong, meaningful relationships
  - Increase social interaction
  - Allow for difficult discussions and complex decision making
  - Keep people focused
- **At their worst:**
  - Lead to excessive socializing
  - Are expensive and show unproven return on investment (when large groups travel)

Face-to-Face Meetings

ALEXANDER RATHS/ISTOCKPHOTO.COM

- **Description:** Audio conference calls for people in two or more locations (often through speakerphone)
- **At their best:**
  - Accommodate one-way and two-way communication
  - Connect multiple people in other locations on one medium
  - Cost little and are easy to set up
- **At their worst:**
  - Cause overlapping conversations because participants lack nonverbal cues
  - Fail when connections are lost
  - Lead to distractions when people multitask or forget to mute the call

Conference Calls

TETRA IMAGES/GETTY IMAGES

- **Description:** Web-based meetings using a service such as WebEx or GoToMeeting
- **At their best:**
  - Allow teams to work on documents together (with screen-sharing capabilities)
  - Provide an inexpensive alternative to a face-to-face presentation (with PowerPoint driven by one or more people)
  - Are free for small groups and limited use
- **At their worst:**
  - Fail because of the technology, which sometimes requires a separate telephone connection
  - Lead to distractions (as with conference calls)

Online Meetings

ANDRESR/ISTOCKPHOTO.COM

- **Description:** Video-based meetings using smartphones, desktop programs, or dedicated services such as telepresence suites
- **At their best:**
  - Provide the best alternative to face-to-face meetings
  - Feel like a face-to-face meeting (telepresence)
  - Cost little (smartphones and desktop systems)
- **At their worst:**
  - Fail because of technology problems (or people using the technology!)
  - Require equipment that's too expensive for most businesses (telepresence)

Videoconferences

JON FEINGERSH/BLEND IMAGES/GETTY IMAGES

vague and doesn't identify a clear outcome. These purpose statements are clearer and more specific:

- To decide whether to implement a new rewards program for the marketing staff
- To finalize the work schedule for July
- To prioritize candidates for the IT analyst position

Determine Whether a Meeting Is Necessary

Sometimes meetings are not the most efficient means of communication. For one-way communication that doesn't require input or feedback, such as a monthly status update, perhaps sending an email or posting a podcast on the intranet is best. Similarly, it doesn't make sense to use the weekly staff meeting of ten people to hold a long discussion involving only one or two of the members. A phone call or smaller meeting would accomplish that task more quickly and less expensively.

Sit-down meetings are particularly difficult for technology workers, who need blocks of time for programming and other work. At GitHub, a start-up that stores computer code, almost no face-to-face meetings take place. At Grouper, a blind-dating company, employees attend a daily morning meeting that lasts only ten minutes, and people are required to stand.[35]

Decide Who Should Attend

Everyone you invite to your meeting should have a specific reason for attending. Ideally, you will include only those people who can contribute to the meeting. Who will make the decision? Who will contribute ideas? Who can provide background information? On the one hand, you want to include all who can contribute to solving the problem; on the other hand, you want to keep the meeting to a manageable number of people. For videoconferences, who is invited is even more important: each connection to a location costs money.

Meeting invitations—like wedding invitations—can cause friction. You may want to keep your meeting small but feel obligated to include someone. Of course, you want to avoid hurt feelings, but you should balance this with your goal: to run an efficient, productive meeting. Speaking with someone ahead of time about whether he or she needs to attend or involving your manager in the decision may be useful.

On the other hand, getting everyone to agree on the same goal can be challenging, but avoid excluding people just to prevent conflict. Instead, speak separately with decision makers and cynics ahead of time to help rally their support during the meeting.

Prepare an Agenda

With your purpose and participants set, you need to decide what topics the meeting will cover and in what order. This list of topics, or agenda, will accomplish two things: it will help you prepare for the meeting, and it will help you run the meeting by keeping everyone focused on the schedule.

Knowing what topics will be discussed will also help participants plan for the meeting by reviewing background information, bringing documentation, and preparing questions. You also may assign topics for participants to lead (with their permission, of course). By doing this, you'll engage more people in the meeting and share some of the responsibility.

Send the agenda before the meeting is scheduled, so people know what to expect and have enough time to prepare. Ideally, you would send the agenda with a calendar invitation that automatically schedules a time when everyone is available. If you schedule the meeting far in advance, you may want to send a reminder a day or two before the date. The sample email in Figure 15, to the team who will select a new IT analyst, encourages people to come to the meeting ready to contribute.

The more specific the agenda you can provide, the better. Figure 16 is an example of a detailed agenda.

Notice that this agenda isn't set for one hour. Although one hour is often the default time, some meetings need more or less time and should be scheduled accordingly. People may be more likely to stick with the agenda if the times are not typical. Also, most of the work will be done outside the meeting. The short time frames keep people focused on why they are meeting: to make a decision.

Emotional INTELLIGENCE

Have you invited someone to a meeting because you felt obligated or didn't want to hurt his or her feelings? Have you been invited to a meeting at which you felt you didn't belong? How did each situation affect how you felt and how the meeting ran?

Figure 15 | Sample Email to Prepare for a Meeting

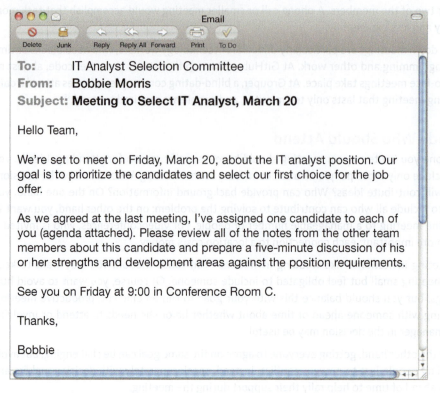

To: IT Analyst Selection Committee
From: Bobbie Morris
Subject: **Meeting to Select IT Analyst, March 20**

Hello Team,

We're set to meet on Friday, March 20, about the IT analyst position. Our goal is to prioritize the candidates and select our first choice for the job offer.

As we agreed at the last meeting, I've assigned one candidate to each of you (agenda attached). Please review all of the notes from the other team members about this candidate and prepare a five-minute discussion of his or her strengths and development areas against the position requirements.

See you on Friday at 9:00 in Conference Room C.

Thanks,

Bobbie

Figure 16 | Sample Detailed Agenda

IT Analyst Selection Team Meeting
Purpose: To prioritize the candidates and select our first choice for the job offer
March 20
Conference Room C
9:00 – 9:45 a.m.

Topic	Who	Timing
Review requirements of the IT analyst position	Yuri	9:00 – 9:05
Candidate 1		
• Review feedback gathered	Kelly	9:05 – 9:10
• Discuss qualifications	Everyone	9:10 – 9:15
Candidate 2		
• Review feedback gathered	David	9:15 – 9:20
• Discuss qualifications	Everyone	9:20 – 9:25
Candidate 3		
• Review feedback gathered	Eun	9:25 – 9:30
• Discuss qualifications	Everyone	9:30 – 9:35
Agree on the top candidate (and possibly a backup)	Everyone	9:35 – 9:40
Recap and agree on next steps	Yuri	9:40 – 9:45

Arrange Logistics

Coordinating a meeting—whether face-to-face or virtual—requires thoughtful preparation. Figure 17 offers suggestions to get your meeting off to a good start.

Communication
TECHNOLOGIES

Logistics for a Well-Planned Meeting | **Figure 17**

FACE-TO-FACE MEETINGS	VIRTUAL MEETINGS
• **Schedule a room.** Choose a room large enough for people to feel comfortable, and include the location in your meeting invitation.	• **Prepare the main meeting room.** If you have several people in one location, use the face-to-face meeting guidelines.
• **Send an online meeting invitation.** Use your company's calendar system or a program such as Doodle (www.doodle.com) to schedule meetings easily.	• **Send instructions with your meeting invitation.** Include detailed instructions for using the technology, and encourage people to log on early.
• **Check the seating arrangement.** Make sure you have enough chairs, and place them to facilitate interaction (facing each other as much as possible).	• **Practice using the technology.** Call a colleague in another room to adjust sound, lighting, and camera positioning. Practice navigating the system seamlessly.
• **Check the technology.** Practice using whatever technology you'll need during the meeting. Make sure everything works properly.	• **Bring all contact numbers.** Have technical support and all participants' emails and phone numbers with you just in case.
• **Send materials in advance.** Help people prepare for the meeting by sending your agenda and perhaps handouts or slides ahead of time.	• **Log on five to ten minutes early.** Greet people as they enter, and make sure they can see and hear.
• **Welcome people.** Greet people as they join the meeting, and introduce people who do not know each other.	• **Have a backup plan.** For a videoconference, bring a speakerphone in case the system fails. For an online meeting, prepare to email materials in case participants can't see them.

3-5c Facilitating the Meeting

After all of the planning, a manager's job is to facilitate the meeting, making sure that goals are met through clear organization and active participation.

Follow the Agenda

Within the first few minutes, you'll set the stage for the meeting. Starting on time tells people you're serious about the topic, value their time, and expect them to be prompt for future meetings. Depending on the organizational culture and people, you may spend a few minutes socializing, but don't let this go on too long. The most efficient meetings get down to business on time and save socialization for just before and a few minutes after the meeting.

Use the agenda as your guide throughout the meeting. Keep track of time and refer to the schedule periodically. Bring copies or display the agenda so that everyone can see the progress you're making. Be respectful of people's time and end when you plan to. People often have back-to-back meetings and need to get somewhere else quickly.

Encourage Participation and Facilitate Discussion

Several strategies will help you keep the meeting focused and productive:

- State the purpose of the meeting and review the agenda upfront.

  Example: "Thank you, everyone, for coming on time. I'm looking forward to hearing your feedback on the three candidates for the IT analyst position. By the end of the meeting, we'll know which candidate will receive an offer—and we may identify a backup candidate. Here are copies of the agenda. I'd like to start by reviewing the job qualifications, and then we'll review each candidate before we agree on our top choice."

- Manage time efficiently but tactfully.

  Example: "Kelly, I'm getting concerned about time. Maybe we should move on to Candidate 2 at this point."

  Example: "It sounds like we're not 100% clear where this position will be located. Why don't I check with HR and follow up with you separately, so we can continue discussing Candidate 3's qualifications?"

- Be flexible to avoid cutting off valuable discussion.

  Example: "We're running a little behind schedule, but I think this discussion is important. Do you want to schedule time for tomorrow, so we can talk more about this?"

- Encourage participation from everyone.

  Example (before the meeting): "David, I'm really looking forward to hearing whether you think these candidates have the technical skills for the job."

  Example (during the meeting): "Eun, what did you think about Candidate 2's interpersonal skills?"

- Summarize the meeting and next steps.

  Example: "So, it sounds like we all agree to extend an offer to Candidate 2. If she doesn't accept, then we'll start a new search. I'll call her today and will let you know by email what she says. Thanks for a productive meeting, everyone."

Participate in the Meeting

Meetings rely on good facilitation and participation. As a meeting participant, follow the guidelines in Figure 18 to be perceived as a professional who is engaged in the conversation—for both face-to-face and virtual meetings.

Figure 18 | Guidelines for Meeting Participants

ALL MEETINGS	VIRTUAL MEETINGS
• Arrive on time and prepared. • Don't bring food. • Turn off your smartphone. • Introduce yourself to new people. • Avoid side conversations. • Participate fully. • Don't interrupt others. • Stick to relevant topics. • Stay focused and engaged. • Support others' comments. • Disagree respectfully.	• Practice with the technology ahead of time to make sure the system works on your computer. • Avoid loud plaid or striped clothing, which can look distorted on video. • Log on a minute or two before the meeting start time. • Minimize background noises such as shuffling papers or tapping on the desk. • Mute your phone when you're not speaking. • Avoid multitasking—you may miss an important point or a question directed to you! • Allow a little extra time before you speak, so you don't overlap others' comments. • State your name when you speak (for teleconference calls without video). • Speak and act naturally—no need to talk loudly or exaggerate your gestures.

During some meeting situations, you may use your smartphone. You may find a text or IM useful to get a quick answer during a meeting—multicommunicating, as we discussed earlier. But you should do this only if your organizational culture allows it. If you are unsure, you might consider asking permission first.

Conference calls are particularly challenging. For example, mute buttons prevent embarrassing situations such as 15 people hearing you flush the toilet (another true story!). A popular video, "A Conference Call in Real Life," pokes fun at conference calls: people entering late, talking over each other, getting cut off, and so on (bit.ly/1mL5gTn).[36]

Communication
TECHNOLOGIES

A study reported in *Harvard Business Review* tells us that people aren't always listening during conference calls (Figure 19). In addition to doing other work or sending an email, 40% of people surveyed admitted to dropping off a call while people assumed they were still connected, and 27% said that have fallen asleep on calls.[37]

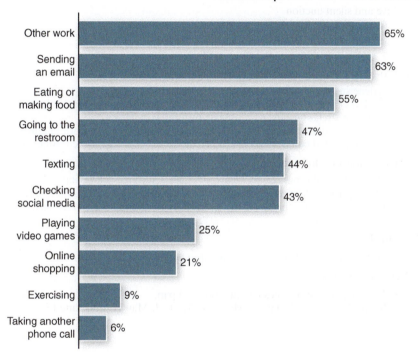

What People Do on Conference Calls | **Figure 19**

Other work	65%
Sending an email	63%
Eating or making food	55%
Going to the restroom	47%
Texting	44%
Checking social media	43%
Playing video games	25%
Online shopping	21%
Exercising	9%
Taking another phone call	6%

Follow Up After the Meeting

Regular or informal meetings may only require a short email as a follow-up to what was decided. Formal meetings or meetings where controversial ideas were discussed may require a more formal summary.

Minutes are an official record of the meeting; they summarize what was discussed, what decisions were made, and what actions participants will take. Generally, they should emphasize what was *decided* at the meeting, not what was *said* by the members.

Figure 20 is an example of meeting minutes—sent by email—for a development committee at a not-for-profit organization. To keep this simple, the writer added minutes in blue type to the agenda. From reading these, you can tell that this group of people meets regularly. Sending

Figure 20 | Sample Meeting Minutes

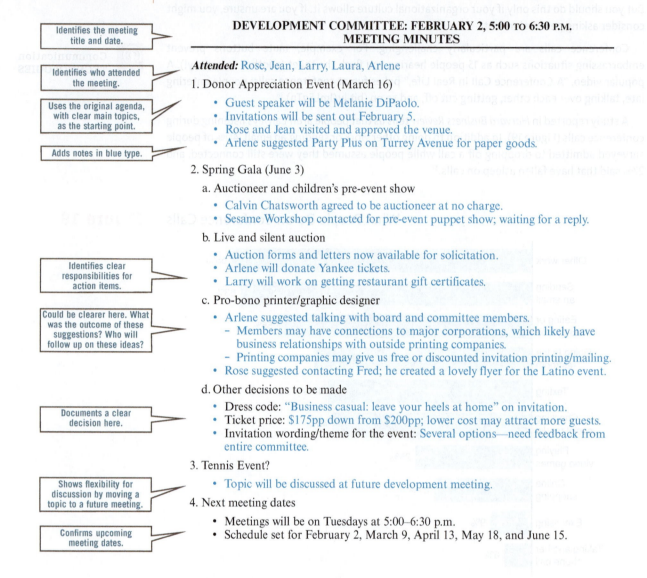

Identifies the meeting title and date.

Identifies who attended the meeting.

Uses the original agenda, with clear main topics, as the starting point.

Adds notes in blue type.

Identifies clear responsibilities for action items.

Could be clearer here. What was the outcome of these suggestions? Who will follow up on these ideas?

Documents a clear decision here.

Shows flexibility for discussion by moving a topic to a future meeting.

Confirms upcoming meeting dates.

DEVELOPMENT COMMITTEE: FEBRUARY 2, 5:00 TO 6:30 P.M.
MEETING MINUTES

Attended: Rose, Jean, Larry, Laura, Arlene

1. Donor Appreciation Event (March 16)

   • Guest speaker will be Melanie DiPaolo.
   • Invitations will be sent out February 5.
   • Rose and Jean visited and approved the venue.
   • Arlene suggested Party Plus on Turrey Avenue for paper goods.

2. Spring Gala (June 3)

   a. Auctioneer and children's pre-event show

   • Calvin Chatsworth agreed to be auctioneer at no charge.
   • Sesame Workshop contacted for pre-event puppet show; waiting for a reply.

   b. Live and silent auction

   • Auction forms and letters now available for solicitation.
   • Arlene will donate Yankee tickets.
   • Larry will work on getting restaurant gift certificates.

   c. Pro-bono printer/graphic designer

   • Arlene suggested talking with board and committee members.
     – Members may have connections to major corporations, which likely have business relationships with outside printing companies.
     – Printing companies may give us free or discounted invitation printing/mailing.
   • Rose suggested contacting Fred; he created a lovely flyer for the Latino event.

   d. Other decisions to be made

   • Dress code: "Business casual: leave your heels at home" on invitation.
   • Ticket price: $175pp down from $200pp; lower cost may attract more guests.
   • Invitation wording/theme for the event: Several options—need feedback from entire committee.

3. Tennis Event?

   • Topic will be discussed at future development meeting.

4. Next meeting dates

   • Meetings will be on Tuesdays at 5:00–6:30 p.m.
   • Schedule set for February 2, March 9, April 13, May 18, and June 15.

minutes within 24 hours shows meeting participants that their contributions are valued. Minutes may be sent by email or posted to an intranet or wiki.

With good planning, strong facilitation, and timely follow-up, you might hold meetings that people *want* to attend.

Listening to Employees' Concerns

>>> PURPOSE

As the CEO of a small company, you have decided to encourage employees to use video calls rather than conference calls. At a staff meeting when you announced the plan, some people were very upset. As a good manager, you need to listen to their concerns.

>>> PROCESS

1. **What is your objective in handling concerns at the meeting?**
   Before deciding anything, I need to understand employees' concerns and fully consider their position.

2. **What limitations do you have in listening to employees?**
   I'm disappointed with employees' response. I feel strongly that video calls will improve communication because people will see each other's body language. I was hoping that employees would feel the same way. I'll try not to let my personal feelings get in the way.

3. **What listening skills will be most useful during the conversation?**
   I will avoid simply repeating what employees say; rather, I'll paraphrase some information and reflect emotion to ensure that I understand their perspective and acknowledge how upset they are.

4. **How will you end the conversation?**
   I will end by making sure everyone agrees to try video calling—or we'll decide on another way to achieve the objectives.

>>> PRODUCT

Here are examples of listening skills that I'll use during the meeting:

- "Some of you are wondering whether getting over the technology hurdles is worth it." (paraphrase)
- "So, it sounds like you don't think that video calls will improve communication." (paraphrase)
- "I hear your concern that video calls are more cumbersome and will take more time to set up." (reflect)
- It seems like some of you are frustrated because I proposed this without considering your views first." (reflect)

3Ps
> IN PRACTICE

Planning a Meeting

>>> PURPOSE

Imagine that you manage the customer service division of a technology company. As part of your job, you're evaluating the "Frequently Asked Questions" on the Customer Support page of the website. You continually update these questions to give customers quick answers and to prevent unnecessary contact with the customer service associates.

You're planning a meeting with two customer service associates at the company headquarters to decide what, if any, changes to make to the current questions. You have some data about which current questions are accessed most frequently on the website, and you would like to hear from the associates what additional questions they typically receive by email and by chat. To plan the meeting, you prepare an email to the associates.

>>> PROCESS

1. What is the purpose of this meeting, and why is a meeting necessary?

2. What is the best format for the meeting (in person, teleconference, online, or videoconference)? Why is this format the best choice?

3. What will you include in the meeting agenda? How can you make sure the agenda is detailed enough?

4. How can you inspire associates to come to the meeting prepared?

5. What else will you include in your email?

>>> PRODUCT

Write an email to the customer service associates.

LO1   Explain the meaning and importance of nonverbal messages.

Nonverbal communication includes body movement, physical appearance, voice qualities, time, touch, and space and territory. Cultures differ greatly in terms of how they interpret nonverbal behavior.

LO2   Listen and show empathy in business situations.

Listening has many positive benefits for business but is the least developed verbal communication skill. Empathy is important to understand another person's feelings, which may differ from your own. Whether listening to a formal presentation or conversing with one or two people, you can learn to listen more effectively by giving the speaker your undivided attention, staying open-minded about the speaker and the topic, avoiding interrupting the speaker, and involving yourself actively in the communication.

LO3   Use social media to build business relationships.

Like listening in person, listening online is important to build business relationships. Companies that truly engage customers and employees through social media develop stronger connections with these audiences and receive more valuable feedback. When companies offer online channels for customers, they must respond—or prepare to lose credibility.

LO4   Use voice technologies and texting effectively in business situations.

Use the telephone for richer communication that requires more cues for understanding and text messaging for short messages. How you present yourself on the phone and while texting will demonstrate your professionalism.

LO5   Plan, facilitate, and participate in business meetings.

Planning a business meeting requires determining your purpose, deciding whether a meeting is necessary, and identifying what format is most appropriate. You must then decide who should attend, prepare your agenda, and arrange logistics. When facilitating and participating in a meeting, follow the agenda and encourage and contribute to discussion. Follow up the meeting with detailed minutes that summarize discussion, decisions, and actions.

> EXERCISES

1. **Identify facial expressions.**

   Find a partner and take turns telling each other a three-minute story. When each of you tells your story, try to exaggerate, as if you were on stage and telling the story to a live audience. As you watch your partner, take notes on facial expressions you see, and identify what emotion each expression conveys (e.g., anger, excitement, and disgust). Pay particular attention to your partner's nose, mouth (lips and tongue), eyes (eyebrows and eyelids), and forehead.

   As an alternative to this exercise, watch a few minutes of your favorite stand-up comedian online. What facial expressions do you see, and which emotions does he or she convey?

   LO1   Explain the meaning and importance of nonverbal messages.

2. **Communicate without talking.**

   This is your big chance to be a star! In front of the class, use only nonverbal communication to convey the following emotions.

   a. Surprise
   b. Anger
   c. Sorrow
   d. Puzzlement
   e. Boredom

See whether the class can guess your emotion. This will give you practice in matching your nonverbal language to your message.

3. **Use your voice tone to convey emotions.**

   With a partner, repeat the following groups of sentences, conveying a different emotion each time. Change the order, and see if your partner can guess which emotion you're expressing.

Today is my birthday. (excited)	I didn't get the Bank of America job. (disappointed)
Today is my birthday. (sad)	I didn't get the Bank of America job. (angry)
Today is my birthday. (anxious)	I didn't get the Bank of America job. (indifferent)
Today is my birthday. (surprised)	I didn't get the Bank of America job. (surprised)

4. **Analyze time norms.**

   Think back to a meeting you attended recently, either at school or at a workplace. Did everyone arrive at the same time? How do you interpret the behavior of those who arrived first and last? Would you draw any conclusions about their status in the group or their culture, which may have influenced their perception of time? How does your own perspective on time factor into your analysis?

5. **Listen to key ideas and compare notes.**

   Watch a few minutes of a news report with the class. As you're listening, take notes about the most important points. In small groups, compare a few examples. In what ways are your notes different or similar? Did you miss important points that your classmates wrote down? If so, why do you think this is the case?

6. **See how nonverbal communication affects a speaker.**

   Working in groups of three or four, have one person tell a three-minute story to the rest of the group. As he or she tells the story, demonstrate negative nonverbal communication: roll your eyes, cross your arms, frown, turn away, and lean back in your chair. Ask the storyteller what effect this had on him or her. Was he or she able to continue the story? It probably didn't feel very good!

   Now give the storyteller a fair chance. This time, when he or she tells a story (the same or a different one), practice good nonverbal listening skills by nodding your head, smiling, and expressing other emotions that track with the story. What effect does your nonverbal communication have on the speaker? (It should encourage him or her to continue talking and want to say more.)

LO2 Listen and show empathy in business situations.

7. **Assess your listening skills and ability to show empathy.**

   Rate yourself on the following dimensions, and consider how you could become a better, more empathic listener.

	Never	Sometimes	Often	Always
I prefer to talk than to listen.				
I have a tough time listening to people whose views are different from mine.				
I have a tough time listening to people complain.				
When someone else is talking, I plan what I'll say next.				
I tend to try to solve problems quickly instead of listening to the whole situation first.				

8. **Observe someone listening.**

Working in groups of three, have one person talk about a difficult decision he or she needs to make. As he or she describes the situation, have a second person listen, using skills discussed in this chapter. The listener does not need to give advice or help the speaker solve the problem; he or she merely needs to listen. The third person in your group should take notes on how the listener uses the skills in Figure 21.

After about five minutes of conversation, have both the speaker and observer give feedback to the listener. Which skills were used most effectively, and which skills could the listener improve?

If you have time, switch roles so everyone has a chance to practice listening skills.

Checklist for Listening Skills Feedback | **Figure 21**

SKILLS	RATING
• Gives the speaker his or her undivided attention	1 2 3 4 5
• Stays open-minded	1 2 3 4 5
• Doesn't interrupt	1 2 3 4 5
• Involves himself or herself by doing the following:	
– Maintains eye contact	1 2 3 4 5
– Nods in agreement	1 2 3 4 5
– Leans forward	1 2 3 4 5
– Uses encouraging phrases ("Uh huh," "I see")	1 2 3 4 5
– Responds (paraphrases and reflects)	1 2 3 4 5

9. **Listen to an employee's explanation.**

In the Write Experience exercise, "A Matter of Convenience," you are Karl Martin, the manager of Crikey, a convenience store. You received several complaints from regular customers that the store was closed for about an hour and a half after opening time. From video footage, you know that Anne Jackson, the employee who was expected to open the store, showed up one and a half hours late. Further, she reported these hours on her timesheet, even though she clearly didn't work the time.

In front of the class, have two students role play a discussion between Karl and Anne. As Anne, admit that you were not at the store, but give the following explanations:

- You had to go to the doctor to follow up on your recent kidney transplant.

- You are a widow and support three children, one of whom has special needs.

- You often work overtime to prepare the store for the next day, and you never claim those hours.

As Karl, you will want to listen to Anne. Be sure to use good paraphrasing and reflecting skills. Also explain that Anne should put in for overtime pay—which she fully deserves—but that she is expected to work regular store hours. Try to solve the problem with Anne to avoid this situation in the future.

Students who observe the interaction should use the checklist provided in Exercise 8.

After the discussion, first have Anne describe how she felt. In what ways did she feel that Karl was empathizing with her? Next, students who were observing the scenario can

Exercise 9 refers to Write Experience, a technology that uses artificial intelligence to score student writing and provide feedback to help them improve. Additional exercises from Write Experience are included in Chapters 7, 9, 10, and 12.

give Karl feedback: for which skills did you rate Karl most highly, and which skills could Karl most improve?

10. **Discuss challenges with empathy.**

    Watch Dr. Brené Brown's TED Talk, "The Power of Vulnerability" (http://bit.ly/1fZuRnC). In groups of three, discuss the video and her how concept of vulnerability relates to empathy. If you're comfortable, take some risks and discuss your personal views of empathy: what do you find easy or difficult about showing empathy towards others?

LO3 Use social media to build business relationships.

11. **Help a company improve how it listens to customers online.**

    Think about one of your favorite companies—or a company where you might like to work—and analyze their social media presence and engagement. Does it have a Facebook page, Twitter account, blog, or other ways to connect with customers online? If it does have a presence, what do you think of the way the company interacts with customers? Does their approach encourage you to contribute? Do you believe that customers feel *listened to* online?

    Write an email to the company's vice president of social media with your recommendations. Submit this to your instructor.

12. **Propose a way to include employees' input.**

    Imagine that you are the vice president of employee communication at a large financial services company. Management is considering redesigning the office space for customer service associates to reduce noise but keep an open environment. As part of the process, you propose an online survey to hear employees' opinions. Write a one- or two-page proposal to the rest of the management team (your peers) to implement a survey on the company's intranet. Convince the rest of the team that this is a good idea by explaining your rationale and providing enough details so that they understand how the survey would work. Be honest about the downsides of your idea; after all, asking employees for their opinions can be risky.

13. **Consider Yammer for a company.**

    In small groups, discuss how Yammer could be used at a company where you have worked. How could employees use the social networking functionality? What could be potential obstacles to implementing it? What could be the benefits and downsides?

LO4 Use voice technologies and texting effectively in business situations.

14. **Leave a voice mail message.**

    Imagine that you applied for a job and received the following voice mail message from the company's HR manager:

This voice mail relates to the Bank on Me company scenario available at www.cengagebrain.com.

> Hello. This is Mariey Catona from Bank on Me. We received your cover letter and résumé, and I'd like to schedule a phone interview with you. Will you please tell me what times you're available this Friday for a half-hour call? You can reach me at 555-1212. Thank you.

    Leave a response on another student's phone. Plan your message in advance, but try to sound natural. You'll want to express your enthusiasm for the interview and give specific times when you're available. Use the checklist in Figure 22 to give each other feedback.

❑ Thanks Ms. Catona for the call

❑ Includes all relevant information:
  ○ First and last name
  ○ Reason for calling (responding to Ms. Catona's message)
  ○ Times available on Friday

❑ Avoids extraneous information and fillers (e.g., overuse of "uh," "um")

❑ Uses an appropriate tone:
  ○ Professional
  ○ Enthusiastic
  ○ Natural
  ○ Confident, but not overly confident

❑ Ends the call clearly and professionally

❑ Other: _____

---

15. Practice texting for business.

Exchange cell phone numbers with a partner, and assign roles of manager and employee. The manager is at a meeting with a client that started at 9:00 a.m. It's 9:05 a.m., and the employee hasn't arrived yet with the design board (large display) that shows fabrics, paint colors, furnishings, and other elements of the conference space that your firm is proposing to redesign. The manager initiates the text conversation. What will each of you say? The employee can invent details (excuses!) for this scenario.

After a few exchanges, give each other feedback on the text messages. Were they clear and professional?

16. Determine the best meeting format.

For each of the following scenarios, identify which format—face-to-face, conference call, online meeting, or videoconference—would work best.

- You want to close a sale with a new client.
- You have a weekly meeting with housekeeping staff at the Arlington, Virginia, hotel.
- You call a meeting to discuss cost-cutting ideas with your counterparts in three different states.
- You need to teach the new IT analyst, who works in a different office, how to operate a proprietary system.
- You need to tell employees who report to you but work in different locations that the company is planning to downsize.

> **LO5** Plan, facilitate, and participate in business meetings.

17. Evaluate a business meeting.

Attend a business meeting at work, a city council meeting in your community, a student organization meeting at school, or some other meeting. Observe the meeting and evaluate how well the facilitator plans and runs the meeting. Write an email to the facilitator to recommend improvements, according to what you learned in this chapter.

18. Plan a business meeting.

Working in groups of five, choose one of these scenarios for the next three exercises. For the scenario you and your team members choose, prepare an email and detailed agenda to send to the other meeting participants.

Scenario 1

Imagine that you are a dean at your college, which does not celebrate Martin Luther King, Jr.'s birthday with a paid holiday. You want the support of the college's four other deans to make the third Monday in January a holiday for all college employees and students. Invite your four colleagues to a meeting.

Scenario 2

Imagine that you work as a sales associate for your local Gap store. The work schedule is always set a month in advance, but you want more flexibility. You ask the four other sales associates in the store to meet with you, so you can convince them to plan the schedule only one week in advance. You would need the store manager's approval to do this, but you decide to get your coworkers on board first.

19. Facilitate a face-to-face meeting.

Use one of the scenarios in the previous exercise to practice facilitating and participating in a meeting.

Have each person assume the role of another participant. Determine who will lead the meeting (the dean or the sales associate calling the meeting). Conduct a ten-minute meeting. Following the meeting, evaluate its effectiveness. Did you achieve your objective? Explain your answer.

20. Write meeting minutes.

To summarize the meeting for your colleagues in the previous scenario, write up the meeting minutes. Each of you in the group should prepare minutes separately. Then, as a group, compare your minutes. Which are best and why?

21. Participate in an online meeting.

Sign up for free versions of WebEx, GoToMeeting, or another service to practice participating in an online meeting. In groups of four or five, have one person take the role of facilitator to schedule a time and send an invitation to the rest of the team.

During the meeting, discuss the benefits and obstacles of using the tool for an organization where you worked recently. In what ways could the service be useful for the organization? In what ways is the service not appropriate for this particular organization?

COMPANY SCENARIO

In the Loop Soup Kitchen

In the Loop is a not-for-profit community kitchen that provides a safe, warm place for locals to get a healthy meal. This scenario presents a crisis situation—someone enters the facility with a gun—and challenges you to do the following:

- Analyze Twitter use in a crisis situation.
- Practice leaving a voice mail message during a crisis.
- Write internal and external messages to address a sensitive situation.
- Take a proactive, strategic approach to crisis communication.

At www.cengagebrain.com, you'll find information about the situation and communications during the crisis, including the tweet written by an intern, shown here.

If you were the assistant director of In the Loop and had to handle this situation in the executive director's absence, what would you do? Your instructor may assign you to do the following to practice your interpersonal communication skills:

- Analyze the intern's use of Twitter in this situation and meet with Chris, the intern, to understand his perspective and to present your own ideas.
- Write a few tweets that would communicate that all is well at In the Loop and to continue building relationships with your key audiences.
- Leave a voice mail message for Emilio, the executive director (in response to his message, which you can listen to online).

These communications—and others for this scenario—will test your ability to build relationships in a difficult situation.

Endnotes

1. Peter F. Drucker, quoted by Bill Moyers in *A World of Ideas* (Garden City: Doubleday, 1990).

2. Pamela Meyer, "How to Spot a Liar," TED Talk, July 2011, www.ted.com/talks/pamela_meyer_how_to_spot_a_liar, accessed April 28, 2015.

3. Judy Foreman, "A Conversation with Paul Ekman: The 43 Facial Muscles That Reveal Even the Most Fleeting Emotions," *New York Times Online*, August 5, 2003, http://nytimes .com/2003/08/05/health/conversation-with-paul-ekman-43 -facial-muscles-that-reveal-even-most-fleeting.html, accessed April 28, 2015.

4. Robin Marks, "The Eyes Have It," *QUEST Community Science Blog*, January 24, 2008, www.kqed.org/quest/blog/2008/01/24 /the-eyes-have-it/, accessed April 28, 2015.

5. Buck Wolf, "The Pinocchio Effect," ABCNews.com Home Page, December 17, 2000, http://abcnews.go.com/sections/us /WolfFiles/wolffiles68.html, accessed April 28, 2015.

6. Timothy A. Judge, Charlice Hurst, and Lauren S. Simon, "Does It Pay to Be Smart, Attractive, or Confident (or All Three)?" *Journal of Applied Psychology* 94 (2009): 742–755.

7. Disa A. Sauter et al., "Cross-Cultural Recognition of Basic Emotions through Nonverbal Emotional Vocalizations," *Proceedings of the National Academy of Sciences of the United States of America*, November 4, 2009, www.pnas.org/ content/107/6/2408, April 28, 2015.

8. David B. Givens, "Tones of Voice," *The Nonverbal Dictionary of Gestures, Signs, and Body Language Cues*, 2002.

9. Curt Suplee, "Get Outta My Face," *Washington Post*, June 9, 1999, p. H-1.

10. "Brené Brown on Empathy," YouTube, published December 10, 2013, www.youtube.com/watch?v=1Evwgu369Jw, accessed February 16, 2015.

11. Jane O'Reilly, Sandra L. Robinson, Jennifer L. Berdahl, and Sara Banki, "Is Negative Attention Better than No Attention? The Comparative Effects of Ostracism and Harassment at Work," *Organization Science*, April 4, 2014, http://pubsonline.informs .org/doi/abs/10.1287/orsc.2014.0900?journalCode=orsc accessed April 28, 2015.

12. Andrew O'Connell, "Being Treated as Invisible is More Harmful than Harassment," *HBR Blog*, June 12, 2014, http://blogs.hbr .org/2014/06/being-treated-as-invisible-is-more-harmful-than -harassment/, accessed April 28, 2015.

13. Judi Brownell, "Fostering Service Excellence through Listening: What Hospitality Managers Need to Know," The Center for Hospitality Research, *Cornell Hospitality Report* 9 (April 2009).

14. Josh Bernoff, "Five Objectives in the Groundswell (Listening)," Forrester's Consumer Forum 2007, April 7, 2008, www.youtube .com/watch?v=xC8JU_aEvgg, accessed April 28, 2015.

15. Charlene Li, Josh Bernhoff, *Groundswell: Winning in a World Transformed by Social Technologies* (Boston: Harvard Business Press, 2011).

16. "The Myth of Social Media," Gallup, June 11, 2014, online.wsj .com/public/resources/documents/sac_report_11_socialmedia _061114.pdf, accessed April 28, 2015.

17. Matt Wilson, "American Airlines Responds to Every Tweet with Original, Non-Scripted Answers," *PR Daily*, August 1, 2012, www.prdaily.com/Main/Articles/12296.aspx, accessed April 28, 2015.

18. Molly Driscoll, "George Takei: Does He Write His Own Facebook Posts?" *CS Monitor*, June 13, 2013, www.csmonitor .com/The-Culture/Culture-Cafe/2013/0613/George-Takei-Does -he-write-his-own-Facebook-posts, accessed April 28, 2015.

19. Marist Research and evolve24, "Twitter Study," September 2011, www.maritzresearch.com/~/media/Files/MaritzResearch/e24 /ExecutiveSummaryTwitterPoll.ashx, accessed April 28, 2015.

20. Seth Fiegerman, Mashable, "Most Top Brands Still Don't Engage with Twitter Followers," Simply Measured Survey, January 21, 2014, http://mashable.com/2014/01/21/twitter-brand-engagement -study/, accessed April 28, 2015.

21. eMarketer, "Twitter Users Want Businesses to Answer Them," June 14, 2011, www.emarketer.com/Article/Twitter-Users-Want -Businesses-Answer-Them/1008440, accessed February 15, 2015.

22. Marist Research and evolve24.

23. Hollis Thomases, "McDonald's Twitter Mess: What Went Wrong," April 28, 2015, www.inc.com/hollis-thomases/mcdonalds -mcdstories-twitter-mess.html, accessed February 15, 2015.

24. Emma Hall, "Brits Mock U.K. Supermarket in Tweets About Shopping at Waitrose," *Ad Age*, September 18, 2012, http:// adage.com/article/global-news/tweets-brits-mock-u-k -supermarket-waitrose/237249, accessed April 28, 2015.

25. Reference crediting: "Best Buy engages young staff through online dialogue," Ragan's HR Communication, December 19, 2011, http://hrcommunication.com/Main/Articles/Best_Buy _engages_young_staff_through_online_dialog_7293.aspx, accessed February 15, 2015.

26. Jillian Berman, "Coca-Cola Employees No Longer Have to Listen to Voice Mails," *Huffington Post*, December 22, 2014, www.msn .com/en-us/news/offbeat/coca-cola-employees-no-longer-have -to-listen-to-voice-mails/ar-BBh7fQq, accessed February 15, 2015.

27. Hubert B. Herring, "Endless Meetings: The Black Holes of the Workday," *New York Times*, June 18, 2006, p. E7.

28. Kelly Services, "Kelly Global Workforce Index," www .smartmanager.us, accessed July 19, 2010.

29. Harvard Business Review Analytic Services, "Managing Across Distance in Today's Economic Climate: The Value of Face-to -Face Communication," June 2009 survey.

30. Endnote crediting: Harvard Business Review Analytic Services, "Managing Across Distance in Today's Economic Climate: The Value of Face-to-Face Communication," June 2009 survey.

31. Harvard Business Review Analytic Services.

32. Global Travel Industry News, "Forecast for the Meeting and Incentive Industry (MICE)," October 17, 2013, www.eturbonews .com/38921/forecast-meeting-and-incentive-industry-mice, accessed February 21, 2015.

33. "Second Life Work/Success Stories," http://wiki.secondlife.com, accessed April 28, 2015.

34. Meeting Cost Counter, Effective Meetings, www.effectivemeetings .com/diversions/meetingclock.asp, accessed June 17, 2014.

35. Mark Milian, "Startups' War on Meetings," *BloombergBusinessweek*, June 7, 2012, www.businessweek.com/articles/2012-06-07/ startups-war-on-meetings, accessed April 28, 2015.

36. Tripp and Tyler, "A Conference Call in Real Life," YouTube, published January 22, 2014, www.youtube.com/watch?v=DYu _bGbZiiQ, accessed February 15, 2015.

37. Gretchen Gavett, "What People Are Really Doing When They're on a Conference Call," *Harvard Business Review*, August 19, 2014, https://hbr.org/2014/08/what-people-are-really-doing-when -theyre-on-a-conference-call, accessed February 15, 2015.

CHAPTER

4

The Writing Process

...

LEARNING OBJECTIVES

After you have finished this chapter, you should be able to

LO1   Analyze the audience for your communication.

LO2   Plan the purpose, content, and organization of your message.

LO3   Compose the first draft of your message.

LO4   Revise for content, style, and correctness.

LO5   Proofread your message.

" *Got accepted, denied, and deferred to Fordham all in less than 24 hours.* "[1]

—Tweet by Ashtyn

CHAPTER INTRODUCTION

Bad Writing Is Bad Business

These examples show how poor writing affects the bottom line and people's lives:

- Fordham University sent acceptance letters to 2,500 students by mistake. In just one year, UCLA sent acceptances to 894 seniors on a wait list, Vassar sent letters to 76 early-decision candidates, and the University of California, Los Angeles, sent letters to 900 wait-list candidates, most of whom were later rejected.[2,3] Fordham's apology email to students is shown here.[4]

- A federal prisoner found a typo in his legal case that almost kept him incarcerated for another three-and-a-half years. It took the president's clemency powers to fix the mistake.[5]

- An attorney and her law firm were hit with a $6.6 million suit because a lease agreement was "inartfully written and done so in a confusing fashion, which lends itself to ambiguities and disagreements."[6]

- A confusing comma almost cost a cable TV company $1 million Canadian. The company won the case on appeal, but not before an unnecessary lawsuit about just one comma in a 14-page contract.[7]

Unclear and sloppy writing hurts organizations and damages professional reputations. In this chapter, you'll learn to write well—from the first step of knowing your audience to the last, proofreading your work.

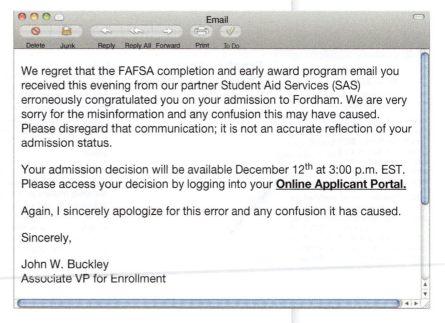

We regret that the FAFSA completion and early award program email you received this evening from our partner Student Aid Services (SAS) erroneously congratulated you on your admission to Fordham. We are very sorry for the misinformation and any confusion this may have caused. Please disregard that communication; it is not an accurate reflection of your admission status.

Your admission decision will be available December 12th at 3:00 p.m. EST. Please access your decision by logging into your **Online Applicant Portal.**

Again, I sincerely apologize for this error and any confusion it has caused.

Sincerely,

John W. Buckley
Associate VP for Enrollment

4-1 An Overview of the Writing Process

When faced with a writing task, some people just start writing. They try to do everything at once: choose the best words, organize into paragraphs, format, proofread—all at the same time. This may seem like the most efficient writing process, but it's not. You might be bogged down with details that will prevent you from moving forward and producing the best product. Instead, writing in steps is the better strategy and will save you time in the long run. For example, spending planning time up front gives you a sense of where you want to go. With clear goals, it's more likely your writing will accomplish those goals. And if you save a separate step for proofreading, you'll catch more errors.

Although you may vary this process for different writing projects, business writers typically perform five steps (see Figure 1).

Figure 1 | The Writing Process

Audience Analysis: Studying the needs, experiences, background, personality, and other aspects of the receiver.

Planning: Determining the purpose of the message, what information you need to give the reader, and in what order to present it.

SEPS Email to All Employees
- Announce the system.
- Describe the purpose.
- List goals achieved.
- Close on a positive note.

Drafting: Composing a first draft of a message.

On behalf of senior managers at Sony, I am pleased to introduce our new performance management process, **SEPS** (**S**ony **E**mployee **P**erformance **S**ystem). We are continuing to focus on employee performance and development by giving you new tools and resources to use for the performance management process.

SEPS will provide a unified, consistent, organizational platform for managing and developing employee performance. This process is consistent with, and reinforces, our existing performance systems; **SEPS** builds upon the performance management needs and philosophies of each of the divisions, while improving consi... divisions. Rather than an off-the...

Proofreading: Checking for content, typographical, and format errors.

Email

To:	All Sony Employees
From:	Warren Saliano
Subject:	SEPS: New Performance Management System

On behalf of senior managers at Sony, I pleased to introduce our new performance management Process SEP (Sony Employee Performance System). We are continuing focus on employee performance and dev ment by giving you new tools nce and for the performance management process.

SEPS will provide a unified, consistent platform for managing and developing employee performance. This process reinforces our existing performance systems; **SEPS** builds on the performance management needs and philosophies of each division, while improving consistency across all groups. Rather than an

---

On behalf of senior managers at Sony, I am pleased to introduce our new performance management process, **SEPS** (**S**ony **E**mployee **P**erformance **S**ystem). We are continuing to focus on employee performance and development by giving you new tools and resources ~~to use~~ for the performance management process.

SEPS will provide a unified, consistent, ~~organizational~~ platform for managing and developing employee performance. The process ~~is consistent with, and~~ reinforces, our our existing performance systems; **SEPS** builds ~~upon~~ on the performance management needs and philosophies of ~~each of the divisions~~ division, while improv... across ~~divisions.~~ all groups. Rat

Revising: Editing for content, style, and correctness.

The amount of time you devote to each step depends on the complexity, length, and importance of the writing project. You may go through all the steps when writing a business plan but not when answering an email inviting you to a meeting.

4-2 Audience Analysis

LO1 Analyze the audience for your communication.

Your first step is to consider your audience for the message—the reader or readers of your writing. Your audience may be just one person or a group of diverse people all over the world. We can't always understand our audience perfectly, but we do our best to anticipate what they need and how they might react to our message. For a strategic-level communication—for example, announcing a big change in a company, such as a merger or acquisition—multiple messages would be sent to different audiences. Here, we'll consider just one message at a time.

An audience analysis will help you understand your message from the reader's perspective. This process gives you a sense of the audience's potential mental filters and how to adjust your message accordingly.

Let's take an example of moving an office from downtown Chicago to a suburb. In Figure 2, you can see how analyzing an audience helps the writer tailor a message.

Audience Analysis Example (Moving the Office to the Suburbs) | Figure 2

Who is the audience?	**What is your relationship with the audience?**	**How will the audience likely react?**	**What does the audience already know?**	**What is unique about the audience?**
• Primary audience: employees in the Chicago office, who will be moving • Secondary audience: employees in the Boston office, who may be concerned that they will move next	• As the Chicago office manager, I know these employees well and have credibility with them. • My tone will be respectful and conversational.	• Employees who live near the new location will be happy, but most will not. This is a big change for everyone. • I will get to the main point quickly and will explain the rationale for the move and include lots of evidence to support the decision.	• Employees know this was a possibility because we have been looking to reduce costs. • I will refer to previous discussions about ways to reduce costs. • I will be honest and say that the Boston location may move as well.	• Many employees don't have cars, so I'll emphasize the public transportation options. • Many employees are paid minimum wage, so I'll emphasize less expensive housing options in the area.

4-2a Who Is the Primary Audience?

When you have more than one audience, you need to identify your primary audience (e.g., the decision maker) and your secondary audience (others who will also read and be affected by your message). Focus on the primary audience, but try to satisfy the needs of the secondary audience as well. If this is too much to accomplish with one message, write separate messages to different audiences. For example, a sales letter to a major client should be tailored to that client's needs.

4-2b What Is Your Relationship with the Audience?

Does your audience know you? If your audience doesn't know you, establish your credibility by assuming a professional tone, and give enough evidence to support your claims. Are you writing to someone inside or outside the organization? If outside, your message may be more formal and contain more background information and less jargon than if you are writing to someone inside the organization.

What is your status in relation to your audience? Because communications to your manager are vital to your success in the organization, typically, these messages are a little more formal, less authoritarian in tone, and more informative than communications to peers or people who

 Emotional **INTELLIGENCE**

When have you found it difficult to consider your audience's perspective? What barriers have prevented you from accepting another's point of view? Recognizing your own judgment may help you appreciate your audience and how to tailor a message.

report to you. Study your manager's own messages to understand his or her preferred style, and adapt your own message accordingly.

When you communicate with people who report to you, be respectful rather than patronizing. Try to instill a sense of collaboration, and include employees in your message rather than talking down to them. For example, use "we" when you refer to the company or department, but avoid platitudes such as, "Employees are our greatest assets." Be sincere and think about how your employees might react to your message. When praising or criticizing, focus on specific behaviors, not the person. As always, praise in public, but criticize in private.

4-2c How Will the Audience Likely React?

If the reader's initial reaction to both you and your topic is likely to be positive, your job is relatively easy. Typically, your message can be short and straightforward, and you can provide little, if any, justification.

But if you expect your reader's reaction—either to your topic or to you personally—to be negative, now you have a real sales job. Your best strategy is to call on external evidence and expert opinion to bolster your position. Use polite, conservative language, and suggest ways the readers can cooperate without appearing to "give in." Begin with the areas of agreement, stress how the audience will benefit, and try to anticipate and answer any objections the reader might have. Through logic, evidence, and tone, build a case for your position.

4-2d What Does the Audience Already Know?

Understanding what the audience already knows helps you decide how much content to include and what writing style is most appropriate. When writing to multiple audiences, adapt to the key decision maker (the primary audience). In general, it is better to provide too much rather than too little information.

4-2e What Is Unique About the Audience?

The success or failure of a message often depends on little things—the extra touches that say to the reader, "You're important, and I've taken the time to learn some things about you." What can you learn about the interests or demographics of your audience that you can build into your message? What questions and concerns can you anticipate and address in your message?

4-2f Example of Audience Analysis

To illustrate the crucial role that audience analysis plays in communication, assume that you are a marketing manager at Seaside Resorts, a chain of small hotels along the California, Oregon, and Washington coasts. You know that many of the larger hotel chains have instituted frequent-stay (or loyalty) programs, which reward repeat customers with free stays or other perks.

You want to write a message recommending a similar plan for your hotel. Assume that Cynthia Haney, your immediate manager and the vice president of marketing, will be the only reader of your email and has the authority to approve or reject your proposal. Let's look at three versions of Haney and how you could adjust your message to each (Figure 3).

As you can see in Figure 3, the type, amount, and organization of information you include in your message reflect what you know (or can learn) about your audience.

Three Versions of Haney, VP of Marketing

Version 1

Haney has 20 years of management experience in the hospitality industry, and she respects your judgment. She likes directness in writing and wants the important information upfront.

Version 2

Haney assumed her position at Seaside Resorts just six months ago and is still "learning the ropes" of the hospitality industry. Up to this point, your relationship with her has been cordial, although she is probably not very familiar with your work.

Version 3

Haney has implied that she doesn't yet completely trust your judgment. In the past, she has been hesitant about accepting your ideas.

Your first paragraph can be short and to the point: "The purpose of this memo is to recommend implementing a frequent-stay plan for a 12-month test period in our three Oregon resorts. This recommendation is based on our competitors' policies and the costs and benefits of instituting a loyalty program."

Your first paragraph might use a less direct approach, in which you discuss your process and present the evidence before making a recommendation: "The attached *Wall Street Journal* article discusses four small hotels that have started frequent-stay plans. The purpose of this memo is to describe these plans and analyze the costs and benefits of a similar plan at Seaside."

You might write a longer introduction, with a second paragraph to establish your credibility: "This proposal is based on a large amount of data collected over two months. I studied several Hotel and Restaurant Association reports, interviewed the person in charge of frequent-stay programs at three hotels, and asked Dr. Kenneth Lowe, professor of hospitality services at Southern Cal, to review and comment on my first draft."

4-3 Planning

Planning involves making conscious decisions about the purpose, content, and organization of the message.

LO2 Plan the purpose, content, and organization of your message.

4-3a Purpose

If you don't know why you're writing the message (i.e., what you hope to accomplish), then you won't know whether you have achieved your goal. In the end, what matters is not how well crafted your message was or how well it was formatted; what matters is whether you achieved your communication objective.

Most writers find it easier to start with a general purpose and then refine it into a specific objective. The objective should state what you expect the reader to do as a result of your message. For the hotel frequent-stay program example, your general purpose might be this:

> *General Purpose:* To describe the benefits of a frequent-stay program at Seaside Resorts.

This goal is a good starting point, but it is not specific enough. It doesn't identify the intended audience or the outcome you expect. If the audience is the marketing vice president, do you want her to simply understand what you've written? Commit resources for more research? Agree to implement the plan immediately? How will you know if your message achieves its objective? This is one example of a more specific communication objective:

> *Specific Purpose:* To persuade Cynthia to approve developing and implementing a frequent-stay plan for a 12-month test period in Seaside's three Oregon resorts.

This purpose is now specific enough to guide you in writing the message and evaluating its success. Figure 4 shows additional examples of general-purpose statements converted to more useful objectives. These communication objectives state what you expect the audience to do and how you hope people will feel after reading your message. A clearly stated objective helps you avoid including irrelevant and distracting information.

Figure 4 | Identifying a Communication Objective

GENERAL-PURPOSE STATEMENT	SPECIFIC COMMUNICATION OBJECTIVE
To communicate the office move.	To explain the rationale and process for the move to employees, while maintaining morale and minimizing employee turnover.
To apply for the sales associate position.	To convince the HR manager to call me for an interview based on my qualifications for the job.
To deny a customer's request for a replacement phone.	To maintain the customer's goodwill by helping her understand the rationale for the decision and convincing her that the denial is reasonable.

4-3b Content

After you analyze your audience and identify the objective of your message, the next step is to decide what information to include. For simple messages, such as a quick text or routine email, this step is easy. However, most communication projects require many decisions about what to include. How much background information is needed? What statistical data best supports the conclusions? Are expert opinions needed? Would examples, anecdotes, or graphics help comprehension? Will research be necessary, or do you have what you need? The trick is to include enough information so that you don't lose or confuse the reader, yet avoid including irrelevant material that wastes the reader's time and obscures important data.

For all but the simplest communications, one thing you should not do is to start drafting immediately, deciding as you write what information to include. Instead, start with at least a preliminary outline of your message—whether it's in your head, in a typed outline, or as notes on a piece of paper.

One useful strategy is brainstorming—jotting down ideas, facts, possible leads, and anything else you think might be helpful in constructing your message. Aim for quantity, not quality.

Don't evaluate your output until you run out of ideas. Then begin to refine, delete, combine, and revise your ideas to form your message.

Another approach is mind mapping (also called *clustering*), a process that avoids the step-by-step limitations of lists. Instead, you write the purpose of your message in the middle of a page and circle it. Then, as you think of possible points to add, write them down and link them with a line either to the main purpose or to another point. As you think of other details, add them where you think they might fit. This visual outline offers flexibility and encourages free thinking. Figure 5 shows an example of mind mapping for the frequent-stay idea.

You may use computer graphics for this process, but many people find writing by hand more freeing. Either way, by putting your ideas down and showing how they relate, you're beginning to organize your message, which is the next step in the planning process.

Consider using SpicyNodes (spicynodes. org), a tool for displaying hierarchical information.

Mind Map of Ideas | **Figure 5**

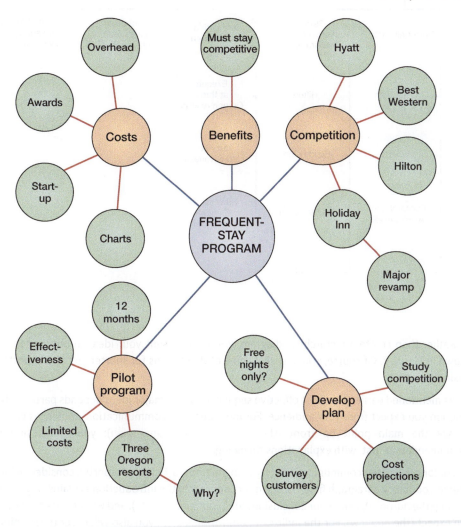

4-3c Organization

After you have brainstormed around a main idea, you need to organize your points into an outline. The organization of a message indicates the order in which you'll discuss each topic.

First, classify or group related ideas. Next, differentiate between the major and minor points so that you can line up minor ideas and evidence to support the major ideas. The diagram in Figure 6 shows the frequent-stay idea shaping up into a well-organized message.

Figure 6 Organization for the Frequent-Stay Message

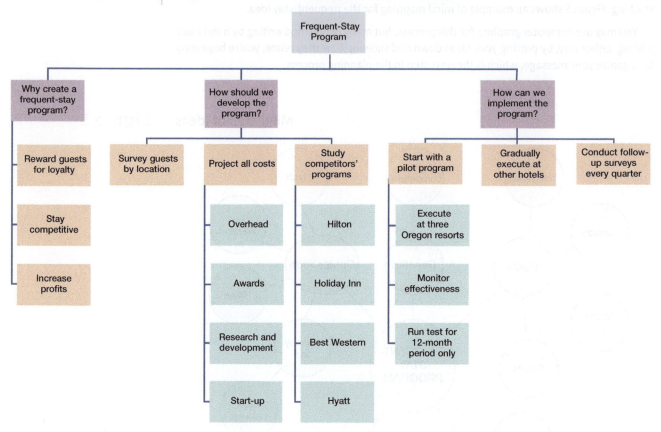

Rather than create a hierarchical diagram, you may present your ideas in outline format, shown in Figure 7. Of course, you may skip some of these steps for shorter and less important business writing.

As mentioned earlier, the most effective sequence for the major ideas depends partly on the reaction you expect from your audience. For most business communication, audiences expect to see the main point up front (the direct organizational plan): your conclusion or recommendation first, with explanations following.

For longer written communications (e.g., long memos, articles, or reports), consider writing your introductory paragraph first. For the direct approach, the introduction explains why you're writing (the purpose), what your conclusions are (your main points), and what topics the reader can expect (the preview). For the indirect organizational plan, you also will cover these points, but you would provide more background information—and discuss your purpose and main points later in the introduction. Compare two approaches for an introductory paragraph for the frequent-stay proposal (Figure 8). These build on our earlier examples of analyzing the audience (Figure 3).

Emotional INTELLIGENCE

Do you prefer a more direct or indirect style of communication? Do you tend to get to the main point right away or give explanations and examples before conveying the main point? Does your own style sometimes get in the way of what's best for the audience and situation?

Message Organization in Outline Format | Figure 7

Frequent-Stay Program Message Outline

Introduction: Include purpose, summary of main points, and preview of topics to be covered.

Section 1: Why should we create a frequent-stay program?
    (1) Reward guests for loyalty
    (2) Stay competitive
    (3) Increase profits

Section 2: How should we develop the program?
    (1) Survey guests by location
    (2) Project all costs
        1. Overhead
        2. Awards
        3. Research and development
        4. Start-up
    (3) Study competitors' programs
        1. Hilton
        2. Holiday Inn
        3. Best Western
        4. Hyatt

Section 3: How can we implement the program?
    (1) Start with a pilot program
        1. Implement at three Oregon resorts
        2. Monitor effectiveness
        3. Run test for 12 months
    (2) Implement at other hotels gradually
    (3) Conduct follow-up surveys on programs every quarter

Conclusion: Summarize points, request action, and provide contact information.

Direct and Indirect Introductory Paragraphs | Figure 8

Direct Approach	Indirect Approach
Background: The VP is experienced and respects you.	*Background: The VP is new and doesn't know you well.*

Direct Approach

Purpose statement → The purpose of this memo is to recommend implementing a frequent-stay plan for a 12-month test period in our three Oregon resorts. This recommendation is based on our competitors' policies and the costs and benefits of instituting a loyalty program. *Main points* → Implementing a similar program will keep us competitive in the Oregon market and may significantly increase guest loyalty and profits. *Preview of topics to be covered* → In this memo, I'll discuss why we should establish a frequent-stay program, how we should develop the program, and how we can implement the program for our guests.

Indirect Approach

A recent *Wall Street Journal* article discusses four small hotels that have started frequent-stay plans. I became interested in this idea for Seaside and would like to share with you my research about these programs. ← *Purpose statement* My research shows that 77% of our competitors have a frequent-stay program, and a recent survey shows that nearly half of the 5,000 respondents choose specific hotels (even if they are more expensive) in order to accrue hotel loyalty points. In this memo, I'll describe frequent-stay plans and then analyze the costs and benefits ← *Preview of topics to be covered* for Seaside. After reviewing this information, I hope that you will ← *Main point* consider piloting a frequent-stay program at our three Oregon resorts.

In the indirect introduction example, notice how much softer the tone is for the reader. The main point is more of an invitation than a recommendation. In Chapter 5, we'll discuss more about paragraph unity, coherence, and length—also important elements of organization.

LO3 Compose the first draft of your message.

4-4 Drafting

After planning your message, you're finally ready to begin drafting—composing a preliminary version of a message. The more work you did to plan and organize your message, the easier this step will be. Again, don't begin writing too soon. People who believe they have weak writing skills tend to jump in and get it over with as quickly as possible. Instead, follow each of the five steps of the writing process to ease the journey and improve your final product.

4-4a Letting Go

Probably the most important thing to remember about drafting is to just let go—let your ideas flow as quickly as possible, without worrying about style, correctness, or format. Separate the drafting stage from the revising stage. Although some people revise as they create, most find it easier to first get their ideas down in rough-draft form, and then revise. It's much easier to polish a page full of writing than a page full of nothing.

Avoid moving from author to editor too quickly. Your first draft is just that—a *draft*. Don't expect perfection, and don't strive for it. Instead, write in narrative form all the points you identified in the planning stage.

4-4b Overcoming Writer's Block

 Emotional INTELLIGENCE

How do you feel about your own writing? Have you been told that you're a good writer or a poor writer? Do you tell yourself that you hate writing? Consider how these messages may cause writer's block. Instead, try to think positively: you can write well.

If a report is due in five weeks, some managers (and students) spend four weeks worrying about the task and one week (or less!) actually writing the report. Similarly, when given 45 minutes to write an email, some people spend 35 minutes anxiously staring at a blank screen and 10 minutes actually writing. These people are experiencing writer's block—the inability to focus on the writing process and to draft a message. Typical causes of writer's block follow:

- *Procrastination*: Putting off what we dislike doing.
- *Impatience*: Getting bored with the naturally slow pace of the writing process.
- *Perfectionism*: Believing that our draft must be perfect the first time.

Once these factors interfere with creativity, writers may start to question their ability, which makes it even harder to tackle writing.

Try the strategies in Figure 9 for avoiding writer's block at least once. Then, choose what works best for you.

4-4c Writing for Different Media

In Chapter 1, we discussed several options for conveying your message. How you draft your message depends on which medium you choose. In this chapter, we'll look at writing guidelines for four typical media choices for business communication: email, memos, letters, and the Internet.

Writing Email Messages

 **Communication TECHNOLOGIES**

Email is so pervasive in organizations that many people don't consider it writing—but of course it is. In business, emails can be one-word confirmations or longer messages with attachments.

Strategies for Overcoming Writer's Block | Figure 9

1 Choose the right environment.
- Go to a quiet library—or a busy computer lab.
- Experiment until you find a place where you write best.

5 Write freely.
- Start by free writing: write without stopping for 5 to 10 minutes.
- Write anything, without judgment; if you get stuck, write, "I'll think of something soon."

2 Minimize distractions.
- Close web browsers to avoid IM notifications and the lure of Facebook!
- Leave your smartphone in another room so you're not tempted to text.

6 Think out loud.
- Picture yourself telling a colleague what you're writing about, and explain aloud the ideas you're trying to get across.
- Sharpen and focus your ideas by speaking rather than writing them.

3 Schedule a reasonable block of time.
- For short writing projects, block out enough time to plan, draft, and revise the entire message in one sitting.
- For long or complex projects, schedule blocks of about two hours, or set milestones, such as writing one section and then taking a break.

7 Avoid perfectionism.
- Think of your writing as a draft—not a final document.
- Don't worry about style, coherence, spelling, or punctuation errors at this point. The artist in you must create something before the editor can refine it.

4 State your purpose in writing.
- Define the objective of your message clearly and concisely.
- Write the objective someplace prominently so you always keep it in mind.

8 Write the easiest parts first.
- Skip the opening paragraph if you're struggling with it.
- Start with a section that's easiest for you to write.

Email is the default communication choice in many organizations, with business people sending and receiving on average 121 messages a day.[8] With people receiving so many messages, how you write emails will determine whether yours are read and understood.

Emails tend to be more concise and—even if sent outside the organization—are often less formal than letters. See guidelines for drafting email messages in Figure 10. The email in Figure 12 meets these criteria.

Every organization has its own conventions for email. When you start working at a company, pay attention to how people open and close messages, who's copied, when emails are sent, and other details.

In addition to conforming to organizational norms for email, you should pay attention to variations by country and region. Cultural differences discussed in Chapter 2 are as apparent in email messages as in any business communication. For example, in cultures that emphasize relationships rather than tasks, you may see longer emails with more personal information. Although an email from a U.S. manager may jump right into the main point, an email from a Latin American manager may start with a longer introduction about the weather or an update about the family. Email presents many challenges for communication—and cultural differences add even more possibilities for misunderstandings.

International **COMMUNICATION**

Figure 10 | Writing Effective Email Messages

Openings and Closings

- Follow your company's standards for salutations. Use "Dear," "Hi," "Hello," or "Good morning" as salutations, depending on what people in your organization typically use. If you're writing an email to a prospective employer, err on the side of formality with "Dear Ms. Unger," followed by a comma. Although a comma after "Hi" as in, "Hi, Jasmine," is technically correct, you may find that few people in your company use this as a convention. Also, most people will skip the salutation (and signature) after one round of emails. It's silly to continue using someone's name for quick response emails.
- Follow conventions for closings and signatures. Similar to salutations, use standard phrases that reflect your organization's culture. See what other people use, for example, "I hope all is well" or "Please let me know if you have any questions." Before you type your name at the end of the email, include a brief closing. For more formal emails, end with "Best regards," "Regards," "All the best," or simply "Best." For less formal emails, you may simply write "Thanks" or nothing before your name. In some organizations or departments, people may omit their name entirely—it just depends on the culture.
- Use a signature line. You may set up a personalized signature line for emails that you send. Typically, this includes your name, title, company, and possibly your phone number. If your company has guidelines, follow what's required. If not, keep your signature line simple and professional: avoid fancy fonts, colors, and backgrounds for business email.

Audience

- Draft your email before you enter the receiver's name in the "To" line. This way, you won't send the email accidentally before you proofread.
- Use an appropriate tone. Emails can be formal or informal. Typically, more formal emails are sent to people you don't know well or those far more senior to you in an organization.
- Don't copy the world. People already receive too many emails, so be respectful and copy only those people who need to know about your message. Consider the people who are copied as your secondary audience, and adjust your message accordingly.
- Use "BCC" (blind carbon copy) sparingly. In some organizations, using BCC to send people a copy of your email without others knowing about it is considered sneaky. This can become an ethical issue—and can come back to bite you if the person on BCC replies to all. A better alternative is to be open about who else is seeing the message or, if you must, forward an email after it has been sent.

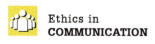

Ethics in
COMMUNICATION

Content

- Provide context. Initiating an email and responding to one require different approaches. When you initiate an email, provide enough context for the reader, just as you would in a memo or letter. Although email is fast, we still need to consider—and clearly communicate—our purpose for writing. When responding, consider including parts of the original email so that the receiver understands your reply.
- Keep emails short. Some managers believe emails should be no longer than what fits on a desktop computer screen; others believe anything more than a paragraph is too much, particularly for emails received on smartphones. For messages longer than about 300 words, consider an attachment instead.

Organization

- Use a descriptive, attention-grabbing subject line, such as those in Figure 11. Research tells us people often delete or read email based on the subject line alone.
- Make emails skimmable. Particularly for email, which people read quickly, make sure your main points are clear and up front. Bulleted lists are common in email.
- Keep paragraphs short. You may lose your audience with dense paragraphs in email. Keep them shorter—even single-sentence paragraphs are acceptable in email—to improve readability.

To celebrate *Harry Potter* author J.K. Rowling's birthday, ThinkGeek sent an email with the subject line, "We solemnly swear, we are up to no good . . ."[9]

Here are more examples of clear, specific subject lines:

- Today's meeting changed from 3:00 to 3:30 p.m.
- Need your input on the proposal revisions by 7/14
- Do you want to include Marjorie in the meeting?
- Customer has a question about shipping fees to Alaska
- Revised performance objectives for your approval

Sample Email | **Figure 12**

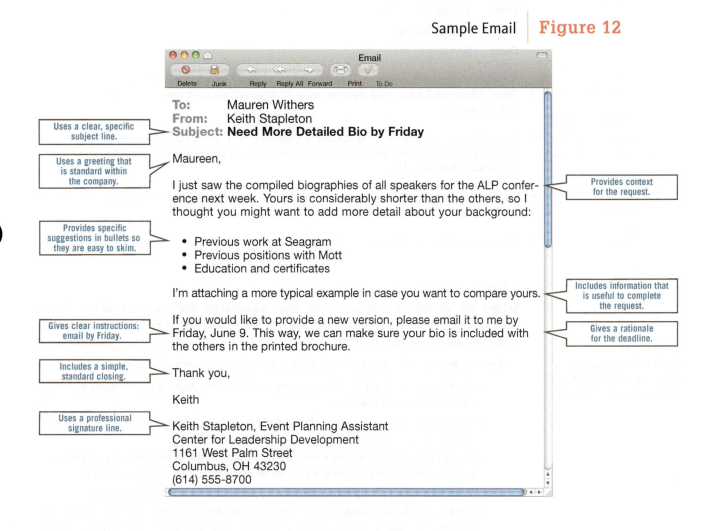

Uses a clear, specific subject line.

Uses a greeting that is standard within the company.

Provides specific suggestions in bullets so they are easy to skim.

Gives clear instructions: email by Friday.

Includes a simple, standard closing.

Uses a professional signature line.

Provides context for the request.

Includes information that is useful to complete the request.

Gives a rationale for the deadline.

> **To:** Mauren Withers
> **From:** Keith Stapleton
> **Subject: Need More Detailed Bio by Friday**
>
> Maureen,
>
> I just saw the compiled biographies of all speakers for the ALP conference next week. Yours is considerably shorter than the others, so I thought you might want to add more detail about your background:
>
> - Previous work at Seagram
> - Previous positions with Mott
> - Education and certificates
>
> I'm attaching a more typical example in case you want to compare yours.
>
> If you would like to provide a new version, please email it to me by Friday, June 9. This way, we can make sure your bio is included with the others in the printed brochure.
>
> Thank you,
>
> Keith
>
> Keith Stapleton, Event Planning Assistant
> Center for Leadership Development
> 1161 West Palm Street
> Columbus, OH 43230
> (614) 555-8700

Writing Memos

Email has replaced almost all memos—written messages to people within an organization. Sometimes *memo* and *letter* are used generically. When the founder and CEO of Mashable posted his message to employees about a new executive, the story was titled "Memo to Staff."[10] But Mashable is a news website and blog; it's highly unlikely that internal documents are printed and mailed.

Today, memos are reserved for more formal and print messages. Memos may be longer than one page (attached to short emails) or short messages that serve as cover notes (attached to printed material), as in the example in Figure 13. In some organizations, memos also may be printed for employees who do not have regular access to a computer at work. See the Reference Manual for an example of a longer memo.

Figure 13 | Sample Short Cover Memo

Is printed on paper with a company logo.

Includes standard memo heading with the writer's initials.

To: Store Managers
From: Andrea Jewel, CEO A.J.
Subject: Spring Catalog
Date: February 8, 2017

Refers to attached printed materials (a good reason to send a printed memo).

Attached is a preview copy of our spring catalog. I'm very proud of our Design Team, who created a beautiful representation of Aggresshop's most unique clothing and accessories.

Asks for feedback by email, which is the more typical communication medium for the company.

You will receive 100 copies of the catalog in your store by February 20. If you would like more than 100 copies, please contact Maryanne (msunger@aggresshop.com) by Wednesday, February 15.

Includes information related to the printed catalogs; this also may be sent by email.

Catalogs will be shipped to customers on February 22—one week earlier this year in response to your requests.

Closes on a positive note.

Best of luck for a successful spring season.

Writing Letters

Letters are written to people outside your organization and are reserved for formal communication. In your business career, you may write cover letters for jobs, sales letters to customers, proposal letters to accompany external reports, or thank-you letters to donors.

See letter examples in Chapters 5, 6, and 12, and in the Reference Manual.

Because letters are for external audiences, a more formal approach is appropriate:

- Use block or modified block format (see the Reference Manual for samples) with your return address and the date.
- Use a formal salutation, typically, "Dear Mr. Patel," followed by a colon (although commas are often used).
- Print your letter on company stationery or with an image of the company's logo. Many organizations will provide image files for you to paste into a document online.
- Write with longer paragraphs (typically 3–7 sentences) and few bulleted lists.
- Use a professional closing, such as "Sincerely" or "Regards," and then leave a few lines to sign your name above your full typed name. Your title and department may follow your name.

Writing for the Web

Web writing takes many forms for business communication: websites, blogs, tweets, Facebook posts, and more. Here, we'll focus on writing for company websites and blogs.

Static websites, intended only for people to retrieve information, can be useful but are least ideal for business communication. Effective online communication from companies today has

Communication **TECHNOLOGIES**

less writing and includes more interactivity—if not social media functionality, then other ways to connect with customers.

Less text is preferable for websites. Typically, people scan web pages, so putting main points in prominent positions—at the top of the page—is critical. Bulleted text, short sentences and paragraphs, simple words, and links to more information will keep your reader engaged rather than overwhelmed.

You can see that the Girls Who Code website (Figure 14), which promotes computing skills, leads with a striking photo. Users can easily find information about programs and how to get involved. Where the site has written content, it's short, as shown in Figure 15. On most websites, and almost all shopping websites, you won't find long blocks of text—only engaging graphics.

Girls Who Code Website Homepage | Figure 14

HTTP://GIRLSWHOCODE.COM/ABOUT-US/

COURTESY OF GIRLSWHOCODE

Girls Who Code Website Text | Figure 15

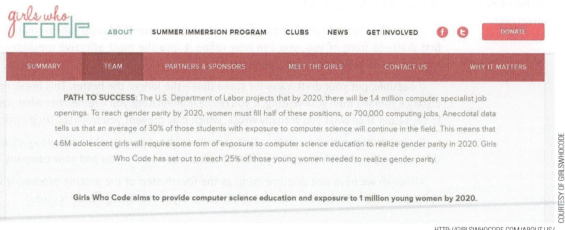

HTTP://GIRLSWHOCODE.COM/ABOUT-US/

COURTESY OF GIRLSWHOCODE

Blogs use far more text than websites and typically allow for customer comments. Although many opinion blogs include longer articles, company blogs—designed to engage customers— more often include short posts or blurbs of information. The writing style for Southwest Airlines' popular "Nuts About Southwest" blog is concise and quite personal (Figure 16). This approach is most likely to encourage interactivity with customers, which we discussed in Chapter 3.

Figure 16 | **"Nuts About Southwest" Blog**

Concise writing, short paragraphs, and a conversational style are hallmarks of writing for the web. Well-written web pages are highly skimmable, with graphics, headings, bullets, and links to encourage people to read more or visit other parts of the company's website.

4-5 Revising

Revising refers to modifying a message to make improvements. Having the raw material—your first draft—in front of you, you can now refine it into the most effective message possible, considering its importance and your time constraints.

If possible, put your draft away for some time—the longer the better. This break helps you distance yourself from your writing. If you revise immediately, you'll remember what you meant to say rather than what you actually wrote, which may prevent you from spotting errors.

For important writing projects, solicit comments about your draft from colleagues as part of the revision process. This step may prevent embarrassment for you and your company.

Although we have discussed revising as the fourth step of the writing process, it involves several substeps. Revise first for content, then for style, and finally for correctness.

4-5a Revising for Content

After an appropriate time interval, first reread your purpose statement and then the entire draft to get an overview of your message. Ask yourself such questions as these:

- Is the content appropriate for the purpose I've identified?
- Will the purpose of the message be clear to the reader?

- Have I been sensitive to how the reader might react?
- Is all the information necessary?
- Is important information missing?
- Is the order of my main points logical?

Although you may be proud of your first draft, don't be afraid of making changes to improve your writing—even if it means striking out whole sections and starting again from scratch. The goal is to produce the best possible message.

4-5b Revising for Style

Next, read each paragraph again (aloud, if possible). Reading aloud gives you a feel for the rhythm and flow of your writing. Long sentences that made sense as you wrote them may leave you out of breath when you read them aloud.

4-5c Revising for Correctness

The final phase of revising is editing, ensuring that the writing conforms to standard English. Editing involves checking for correctness—identifying problems with grammar, spelling, punctuation, and word usage. Unfortunately, you can't rely solely on your computer's grammar and spellchecker. These tools aren't 100% accurate, and they miss the context of your writing. Take responsibility to catch your own errors that may reflect negatively on your credibility or cause misunderstandings, as we saw in the introduction to this chapter.

See the Language Arts Basics section of the Reference Manual for editing guidelines.

4-6 Proofreading

Proofreading is the final quality-control check for your message. A reader may not know whether an incorrect word resulted from a simple typo or from the writer's ignorance of correct usage. During the Scribes National Spelling Bee, ESPN misspelled "South American" as "Soouth American" in a word definition. This was embarrassing for the network—particularly because it's not a hard word.[11]

Make sure your final product is the best possible reflection of you. Proofread for content, typographical, and formatting errors.

- **Content Errors**: First, read through your message quickly, checking for content errors. Was any material omitted unintentionally? As you revise, you may move, delete, or duplicate text. Check to be sure that your message makes sense.
- **Typographical Errors**: Next, read through your message slowly, checking for typographical errors. Look carefully for these hard-to-spot errors:

> Look for Hard-to-Spot Errors
>
> - Misused words that spellcheckers won't flag—for example, "I took the data form last month's report."
> - Repeated or omitted words, such as articles (the, a, an).
> - Proper names and numbers.
> - Titles and headings, particularly if you use "all caps," which some spellcheckers skip (although you can change this option).

- **Formatting Errors**: Visually inspect the message for appropriate format. Are all the parts included and in the correct position? Does the message look attractive on the page or online?

LO5 Proofread your message.

Emotional INTELLIGENCE

Do you take time to proofread? If not, what gets in the way? Try to be honest about the obstacles: lack of planning, procrastination, not feeling good about your writing, or something else.

Use the following tips to catch more errors in your writing:

> **Catch More Errors**
>
> - Proofread in print—never on the computer screen.
> - Print on yellow or pink paper to see your work differently.
> - Wait a few hours or overnight after your last revision before you start proofreading.
> - Use a ruler to guide and slow down your eyes as you proofread.
> - Read backwards, one sentence at a time.

After you make changes, be sure to proofread again. By correcting one mistake, you might inadvertently introduce another. You're finished proofreading only when you read through the entire message without making any changes.

The Checklist for the Writing Process summarizes the five steps discussed in this chapter.

Checklist for the Writing Process

1. AUDIENCE ANALYSIS

☑ Who is the primary audience?

☑ What is your relationship with the audience?

☑ How will the audience likely react?

☑ What does the audience already know?

☑ What is unique about the audience?

2. PLANNING

☑ Determine the specific purpose of the message. What response do you want from the reader?

☑ Determine what information to include in the message, given its purpose and your analysis of the audience.

☑ Organize the information according to the reader's expected reaction:

  ☑ Direct approach (expected positive or neutral reaction): present the major idea first, followed by supporting details.

  ☑ Indirect approach (expected negative reaction): present the reasons first, followed by the major idea.

3. DRAFTING

☑ Choose a productive work environment, and schedule a reasonable block of time to devote to the drafting phase.

☑ Let your ideas flow as quickly as possible, without worrying about style, correctness, or format. If helpful, write the easiest parts first.

☑ Do not expect a perfect first draft; avoid the urge to revise at this stage.

☑ If possible, leave a time gap between writing and revising the draft.

4. REVISING

☑ Revise for content: check for unnecessary information, omitted information, and organization.

☑ Revise for style: try reading your message aloud.

☑ Revise for correctness: use correct grammar, mechanics, punctuation, and word choice (see the Reference Manual).

5. PROOFREADING

☑ Proofread for content, typographical, and formatting errors.

Responding to a Reporter's Inquiry

>>> PURPOSE

Imagine that you are the head of enrollment at Fordham University, and you are responsible for handling fallout from the acceptance letter mistakenly sent to applicants (described in the chapter introduction).

When you check your email, in addition to dozens of emails from frustrated students and parents, you see this message from a local reporter.

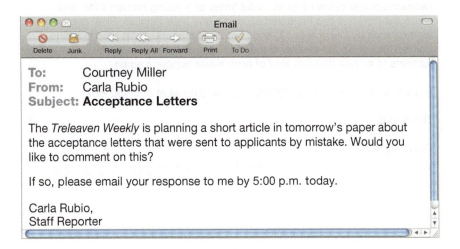

To: Courtney Miller
From: Carla Rubio
Subject: **Acceptance Letters**

The *Treleaven Weekly* is planning a short article in tomorrow's paper about the acceptance letters that were sent to applicants by mistake. Would you like to comment on this?

If so, please email your response to me by 5:00 p.m. today.

Carla Rubio,
Staff Reporter

You decide to respond so that the article will include your perspective.

>>> PROCESS

1. **What is the purpose of your message?**
   To restore the university's credibility.

2. **Describe your primary audience.**
   Carla Rubio, the reporter. She is on a deadline and wants my perspective for a well-balanced story.

3. **Do you have other audiences for your email? If so, describe these groups.**
   Yes, the entire university community who may read the article: prospective students and their families, current students and their families, faculty, staff, alumni, and administrators at other universities.

4. **Considering your purpose, what are your main points for the response to the reporter?**
   - *Thank her for the opportunity to respond.*
   - *Express my empathy for students, and apologize to everyone affected by this embarrassing mistake.*
   - *Explain what happened, including Student Aid Services (SAS)'s role. But I can't shirk responsibility either.*
   - *Tell prospective students and their families how and when they can find correct information.*

5. **What medium will you use for your message?**
   I'll reply to the reporter's email, as she requested. If I don't get a confirmation by 4:30 p.m., I will call her to make sure she received it in time.

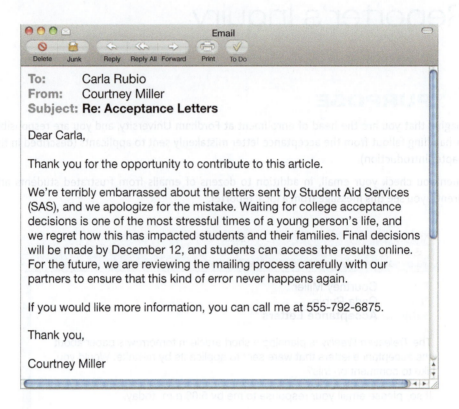

To: Carla Rubio
From: Courtney Miller
Subject: Re: Acceptance Letters

Dear Carla,

Thank you for the opportunity to contribute to this article.

We're terribly embarrassed about the letters sent by Student Aid Services (SAS), and we apologize for the mistake. Waiting for college acceptance decisions is one of the most stressful times of a young person's life, and we regret how this has impacted students and their families. Final decisions will be made by December 12, and students can access the results online. For the future, we are reviewing the mailing process carefully with our partners to ensure that this kind of error never happens again.

If you would like more information, you can call me at 555-792-6875.

Thank you,

Courtney Miller

Solving the Mailing Mistake

>>> PURPOSE

As the head of enrollment at Fordham University, you were embarrassed about acceptance letters mistakenly sent to students, and you want to make sure this never happens again. You decide to write an email to the director of SAS to start the conversation.

>>> PROCESS

1. What is the purpose of your message?

2. Describe your audience. Consider how the organization feels about the mistake and how this might impact their response to your email. Also consider your relationship with the group as your partner, rather than an employee.

3. How will you briefly explain your purpose? Try to summarize the issue in a couple of sentences.

4. How will you share the responsibility without taking full responsibility or blaming SAS? This is a delicate balance.

5. What next steps will you propose? How will you encourage the director to respond?

6. What will you use as your subject line?

>>> PRODUCT

Prepare an email message to the SAS director.

LO1   Analyze the audience for your communication.

Before writing, carefully analyze your audience. Identify who the audience is (both primary and secondary), determine what the audience already knows, consider your relationship with the audience, anticipate the audience's likely reaction, and identify any unique characteristics of the audience.

LO2   Plan the purpose, content, and organization of your message.

Identify the general purpose and then the specific purpose of your message. Based on your audience analysis, determine what information to include and in what order.

LO3   Compose the first draft of your message.

Select an appropriate environment for drafting, and schedule enough time. Concentrate on getting the information down without worrying about style, correctness, or format. Leave a time gap between writing and revising the draft. Adjust your writing for different media. Follow organizational conventions for email, write memos for longer messages and when email is not practical, use a more formal style for letters, and work toward interactivity for the web.

LO4   Revise for content, style, and correctness.

Revise first for content to determine whether the right amount of information is included in a logical order. Then revise for style to ensure that your message reads well for your audience. Finally, revise for correctness, being sure to avoid any errors in grammar, mechanics, punctuation, and word choice.

LO5   Proofread your message.

Read through your message carefully to catch content, typographical, and formatting errors.

> EXERCISES

LO1   Analyze the audience for your communication.

1. **Complete an audience analysis of housekeeping staff.**

   Imagine that you work for a small, independent hotel. Management has decided to change housekeepers' hours from 8:00 a.m–4:00 p.m. to 8:30 a.m.–4:30 p.m. Using the five audience analysis questions in Figure 2, analyze the housekeeping staff. How does your analysis affect your approach for communicating the message?

2. **Analyze an instructor as the audience.**

   If you were a business communication instructor and received this email from a student, how would you react? Analyze your instructor as an audience for this student's message, and consider changes the student might make to achieve his or her purpose.

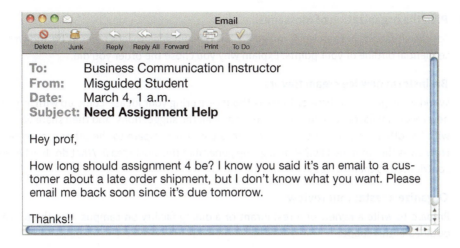

To: Business Communication Instructor
From: Misguided Student
Date: March 4, 1 a.m.
Subject: Need Assignment Help

Hey prof,

How long should assignment 4 be? I know you said it's an email to a customer about a late order shipment, but I don't know what you want. Please email me back soon since it's due tomorrow.

Thanks!!

3. **Evaluate audience focus in a company invitation.**

   The Century Aurora 16 theater in Colorado, where 12 people were killed and 58 injured, reopened a few months after the horrific shooting incident. To encourage people to return, the theater sent invitations to the victims' families, for a "special evening of remembrance" with a movie showing. The families didn't appreciate the gesture. In a letter to the theater company, they called the invitation "disgusting" and "wholly offensive to the memory of our loved ones." Coming just two days after Christmas, the invitation stung even worse for some families.

   You can read the invitation and families' letter at bit.ly/Zt3f4s. In small groups, discuss your perspective:

   - What's your view of the theater's invitation: a nice gesture, an insensitive ploy to recoup revenue, or something else?

   - What could have been a better approach for the theater?

   - How well does the families' letter express their perspective? What suggestions, if any, do you have for a revision?

   - In the families' letter, they say that the theater has refused to meet with them. How, if at all, does this influence your perspective of the invitation?

4. **Identify general-purpose statements and communication objectives for several situations.**

   LO2 Plan the purpose, content, and organization of your message.

   Read the following situations and write a general-purpose statement and a specific communication objective—the results you want—for each.

   - As the manager of a small retail-clothing store, you write an email to let employees know they're getting a $1 per hour wage increase.

   - As the assistant manager of a movie theater, you write an email to tell a customer you found the earring she lost the night before.

   - As a newly hired advertising director, you write an email to the president of the company requesting a 10% increase in your advertising budget.

   - As a CEO, you write a blog post on your investor website about your company's falling stock price.

   - As a marketing manager, you write a letter to customers announcing a new product that will be available in your store starting next month.

   - As a student, you write a letter to your college newspaper editor about the increase in tuition costs.

   - As a warehouse manager, you write an email to an employee about the facility being left unlocked last night.

5. **Plan the organization of messages.**

   For the situations in Exercise 4, imagine what the audience reaction might be and write a sequential outline of your points. Explain why you chose the order you did.

6. **Brainstorm new ice cream flavors.**

   Workings in groups of three or four—without censoring your ideas—come up with as many new ice cream flavors as you can. Make a list of all the suggestions, and then share your list with the other groups in the class. How does your list compare to the other groups' lists? How big is the combined list? Which group generated the most ideas? What do they believe contributed to their success?

7. **Organize a restaurant review.**

   Prepare to write a review of a restaurant or a dining facility on campus. Use the process outlined in this chapter:

   • Brainstorm ideas. What do you think is important to include in your review? Draw a mind map.
   • Create a hierarchy of ideas. How will you organize your main and supporting points?
   • Develop an outline. Write a more detailed, sequential plan for your restaurant review.

LO3 Compose the first draft of your message.

8. **Assess how you feel about writing.**

   Rate how you feel about yourself as a writer and about the process of writing.

	Mostly True	Mostly False
I've been told I'm a good writer.		
I've been told I'm a poor writer.		
I feel good about myself when I'm writing.		
I enjoy writing.		
Writing causes me stress.		
It takes me a long time to write anything.		
I experience writer's block.		
I prefer writing assignments to doing other types of work.		

When you finish, consider how your responses affect your writing. How can you dispel negative messages and shift your thinking about yourself and your writing?

9. **Practice free writing.**

   Without judgment, write for five minutes without stopping. Write anything. If you get stuck, write about the process of writing. After five minutes, review what you wrote and make a list of only positive aspects of your writing. Focus on your penmanship, word choice, sense of humor, sentence structure, creativity—anything that recognizes your strengths as a writer, even when you're not trying too hard.

10. **Write a draft restaurant review.**

    Now that you have your outline for Exercise 7, draft your restaurant review. Practice free writing for this activity to avoid moving to the revision stage too quickly. Don't worry about formatting for this exercise; just practice moving from an outline to a written document.

11. **Write a draft email to the sales team at Herman Miller.**

    Using the principles discussed for effective email communication, write a draft email to a team of sales associates. Imagine that you work for Herman Miller, a company that sells high-end office furniture. Today, the associates typically make phone calls and send online brochures to prospective clients. You believe that you can increase sales if the associates make personal visits instead. In your email, encourage associates to visit at least three businesses each week.

    Use a respectful, encouraging tone, and provide enough reasons to convince the sales associates that personal visits will increase business. Invent whatever details you need to make your email realistic.

12. **Write a company memo to announce a new organizational structure.**

    Imagine that you have just acquired a company and have brought in an entirely new management team—five of your classmates. In a separate message to employees, you have communicated the rationale for the changes. Now, you would like to introduce your new team to the rest of the organization.

    Write a two-page memo. After a brief introduction, in which you refer to previous communications about the change, include one short paragraph (about 50 words) for each of the five new executive team members. In each paragraph, include the following information: executive's name, new title, and previous experience. You may invent whatever details you would like.

13. **Format a letter.**

    You have just finished collecting donations for the American Cancer Society. To thank people for donating, you will send individual letters. Using guidelines in this chapter and in the Reference Manual, format your letter. You do not need to write the letter; just create the template with the date, addresses, salutation, and closing. You may create your own letterhead or use a standard return address.

14. **Write blog posts.**

    Imagine that you work for Southwest Airlines and have been asked to write a few entries on their "Nuts About Southwest" blog. Write three short posts (about 50 words each). Write one post about a recent national holiday, one post to encourage viewers to visit your website, and one post to link to a recent news story about the company.

15. **Set goals to overcome writer's block.**

    In this chapter, you read about ways to overcome writer's block. Choose two or three strategies from Figure 9 to improve your writing process. Try them out, and then send an email to your instructor assessing your results. What worked well for you that you can use in the future?

16. Revise your email to sales associates at Herman Miller.

Revise your draft email to Herman Miller sales associates (from Exercise 11). What changes will you make to improve the message? Follow these steps for the revision process:

    a. Read the email once, revising for content. Make sure that all needed information is included, no unnecessary information is included, and the information is presented in a logical sequence.

    b. Read the email a second time, revising for style. Make sure that the words, sentences, paragraphs, and overall tone are appropriate.

    c. Read the email a third time, revising for correctness. Make sure that grammar, mechanics, punctuation, and word choice are error free.

17. Revise another student's Herman Miller email.

Exchange draft Herman Miller emails with other students in class (so that you're not revising the paper of the person who is revising yours). Using the process described in Exercise 16, revise the other student's message, and then return the paper to the writer with your changes.

18. Revise a previous message.

Bring in a one-page message (email, memo, or letter) you have written in the past. Exchange papers with other students (so that you're not revising the paper of the person who is revising yours). Spend a few minutes asking the writer to give you background information about the message: purpose, audience, and so on. Then, follow the three-step revision process described in Exercise 16.

Return the paper to the writer. Then, using the revisions of your paper as a guide only (after all, you are the author), prepare a final version of the message. Submit both the marked-up version and the final version of your paper to your instructor.

19. Revise an email gone wrong.

When you read this email, you'll know it was sent in anger. (This is adapted from a real email stemming from a similar situation.) Use the process described in Exercise 16 to revise this email.

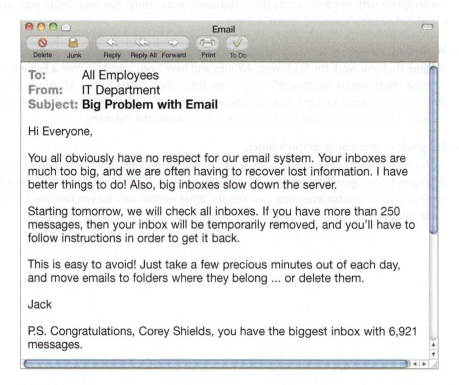

```
To:      All Employees
From:    IT Department
Subject: Big Problem with Email

Hi Everyone,

You all obviously have no respect for our email system. Your inboxes are
much too big, and we are often having to recover lost information. I have
better things to do! Also, big inboxes slow down the server.

Starting tomorrow, we will check all inboxes. If you have more than 250
messages, then your inbox will be temporarily removed, and you'll have to
follow instructions in order to get it back.

This is easy to avoid! Just take a few precious minutes out of each day,
and move emails to folders where they belong ... or delete them.

Jack

P.S. Congratulations, Corey Shields, you have the biggest inbox with 6,921
messages.
```

20. Revise another email gone wrong.

Another angry writer sent the email below to employees of a news agency. (This is adapted from a real message—and the original was much longer.) Use the same process as in Exercise 16 to revise this email.

First, discuss the issues in class. What went wrong? How would the audience likely have reacted to this message? What was the intended communication objective? Did it likely achieve that objective?

Next, revise the message. The purpose is legitimate: to improve how people file expense reports. But the approach and tone could be much improved.

Finally, compare your version with two others drafted by your classmates. How do they differ? What are the best parts of each version?

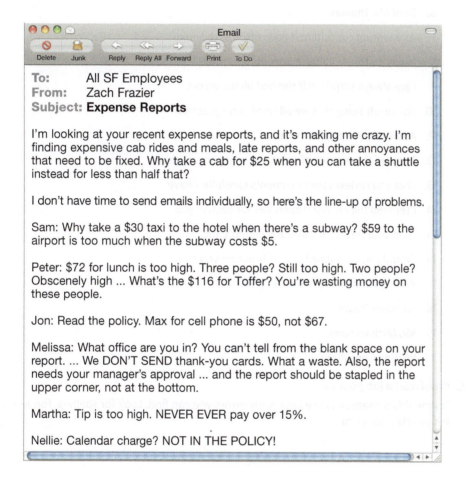

To: All SF Employees
From: Zach Frazier
Subject: Expense Reports

I'm looking at your recent expense reports, and it's making me crazy. I'm finding expensive cab rides and meals, late reports, and other annoyances that need to be fixed. Why take a cab for $25 when you can take a shuttle instead for less than half that?

I don't have time to send emails individually, so here's the line-up of problems.

Sam: Why take a $30 taxi to the hotel when there's a subway? $59 to the airport is too much when the subway costs $5.

Peter: $72 for lunch is too high. Three people? Still too high. Two people? Obscenely high ... What's the $116 for Toffer? You're wasting money on these people.

Jon: Read the policy. Max for cell phone is $50, not $67.

Melissa: What office are you in? You can't tell from the blank space on your report. ... We DON'T SEND thank-you cards. What a waste. Also, the report needs your manager's approval ... and the report should be stapled in the upper corner, not at the bottom.

Martha: Tip is too high. NEVER EVER pay over 15%.

Nellie: Calendar charge? NOT IN THE POLICY!

21. Proofread a letter.

Proofread the following lines of a letter, using the line numbers to indicate the position of each error. Proofread for content, typographical errors, and format. For each error, indicate by a "yes" or "no" whether the error would have been identified by a computer's spelling checker. How many errors can you find?

1. April 31 2017

2. Mr. Thomas Johnson, Manger

3. JoAnn @ Friends, Inc.

4. 1323 Charleston Avenue

5. Minneapolis, MI 55402

6. Dear Mr. Thomas:

7. As a writing consultant, I have often asked auld-

8. iences to locate all the errors in this letter.

9. I am always surprised if the find all the errors.

10. The result being that we all need more practical

11. Advise in how to proof read.

12. To avoid these types of error, you must ensure that

13. That you review your documents carefully. I have

14. Prepared the enclosed exercises for each of you

15. To in your efforts at JoAnne & Friend's, Inc.

16. Would you be willing to try this out on you own

17. Workers and let me know the results.

18. Sincerely Yours

19. Mr. Michael Land,

20. Writing Consultant

22. Proofread a job posting.

Review this passage, and see how many errors you can find. Look for spelling, formatting, and punctuation errors.

Finance Management Trainee

Program Overview

Bank on Me; a financial services company based in NYC; is now recruit a select number of candidates for its finance management training program. This is a comprehensive two year financial training program to provide you with experience in the magor financial areas of the bank.

In addition to ongoing classroom training, the trainees complete projects in one or more of the following area:
- Analyzing and reporting on internal operations
- Forecasting financial trends
- Developing models and performing financial analyze of investments
- Supporting the corporations internal planning and management accounting functions
- Prepare external reports for shareholders and regulatory authorities
- Providing guidance on acounting policy issues and/or taxation issues

Position Qualification
- Associates or bachelors degre
- Financial course work
- At least on summer of finance related experience
- Minimum 3.5 GPA
- Demonstrated leadership experience
- Spanish language, a plus
- Microsoft Excel proficiency
- Strong comumnication skills
- Excellent attention detail

About Bank on Me

Founded in 1964, Bank on Me offer consumer and commercial banking services at 630 branches throughout the North east U.S. We offer personal and busines checking accounts, loans, credit cards, and other financial products. We also provide home loans and assistance to commercial property owners and investors. At Bank on Me we prid ourselves on superior customer service and have won several service awards that demonstrate this commitment.

Contact Information

Please send your cover letter and resume to the following:
Marley Catona
Recruting Officer
Bank on Me
555 New York Ave.
New York, NY 10022

COMPANY SCENARIO

Writeaway Hotels

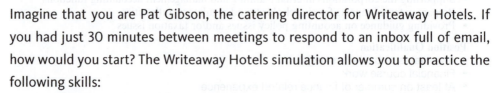

Imagine that you are Pat Gibson, the catering director for Writeaway Hotels. If you had just 30 minutes between meetings to respond to an inbox full of email, how would you start? The Writeaway Hotels simulation allows you to practice the following skills:

- Reading and prioritizing email
- Making decisions about whether and how to respond to email
- Writing messages under pressure
- Evaluating the effectiveness of email you receive

Your instructor may assign a role for you to play from the Writeaway Hotels group.

To practice drafting email messages, you can start by responding to these. If you were Pat Gibson and received these messages, how would you respond? The first is from an upset client; the second is from your general manager.

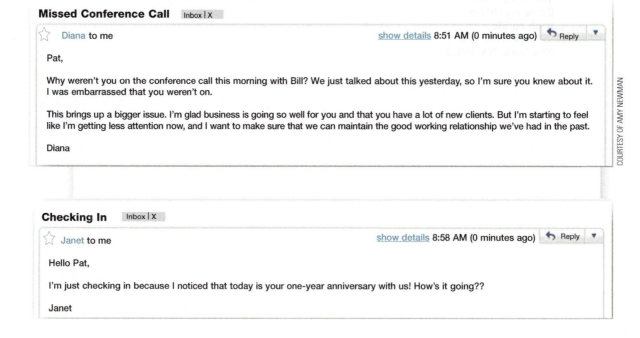

Missed Conference Call   Inbox | X

☆ Diana to me   show details 8:51 AM (0 minutes ago) ↩ Reply ▾

Pat,

Why weren't you on the conference call this morning with Bill? We just talked about this yesterday, so I'm sure you knew about it. I was embarrassed that you weren't on.

This brings up a bigger issue. I'm glad business is going so well for you and that you have a lot of new clients. But I'm starting to feel like I'm getting less attention now, and I want to make sure that we can maintain the good working relationship we've had in the past.

Diana

Checking In   Inbox | X

☆ Janet to me   show details 8:58 AM (0 minutes ago) ↩ Reply ▾

Hello Pat,

I'm just checking in because I noticed that today is your one-year anniversary with us! How's it going??

Janet

COURTESY OF AMY NEWMAN

COURTESY OF ED MARION, EDMARION.COM

Writeaway Hotels

Endnotes

1. Corinne Lestch, "Fordham University Revokes 2,500 Acceptance Letters After Embarrassing Email Error," *NY Daily News*, December 13, 2013, www.nydailynews.com/new-york/education/fordham-revokes-2-500-acceptance-letters-mix-up-article-1.1546679, accessed March 7, 2015.

2. Corinne Lestch.

3. Amy Newman, "Fordham Accidentally Accepts 2500 Students," *BizCom in the News*, December 16, 2013, www.bizcominthenews.com/bizcom_in_the_news/2013/12/fordham-accidentally-accepts-2500-students.html, accessed March 7, 2015.

4. "Fordham Mistakenly Tells 2,500 Applicants They Were Accepted to University," *Time Warner Cable News NY 1*, December 12, 2013, http://bronx.ny1.com/content/news/200270/fordham-mistakenly-tells-2-500-applicants-they-were-accepted-to-university, accessed June 17, 2014.

5. Peter Baker, "Obama Commutes a Prisoner's Sentence, Lengthened More than 3 Years by a Typo," *The New York Times*, April 15, 2014, www.nytimes.com/2014/04/16/us/politics/obama-commutes-a-sentence-lengthened-by-a-typing-error.html, accessed March 7, 2015.

6. Shannon P. Duffy, "Attorney Hit With $6.6 Million Malpractice Verdict," Law.com, April 23, 2007, www.law.com/jsp/article.jsp?id=900005479433&slreturn=1&hbxlog, accessed January 19, 2013.

7. "The, Case, of, the, Million, Dollar, Comma," *The Register*, October 26, 2006, www.theregister.co.uk/2006/10/26/the_case_of_the_million_dollar_comma/, accessed March 7, 2015.

8. Radicati, "Business User Survey 2014," The Radicati Group, Inc., www.radicati.com/wp/wp-content/uploads/2014/01/Email-Statistics-Report-2014-2018-Executive-Summary.pdf, accessed March 7, 2015.

9. Chad White, "The Last Word on July 2013," Email Marketing Rules, August 2, 2013, www.emailmarketingrules.com/the-last-word-on-july-2013/, accessed March 7, 2015.

10. Pete Cashmore, "Memo to Staff: An Exciting Future for Mashable," LinkedIn, October 30, 2013, www.linkedin.com/today/post/article/20131030165111-1863151-memo-to-staff-an-exciting-future-for-mashable, March 7, 2015.

11. Tony Manfred, "FAIL: ESPN Just Misspelled 'South' During the Spelling Bee," May 31, 2012, www.businessinsider.com/espn-spelling-bee-fail-2012-5, accessed March 7, 2015.

CHAPTER

5 | Improving Your Writing Style

LEARNING OBJECTIVES

After you have finished this chapter, you should be able to

LO1   Choose the right words for your message.

LO2   Write effective sentences.

LO3   Develop logical paragraphs.

LO4   Convey an appropriate tone.

" It's not just that the bank uses jargon but that it talks about branch counts in key areas as being representative of optimism and growth. " [1]

—*Julia La Roche, Business Insider*

CHAPTER INTRODUCTION

Citigroup Blunders a Press Release

To announce 11,000 employee layoffs, Citi issued a press release titled, "Citigroup Announces Repositioning Actions to Further Reduce Expenses and Improve Efficiency."[2] Critics called the company's release "classically bad" and "lacking any trace of humanity."[3]

Layoffs usually are good news for Wall Street, but the real damage is to employees, not mentioned until late in the release and suspiciously absent from the statement introduction. Although Citi clearly wants to present the news positively, too much spin disregards the effect on so many people.

The company also used the word "repositioning" an astonishing 17 times in the 1070-word press release, starting in the introductory paragraph:

> Citigroup today announced a series of repositioning actions that will further reduce expenses and improve efficiency across the company while maintaining Citi's unique capabilities to serve clients, especially in the emerging markets. These actions will result in increased business efficiency, streamlined operations, and an optimized consumer footprint across geographies.

The text doesn't exactly roll off the tongue. A revision with simpler language that focused on all of the bank's audiences—including employees—may have been better received.

Do you have a particular writing style? If so, how would you describe it, and what does it say about you?

See the Reference Manual for a review of Language Arts Basics (LAB) modules.

5-1 What Do We Mean by *Style?*

When you think of "style," what comes to mind? Someone with fashionable clothes? A sports car? A good haircut? At W Hotels, housekeepers are called "room stylists." They clean and rearrange items to make the room visually appealing to guests. When you "style" your business writing, you're working towards a clear, professional message for your audience.

When we talk about writing style, we mean how an idea is expressed. Style is everything but the content (or the message substance) and mechanics. Mechanics are elements in communication that show up only in writing, for example, spelling, punctuation, abbreviations, capitalization, number expression, and word division. In this chapter, you'll learn to create an effective style by choosing the best words and then arranging them into sentences, paragraphs, and complete messages.

In what ways does the thank-you email in Figure 1, which is based on a real email, lack style? It's grammatically correct and easy to read, but what's the problem? Apply the principles of style shown in Figure 2 as you revise your business messages.

Figure 1 | Thank-You Email Lacking Style

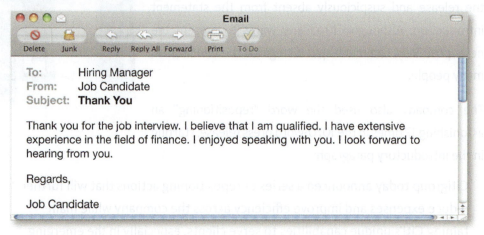

Figure 2 | Principles of Style

Words	Sentences	Paragraphs	Tone
• Write clearly. • Write concisely.	• Use a variety of sentence types. • Use active and passive voice appropriately. • Use parallel structure.	• Keep paragraphs unified and coherent. • Control paragraph length.	• Write confidently. • Use a courteous and sincere tone. • Use appropriate emphasis and subordination. • Use positive language. • Stress the "you" attitude.

5-2 Choosing the Right Words

LO1 Choose the right words for your message.

As the building blocks for writing, words can make or break your message. Clear, concise writing is essential for business communication.

5-2a Write Clearly

The most basic guideline for writing is to write clearly—to write messages the reader can understand and act on. You can achieve clarity by following these guidelines:

- Be accurate and complete.
- Use familiar words.
- Use specific, concrete language.
- Avoid dangling expressions.
- Avoid clichés, slang, and unnecessary jargon.

Be Accurate and Complete

Your credibility as a writer depends on the accuracy of your message. If a writer is careless, doesn't prepare, or intentionally misleads the reader, the damage is immediate and long lasting. The headlines in Figure 3 use correct grammar, but are they accurate?[4]

Headlines Gone Wrong | **Figure 3**

Iraqi Head Seeks Arms
Police Begin Campaign to Run Down Jaywalkers
Red Tape Holds Up New Bridges
Farmer Bill Dies in House
Teacher Strikes Idle Kids
New Study of Obesity Looks for Larger Test Group
Kids Make Nutritious Snacks
Typhoon Rips Through Cemetery; Hundreds Dead

The accuracy of a message depends on what is said, how it is said, and what is left unsaid. Competent writers assess the ethical dimensions of their writing and use integrity, fairness, and good judgment to make sure their communication is ethical. When the oil spill disaster in the Gulf of Mexico became public, Tony Hayward, former CEO of British Petroleum, said, "The Gulf of Mexico is a very big ocean. The amount of volume of oil and dispersant we are putting into it is tiny in relation to the total water volume."[5] Hayward was highly criticized for this comment. Can you understand why?

Closely related to accuracy is completeness. A message that lacks important information may create inaccurate impressions. A message is complete when it contains all the information the reader needs—no more and no less—to react appropriately.

Ethics in
COMMUNICATION

Use Familiar Words

To make your message easy to understand, use words familiar to you and your readers. A Princeton University study, "Consequences of Erudite Vernacular Utilized Irrespective of Necessity: Problems with Using Long Words Needlessly," found that undergraduates use more complex words in papers to sound more intelligent. However, according to the researcher, this strategy achieves the opposite effect:

> It turns out that somewhere between two-thirds and three-quarters of people...admit to deliberately replacing short words with longer words in their writing in an attempt to sound smarter....The problem is that this strategy backfires—such writing is reliably judged to come from less intelligent authors.[6]

Short and simple words are more likely to be understood, less likely to be misused, and less likely to distract the reader. Literary authors often write to *impress*; they select words to amuse, excite, or anger. Business writers, on the other hand, write to *express*; they want to achieve *comprehension*. They want their readers to focus on their information, not on how they convey their information.

The "before" example in Figure 4 uses unnecessarily long words, and the "after" version shows simplified words. You may still use long words, but use them in moderation. And when a shorter word works just as well, choose that one for business writing.

Figure 4 | Before and After Track Changes

Before Track Changes	After Track Changes
After ascertaining that the modification of the plan was too onerous, we enumerated the substantial number of reasons to terminate the accord. On Tuesday, we'll initiate deliberations to utilize a more undemanding course of action in the future.	After ~~ascertaining~~ learning that ~~the modification of~~ changing the plan was too ~~onerous~~ difficult, we ~~enumerated~~ listed the ~~substantial number of~~ many reasons to ~~terminate~~ end the ~~accord~~ contract. On Tuesday, we'll ~~initiate~~ start ~~deliberations~~ talking about ~~to utilize a more undemanding course of action~~ an easier process ~~in~~ for the future.

Communication TECHNOLOGIES

The "Track Changes" feature in Microsoft Word or similar programs is particularly useful for team writing, as discussed in Chapter 2. Under "Change Tracking Options," you can select colors and other ways revisions are displayed in a document, for example, whether you show comments within the text or as "balloons" (Figure 5).

Use Specific, Concrete Language

In Chapter 1, we discussed the communication barriers caused by overabstraction and ambiguity. When possible, choose *specific* words (words that have a definite, unambiguous meaning) and *concrete* words (words that bring a picture to your reader's mind).

☒ NOT   The vehicle broke down several times recently.

☑ BUT   The delivery van broke down three times last week.

In the first version, what does the reader imagine when he or she reads the word *vehicle*—a golf cart? Automobile? Boat? Space shuttle? And how many times is *several*—two? Three? Fifteen? What is *recently*? The revision tells precisely what happened.

Sometimes we don't need such specific information. For example, in, "The president answered *several* questions from the audience," the specific number of questions is probably not important. But in most business situations, you should watch out for words like *several, recently, a number of, substantial, a few*, and *a lot of*. You may need to be more exact.

Concrete words translate an idea for the reader. Compare these descriptions; how persuasive is each version?

NOT	BUT
Friendly's Mac & Cheese Quesadilla meal for kids has a lot of calories.	Friendly's Mac & Cheese Quesadilla meal for kids has 2,270 calories—the equivalent of 45.5 Glazed Munchkins from Dunkin' Donuts.
Airbnb will save the planet!	"In one year alone, Airbnb guests in North America saved the equivalent of 270 Olympic-sized pools of water while avoiding the greenhouse gas emissions equivalent to 33,000 cars on North American roads."[7]

Track Changes Options in Microsoft Word | **Figure 5**

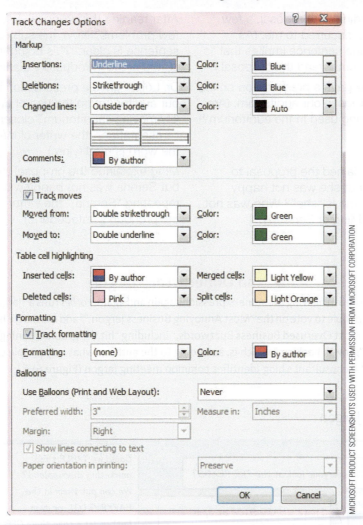

MICROSOFT PRODUCT SCREENSHOTS USED WITH PERMISSION FROM MICROSOFT CORPORATION

Of course, the versions on the right are more specific and concrete. Providing the number of calories gives parents more information about a meal they may—or may not!—order for their child. Claiming to save the planet isn't credible, but when Airbnb compared water savings and reduced emissions to swimming pools and cars, people paid attention.

☒ NOT   The vice president was bored by the presentation.

☑ BUT   The vice president kept yawning and looking at her watch.

Bored is an abstract concept. "Yawning and looking at her watch" paints a more vivid picture.

Specific terms tell readers how to react. Watch out for terms like *emotional meeting* (anger or gratitude?), *bright color* (red or yellow?), *new equipment* (projector or computer?), and *change in price* (increase or decrease?).

Avoid Dangling Expressions

A dangling expression is any part of a sentence that doesn't logically fit in with the rest of the sentence. Its relationship with the other parts of the sentence is unclear; it *dangles*. The two most common types of dangling expressions are misplaced modifiers and unclear antecedents.

NOT	BUT
After reading the proposal, a few problems occurred to me. (As written, the sentence implies that "a few problems" read the proposal.)	After reading the proposal, I noted a few problems. (Now, the subject of the sentence is clear: "I" is doing the action stated in the introductory clause.)
Dr. López gave a presentation on the use of drugs in our auditorium. (Are drugs being used in the auditorium?)	Dr. López gave a presentation in our auditorium on the use of drugs. (By moving "auditorium" closer to "presentation," the writer clarifies what the word is modifying.)
Ming explained the proposal to Serena, but she was not happy with it. (Who is "she"? Who was not happy—Ming or Serena?)	Ming explained the proposal to Serena, but Serena was not happy with it. (By repeating "Serena," the writer clarifies the pronoun's antecedent.)

Avoid Clichés, Slang, and Unnecessary Jargon

People get tired of hearing the same expressions again and again. *Forbes* runs a "Jargon Madness" contest for people to vote on the "Most Annoying Business Jargon,"[8] and Mashable has published the "The 12 Most Overused Business Buzzwords," including "hit the ground running," "paradigm shift," and "growth hacking," which is, according to the author, "what lazy people call an expert marketer."[9] A consultant's blog identifies common meeting jargon (Figure 6).[10]

Figure 6 | Meeting Jargon

A cliché is an expression that has become trite through overuse. Because audiences have heard a cliché many times, using clichés may send the message that the writer is unoriginal—and couldn't be bothered to tailor the message to the audience.

> ☒ NOT   Enclosed please find an application form that you should return at your earliest convenience.

> ☑ BUT   Please return the enclosed application form before May 15.

Avoid these overused expressions in your writing:

According to our records	Our records indicate that
Company policy requires	For your information
Thank you for your attention to this matter	Please be advised that
Do not hesitate to	If you have any other questions

Picture a person seeing "Thank you for your recent letter" in all 15 letters he or she reads that day. How sincere and original does it sound?

As discussed in Chapter 1, slang is an informal expression, often short-lived, that is identified with a specific group of people. If you understand each word in an expression but still don't understand what it means in context, chances are you're having trouble with a slang expression. Slang is particularly challenging for nonnative English speakers, who may think the writer of the following sentence is in a great deal of pain.

> ☒ NOT   It turns my stomach the way you can break your neck and beat your brains out around here, and they still stab you in the back.

> ☑ BUT   I am really upset that this company ignores hard work and loyalty when making promotion decisions.

Jargon is technical vocabulary used within a special group. Every field has its own specialized words, and jargon offers a precise and efficient way of communicating with people in the same field. But problems arise when jargon is used to communicate with someone who doesn't understand it. For example, does the NRA refer to the National Rifle Association or the National Restaurant Association?

Closely related to jargon are *buzzwords*, which are important-sounding expressions used mainly to impress other people. Because buzzwords are so often used by government officials and high-ranking business people—people whose comments are "newsworthy"—these expressions get much media attention. They become instant clichés and then go out of fashion just as quickly. Be careful of turning nouns and other types of words into tiresome verbs by adding *–ize*: *operationalize, prioritize, commoditize,* and *maximize*.

International COMMUNICATION

5-2b Write Concisely

To develop a concise writing style, Purdue University's "Online Writing Lab" (OWL; see https://owl.english.purdue.edu/owl/) suggests we "interrogate every word" in a sentence. The example in Figure 7 is reduced from 67 to only six words.[11] Is anything lost in translation? Not much. When you revise, avoid redundancy, wordy expressions, hidden verbs and nouns, and other "space eaters."

Avoid Redundancy and Wordy Expressions

A redundancy is the repetition of an idea that has already been expressed or intimated.

> ☒ NOT   Signing both copies of the lease is a necessary requirement.

> ☑ BUT   Signing both copies of the lease is necessary.

> ☒ NOT   Combine the ingredients together.

> ☑ BUT   Combine the ingredients.

Emotional INTELLIGENCE

Do you sometimes add "fluff" to your writing? If so, how can you challenge yourself to develop a more concise style?

Figure 7 | Revision for Conciseness

(67 words)

Wordy: Many have made the wise observation that when a stone is in motion, rolling down a hill or incline, that that moving stone is not as likely to be covered all over with the kind of thick green moss that grows on stationary unmoving things and becomes a nuisance and suggests that those things haven't moved in a long time and probably won't move any time soon.

(6 words)

Concise: A rolling stone gathers no moss.

COURTESY OF GOOGLE, INC.

Don't confuse redundancy and repetition. Repetition—using the same word more than once—is occasionally effective for emphasis (as we'll discuss later in this chapter). Redundancies, however, serve no purpose and should always be avoided.

Although wordy expressions are not necessarily writing errors (as redundancies are), they do slow the pace of the communication. Substitute one word for a phrase whenever possible.

NOT	BUT
ATM machine	ATM
PIN number	PIN
new innovation	innovation
divide up	divide
any and all	any *or* all
11:00 a.m. in the morning	11:00 a.m.
free gift	gift

☒ NOT   In view of the fact that the model failed twice during the time that we tested it, we are at this point in time searching for other options.

☑ BUT   Because the model failed twice when tested, we are searching for other options.

The original sentence contains 28 words; the revised sentence, 13. You've "saved" 15 words. In his book *Revising Business Prose*, Richard Lanham speaks of the "lard factor": the percentage of words saved by getting rid of the lard in a sentence. In this case, 54% of the original sentence was lard:

$$28 - 13 = 15$$

$$15 / 28 = 54\%$$

Lard fattens a sentence without providing any nutrition. Lanham suggests, "Think of a lard factor (LF) of 1/3 to 1/2 as normal, and don't stop revising until you've removed it."[12]

NOT	BUT
are of the opinion that	believe
in the event of	if
due to the fact that	because
pertaining to	about
for the purpose of	for *or* to
with regard to	about
in order to	to

Overusing prepositions also can cause wordiness. Consider these examples and their shorter equivalents:

NOT	BUT
The cover of the book	The book cover
Department of Human Resources	Human Resources Department
The tiles on the floor	The floor tiles
Our benefits for employees	Employee benefits
The battery in my smartphone	My smartphone battery

In these examples, nouns (for example, book) are used as adjectives. This strategy also is useful to condense your writing:

NOT	BUT
This brochure, which is available free of charge	This free brochure
The report with sales numbers for July	The July sales report

Avoid Hidden Verbs and Hidden Subjects

A hidden verb is a verb that has been changed into a noun, which weakens the action. Verbs are *action* words and should convey the main action in the sentence. They provide interest and forward movement.

☒ NOT   Carl made an announcement that he will give consideration to our request.

☑ BUT   Carl announced that he will consider our request.

What is the real action? It is not that Carl *made* something or that he will *give* something. The real action is hiding in the nouns: Carl *announced* and will *consider*. These two verb forms, then, should be the main verbs in the sentence. Notice that the revised sentence is much more direct—and four words shorter (LF = 33%).

Here are more actions that should be conveyed by verbs instead of being hidden in nouns:

NOT	BUT
arrived at the conclusion	concluded
has a requirement for	requires
came to an agreement	agreed
held a meeting	met
gave a demonstration of	demonstrated
made a payment	paid

Like verbs, subjects play a prominent role in a sentence and should stand out, rather than be obscured by an expletive. An expletive (not to be confused with profanity) is an expression, such as *there is* or *it is*, that begins a clause or sentence and for which the pronoun has no antecedent. Avoid expletives for clearer subjects and conciseness.

> ☒ NOT   There was no indication that it is necessary to include John in the meeting.

> ☑ BUT   No one indicated that John should be included in the meeting.

Business writers sometimes use expletives to avoid a clear subject. Consider the variations in Figure 8, with particular attention to the changes in subjects and verbs.

Figure 8 | Changing a Sentence to Avoid an Expletive

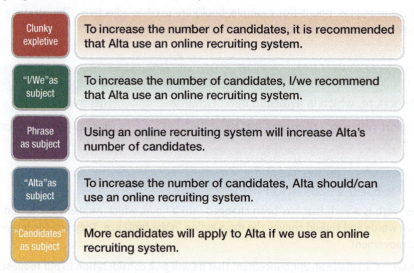

All of these variations are grammatically correct—but they emphasize different subjects. For example, the first variation, with no clear subject, might be used to distance the source from the advice, which may be appropriate in some situations. In the second variation, the source takes ownership for the advice. The third, fourth, and fifth variations all clarify the subject and avoid the expletive in the first sentence. Notice how each of these three variations emphasizes using the online recruiting system, Alta, and candidates, respectively. You would choose the version that achieves your communication objective.

5-3 Writing Effective Sentences

LO2 Write effective sentences.

A sentence has a subject and predicate and expresses at least one complete thought. Beyond these attributes, however, sentences vary widely in style, length, and effect.

Sentences are also very flexible; you can move sentence parts around, add and delete information, and substitute words to express different ideas and emphasize different points. To build effective sentences, use a variety of sentence types, use active and passive voice appropriately, and use parallel structure.

5-3a Use a Variety of Sentence Types

The three sentence types—simple, compound, and complex—are all appropriate for business writing. Only simple sentences were used in the thank-you email in Figure 1 at the beginning of this chapter. Rewriting the email using a variety of sentence types is one way to give the email more style (Figure 9).

Thank-You Email with Style | **Figure 9**

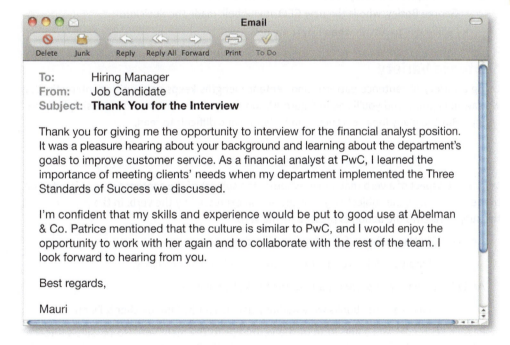

To: Hiring Manager
From: Job Candidate
Subject: **Thank You for the Interview**

Thank you for giving me the opportunity to interview for the financial analyst position. It was a pleasure hearing about your background and learning about the department's goals to improve customer service. As a financial analyst at PwC, I learned the importance of meeting clients' needs when my department implemented the Three Standards of Success we discussed.

I'm confident that my skills and experience would be put to good use at Abelman & Co. Patrice mentioned that the culture is similar to PwC, and I would enjoy the opportunity to work with her again and to collaborate with the rest of the team. I look forward to hearing from you.

Best regards,

Mauri

Simple Sentences

A simple sentence contains one independent clause (i.e., a clause that can stand alone as a complete thought). Because it presents a single idea and is usually short, a simple sentence is often used for emphasis. Although a simple sentence contains only one independent clause, it may have a compound subject or compound verb (or both). All of the following sentences are simple:

- I quit.
- Employees can enroll in the company's 401(k) plan.
- Both part- and full-time employees can enroll in the company's 401(k) plan and in an Individual Retirement Account.

Compound Sentences

A compound sentence contains two or more independent clauses. Because each clause presents a complete idea, each idea receives *equal* emphasis. (If the two ideas are not closely related, they should be presented in two separate sentences.) Here are three compound sentences:

- Stacey listened, and I nodded.
- Morris Technologies made a major acquisition last year, but it turned out to be a mistake.
- Westmoreland Mines moved its headquarters to Prescott in 1984; however, it stayed there only five years and then moved back to Globe.

Complex Sentences

A complex sentence contains one independent clause and at least one dependent clause. For example, in the first sentence below, "the scanner will save valuable input time" is an independent clause because it makes sense by itself. "Although it cost $235" is a dependent clause because it does not make sense by itself. The dependent clause provides additional, but *subordinate*, information related to the independent clause.

- Although it cost $235, the scanner will save valuable input time.
- George Bosley, who is the new CEO at Hubbell, made the decision.
- I will move to Austin when I start my new job.

Sentence Variety

Using a variety of sentence patterns and sentence lengths keeps your writing interesting. As we saw in Figure 1, and you'll see in Figure 10, too many short sentences sound simplistic and choppy. But too many long sentences can be boring and difficult to read.

Emotional INTELLIGENCE

Sometimes people use passive voice to avoid taking responsibility. In what situations might this be appropriate—and inappropriate?

5-3b   Use Active and Passive Voice Appropriately

Voice is the aspect of a verb that shows whether the subject of the sentence acts or is acted on. In the active voice, the subject *performs* the action expressed by the verb. In the passive voice, the subject *receives* the action expressed by the verb.

Active   Old Navy offers a full refund on all orders.

Passive   A full refund on all orders is offered by Old Navy.

Active   Shoemacher & Doerr audited the books last quarter.

Passive   The books were audited last quarter by Shoemacher & Doerr.

Passive sentences add some form of the verb *to be* to the main verb, so passive sentences are always somewhat longer than active sentences. In the first set of sentences, for example, compare *offers* in the active sentence with *is offered by* in the passive sentence.

In active sentences, the subject is the doer of the action; in passive sentences, the subject is the receiver of the action. Because the subject gets more emphasis than other nouns in a sentence, active sentences emphasize the doer, while passive sentences emphasize the receiver. In the second set of sentences, both versions are correct, depending on whether the writer wanted to emphasize *Shoemacher & Doerr* or *the books*.

Use active sentences most of the time in business writing, just as you naturally use active sentences in most of your conversations. Note that verb *voice* (active or passive) has nothing to do with verb *tense*, which shows the time of the action. As the following sentences show, the action in both active and passive sentences can occur in the past, present, or future.

☒ NOT A very logical argument was presented by Hal. (*Passive voice, past tense*)

    ☑ BUT Hal presented a very logical argument. (*Active voice, past tense*)

☒ NOT An 18% increase will be reported by the eastern region. (*Passive voice, future tense*)

    ☑ BUT The eastern region will report an 18% increase. (*Active voice, future tense*)

Sentence Variety for Greater Interest and Easier Reading | Figure 10

Too Choppy:

Golden Nugget will not purchase the Claridge Hotel. The hotel is 60 years old. The asking price was $110 million. It was not considered too high. Golden Nugget had wanted some commitments from New Jersey regulators. The regulators were unwilling to provide such commitments. Some observers believe the refusal was not the real reason for the decision. They blame the weak Atlantic City economy for the cancellation. Golden Nugget purchased the Stake House in Las Vegas in 2000. It lost money on that purchase. It does not want to repeat its mistake in Atlantic City.

(Average sentence length = 8 words)

Too Difficult:

Golden Nugget will not purchase the Claridge Hotel, which is 60 years old, for an asking price of $110 million, which was not considered too high, because the company had wanted some commitments from New Jersey regulators, and the regulators were unwilling to provide such commitments. Some observers believe the refusal was not the real reason for the decision but rather that the weak Atlantic City economy was responsible for the cancellation; and since Golden Nugget purchased the Stake House in Las Vegas in 2000 and lost money on that purchase, it does not want to repeat its mistake in Atlantic City.

(Average sentence length = 50 words)

The sentences in these paragraphs should be revised to show relationships between ideas more clearly, to keep readers interested, and to improve readability. Use simple sentences for emphasis and variety, compound sentences for coordinate (equal) relationships, and complex sentences for subordinate relationships.

More Variety:

Golden Nugget will not purchase the 60-year-old Claridge Hotel, even though the $110 million asking price was not considered too high. The company had wanted some commitments from New Jersey regulators, which the regulators were unwilling to provide. However, some observers blame the cancellation on the weak Atlantic City economy. Golden Nugget lost money on its 2000 purchase of the Stake House in Las Vegas, and it does not want to repeat its mistake in Atlantic City.

(Average sentence length = 20 words)

The first two sentences in the revision are complex, the third is simple, and the last sentence is compound. The lengths of the four sentences range from 12 to 27 words. To write effective sentences, use different sentence patterns and lengths. Most sentences in good business writing range from 16 to 22 words.

Passive sentences are most appropriate when you want to emphasize the *receiver* of the action, when the person doing the action is either unknown or unimportant, or when you want to be tactful in conveying negative information. All the following sentences are appropriately stated in the passive voice:

- Protective legislation was blamed for the drop in imports. (*Emphasizes the receiver of the action*)
- Transportation to the construction site will be provided. (*Downplays the unimportant doer of the action*)
- Several complaints have been received regarding the new policy. (*Conveys negative news tactfully*)

5-3c Use Parallel Structure

The term parallelism means using similar grammatical structure for similar ideas—that is, matching adjectives with adjectives, nouns with nouns, infinitives with infinitives, and so on. Widely quoted writing often uses parallelism—for example, Julius Caesar's "I came, I saw, I conquered" and Abraham Lincoln's "government of the people, by the people, and for the people." Parallel structure links ideas and adds a pleasing rhythm to sentences and paragraphs, which enhances coherence.

☒ NOT The new dispatcher is competent and a fast worker.

    ☑ BUT The new dispatcher is competent and fast.

☒ NOT The new grade of paper is lightweight, nonporous, and it is inexpensive.

    ☑ BUT The new grade of paper is lightweight, nonporous, and inexpensive.

☒ NOT The training program will cover vacation and sick leaves, how to resolve grievances, and managing your workstation.

    ☑ BUT The training program will cover vacation and sick leaves, grievance resolution, and workstation management.

☒ NOT One management consultant recommended either selling the children's furniture division or its conversion into a children's toy division.

    ☑ BUT One management consultant recommended either selling the children's furniture division or converting it into a children's toy division.

☒ NOT Gwen is not only proficient in Microsoft Word but also in Excel.

    ☑ BUT Gwen is proficient not only in Microsoft Word but also in Excel.

In the last two sets of sentences, note that correlative conjunctions (such as both/and, either/or, and not only/but also) must be followed by words in parallel form.

Also use parallel structure in report headings and presentation slide titles that have equal weight and in numbered and bulleted lists (Figure 11).

Figure 11 | Revising for Parallel Phrasing

Before	After
Agenda: Planning for Independent Research • What is independent research? • Reasons we should use independent research for this project • Starting the process	**Agenda: Planning for Independent Research** • What is independent research? • Why is independent research appropriate for this project? • How should we begin the research process?
What is the process for conducting independent research? • Pick a topic • Faculty sponsor • Setting up a timeline • Resources • Figure out a method • Data study • You should deliver results	**What is the process for conducting independent research?** **D.I.S.C.U.S.S.** • Discover topic • Identify faculty sponsor • Set up timeline • Consult resources • Use methods • Study data • Shape deliverables

5-4 Developing Logical Paragraphs

LO3 Develop logical paragraphs.

A paragraph is a group of related sentences that focus on one main idea. The main idea is often identified in the first sentence of the paragraph—the topic sentence. The body of the paragraph supports this main idea by giving more information, analysis, or examples. A paragraph is typically part of a longer message, although one paragraph may be an entire email.

Paragraphs organize a topic into manageable units of information for the reader. Readers need a cue to tell them when they have finished a topic so they can pause and refocus their attention on the next topic. Effective paragraphs are unified, coherent, and an appropriate length.

5-4a Keep Paragraphs Unified and Coherent

Although closely related, unity and coherence are not the same. A paragraph has unity when all of its parts work together to develop a single idea consistently and logically. A paragraph has coherence when each sentence links smoothly to the sentences before and after it.

Unity

A unified paragraph gives information that is directly related to the topic, presents this information in a logical order, and omits irrelevant details. The following excerpt is a middle paragraph in a memo arguing against the proposal that Collins, a baby-food manufacturer, should expand into producing food for adults:

> ☒ NOT [1] We cannot focus our attention on both ends of the age spectrum. [2] In a recent survey, two-thirds of the under-35 age group named Collins as the first company that came to mind for the category "baby-food products." [3] For more than 50 years, we have spent millions of dollars annually to identify our company as the baby-food company, and market research shows that we have been successful. [4] Last year, we introduced Peas 'n' Pears, our most successful baby-food introduction ever. [5] To now seek to position ourselves as a producer of food for adults would simply be incongruous. [6] Our well-defined image in the marketplace would make producing food for adults risky.

Before reading further, rearrange these sentences to make the sequence of ideas more logical. As written, the paragraph lacks unity. You may decide that the overall topic of the paragraph is Collins' well-defined image as a baby-food producer. So Sentence 6 would be the best topic sentence. You might also decide that Sentence 4 brings in extra information that weakens paragraph unity and should be left out. The most unified paragraph, then, would be Sentences 6, 3, 2, 5, and 1, as shown here:

> ☑ BUT Our well-defined image in the marketplace would make producing food for adults risky. For more than 50 years, we have spent millions of dollars annually to identify our company as the baby-food company, and market research shows that we have been successful. In a recent survey, two-thirds of the under-35 age group named Collins as the first company that came to mind for the category "baby-food products." To now seek to position ourselves as a producer of food for adults would simply be incongruous. We cannot focus our attention on both ends of the age spectrum.

A topic sentence is especially helpful in a long paragraph, for the reader as well as the writer. Placed at the beginning of the paragraph, the topic sentence tells the reader the main point of the paragraph and encourages the writer to stay focused on one topic to ensure paragraph unity.

Coherence

A coherent paragraph weaves sentences together so that the discussion is integrated. The reader never needs to pause to puzzle out the relationships or reread to get the intended meaning. To achieve coherence, use transitional words, use pronouns, and repeat key words and ideas.

Transitional words help the reader see relationships between sentences. Such words may be as simple as *first* and other indicators of sequence.

> Ten years ago, Collins tried to overcome market resistance to its new line of baby clothes. *First*, it mounted a multimillion-dollar ad campaign featuring the Mason quintuplets. *Next*, it sponsored a Collins Baby look-alike contest. *Then*, it sponsored two network specials featuring Dr. Benjamin Spock. *Finally*, it brought in the Madison Avenue firm of Morgan & Modine to broaden its image.

The words *first, next, then*, and *finally* clearly signal step-by-step movement. Now note the use of transitional words in the following paragraph:

> I recognize, *however*, that Collins cannot thrive on baby food alone. *To begin with*, since we already control 73% of the market, further gains will be difficult. *Also*, the current baby boom is slowing. *Therefore*, we must expand our product line.

These transitional words act as road signs, indicating where the message is headed and letting the reader know what to expect. Figure 12 shows commonly used transitional expressions for the relationships they express.

Figure 12 | Common Transitional Expressions

RELATIONSHIP	TRANSITIONAL EXPRESSIONS
addition	also, besides, furthermore, in addition, too
cause and effect	as a result, because, consequently, therefore
comparison	in the same way, likewise, similarly
contrast	although, but, however, nevertheless, on the other hand, still
illustration	for example, for instance, in other words, to illustrate
sequence	first, second, third, then, next, finally
summary/conclusion	at last, finally, in conclusion, therefore, to summarize
time	meanwhile, next, since, soon, then

A second way to achieve coherence is to use pronouns. Because pronouns stand for words already named, using pronouns binds sentences and ideas together. The pronouns are italicized here:

> If Collins branches out with additional food products, one possibility would be a fruit snack for youngsters. Funny Fruits were tested in Columbus last summer, and *they* were a big hit. Roger Johnson, national marketing manager, says *he* hopes to build new food categories into a $200 million business. *He* is also exploring the possibility of acquiring other established name brands. *These* acquired brands would let Collins expand faster than if *it* had to develop a new product of *its* own.

A third way to achieve coherence is to repeat key words. In a misguided attempt to appear interesting, writers sometimes use different terms for the same idea. For example, in discussing a proposed merger, a writer may at different points use *merger, combination, union, association*, and *acquisition*. Or a writer may use the words *administrator, manager, supervisor*, and *executive* all to refer to the same person. Such "elegant variation" only confuses the reader, who has no way of knowing whether the writer is referring to the same concept or to slightly different variations of that concept.

Avoid needless repetition, but use purposeful repetition to link ideas and thus promote paragraph coherence. Here is a good example:

> Collins has taken several *steps* recently to enhance profits and project a stronger leadership position. One of these *steps* is streamlining operations. Collins' line of children's clothes was *unprofitable*, so it discontinued the line. Its four produce farms were also *unprofitable*, so it hired an outside professional *team* to manage them. This *team* eventually recommended selling the farms.

Ensure paragraph unity by developing only one topic per paragraph and by presenting the information in logical order. Ensure paragraph coherence by using transitional words and pronouns and by repeating key words.

5-4b Control Paragraph Length

How long should a paragraph of business writing be? Long blocks of unbroken text look boring and may unintentionally obscure an important idea buried in the middle. On the other hand, a series of extremely short paragraphs can weaken coherence by obscuring underlying relationships. Compare the messages in Figure 13. Which is more inviting to read? Information is easier to digest when broken into small chunks with paragraph breaks, headings, bullets, and in this example, sub-bullets.

See the Reference Manual for a full version of the memo in Figure 13.

There are no fixed rules for paragraph length, and occasionally one- or ten-sentence paragraphs might be effective. However, most paragraphs of good business writers fall into the 60- to 80-word range—long enough for a topic sentence and three or four supporting sentences.

A paragraph is both a logical unit and a visual unit: logical because it discusses only one topic, and visual because the end signals readers to pause and digest the information. Although a single paragraph should never discuss more than one major topic, complex topics may need to

Comparing Paragraph Length: Which Is More Inviting to Read? | Figure 13

Our goal is to transition the organization as smoothly as possible. Over the next 90 days, we will implement the transition plan. By October 15, we will transfer sales representatives to new divisions. Each sales representative will be moved from our current regional teams to a new team: consumer, small business, or corporate. Managers will work closely with representatives to determine strengths, experience, and preferences. By October 31, we will identify account type. All sales representatives will categorize current accounts for the new divisions: consumer, small business, and corporate. By November 30, we will transition accounts to new teams. Where accounts are changing sales representatives, we will follow this process. For small business accounts, the former and new sales representative will send an email to the account contact, followed by a phone call and visit (if possible) by the new sales representative. For corporate accounts, the former sales representative will send an email and schedule a conference call or visit by the account contact and new sales representative.

Our goal is to transition the organization as smoothly as possible. Over the next 90 days, we will implement the transition plan:

- **Transfer sales representatives to new divisions (by October 15)**
  Each sales representative will be moved from our current regional teams to a new team: consumer, small business, or corporate. Managers will work closely with representatives to determine strengths, experience, and preferences.

- **Identify account type (by October 31)**
  All sales representatives will categorize current accounts for the new divisions: consumer, small business, and corporate.

- **Transition accounts to new teams (by November 30)**
  Where accounts are changing sales representatives, we will follow this process:
  - For small business accounts, the former and new sales representative will send an email to the account contact, followed by a phone call and visit (if possible) by the new sales representative.
  - For corporate accounts, the former sales representative will send an email and schedule a conference call or visit by the account contact and new sales representative.

be divided into several paragraphs. Your purpose and the needs of your reader should ultimately determine paragraph length.

5-5 Creating an Appropriate Tone

Tone in writing refers to the writer's attitude toward both the reader and the subject of the message. The overall tone of your written message affects your reader, just as your tone of voice affects your listener during a conversation.

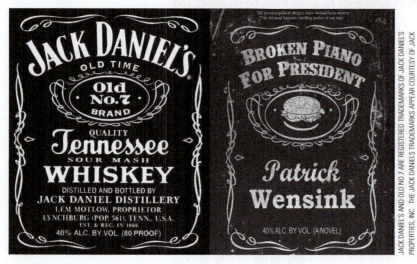

The book cover (right) looks very similar to the Jack Daniel's bottle label.

Jack Daniel's "cease-and-desist letter" in Figure 14 is a good example of focusing on the audience. Unlike most legal requests, this letter uses guidelines to achieve an appropriate tone in business writing:

- Write confidently.
- Use a courteous and sincere tone.
- Use appropriate emphasis and subordination.
- Use positive language.
- Stress the "you" attitude.

Compare the Jack Daniel's letter to language used in a U.S. Olympic Committee letter to a group of knitters who staged a "Ravelympics":

> We believe using the name "Ravelympics" for a competition that involves an afghan marathon, scarf hockey, and sweater triathlon, among others, tends to denigrate the true nature of the Olympic Games. In a sense, it is disrespectful to our country's finest athletes and fails to recognize or appreciate their hard work.[13]

Knitters were outraged, and a spokesperson for the Olympic Committee admitted that the letter "was definitely too strident in its tone."[14]

5-5a Write Confidently

Emotional INTELLIGENCE

Do you tend to sound overconfident or unsure of yourself? What challenges do you face in striking the right tone?

To achieve your communication objective, your message should convey a professional, confident attitude. The more confident you are about your writing, the more likely your audience will understand your explanation, accept your decision, or complete your request.

Avoid using language that makes you sound unsure of yourself. Be especially wary of beginning sentences with "I hope," "If you agree," "I think," and other self-conscious terms.

☒ NOT   If you'd like to take advantage of this offer, call our toll-free number.

☑ BUT   To take advantage of this offer, call our toll-free number.

☒ NOT   I hope that you will agree that my qualifications match your job needs.

☑ BUT   My qualifications match your job needs in the following respects.

In some situations, the best strategy is simply to omit information. Why focus on your lack of work experience in a cover letter or imply that your product may need to be returned?

☒ NOT   Let us know if you experience any other problems.

☑ BUT   Your Skullcandy headphones should now provide you with several years of clear audio enjoyment.

July 12, 2012   VIA EMAIL ONLY

Mr. Patrick Wensink
Louisville, KY
patrickwensink@gmail.com

Re: Mark: **JACK DANIEL'S**
        Subject: Use of Trademarks

Dear Mr. Wensink:

> **Starts with a friendly introduction and background information about the trademark.**

I am an attorney at Jack Daniel's Properties, Inc. ("JDPI") in California. JDPI is the owner of the JACK DANIEL'S trademarks (the "Marks") which have been used extensively and for many years in connection with our well-known Tennessee whiskey product and a wide variety of consumer merchandise.

> **Uses objective language to describe the concern.**

It has recently come to our attention that the cover of your book *Broken Piano for President*, bears a design that closely mimics the style and distinctive elements of the JACK DANIEL'S trademarks. An image of the cover is set forth below for ease of reference.

> **Uses courteous language and a positive tone.**

We are certainly flattered by your affection for the brand, but while we can appreciate the pop culture appeal of Jack Daniel's, we also have to be diligent to ensure that the Jack Daniel's trademarks are used correctly. Given the brand's popularity, it will probably come as no surprise that we come across designs like this on a regular basis. What may not be so apparent, however, is that if we allow uses like this one, we run the very real risk that our trademark will be weakened. As a fan of the brand, I'm sure that is not something you intended or would want to see happen.

> **Builds understanding by relating to the author's own situation.**

As an author, you can certainly understand our position and the need to contact you. You may even have run into similar problems with your own intellectual property.

> **Offers reasonable alternatives.**

In order to resolve this matter, because you are both a Louisville "neighbor" and a fan of the brand, we simply request that you change the cover design when the book is re-printed. If you would be willing to change the design sooner than that (including on the digital version), we would be willing to contribute a reasonable amount towards the costs of doing so. By taking this step, you will help us to ensure that the Jack Daniel's brand will mean as much to future generations as it does today.

> **Continues using positive language, yet confidently requests a response.**

We wish you continued success with your writing and we look forward to hearing from you at your earliest convenience. A response by **July 23, 2012** would be appreciated, if possible. In the meantime, if you have any questions or concerns, please do not hesitate to contact me.

Sincerely,

Christy Susman

Christy Susman
Senior Attorney - Trademarks

JACK DANIEL'S PROPERTIES, INC.
4040 CIVIC CENTER DRIVE • SUITE 528 • SAN RAFAEL, CALIFORNIA 94903
TELEPHONE: (415) 446-5225 • FAX (415) 446-5230

To clarify the modifier in the third paragraph in Figure 8, rewrite, "As a fan of the brand, you . . ."

A word of caution: Do not appear *overconfident;* avoid sounding presumptuous or arrogant. Be especially wary of using such strong phrases as "I know that" and "I am sure you will agree that."

    ☒ NOT   I'm sure that you'll agree our offer is reasonable.

         ☑ BUT   This solution should give you the data you need while still protecting the privacy of our clients.

Competent communicators are *confident* communicators. They write with conviction, yet avoid appearing pushy or presumptuous.

5-5b   Use a Courteous and Sincere Tone

A tone of courtesy and sincerity builds goodwill for you and your organization and increases the likelihood that your message will achieve its objective. For example, lecturing the reader or filling a letter with platitudes (trite, obvious statements) implies a condescending attitude. Also, readers are likely to find offensive such expressions as "you failed to," "we find it difficult to believe that," "you surely don't expect," or "your complaint."

☒	NOT	Companies like ours cannot survive unless our customers pay their bills on time.
☑	BUT	By paying your bill before May 30, you will maintain your excellent credit history with our firm.
☒	NOT	You sent your complaint to the wrong department. We don't handle shipping problems.
☑	BUT	We have forwarded your letter to the shipping department. You should be hearing from them within the week.

Your reader is sophisticated enough to know when you're being sincere. To achieve a sincere tone, avoid exaggeration (especially using too many modifiers or too strong modifiers), obvious flattery, and expressions of surprise or disbelief.

☒	NOT	Your satisfaction means more to us than making a profit, and we will work night and day to see that we earn it.
☑	BUT	We value your goodwill and have taken these specific steps to ensure your satisfaction.
☒	NOT	I'm surprised you would question your raise, considering your overall performance last year.
☑	BUT	Your raise was based on an objective evaluation of your performance last year.

The best way to achieve an appropriate tone is to genuinely think well of your reader.

5-5c Use Appropriate Emphasis and Subordination

Let's say you work for a large mutual fund company and have been asked to recommend an iPhone case for 150 employees. You were given two popular cases to compare: LifeProof and Bandbox. Through your research, you find that, although LifeProof is waterproof and comes in more colors, these features aren't important to your staff. You decide to recommend Bandbox because it's less expensive.

Feature	LifeProof	Bandbox
Waterproof?	Yes	No
Price	$80	$65
Color Selection	10	3

As you plan an email to your manager, consider ways to show the relative importance of each feature. To emphasize an idea, use the strategies in Figure 15. To subordinate an idea, simply use the opposite strategy.

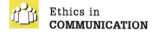

Ethics in COMMUNICATION

Use emphasis and subordination to show your reader how important you consider each idea. Your goal is not to mislead the reader. If you believe that the Bandbox is the *slightly* better choice, avoid intentionally misleading your reader into concluding that it is *clearly* the better choice. Achieve your communication objectives using fair tactics and sound business judgment.

5-5d Use Positive Language

You are more likely to achieve your objectives with positive instead of negative words. Positive language builds goodwill and usually provides more information to your reader. Note the differences in tone and detail in the following sentences:

| ☒ | NOT | The briefcase is not made of cheap imitation leather. |
| ☑ | BUT | The briefcase is made of 100% belt leather for years of durable service. |

☒ NOT   I do not yet have any work experience.

☑ BUT   My two terms as secretary of the Management Club taught me the importance of accurate recordkeeping and gave me experience in working as part of a team.

Ways to Emphasize Ideas | **Figure 15**

Put the idea in a short, simple sentence. However, if you need a complex sentence to convey all of the information, put the more important idea in the independent clause. (The ideas communicated in each independent clause of a *compound* sentence receive *equal* emphasis.)

- **Simple** *Bandbox is the best case for our use.*
- **Complex** *Although LifeProof is waterproof, it will be less expensive for us to replace phones in the few "flushing" incidents.* (The independent clause emphasizes that water protection is not a crucial consideration.)

Place the major idea first or last. The first paragraph of a message receives the most emphasis, the last paragraph receives less emphasis, and the middle paragraphs receive the least emphasis. Similarly, the middle sentences within a paragraph receive less emphasis than the first sentence in a paragraph.

The cost difference is significant. LifeProof costs $100 per case. But Bandbox offers discounts for large orders and will cost us $65 per case, or 35% less.

Make the noun you want to emphasize the subject of the sentence. In other words, use active voice to emphasize the doer of the action and passive voice to emphasize the receiver.

- **Active** *Bandbox costs 35% less than LifeProof.* (Emphasizes Bandbox rather than LifeProof)
- **Passive** *The costs of the two cases were compared first.* (Emphasizes the costs rather than the two cases)

Devote more space to the idea.

Cost is the most important consideration. At 35% less, Bandbox will cost us $9,750 instead of $15,000 for a $5,250 savings. Given our current budget constraints, this savings is significant.

Use language that directly implies importance, such as *most important, major*, or *primary*. Use terms such as *least important* or *a minor point* to subordinate an idea.

The most important factor for us is cost. Color selection is a minor concern.

Use repetition (within reason).

Bandbox will save money—money that could be used to upgrade our service plans.

Use bullets, italics, colors, indenting, or other design elements to emphasize key ideas.

*But the most important criterion is cost, and Bandbox costs **35%** less than LifeProof.*

Expressions like *cannot* and *will not* are not the only ones that convey negative messages. Stress what *is* true and what *can* be done rather than what is not true and cannot be done. Other words, like *mistake, damage, failure, refuse,* and *deny*, also carry negative connotations and should be avoided when possible.

☒ NOT   We can't replace the blender because the warranty has expired.

☑ BUT   Although the warranty expired, we can offer you a replacement blender.

☒ NOT   Failure to follow the directions may cause the blender to malfunction.

☑ BUT   Following the directions will ensure many years of carefree service from your blender.

The head of a Cleveland-based job bank surprised her colleagues when her negative language in emails became public. When people wrote to her for advice and for access to her Yahoo group for employers and job seekers, she responded harshly (Figure 16). A year earlier, she had won a "Communicator of the Year" award.

Negative language also often has the opposite effect of what is intended. "Do not think of elephants." What are you thinking of now?

Figure 16 | Part of a Negative Email

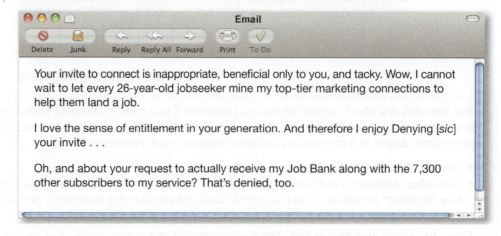

> Your invite to connect is inappropriate, beneficial only to you, and tacky. Wow, I cannot wait to let every 26-year-old jobseeker mine my top-tier marketing connections to help them land a job.
>
> I love the sense of entitlement in your generation. And therefore I enjoy Denying [*sic*] your invite . . .
>
> Oh, and about your request to actually receive my Job Bank along with the 7,300 other subscribers to my service? That's denied, too.

The woman did apologize. But she could have avoided the embarrassment by using more positive, encouraging language and, as we'll discuss next, stressing the "you" attitude, rather than her own perspective—just as she's asking the job seeker to do.

5-5e Stress the "You" Attitude

If you're like most people reading or hearing a message, your reaction probably is, "What's in it for me?" To focus on the reader, adopt the "you" attitude.

The "you" attitude emphasizes what the *receiver* (the listener or the reader) wants to know and how he or she will be affected by the message.

☒ NOT   I am shipping your order this afternoon.

      ☑ BUT   You should receive your order by Friday.

☒ NOT   We will be open on Sundays from 1:00 p.m. to 5:00 p.m., beginning May 15.

      ☑ BUT   You will be able to shop on Sundays from 1:00 p.m. to 5:00 p.m., beginning May 15.

An important component of the "you" attitude is the concept of receiver benefits—emphasizing how the reader or the listener will benefit from doing as you ask. Sometimes, especially when asking a favor or refusing a request, the best we can do is to show how *someone* (not necessarily the reader) will benefit. But whenever possible, we should show how someone *other than ourselves* benefits from our request or from our decision.

☒ NOT   We cannot afford to purchase an ad in your organization's directory.

      ☑ BUT   Advertising exclusively on television allows us to offer consumers like you the lowest prices on their cosmetics.

☒ NOT   Our decorative fireplace has an oak mantel and is portable.

      ☑ BUT   Whether entertaining in your living room or den, you can still enjoy the ambience of a blazing fire because our decorative fireplace is portable. Simply take it with you from room to room.

The revised sentences are longer than the original sentences because they contain *more information*. But they do not contain unnecessary words. You can add information and still write concisely.

Stressing the "you" attitude focuses the attention on the reader, which is right where the attention should be—most of the time. However, when you refuse someone's request, disagree with someone, or talk about someone's mistakes or shortcomings, avoid connecting the reader too closely with the negative information. In these situations, avoid second-person pronouns (*you* and *your*), and use passive sentences or other subordinating techniques to stress the receiver of the action rather than the doer.

☒ NOT   You should have included more supporting evidence in your presentation.

☑ BUT   Including more supporting evidence would have made the presentation more convincing.

☒ NOT   You failed to return the merchandise within the 10-day period.

☑ BUT   We are happy to give a full refund on all merchandise that is returned within 10 days.

Note that neither of the revised sentences contains the word *you*. Instead, the revisions separate the reader from the negative information, making the message more tactful and palatable.

The Checklist for Revising Your Writing summarizes principles of style, which goes beyond *correctness*. Style involves choosing the right words, writing effective sentences, developing logical paragraphs, and setting an appropriate tone.

At first, you may find it difficult and time-consuming to revise your writing using these criteria. But your time spent will pay off: soon, you'll apply these principles unconsciously and will see a big improvement in your writing.

Checklist for Revising Your Writing

WORDS

☑ **Write clearly.** Be accurate and complete; use familiar words; use specific, concrete language; avoid dangling expressions; and avoid clichés, slang, and unnecessary jargon.

☑ **Write concisely.** Avoid redundancy and wordy expressions, avoid hidden subjects and hidden verbs, and imply or condense when appropriate.

SENTENCES

☑ **Use a variety of sentence types.** Use simple sentences for emphasis, compound sentences for coordinate relationships, and complex sentences for subordinate relationships.

☑ **Use active and passive voice appropriately.** Use active voice in general and to emphasize the doer

of the action; use passive voice to emphasize the receiver.

☑ **Use parallel structure.** Match adjectives with adjectives, nouns with nouns, infinitives with infinitives, and so on.

PARAGRAPHS

☑ **Keep paragraphs unified and coherent.** Develop a single idea consistently and logically; use transitional words, pronouns, and repetition when appropriate.

☑ **Control paragraph length.** Use a variety of paragraph lengths.

OVERALL TONE

☑ **Write confidently.** Avoid sounding self-conscious, but also avoid sounding arrogant or presumptuous.

☑ **Use a courteous and sincere tone.** Avoid platitudes, exaggeration, obvious flattery, and expressions of surprise or disbelief.

☑ **Use appropriate emphasis and subordination.** Emphasize and subordinate through the use of

sentence structure, position, verb voice, amount of space, language, repetition, and mechanical means.

☑ **Use positive language.** Stress what you *can* do or what *is* true rather than what you cannot do or what is not true.

☑ **Stress the "you" attitude.** Emphasize what the receiver wants to know and how the receiver will be affected by the message; stress receiver benefits.

Revising a Press Release for Citigroup

>>> PURPOSE

Imagine that you work for Citigroup as the vice president of corporate communication. You receive a draft press release from the director of investor relations, announcing 11,000 employee layoffs. The release starts with this introductory paragraph:

> "Citigroup today announced a series of repositioning actions that will further reduce expenses and improve efficiency across the company while maintaining Citi's unique capabilities to serve clients, especially in the emerging markets. These actions will result in increased business efficiency, streamlined operations, and an optimized consumer footprint across geographies."

You are not happy with this opening and plan to revise it.

>>> PROCESS

You ask yourself the following questions as you start this revising job.

1. **What do you want to accomplish with the press release?**
   I want to explain the changes we have planned and the rationale for them. My hope is to maintain readers' confidence in the company, but I also want to be respectful to the 11,000 employees who are losing their jobs.

2. **Who are your primary and secondary audiences?**
   Investors, the media, and customers are my primary audience; employees are my secondary audience.

3. **What tone is appropriate for the press release?**
   A professional tone is important, and I need to balance empathy with a positive outlook. This real challenge is addressing investors, who probably will like the news of layoffs, and employees and others, who may be critical of the company's values. My language should be clear and concise.

4. **How else can you improve the introduction?**
   I can remove jargon and simplify the language. I'll also mention the layoffs up front—this is the major news and deserves attention.

5. **What changes will you make to the introduction?**

> Today, Citigroup ~~today~~ announced ~~a series of repositioning actions~~changes that ~~will~~ to further reduce expenses, streamline operations, and improve efficiency across the company. Although these changes include significant employee reductions, we will ~~while~~ maintaining ~~Citi's~~ our unique capabilities to serve clients, especially in the emerging markets. ~~These actions will result in increased business efficiency, streamlined operations, and an optimized consumer footprint across geographies.~~

>>> PRODUCT

Today, Citigroup announced changes to further reduce expenses, streamline operations, and improve efficiency across the company. Although these changes include significant employee reductions, we will maintain our unique capabilities to serve clients, especially in the emerging markets.

Revising an Email to Employees

>>> PURPOSE

Imagine that you work as the director of human resources for a division of a major bank and have asked an intern to draft an email to employees about a summer dress code. The email will be distributed to 300 employees in the divisional office. You will allow employees to dress more casually during the warm weather, but you also want to give them clear guidelines on what is and is not acceptable to wear in the office. You receive the draft from the intern, but it needs work.

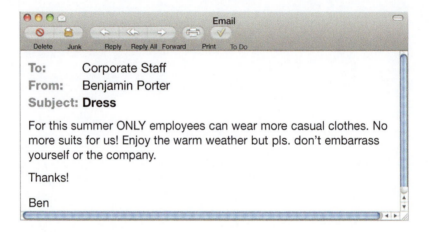

To: Corporate Staff
From: Benjamin Porter
Subject: **Dress**

For this summer ONLY employees can wear more casual clothes. No more suits for us! Enjoy the warm weather but pls. don't embarrass yourself or the company.

Thanks!

Ben

>>> PROCESS

1. What do you want to accomplish with this email?

2. What, specifically, do employees need to know?

3. What works well in this email draft?

4. What could be improved in this message?

>>> PRODUCT

Rewrite the draft email for employees.

> SUMMARY

LO1   Choose the right words for your message.

Achieve clarity by making your message accurate, by using familiar words, and by avoiding dangling expressions and unnecessary jargon. Write to express—not to impress. Use longer words only if they express your idea more clearly. Use specific, concrete language and avoid clichés, slang, and buzzwords.

To achieve conciseness, make every word count. Avoid redundancy, wordy expressions, and hidden verbs and subjects. Sometimes you may imply rather than explicitly state certain information. In other situations, use adjectives or adverbs instead of clauses to convey information more concisely.

LO2   Write effective sentences.

Because they present a single idea and are usually short, prefer simple sentences for emphasis. Use compound sentences to communicate two or more ideas of equal importance. When communicating two or more ideas of unequal importance, choose complex sentences and place the subordinate idea in the dependent clause.

Use active voice to emphasize the doer of the action and passive voice to emphasize the receiver of the action. Express similar ideas in similar grammatical structure. Be especially careful to use parallel structure in report headings and in numbered lists.

LO3   Develop logical paragraphs.

Your paragraphs should be unified and coherent. Develop only one topic per paragraph, and use transitional words, pronouns, and repetition to move smoothly from one idea to the next. Although you should vary paragraph lengths, most range from 60 to 80 words.

LO4   Convey an appropriate tone.

Convey competence in your writing and confidence that your reader will do as you ask or will accept your decision. However, avoid sounding presumptuous or arrogant. Use a tone of courtesy and sincerity to build goodwill and to help you achieve your objectives.

Use emphasis and subordination to develop a common frame of reference between you and the reader. Positive rather than negative words are more likely to help you achieve your communication objective. Keep the emphasis on the reader—stressing what the reader needs to know and how the reader will be affected by the message.

LO1 Choose the right words for your message.

1. Improve writing style.

Rewrite this company's description to improve style and correct errors.

| SELECT COLOR | PHOTO GALLERY | DESCRIPTION | OPTIONS | SPECIFICATIONS | HOW TO INSTALL | REVIEWS |

More information about Motorized Solar Shades

Shades Shutters Blinds offers a wide selection of window coverings, including Timber Remote Solar Shades- Radio. If you are not sure which window coverings will look best, you can get a free sample of any design. This can give a person ease of mind when they place their order, because it gives them a better idea about what they will be getting. Another advantage of shopping with this company is that they offer free standard shipping.

The solar shades available from Shades Shutters Blinds come with an openness factor of between 1% and 14%. They come in various colors, including many that have a grayish tint. There also come in varieties of black and white. The Vienne Collection has soft earth tones, and the Sheerweave 5000 Collection has many interesting patterns and textures.

One of the mounting options available for these window treatments is a fascia valance, a metal valance that is installed at the top of the window. When the shade is rolled up, the roll is hidden behind the valance. It is designed for long windows and is available in five different colors.

Timber Remote Solar Shades- Radio is a good product to consider when you are trying to decide on a window covering. Shades Shutters Blinds is a customer oriented company that will deliver a quality product.

WWW.SHADESSHUTTERSBLINDS.COM

2. Announce a new initiative using clear, simple language.

As the CEO of a growing business, you want to help employees save for retirement. Many of your employees receive minimum wage and have little experience with investing money. Write a simple, clear email to employees explaining what a 401(k) plan is, why employees should participate, and how it will work at your company. You may need to research 401(k) plans first; you will find information at sites such as www.irs.gov.

For this new initiative, you will probably have in-person meetings, too, to explain the new plan. Imagine that this email is a starting point.

3. Write clearly and avoid slang.

These two sentences are filled with business slang and clichés. Revise them using simple, clear language.

> Using the synergies amongst our competitors, we can formulate a program that not only capitalizes on the strengths of each of our respective constituencies but that raises the bar to a new level for each and every one of us.
>
> At the end of the day, we need to think outside the box to look for low-hanging fruit, or we'll never reach our end goal.

4. Revise to eliminate dangling expressions.

Revise these sentences to eliminate dangling expressions.

a. Driving through Chicago in the fog, the street signs were hard to read.

b. The Federal Reserve banks maintain excellent relations with the major financial institutions, but they are still not doing as much as they had expected.

c. To become law, the governor must sign the bill by the end of the session.

d. While drilling a hole to bring in the wiring, a crack was created in the wall.

e. After attending the meeting, the minutes were prepared by the administrative assistant.

f. After resting in bed for several weeks, the doctor told the actor the plastic surgery was successful.

g. Although the owners have changed, they continue to expand.

h. Sitting in a diner on Main Street, hamburgers were enjoyed by the soccer team.

i. Purchased in Italy, I brought home several bottles of fantastic red wine.

j. To try out for *American Idol*, an entry form must be completed while you wait in line.

5. **Use concrete language.**

Imagine that you work for a middle school and want to help teens develop healthier habits. How could you present these descriptions in more concrete terms? To what can each be compared? You might consider illustrating some of these with consumption over time (for example, a pack of cigarettes per day for a month or a year).

a. A pack of cigarettes can cost $14.50 in New York City.

b. Average food orders at Chipotle have 1,070 calories and 2,400 milligrams of sodium.[15]

c. A 16-ounce bottle of soda can have 44 grams of sugar.

d. According to the National Institutes of Health, "More than 190,000 people under age 21 visited an emergency room for alcohol-related injuries."[16]

6. **Analyze a simple explanation of a complex topic.**

Watch one or two videos by the company Common Craft, which creates short videos to make complex topics easy to understand.[17] Go to www.commoncraft.com or search YouTube for "Common Craft," and choose a topic that interests you. What about the video helps you understand the topic? Consider the use of words and graphics to explain abstract topics. Giving specific examples from the video, write a one-page analysis and submit it to your instructor.

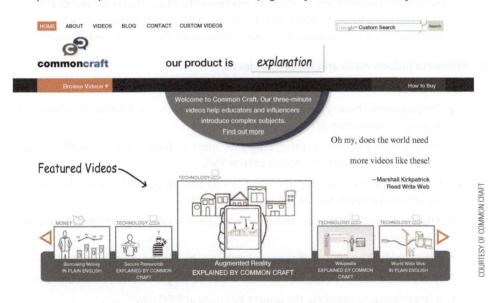

7. **Use simple language.**

Revise this paragraph to make it more understandable.

> The privileged juvenile was filled with abundant glee when her fashion mogul employer designated her as the contemporary representative of an ostentatious couture line. Although she was temporarily employed for the summer for an internship in the design department, her adolescent ambition was to enrich her life as a model. Subsequent to altering her hair, administering makeup, and adorning herself with the fashion designer's creations, she advanced in front of the photographer's lenses, beginning the succession of fulfilling her dreams.

8. **Eliminate wordy expressions.**

Revise the following sentences to eliminate wordy phrases by substituting a single word wherever possible. You may find other opportunities to tighten for conciseness.

  a. Push the red button in the event that you see smoke rising from the cooking surface.

  b. More than 40% of the people polled are of the opinion that government spending should be reduced.

  c. Please send me more information pertaining to your new line of pesticides.

  d. Due to the fact that two of the three highway lanes were closed for repairs, I was nearly 20 minutes late for my appointment.

  e. Chef Ramsay, who was formerly my instructor at culinary school, is in today's society the owner of several restaurants, which are all over the world.

  f. The newest sports automobile trend is to install seats made out of leather.

  g. Google is now taking applications for job positions at this point in time, in spite of the fact that they just laid off employees.

  h. We have the ability to vote for the best performer on TV by text messaging the on-screen telephone number.

9. **Tighten a paragraph for conciseness.**

By how many words can you reduce this paragraph without changing the meaning?

New York City is the most natural choice of a location for an innovative restaurant like Fellerton. It is no secret that New York City is a world capital in restaurant innovation. In fact, New York City residents and locals alike consider themselves the most experimental eaters in the country as well as the top foodies. It is also home to Restaurant Week, which has since spread to cities all over the world. The fact that people living in New York City are adventurous eaters means they are more likely to accept and praise an unheard of restaurant concept like Fellerton.

10. **Eliminate hidden verbs and hidden subjects.**

Revise the following sentences to eliminate hidden verbs and hidden subjects.

  a. The jury needs to carry out a review of the case to make a decision about whether the actress has a violation of her alcohol probation.

  b. For our road trip during spring break, we must undertake the calculations of our driving travel time from California to New York.

  c. If you cannot make the payment for the $135 tickets, you will not be able to make backstage visitations for the Lollapalooza concerts.

  d. After much deliberation, the group came to a decision about how to make a response to the lawsuit.

  e. Although Hugh wanted to offer an explanation of his actions, his boss refused to listen.

  f. If confused about the assignment, there are some diagrams that you should review.

  g. It is our intent to complete the project by Friday at 3:00 p.m.

  h. There are four principles of marketing that we need to consider.

LO2 Write effective sentences.

11. **Identify types of sentences.**

What type of sentence—simple, compound, or complex—is each of the following? Internal punctuation has been omitted to avoid giving hints. Compare your answers to others' in the class.

  a. Now that she has found her true love "The Bachelorette" wants women everywhere to know that it is worth it to wait for the right guy.

  b. Hillary went to see the new branch manager but the manager had gone to lunch.

c. The new single from the band's album is out on Tuesday while the demo version which you can download on iTunes will be available on Monday.

d. You will have 12 hours to complete the job.

e. I will try to get the project finished and shipped to you by tomorrow.

f. Everyone seems to be feeding off the intensity at the physically challenging football camp particularly the defensive tackles who often sport aggressive expressions.

g. The milestone homer provided an encouraging lift during a trying stretch for the baseball team.

h. Walking down the street with my sister I saw two men dressed in dark suits running out of the bank.

i. See the coach and turn in your gear.

j. Please clean your room when you have finished your homework.

k. The fifth order arrives today it should be the last one.

12. **Practice writing different types of sentences.**

Write a simple, a compound, and a complex sentence that incorporates both items of information in each bullet. For the complex sentences, emphasize the first idea in each item.

a. The new smartphone will be available on Wednesday / The smartphone will have more features than the older model.

b. The captain got promoted to a major today / He will lead the army into battle.

c. Tim was promoted / Tim was assigned additional responsibilities.

d. Eileen is our corporate counsel / Eileen will draft the letter for us.

13. **Practice sentence variety.**

Rewrite the following paragraph by varying sentence types and sentence lengths to keep the writing interesting.

Smartfood was founded by Ann Withey, Andrew Martin, and Ken Meyers in 1984. The product was the first snack food to combine white cheddar cheese and popcorn. Ann Withey perfected the Smartfood recipe in her home kitchen after much trial and error. Smartfood sales were reportedly only $35,000 in 1985. During that time, the product was available only in New England. By 1988, sales had soared to $10 million. This attracted the attention of Frito-Lay. The snack-food giant bought Smartfood in 1989 for $15 million. Since the purchase, Frito-Lay has not tampered with the popular Smartfood formula. It has used its marketing expertise to keep sales growing, despite the growing number of challengers crowding the cheesy popcorn market.

14. **Vary sentence length.**

Write a long sentence (40 to 50 words) about a company or person you admire. Then revise the sentence so that it contains 10 or fewer words. Finally, rewrite the sentence so that it contains 16 to 22 words. Which sentence is the most effective? Why?

15. **Use active and passive voice.**

Working in groups of three, identify whether each of the following sentences is active or passive. Then, discuss whether the sentence uses active or passive voice appropriately and why. Next, change the sentences that use an inappropriate voice.

Sentence Example	Active or Passive Voice?	Appropriate Use?(If not, then rewrite the sentence.)
a. A very effective sales letter was written by Paul Mendelson.		
b. Our old office will be sold to a real estate developer.		
c. You failed to verify the figures on the quarterly report.		
d. The website designed by Catalina Graphics did not reflect our company's image.		

16. **Check and revise sentences for parallel structure.**

Determine whether the following sentences use parallel structure. Revise sentences as needed to make the structure parallel.

a. The executive at Ernst & Young writes reports quickly, accurately, and in detail.

b. The bride hates wearing heels, and on her wedding day, she just wanted to wear flats, be able to dance around, and be comfortable.

c. The store is planning to install a new point-of-sale system that is easier to operate, easier to repair, and cheaper to maintain than the current system.

d. Angelina's children like to go swimming, biking, and play tennis.

e. According to the survey, most employees prefer either holding the employee cafeteria open later or its hours to be kept the same.

f. The quarterback is expert not only in calling plays but also in throwing passes.

g. Our career guide will cover writing résumés, cover letters, and techniques for interviewing.

LO3 Develop logical paragraphs.

17. **Order sentences into a logical paragraph (Honda Accord).**

Place a number (from 1 to 7) next to each sentence to represent its position within the paragraph. *Hint:* The broadest statement will be the first sentence.

The Accord has 17-inch alloy wheels.	
The car's wide-opening doors provide easy access to the interior.	
With an automatic reverse feature, the moonroof is safe.	
The Accord is a good choice for today's active driver.	
The Honda Accord is a well-designed, functional car that will attract attention.	
In a variety of colors, the Accord will stand out in the crowd.	
The one-touch power moonroof with tilt is easy to operate.	

18. **Order sentences into a logical paragraph (Nick's Pizza).**

    Place a number (from 1 to 8) next to each sentence to represent its position within the paragraph. *Hint:* The broadest statement will be the first sentence.

But, as Nick says, "I decided I needed to do what felt like the right thing to do: communicate openly, clearly, and honestly."	
Going against the advice of his publicist and his banker, Nick decided to send an email explaining the situation to his customers and asking for their patronage.	
Analysts credit Nick's transparency and authenticity for saving the business.	
Some started a Facebook page, while others frequented Nick's Pizza and spread the word.	
This strategy also defies conventional wisdom, which warns of suppliers cutting off a potentially failing business and customers avoiding a place in trouble.	
When Nick's Pizza & Pub was going out of business, Nick turned to his customers for support—and he got it.	
Nick saw an immediate increase in sales, and today it's still a viable restaurant.	
Customers responded.	

19. **Use transitions for paragraph coherence.**

    Revisit the Honda Accord paragraph in Exercise 17. Now that you have sentences in a logical order, add transitions to improve coherence.

20. **Insert transitions for paragraph coherence.**

    Insert logical transitions in the blanks to give the following paragraph coherence.

    Bits 'n' Bytes is widening its lead over Desktop Computing in the computer-magazine war. _____ its revenues increased 27% last year, whereas Desktop Computing's increased only 16%. _____ its audited paid circulation increased to 600,000, compared to 450,000 for Desktop Computing. _____ Desktop Computing was able to increase both the ad rate and the number of ad pages last year. One note of worry _____ is Desktop Computing's decision to shut down its independent testing laboratory. Some industry leaders believe much of Desktop Computing's success has been due to its reliable product reviews. _____ Bits 'n' Bytes has just announced an agreement whereby Stanford University's world-famous engineering school will perform product testing for Bits 'n' Bytes.

21. **Adjust paragraph length.**

    Read the following paragraph and determine how it might be divided into two or more shorter paragraphs to help the reader follow the complex topic being discussed.

    Transforming a manuscript into a published book requires several steps. After the author submits the manuscript, the copy editor makes any needed grammatical or spelling changes. The author reviews these changes to be sure that they haven't altered the meaning of any sentences or sections. Next, the publisher begins the design process. At this point, designers select photographs and other artwork and create page layouts, which show how the pages will look when printed. The author and publisher review these page proofs for any errors. Only after all corrections have been made does the book get published. From start to finish, this process can take as long as a year.

22. Revise a paragraph to convey an appropriate tone.

Revise the paragraph to create a more confident, less presumptuous tone.

> If you believe my proposal has merit, I hope that you will allocate $50,000 for a pilot study. It's possible that this pilot study will achieve my profit estimates so that we can implement the idea in other locations. Even though you have several other worthwhile projects to consider for funding, I know you will agree the proposal should be funded prior to January 1. Please call me before the end of the week to tell me that you've accepted my proposal.

23. Revise sentences to convey a confident tone.

Revise the following sentences to convey an appropriately confident attitude.

a. Can you think of any reason not to buy a wristwatch for dressy occasions?

b. I hope you agree that my offer provides good value for the money.

c. Of course, I am confident that my offer provides good value for the money.

d. You might try to find a few minutes to visit our gallery on your next visit to galleries in this area.

24. Revise this passage to avoid platitudes, obvious flattery, and exaggeration.

> You, our loyal and dedicated employees, have always been the most qualified and the hardest working in the industry. Because of your faithful and dependable service, I was quite surprised to learn yesterday that an organizational meeting for union representation was recently held here. You must realize that a company like ours cannot survive unless we hold labor costs down. I cannot believe that you don't appreciate the many benefits of working at Allied. We will immediately have to declare bankruptcy if a union is voted in. Please don't be fooled by empty rhetoric.

25. Vary emphasis in a memo.

Assume that you have evaluated two candidates for the position of sales assistant. This is what you have learned:

- Carl Barteolli has more sales experience.
- Elizabeth Larson has more appropriate formal training (earned a college degree in marketing and attended several three-week sales seminars).
- Elizabeth Larson's personality is a better fit for the corporate culture.

You must write a memo to Robert Underwood, the vice president, recommending one of these candidates. First, assume that personality is the most important criterion, and write a memo recommending Elizabeth Larson. Second, assume that experience is the most important criterion, and write a memo recommending Carl Barteolli. Use appropriate emphasis and subordination in each message. You may make up any reasonable information needed to complete the assignment.

26. Use positive language.

Revise the following paragraph to eliminate negative language.

> We cannot issue a full refund at this time because you did not enclose a receipt or an authorized estimate. I'm sorry that we will have to delay your reimbursement. We are not like those insurance companies that promise you anything but then disappear when you have a claim. When we receive your receipt or estimate, we will not hold up your check. Our refusal to issue reimbursement without proper supporting evidence means that we do not have to charge you outlandish premiums for your automobile insurance.

27. **Make a positive impression.**

Revise the following signs often seen in stores:

    a. "No shirt, no shoes, no service."

    b. "American Express cards not accepted."

    c. "No returns without receipts."

    d. "No smoking."

    e. "No dogs allowed."

28. **Stress the "you" attitude in a paragraph.**

Revise the following paragraph to make the reader the center of attention.

> We are happy to announce that we are offering for sale an empty parcel of land at the corner of Mission and High Streets. We will be selling this parcel for $89,500, with a minimum down payment of $22,500. We have had the lot rezoned M-2 for student housing. We originally purchased this lot because of its proximity to the university and had planned to erect student housing, but our investment plans have changed. We still believe that our lot would make a profitable site for up to three 12-unit buildings.

29. **Use a "you" attitude and positive language.**

Rewrite this email from a facilities manager to country club members. How can you stress the "you" attitude and focus on good news without misleading members?

30. **Emphasize receiver benefits.**

Revise the following sentences to emphasize receiver benefits.

    a. We have been in the business of repairing sewing machines for more than 40 years.

    b. We need donations so that we can expand the free-food program in this community.

    c. Company policy requires us to impose a 2% late charge when customers don't pay their bills on time.

    d. Although the refund department is open from 9:00 a.m. to 5:00 p.m., it is closed from 1:00 p.m. to 2:00 p.m. so that our employees can take their lunch breaks.

COMPANY SCENARIO

Writeaway Hotels

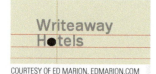

COURTESY OF ED MARION, EDMARION.COM

Even in a fast-paced company like Writeaway Hotels, your writing reflects on your credibility as a business professional. Take this opportunity to revise some of the emails you created for this simulation in Chapter 4.

To do this, you might look over your sent messages and choose a few to edit. Or, you might sign into another student's email—for the character he or she played—and choose a few messages to edit. How can you improve your writing now that you have more time?

Another option is to practice by revising the following emails, which were sent by students who participated in this simulation in the past. For their future writing, what advice would you give these students? In the first email exchange, Pat responds to Diana, the upset client; in the second email, Pat responds to Ron, the HR manager. For the response to Ron, you might consider lessons learned about potential legal consequences of communication, discussed in Chapter 1.

Missed Conference Call   Inbox | X

⭐ ● Diana1 Chavez to me   show details 9:45 AM (0 minutes ago) ↩ Reply ▼

Pat,

Why weren't you on the conference call this morning with Bill? We just talked about this yesterday, so I'm sure you knew about it. I was embarrassed that you weren't on.

This brings up a bigger issue: I'm glad business is going so well for you and that you have a lot of new clients. But I'm starting to feel like I'm getting less attention now, and I want to make sure that we can maintain the good working relationship we've had in the past.

Diana

↩ Reply   → Forward   ● Diana1 is not available to chat

⭐ ● Pat2 Gibson to Diana1   show details 9:46 AM (0 minutes ago) ↩ Reply ▼

Diana Banana,

You know I love ya, babe! I had family issue that required my immediate attention. It won't happen again.

Pat

↩ Reply   → Forward   ● Diana1 is not available to chat

Confidential   Inbox | X

⭐ ● Ron1 Harrison to me   show details 9:32 AM (15 minutes ago) ↩ Reply ▼

Dear Pat,

We need to talk. Someone in your department filed a sexual harassment complaint, and I'd like to discuss it with you. Are you available tomorrow at 10:00? That time would work best for me. Please let me know asap.

Regards,
Ron

↩ Reply   → Forward   ● Ron1 is not available to chat

⭐ ● Pat11 Gibson to Ron1   show details 9:33 AM (14 minutes ago) ↩ Reply ▼

Hello Mr. Harrison,

Yes, that incident did occur in my department. I will definitely discuss the matter with you tomorrow morning at 10:00.

↩ Reply   → Forward   ● Ron1 is not available to chat

Endnotes

1. Julia La Roche, "Citigroup's Press Release About Cutting 11,000 Jobs Gets a Gold Medal for Over-The-Top PR Speak," *Business Insider*, December 5, 2012, www.businessinsider.com/citigroups-press-release-corporate-speak-2012-12#ixzz2FubAbtc4, accessed March 15, 2015.

2. "Citigroup Announces Repositioning Actions to Further Reduce Expenses and Improve Efficiency," Citigroup Website, News, December 5, 2012, www.citigroup.com/citi/news/2012/121205a.htm, accessed March 15, 2015.

3. Michael Sebastian, "'Classically bad' press release leaves Citi vulnerable," *PR Daily Europe*, December 6, 2012, www.prdaily.eu/PRDailyEU/Articles/13318.aspx, accessed March 15, 2015.

4. "Funny Headlines," www.plainlanguage.gov/examples/humor/headlines.cfm, accessed July 2, 2014.

5. Tim Webb, "BP Boss Admits Job on the Line over Gulf Oil Spill," *The Guardian*, May 14, 2010, www.guardian.co.uk, accessed March 15, 2015.

6. Daniel M. Oppenheimer, "Consequences of Erudite Vernacular Utilized Irrespective of Necessity: Problems with Using Long Words Needlessly," *Applied Cognitive Psychology*, vol. 20, pp. 139–156 (2006). Quoted in Richard Morin, "Nerds Gone Wild," The 2006 Ig Nobel Awards, Pew Center Research Publications, October 6, 2006, http://pewresearch.org/pubs/72/nerds-gone-wild, accessed March 15, 2015.

7. "New Study Reveals a Greener Way to Travel: Airbnb Community Shows Environmental Benefits of Home Sharing," Airbnb, July 31, 2015, www.airbnb.com/press/news/new-study-reveals-a-greener-way-to-travel-airbnb-community-shows-environmental-benefits-of-home-sharing, accessed March 14, 2015.

8. "Most Annoying Business Jargon," *Forbes*, 2015, www.forbes.com/pictures/ekij45gdh/most-annoying-business-jargon/, accessed March 10, 2015.

9. Scott Gerber, "The 12 Most Overused Business Buzzwords," Mashable, June 22, 2014, http://mashable.com/2014/07/22/stop-using-jargon, accessed March 10, 2015.

10. "Consulting Jargon, Slang and Double-Speak That Drives Clients Crazy," Consultants Mind, October 7, 2012, http://consultantsmind.com/2012/10/07/consultant-jargon/, accessed March 10, 2015.

11. "Conciseness," Purdue University Online Writing Lab, February 27, 2013, https://owl.english.purdue.edu/owl/resource/572/01/, accessed March 10, 2015.

12. Richard A. Lanham, *Revising Business Prose* (New York: Scribner, 1981), p. 2.

13. Adrian Chen, "Knitters Outraged After U.S. Olympic Committee Squashes Knitting Olympics—and Disses Knitters," Gawker, June 20, 2012, http://gawker.com/5920036/us-olympics-committee-is-mad-at-knitting-olympics-for-denigrating-real-athletes, accessed March 15, 2015.

14. Kevin Allen, "U.S. Olympics PR Chief Shares Lessons from Knitting Controversy," *PR Daily Europe*, June 26, 2012, www.prdaily.eu/PR Daily EU/Articles/12006.aspx, accessed July 2, 2014.

15. L.V. Anderson, "Yes, Chipotle Is High in Calories. That Doesn't Mean It's Not Good for You" *Slate*, February 20, 2015, www.slate.com/blogs/browbeat/2015/02/20/chipotle_high_in_calories_as_new_york_times_shows_but_that_doesn_t_mean.html, accessed March 14, 2015.

16. "Underage Drinking," The National Institute on Alcohol Abuse and Alcoholism, www.niaaa.nih.gov/alcohol-health/special-populations-co-occurring-disorders/underage-drinking, accessed March 14, 2015.

17. Common Craft Home Page, www.commoncraft.com, accessed March 15, 2015.

CHAPTER

6 | Neutral and Positive Messages

LEARNING OBJECTIVES

After you have finished this chapter, you should be able to

LO1   Compose a neutral message.

LO2   Respond to a neutral message.

LO3   Compose a goodwill message.

LO4   Address customer comments online.

66 *When Jimmy Fallon sits down to write his weekly thank-you notes on 'The Tonight Show,' he is both ribbing and breathing life into a custom many felt was headed the way of the dodo.* 99 [1]

—Guy Trebay, *The New York Times*

CHAPTER INTRODUCTION

The Handwritten Note

Handwriting seems to be a dying art, but a handwritten note in certain business situations may differentiate you. On "The Tonight Show," Jimmy Fallon writes thank-you notes as a joke, but he also honors the tradition. On a recent show, he wrote a thank-you note to WuShock, Wichita State University's mascot, for "looking like a Muppet Gordon Ramsay."[2]

COURTESY OF YOUTUBE

In a *New York Times* opinion piece, "The Lost Art of the Condolence Letter," Saul Austerlitz writes about the value of a handwritten condolence letter:

> The letter is a lost art, subsumed by the email and the text message, but the condolence letter trudges on, alongside the thank-you note and the love letter, remnants of an older time. A condolence letter is a formal enterprise, its content secondary to the physical act of its writing, the sealing of its envelope, its mailing. It is a product whose labor is intentionally visible. A condolence email—let alone a condolence text—cannot bear the same weight, however carefully crafted.[3]

A New York fashion publicist also explains the value of a written note:

> "It is so important, in a digital world, to have the dignity to sit down and write something in your own hand. . . . It not only strengthens the bonds between people, in your personal life and in business, it also rings an emotional chord."[4]

In business, a handwritten thank-you card with a special message would likely be appreciated by someone who sponsored you for a scholarship, recommended you for a job, or took you out for a nice dinner. Thank-you emails after job interviews are best for expediency, but a handwritten note to someone you connected with personally could set you apart during the selection process.

Goodwill messages are rare enough; don't miss an opportunity to take the extra step to personalize a message and show how much you value the relationship.

6-1 Types of Neutral and Positive Messages

Business communication is often about routine topics. A small business owner asks for information from a supplier, a manager at a large corporation sends an email about a minor policy change, a customer calls a store for product information, a manager compliments an employee, or a customer writes positive comments about a company online. Although routine, these messages are important to run a business.

To distinguish these examples from more difficult communication—persuasive and bad-news messages covered in the next chapters—we'll refer to these as neutral or positive messages. These communications can be internal or external and may be presented in any communication medium.

6-2 Planning a Neutral or Positive Message

When a message conveys neutral or positive information to an audience who will likely be interested in what we have to say, we use the direct organizational plan. The main idea is stated first, followed by explanations and details, and then a friendly closing. Most neutral and positive messages follow the direct plan. Figure 1 shows the first paragraph of three company announcements with the main point clearly up front.

Figure 1 | Main Points in the First Paragraph of Company Announcements

Although job titles do not need to be capitalized unless they precede a name, these examples use capitalization by convention.

Press Release:
Redmond, Wash. Microsoft Corp. today announced that its Board of Directors has appointed Satya Nadella as Chief Executive Officer and member of the Board of Directors effective immediately. Nadella previously held the position of Executive Vice President of Microsoft's Cloud and Enterprise group.[5]

Website Post:
Diane Dickerson Chosen to Be New CEO of the Y
The Board of Directors of The Bangor YMCA announced that they have chosen Diane Dickerson as its new CEO. Diane has been with the Y for the past year, serving as Executive Vice President of Marketing, Development, and Community Engagement.

Email to Staff:
Team Mashable,
Today we are announcing an important and exciting addition to our family—Jim Roberts. Jim joins our team as Executive Editor and Chief Content Officer.[6]

A written message is not always the best medium for achieving your objective. As we discussed earlier, email is often overused in organizations; calling someone or walking down the hall to a colleague's office may work better in some cases. For quick interactions, an instant message or a text message may be enough.

However, for many situations, a written message will be the best choice. When you need to reach many employees, or you need a record of your conversation, follow these guidelines for organizing your written message.

6-3 Organizing a Neutral Message

LO1 Compose a neutral message.

A message is neutral if you anticipate that the reader will do as you ask without having to be persuaded. For example, a request for specific information about an organization's product is neutral because all organizations appreciate the opportunity to promote their products. However, a request for free product samples might require a persuasive message to convince the company to do something that will cost money.

6-3a Major Idea First

When making a routine request, present the major idea—your request—clearly and directly in the first sentence or two. You may use a direct question, a statement, or a polite request to present the main idea. A polite request can take a period instead of a question mark, such as, "May I please have your answer by March 3." Use a polite request when you expect the reader to respond by acting rather than by actually giving a yes-or-no answer.

Always pose your request clearly and politely, and give any background information needed to set the stage. Following are examples of effective routine requests:

> **Direct Question**
>
> Does Black & Decker offer educational discounts? Blair Junior High School will soon replace approximately 50 portable electric drills used by our industrial technology students.

> **Statement**
>
> Please let me know how I might invest in your deferred money-market fund. As an American currently working in Bangkok, Thailand, I cannot easily take advantage of your automatic monthly deposit plan.

> **Polite Request**
>
> Would you please answer several questions about the work performance of Janice Henry. She has applied for the position of financial analyst at Citibank and gave your name as a reference.

Decide in advance how much detail you need. If you need only a one-sentence reply, phrase your request to elicit that response.

☒ NOT   Please explain the features of your Google Docs program.

☑ BUT   Does your Google Docs program automatically number lines and paragraphs?

Remember that you are imposing on the goodwill of the reader. Ask as few questions as possible—and never ask for information that you can easily get on your own. If many questions *are* necessary, number them; most readers will answer questions in order and will be less likely to skip one unintentionally. Yes-or-no questions or short-answer questions are easy for the reader to answer, but when you need more information, use open-ended questions.

Arrange your questions in logical order (for example, order of importance, chronological order, or simple-to-complex order), word each question clearly and objectively (to avoid bias), and limit the content to one topic per question. If appropriate, assure the reader that the information provided will be treated confidentially.

6-3b Explanation and Details

Most of the time, you'll need to explain your initial request. Include background information (the reason for asking) either immediately before or after making the request.

For example, suppose you received the polite request asking about Janice Henry's job performance. Unless you were also told that the request came from a potential employer and that Janice Henry had given your name as a reference, you might be reluctant to provide such confidential information.

Or assume that you're writing to a former employer or professor asking for a letter of recommendation. You might need to give some background about yourself to jog the reader's memory. Put yourself in the reader's position. What information would you need to answer the request accurately and completely?

A reader is more likely to cooperate if you can show how responding to the request will benefit him or her.

> Will you please complete our five-minute survey about your online banking needs.
> We're revamping our website to make it easier for you to navigate.

You can skip the benefits when they're obvious. An email asking employees to recycle their paper would probably not need to discuss the value of recycling, which most people already know.

6-3c Friendly Closing

Use a friendly, positive tone in your last paragraph. In your closing, express appreciation for the assistance, state and justify any deadlines, or offer to reciprocate. Make your closing specific to the purpose and original.

> ☒ NOT   I need the information by October 1.
>
> > ☑ BUT   May I please have the product information by October 1, so I can include Kodak products in the next catalog.
>
> ☒ NOT   Thank you in advance for your assistance in this matter.
>
> > ☑ BUT   Thank you for providing this information, which will help us make a fairer evaluation of Janice Henry's qualifications for this position.
>
> ☒ NOT   Let me know how I can help you in the future.
>
> > ☑ BUT   Please let me know if I can return the favor by attending the meeting with Gupta Associates next week.

From the audience's perspective, what are the issues with the request in Figure 2? Consider the timing, tone, and Johara's potential concerns. For an improved version, see Figure 3.

Figure 2 | Ineffective Email Request

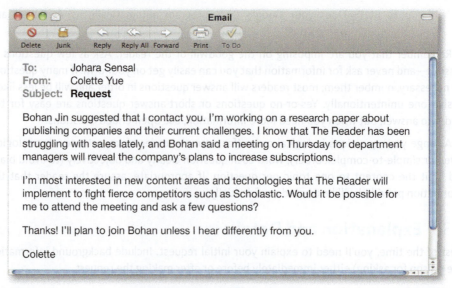

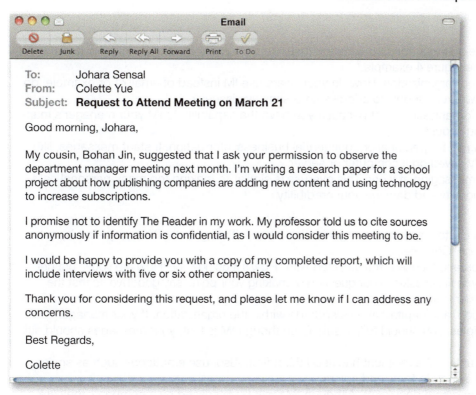

Figure 3

6-4 Sending Instant Messages for Neutral Messages

Instant messaging (IM) is a good choice for simple, neutral messages that require quick responses. The example in Figure 4 is an IM from a major global consulting organization.

Communication
TECHNOLOGIES

This conversation, like most instant messages, took less than a minute to complete. Although proper grammar isn't used here, this is acceptable for communicating with coworkers you know well (but may not be appropriate in all situations). Follow the guidelines in Figure 5 for effective IM use at work.

Many of these guidelines also apply to texting at work. Observe your company's norms, and send texts as others do in certain situations and to appropriate people.

Sample IM for a Neutral Message | **Figure 4**

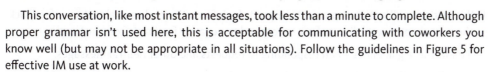

Employee 1: do you know how to undo split screens?
Employee 1: on excel?
Employee 2: yup
Employee 1: how?
Employee 2: go into ... one sec
Employee 2: ok highlight the column or row where the split is
Employee 2: go into Window
Employee 2: click freeze panes
Employee 2: that should do it
Employee 1: thanks!
Employee 2: no prob

Figure 5 | IM Use at Work

When to IM at Work

- Send an IM when you have a straightforward question, need to convey information quickly, or need help with a simple task, as in the Figure 4 example.[7]
- Follow the culture within your organization. How do your peers use IM instead of email? For example, do they IM only with close coworkers or only to address time-sensitive issues?
- Respect levels within your organization. Just because you have the capability to IM your manager's manager doesn't mean that you should.
- Avoid using instant messaging for personal or confidential business information. Instant messages, like email, can be automatically saved on a computer or server.
- Avoid excessive personal messaging at work. This overuse is similar to making too many personal calls and may affect your productivity and damage your credibility.

How to IM at Work

- Follow the communication custom within your organization when initiating an IM. You may start by asking, "Is this a good time?" or "Got a sec?"
- Keep instant messages short and focused. You can start with "How's it going?" or "How are you?" but get to the point quickly. When you finish asking your question or making your point, say goodbye so that the recipient can get back to other work.
- Follow grammar, punctuation, and capitalization standards within the organization. If your manager follows good writing principles, you should follow suit. Even though IM is fast, your messages should still be reasonably error free.
- Avoid using abbreviations unless the recipient has used them first. Also, use emoticons such as smiley faces sparingly, and avoid elaborate fonts and colors.
- Save important IMs into a separate document. Although IMs can be accessed by a company, they are not always easy for the sender or receiver to retrieve.
- Follow your company's IM policy, and be aware of viruses and security risks. Avoid accepting IMs from people you don't know and—as with email—don't open attachments unless you trust the source.

LO2 Respond to a neutral message.

6-5 Responding to a Neutral Message

In this section, we'll look at responses to requests for information and neutral customer feedback. In the next chapter, we'll discuss how to respond to negative feedback from customers.

Follow these guidelines when responding to requests and other neutral messages:

- Respond promptly. You'll want prospective customers to receive your information before they make a purchase decision—and possibly go to a competitor. Research shows that customers expect a response within 24 hours, and satisfaction levels drop sharply if responses take longer.[8] However, quicker responses are best. For requests posted online, for example, on Twitter, customers may expect a response within just an hour or two.
- Respond courteously. Your response represents the organization. A reply that sounds terse or burdened misses an opportunity to build goodwill.

☒ NOT   Although we do not generally provide the type of information you requested, we have decided to do so in this case.

☑ BUT   We are happy to provide the information you requested.

- Use a direct organizational plan. Make it easy for the reader to understand your response by putting the "good news"—the fact that you're responding favorably—up front. This pattern is the same as a neutral request.

☒ NOT   I have received your request of June 26 asking me to speak at the meeting.

☑ BUT   I would be pleased to speak at your Engineering Society meeting on August 8. Thank you for thinking of me.

- Answer all the questions asked or implied, using objective and clearly understood language.
- Personalize your response. Even if you start with a form letter, include your reader's name and tailor the message to specific requests.
- Promote your company, products, or services—within reason. You may choose a subtle sales approach when responding to simple requests.
- Close your response on a positive, friendly note. Avoid such clichés as, "If you have additional questions, please don't hesitate to let me know." Use original wording, personalized especially for the reader.

In the next example, Southside Brewery responds to a customer inquiry with personalized, thorough information (Figure 6).

Personalized Response to a Customer's Inquiry | Figure 6

September 5, 2017

Mr. Derek Morris
13 Barnes Street
Dallas, TX 75202

> *Uses the standard block-letter format on company stationery.*

Dear Mr. Morris:

> *Includes the standard letter salutation.*

Southside Brewery would be delighted to host Moniker's office party. Thank you for thinking of us for your event. Yes, we have a private room that will accommodate up to 25 people, and we do have availability on December 9.

> *Immediately addresses the customer's inquiry about a function on a specific date.*

We offer two options for private parties: a full menu or a fixed-price limited menu. For the full menu, your guests would simply order from our regular lunch menu, and we would charge you accordingly. I have enclosed a menu for your reference. If you prefer a limited menu, we could offer a fixed price depending on the items you choose. For example, for $15 per person (not including beverages and dessert), your guests could choose from these items:

> *Explains two options to meet the customer's needs.*

> *Attaches relevant information.*

- Southwest Chicken Salad
- Salmon Teriyaki
- Ground Beef Burger

> *Offers sample menu items in easy-to-read bullets.*

If you prefer different menu items, we can work up pricing based on your preferences.

> *Encourages more customization.*

You also asked about a special occasion cake, and we certainly can arrange this for you. We work closely with a bakery that would create something according to your specifications.

> *Addresses another specific request.*

I would be happy to meet with you to talk about your requirements and to finalize arrangements.

Thanks again for your inquiry, and I hope to speak with you soon. You can call me at (215) 555-6760 or email me at ron@southsidebrewery.com.

> *Closes on a positive note after an offer to meet in person.*

Sincerely,

> *Includes the standard letter closing with signature.*

Ron Ramone

Enclosure

6-6 Composing Goodwill Messages

People send goodwill messages out of a sense of kindness and to maintain or build relationships. With no true business objective, these messages convey congratulations, appreciation, or sympathy. Goodwill messages achieve their objective precisely because they have no ulterior motive. Even subtle sales promotion would make receivers suspect the sincerity of your message.

Of course, businesses may reap advantages from goodwill messages. Customers like to deal with people who take the time to acknowledge what's important to them. But this is not the goal of a sincere goodwill message.

Goodwill messages vary by culture. What may be appropriate, even expected, in one country may be improper in another. Also, what is emphasized in a goodwill message may differ by culture. In a study comparing Chinese and American graduation cards, Chinese messages reflected far more "process-focused themes" of hard work and continuous self-improvement, whereas American cards emphasized "person-focused themes," such as individual traits.[9] Ask your international host or a local colleague before writing goodwill messages to people from cultures you don't know well.

You may send a goodwill message by calling instead of writing—especially for minor occasions. But a written message, including a handwritten note, is more thoughtful, more appreciated, and more permanent. Because they require extra effort, and people receive fewer of them, written goodwill messages may be more meaningful than a phone call. To write effective goodwill messages, follow the guidelines in Figure 7.

Figure 7 | Guidelines for Goodwill Messages

Be prompt.
Send a goodwill message while the reason is still fresh in the reader's mind. A welcome note to a new employee, for example, should be sent within his or her first few days on the job.

Be direct.
State the major idea in the first sentence or two, even for sympathy notes; because the reader already knows the bad news, you don't need to shelter him or her from it.

Be specific.
If you're thanking or complimenting someone, mention a specific incident or anecdote. Personalize your message to avoid having it sound like a form letter.

Be sincere.
Avoid language that is too flowery or too strong (for example, "awesome" or "the best I've ever seen"). Use a conversational tone, as if you were speaking to the person directly, and focus on the reader—not on yourself. Take special care to spell names correctly and to make sure your facts are accurate. You may use exclamation marks, but don't overdo it.

Be brief.
You may not need an entire page to get your point across. A personal note card or a one-paragraph email may be plenty.

6-6a Recognition Notes

Most employees believe they don't receive enough positive feedback at work. Messages should be sent to recognize when someone does a particularly good job. An email to specify what the person did and how it benefited the organization will go a long way in showing people how they're valued and improving employee morale. When appropriate, you might copy an employee's immediate supervisor.

Dear Javier,

You did a terrific job on the feasibility study for Barker Associates. Ron called me this morning to tell me it was the most thorough, detailed analysis he had received in years. He also complimented the easy-to-read report format.

I really appreciate your work on this project. You put in long hours in the past three months, and your dedication has certainly paid off. When Ron has another project in the pipeline, he'll definitely call us for the job!

Keep up the good work,

Maurice

6-6b Congratulatory Notes

Congratulatory notes should be sent for major business achievements—receiving a promotion, winning new business, announcing a retirement, receiving an award, opening a new branch, or celebrating an anniversary with the company. These notes are also appropriate for personal milestones—engagements, weddings, births, graduations, and other occasions. Congratulatory notes should be written to employees within the company and to customers, suppliers, and others outside your company.

Congratulations, Tom, on being elected president of the United Way of Alberta County. I was happy to see the announcement in this morning's newspaper and to learn of your plans for the upcoming campaign.

Best wishes for a successful fund drive. This important community effort surely deserves everyone's full support.

Daniel

Dear Melody,

Congratulations on your new house. Thad sent me the listing, and it looks like a great spot—move-in ready!

I hope you and Thad enjoy many happy years there.

Best,

Sam

6-6c Thank-You Notes

A note of thanks or appreciation may be valued more than a monetary reward. Thank-you notes should be sent whenever someone does you a favor—sends you a gift, writes a recommendation letter for you, gives you a scholarship, or interviews you for a job. The example in Figure 8 is from a not-for-profit organization.

Figure 8 | Thank-You Note from a Not-for-Profit Organization

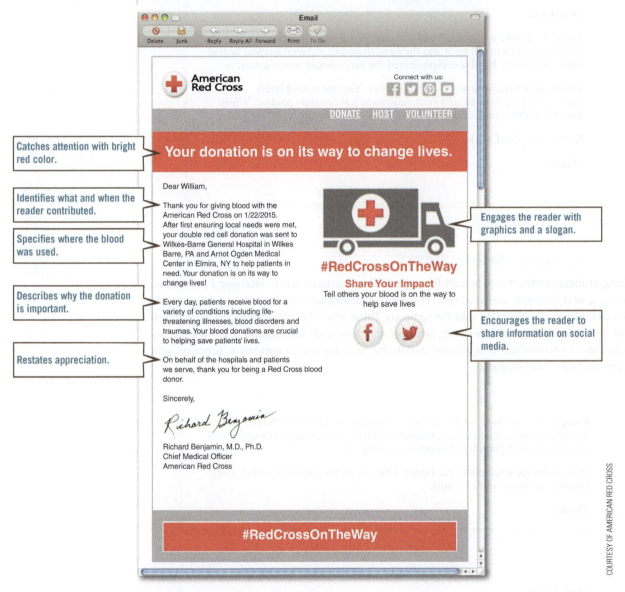

Catches attention with bright red color.

Identifies what and when the reader contributed.

Specifies where the blood was used.

Describes why the donation is important.

Restates appreciation.

Engages the reader with graphics and a slogan.

Encourages the reader to share information on social media.

6-6d Sympathy Notes

Expressions of sympathy or condolence to a person who is having a difficult time personally are especially tough to write but are also especially appreciated. People who have experienced serious health problems, a severe business setback, or the death of a loved one need to know that others are thinking of them and that they are not alone.

Some of the most difficult messages to write are those expressing sympathy over someone's death. These notes should be handwritten, whenever possible. They should not avoid mentioning the death, but they need not dwell on it. Most sympathy notes are short. Begin with an expression of sympathy, mention some specific quality or memory about the deceased, and then close with an expression of comfort and affection. An offer to help, if genuine, is appropriate. Figure 9 expresses sympathy to the wife of a coworker who died.

Sympathy Note to an Employee's Spouse | **Figure 9**

Uses company letterhead. (Personal stationery or a store-bought card are also appropriate.)

November 14, 2017

Begins with an expression of sympathy and expresses the impact of the death.

Dear Katrina,

I was so sorry to hear about Alan's death. This came as a terrible shock to his Southside friends and co-workers, many of whom knew Alan since our opening in 2001.

Mentions specific qualities and a personal remembrance.

Alan will always be remembered for his diligence, his willingness to help others, and his sharp sense of humor. Alan's co-workers have been talking about his memorable speech at Southside's 10th Anniversary Dinner — what a great time that was for everyone, and Alan was a big part of it.

Closes with a genuine, specific offer of help.

I wish you well during this difficult time and would like to help in any way I can. I know that you have been in touch with our HR department; if I can smooth the process, please call me directly at 555-7037.

Sincerely,
Victor

114 W. 115th Street
Chicago, IL 60628

Communication **TECHNOLOGIES**

6-7 Addressing Customer Comments Online

So far, we have discussed one-to-one requests and responses. But communication is often far more complex. For online customer communication—public comments on review sites, blogs, and social networks—the opportunities are greater and the stakes higher. Companies can win customers and build a positive reputation online, but slow and poorly written responses can lose customers and damage a company's image—with potentially millions of people watching.

6-7a Deciding Whether to Respond

Smart companies monitor the constant stream of social media posts and decide whether and how to respond to each. For large companies that can afford them, aggregators scan the web for comments about the company. These programs automatically collect and analyze the online messages. Smaller companies have staff members who use tools such as Google Alerts to search the web for conversations about their company.

The flowchart shown in Figure 10, typical for organizations that pay attention to online customer feedback, helps guide a company's response. As you can see from the flowchart, companies won't necessarily respond to every online post. For "happy" customers whose posts

Figure 10 | Social Media Response Guidelines

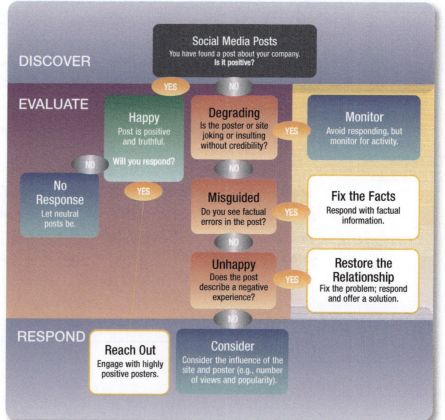

are positive and truthful, you may or may not respond. However, if a post is *highly* positive, you may want to reply to engage the sender and highlight the good feedback.

For comments such as those in Figure 11, posted on the review site Yelp, management *could* respond but does not. This post can stand alone without negative repercussions for the company—or a missed opportunity to build on positive feedback.

Negative posts require more attention. We'll discuss these in Chapter 7.

Neutral Customer Online Post | **Figure 11**

26
67
Tiffany P.
Stockton, CA

We tend to forget this place exists, but then a special occasion comes up, and we are reminded again. We've attended a wedding rehearsal dinner here, had an anniversary dinner here, and even had our engagement dinner here. It's a cozy little place with exceptionally good service. The food is delicious although sometimes lacks in quantity. But they offer a full bar and a great variety of food as well as lovely desserts. This is a great place all around.

YELP.COM. REPRINTED BY PERMISSION.

6-7b Responding to Positive Reviews

The online comment shown in Figure 12 is highly positive and does warrant a management response to acknowledge the feedback.

The Plymouth manager's response (at the bottom of Figure 12) could be more substantive, but her response is brief and funny. For informal social media interactions, this works just

Highly Positive Online Post and Management's Response | **Figure 12**

0
5
Erik H.
Plymouth, MI

My favorite hangout in Plymouth. It's got a great European warm modern feel, and the staff is very friendly and professional. The food is very tasty and interesting.
A great place to meet with friends who are wine drinkers!
Another hidden gem that is uniquely a part of Plymouth!

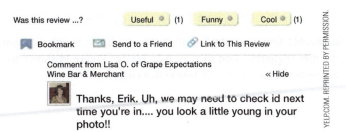

Was this review ...?   Useful (1)   Funny   Cool (1)

Bookmark   Send to a Friend   Link to This Review

Comment from Lisa O. of Grape Expectations
Wine Bar & Merchant   « Hide

Thanks, Erik. Uh, we may need to check id next time you're in.... you look a little young in your photo!!

YELP.COM. REPRINTED BY PERMISSION.

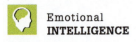
fine to connect with the writer and other prospective customers. Considering the reviewer's casual post, it might look odd for the manager to respond with something longer and more formal.

Yelp offers the example in Figure 13 with good advice for responding to positive feedback online. For an authentic approach, personalize the response: provide a photo and your own name (not just the company's name), mention the writer's name, thank the writer for the post, address specific comments from the post, and offer solutions or other ways to stay in touch.

Figure 13 | Yelp's Advice to Managers for Responding to a Positive Customer Post

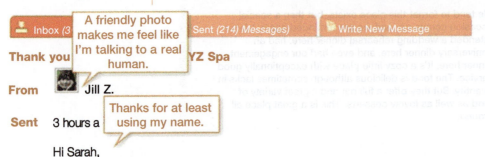

A friendly photo makes me feel like I'm talking to a real human.

Thanks for at least using my name.

Hi Sarah,

I wanted to personally thank you for sharing your positive experience with XYZ Spa on Yelp. Our staff works hard to ensure that you enjoy your time there, so it's most rewarding to hear that our treatments helped to make your birthday special.

Wow! You really read my review!

Please feel free to ask for me if and when you are next coming in—it would be my pleasure to meet and thank you again in person. In the meantime, please let me know if you have any suggestions for us, as we are continuously trying to improve.

They really care what I think.

Best wishes,

Jill Zeffers
jill@spas.com
XYZ Spas & Salons

(Reply) (Delete) (Block User)

6-7c Anticipating Customer Needs Online

Sometimes simply responding to customers isn't enough. Companies can *anticipate* requests and offer suggestions on sites such as Twitter. Figure 14 shows an example of Wynn Encore in Las Vegas proactively interacting with a customer.[10,11]

- Shean702 tweets this message about his weekend plans in Las Vegas:

This weekend = room @venetianvegas dinner & drinks
@LavoLasVegas on Friday. Saturday is dinner @EncoreLasVegas
drinks @SurrenderVegas #Vegas
about 22 hours ago via twidroid

- With the tag "@EncoreLasVegas," the Wynn Encore Tweeter finds the tweet and asks a follow-up question:

@shean702 where are you dining at Encore on Saturday? ^JB
about 14 hours ago via CoTweet in reply to shean702

Following

- Shean responds with the name of the restaurant, Switch Steak:

@WynnLasVegas switch steak! I have heard great things but
never been! #staycation
about 13 hours ago via twidroid in reply to WynnLasVegas

- The Wynn Tweeter then makes an unsolicited recommendation:

EXPLORE
DISCOVE

Wynn Las Vegas
designed to be e
discovered, to ex
of each and ever

@shean702 try the Kobe-style beef
carpaccio, grilled baby octopus, dry-
aged NY strip w/bacon-mushroom
crust, or Montana bison rib-eye. ^JB
about 12 hours ago via UberTweet in reply to shean702

award-winning rooms &
suites, signature restaurants,
exciting leisure activities &
nightly entertainment.

800	346,037	1,744
following	followers	listed

Tweets   3,852

- Shean responds with his gratitude:

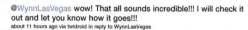

@WynnLasVegas wow! That all sounds incredible!!! I will check it
out and let you know how it goes!!!
about 11 hours ago via twidroid in reply to WynnLasVegas

TWITTER.COM

Speed is critical in online communication. This Wynn interaction takes place within 11 hours—slower than a phone conversation but probably faster than an email exchange for several messages. Responses are even faster with location-based apps such as Foursquare, which tell companies when potential customers are near their store. Companies have to decide how "proactive" to be without being intrusive. These decisions will only get more complex as new apps are developed and privacy is increasingly challenged.

3Ps
< IN ACTION

Acknowledging a Woman's Life

>>> **PURPOSE**

Imagine that you're a doctor who has treated a woman who died. You were so touched by her that you write a handwritten note to her husband. (This is a true story you can read more about here: yhoo.it/1owvj2x.)

Dear Mr. ▮▮▮,

I am the Emergency Medicine physician who treated your wife Mrs. ▮▮▮▮▮▮▮ last Sunday in the Emergency Department at the New York Presbyterian Hospital. I learned only yesterday about her passing away and wanted to write to you to express my sadness. In my twenty years as a doctor in the Emergency Room, I have never written to a patient or a family member, as our encounters are typically hurried and do not always allow for more personal interaction. However, in your case, I felt a special connection to your wife ▮▮▮▮ who was so engaging and cheerful in spite of her illness and trouble breathing. I was also touched by the fact that you seemed to be a very loving couple. You were highly supportive of her, asking the right questions with calm, care and concern. From my experience as a physician, I find that the love and support of a spouse or a family member is the most soothing gift, bringing peace and serenity to those critically ill.

I am sorry for your loss and I hope you can find comfort in the memory of your wife's great spirit and of your loving bond. My heartfelt condolences go out to you and your family.

▮▮▮▮▮▮▮, MD

COURTESY OF IMGUR

>>> **PROCESS**

1. **What is the purpose of your note?**
   I want to honor the woman's life and express my feelings about her to her husband.

2. **Describe your audience.**
   My primary audience is the woman's husband, but this is for the rest of her family too.

3. **What information will you provide in your message?**
   - How rare it is for me to write this type of note—how much she touched me.
   - The wonderful qualities I saw in her and in her husband's care.

>>> **PRODUCT**

Writing a Thank-You Note

>>> PURPOSE

Think about someone who has been important to you—a teacher, a manager, a friend, a family member. Write a handwritten note to show your gratitude.

>>> PROCESS

1. Describe the person. What is it about that person or how she or she has helped you that makes you want to write the note?

2. What specific information will you include? Think about examples of what he or she did and how you were affected.

3. How do you expect him or her to react? Thinking about the response may help you shape the message.

4. Will you send the note? Why or why not?

>>> PRODUCT

Write the handwritten note. You may find typing it first easier for revising the final product.

LO1 Compose a neutral message.

When writing a neutral message, such as to request action or ask a question, present the major request early, along with reasons for making the request. Word your questions so that they are clear and easy to answer. Close on a friendly note.

LO2 Respond to a neutral message.

Answer neutral messages promptly and graciously. Grant the request early and answer all questions asked. Close on a positive and friendly note, and use original language.

LO3 Compose a goodwill message.

Write goodwill messages to express congratulations, appreciation, or sympathy. Write promptly, using a direct pattern, and be sincere, specific, and brief.

LO4 Address customer comments online.

Follow a strategy for responding to online comments. Highly positive comments may deserve a response, while neutral comments can be left alone.

> EXERCISES

LO1 Compose a neutral message.

1. **Request alumni organization membership information.**

   Whether you're graduating this year or a few years from now, you may want to join a local alumni organization. Write an email to the head of the alumni association in the area you might live. Include specific questions about membership fees, club activities, benefits of joining, and the process for enrollment.

   Compare the email you receive from the association with emails your classmates receive. Is the alumni association communicating consistently across regions (if there are multiple locations), and are representatives of the organization customizing emails to each of you?

2. **Request health club membership information.**

   Research a local health club online. Look at all of the information on the club's website, and find one question that isn't answered online. For example, you might ask a question about cancelling membership, suspending membership temporarily, getting discounts for bringing in new members, or parking facilities. Write an email—or complete the club's online form—to submit your question. Before you send the question, print a copy for your instructor.

3. **Request information about a product.**

   Research a product that you would like to buy. Look at the product description on the company's website, and read consumers' product reviews online. Think of one or two questions that you would like to know before deciding to buy the product. For example, you may find a functionality issue identified in one of the product reviews, and you want the company's response. Or, you may have a specialized need for the product, and you want to make sure you can use it in a certain way.

   Using a contact form or email address on the company's website, write a message to ask your question(s). Copy the message into a new document and give it into your instructor.

4. **Write an email to request repair or maintenance.**

   Is something broken where you live? Try to get it fixed by sending an email to the building manager. Specify the problem and why it's important to repair. Or you could ask for other services, such as better garbage removal or more heat. In class, compare the responses you receive. How do landlords respond to your issues—or not?

5. **Write an email to employees about new security procedures.**

Imagine that you work for a news organization. Because of recent bomb threats to your building, facility management will implement new security procedures. In the past, employees would walk to the elevators freely, but starting two weeks from today, employees will have to swipe ID cards to get access to the elevators.

Write an email to employees explaining the rationale for the new procedure, where to get an ID card, and how the process will work. Invent whatever details you believe employees will need in order to understand the change.

6. **Respond to a request for information about school.**

Imagine that you receive an email from a student at your former high school, asking you about life at your college. Read the message below, and then write a response.

LO2 Respond to a neutral message.

```
●●● ✉                          Email                              ⊖
 ⊘      🖫      ↶      ↞      ⇥      🖨      ✓
Delete  Junk  Reply Reply All Forward  Print  To Do
```

To: _____
From: Penny Garzon
Subject: Questions About College Life

Hello _____,

I'm a sophomore at _____ high school, and I'd like to know more about _____ [college or university]. You might remember my sister, Marguerite Garzon, who graduated with you. She went to Ohio State University, but I'm looking at other options.

Will you please tell me how you like school and answer a few questions for me:
- How difficult is the work? Is the workload much more than what we have in high school? Is it manageable if I also have a part-time job during school?
- How accessible are the instructors at your school? Do they have time for you one-on-one?
- What's the social life like at your school? Are fraternities and sororities popular? What do people do for fun?
- Does your school have a debate club? I'm on the debate team in high school, and I'd like to join a club in college. What are my options?

Thanks for giving me your perspective. This will help me make a decision about whether to apply to your school.

Penny Garzon

---

7. **Evaluate responses to the request for information about school.**

Compare responses to the previous exercise. When you look at two other students' responses to the same request for information, you'll likely see differences. Some differences may reflect high school experiences; you'll provide different information when using your high school as a common point of reference. Other differences may be because of your perceptions about college life.

Still other differences may reflect your writing style and the level of detail you provided. What differences do you see in your responses, and which versions work best and why?

8. **Respond to a speaking request.**

Imagine that your former employer invites you back to speak to their human resources department. They want to know your perspective as a former employee or intern. Read the following email, and write a response accepting the invitation.

9. **Respond to a child's request for a LEGO set.**

   For two years, James Groccia, an 11-year-old boy with Asperger's Syndrome, saved up for his dream LEGO train set, only to learn that the set had been discontinued. James wrote a letter to LEGO, hoping for the set or a lead to find one.[12]

   > For two years I kept all the money I got for birthday and holiday gifts, some of my allowance and some money I got for participating in a research project. At last, a couple of months ago I had my $100 and was ready to buy the LEGO set of my dreams.
   >
   > My mom started looking for it online and could not find any. We checked the LEGO store in our area and they didn't have it either. I was completely crushed. You've stopped making it! It seems the only way to get one now is to pay $250 on Amazon or eBay, since now it is considered collectible.
   >
   > I got another LEGO set, thinking I could forget about the Emerald Night, but every time I see it anywhere online I get very sad and disappointed. I still want the Emerald Night so badly, but there are none to be found.
   >
   > Do you have any at your corporate headquarters? Perhaps I could get one that way? If you have any other ideas, I would be happy to hear them. I have never wanted a LEGO set so badly ever in my life.

   Imagine that you're a consumer services advisor at LEGO and are sending James the Emerald Night train. Write a letter to James that will accompany the package.

   Compare your draft with the actual letter LEGO sent (bit.ly/Vsbk3e). Discuss the similarities and differences in class, paying particular attention to how your message is organized. Which approach works better and why?

10. **Write a team response to a request.**

You are a member of the Presidents' Council, which consists of the presidents of all on-campus student organizations. You just received a memo from Dr. Robin H. Hill, dean of students, wanting to know what types of service projects the student organizations on campus have been engaged in during the past year. The dean must report to the board of trustees on the important role played by student organizations—both in the life of the university and community and in the development of student leadership and social skills. She wants to include such information as student-run programs on drug and alcohol abuse, community service, and fundraising.

Working in groups of four, identify and summarize the types of service projects that student organizations at your institution have completed this year. Then organize your findings into a one-page memo to Dr. Hill. After writing your first draft, have each team member review and comment on the draft. Then revise as needed and submit. Use only factual data for this assignment.

11. **Write a congratulations note.**

Imagine that your former boss just won a "Manager of the Year" award. Handwrite a note congratulating the manager, and make it meaningful by referring to your own experience as his or her employee. Include whatever details and examples you believe are relevant when congratulating your boss for the award.

LO3 Compose a goodwill message.

12. **Write a recognition email.**

Imagine that you're a store manager for a local Costco. Brian, one of the sales associates who reports to you, has a reputation of going above and beyond to help customers. You just received a copy of this note, which a customer sent to Brian:

> Dear Brian,
>
> Thank you so much for your help with the Panda curtains. Thanks to your diligent follow-up, I found the size and color I wanted at the Birmingham store.
>
> I appreciate that you remembered to call me with the information, and even more, I appreciate your cheerful personality. In other stores, I sometimes feel like a burden to the sales staff, but you treated me like a real customer—someone who is important to Costco. I'll remember this next time I redecorate my house!
>
> Best wishes,
>
> Annan Pongsudhirak

As a good manager who takes the time to recognize employees' work, you write your own email to Brian. In addition to acknowledging this customer's feedback, include other examples of Brian's performance (which you can invent).

13. **Write a thank-you note.**

Imagine that you work for In the Loop Soup Kitchen, a local food pantry. Earlier this week, a man came into the facility with a gun. Fortunately, no one was hurt, but people were frightened. Write a note to your local police department thanking them for their quick response and adept handling of the situation.

You'll find more information about the company scenario, In the Loop, on www.cengagebrain.com

14. **Decide whether to respond to online reviews.**

Read three tweets about Gap. If you were in charge of customer service, to which, if any, of these reviews would you respond? Why or why not? In small groups, discuss your rationale for whether to respond to each review. If you do choose to respond, what would you hope to accomplish with each reply?

LO4 Address customer comments online.

Terri Griffith
@terrigriffith

⚙ 👤 Follow

.@Gap first F500 co in America to be independently certified as paying women & men equally" & results only work!
terri.es/1FUJN2C

TWITTER.COM

Heather Desserud
@UptownHeather

⚙ 👤 Follow

Okay @Gap. Your #SpringIsWeird campaign got me. Ordered the navy utility jacket.
gap.secondfunnel.com/springisweird/...

TWITTER.COM

PayForward
@JoinPayForward

⚙ 👤 Follow

Get 10% cash back at select merchants at @WestfieldVTC, including @Gap, @VictoriasSecret & @TGIFridays.
facebook.com/events/1425249...
#PayForward

TWITTER.COM

15. **Respond to a positive customer online post.**

Imagine that you're the general manager of the Hotel Urbano in Miami and find this review on TripAdvisor. Use the Yelp guidelines in Figure 13 to write a response that would be posted on TripAdvisor.

teresa m
Chicago, Illinois

Reviewer
☆ 5 reviews
🛏 5 hotel reviews
🌐 Reviews in 2 cities
🎖 4 helpful votes

"Different but delightful"

⬤⬤⬤⬤◯ Reviewed 2 weeks ago

This hotel is quite different from other miami hotels I have stayed at. I am not particularly an art lover but I was delighted by the art inside this hotel. It reminds me of the Galleria Park Hotel in San Francisco. Galleria also puts information about their artwork in a digital eGuest Directory that you can access on the app Foli. It also offers digital magazines and eBooks which I love. It'd be great if this hotel did the same. They could offer more information about the artwork digitally and save paper! Other than that, the location is a little far but the staff is very friendly, I'll definitely recommend this hotel to friends and family.

Stayed February 2015, traveled on business

  Rooms
 Cleanliness
  Service

COURTESY OF TRIPADVISOR

16. **Send an email response to a highly positive customer comment.**

Imagine that you just found this comment about your new dog-training company online. Using the Yelp guidelines in Figure 13, write a response that shows appreciation for the comment.

 ★★★★★ **The Best $ You Could Spend**
February 21, 2017 See all my reviews

Doggie Do is the best! My Doberman, Oscar, wasn't house trained and took frequent nips at my 11-year-old son, but now he's a new dog. Amelia at Doggie Do immediately took control, and now Oscar is a well-behaved little pooch—and the rest of the family is much happier. I'd recommend Amelia to anyone having trouble breaking in a new pet.

AMY NEWMAN

17. **Evaluate a company response to comments online.**

Imagine that you are a manager at the department store JCPenney. A new employee, Marni, is responding to customer comments online and wants your advice on her draft. She says that she wants to keep responses short and doesn't see the point of adding anything. In an email to Marni, provide your feedback on her draft—and rewrite the response. Consider how you can personalize the response and perhaps engage the customer to tell you more about his or her experience.

Original post: "Ordering online with JCPenney is a breeze! What a great website—easy to find anything and easy to navigate. I love JCPenney!"

Draft company response: "Thank you. This is nice to read."

18. **Anticipate a customer's needs.**

Imagine that you manage the Twitter account for Nike. At least twice a day, you search for mentions of the company and questions about products and services. Today, you found this tweet.

 chrisbushkin Chris Bush
does anyone know where i can get **Nike** Total 90 Supremacy's from .. Size 11 FB ..
18 seconds ago

TWITTER.COM

This is a great opportunity to reach out to a potential customer proactively. You may invent information to include about the product. Just be sure to stay within Twitter's 140-character limit. If you want to refer to a web address, you may include a shortened link (using the web address "bit.ly").

COMPANY SCENARIO

In the Loop

In The Loop
Soup Kitchen

Let's revisit In the Loop, the soup kitchen in the midst of a crisis. You may recall that a gunman entered the facility, and fortunately, no one was hurt. Now it's your job, as the assistant director, to get the agency back to normal so that you can continue to serve the community. Encouraging people to return to In the Loop is crucial for the organization to fulfill its mission.

Your instructor may assign the following for you to practice communicating neutral/positive messages:

- Write a news release to be posted on the In the Loop website and sent to news agencies. Your instructor may provide a sample template for you to use.
- Write an internal email to explain the situation to volunteers and encourage them to return to In the Loop.
- Create a crisis communication plan for handling potential situations in the future. You may use the template below.

In The Loop
Soup Kitchen

» About *In the Loop* Soup Kitchen

Mission

Our mission is to serve people in the Olpine community who need food and warmth. Through direct service and education, we strive to help people meet basic needs for survival.

Organizational Structure

Working on a tight budget, *In the Loop* has only three full-time employees:

- Emilio, Executive Director
- Jennifer [you], Assistant Director
- Peggy, Volunteer Coordinator

The organization relies on volunteers who help with administration, purchasing, cooking, serving, cleaning, and more.

pages

» In The Loop Soup Kitchen: Crisis Communication Simulation
» About In the Loop Soup Kitchen

COURTESY OF AMY NEWMAN

Communication Plan Template				
Audience	Communication Objectives	Audience Background	Communication Medium	Message Timing

Endnotes

1. Guy Trebay, "The Found Art of Thank-You Notes," *The New York Times*, April 4, 2014, www.nytimes.com/2014/04/06/fashion/the-found-art-of-thank-you-notes.html, accessed March 22, 2015.

2. "Thank You Notes: Hand Warmers, Kraft Singles," YouTube, *The Tonight Show Starring Jimmy Fallon*, March 21, 2015, www.youtube.com/watch?v=bltTk923DWk, March 21, 2015

3. Saul Austerlitz, "The Lost Art of the Condolence Letter," *The New York Times*, February 10, 2014, http://opinionator.blogs.nytimes.com/2014/02/10/the-lost-art-of-the-condolence-letter, accessed March 22, 2015.

4. Cristiano Magni quoted in Guy Trebay.

5. "Microsoft Board names Satya Nadella as CEO," Microsoft.com, February 4, 2014, www.microsoft.com/en-us/news/press/2014/feb14/02-04newspr.aspx, accessed March 22, 2015.

6. Pete Cashmore, "Memo to Staff: An Exciting Future for Mashable," LinkedIn, www.linkedin.com/today/post/article/20131030165111-1863151-memo-to-staff-an-exciting-future-for-mashable, accessed March 22, 2015.

7. Pilar Pazos, Jennifer Chung, and Marina Micari, "Instant Messaging as a Task-Support Tool in Information Technology Organizations," *Journal of Business Communication* 50, 2013: 68–86.

8. Yoram M.Kalman and Sheizaf-Rafaeli, "Email Chronemics: Unobtrusive Profiling of Response Times," Proceedings of the 38th Hawaii International Conference on System Sciences, 2005.

9. Karen Choi and Michael Ross, "Cultural Differences in Process and Person Focus: Congratulations on Your Hard Work Versus Celebrating Your Exceptional Brain," *Journal of Experimental Social Psychology*, 2010, www.sciencedirect.com/science/article/pii/S0022103110002581, accessed March 22, 2015.

10. @Shean702, Twitter, August 4, 2010, http://twitter.com/shean702, accessed August 5, 2010.

11. @WynnLasVegas, Twitter, August 4, 2010, http://twitter.com/wynnlasvegas, accessed August 5, 2010.

12. Hayley Hudson, "James Groccia, Massachusetts Boy, Receives Dream LEGO Set After Sending Heartwarming Letter," *Huffington Post*, November 30, 2012, www.huffingtonpost.com/2012/11/30/james-groccia-massachuset_n_2213788.html, accessed March 22, 2015.

Persuasive Messages

LEARNING OBJECTIVES

After you have finished this chapter, you should be able to

LO1   Plan a persuasive message for your audience.

LO2   Write a short persuasive message.

LO3   Write a sales letter.

LO4   Write and respond to negative customer and public feedback.

" *SeaWorld is becoming the textbook case of what not to do in a crisis.* " [1]

—David E. Johnson, CEO, *Strategic Vision, LLC*

CHAPTER INTRODUCTION

SeaWorld Mishandles *Blackfish* Controversy

The director of the movie *Blackfish* says she didn't intend to cripple SeaWorld, but that's exactly what happened.[2] The documentary criticized the theme park for mistreating orca whales, blaming their captivity for trainer deaths.

For months, SeaWorld ignored negative comments on social media hoping the controversy would settle down. Instead, celebrities and animal rights activists continued their attacks, which damaged SeaWorld's image and caused declining park attendance.

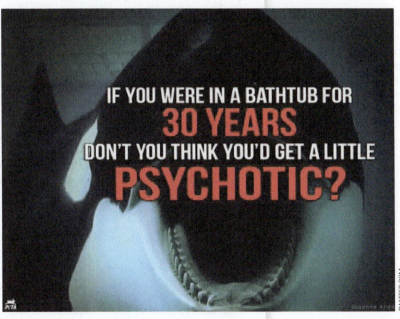

Finally, the company took action. On Facebook, Twitter, and Instagram, SeaWorld defended its position with videos, statements, and images of animal rescues.

But SeaWorld still struggled with its response. Twitter campaigns, such as #Love dolphins? and #AskSeaWorld, backfired. For the latter, People for the Ethical Treatment of Animals (PETA) posted the tweet shown here.

A writer for *Slate* magazine called the campaign "a terrible idea."[3] When companies mishandle negative feedback, they only exacerbate a bad situation.

7-1 Planning Persuasive Messages

We use persuasion to motivate someone to do something or believe something that he or she would not otherwise have done or believed. Every day people try to persuade you: companies advertise their products, friends convince you to go to the movies, and instructors encourage you to learn new concepts.

As a manager, you need to persuade others to do what you want. To be successful, you must overcome resistance. People may resist your ideas for many reasons. Following are a few examples of persuasive messages and the resistance you may encounter.

Emotional INTELLIGENCE

How comfortable are you overcoming resistance from others? Do you tend to shy away from persuasion, or do you embrace the opportunity to convince others of your point of view?

Persuasive Message	Possible Resistance
You want your manager to give you a promotion.	Your manager may have budget restrictions or may believe your performance doesn't warrant a promotion.
You want to sell a new product to an existing customer.	The customer may be happy with the current product or may not want to spend more money.
You want an employee to work overtime.	The employee may have other plans or may believe your request is unfair or unnecessary.
You want a supplier to give you a discount on products.	The supplier may have sales targets he or she needs to reach, may not have authority to grant your request, or may be concerned about fairness to other customers.
You want a business to provide better service.	The business may not believe your negative feedback or may have national standards that can't be changed (for example, how many people work in local stores).
You want to improve your company's image after negative publicity.	The public may not trust the brand after a crisis situation, particularly if the company didn't handle it well.

In each of these situations, you must find ways to overcome the resistance. This process begins with analyzing your audience.

7-2 Analyzing Your Audience

You'll have the best chance of persuading your audience if you know your audience and adapt your message to them.

7-2a Knowing Your Audience

One distinction between advertising and persuasion is that persuasion is more personalized. Although advertisers can target a consumer based on, for example, other online purchases and websites visited, managers who know their audience personally can tailor a persuasive message to their specific needs.

In Chapter 4, you learned an approach for analyzing your audience. These five questions, shown again in Figure 1, are particularly useful for persuasive messages.

Let's say you manage a team of eight employees and—because of cutbacks—need to persuade each of them to take on additional responsibilities.

Audience Analysis

| Who is the primary audience? | What is your relationship with the audience? | How will the audience likely react? | What does the audience already know? | What is unique about the audience? |

Example of Tailoring a Persuasive Message to Different Employees

For an employee who . . .	*You might focus on how taking on additional responsibilities will . . .*
Is ambitious and wants to be promoted.	Make him or her eligible for higher-level positions in the future.
Is social and cares about the team.	Help the overall team performance.
Has a strong work ethic.	Increase his or her contribution to the organization.
Is an underperformer.	Maintain his or her status in the organization (by understanding that the new responsibilities are essential to the job).

Stress the "you" attitude to achieve the results you want. Audiences need to know, "What's in it for me?" and you can address this if you know your audience well. Your job is to let the reader know the benefits of doing as you ask. Emphasize the reader, not your request or product.

☒ NOT   Our firm would like to do an energy audit of your business.

☑ BUT   An energy audit will tell you which investments will save the most money over time.

7-2b Applying Persuasion Principles

In his work *Rhetoric,* Aristotle identified three methods by which people can be persuaded:

- Ethos, an appeal based on credibility
- Pathos, an appeal based on emotion
- Logos, an appeal based on logic

These methods remain as relevant today as they were when Aristotle wrote about them more than two thousand years ago. As part of your process of analyzing your audience, you might consider which of these methods—or what combination—will work best to persuade each person or group.

Ethos: Appeal Based on Credibility

To persuade an audience who is skeptical about your character or ethics, focus on your credibility. In these situations, your audience may not know you well or may question your motives. You might hear clues about your audience's resistance to your credibility—for example, you might get questions such as, "What's your background?" or "How long have you been working with Wells Fargo?"

To address these concerns, demonstrate your good character. Consider discussing your background up front, sending your bio ahead of time, bringing a more experienced person with you to a meeting, showing examples of your work, or providing references. The more your audience connects with you as a person, the more they may trust you and your opinions.

Emotional **INTELLIGENCE**

In what ways do you feel credible as a business professional, and in what ways do you feel deficient? Consider your view of yourself and how you can strengthen how others perceive you.

The Society for the Prevention of Cruelty to Animals (SPCA), whose mission is "the advancement of safety and well-being of animals," uses credibility in this example by identifying the organization with famous celebrities, a common approach in advertising.

On Saturday, July 11, actresses Mary Tyler Moore and Bernadette Peters honored SPCA International at the annual "Broadway Barks" – a star-studded dog and cat adopt-a-thon in New York City hosted by Broadway Cares.

Pathos: Appeal Based on Emotion

Some audiences are more persuaded by emotional appeals—and some topics lend themselves to more emotional appeals. As you might imagine, the SPCA often uses this approach to get people to adopt pets and donate money. Adorable—and tragic—stories and images of animals appeal to the SPCA's audience on an emotional level. Notice how pets' names are used in this story to personalize the animals. You also can connect with people emotionally through vivid language and, for an oral presentation, dynamic delivery.

Another Mission Complete!

After a long summer of sweltering heat that forces airlines to impose restrictions on animal travel in the Middle East, SPCA International's rescue experts were able to go back to Baghdad last week and save 18 U.S. soldiers' companions. Dusty, Zada, Demon, Stryker, Dude, Maggie, Stinky, and DH, along with twelve others, landed safely at Dulles International Airport in Virginia. Stryker (pictured here) has an especially sweet story of rescue and survival.

Logos: Appeal Based on Logic

To persuade some audiences, logical appeals—solid evidence and reasoning—work best. When an audience challenges your argument ("How can you be sure we'll get the results you promise?") or asks for data ("What's the return on investment for your proposal?"), focus on logical appeals. In this example, the SPCA uses evidence and reasoning to show—in concrete terms—the consequence of one unspayed animal and what your donation will achieve.

Your donation will make a difference!

| Operation Baghdad Pups | One Cat, One Day | Emergency Shelter Grants | Spay and Neuter |

An unspayed cat and her offspring can produce more than 400,000 cats. An unspayed dog and her offspring can product over 6,000 puppies. SPCA International supports free and low-cost spay and neuter clinics worldwide. **Your donation of $75 can neuter a low-income family's male cat; $100 can spay their female cat; $100 can help neuter their male dog; $125 can spay their female dog.** Donate Now!

For many business communication situations, logic is the most effective form of persuasion. Aristotle defined the three aspects of logic this way:

- **Fact:** indisputably true
- **Inference:** probably true
- **Opinion:** possibly true

Factual data is most persuasive; however, inferences drawn on available data and expert opinion also may convince your audience.

Ethical Persuasion

Persuasion is not coercion. In some cases, people may be forced to do something, but they can't be forced to believe something. They must be persuaded in ways that are acceptable to them.

As business communicators, we have a responsibility to act ethically in building relationships with our audience. Imagine trying to rent an apartment when you're in a desperate situation: you have only one day to find a new place. Knowing this, the landlord tells you that three other people are coming to see it later in the day, even though that's not true.

People who prey on others' limitations just to make a sale are not acting ethically. Ethical communicators know their audience—and ensure that their audience knows them—but never take advantage of this relationship.

Let's look at an example of questionable ethics in persuasive writing. You probably heard of scam emails that con people into sending money, either to help someone in trouble or in exchange for a large inheritance. Notice how the writer uses ethos, pathos, and logos to persuade the audience in the email example in Figure 2.

Ethics in **COMMUNICATION**

Emotional **INTELLIGENCE**

Have you been in situations where you felt gullible? Have you fallen for a scam and realized too late? What influenced you, and how can you avoid this in the future?

Scam Email Uses Principles of Persuasion | **Figure 2**

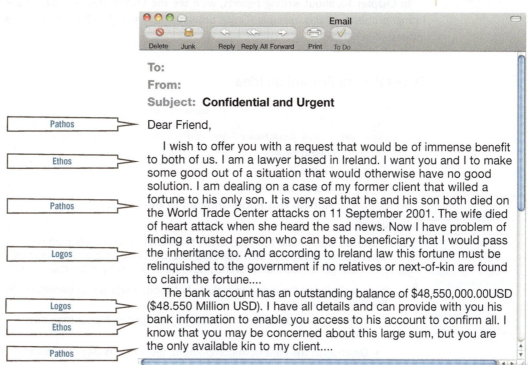

This email goes on to promise a 40% share of the $48 million, but of course, there's a catch. When readers get in touch with the sender, they are asked for a "transaction fee" before they can receive the money. This could be a few thousand dollars—not much if you're expecting millions in return. In a similar scam, a 76-year-old Floridian sent $30,000 to someone in New York and $12,000 to what she believed to be the Central Bank of Nigeria.[4]

The many grammatical errors and awkward sentences should cause the receiver to question the writer's credibility.

You might find it unbelievable that so many people fall for this blatant fraud. But this is persuasion at its worst. With an adept use of ethos, pathos, and logos, thousands of similar schemes swindle people out of millions of dollars. One scam-prevention organization estimates that people lose $200 million each year because of such emails.[5]

LO2 Write a short persuasive message.

7-3 Writing a Short Persuasive Message

In business, you'll write many types of persuasive messages. In this section, we'll discuss how to write a short message, for example, to present an idea or to request action. In later sections, we'll explore approaches to sales letters and negative customer feedback—also challenging situations for persuasive writing.

To help you write messages to persuade an audience to accept your idea or fulfill your request, we'll discuss how to start the message, capture the reader's attention, justify your idea or request, deal with obstacles, and motivate action.

7-3a Determining How to Start the Message

Most persuasive messages in the United States have the main point up front with the direct organizational plan. However, depending on the audience and situation, you may choose a more indirect organizational plan, with explanations before the main point.

In the example in Figure 3, a restaurant employee uses the direct plan to present an idea to improve the owner's business. She states her recommendation up front (adding hot food items), mentions the problem (declining sales), and then provides evidence to support her idea.

In Chapter 10, about writing reports, we'll see the Jason's Deli example as a longer, more formal proposal. In this example, Grace provides just enough information to get the owner interested in her idea.

Figure 3 | Direct Plan to Present an Idea

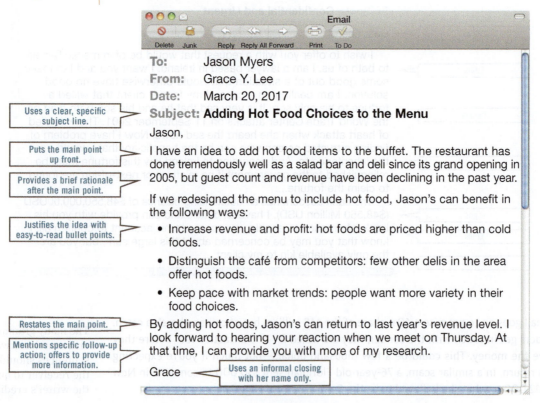

Consider using the direct organizational plan for persuasive messages in these situations:

- You're writing to people who prefer the direct approach and may not read your entire message (e.g., senior-level managers).
- The idea does not require strong persuasion (i.e., there are no major obstacles).
- The idea is long or complex (a reader may become impatient if your main point is buried in a long report).

To use the direct style, present your recommendation and brief rationale in the first paragraph, followed by supporting evidence.

☒ NOT   I recommend we hold our Pittsburgh sales meeting at the Mark-Congress Hotel.

☑ BUT   I have evaluated three hotels as possible meeting sites for our Pittsburgh sales conference and recommend we meet at the Mark-Congress Hotel. The Mark-Congress is centrally located, has the best meeting facilities, and is moderately priced.

Consider using the indirect organizational plan in these situations:

- You're writing to someone who resists your message but is likely to read your entire message (e.g., employees who report to you).
- You know that your reader prefers the indirect plan (e.g., someone from a high-context culture).

International
COMMUNICATION

For the indirect style, you might avoid disclosing your purpose immediately. For a PowerPoint presentation, for example, compare the three title slides in Figure 4. The first may be too specific for an idea that will probably meet resistance (to sell a division of the business to reduce headcount). The second title, "Roper Division," is too general and tells the audience nothing about your idea. The third is probably best for the topic: the title provides context for the presentation but does not reveal the conclusion up front.

Direct and Indirect Title Slides | **Figure 4**

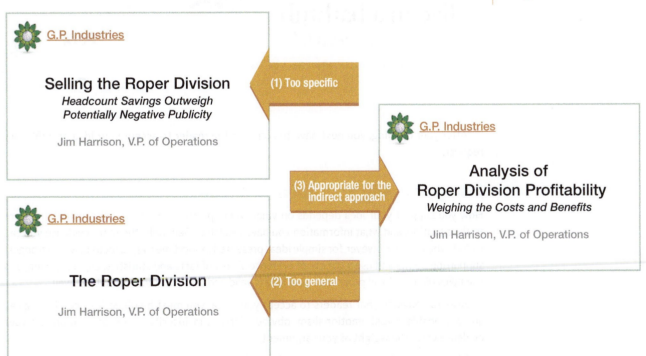

7-3b Capturing the Reader's Attention

To capture your audience's attention, use a catchy opening. An opening that is interesting, relevant, and short will entice your audience to continue reading.

- **Interesting**: A good opening sentence in a persuasive message grabs and keeps the reader's attention. A rhetorical question gets the reader thinking about the topic of your message but doesn't elicit a literal answer. Of course, yes-or-no questions or questions with obvious answers won't motivate someone to read on and may insult the reader's intelligence. An effective rhetorical question is, "How much weight does the average Cedar Fitness Center member lose within a month of joining?" An unusual fact or unexpected statement also may draw the reader into the message. Or, you might want to write something that immediately establishes common ground between you and the reader.
- **Relevant**: Your opening statement must also be relevant to the purpose of your message. If it is too far off the topic or misleads the reader, you risk losing goodwill, and the reader may simply stop reading. At the very least, the reader will feel confused or deceived, making persuasion more difficult.
- **Short**: Often an opening paragraph of just one sentence will make the message inviting to read. Few readers have the patience to wade through a long introduction to figure out the purpose of the message.

Showing one of the "Real Housewives" in a bathtub, the billboard in Figure 5 was part of PETA's campaign to improve how orca whales are treated, which you read in the chapter introduction. The rhetorical question attracts attention and encourages you to learn more.

Figure 5 | Rhetorical Question Captures Attention

After your opening, you next have to convince the reader to accept your idea or fulfill your request.

7-3c Justifying Your Idea or Request

How you support your idea depends on what would persuade your audience, what is relevant to the situation, and what information you have available. Generally, the more evidence you can include, the better. However, for simple ideas presented in short messages, focus on your strongest supporting points and use a variety of evidence. A mix of facts and statistics, expert opinion, and examples (Figure 6) will prove that your idea is valid and that you know the subject well.

Also, to convince your readers to accept your idea, you must be objective, specific, logical, and reasonable. Avoid emotionalism, obvious flattery, insincerity, and exaggeration. Let your evidence carry the weight of your argument.

☒ NOT   Moving our plant to Norfolk would result in considerable savings.

☑ BUT Moving our plant to Norfolk would save nearly $175,000 annually.

☒ NOT   Why should it take a thousand phone calls to convince your computer to credit my account for $37.50?

☑ BUT   Even after five phone calls over the past three weeks, $37.50 has still not been credited to my account.

Types of Evidence | **Figure 6**

Facts and Statistics: Use objective statements and statistics that can be verified. Choose a few relevant data points to avoid overwhelming the reader.

Example: The Roper Division represents 34% of our overhead expenses.

Expert Opinion: Include experts to support your points, particularly if your credibility is in question.

Example: According to a recent study by Accenture's Supply Chain Management group...

Examples: Use relevant, representative cases or incidents to illustrate your points.

Example: When Maximus outsourced its logistics last year, the company saved...

When Beef Products Inc. was accused of making "pink slime," a beef additive treated with ammonia, the company fought back. But the tone in a statement and marketing materials was defensive. The CEO's message attacked the media for the "campaign of lies and deceit that have [*sic*] been waged against our company." The statement provided evidence about product safety: the company had been in business for 30 years and produced millions of meals (facts) and was supported by credible organizations (expert opinion). But the company lost credibility because of the tone and the threat of lost jobs.[6]

7-3d Dealing with Obstacles

Most business audiences are smart enough to know potential downsides of your idea. If you ignore obvious obstacles, you miss an opportunity to address them—and could insult your audience.

In most cases, you can devote relatively little space to address potential concerns. Include these points in the same sentence as benefits to the reader, or in mid-paragraph.

However, if the obstacles are pressing—or you have a good response to them—you might address them up front. On its website, The Strebel Planning Group directly addresses cynicism about the finance industry (Figure 7).

Addressing Potential Obstacles | **Figure 7**

The Strebel Planning Group takes a "whole person" approach to the business of money.

The Strebel Planning Group is different from other area providers in so many ways. Most important of all, we believe, is that we are locally owned and completely independent. This means that we don't answer to a home office, don't have sales quotas that result in our recommending products that are not quite right for you, and have the ability to create client fulfillment processes in response to client's needs, not those of some bureaucrat who has no understanding of our community. We subscribe to a fiduciary standard not required or aspired to by the vast majority of firms out there. Read more about "How We Differ"...

7-3e Motivating Action

After providing background information and reader benefits, give a direct statement to motivate action. Make the specific action clear and easy to fulfill. Provide specific instructions on how and when the reader can complete the task—for example, ask for a meeting to discuss an idea in more detail, or state when a request is needed.

You may use compliments, but only when they're sincere. Readers are rightfully suspicious when they receive a form letter saying they have been "selected" (along with thousands of others). Instead, a personalized request may be more persuasive: "We have selected only five advertising firms to participate on our panel. We included Madison Clark because of your 24 years of experience and your strong service reputation in the industry."

In some ways, justifying a persuasive request is more challenging because reader benefits are not always obvious. Use a confident, polite tone to ask for the desired action. You might acknowledge, "I know this is a busy time for you," but avoid weak statements, such as, "If you don't want to do this, I understand." Don't let the reader off the hook too easily. End on a positive tone by reinforcing the "you" attitude and the action you want the reader to take.

Possibly most important, keep your request reasonable and show your appreciation. Don't ask someone else to do something that you can or should do yourself. And remember to thank the person after the request is fulfilled.

The Checklist for Short Persuasive Messages summarizes these guidelines. Although you will not be able to use all of these suggestions in each persuasive request, you should use them as an overall framework for structuring your persuasive message.

Checklist for Short Persuasive Messages

DETERMINE HOW TO START THE MESSAGE

☑ State your main points up front for most persuasive messages (the direct organizational plan).

☑ Consider an indirect organizational plan when your audience may resist your message or would prefer a less direct style.

CAPTURE THE READER'S ATTENTION

☑ Use a catchy opening to entice the reader to continue.

☑ Choose an interesting, relevant, and short opening.

JUSTIFY YOUR IDEA OR REQUEST

☑ Devote the major part of your message to justifying your message. Give enough background and evidence to enable the reader to make an informed decision.

☑ Use facts and statistics, expert opinion, and examples to support your points.

☑ Use an objective, logical, reasonable, and sincere tone.

☑ Present the evidence in terms of reader benefits.

DEAL WITH OBSTACLES

☑ Do not ignore obstacles or any negative aspects of your message. Instead, address them directly.

☑ In most cases, subordinate the discussion of obstacles by position and amount of space devoted to the topic.

ASK CONFIDENTLY FOR ACTION

☑ State (or restate) the specific idea or request late in the message—after most of the benefits have been discussed.

☑ Make the desired action clear and easy for the reader to take, use a confident tone, and do not provide excuses.

☑ End on a forward-looking note, continuing to stress reader benefits.

7-4 Writing a Sales Letter

LO3 Write a sales letter.

The heart of most business is sales—selling a product or service. Individual letters and form letters are common to reach prospective customers. In your career, you may write letters as a sales manager for a large company, as a development officer for a not-for-profit organization, or as the owner of a start-up company. All of these situations require a special approach to persuasion—and involve ethical challenges.

Sales letters are an important part of Relay For Life's annual campaign, which involves more than 4 million people and raises more than $400 million for cancer research and awareness each year. A template fundraising letter that Relay For Life gives to its volunteers is shown in Figure 8.[7]

Sample Relay For Life Fundraising Letter | **Figure 8**

Dear friends and family,

> Introduces the selling theme up front: fighting against cancer.

The fight against cancer goes on. There is no one I know who can say they DO NOT have a friend or relative who has battled this terrible illness.

> Immediately captures attention.

> "No one" should take a singular pronoun, but "they" may be acceptable to most readers of a personal letter.

> The Comic Sans typeface is a bit overused but may be appropriate for Relay For Life's casual letters.

I have found a way I can fight this disease—through the American Cancer Society's Relay For Life. I am dedicating my walk this year to those I know who have cancer right now or have lost the battle.

The American Cancer Society Relay For Life raises hundreds of millions of dollars each year in the fight against cancer. Millions of people will walk or run through the night to raise money to fight cancer. Relay For Life builds awareness of this dreaded disease and makes a difference in the lives of those affected by cancer HERE AND NOW!

> Uses the word "fight" six times in this short letter.

> Includes a strong sense of urgency.

> Balances logical arguments with emotional appeal.

My goal is to raise (*your goal $$$*) to help fight cancer. I am asking for your support. Your tax-deductible contribution of $25 or more will help our community step up the fight against cancer. Please send a check, payable to the American Cancer Society, to my address today:

(*your address, city, state*)

Thanks in advance for your thoughtfulness and generosity!

Sincerely,

(*your name here*)

Typically, the indirect organizational plan is used for sales letters. It is sometimes called the *AIDA* plan, because you first gain the reader's *attention,* then create *interest* in and *desire* for the benefits of your product, and finally motivate *action.*

7-4a Selecting a Central Selling Theme

Your first step is to become thoroughly familiar with your product, its competition, and your audience. Then, you must select a central selling theme for your letter. Rather than focus on all of your product's features, find one major reader benefit that you introduce early and emphasize throughout the letter.

With a sales letter, you have only a short time to make a lasting impression on your reader. Introduce your central selling theme early (in the opening sentence, if possible), and keep referring to it throughout the letter.

7-4b Gaining the Reader's Attention

A reply to a request for product information from a potential customer is called a solicited sales letter. An unsolicited sales letter, on the other hand, promotes a company's products and is mailed to potential customers who have not expressed any interest. (Unsolicited sales letters are also called *prospecting letters.* You might call them *spam* or *junk mail.*)

As we discussed earlier, you have only a line or two to grab the reader's attention. Then, you're lucky if the reader skims the rest of your message—either out of curiosity or because the opening sentence was especially intriguing.

These opening sentences have proven effective, particularly for sales letters. They may stand alone as the first paragraph, but avoid irrelevant, obvious, or overused statements.

Technique	Item Promoted	Example
Rhetorical question	A high-priced car	*What is the difference between extravagance and luxury?*
Thought-provoking	An early-morning television news program	*Most of what we had to say about business this morning was unprintable.*
Unusual fact	A laundry detergent	*If your family is typical, you will wash one ton of laundry this year.*
Current event	A real estate company	*The new Arrow assembly plant will bring 1,700 new families to White Rock within three years.*
Anecdote	A weekly business magazine	*During six years of college, the one experience that helped me the most did not occur in the classroom.*
Direct challenge	A no-blot ballpoint pen	*Drop the enclosed Pointer pen on the floor, writing tip first, and then sign your name with it.*

Sales letters, unlike other persuasive messages, may stretch sincerity—within reason. In another sample Relay For Life letter, the author writes, "Hundreds of people will be walking for 12 hours to help raise money to fight cancer." We may question whether everyone is walking for all 12 hours, but this is probably acceptable for the purpose and audience.

Ethics in COMMUNICATION

Still, be careful about crossing an ethical line to draw people in. Phishing scams, as we saw earlier, lure people into giving personal information, such as bank account numbers, computer passwords, or social security numbers. Today, because people are more attuned to this type of fraud, they may react negatively to a sales letter with a questionable introduction, even if the business is legitimate.

For solicited sales letters, which respond to a customer inquiry, an attention-getting opening is not as crucial. Instead, you might begin by expressing appreciation for the customer's inquiry and then introduce the central selling theme.

7-4c Creating Interest and Building Desire

If your opening sentence is directly related to your product, transitioning to features and reader benefits will be smooth and logical.

Interpreting Features

Most of your letter (typically, several paragraphs) will probably be devoted to creating interest and building desire for your product. An American Express letter offering a credit card does this well, with easy-to-skim bullets. The writer *interprets* services by showing how each aspect of the program benefits members. The American Express letter focuses on benefits rather than features (how the card works), making the reader—not the product—the subject of the letter.

Marketers refer to the benefit a user receives from a product or service as the derived benefit. In the American Express example, the company doesn't sell cards; it sells exclusivity.

Although emphasizing the derived benefit rather than product features is generally the preferred strategy, two situations call for emphasizing product features instead: when promoting a product to experts and when promoting expensive equipment. For example, if the car you're promoting to sports car enthusiasts achieves a maximum torque of 138 ft-lb at 3,000 rpm or produces 145 hp at 5,500 rpm, tell the reader that. You would sound condescending if you explained to such experts what this means.

Using Vivid Language and Graphics

Because people are bombarded with advertising today, novel approaches are essential to differentiate your product or service from the pack. Other Relay For Life letter examples reflect personal stories and show pictures for visual and emotional appeal. One is written from the perspective of a dog:[8]

Dear Friend,

Greetings, salutations, and a wag of my tail from [YOUR TOWN HERE] in [YOUR STATE HERE]! I am writing to you today because I know that my master needs my help. As you probably know, Robert has always managed to get himself in some real jams. Well, this is no exception. In my three short years with him, he has managed to come up with some doozies. Do you know what he has done this time? He has promised to raise at least $1,000 in sponsorship for the upcoming 24-Hour Relay For Life to benefit the American Cancer Society. . . .

Another sample letter is written from a child's perspective and includes a picture of a baby (who doesn't love that!) and colorful text:

> Hello to all my family and friends!
>
> My name is Kal. I'm about to participate in my first **Relay For Life**. Now, I've been to a lot of Relays with my mom and dad. Mom says she takes me to **Relays** for two reasons: (1) it's her job—she works for the **American Cancer Society**, and (2) it's a chance to pay tribute to the memory of my **Grammy**. . . .

Use action verbs when talking about the product's features and benefits. Within reason, use colorful adjectives and adverbs and positive language, stressing what your product *is,* rather than what it is *not.*

☒ NOT   The ski lodge isn't in one of those crowded resort areas.

    ☑ BUT   The private ski lodge sits on the snow-capped peaks of the Canadian Rocky Mountains.

☒ NOT   A serving of our baked potato chips doesn't have high calories like the original chips.

    ☑ BUT   Our baked potato chips have 140 calories per serving—40% less than the original chips.

Using Objective, Ethical Language

Ethics in COMMUNICATION

To be convincing, you must present specific, objective evidence. For sales letters, even more than other persuasive messages, simply saying that a product is great is not enough. You must provide evidence to show *why* or *how* the product is great. Here is where you'll use all the data you gathered before you started to write. Avoid generalities, unsupported superlatives and claims, and too many or too strong adjectives and adverbs. Avoid stating or implying something your product is not, so your letter doesn't cross an ethical line.

☒ NOT   At $795, the Sherwood scooter is the best buy on the market.

    ☑ BUT   The May issue of *Independent Consumer* rated the $795 Sherwood scooter the year's best buy.

☒ NOT   Everyone enjoys the convenience of our Bread Baker.

    ☑ BUT   Our Bread Baker comes with one feature we don't think you'll ever use: a 30-day, no-questions-asked return policy.

Emotional INTELLIGENCE

Have you crossed an ethical line when trying to persuade others? What was the situation, and how do you feel about it in retrospect? Would you do anything differently next time?

Similar to a message proposing an idea, a sales letter should include a variety of evidence. If you were selling a Kindle, for example, you might include the evidence shown in Figure 9.[9,10]

Mentioning Price

If price is your central selling theme, introduce it early and emphasize it often. In most cases, however, price is not the central selling theme and should therefore be subordinated. Introduce the price late in the message, after most of the advantages of owning the product have been

Facts and Statistics

Weighing only 8.7 ounces, the Amazon Kindle stores up to 3,500 books.

Expert Opinion

According to David Pogue, technology writer and commentator, "The Kindle is, of course, the world's most popular electronic book reader.... What makes the Kindle successful is the effortlessness of it.... The convenience is amazing."

Examples

As one customer says, "For years, I was unable to read regular books because of problems with my hands and failing eyesight, so the Kindle has been a great investment for me. Plus, the cost of books I currently own on my Kindle, had I bought them in the store, would have been $527.98; however, the cost of those books in electronic format was approximately $140—almost $390 in savings in less than a year!"

discussed. State it in a long complex or compound sentence, perhaps in a sentence that also mentions a reader benefit.

Presenting the price in small units and comparing it to a familiar object may soften the expense. You can see this technique used in the website image shown in Figure 10, which seeks donations for Rottweilers. By comparing the amount to the price of a cup of coffee, the organization makes a convincing argument for donating to its cause.

Comparing Donations to Small, Everyday Purchases | **Figure 10**

COURTESY OF YOUCARING

Referring to Enclosures

Sometimes, an enclosure explains your product or service or inspires action. If you include an enclosure, subordinate your reference to it, and refer to some specific item in the enclosure to increase the likelihood of its being read.

☒ NOT   I have enclosed a sales brochure on this product.

     ☑ BUT   Take a look at our clearance items on page 7 of the enclosed brochure.

☒ NOT   I have enclosed an order blank for your convenience.

     ☑ BUT   Use the enclosed order blank to send us your order today. Within a week, you'll be wearing your new waterproof boots!

7-4d Motivating Action

Although the purpose of your letter should be apparent right from the start, delay making your specific request until late in the letter—after you have created interest and built desire for the product. Then state the specific action you want. In a State Farm vehicle loan offer, the requested action is clear in the last paragraph: "The process is quick, and you'll get a decision the same day in most instances." Follow these suggestions to motivate your reader to take action:

- Make the action easy by including a toll-free number, a website link, or an order form. For high-end items, get the reader to take just a small step toward purchasing. It's unlikely that someone would phone in an order for a new car after reading a sales letter, so encourage them to visit a dealership for a test drive, call for more information, or ask a sales representative to follow up.

- Provide an incentive for prompt action, for example, by offering a gift to the first 100 people who respond or by stressing the need to buy early while there is still a good selection, before the holiday rush, or during the three-day sale. But make your push for action *gently*. Any tactic that smacks of high-pressure selling is likely to increase reader resistance and, again, may lead the reader to question your ethics.

☒ NOT   Hurry! Hurry! Hurry! These sale prices won't be in effect long.

☑ BUT   Call before September 30 to take advantage of our lowest prices of the year.

- Use confident language when asking for action, avoiding such hesitant phrases as, "If you want to save money" or "I hope you agree that this product will save you time." When asking the reader to part with money, mention a reader benefit in the same sentence.

☒ NOT   If you agree that this ice cream maker will make your summers more enjoyable, you can place your order by telephone.

☑ BUT   To use your Jiffy Ice Cream Maker during the upcoming July 4 weekend, simply call our toll-free number today.

- Consider putting an important marketing point in a postscript (P.S.). The State Farm letter uses a P.S. to encourage a response: "You can also use this special offer to purchase a new or used vehicle. Call me at (607) 257-xxxx for details." Some studies have shown that people first read their name, then who signed the letter, and then the postscript—all before reading the introductory paragraph on the first page.[11] Because of this reading pattern, the P.S. should contain new and interesting information, as the State Farm letter does.

Use the Checklist for Sales Letters to make your letters as persuasive as possible. With a well-written letter, you'll have a better chance of achieving your goals.

Checklist for Sales Letters

SELECT A CENTRAL SELLING THEME

☑ Highlight your product's most distinguishing feature—and refer to this throughout the letter.

GAIN THE READER'S ATTENTION

☑ Make your opening brief, interesting, and original. Avoid obvious, misleading, and irrelevant statements.

☑ Use any of these openings: rhetorical question, thought-provoking statement, unusual fact, current event, anecdote, direct challenge, or some similar attention-getting device.

- ☑ Introduce (or at least lead up to) the central selling theme in the opening.
- ☑ If the letter is in response to a customer inquiry, begin by expressing appreciation for the inquiry, and then introduce the central selling theme.

CREATE INTEREST AND BUILD DESIRE

- ☑ Make the introduction of the product follow naturally from the attention-getter.
- ☑ *Interpret* the features of the product; instead of just describing the features, show how the reader will benefit from each feature. Let the reader picture owning, using, and enjoying the product.
- ☑ Use action-packed, positive language and engaging graphics. Provide objective, convincing evidence to support your claims—specific facts
- and figures, independent product reviews, endorsements, and so on.
- ☑ Continue to stress the central selling theme throughout.
- ☑ Subordinate price (unless price is the central selling theme). State price in small terms, in a long sentence, or in a sentence that also talks about benefits.

MOTIVATE ACTION

- ☑ Make the desired action clear and easy to take.
- ☑ Ask confidently, avoiding the hesitant "If you'd like to. . ." or "I hope you agree that. . . ."
- ☑ Encourage prompt action (but avoid a hard-sell approach).
- ☑ End your letter with a reminder of a reader benefit.

7-5 Writing and Responding to Negative Customer and Public Feedback

LO4 Write and respond to negative customer and public feedback.

Wouldn't it be great if all customers were happy all the time? Of course, this isn't the case. Throughout your career—both as a customer and as a provider of a product or service—you will have to address situations when expectations are not met. To convince a business that its product is faulty or to convince a customer that your product is *not* faulty requires another type of persuasion.

Sometimes, negative feedback is best handled in person or with a phone call. If you work for McKinsey Consulting and have a two-year relationship with a client for potentially millions of dollars in consulting fees, you would hope that the client would call with a complaint rather than post a rant on YouTube. Also, if you receive a complaint from a customer, you might call her rather than respond by letter to explain how you'll fix the problem. How you communicate your response is critical to service recovery—ideally, turning an upset customer into a loyal one. In situations such as these, you might improve your chances of rebuilding a relationship with personal communication.

However, for more transactional, high-volume businesses, where you don't necessarily know your customer, you may be more likely to see comments posted on social media sites. As we discussed in Chapter 6, responding to positive comments online is important, but the stakes are even higher with negative online feedback.

 Communication **TECHNOLOGIES**

How well you handle negative customer feedback affects your company's image. When a customer has a negative service experience, the situation may be exacerbated in two ways: the customer writes about the experience on a public website, and the company mishandles the online comment.

Failing to respond well to criticism, companies often create their own crisis situation—a significant threat to the organization—which we might say about SeaWorld. A MarketWatch article describes the company's response to PETA's hijacking the #AskSeaWorld campaign (Figure 11).[12] Blaming those who criticize you is rarely a good choice.

In this section of the chapter, we'll look at principles for writing complaints and responding to negative feedback.

Figure 11 | SeaWorld Blames PETA

 MarketWatch

SeaWorld blames PETA for spamming its outreach campaign

AFP/Getty Images

SeaWorld's campaign comes after a documentary alleged mistreatment of orca whales at the parks.

By
**CAITLIN
HUSTON**

NEW YORK (MarketWatch) — SeaWorld is blaming PETA activists for derailing their #AskSeaWorld campaign with fake accounts and repeat questions about the treatment of animals in its water parks.

COURTESY OF MARKETWATCH

7-5a Writing Complaints and Online Reviews

To present yourself as a credible customer with a complaint worth the company's attention, follow these principles for writing a complaint letter or negative online review:

- Consider an indirect style. Although you'll want to get to the issue quickly, asking for compensation in your first paragraph may turn off the reader. Instead, build your case gradually to convince the reader to fulfill your request.

  ☒ NOT Recently, I planned to take the bus to Houston, but it left early, and I'd like my $55 refunded.

  ☑ BUT Recently, I planned to take the bus to Houston, but I missed it because it left early.

- Give specific evidence about what went wrong. For the bus example, giving the specific location, date, and time—and witnesses—makes your argument more credible and persuasive. Avoid generalizations and vague descriptions.

  ☒ NOT The bus always leaves early.

  ☑ BUT On Thursday, September 14, I was scheduled to take the bus at 3:15 from Minor Hall. When I arrived at 3:05 with my luggage, two people told me they saw the bus leave at 3:00.

- Maintain a calm, objective tone. Your anger may be understandable, but it could hinder your ability to get a positive response from the company. Consider asking a friend for feedback or waiting a day before you send email or post angry feedback online.

 Emotional
INTELLIGENCE

What could get in the way of your using a calm, objective tone when writing a complaint? How can you avoid writing something that could hinder your ability to get a positive response?

☒ NOT   What's the deal with this? Even Amanda, at your central office, said the bus left early, and she was upset about it too!

        ☑ BUT   I called the central office and spoke with Amanda, who called the driver on the other line and confirmed that the bus had left at 3:00. She said she was surprised the bus left before 3:15, which was its scheduled departure.

- Close with a confident, respectful tone. After you provide details, ask for reasonable compensation and a response.

☒ NOT   I hope you'll send me the $55 I paid for the ticket and $200 for my waiting time until I could catch a ride with a friend.

        ☑ BUT   I enclose the ticket and respectfully request $55 as reimbursement. Please send the check to my home address: 525 Simpson Hall, Dallas, TX, 74205.

With such clear explanations and an appropriate tone, this is a persuasive message to which any reasonable company would respond.

If you weren't requesting compensation for a dissatisfying bus experience, you could have instead posted a review online. Whether you post on the company's Facebook page or a public review site, such as Yelp, the audience is slightly different: a company representative may read your post, but your primary audience is the public—including people considering taking the bus.

The same principles of organization, evidence, and tone apply for online reviews, but respect may be even more important for public comments. If your post is unreasonable or angry, you may embarrass yourself and regret it later. Also, you might want to give the company the opportunity to address major concerns more privately through a phone call, email, letter, direct message on Twitter, or feedback form on the company's website.

The review about a television, shown in Figure 12, is honest, measured, and reasonable. The customer isn't happy, but the feedback is clear and useful for other consumers—and the manufacturer.

Negative Online Review for a TV | **Figure 12**

⭐ **Good Color, but Terrible Visibility** ← Includes a specific title for the post.

February 4, 2017

Uses the direct plan with the main point up front. This is appropriate for the public audience. →

Includes relevant positive information. Provides specific measurements to justify the point. →

Offers a comparison to explain the results. →

The color is nice on this 40-inch TV, but it's difficult to see. The colors are accurate, but I can't see the picture from all angles. I see fine if I move from left and right of the set (at up to a 75-degree angle), but I can't watch TV in bed (at more than 20 degrees below eye level). I see only dark, muted colors, almost like a negative of a photo. I wouldn't buy this brand again, and I don't recommend this TV at all. ← Ends with a clear recommendation.

7-5b **Responding to Negative Feedback**

Hearing negative feedback can be difficult but is a good opportunity to improve the business and rebuild relationships. As we know by now, ignoring the feedback or responding rudely will surely lose one already angry customer and may lose even more if the feedback is posted online. We want to avoid situations from escalating—and to handle them well when they do, inevitably, turn into crises.

Addressing Negative Reviews and Other Feedback

Worse than not responding to negative feedback is actively discouraging social media posts. The Union Street Guest House in Hudson, New York, tried to fine people $500 for each negative review posted by one of their wedding guests.[13] Clearly, the management isn't "engaging" customers, as we discussed in Chapter 3; they're pushing them away and embarrassing the organization.

Let's look at a better example of responding to negative reviews. If you owned the Lakes Inn and saw the online travel review in Figure 13, how would you respond?

Figure 13 | Lakes Inn Review

> ### "Beautiful location but smells"
>
> Courtney
>
> March 11
>
> This inn is at the top of Twin Lake, the perfect spot for boating and a terrific view of the lake and surrounding areas. But I noticed a musty smell throughout the inn. This wasn't as noticeable in our room, but it was very prevalent in the lobby and the restaurant. It was a real turn-off.

Overall the review is positive, but the guest makes one negative comment that should be addressed. According to the Social Media Response Guidelines presented in Chapter 6, this guest could be considered "Unhappy." Also, it's smart to respond because a negative review may influence the decisions of millions of travelers.

Follow these guidelines when responding to negative online reviews and other feedback:

- Show appreciation for the feedback. Thank the writer for the feedback—even negative comments give you the opportunity to respond and restore your company's reputation.
- Reinforce positive aspects of the feedback. Many comments will include some positive points; highlight those for other readers.
- Address negative aspects directly. Explain what you will do to correct the situation. Then, follow through to use negative feedback to improve operations or service.
- Invite the customer to experience your product or service again. If you can contact the writer directly, you might offer a special discount to entice him or her to try your company again—and to have a better experience.

The manager of the Lakes Inn uses these principles to respond to the guest's review in Figure 14.

Handling Crisis Situations

Sometimes, despite management's best efforts, situations spiral out of control. People aren't always fair on social media sites: the anonymity and mob mentality get the best of them. When a company's reputation is at risk, companies need to apply crisis communication principles to protect and defend the brand and, when appropriate, apologize.

When SeaWorld came out of denial about the effects of *Blackfish*, the company made some positive moves. For the first time during the crisis, SeaWorld took real action for the whales: improved their living conditions and promised investment in research (Figure 15).[14] This is the type of genuine change critics wanted to see.

A search of BizCom in the News for "apologize" reveals a whopping 96 stories over three and a half years.

In other situations, companies have to admit wrongdoing. When companies apologize, they take full responsibility for the crisis and ask for forgiveness.[15] Apologies are becoming more common and, particularly in politics, can be met with cynicism. But apologies can increase the company's credibility, move the business forward, and improve the outcome of litigation.[16]

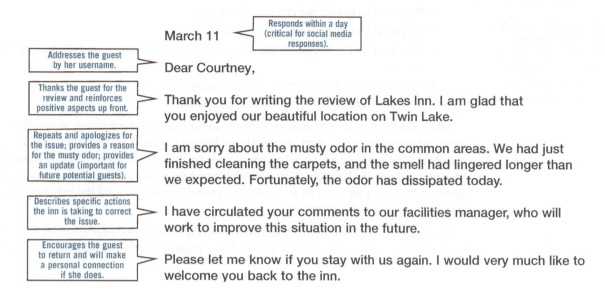

March 11 ◄ *Responds within a day (critical for social media responses).*

Addresses the guest by her username. ⟩ Dear Courtney,

Thanks the guest for the review and reinforces positive aspects up front. ⟩ Thank you for writing the review of Lakes Inn. I am glad that you enjoyed our beautiful location on Twin Lake.

Repeats and apologizes for the issue; provides a reason for the musty odor; provides an update (important for future potential guests). ⟩ I am sorry about the musty odor in the common areas. We had just finished cleaning the carpets, and the smell had lingered longer than we expected. Fortunately, the odor has dissipated today.

Describes specific actions the inn is taking to correct the issue. ⟩ I have circulated your comments to our facilities manager, who will work to improve this situation in the future.

Encourages the guest to return and will make a personal connection if she does. ⟩ Please let me know if you stay with us again. I would very much like to welcome you back to the inn.

SeaWorld's Effective Crisis Communication Response | **Figure 15**

The best apologies are authentic and demonstrate real change. A writer for *The New York Times*, tired of reading surface apologies, identified these characteristics of a sincere apology:

- They must be painful and create vulnerability.
- They must be authentic and not an excuse.
- They must probe deeply into the personal or organizational values that permitted the offense.
- They must encourage feedback from the aggrieved.
- They must turn regret into a real change in behavior.[17]

When the Twitter account manager for DiGiorno Pizza used a hashtag about domestic violence to promote the product, he quickly apologized (Figure 16).[18] Within minutes, he sent customized messages to people who complained. According to *Adweek*, "Each response has been personalized and is clearly sincere, which is a nice reprieve from the usual copy-and-paste approach to dealing with bad PR in social." His apology worked to quell the criticism and get back to the business of making pizza.

Responding to negative feedback is a make-or-break situation for business professionals. If handled well, you can win over a customer for life. If handled poorly, you risk losing much more than one dissatisfied customer.

Figure 16 | Digiorno's Quick, Authentic Apology

Writing a Press Release About SeaWorld's New Spaces for Whales

3Ps
‹ IN ACTION

>>> PURPOSE

Imagine that you're the vice president of corporate communications for SeaWorld and want to announce new programs for whales.

>>> PROCESS

To plan your press release, you first answer the following questions.

1. **Who is my audience, and what do I know about them?**
   My audience includes all constituencies of the park: customers, employees, shareholders, animal rights activities, and so on. Many are skeptical of the company, having seen the movie *Blackfish* and heard about trainer deaths and conditions for our whales in captivity.

2. **What do I want to accomplish with my response?**
   My main goal is to rebuild the company's image as a responsible park that cares about killer whales. To do this, I'll announce our plans for larger spaces for the animals and funding for research and to improve ocean health.

3. **How will I organize the message?**
   I'll use the direct organizational plan with my main points up front. Then, I'll use headings to distinguish main sections.

4. **Will I address potential obstacles?**
   In the press release, it's not appropriate for me to directly address obstacles. Instead, I'll keep the tone positive and focus on our good news.

⟩⟩⟩ PRODUCT

The first two paragraphs of SeaWorld's press release are below. Read the entire statement at bit.ly/1Fi2Mop.

SeaWorld — Realm | Education | Research | Partnerships

SeaWorld Announces First-Of-Its-Kind Killer Whale Environment and More Than $10 Million In New Funding For Research and Conservation Projects

SAN DIEGO (Aug. 15, 2014) – SeaWorld Entertainment, Inc. announced today that it plans to build new, first-of-its-kind killer whale environments and that it will fund new programs to protect ocean health and killer whales in the wild. The new projects will build on SeaWorld's legacy of providing state-of-the- art, innovative homes for its animals, and will offer park guests unique and inspiring killer whale encounters for generations to come. As part of its vision for the future, the company also pledged $10 million in matching funds for killer whale research and is embarking on a multi-million dollar partnership focused on ocean health, the leading concern for all killer whales and marine mammals.

"For 50 years, SeaWorld has transformed how the world views marine life. The unprecedented access to marine mammals that our parks provide has increased our knowledge of the ocean and inspired generations," said Jim Atchison, Chief Executive Officer and President of SeaWorld Entertainment, Inc. "Our new killer whale homes and research initiatives have just as bold a vision: to advance global understanding of these animals, to educate, and to inspire conservation efforts to protect killer whales in the wild."

Write a Sales Letter to SeaWorld Customers

>>> PURPOSE

Imagine that you're the head of marketing for SeaWorld and want to encourage former customers to return to the park. You'll write a letter to people who have visited in the past five years.

>>> PROCESS

To plan your letter, answer the following questions.

1. Describe your audience. What do you know about past visitors that will help you tailor your message?

2. What are your communication objectives? What, specifically, do you want people to do after they read your letter?

3. How will you create interest? What new information can you provide, or what can you offer, that will entice people to return to the park?

4. How can you justify your request? What evidence will you present to support your points?

5. What obstacles, if any, should you address in your letter? Will you tackle the controversy about killer whales, or avoid it?

6. Write your opening paragraph. How will you describe your purpose and main points up front?

7. How will you summarize your main points and inspire action in your closing?

>>> PRODUCT

Draft, revise, format, and proofread your letter. Then submit your letter and your responses to the process questions to your instructor.

LO1   Plan a persuasive message for your audience.

The more you know your audience, the more likely you can persuade them. Consider possible resistance and adapt your message accordingly. Use a mix of credibility, emotional appeal, and logical arguments, depending on your audience and the situation. However, be mindful about ethical lines. Never misuse someone's trust to persuade someone to do something that is ultimately not in his or her best interest.

LO2   Write a short persuasive message.

Use a direct writing style for most persuasive messages. Present the idea or request, along with the criteria or a brief rationale, in the first paragraph. Use the indirect style when you expect considerable resistance and for people who prefer this style. Capture the reader's attention by using an opening paragraph that is relevant, interesting, and short. Then provide a variety of evidence—facts, expert opinion, and examples—to support your points. Discuss and minimize any obstacles to your idea, and finally, motivate action.

LO3   Write a sales letter.

For sales letters, introduce a central selling theme early and build on it throughout the message. Devote most of the message to showing how the reader will specifically benefit from owning the product or using the service. Subordinate the price, unless price is the central selling theme.

LO4   Write and respond to negative customer and public feedback.

Negative customer feedback presents an opportunity for businesses to improve but can be difficult to address online. To write a complaint or negative review as a customer, use an appropriate tone and provide enough evidence to support your points. When responding to negative feedback, consider a personal approach if you know the customer; otherwise, respond online promptly, thank the customer, acknowledge the feedback, apologize where appropriate, explain how the problem will be fixed, and ask for repeat business. If faced with a crisis situation, protect and defend the company's reputation and, if appropriate, make an authentic apology that reflects real change.

> EXERCISES

LO1   Plan a persuasive message for your audience.

1. **Assess what is important to team members.**

   Think about a team you know well. It could be a volunteer organization, a small group at work, or a sports team. If you were introducing a new idea—one that team members might resist—what would be important to know about each team member that might influence how you tailor your message? You might consider questions such as the following:

   - How long has this person been a part of the team?
   - How important is the team to the person?
   - What level of commitment to the team—rather than to him- or herself—do you see?
   - How might the person react to your idea?
   - How will this person, specifically, be affected by the change?
   - What questions or objections would this person have?

2. **Analyze use of ethos, pathos, and logos in a sales call.**

   In the movie *Boiler Room,* Giovanni Ribisi's character (Seth) is a trainee working at a "chop shop"—a shady brokerage firm that sells stock in fake companies. The movie is based on a real company, previously on Long Island. During a sales call to a prospective customer (Harry), Seth uses credibility (ethos), emotional appeals (pathos), and logical arguments (logos)—but not in a professional, ethical way.

You'll find the clip under "Videos" on the author's blog (www.bizcominthenews.com) and at bit.ly/1CTSR8E.

As you watch the scene, how do you see Seth using credibility, emotional appeals, and logic to convince Harry to buy stock? Write down specific text that represents each strategy for persuasion. You may use this form for your notes.

Ethos	Pathos	Logos

3. **Analyze use of ethos, pathos, and logos in a speech.**

Karim Abouelnaga, founder and CEO of the mentoring group Practice Makes Perfect, delivered a speech at the United Nations about his organization. Watch the video at http://bit.ly/1BRiQd8 and, using the format from the previous exercise, identify examples of credibility (ethos), emotional appeals (pathos), and logical arguments (logos).

Inspiring Voices at the United Nations

Practice Makes Perfect

Subscribe 22

253 views

4. **Discuss the ethics of an advertisement.**

    On its website (Figure 17), a company promises to deposit cash into a customer's bank account within 24 hours. In small groups, discuss tactics this company uses to persuade its audience. How do you see credibility (ethos), emotional appeals (pathos), and logical arguments (logos) used? What is *not* being said that may ultimately turn out badly for a customer?

Figure 17 | Website Using Questionable Ethics

5. **Write an article on a blog to warn people about quick cash businesses.**

    To discourage people from signing up at the Promise/Cash Center site discussed in Exercise 4, write an online article. Imagine that you'll post your article on a site that warns consumers about questionable business practices. Your objective is to convince people that—even though fast cash sounds good—it's not in their best interest in the long term.

    Consider these questions as you draft your article:

    a) What evidence will you use? Research outside sources to support your view. Include data, expert opinion, and examples where relevant.

    b) What will you write up front to capture and keep the reader's attention?

    c) How will you address potential obstacles or objections from readers?

    d) What is a catchy title for your article?

6. **Identify the organization of a persuasive letter.**

    When you graduate, you may receive communications from your school's alumni office. For example, the "Open Letter" from Georgia Tech's School of Electrical and Computer Engineering is posted on the school's website (Figure 18).[19]

    How is the letter organized—using the direct or indirect approach? What specific examples in the text tell you it's organized in this way? Do you believe this is the best approach for this letter? Why or why not? Write a one-page summary of your analysis.

LO2 Write a short persuasive message.

COLLEGE OF ENGINEERING

Georgia Tech

School of Electrical and Computer Engineering

Great Minds Think Differently

Expand All | Collapse All

alumni & external relations

+ About ECE

+ Academics

+ Academic Enrichment

+ Research

+ Faculty & Staff

+ Alumni & External Relations

Open Letter from the Chair

Update Your Information With Us

GT Alumni Association

Professional Education

Advisory Board

Corporate Affairs Partnerships (CAP)

Gift Opportunities

Direct Involvement

+ Campuses

+ Media & Calendar

ECE Home

An Open Letter to Alumni of the School of Electrical and Computer Engineering (ECE)

Dear Fellow Alumnus/Alumna,

Thank you for visiting ECE's web site. Like me, you are a member of a rarified group of people who received a degree from our School. This community of people, now numbering over 15,500, continues to make significant and distinctive contributions to our profession and to many related fields.

What you have collectively accomplished is in large measure responsible for the ever-growing tradition and reputation of Georgia Tech and our School as one of the best engineering education and research institutions in the world. In like measure, that reputation enhances the value of all our degrees.

ECE has been working to strengthen its connection with our alumni over the past years. As the School Chair, I am committed to continuing this work, with the goal of making your connection with ECE a lifelong one that will be mutually beneficial.

You can remain involved with the School in many ways. First and foremost, please keep us posted on where you are and what you are doing through our Contact Alumni Affairs at ECE page. Also, keep abreast of what is going on at ECE through our biannual alumni newsletter, *ECE Connection*, and our online newsletter *ECE Highlights*. Visit the institute's Alumni Affairs web site to find out about institute-wide events, continuing education opportunities, and local alumni clubs and activities.

Of course, financial support is always welcome. In fact, the financial contributions of ECE alumni represent a vital resource for the School's programs and services. If you would like to make a contribution, or have an idea for an innovative gift, please contact Martina Emmerson at 404.894.0274 or at martina.emmerson@ece.gatech.edu.

I appreciate your support and honor your continued involvement with the ECE family of faculty, students, staff, and alumni.

Best regards,

Gary S. May,
Professor and Steve W. Chaddick School Chair

Last revised on April 23, 2010

Van Leer Electrical Engineering Building • 777 Atlantic Drive NW • Atlanta, GA 30332-0250 • 404.894.2901 • Fax 404.894.4641
1994-2010, School of Electrical and Computer Engineering at the Georgia Institute of Technology
GT Legal & Privacy Information

 Internet | Protected

7. **Write an email requesting a recommendation.**

Imagine that you're interviewing for your ideal job. You're doing well in the process, and the HR manager has asked you for a letter of recommendation from one of your instructors. Write an email to the instructor who knows you best. You may invent details about the job for which you're interviewing.

8. **Write an email to suggest an idea.**

Similar to Grace Lee's suggestion in Figure 3, write an email to a current or previous employer. Think of an idea that would improve the business: a new procedure, an upgraded system, an innovative product, or some other way to increase sales, improve service, or increase operational efficiencies. Choose something simple enough to convey in a short message. Put your main point up front, and be sure to use a clear, specific subject line to capture attention.

LO3 Write a sales letter.

9. **Write a magazine subscription letter.**

Imagine that you work for your favorite magazine. Write a sales letter to encourage new subscriptions. As you're planning your letter, think carefully about your audience:

- Why would they want to subscribe to the magazine? What benefits would they gain?
- What can you offer to make a subscription attractive?
- What are the potential obstacles to your sale? How can you overcome them?
- How can you personalize the letter to your audience?
- What creative opening would capture attention?

10. **Write a fundraising letter to recent alumni.**

Imagine that you're working for your college's alumni office. You're asked to write a letter to recent graduates (within the past three years) to inspire them to donate to your school. You may use the Georgia Tech example in Figure 18, but tailor the letter to your school—and to recent graduates. You also may consider that your letter will be sent directly to graduates; this is different from the Georgia Tech example, which is posted on the school website. Consider how this difference might affect the order, content, and tone of your letter.

11. **Write a fundraising letter to older alumni.**

Now rewrite the letter you wrote for Exercise 10. Adapt it for a new audience: people who graduated between 30 and 40 years ago. What will you change to persuade this cohort to donate to your school?

12. **Analyze a sales letter or email you receive.**

Be on the lookout for sales letters you receive at home or through email. Bring one to class so you can discuss the example with other students.

In small groups, discuss how the letter or email uses persuasion tactics discussed in this chapter. What works best about the example, and what could be improved? Will you—or did you—purchase the product or service being promoted? Why or why not?

Agree on the best letter or email within your group, and share it with the rest of the class.

LO4 Write and respond to negative customer and public feedback.

13. **Write a complaint letter to a business owner.**

Think about a negative customer service experience you had recently. Write a letter to the business owner or the company's customer service department explaining what happened. Be sure to use a credible tone and specific examples to persuade the owner that your experience is valid.

Also find a way to encourage a response from the company. You may ask for reasonable compensation, if appropriate.

14. Give feedback on someone else's letter.

After you complete Exercise 13, switch letters with a partner. Imagine that you're the business owner receiving this complaint. Use the following form to give feedback to your partner. Circle a rating for each question.

Feedback on a Customer Service Letter				
	Not at All	Somewhat	Yes	Definitely
1. The organization works well for the purpose. COMMENTS:	1	2	3	4
2. The tone is appropriate for the audience. COMMENTS:	1	2	3	4
3. Enough details and examples explain the situation. COMMENTS:	1	2	3	4
4. Requests for compensation are reasonable. COMMENTS:	1	2	3	4
5. Correct grammar and punctuation make the letter credible. COMMENTS:	1	2	3	4

15. Respond to a complaint letter.

Imagine that you own the business that is the subject of your peer's complaint in Exercise 13. Respond to the letter using principles discussed in this chapter. You may invent whatever details are necessary to win over the customer.

16. Write a negative review online.

Rewrite your customer complaint letter from Exercise 13 for an online review. For your post to an online review site, you have a different audience: the public. Consider making changes for a broader audience, who, like the business owner, cares about your credibility, tone, and details. But, unlike the business owner, this audience may make a buying decision based on your review.

17. Respond to another student's review.

Give the review you completed in the previous exercise to a partner in class. Imagine that you're the proprietor of the business—the owner or a manager who would be responsible for responding to online reviews. First, decide how you would respond to this post. Would you ignore it, write an online response, or try to call or email the customer directly? Then, talk with your partner about your decision. Is this what he or she would prefer? Why or why not?

Next, assume that you'll write a response online. Draft your response, and again ask your partner for feedback. Would he or she be satisfied with the response?

Finally, rewrite the response to perfect it with feedback from your partner.

18. Write a letter to respond to illness at a restaurant.

Imagine that you are the customer service manager for a restaurant. Recently, several of your customers became ill, some seriously, from an ingredient that was mishandled by your supplier. Write a letter to the media to communicate your company's position on this matter and restore the public's confidence in your restaurant. In your letter, be sure to describe the source of the problem and your company's response.

For Exercises 18–20, refer to Write Experience, a technology that uses artificial intelligence to score student writing and provide feedback to help them improve. In Write Experience, Exercise 18 is referred to as a "press release," but use the letter format instead.

19. Write an email reply to a customer demanding a refund.

You are the customer service manager at a small company, and one of your employees has escalated a customer complaint to your attention. The customer reported that an expensive, customized product he purchased does not function as advertised, and he is demanding his money back. Write an email to this customer to explain your company's refund policy, describe what action will be taken to fix the problem, and restore the customer's confidence in your company.

20. Write a letter to complain about damaged equipment.

You have just received an order from an Internet retailer for some equipment that you need for a business presentation. Unfortunately, some of the equipment is damaged. Write a letter to the retailer to explain the damage, express your dissatisfaction with the shipment, and describe what you want the retailer to do to fulfill your shipment.

21. Write an email to a customer who posted negative feedback.

Exercise 21 refers to the Colonnade Hotel scenario at bit.ly/UwHvjd.

Imagine that you work for the Colonnade Hotel and Resort, and a customer posted a video of his negative experience checking into the hotel (Figure 19). The customer also posted a negative review of the hotel on a travel website (Figure 20).

Prepare an email to the customer, addressing his concerns. How can you win over this very angry customer?

Figure 19 | Dissatisfied Customers at the Hotel

COURTESY OF AMY NEWMAN

Figure 20 | Negative Review of the Colonnade Hotel and Resort

---

Colonnade Hotel and Resort

"No available room for our parents' 50th anniversary!"

kward55

What a scam! My whole family (15 of us) made plans 8 months ago to celebrate my parents' anniversary together. We heard great things about the CHR (and it was beautiful), but when my wife, son, and I arrived at 10 p.m., we were told the hotel was overbooked, and we had to stay at another hotel 15 miles away. The front desk agent was nice enough (although she didn't look too happy about the situation), and CHR paid for our first night, but what a hassle! And my poor parents—this was their dream . . . to celebrate their 50th with their 3 children and 7 grandchildren from all over the country. My brother came in later than we did, and he and his wife were sent to yet another hotel in another direction. What's the point of making reservations far in advance and reserving with a credit card?? Every day, we were on the phone trying to make plans and taking taxis to and from the hotel to see each other. It was crazy. Check out our video on YouTube: www.youtube.com/watch?v=0qPeva-fiNA

---

22. **Write an apology tweet and blog post.**

Progressive Insurance was criticized for "robo-tweets" when the company fought an insurance claim for a woman who died in a car accident. The Twitter account manager tweeted the same message several times (Figure 21). Read more about the case at bit .ly/1EKKsqi, and write a few customized tweets and a blog post to extend your sympathy and convey the company's position.

Progressive Insurance's "Robo-Tweets" | **Figure 21**

Progressive @Progressive   14h
@mbeckler This is a tragic case, and our sympathies go out to Mr. Fisher and his family for the pain they've (cont) tl.gd/iqv5qi
Expand

Progressive @Progressive   14h
@alexblagg This is a tragic case, and our sympathies go out to Mr. Fisher and his family for the pain they've (cont) tl.gd/iqv2sf
Expand

Progressive @Progressive   14h
@pkollar This is a tragic case, and our sympathies go out to Mr. Fisher and his family for the pain they've (cont) tl.gd/iqv253
Expand

Progressive @Progressive   14h
@MissObdurate This is a tragic case, and our sympathies go out to Mr. Fisher and his family for the pain (cont) tl.gd/iqurqn
Expand

Progressive @Progressive   15h
@mhebrank This is a tragic case, and our sympathies go out to Mr. Fisher and his family for the pain they've (cont) tl.gd/iqumb2
Expand

Progressive @Progressive   15h
@TheWookieWay This is a tragic case, and our sympathies go out to Mr. Fisher and his family for the pain (cont) tl.gd/iqulab
Expand

Progressive @Progressive   15h
@patrickjd This is a tragic case, and our sympathies go out to Mr. Fisher and his family for the pain they've (cont) tl.gd/iqujfk
Expand

TWITTER.COM

COMPANY SCENARIO

PersuadeCafé

COURTESY OF ED MARION, EDMARION.COM

PersuadeCafé, a 220-store coffee and pastry company, is facing several challenges. The company is asking you—one of their smart, new employees—for ideas to improve the business. This scenario encourages you to do the following:

- Analyze company information to determine business priorities.
- Apply persuasive communication strategies to oral and written messages.
- Evaluate messages based on given criteria.
- Adjust communications based on feedback provided.
- Create visuals and a written proposal, including quantitative data, to support an argument.

On www.cengagebrain.com, you'll see PersuadeCafé's employee intranet site, shown below. The intranet includes information to help you propose a new business idea:

- Presentation by the company CEO and president, Jacqueline Marcus (PowerPoint and audio)
- Company background and menu
- Customer and employee survey results
- Executive profiles
- Assignment instructions

You can start by thinking of an idea you might propose to management and by analyzing the executive who will be most interested in your proposal. Your instructor may assign you to write a pitch memo and provide feedback to another student.

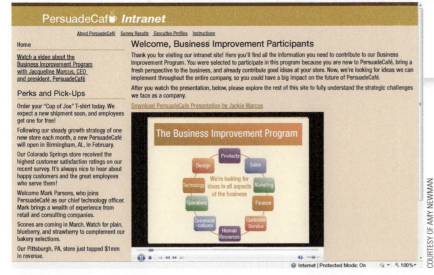

COURTESY OF AMY NEWMAN

Endnotes

1. David E. Johnson, "SeaWorld Crisis Management: The Textbook Case of What NOT To Do," January 4, 2014, www.commpro.biz /corporate-communications/crisis-communications-corporate -communications/seaworld-crisis-managment-textbook-case/, accessed April 2, 2015.

2. Eric Kohn, "Sundance Interview: 'Blackfish' Director Gabriela Cowperthwaite Discusses Suffering Orcas, Trainer Death, and Why SeaWorld Hasn't Seen the Movie," Indiewire, January 26, 2013, www.indiewire.com/article/sundance-interview-blackfish -director-gabriela-cowperthwaite-discusses-suffering-orcas -trainer-death-and-why-seaworld-hasnt-seen-the-movie, accessed March 31, 2015.

3. Alison Griswold, "Why Would Companies Ever Think a Campaign Like #AskSeaWorld Is a Good Idea?" *Slate*, March 27, 2015, www.slate.com/blogs/moneybox/2015/03/27 /_askseaworld_twitter_amas_are_a_terrible_idea_and_yet _companies_do_them.html, accessed March 31, 2015.

4. Cassie Carothers, "Victims Still Falling Prey to Nigerian Email Scam," Fox News, November 29, 2006, www.foxnews.com /story/0,2933,232500,00.html, accessed April 2, 2015.

5. Cassie Carothers.

6. Eldon Roth, "'Pink Slime' Libel to Cost This Country Jobs," Beef Products Inc. Website, *Wall Street Journal* Advertisement, March 23, 2012, http://beefproductsinc.files.wordpress .com/2012/03/beef-products_wsj_ad-fnl1.pdf, accessed April 2, 2015.

7. Relay For Life, American Cancer Society, "Why We Fundraise" and "10 Fundraising Letters," http://relay.acsevents.org, accessed August 1, 2013.

8. Relay for Life, American Cancer Society, "Fundraising Guidebook," http://training.relayforlife.org/courses/team /resources/Lesson%202/fundraising%20guidebook.pdf, accessed March 31, 2015.

9. Amazon.com, Kindle Store, www .amazon.com, accessed August 11, 2010.

10. David Pogue, *Pogue's Posts*, "Kindle Tag," *New York Times* blog, March 5 and July 2, 2009, http://pogue.blogs.nytimes.com/tag /kindle, accessed February 21, 2013.

11. "Understanding How People Read Your Direct Mail Results in Higher Response Rates," The Lead Tree, May 6, 2010, www .theleadtree.com, accessed August 16, 2010. Original study in German: Professor Siegfried Vögele, "Eye Tracking," Institute for Direct Marketing in Munich, Germany, March 2005, www .braatz-text.de/INSIGHT_10_Augenkamera.pdf, accessed April 2, 2015.

12. Caitlin Huston, "SeaWorld Blames PETA for Spamming Its Outreach Campaign," MarketWatch, March 30, 2015, www .marketwatch.com/story/seaworld-blames-peta-for-spamming -its-outreach-campaign-2015-03-30, accessed April 1, 2015.

13. Mara Siegler, "Hotel Fines $500 for Every Bad Review Posted Online," NYPost.com, Page Six, August 4, 2014, http://pagesix .com/2014/08/04/hotel-charges-500-for-every-bad-review -posted-online/, accessed April 1, 2015.

14. "SeaWorld Announces Bold Vision," SeaWorld, 2014, http://links.connect.seaworld.com/servlet/MailView? ms=NjkxNzcxOAS2&r=NTgyMTY2NDY4MDIS1&j =NTAxNTkwMzQzS0&mt, accessed April 1, 2015.

15. W. Timothy Coombs, "Crisis Management and Communications," Institute for Public Relations, January 6, 2011, www.instituteforpr .org/crisis-management-and-communications/, accessed April 1, 2015.

16. David B. Wooten, "Say the Right Thing: Apologies, Reputability, and Punishment," *Journal of Consumer Psychology*, vol. 19, pp. 225–235 (2009).

17. Dov Seidman, "Calling for an Apology Cease-Fire," *The New York Times*, February 3, 2014, http://dealbook.nytimes.com/ 2014/02/03/calling-for-an-apology-cease-fire/?_php, accessed April 1, 2015.

18. David Griner, "DiGiorno Is Really, Really Sorry About Its Tweet Accidentally Making Light of Domestic Violence," *Adweek*, September 4, 2014, www.adweek.com/adfreak/digiorno-really -really-sorry-about-its-tweet-accidentally-making-light -domestic-violence-159998, accessed April 1, 2015.

19. Gary S. May, "An Open Letter to Alumni of the School of Electrical and Computer Engineering (ECE)," Georgia Tech, www.ece.gatech.edu /alumni-exrel/letter.html, accessed October 9, 2010.

LEARNING OBJECTIVES

After you have finished this chapter, you should be able to

LO1   Plan a bad-news message.

LO2   Write components of a bad-news message.

LO3   Write a bad-news reply.

LO4   Write a bad-news announcement.

LO5   Give and receive constructive performance feedback.

> " *I have just been diagnosed with throat cancer.* " [1]

—Jamie Dimon, CEO, JPMorgan

CHAPTER INTRODUCTION

JPMorgan CEO Reveals Cancer

When Jamie Dimon, CEO, JPMorgan, announced that he has throat cancer, he sent a public message.[2] Posted on Business Wire, the notice is called a press release, a memo, a letter, and a note in various news articles. Intended for a broad audience of employees, investors, and customers, the message is well described as all of the above. The style is direct, and Dimon's objective is to reassure all constituencies of his and the bank's health.

Press Release

Sharing Some Personal News
to all colleagues and shareholders

I wanted to let you know that I have just been diagnosed with throat cancer. The good news is that the prognosis from my doctors is excellent, the cancer was caught quickly, and my condition is curable. Following thorough tests that included a CAT scan, PET scan and a biopsy, the cancer is confined to the original site and the adjacent lymph nodes on the right side of my neck. Importantly, there is no evidence of cancer elsewhere in my body.

Jamie Dimon

The news comes after the bank paid more than $20 billion dollars in settlements over regulatory issues, leading to criticism of Dimon's leadership. At the same time, the bank has been done well by shareholders, earning $17.9 billion in profit,[3] which could explain why Dimon has continued in the role. Still, according to a JPMorgan board representative, a succession plan was in place before Dimon's diagnosis.

This is an unusual message from a corporate executive but an essential one to avoid rumors and answer questions long before they are asked.

Emotional INTELLIGENCE

How do you feel about giving bad news? Understanding what makes you uncomfortable may help you improve how you communicate these messages.

8-1 Planning the Bad-News Message

At some point, we'll all be senders and receivers of bad news. Closing an office, discontinuing a product, denying credit, rejecting an offer—bad news is part of running a business.

Just as people don't like hearing bad news, few enjoying giving it—and most people don't do it well. Like persuasive messages, bad-news messages require careful planning. According to Andrew Grove, a founder of Intel Corporation, "The worse the news, the more effort should go into communicating it."[4] Grove should know: Intel, like most companies, has communicated its share of bad news, including thousands of layoffs.

How you write your messages won't change the news, but it may determine how your reader responds. The potential negative consequences are serious: people who don't like the news or the way you present it are more likely to tell others.

You have several goals in communicating bad news:

- Make your decision clear.
- Help your audience accept the message.
- Maintain a goodwill relationship.
- Prevent further unnecessary discussion.
- Preserve the company's image.
- Protect the company against lawsuits.

To achieve these goals, we need to revisit components of the communication model presented in Chapter 1: the communication context, audience analysis, and media choice.

8-1a Communication Context

When managers are faced with communicating bad news, they first consider the context for the message. Is the message minor (e.g., an unimportant delayed shipment) or major (e.g., a significant company reorganization)? How formal is the company culture? A more formal culture may require longer messages and a more formal tone. What are the legal and ethical considerations? Should corporate attorneys review the message? If so, can you maintain a personal tone and empathy toward the reader, while meeting legal requirements? What is the urgency of the message? Does your audience need to know the information and take action quickly?

Rarely is bad news given in a vacuum. At the end of the chapter, we'll look at examples of layoff emails, arguably the worst news employees can hear. But long before these decisions are communicated, managers can keep employees informed about organizational problems, such as declining revenue, so they aren't blindsided by the news. Explaining decisions before they're finalized connects employees to the company and positions bad news within a larger organizational context.[5] In addition to assessing the context for your communication, you'll want to analyze your audience.

8-1b Audience Analysis

Review the audience analysis questions in Chapter 4.

Understanding your audience's perspective is a critical step, particularly when communicating bad news. The audience analysis questions in Chapter 4, Figure 2, help us determine how to convey the message so it's as well received as possible.

In a bold move, Founder, Chairman, and Interim CEO of RealNetworks Rob Glaser posted his layoff email to employees on his personal Facebook page after sending it internally.[6] He did the same when the company laid off employees two years prior.[7] Glaser probably realized that the emails would be leaked anyway, so why not publish them himself (Figure 1)? By doing so, Glaser considers both his primary audience—employees—and secondary audiences, such as customers, investors, and the media, who would be interested in the news.

8-1c Media Choice

As we discussed in Chapter 1, the medium you choose for your message is critical. Most people prefer to give and receive bad news in person.[8] But this doesn't always happen. When Yahoo!'s former CEO Carol Bartz was terminated, she sent an email to all employees: "I am very sad to tell you that I've just been fired over the phone. . . ." Known as an abrasive manager, Bartz sounded angrier than usual.[9]

When communicating bad news, you may achieve your purpose better with a personal visit or phone call than with a written message. Particularly if the news has serious consequences—for example, an employee's promotion wasn't approved, or his or her job has been relocated to another state—then a face-to-face meeting is most appropriate.

However, in-person meetings are not always practical. When meeting in person is too expensive because of travel, or when the news needs to be delivered quickly to many people, we have to choose another medium. For these and other situations, email may be the best option.

 Communication **TECHNOLOGIES**

 Emotional **INTELLIGENCE**

Do you avoid giving bad news in person? Have you hid behind technology rather than confront someone face-to-face? What were the consequences?

Email is so pervasive in business that it is often used for communicating bad news. Compared to face-to-face meetings, email has the following advantages for delivering bad news:

- Allows the sender to determine precise wording.
- Gives the reader time to absorb and understand the message before reacting.
- Ensures a consistent message when sent to many people.
- Controls the message timing when sent to many people.
- Provides a permanent record of what was communicated.
- Ensures a more accurate and complete message.

This last point is a particularly interesting one, based on a study about delivering bad news by email rather than in person or by phone. The study authors hypothesize that because communicating bad news is difficult, the sender often delays, distorts, or incompletely communicates the message. Email may provide just enough distance to help senders communicate more clearly.[10]

When deciding which medium to use for your message, you might consider how the original message was sent. For example, if you received a request over the phone, it's probably best to respond with a phone call rather than an email; otherwise, the receiver may think you're avoiding a more genuine response. But a quick IM request ("Can you please join the meeting at 2?") needs only a quick IM reply ("Sorry, I'm meeting with Ted at 2 and don't want to change it").

For complex decisions and significant organizational changes, several messages are sent through various channels to both internal and external audiences.

LO2 Write components of a bad-news message.

8-2 Components of Bad-News Messages

Bad-news messages are so varied and potentially sensitive that no one structure or approach applies. To achieve your objectives and meet audience needs, you'll want to consider how to organize the message, explain the decision, give the bad news, and close the message.

8-2a Organizing the Message

Emotional INTELLIGENCE

Do you prefer to hear bad news directly or more indirectly, perhaps after an explanation of the decision? Does your own style get in the way of how you deliver bad news to others? In other words, do you use your preferred style rather than what might be best for your audience?

How you open your bad-news message depends on the content of the message, your relationship with the reader, the reader's expectations, and other factors.[11] Will you present the news right up front or wait until the very end? Often, something in between will work best. The decision is even more complicated with email: is your message in the subject line or within the body of the email? You may choose a subject that hints at bad news but isn't too specific, as in Jamie Dimon's message in the chapter introduction: "Sharing some personal news."

Most U.S. messages about bad news use the direct organizational plan, with the news fairly quickly up front. We see this approach in Jamie Dimon's message. But business is complex and requires us to consider options along a continuum of direct and indirect organizational plans.[12] When deciding how quickly to present the bad news, consider these questions:

- **What is the content of your message?** If the bad news is a small, insignificant issue, then consider presenting the news up front and following with a brief rationale. If the news affects people personally and may elicit an emotional reaction, you may want to provide your rationale before delivering the bad news. And if the situation is highly complex, you may need to provide more explanations before you state the news.
- **How important is the news?** In a crisis situation or when the news may prevent harm, the news should be right up front. When responding to repeated, unreasonable requests or in other situations when a forceful "no" is in order, also present the news clearly and early on.

- **What are the reader's expectations?** Even in worst-case scenarios, such as layoffs, if employees know the news is coming, a more direct approach may work best. Delaying the inevitable may feel manipulative and will frustrate the reader. But if an employee is expecting a positive response about a proposal, a softer approach with your rationale first may be more appropriate. Cultural expectations, as discussed in Chapter 2, also affect structure; people in high-context cultures may prefer a less direct style than people in low-context cultures.

International
COMMUNICATION

- **What is your relationship with the reader?** When writing to people who report to you, you might choose a less direct style: employees likely will read your entire message, and you can explain the rationale to help them understand a decision that affects them negatively. On the other hand, senior-level managers may prefer news up front to avoid too much reading. Also consider how well you know your audience. For people you communicate with regularly, a more direct style may be acceptable, while people you don't know well may need more relationship building that happens in indirect messages.

To ease into a bad-news message, some writers start with a one- or two-sentence, neutral buffer before stating the bad news. Research is mixed about whether buffers really soften the blow of bad news,[13,14] but buffers are commonly used when writing to customers and job applicants. Effective buffers that are neutral, interesting, relevant, short, and supportive can provide a more subtle approach to bad news (Figures 2 and 3).

Characteristics of Effective Opening Buffers | **Figure 2**

Situation: A manufacturer of home theater systems denies a request from a store owner (Parker Electronics) to provide a demonstration model for the store.

Neutral
- Does not convey the news immediately.
- Resists implying positive news, which is misleading.

Not neutral: "Stores like Parker benefit from our policy of not providing demos of our home theater systems."
Misleading: "Your store would be a great venue for a demo product."

Interesting
- Motivates the receiver to continue reading.
- Avoids obvious information.

Obvious: "We have received your request for an in-store demo model."

Relevant
- Provides a smooth transition to the reasons that follow.
- Refers to the original request.

Irrelevant: "Our new V12 system has received rave reviews from the December issue of *Consumer Reports*."

Short
- Gets to the main point quickly.

Too Long: "As you may remember, for many years we provided in-store demos of our audio systems. We were happy to do this because we felt that customers needed to hear the surround effects and superior quality compared to competitors' systems. We discontinued this practice last year because ..."

Supportive
- Establishes compatibility between the reader and writer.
- Avoids controversy and condescension.

Not supportive: "You must realize how expensive it would be to supply a demo for every store that sells our products."

We use a buffer in a sincere effort to help the reader accept the disappointing news, not to manipulate or confuse the reader. Imagine a situation where an employee is called into a manager's office and doesn't know what to expect. In the exchange in Figure 4, does the manager use buffers well, or is the employee simply rebuffed? A long, false buffer is not ethical communication.

Ethics in
COMMUNICATION

Figure 3 Types of Buffers

BUFFER TYPE	EXAMPLE
Agreement	We both recognize the promotional possibilities of having in-store demos.
Appreciation	Thanks for letting us know of your success in selling our V12 Home Theater System. (*Avoid, however, thanking the reader for asking you to do something that you're going to refuse to do, which would sound insincere.*)
Compliment	Congratulations on having served the community of Greenville for ten years.
Facts	Three-fourths of our distributors sold at least 50% more V12 systems than the older A19 model.
General principle	We believe in giving our distributors a wide range of support in promoting our products.
Good news	Our upcoming 20% off sale will be heavily advertised and will likely increase traffic for the holiday season.
Understanding	We want to help you boost sales of the V12.

Figure 4 Buffered or Rebuffed?

1 **Manager:** "Hi, Melissa, how are you doing today?"

2 **Employee:** "Great. I finished the Gap proposal yesterday, and I'm waiting for their response."

3 **Manager:** "How do you think the proposal turned out? You're so good at pricing and figuring out exactly what the client needs."

4 **Employee:** "Thank you. I enjoy writing proposals, and I'm confident about Gap."

5 **Manager:** "That's great. I'm glad to hear it. But . . ."

6 **Employee:** "Yes? Is something wrong?"

7 **Manager:** "Well, no, nothing is wrong, but Paul called, and we didn't get the Gap project."

8 **Employee:** "We didn't? Why didn't you just say so?"

8-2b Explaining the Decision

Presumably, you have good reasons for reaching your negative decision. Whether you presented the news up front or later in your message, explaining your reasons may help your audience accept the decision—and providing your rationale is the right thing to do as an ethical communicator. Most of your message should focus on the reasons rather than on the bad news itself.

For bad-news messages about unimportant issues and in crisis situations, provide the reasons concisely and matter-of-factly. In emergency situations, no one has time for long explanations—these can come later.

Bad-news messages that affect people personally and may face resistance require more careful planning because the stakes are typically greater. Present the reasons honestly and convincingly. If possible, explain how the reasons benefit the reader or, at least, benefit someone other than your organization, as illustrated in these examples:

- You don't provide copies of company documents in order to protect the confidentiality of customer transactions.
- You raised prices of a product in order to use a greener manufacturing process.
- You don't exchange worn garments in order to offer better quality merchandise to your customers.

To help readers accept your decision when using the direct plan, present a brief rationale along with the bad news in the first paragraph. When Hostess Brands announced its bankruptcy, the company issued a statement blaming a union strike for dooming the maker of beloved Ho Hos, Ding Dongs, Sno Balls, and Twinkies.[15] The main point—the company closure—was up front in the summary paragraph: "We are sorry to announce that Hostess Brands Inc. has been forced by a Bakers Union strike to shut down all operations and sell all company assets."[16] (If you're worried that you may never again taste a Twinkie, fear not: the company has since been purchased.[17])

The New York Museum of Modern Art took a softer approach when rejecting an offer from Andy Warhol, one of the most popular and successful artists of our time. In a letter from 1956 (Figure 5), the museum starts with a one-sentence buffer and explains that the decision is based on their "severely limited gallery and storage space." This is a convincing argument—and much kinder than giving personal negative opinions about the drawing. Of course, the rejected drawing would be worth quite a bit of money today.

Presenting reader benefits keeps your decision from sounding selfish. Sometimes, however, granting the request is simply not in the company's best interests. In such situations, don't invent false reader benefits; instead, just provide whatever short explanation you can and let it go at that.

> Because this data would be of strategic importance to our competitors, we treat the information as confidential. Similar information about our entire industry (SIC Code 1473), however, is collected in the annual U.S. Census of Manufacturing. These census reports are available online for public access.

Show the reader that your decision was a *business* decision, not a personal one. Also show that the request was taken seriously, and don't hide behind company policy. People are turned off by hearing "That's just our policy" if it doesn't make sense to them. If the policy is a sound one, it was established for good reasons; therefore, explain the rationale for the policy.

☒ NOT   Company policy prohibits our providing an in-store demonstration product.

> ☑ BUT   We surveyed our dealers three years ago and found that the space taken up by in-store demos and the resulting traffic problems were not worth the effort. Dealers also had trouble selling demo products, even with large discounts.

The reasons justifying your decision should take up the major part of the message, but be concise, or your readers may become impatient. Do not belabor a point, and do not provide more background than is necessary. If you have several reasons for refusing a request, present the strongest ones first—where they will receive the most emphasis—and omit weak reasons. Why invite a rebuttal? Stick with your most convincing arguments.

Figure 5 | Andy Warhol Rejection Letter

THE MUSEUM OF MODERN ART

NEW YORK 19

11 WEST 53rd STREET
TELEPHONE: CIRCLE 5-8900
CABLES: MODERNART, NEW-YORK

THE MUSEUM COLLECTIONS

October 18, 1956

Dear Mr. Warhol:

Last week our Committee on the Museum Collections held its first meeting of the fall season and had a chance to study your drawing entitled Shoe which you so generously offered as a gift to the Museum.

I regret that I must report to you that the Committee decided, after careful consideration, that they ought not to accept it for our Collection.

Let me explain that because of our severely limited gallery and storage space we must turn down many gifts offered, since we feel it is not fair to accept as a gift a work which may be shown only infrequently.

Nevertheless, the Committee has asked me to pass on to you their thanks for your generous expression of interest in our Collection.

Sincerely,

Alfred H. Barr, Jr.
Director of the Museum Collections

Mr. Andy Warhol
242 Lexington Avenue
New York, New York

AHB:bj

P.S.   The drawing may be picked up from the Museum at your convenience.

8-2c Giving the Bad News

If you explained the reasons well, the decision will appear logical and reasonable—the *only* logical and reasonable decision that could have been made under the circumstances.

To retain the reader's goodwill, state the bad news in positive or neutral language, stressing what you *can* do rather than what you *cannot* do. Avoid writing *cannot, are not able to, impossible, unfortunately, sorry*, and *must refuse*.

☒ NOT   Your financial consulting firm is not appropriate for our type of business.

☑ BUT   To maintain confidentiality for our clients, we prefer to handle our financial analysis internally.

Phrase the bad news in impersonal language. Avoid *you* and *your* to distance the reader from the bad news; otherwise, the news may feel like a personal rejection. Also avoid *but* and *however* to introduce the bad news; most readers won't remember what was written before the *but*— only what was written after it.

Avoid giving the receiver opportunities to debate the decision. Present the news as final.

⊠ NOT   The contract is scheduled to end on April 2, but if you need more time, let us know.

☑ BUT   The contract will end on April 2.

8-2d Closing the Message

Any refusal, even when handled skillfully, has negative overtones. Therefore, you need to end your message on a more pleasant note. Figure 6 provides approaches to avoid and techniques to use when closing a bad-news message.

Closing a Bad-News Message | **Figure 6**

Approaches to Avoid

Anticipating Problems
If you run into other problems, please write to me directly.

Inviting Needless Communication
If you have any further questions, please let me know.

Repeating the Bad News
Although we are unable to supply an in-store demo model, we do wish you much success during your holiday season.

Using a Cliché
If we can be of any further help, please don't hesitate to call us.

Revealing a Doubt
I trust that you now understand why we made this decision.

Sounding Selfish
Don't forget to feature the V12 prominently in your holiday display.

Techniques to Use

Offering Best Wishes
Best wishes for success during the holiday season. We have certainly enjoyed our ten-year relationship with Parker and look forward to continuing to serve your needs in the future.

Suggesting a Counterproposal
To provide increased publicity during the holidays, we would be happy to include a special 2-by-6-inch boxed notice of your sale in the *Greenville Courier* edition of our ad on Sunday, February 8. Just send us your copy by January 26.

Directing to Other Sources
To provide increased publicity for the holiday season, we would be happy to provide a demo of the A19 model.

Referring to Sales Promotions
You can be sure that the V12 we're introducing this month will draw many customers to your store during the holidays.

To sound sincere and helpful, make your ending original and positive. If you provide a counterproposal or offer other sources of help, provide all information the reader needs to follow through.

The Checklist for Bad-News Messages summarizes guidelines for writing these difficult messages. The rest of this chapter discusses strategies for writing bad-news replies, writing bad-news announcements, and giving and receiving constructive feedback.

Checklist for Planning and Writing Components of Bad-News Messages

ASSESS THE COMMUNICATION CONTEXT

Consider the content of the message, the organizational culture, ethical responsibilities, legal requirements, level of urgency, and other factors.

ANALYZE THE AUDIENCE

Use the questions from Chapter 4, Figure 2, to increase the chances that your audience will react positively to your message.

CHOOSE THE MEDIUM

Most people prefer to receive bad news in person. However, email may be used to control the message and when face-to-face conversations aren't possible.

WRITE COMPONENTS OF THE MESSAGE

Organize the Message
- ☑ Consider more direct approaches (with the news up front) for insignificant news, in urgent situations, and when you expect little audience resistance.
- ☑ Consider more indirect approaches (with the news later) for complex situations, when you expect more audience resistance, and when your audience prefers this style.

Explain the Decision
- ☑ State reasons in positive language.
- ☑ Avoid relying on "company policy"; instead, explain the reason behind the policy.
- ☑ State reasons concisely; do not over explain.
- ☑ Present the strongest reasons first; avoid discussing weak reasons.

Give the Bad News
- ☑ Present the bad news as a logical outcome of the reasons given.
- ☑ State the bad news in positive and impersonal language. Avoid terms such as *cannot* and *your*.
- ☑ Make the refusal final.

Close the Message
- ☑ Make your closing original, friendly, off the topic of the bad news, and positive.
- ☑ Consider expressing best wishes, offering a counterproposal, or suggesting other sources of help.
- ☑ Avoid anticipating problems, inviting needless communication, referring to the bad news, repeating a cliché, revealing doubt, or sounding selfish.

LO3 Write a bad-news reply.

Emotional INTELLIGENCE

How resilient are you when receiving bad news? Does it tend to discourage you or inspire you to improve?

8-3 Composing Bad-News Replies

Even the best written bad-news message can test a reader's goodwill, particularly when the reader has made a request that you reject. In this section, you'll learn principles for writing five types of negative replies while maintaining a positive relationship:

- Rejecting an idea
- Refusing a favor
- Refusing a customer's request
- Declining a job offer
- Turning down a job candidate

8-3a Rejecting an Idea

One of the more challenging bad-news messages to write is one that rejects someone's idea or proposal. Put yourself in the role of the person making the suggestion, for example, Grace Lee, who recommended that Jason's Deli and Restaurant add hot food items (presented in Chapter 7, Figure 3). Grace was excited about her idea and wants her suggestion to be accepted.

If Jason decides to reject Grace's idea, he'll be in a tough spot. He needs to explain his decision without discouraging Grace from submitting ideas in the future. If his communication is successful, Jason will achieve the following:

- Recognize Grace's hard work.
- Educate Grace by explaining business realities she may not know.
- Focus on business—not personal—reasons for the decision.

Let's see how Jason's message turned out (Figure 7). His email communicates bad news, but it's also a *persuasive* message. Like all bad-news messages, the email persuades the reader that the writer's position is reasonable.

Rejecting an Idea | Figure 7

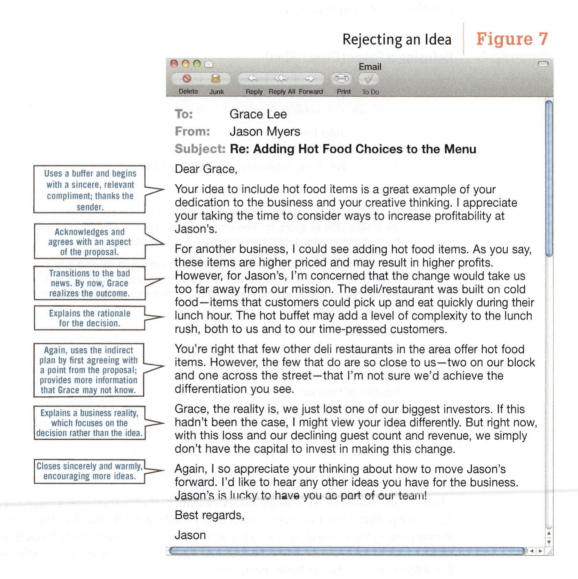

Uses a buffer and begins with a sincere, relevant compliment; thanks the sender.

Acknowledges and agrees with an aspect of the proposal.

Transitions to the bad news. By now, Grace realizes the outcome.

Explains the rationale for the decision.

Again, uses the indirect plan by first agreeing with a point from the proposal; provides more information that Grace may not know.

Explains a business reality, which focuses on the decision rather than the idea.

Closes sincerely and warmly, encouraging more ideas.

To: Grace Lee
From: Jason Myers
Subject: Re: Adding Hot Food Choices to the Menu

Dear Grace,

Your idea to include hot food items is a great example of your dedication to the business and your creative thinking. I appreciate your taking the time to consider ways to increase profitability at Jason's.

For another business, I could see adding hot food items. As you say, these items are higher priced and may result in higher profits. However, for Jason's, I'm concerned that the change would take us too far away from our mission. The deli/restaurant was built on cold food—items that customers could pick up and eat quickly during their lunch hour. The hot buffet may add a level of complexity to the lunch rush, both to us and to our time-pressed customers.

You're right that few other deli restaurants in the area offer hot food items. However, the few that do are so close to us—two on our block and one across the street—that I'm not sure we'd achieve the differentiation you see.

Grace, the reality is, we just lost one of our biggest investors. If this hadn't been the case, I might view your idea differently. But right now, with this loss and our declining guest count and revenue, we simply don't have the capital to invest in making this change.

Again, I so appreciate your thinking about how to move Jason's forward. I'd like to hear any other ideas you have for the business. Jason's is lucky to have you as part of our team!

Best regards,

Jason

8-3b Refusing a Favor

People rely on friends and coworkers in companies for favors. We do favors for each other out of service and because we may need a favor in return some day. But, for business or personal reasons, we cannot always accommodate requests.

How you write your message refusing a favor depends on the circumstances. If someone asks for a favor that requires a large time commitment, he or she probably wrote a thoughtful message trying to persuade you. In this case, a longer, more thoughtful response is appropriate.

Most requests for favors, however, are routine, and you may write your response using the direct organizational plan. A colleague asking you to attend a meeting in her place, an employee asking for a deadline extension, or a business associate inviting you to lunch will not be deeply disappointed if you decline. The writer probably has not spent a great deal of energy composing the request; he or she simply wants a "yes" or "no" response.

Imagine a situation where an employee requests free conference admission for a planning committee. In Figure 8, Swati Mellone uses the direct plan to give her refusal in the first paragraph. After denying the request, she gives clear reasons for the decision and offers a possible alternative without making promises.

Figure 8 | Refusing a Favor (Direct Plan)

To: Julia Foreman
From: Swati Mellone
Subject: Re: Free Admission to the Conference?

Hi Julia,

You did such a great job managing the budget for the conference that we'll have little to spare for free employee admission. Also, one of the budget assumptions was that employees would pay their own way.

The conference is still a few weeks away, so we could receive a few more donations. If this happens, I will certainly discuss your request with the other executive members. As the conference date approaches, I'll keep you updated.

Best regards,

Swati

Swati Mellone
Director of Finance
Tarmot Intelligence, Inc.
818-555-3854

8-3c Refusing a Customer Request

A buffer, as mentioned earlier, is almost always used when refusing a customer's request because the reader (a dissatisfied customer) is emotionally involved in the situation. The customer is already upset by the failure of the product or service to live up to expectations. If you refuse the request immediately, you risk losing the customer's goodwill—and, as discussed earlier, having the situation go viral through social media sites.

Listen to the Comcast call at bit.ly/1qbeNaY.

When a customer tried to cancel his Comcast cable subscription, the service representative did such a poor job that the call went viral. The Comcast agent demanded an explanation and refused to cancel the account without one. The call took 18 minutes and prompted an apology from the company's chief operating officer: "We are embarrassed by the tone of the call and the lack of sensitivity to the customer's desire to discontinue service."[18] Comcast still lost the account—and possibly many more.

Companies don't have to grant all requests, but they do have to handle the communication well. Always use a respectful tone with customers—even when the customer is at fault. To separate the reader from the refusal, begin with a buffer, using one of the techniques presented earlier (e.g., showing understanding).

When explaining the reasons for denying the request, do not accuse or lecture the reader. At the same time, however, don't appear to accept responsibility for the problem if the customer is at fault. Use impersonal, neutral language to explain why the request is being denied.

> ☒ NOT The reason the handles ripped off your Samsonite luggage is that you overloaded it. The tag on the luggage clearly states that you should use the luggage only for clothing, with a maximum of 40 pounds. However, our engineers concluded that you had put at least 65 pounds of items in the luggage.

> ☑ BUT On receiving your piece of Samsonite luggage, we sent it to our testing department. The engineers there found stretch marks on the leather and a frayed nylon stitching cord. They concluded that such wear could have been caused only by contents weighing substantially more than the 40-pound maximum weight that is stated on the luggage tag. Such use is beyond the "normal wear and tear" covered in our warranty.

Note that in the second example, the pronoun *you* is not used at all when discussing the bad news. By using third-person pronouns and the passive voice, the example avoids directly accusing the reader of misusing the product. The actual refusal, given in the last sentence, is conveyed in neutral language.

As with other bad-news messages, close on a friendly, forward-looking note. If you can offer a compromise, it will take the sting out of the rejection and show the customer that you are reasonable. Compromises also help the customer save face. Be careful, however, not to take responsibility.

> Although we replace luggage only when it is damaged in normal use, our repair shop tells me the damaged handle can easily be replaced. We would be happy to do so for $38.50, including return shipping. If you would like us to do this, please respond to this email, and we will return your repaired luggage within two weeks.

Somewhere in your letter you might include a subtle pitch for resale. Although the customer has had a negative experience with your product, you might remind him or her why he or she bought the product in the first place. But use this technique carefully; a strong pitch may simply annoy an already-unhappy customer.

8-3d Declining a Job Offer

When you're fortunate enough to have more than one job offer, you'll need to gracefully decline one (or more) opportunities. This may seem easy, but you never know where you'll work in the future, and how you turn down the job may affect your prospects with the company down the road. Consider these questions as you decide how to communicate your decision:

- What relationships did you build during the selection process? Did you make a special connection with anyone? Did someone go out of his or her way to make you feel comfortable? Express your appreciation in a way that respects the time the employer invested and how well they accommodated you throughout the process.
- Did you meet with multiple people? Did they reimburse your travel expenses? In these situations, you'll want to take extra care in how you tell your main contact that you won't accept the job. You also may want to reach out (typically, through email) to others who interviewed you.

- What is your reason for declining the job? Try to be tactful in how you explain your decision. Saying that another company offered you more money may be off-putting. Is the other job in a city where you prefer to work? Are the job responsibilities closer to what you hoped to be doing?

In most cases, email will be the most appropriate way to decline an offer. The emails in Figure 9 are from a candidate who is in a particularly delicate situation: a good family friend recommended her for the position. Both emails maintain good relationships—and you can tell that the candidate has been in continuous communication with everyone involved.

<table>
<tr><td>Figure 9</td><td>Declining a Job Offer</td></tr>
</table>

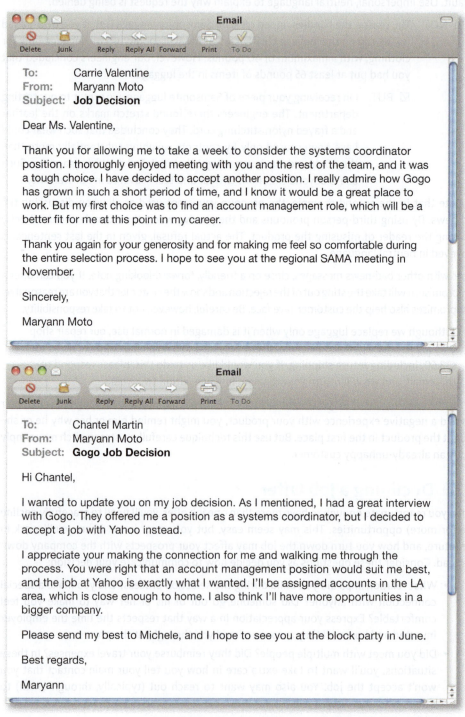

To: Carrie Valentine
From: Maryann Moto
Subject: **Job Decision**

Dear Ms. Valentine,

Thank you for allowing me to take a week to consider the systems coordinator position. I thoroughly enjoyed meeting with you and the rest of the team, and it was a tough choice. I have decided to accept another position. I really admire how Gogo has grown in such a short period of time, and I know it would be a great place to work. But my first choice was to find an account management role, which will be a better fit for me at this point in my career.

Thank you again for your generosity and for making me feel so comfortable during the entire selection process. I hope to see you at the regional SAMA meeting in November.

Sincerely,

Maryann Moto

To: Chantel Martin
From: Maryann Moto
Subject: **Gogo Job Decision**

Hi Chantel,

I wanted to update you on my job decision. As I mentioned, I had a great interview with Gogo. They offered me a position as a systems coordinator, but I decided to accept a job with Yahoo instead.

I appreciate your making the connection for me and walking me through the process. You were right that an account management position would suit me best, and the job at Yahoo is exactly what I wanted. I'll be assigned accounts in the LA area, which is close enough to home. I also think I'll have more opportunities in a bigger company.

Please send my best to Michele, and I hope to see you at the block party in June.

Best regards,

Maryann

8-3e Turning Down a Job Candidate

Almost everyone will apply for a job but not get an offer. This can be a painful process and should be handled sensitively.

Employers seldom give job candidates feedback. They fear discrimination lawsuits and having to further explain the decision.[19] Figure 10 is a template job rejection email recommended by the Society for Human Resource Management.[20] As a manager, you may customize this to sound more personal.

Form Rejection Email | **Figure 10**

> To:
> From:
> Subject:
>
> Dear [Insert Name],
>
> It was a pleasure meeting with you to discuss your background and interest in the [job title] position within our organization. We appreciate your time, attentiveness, and patience throughout the interview process. We did have several highly qualified candidates for the position, and it has been a difficult decision, but we have chosen to pursue another candidate for this position who we feel is best qualified.
>
> We do thank you for your interest in [Company Name], and we wish you good luck in your future endeavors.
>
> Sincerely,
>
> [Name]
> [Title]
> [Company Name]

With your employer's consent, you may choose to give feedback to candidates despite the risks. For an internal candidate, feedback will be expected and is important to the person's development. For students—as you can imagine—it's nice to get feedback to improve your chances for other jobs. If you made a personal connection with someone and want to give more specific reasons, have a phone conversation rather than send email. Also focus on specific job qualifications (e.g., "We had other candidates with more management experience" or "who had previous accounting internships") rather than vague, personal issues (e.g., "You didn't seem to be very motivated" or "We hired someone who seemed more confident"). Can you see how these last two statements could leave a candidate feeling that the decision was subjective?

Have you ever applied for a job, even interviewed with the company, and not heard back at all? When you're on the other side of the hiring decision, as a manager, be sure to communicate decisions with candidates as soon as you can so they can move on to other potential jobs. As with all bad news, avoiding it only makes it worse for the receiver.

8-4 Announcing Bad News

We just discussed strategies for writing negative replies. Often, however, we're presenting bad news about a new situation. Quite often, these messages go to a large internal or external audience. These are just some of the many examples of bad news that companies need to communicate:

- The company suffered a bad fiscal quarter.
- An executive is leaving.
- Employees will be laid off.
- A product is being discontinued.
- Prices are increasing.
- Stores will be closed or departments consolidated.
- The company has been acquired.
- The company is accused of wrongdoing.
- The company lost a big lawsuit.
- A product is being recalled.
- Service cannot be fulfilled.
- A fire caused damage.

Not every organizational change is negative for all audiences—for example, a company acquisition may be good news to shareholders and executives who will be retained, but bad news for employees who will be made redundant (a euphemism for fired). For this reason, messages about corporate change must be tailored to each audience affected, with particular attention paid to those affected negatively.

8-4a Bad News About Normal Operations

Let's look at how a cabin tent manufacturer might communicate a price increase to different audiences (Figure 11). The increase is a routine message for the order department but requires more explanation for wholesalers and end users. Of course, a smart company would provide its order department with all communications so that customer service representatives can answer questions about the change properly.

8-4b Bad News About the Organization

If your organization is experiencing serious problems, your employees, customers, and investors should hear the news from you—not from a newspaper, a blog, or the grapevine. For serious problems that receive widespread attention, the company's public relations department will issue a news release. In a crisis situation, the management team will have a crisis communication plan to ensure clear, consistent messages to all internal and external audiences.

Anything you write may be made public and could be taken out of context. When writing bad news about the company, choose your words carefully, but also recognize that you can't always control how your message is interpreted, as in the example in Figure 12.

The last sentence of the president's statement would have been more effective had it been worded in positive, impersonal language: "Fences are unnecessary in such isolated sites and, in fact, can cause safety hazards of their own. For example. . . ."

If the reader has already learned about the situation from other sources, your best strategy is to use a direct organizational plan. Confirm the bad news quickly, and immediately provide information to help the reader understand the situation: "When you entered the building this morning, you probably saw the broken window in the lobby. I'd like to tell you exactly what happened and what we're doing to ensure the safety of our employees who work during evening hours."

> **Situation: Management has decided to increase by 10% the price of the Danforth cabin tent you manufacture. You have to notify your order department, your wholesalers, and a special retail customer. How would you adapt your message to these different audiences?**

Order Department

To this group, the price change is routine. What matters most is how the procedures need to change, so you can probably send an email using the direct plan.

Effective March 1, the regular price of our Danforth cabin tent (Item R-885) changes from $148.99 to $164.99, an increase of 10%. Any order postmarked before March 1 should be billed at the lower price, regardless of when the order is actually shipped.

The new price will be shown in our spring catalog, and a notice is being sent immediately to all wholesalers. If you receive orders postmarked on or after March 1 but showing the old price, please notify the wholesaler before filling the order.

Wholesalers

Wholesalers probably won't be personally disappointed, so you may use the direct approach, but you do need to justify the price increase. The bad news is cushioned by presenting the reason (which is beyond your control) and including resale in the closing paragraph.

Because of the prolonged strike in South African mines, we now must purchase the chrome used in our Danforth cabin tent elsewhere at a higher cost. Thus, effective March 1, the regular price of the Danforth tent (Item R-885) will change from $148.99 to $164.99.

As a courtesy to our wholesalers, however, we are billing any orders postmarked prior to March 1 at the old price of $148.99. Please use the online form or call us at 800-555-9843 to place your order for what American Camper calls the "sock-it-to-me" tent.

Association for Backpackers and Campers

You have an exclusive marketing agreement with this organization. It promotes the Danforth cabin tent in each issue of *Field News,* its quarterly magazine, at no cost to you in exchange for your offering ABC members the wholesale price of $148.99 (a 26% savings).

This is a critical audience who may respond particularly negatively to the news. Use the indirect plan to communicate the price increase.

The popularity of the Danforth cabin tent that you feature in each issue of *Field News* is based partly on our exclusive use of a chrome frame. Chrome is twice as strong as aluminum, yet it weighs about the same.

Because of the prolonged strike in South African mines, we were faced with the choice of either switching to aluminum or securing the needed chrome elsewhere at a higher cost. We elected to continue using chrome in our tent. This decision to maintain quality has resulted in a change in the wholesale price of the Danforth cabin tent (Item R-885) from $148.99 to $164.99.

The Danforth tent promotion in the spring issue of *Field News* should be changed to reflect this new price. Because the spring issue usually arrives the last week of February, we will bill any orders postmarked before March 1 at the lower price of $148.99.

We have enjoyed serving ABC members, and we extend best wishes to your organization for another successful year of providing such valuable service to American backpackers and campers.

If the reader is hearing the news for the first time, your best strategy is to use a less direct approach, using a buffer opening and stressing the most positive aspects of the situation (in this case, the steps you're taking to prevent a recurrence of the problem): "We are increasingly concerned about the safety and well-being of our night-shift employees. We're taking several steps as a result of an incident last night. . . ."

8-4c Bad News About Jobs

One of the toughest parts of a manager's job is communicating bad news about employees' jobs. When decisions affect people personally—particularly their livelihood and their self-esteem—no one wants to be the messenger.

Figure 12 | Misinterpreting a President's Message

Company President's Original Message	Reported as a News Item
Unlike several other firms in the area, we have always had a strict policy of not allowing any digging in residential areas. In fact, all our excavation sites are at least two miles from any paved road and are well marked by 10-foot signs. Because these sites are so isolated, our company does not require fences around these sites.	Although other drilling companies in the area erect 8-foot fences around their excavation sites, Owens-Ohio President Robert Leach admitted in a letter to shareholders yesterday that "our company does not require fences around these sites."

Companies regularly make decisions that have negative results for employees: they reduce benefits, relocate, change policies, and lay off employees. Maintaining employees' goodwill in these situations is just as important as maintaining customers' goodwill. Employees have the same ability to use traditional news channels and social media to gossip about the company, and with or without cause, they can sue you. In addition, of course, treating employees with respect is the right thing to do. At some point, your company hired these employees, hoping for a promising future with them.

In layoff emails, we see a range of approaches, some more effective than others if we think of them along a continuum of direct-indirect organizational plans (Figure 13). The direct plan, with the bad news up front, is most common in layoff emails, such as those of RealNetworks (shown in Figure 1) and Intel.[21] But an example from Starbucks is written in the indirect style. The CEO may have chosen this approach because of his management style, because of the organizational culture, or because employees were hearing the news for the first time and needed more context to understand the decision.[22] At the other end of the continuum is the Daily Voice email—a painfully indirect approach.[23]

Read the full Daily Voice email at bit.ly/YLpuA9.

Many different approaches work equally well for bad-news announcements about jobs, as long as employees are treated with dignity and respect.

LO5 Give and receive constructive performance feedback.

8-5 Giving and Receiving Constructive Performance Feedback

Another challenging situation for managers and employees is giving and receiving negative (or constructive) feedback about job performance. Managers who avoid telling employees that their performance isn't measuring up may think they're being nice, but they're doing employees a disservice, denying them the chance to improve. According to a recent international study, people want constructive feedback much more than they want positive feedback.[24]

On the other hand, managers may avoid giving constructive feedback because employees don't receive it well. How you react may improve how much feedback you receive—and in turn, how well it's delivered.

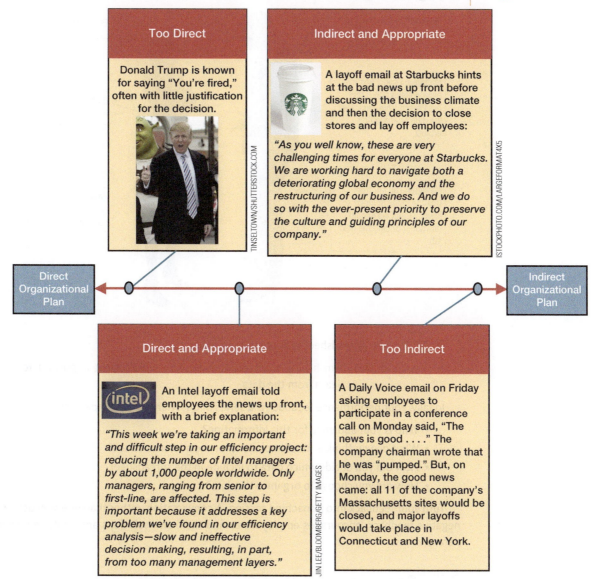

Too Direct

Donald Trump is known for saying "You're fired," often with little justification for the decision.

TINSELTOWN/SHUTTERSTOCK.COM

Indirect and Appropriate

A layoff email at Starbucks hints at the bad news up front before discussing the business climate and then the decision to close stores and lay off employees:

"As you well know, these are very challenging times for everyone at Starbucks. We are working hard to navigate both a deteriorating global economy and the restructuring of our business. And we do so with the ever-present priority to preserve the culture and guiding principles of our company."

ISTOCKPHOTO.COM/LARGEFORMAT4X5

Direct Organizational Plan ← → Indirect Organizational Plan

Direct and Appropriate

An Intel layoff email told employees the news up front, with a brief explanation:

"This week we're taking an important and difficult step in our efficiency project: reducing the number of Intel managers by about 1,000 people worldwide. Only managers, ranging from senior to first-line, are affected. This step is important because it addresses a key problem we've found in our efficiency analysis—slow and ineffective decision making, resulting, in part, from too many management layers."

JIN LEE/BLOOMBERG/GETTY IMAGES

Too Indirect

A Daily Voice email on Friday asking employees to participate in a conference call on Monday said, "The news is good . . . ." The company chairman wrote that he was "pumped." But, on Monday, the good news came: all 11 of the company's Massachusetts sites would be closed, and major layoffs would take place in Connecticut and New York.

8-5a Giving Constructive Feedback

As a manager, when you meet with an employee to give negative feedback, don't beat around the bush. In a *Harvard Business Review* blog post, Peter Bregman supports this direct approach:

> Next time you have a conversation you're dreading, lead with the part you're dreading. Get to the conclusion in the first sentence. Cringe fast and cringe early. It's a simple move that few of us make consistently because it requires emotional courage. At least the first time.

> But the more you do it, the easier and more natural it becomes. Being direct and up front does not mean being callous or unnecessarily harsh. In fact, it's the opposite; done with care, being direct is far more considerate.[25]

Let's take a new look at the dialog in Figure 4, with the manager giving the employee the news more directly (Figure 14).

The best feedback is actionable, meaning the employee can do something about it. Be specific and use principles for giving constructive feedback to team members discussed in Chapter 2.

Figure 14 | Giving Direct Feedback

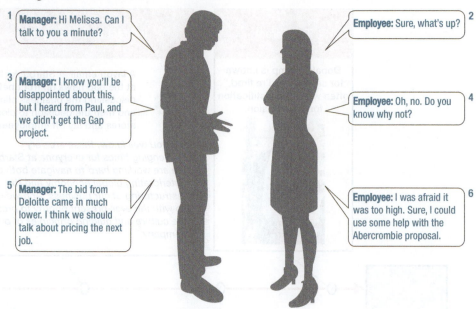

1 Manager: Hi Melissa. Can I talk to you a minute?

2 Employee: Sure, what's up?

3 Manager: I know you'll be disappointed about this, but I heard from Paul, and we didn't get the Gap project.

4 Employee: Oh, no. Do you know why not?

5 Manager: The bid from Deloitte came in much lower. I think we should talk about pricing the next job.

6 Employee: I was afraid it was too high. Sure, I could use some help with the Abercrombie proposal.

☒ **NOT** Your spreadsheet is impossible to read.

☑ **BUT** I'm having trouble understanding what's most important for me to learn from the data.

Ideally, your performance feedback is a series of questions to the employee:

- Who is your audience for this information?
- What do you think is most important for the audience to see?
- How did you decide which data to include in the spreadsheet?
- How did you choose to organize the data?

Turn your feedback into a coaching session. A conversation, rather than one-way delivery of negative feedback, encourages employees to find their own solutions and could reduce their defensiveness.

8-5b Receiving Constructive Feedback

You know that constructive feedback is necessary for your development, but how do you react when you hear it? Knowing that we all have some negative reactions to constructive feedback, answer the questions in Figure 15. Of course, how you receive it depends on how the feedback is delivered, how well you respect your manager, how confident you are about your work, and so on. Try to think about your typical response.

What did you learn about yourself that can help you improve how you receive feedback? Next time you hear constructive feedback, try these strategies:

- **Resist your first reaction.** Naturally, your instinct may be fear or anger. Take a breath and just listen without commenting for a while.
- **Demonstrate good listening skills.** Use the skills you developed from Chapter 3: pay attention; stay open-minded; don't interrupt; and involve yourself by taking notes, asking questions, nodding, and paraphrasing.
- **View the feedback as an opportunity.** Improving your job performance may improve how you feel about yourself and your work. Also, understanding and acting on constructive feedback may improve your relationship with your manager and your coworkers.

Emotional
INTELLIGENCE

When you look at your responses to the questions in Figure 15, which, if any, would you consider working on for yourself personally and professionally?

1. Feel personally attacked. ("She doesn't like me." "We never got along.")	Never	Sometimes	Always
2. Think the worst. ("I'm going to get fired." "They're going to give this project to someone else.")	Never	Sometimes	Always
3. Blame yourself too harshly. ("I'm terrible at this." "This job is too hard for me.")	Never	Sometimes	Always
4. Blame others. ("Why is this *my* fault?" "Why isn't he talking to xx about this?")	Never	Sometimes	Always
5. Argue with the feedback. ("That's not what happened." "She doesn't know the situation.")	Never	Sometimes	Always
6. Shut down. ("If he doesn't like my work, I won't continue on the project." "This is hopeless.")	Never	Sometimes	Always
7. Ignore the feedback. ("I'm just going to continue working the way I have been." "Time for a new job.")	Never	Sometimes	Always

- **Know that your reaction has consequences.** We've talked about negative reactions to feedback, but what about positive reactions? If you respond well to feedback, your manager will likely tell you more ways to improve and will view you as someone who can be coached and promoted within the organization.
- **Thank your manager.** We know that constructive feedback isn't easy to give. Consider saying something like, "I appreciate your telling me this. It was tough to hear, but it's important for me to know, and I'll definitely work on it."

Make it easy for your manager to give you the feedback you need to improve. Encourage him or her by asking for feedback about a specific project or task rather than general feedback—and by reacting positively when you hear it.

Announcing a CEO's Illness

>>> PURPOSE

Imagine that you are Jamie Dimon, CEO of JPMorgan. You need to tell employees and shareholders about the throat cancer diagnosis. (You read the beginning of the message in the chapter introduction.)

>>> PROCESS

1. **Describe your audiences for your message.**
   My primary audiences are employees and shareholders, but customers and others will read the news in the media.

2. **What are the objectives of your message?**
   I want people to know the diagnosis, so I can prevent rumors, but they must know that the prognosis is good. I want people to feel confident about the bank's future and continue to invest in the bank and use the bank's services.

3. **What main points will you include in your message?**
   - The diagnosis is throat cancer, and the prognosis is good.
   - The treatment will take about eight weeks.
   - I'll continue in my role, and the Board is supportive.
   - I'm proud of our employees and know that the bank will operate as successfully as it always does.
   - I'll provide updates as I have more information.

4. **How will you close the message?**
   I'll express my appreciation and end on a positive note.

>>> PRODUCT

Subject line: Sharing some personal news

Dear Colleagues and Shareholders –

I wanted to let you know that I have just been diagnosed with throat cancer. The good news is that the prognosis from my doctors is excellent, the cancer was caught quickly, and my condition is curable. Following thorough tests that included a CAT scan, PET scan and a biopsy, the cancer is confined to the original site and the adjacent lymph nodes on the right side of my neck. Importantly, there is no evidence of cancer elsewhere in my body.

My evaluation and treatment plan are still being finalized, but at this time it appears I will begin radiation and chemotherapy treatment shortly at Memorial Sloan Kettering Hospital, which should take approximately eight weeks. While the treatment will curtail my travel during this period, I have been advised that I will be able to continue to be actively involved in our business, and we will continue to run the company as normal. Our Board has been fully briefed and is totally supportive.

As you all know, we have outstanding leaders across our businesses and functions—the best team I've ever had the privilege of working with—so our company will move forward together with confidence as we continue to deliver first-class results for our customers, communities and shareholders.

I feel very good now and will let all of you know if my health situation changes.

I appreciate your support and want to thank our employees for the amazing work they do day-in and day-out. I'm very proud to be part of this company and honored to be working with such an exceptional group of people.

Jamie

Telling Employees About a Settlement

>>> PURPOSE

Imagine that you are the head of internal communication for JPMorgan. The bank has been charged with criminal activity connected to Bernard L. Madoff, who orchestrated an elaborate Ponzi scheme that lost billions of investors' dollars. (Read more about the JPMorgan settlement here: nyti.ms/1eGQyaF.)

This is bad news for JPMorgan, and employees need to understand the decision from the company's point of view. You decide to send an internal email to all staff.

>>> PROCESS

1. What is the purpose of your message?

2. Describe your audience.

3. At what point in the message will you convey the bad news?

4. Write the first sentence of your email. Be honest about the settlement, but try to put the bad news into perspective.

5. How will you explain the reasons for the decision? Don't hide facts, but you don't have to belabor them either.

6. Write the last sentence of your email. Strive for a forward-looking approach. How can you express optimism, despite the bad news?

>>> PRODUCT

Draft, revise, format, and proofread your email. Then submit both your answers to the process questions and your final email to your instructor.

LO1 Plan a bad-news message.

When writing a bad-news message, your goal is to convey the bad news and, at the same time, maintain the reader's goodwill. Consider the communication context, audience, and media choice before writing your message.

LO2 Write components of a bad-news message.

As you begin drafting, decide how to organize the message based on the content, importance, reader's expectations, and your relationship with the reader. Explain the decision by focusing on the reasons and reader benefits. Deliver the news using positive or neutral language, and close on a friendly, helpful note.

LO3 Write a bad-news reply.

When rejecting someone's idea, tact is especially important. Devote most of your message to presenting reasons based on business, not personal, beliefs. Most requests for favors are routine and should receive a routine response written in the direct organizational plan. Typically use the indirect plan when refusing a customer's request. The tone of your refusal must convey respect and consideration for the customer, even when the customer is at fault. When rejecting a job offer, maintain professionalism and consider the relationships you developed during the selection process. As a manager, follow up with everyone who interviewed for an open position. You may use a form rejection letter unless your employer has a different process.

LO4 Write a bad-news announcement.

Announcements of bad news may be either internal (addressed to employees) or external (addressed to those outside the organization) and may be about normal operations, the organization, or jobs. When people are affected personally, more time and care needs to be put into crafting a message that treats the reader with respect and dignity.

LO5 Give and receive constructive performance feedback.

Telling employees what they could do differently gives them the chance to improve their job performance. Use a direct approach and allow for a conversation in which the employee has time and space to react. When receiving feedback, try to stay open-minded and view the feedback as a good learning opportunity, even if it's painful or you don't, at first, agree with what you hear.

> EXERCISES

1. **Analyze a situation when you received bad news.**

   In groups of three or four, discuss a time when you received bad news. This could be anything work related or personal that is appropriate for you to discuss in class. What communication context is relevant to the message (organizational culture, ethical responsibilities, legal requirements, level of urgency, and so on)? What is important about the audience that should have been considered? What medium (or media) was used to convey the message?

   Given this background information, did you find the message effective? Why or why not? If not, what would have been a better approach?

   LO1 Plan a bad-news message.

2. **Analyze an audience to receive bad news.**

   For the situation you discussed in Exercise 1, complete an audience analysis using the questions from Chapter 4: Who is the audience? What is your relationship with the audience? How will the audience likely react? What does the audience already know? What is unique about the audience?

If these questions had been considered, how might they have influenced how the communication was handled?

3. **Consider media choices for bad-news message.**

   Discuss these situations in small groups, and decide what medium to use for each message. There are no perfect answers; just listen to each other's perspective and try to come to consensus.

   - If you managed a restaurant and had to tell 18 employees that the restaurant would be closed tonight because of allegations of food poisoning, how would you deliver the news?

   - If you lay off a manager and his or her entire department of eight people who work in four different countries, how would you deliver the news to the employees?

   - If an employee works in California, and you (the manager) work in New York, how would you tell her that you're leaving the company?

   - If you were a manager visiting a client in Qatar and learned from Human Resources that one of your employees in Boston was hospitalized, how would you communicate with the employee? How would you communicate with his coworkers?

LO2   Write components of a bad-news message.

4. **Organize a bad-news message.**

   For the following situations, would you use a more direct or a more indirect organizational plan for a written message? When you choose an organizational plan, you're making assumptions about your readers and how they might react. Discuss your ideas in small groups.

   - After three on-site job interviews, you decline an offer for a summer internship with an alumnus of your college.

   - After meeting a CEO at an on-campus job fair, you decline an interview with the company because it is not in your hometown.

   - You decline a lunch invitation from a college friend who works for a competitor.

   - You decline an employee's vacation request because he wants to be away during your busy season.

   - You inform a supplier that you do not plan to renew your contract.

   - You inform customers that a product has been discontinued.

5. **Practice writing buffers.**

   For the situations in Exercise 4 for which you chose a more indirect plan, write a buffer statement. Then compare your buffers with those of two other students. Which work best and why?

6. **Rewrite a layoff email.**

   When Microsoft sent an email to employees announcing layoffs, the company was criticized for using an indirect style.[26] Analyze the message and read a reporter's critique at nym.ag /WjXnvU. Then, rewrite the email using a more direct style that employees might better receive.

LO3   Write a bad-news reply.

7. **Send an email rejecting an idea for online ordering.**

   Imagine that you run a local used bookstore, where you receive this email from a new employee:

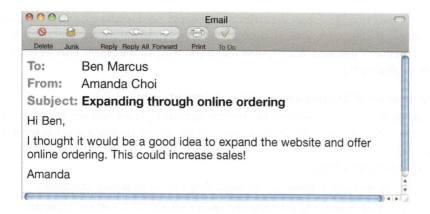

To: Ben Marcus
From: Amanda Choi
Subject: **Expanding through online ordering**

Hi Ben,

I thought it would be a good idea to expand the website and offer online ordering. This could increase sales!

Amanda

Write an email response to this employee rejecting the suggestion. You can invent whatever rationale you'd like, and keep in mind that this employee did not put a lot of thought into the suggestion.

8. **Write an email refusing an employee's request.**[27]

You manage the conventions department for a hotel, where you supervise an employee named Robert. Robert is responsible for meeting with companies that hold events at the hotel. This morning, you received the following email from Robert:

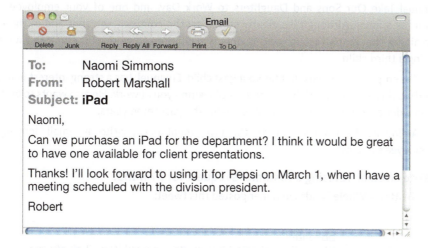

To: Naomi Simmons
From: Robert Marshall
Subject: **iPad**

Naomi,

Can we purchase an iPad for the department? I think it would be great to have one available for client presentations.

Thanks! I'll look forward to using it for Pepsi on March 1, when I have a meeting scheduled with the division president.

Robert

You won't be able to approve this request for the following reasons:

- You have no budget for this capital expense. It's possible to budget for this next year, but you're not sure an iPad just for client presentations would be worth the expense. You really don't see the point because you recently spent a lot on printing beautiful materials, which Robert takes to clients with him.

- Robert started work at your company only one month ago. Although you encourage ideas, you do not like Robert's presumptuous tone.

- Also, you'd like to encourage Robert to put more time and thought into his ideas. Although not a huge expense, an iPad for your department would need to be justified—and Robert would benefit from supporting his suggestions more convincingly.

- His preliminary marketing plan was due two days ago, but he hasn't submitted it yet. You'd like him to focus on his current responsibilities as a priority.

- On the other hand, you hired Robert because of his strong work background and excellent skills, and you *hope* he will have a long career with your company. Also, the hiring process was lengthy and expensive, and you have no desire to go through it again. You don't want to discourage him.

Write an email to Robert that rejects his request. Next, exchange emails with another student. At this point, your instructor may give you more information about Robert's perspective. If you were Robert, how would you react to the email? Provide feedback to the original writer.

9. **Write an email denying a request for a salary advance.**

Imagine that you own a website design firm, and an employee asks you for a favor: a one-month salary advance. This is one of your best employees, someone who has worked with you for more than five years, and you know she's buying a house. But you cannot advance her the money for these reasons:

- It's against your company policy (according to your employee handbook).
- You want to be fair to everyone and cannot accommodate others' requests.
- You don't want to set a precedent for this employee.
- You don't believe it's your responsibility.

Decide how you'll organize the email and which of these reasons you will present to the employee. You don't need to include everything unless you believe it will explain your rationale and maintain the employee's goodwill.

10. **Write an email rejecting an exception.**

Imagine that you work for a *Fortune* 500 investment bank. It's two weeks before the annual Take Our Sons and Daughters to Work Day, and one of your employees asks you for a favor. Although it's clearly stated on the company intranet and in the email reminder that employees may bring only two children to work, this employee wants to bring a third child.

The employee explains that his youngest child, Emanuel, has a strong interest in finance and would get a lot out of the experience of visiting you at work. He also wants to bring his two older children, who have participated for the past three years.

Acting as the HR Director for the investment bank, write an email denying the employee's request.

11. **Write an email refusing a customer's request for a refund.**

On Twitter, a Whole Foods customer posted this tweet:

bbkendel Barb Kendel
Whole Foods' salad bar made me sick! Was ill all afternoon at work. Want $9.59 back.
5 Jun

As a representative for Whole Foods, you find this tweet and send the customer a direct message (DM). In your message, reject her request for a refund. You may invent your own rationale for the decision. Also try including a subtle sales promotion in your closing paragraph.

Exchange drafts with a partner in class and give each other feedback on your approach.

12. **Write an email refusing a customer's request to waive a fee.**

Imagine that you work for Bank of America's credit card division, and you're trying to resolve a complaint from a customer. Through an online form on the website, you receive a customer's message, requesting that the bank waive $75 of overdraft fees accrued over the past three months.

Your policy doesn't require you to waive these fees, although you have for some customers. However, you deny this customer's request for two primary reasons:

- The customer had similar overdraft fees in the previous quarter, so the customer is aware of these fees.
- The customer's account is overdue; a bill has not been paid in two months.

Write an email to communicate your decision to the customer.

13. Decline a job offer.

Imagine that you interviewed for your dream job, but alas, you received an offer to be the supporting actor for a movie starring Jennifer Lawrence. You cannot pass up the opportunity. Write an email to the hiring manager turning down the job. Invent whatever details you would like.

14. Write a job rejection email—to yourself.

Think about a recent job for which you applied but weren't offered a position. If you received a generic or template rejection, write something more specific and personal. Even if you weren't the best candidate for the job, what would you have liked to have received from the employer?

15. Write a memo announcing employee layoffs.

You are the SVP of human resources for a financial software company that has 7,500 employees. The company has decided to sell AccountSoft, one of its major products. The software has suffered declining sales for the past two years, and it no longer fits with the new mission of the company, which is to sell to small businesses and individuals, rather than larger accounting firms (currently 95% of AccountSoft's buyers).

> **LO4** Write a bad-news announcement

You will have individual conversations with employees who are affected by the layoffs, but first you advise the CEO to send an email to all employees to announce the decision to sell AccountSoft and to prepare employees for the downsizing and what will happen next.

As you write this memo for the CEO to send under his name, consider that not all employees from the AccountSoft division will be laid off. The sales and marketing staff (about 150 people) will be leaving the firm, but the software developers will go to the acquiring firm, Accounting Support Services, Inc. This was your agreement with Accounting Support Services, as part of the acquisition deal.

Write the memo to communicate the decision clearly and help employees understand and accept the message.

16. Write an email to tell employees about a product recall.

As the vice president of public relations at Wilton Industries, you need to communicate to staff that one of your products has been recalled. The notice from the U.S. Consumer Product Safety Commission explains the potential burn hazard associated with your Chefmate Tea Kettle. Customers should return the kettle to Target to receive a full refund. Address an email to all Wilton employees to explain the situation.

17. Write a memo announcing no bonus.

You are the manager of a fitness equipment manufacturing plant called Muscles Galore. The plant has been in operation for seven years. Over the years, your employees have been very productive, and sales have been high. Therefore, Muscles Galore has been able to give generous holiday bonuses (usually more than $1,000) to all of its employees for the last five years.

This year, however, because of a slow economy, you will not be able to offer the holiday bonus. Although the workers have been very productive, fitness equipment sales are down about 15% from last year. Your projections indicate that the economy is recovering, and sales should be up about 20% next year. If the projections are accurate, you should be able to offer the bonus again next year—but you won't make any promises.

Write an email to your employees letting them know the bad news. Add details to make your message complete.

18. **Write a letter announcing a decision not to renew a lease.**

Assume the role of Gene Harley, the leasing manager of Northern Shopping Plaza. You have decided not to renew the lease of T-shirts Plus, which operates a tiny T-shirt decorating outlet in the mall. Three times in the past 13 months, the store's employees have left their heat-transfer machinery switched on after closing. Each time, the smoke activated the mall's smoke alarms and brought the fire department to the mall during the late-night hours. Although no damage has occurred, your insurance agent warns that the mall's rates will rise if this situation continues.

The lease that T-shirts Plus signed five years ago specifies that either party can decide not to renew. All that is required is written notification to the other party at least 90 days in advance of the yearly anniversary of the contract date. By writing this week, you will be providing adequate notice. Convey this information to the store's manager, Henry D. Curtis.

19. **Write an email about a party cancellation.**

Nobody likes a party more than Edgar Dunkirk, the president of Rockabilly Enterprises, a record label. In the early days, the company's holiday parties were legendary for their splendid food arrangements and outstanding entertainment (featuring the label's popular singing stars). Employees performed elaborate skits and competed for valuable prizes. These days, however, sales of the company's country and rockabilly recordings are down. In fact, Dunkirk recently had to lay off 150 of the company's 350 employees, the most severe austerity measure in the company's history.

Because so many employees had to be let go, including some who had helped Dunkirk found the company a decade ago, the president has decided that a lavish party would be inappropriate. He has therefore canceled the traditional holiday party. As Dunkirk's vice president of human resources, write an email communicating the news to Rockabilly's employees.

20. **Role-play giving and receiving feedback.**

Imagine that you own one of the Aggresshop stores you read about in the Company Scenario in Chapter 1 (and at the end of this chapter). Management changed the compensation plan that was too generous, which was causing sales associates to be overly aggressive with customers. At your store, you have encouraged associates to take a more service-oriented approach, and most have—offering help but not pushing unless customers ask for more personalized attention.

However, Brittany is still making customers feel uncomfortable in the store. Yesterday, you saw her ask someone twice if she needed help, and when the customer said, "No, thanks. I'm just looking," Brittany brought over an item for her to consider. Even after the customer refused the item, Brittany brought two more. The customer then said, "I'd like to look on my own. Is that OK here?" Then Brittany was curt with her, saying, "Well, OK. I was just trying to help you." The woman left the store soon after.

You would like to talk to Brittany about her idea of customer service and coach her to see the customer's perspective.

Role-play this situation with another student playing the role of Brittany. Have a third student observe the interaction, take notes, and give feedback using principles for giving and receiving feedback discussed in the chapter.

21. **Reflect on feedback you received in the past.**

In groups, talk about a time when you received negative performance feedback from a manager. How well did he or she convey the feedback, and how well did you receive it? Consider the questions in Figure 15. In retrospect, could you have handled the feedback differently?

COMPANY SCENARIO

Aggresshop

Let's revisit Aggresshop, the company struggling to improve customer service in its retail stores. As you read at the end of Chapter 1 and online, Aggresshop has received several customer complaints, and CEO Andrea Jewel is taking action.

Imagine that you are part of the company management team and receive this email from Andrea about a change in compensation structure:

COURTESY OF AMY NEWMAN

You'll find the Aggresshop situation at www .bizcominthenews.com/ aggresshop.

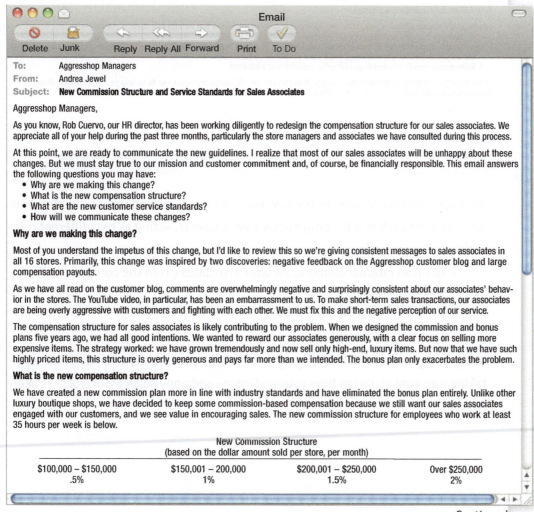

> **Email**
>
> Delete Junk   Reply Reply All Forward   Print To Do
>
> **To:** Aggresshop Managers
> **From:** Andrea Jewel
> **Subject:** New Commission Structure and Service Standards for Sales Associates
>
> Aggresshop Managers,
>
> As you know, Rob Cuervo, our HR director, has been working diligently to redesign the compensation structure for our sales associates. We appreciate all of your help during the past three months, particularly the store managers and associates we have consulted during this process.
>
> At this point, we are ready to communicate the new guidelines. I realize that most of our sales associates will be unhappy about these changes. But we must stay true to our mission and customer commitment and, of course, be financially responsible. This email answers the following questions you may have:
> - Why are we making this change?
> - What is the new compensation structure?
> - What are the new customer service standards?
> - How will we communicate these changes?
>
> **Why are we making this change?**
>
> Most of you understand the impetus of this change, but I'd like to review this so we're giving consistent messages to sales associates in all 16 stores. Primarily, this change was inspired by two discoveries: negative feedback on the Aggresshop customer blog and large compensation payouts.
>
> As we have all read on the customer blog, comments are overwhelmingly negative and surprisingly consistent about our associates' behavior in the stores. The YouTube video, in particular, has been an embarrassment to us. To make short-term sales transactions, our associates are being overly aggressive with customers and fighting with each other. We must fix this and the negative perception of our service.
>
> The compensation structure for sales associates is likely contributing to the problem. When we designed the commission and bonus plans five years ago, we had all good intentions. We wanted to reward our associates generously, with a clear focus on selling more expensive items. The strategy worked: we have grown tremendously and now sell only high-end, luxury items. But now that we have such highly priced items, this structure is overly generous and pays far more than we intended. The bonus plan only exacerbates the problem.
>
> **What is the new compensation structure?**
>
> We have created a new commission plan more in line with industry standards and have eliminated the bonus plan entirely. Unlike other luxury boutique shops, we have decided to keep some commission-based compensation because we still want our sales associates engaged with our customers, and we see value in encouraging sales. The new commission structure for employees who work at least 35 hours per week is below.
>
> **New Commission Structure**
> (based on the dollar amount sold per store, per month)
>
> | $100,000 – $150,000 | $150,001 – 200,000 | $200,001 – $250,000 | Over $250,000 |
> |---|---|---|---|
> | .5% | 1% | 1.5% | 2% |

Continued

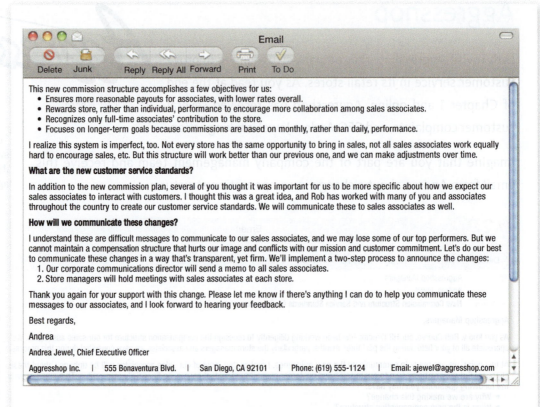

This new commission structure accomplishes a few objectives for us:
- Ensures more reasonable payouts for associates, with lower rates overall.
- Rewards store, rather than individual, performance to encourage more collaboration among sales associates.
- Recognizes only full-time associates' contribution to the store.
- Focuses on longer-term goals because commissions are based on monthly, rather than daily, performance.

I realize this system is imperfect, too. Not every store has the same opportunity to bring in sales, not all sales associates work equally hard to encourage sales, etc. But this structure will work better than our previous one, and we can make adjustments over time.

What are the new customer service standards?

In addition to the new commission plan, several of you thought it was important for us to be more specific about how we expect our sales associates to interact with customers. I thought this was a great idea, and Rob has worked with many of you and associates throughout the country to create our customer service standards. We will communicate these to sales associates as well.

How will we communicate these changes?

I understand these are difficult messages to communicate to our sales associates, and we may lose some of our top performers. But we cannot maintain a compensation structure that hurts our image and conflicts with our mission and customer commitment. Let's do our best to communicate these changes in a way that's transparent, yet firm. We'll implement a two-step process to announce the changes:
1. Our corporate communications director will send a memo to all sales associates.
2. Store managers will hold meetings with sales associates at each store.

Thank you again for your support with this change. Please let me know if there's anything I can do to help you communicate these messages to our associates, and I look forward to hearing your feedback.

Best regards,

Andrea

Andrea Jewel, Chief Executive Officer

Aggresshop Inc. | 555 Bonaventura Blvd. | San Diego, CA 92101 | Phone: (619) 555-1124 | Email: ajewel@aggresshop.com

Your role is to communicate the bad news, as we discussed in this chapter. Your instructor may ask you to complete two assignments, acting as two different roles within the organization:

- Write an internal memo to all sales associates (from the corporate communication director).
- Hold a face-to-face meeting with sales associates at one store (led by a store manager).

These assignments will challenge you to adjust your content for each message, taking into consideration how your audience—unhappy sales associates—is likely to react.

Endnotes

1. Steve Schaefer, "JPMorgan's Jamie Dimon Reveals Throat Cancer Diagnosis," *Forbes*, July 1, 2015, www.forbes.com/sites/steveschaefer/2014/07/01/jpmorgan-ceo-jamie-dimon-reveals-throat-cancer-diagnosis-in-internal-memo, accessed April 9, 2015.

2. Steve Schaefer.

3. Jessica Silver-Greenberg, "JPMorgan's Jamie Dimon Has Throat Cancer That He Calls 'Curable'," *The New York Times*, Dealbook, July 1, 2014, http://dealbook.nytimes.com/2014/07/01/jamie-dimon-of-jpmorgan-diagnosed-with-throat-cancer, accessed April 9, 2015.

4. Dianna Booher, *Communicate with Confidence: How to Say It Right the First Time and Every Time* (New York: McGraw-Hill, 1994).

5. Sandra L. French and Tracey Quigley Holden, "Positive Organizational Behavior: A Buffer for Bad News," *Business Communication Quarterly* 75, no. 2 (June 2012): 208–220.

6. "RealNetworks" Layoffs, *Facebook Newswire*, August 12, 2014, www.facebook.com/FBNewswire/posts/757267250978065, accessed April 10, 2015.

7. Nick Wingfield, "When Chief Executives Share Company News on Facebook," *The New York Times*, August 28, 2012, http://bits.blogs.nytimes.com/2012/08/28/when-chief-executives-share-company-news-on-facebook/, accessed January 10, 2013.

8. Rana Tassabehji and Maria Vakola, "Business Email: The Killer Impact," Communications of the ACM 48, no. 11 (November 2005): 64–70.

9. Verne G. Kopytoff and Claire Cain Miller, "Yahoo Board Fires Chief Executive," *The New York Times*, September 6, 2011, www.nytimes.com/2011/09/07/technology/carol-bartz-yahoos-chief-executive-is-fired.html, accessed January 10, 2013.

10. Stephanie Watts Sussman and Lee Sproull, "Straight Talk: Delivering Bad News Through Electronic Communication," *Information Systems Research* 10, no. 2 (June 1999): 150–166.

11. Gerald J. Alred, "'We Regret to Inform You': Toward a New Theory of Negative Messages," in Brenda R. Sims (Ed.), *Studies in Technical Communication: Selected papers from the 1992 CCCC and NCTE Meetings* (Denton: University of North Texas Press), 17–36.

12. Valerie Creelman, "The Case for 'Living' Models," *Business Communication Quarterly* 75, no. 2 (June 2012): 176–191.

13. Valerie Creelman.

14. Kitty O. Locker, "Factors in Reader Responses to Negative Letters," *Journal of Business and Technical Communication* 13 (1999): 5–48.

15. Rachel Feintzeig and Mike Spector, "Hostess Union Clings to Hope," November 18, 2012, *The Wall Street Journal*, www.wsj.com/articles/SB10001424127887323622904578127281230173980, accessed April 9, 2015.

16. "Hostess Brands Is Closed," Hostess Brands Website, November 21, 2013, http://hostessbrands.com/Closed.aspx, accessed March 18, 2013.

17. "Twinkies Return Expected by Summer, New Hostess Owner Says," *Chicago Tribune*, March 13, 2013, http://articles.chicagotribune.com/2013-03-13/business/chi-new-hostess-owner-eyes-twinkies-summer-return-20130312_1_twinkies-return-hostess-dean-metropoulos, accessed April 9, 2015.

18. Chris Morran, "Comcast Memo: Rep From 'Painful' Retention Call Was Doing 'What We Trained Him To Do'," *Consumerist*, July 21, 2014, http://consumerist.com/2014/07/21/comcast-memo-rep-from-painful-retention-call-was-doing-what-we-trained-him-to-do/, accessed April 9, 2015.

19. "Rejecting Candidates: What Should an Employer Tell a Candidate Who is Not Selected for the Position?" SHRM, May 8, 2014, www.shrm.org/templatestools/hrqa/pages/whatshouldanemployertellarejectedcandidate.aspx#sthash.fRTXEZAW.dpuf, accessed July 24, 2014.

20. "Interview: Rejection Letter - Position Filled," SHRM, www.shrm.org/templatestools/samples/hrforms/articles/pages/1cms_022524.aspx, accessed July 24, 2014.

21. Paul Otellini, "Making Intel More Efficient," *eWEEK*, posted July 14, 2006, www.eweek.com/c/a/Desktops-and-Notebooks/Otellini-Memo-Making-Intel-More-Efficient/, accessed April 9, 2015.

22. Howard M. Schultz, Memo to Employees, from Meg Marco, "300 Starbucks Will Close, Brand New Fancy Jet Will Be Sold," *Consumerist*, February 2, 2009, http://consumerist.com/2009/02/300-starbucks-will-close-brand-new-fancy-jet-will-be-sold.html, accessed April 9, 2015.

23. Camille Dodero, "How Not to Hold Layoffs: Company-Wide Email Promises 'Good' News on Friday, Bloodbath Ensues Monday," *Gawker*, http://gawker.com/5988606/how-not-to-hold-layoffs-company+wide-email-promises-good-news-on-friday-bloodbath-ensues-monday, accessed April 9, 2015.

24. Jack Zenger and Joseph Folkman, "Your Employees Want the Negative Feedback You Hate to Give," *Harvard Business Review Blog*, January 15, 2014, http://blogs.hbr.org/2014/01/your-employees-want-the-negative-feedback-you-hate-to-give/, accessed April 9, 2015.

25. "How to Start a Conversation You're Dreading," HBR Blog Network, July 7, 2014, http://blogs.hbr.org/2014/07/how-to-start-a-conversation-youre-dreading, accessed April 9, 2015.

26. Kevin Roose, "Microsoft Just Laid Off Thousands of Employees With a Hilariously Bad Memo," *New York*, July 17, 2014, http://nymag.com/daily/intelligencer/2014/07/microsoft-lays-off-thousands-with-bad-memo.html, accessed April 9, 2015.

27. Adapted and used with permission from David Lennox, Cornell University, School of Hotel Administration.

Planning the Report and Managing Data

LEARNING OBJECTIVES

After you have finished this chapter, you should be able to

LO1 Find relevant sources for a report.

LO2 Evaluate the quality of data.

LO3 Develop a questionnaire and cover letter.

LO4 Display quantitative information.

LO5 Interpret data for the report reader.

" *Cancer envy: I'd never have thought I would be envious of anyone with breast cancer, but I was.* "[1]

– Ali Stunt, CEO and Founder of Pancreatic Cancer Action

CHAPTER INTRODUCTION

Controversial Advertising Campaign Uses Surprising Data

An ad campaign from Pancreatic Cancer Action, a British organization, caused an uproar with the slogan, "I wish I had breast cancer."[2] The marketers knew what they were doing. Planning for outrage, Founder Ali Stunt introduced the campaign in a website post, "No Cancer Advert That Saves a Single Life Can Be Accused of Going Too Far." The post includes survival rates for cancers, with pancreatic at a sad 3%.[3]

Criticism of the campaign has been harsh, including this retort on the site IHateBreastCancer.com:

> Oh boy. Because obviously the best way to call attention to one disease is at the expense of another. . . . our research situation is much like yours: it sucks. Metastatic breast cancer is responsible for 90 percent of the morbidity and mortality, but gets less than 5 percent of the research budget.[4]

Data can be messy. The Pancreatic Cancer Action's statistics may be accurate, but do they tell the whole story? Similarly, do the breast cancer numbers give an accurate picture of public awareness and funding? Oversimplifying data may help get your point across but may lose the cause the long run.

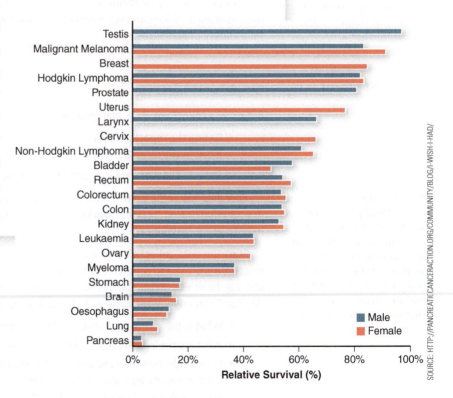

SOURCE: HTTP://PANCREATICCANCERACTION.ORG/COMMUNITY/BLOG/I-WISH-I-HAD/

9-1 Who Reads and Writes Reports

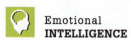

Emotional INTELLIGENCE

How do you feel about reading reports? Have you found them useful? Consider your own experiences and how that might affect your approach to writing reports.

Managers need information to make good business decisions, such as the following:

- A sales manager at General Motors headquarters uses information provided by field representatives to make sales projections. If hybrid car sales are up, manufacturing will ramp up to produce more.
- A vice president of information technology at CVS asks store managers to track wait times to determine how many cash registers are needed in each store.
- A human resources manager at The Home Depot surveys staff to pinpoint causes of low morale. If employees are unhappy with their opportunities for advancement, HR may implement a career development program.
- A product manager for Ben & Jerry's Ice Cream conducts market research to test a new flavor.
- A business development manager at Kroger studies a pilot gas station. If usage is high enough, the manager will recommend implementing stations at all stores.

These situations show why reports are essential to today's organization. Because managers don't always have the time, resources, or expertise, they often rely on others for information, analysis, and recommendations to help make decisions and solve problems. Reports travel upward, downward, and laterally within the organization, so reading and writing reports is a typical part of nearly every manager's responsibilities.

In any organization, unique problems and opportunities require situational reports, which are produced only once. These reports are often more challenging than ongoing reports, such as a weekly time log or monthly sales analysis, because they require the writer to start from scratch. For each report, writers need to determine what and how much information to include, and how best to organize and present the findings. These one-of-a-kind projects will be the focus of this chapter (see Figure 1 for an example).[5]

For our purposes, we define a business report as an organized presentation of information used to make decisions and solve problems (Figure 2). At work, you're likely to see many reports for a variety of audiences.

For guidelines on preparing other types of business reports, see Common Types of Business Reports in the Reference Manual at the end of this book.

9-2 Finding Sources for Your Report

LO1 Find relevant sources for a report.

Before you collect any data, plan your approach:

- Define the report purpose.
- Analyze the intended audience.
- Determine what data is needed to solve the problem or make a decision.

Your data will come from several sources. You may include data that you already have (either in your mind or from previous work), you may need to find data from other sources, or you may have to generate your own data.

Although the word *data* is technically the plural form of *datum*, in most cases in this text the term is used as a collective noun and takes a singular verb. The Usage Panel for the American Heritage Dictionary endorses this position.

Start the data-collection phase by factoring your problem—breaking it down to determine what data you need to collect. Let's say you own a small chain of restaurants and are considering offering healthier menu choices for children. What information would you need to make a decision? You might want answers to the following questions:

- What is the nutritional content of our current menu options for kids?
- What are the industry trends? How prevalent is the move toward healthier menus for kids?
- How might customers respond to the change? Will they choose healthier meals? If so, what kinds of meals would they prefer?
- How much would healthier food cost?

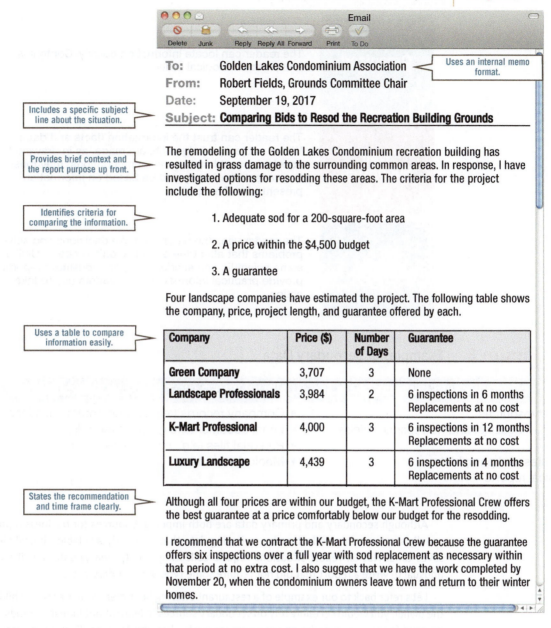

In addition to guiding your research, your questions may ultimately serve as the major divisions of your report.

Research and report writing are a cost, just like other corporate expenses. How much information do you need to make a good decision? You do not want to provide a $100 answer to a $5 question, but neither do you want to provide a $5 answer to a $100 question. A sensible approach to research will keep you focused on your goal: providing enough information to feel confident in your decision.

9-2a Identifying Types of Data

The two major types of data you will use are secondary and primary data. Secondary data is collected by someone else for some other purpose; it may be published or unpublished (Figure 3).

Primary data is collected by the researcher to solve a specific problem. Because you are collecting the data yourself, you have more control over its accuracy, completeness, objectivity, and relevance. The three main methods of primary data collection are surveys, observation, and experimentation.

Figure 2 | Criteria for a Business Report

| Organized | The reader can locate information quickly. Content is presented in a logical order. |

| Well Supported | The reader can trust the information (facts and data). Where subjective judgments are made, as in drawing conclusions and making recommendations, they must be presented ethically and be based on information presented in the report. |

| Useful | The reader uses the report to make decisions and solve problems that affect the organization's success. Unlike some scientific and academic reports, business reports provide practical information that readers use to take action. |

Figure 3 | Examples of Secondary Data

PUBLISHED (WIDELY DISSEMINATED)	UNPUBLISHED (NOT WIDELY DISSEMINATED)
• Internet resources • Journal, magazine, and newspaper articles • Books • Brochures and pamphlets • Technical reports	• Company records (reports and communications) • Legal documents (e.g., court records) • Personal files (e.g., expense records) • Medical records

Although secondary and primary data are both important sources for business reports, we usually start our data collection by reviewing data that is already available—it costs less and saves time. Not all report situations require collecting new (primary) data, but it would be unusual to write a report that did not require some type of secondary data.

Let's refer back to our example of a restaurant offering healthier menu items for children. As the owner, you would certainly rely on secondary sources to learn about industry trends. There's no need for you to commission your own research when the National Restaurant Association and industry publications probably have published studies and articles about the topic. Also, studying secondary data can provide sources for additional published information and provide guidance for possible primary research.

For these reasons, our discussion of data collection first focuses on secondary sources. Secondary data is neither better than nor worse than primary data; it is simply *different*. One of the challenges is finding secondary data that is appropriate for your purpose.

9-2b Searching for Relevant Sources

You may be tempted to start all searches by Googling keywords, but you have better options available. Particularly as a student, you can access subscription-based information through your school's library. Databases such as Business Source Premier, ProQuest, and LexisNexis are good choices for business-related newspapers, magazines, and journals for your research. Figure 4 compares search results for Google, Google Scholar, and EBSCO.

Situation: As a restaurant owner who is considering healthy menu choices, you could search for terms such as *healthy*, *food*, *trend*, and *children*.

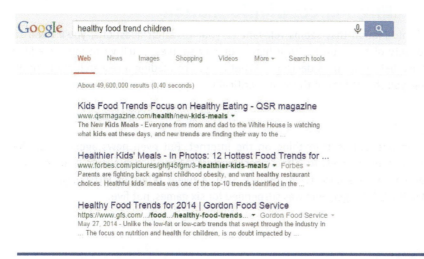

Worst: This Google search yields an overwhelming 49.6 million results from companies, consumer organizations, and government agencies—too many and too varied to reasonably sort through. Advertisements on Google probably will not provide useful information for your search. You could limit your results by using Advanced Search or by changing your search terms, but using Google is still an unrefined approach, which may cause you to spend more time than you'd like finding reliable data.

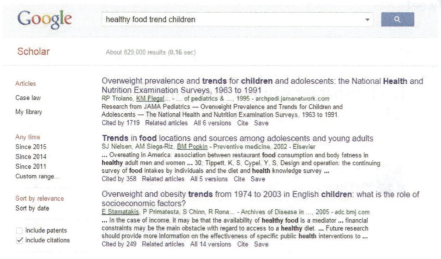

Better: Entering the same search terms in Google Scholar yields 829,000 results, which is still too many to read, but this list is prescreened for you with only academic articles. You also can more easily narrow your search by selecting dates and subject area (e.g., business).

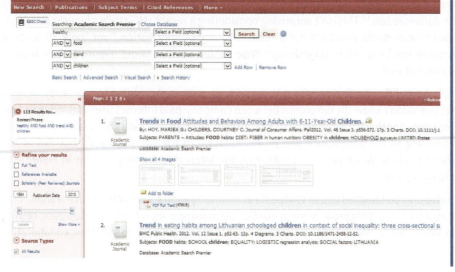

Best: A library database, such as EBSCO, yields a manageable 113 articles,which can be sorted by date and type of publication. Like Google Scholar results, these articles are prescreened and more likely to be reliable sources.

Clearly, this is your best bet for finding relevant, reliable sources.

Getting into Google may be easier than a library database, but you never know what you'll get. Library databases include information already evaluated by scholars and publishers. In the long run, a database will save you time and give you the best results for your report.

LO2 Evaluate the quality of data.

9-2c Evaluating Sources of Information

Once you find information that seems relevant to your research questions, you'll need to evaluate the quality of the sources. With higher quality sources, you'll write more credible reports and make better business decisions. Whether you're reading a research study or an article on a blog, you should look at the source critically.

Evaluating Internet Resources

Communication TECHNOLOGIES

We know that anyone can post anything on the Internet. But even news agencies can be sloppy in checking their sources. As a fact-checking test, Mike Wise, a sports columnist for *The Washington Post*, sent a false tweet (Figure 5). The tweet refers to Pittsburgh Steelers quarterback Ben Roethlisberger, who was suspended for six games, not five.

Figure 5 | False Tweet

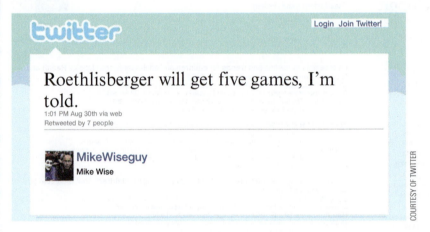

COURTESY OF TWITTER

Emotional INTELLIGENCE

Do you tend to believe what you read on the Internet? How can you be more careful about accepting information that isn't substantiated?

The Washington Post didn't appreciate Wise's joke and suspended him for one month. However, the fake tweet was picked up by several media outlets, including *The Miami Herald* and *The Baltimore Sun*.[6,7] This isn't surprising considering a recent ING study of journalists: one-third said "social media posts are not a reliable source of information," yet "only 20 percent always check the facts before publishing."[8] Wise posted another tweet (Figure 6), which sums up the incident well.

People have difficulty distinguishing the quality of sources. According to one study, 40% of Internet users don't know the difference between company-paid Internet sites and independent Internet sites. Another study concluded that people tend to evaluate the quality of Internet data according to the appearance and professionalism of the website itself,[9] but this is not a sufficient method. When you find content on the Internet, ask the questions in Figure 7 to evaluate the resource.[10]

You also may be tempted to use Wikipedia as an information source. Although librarians may advise against using Wikipedia, several studies demonstrate its reliability.[11] However, relying *only* on Wikipedia is sloppy for two reasons. First, anyone can post to this free, collaborative

twitter   Home Profile Find People Settings Help Sign Out

But in the end, it proved two things: 1. I was right about nobody checking facts or sourcing and 2. I'm an idiot. Apologies to all involved.

3:02 PM Aug 30 via web
Retweeted by 12 people

⬠Reply ⟳Retweet

MikeWiseguy
Mike Wise

COURTESY OF TWITTER

Evaluating Web Sources | **Figure 7**

Authority

- Is the author or organization identifiable? Look for links that say "Who We Are," "About This Site," or something similar.
- How credible are the site owners (e.g., experience, credentials, publications, press)?
- What other sites are linking to this site (search for "link: [site name]")?
- Do links on this site lead to other reputable sites?
- Is the domain extension (e.g., .edu, .gov, .org) appropriate for the content?

Accuracy and Reliability

- Have research sources been properly documented and cited?
- Do you find spelling errors or incorrect uses of grammar?
- Can background information be verified for accuracy?
- How long has the site been in existence (use the Internet Archive to check: www.archive.org)?

Purpose/Objectivity

- What is the purpose or motive for the site (e.g., educational, commercial, entertainment)? Is the site trying to sell you something?
- Do you see a clear distinction between opinion and fact?
- Who is the intended audience, and how is this reflected in the organization and presentation of the site?

Coverage

- Does the site cover a specific time period?
- Does the site cover one aspect of the topic, or does it cover the topic in depth?
- What information is included? What is omitted?
- Is the page completed or "under construction"?

Currency

- When was the site last updated or revised?
- How often is the site updated?
- Do you notice any dead links?

encyclopedia, so it may be a good starting point for research, but you should check all sources in the footnotes yourself. Second, you'll want a variety of sources; citing Wikipedia directly for anything other than definitions may tell your reader you didn't do your homework.

Evaluating Research Studies

Research studies may be a better source than web sources for a report, but they may not be appropriate for your purpose. Ask yourself the questions in Figure 8 about research you consider incorporating into your report.

Data that fails even one of these five tests should probably not be used in your report. At the very least, such data requires extra scrutiny and perhaps extra explanation in the report itself if you do choose to use it.

Figure 8 | Evaluating Research Studies

What was the purpose of the study?

People who have a vested interest in the outcome of a study may take shortcuts to get the answer they want. But people who approach research with a genuine interest in answering a question are more likely to select their samples carefully, ask clear and unbiased questions, and analyze data objectively.

Example: Which study about children's food preferences is more trustworthy—one conducted by the U.S. National Institute of Health or one conducted by Sabrett Hot Dogs?

How was the data collected?

Were appropriate procedures used? Even if you're not an experienced researcher, you can make sure data was collected properly and from a large enough, representative sample.

Example: If you want to learn your customers' reactions to healthier menu items, you wouldn't ask only two guests who visited the restaurant on Saturday. You would ask a large percentage of your customers and include individuals and families, early and late diners, and so on.

How was the data analyzed?

As we'll see later in this chapter, how we analyze data depends on the type of data we collect. In some situations, even though the analysis is appropriate for the original study, it may not be appropriate for your particular purposes.

Example: Let's say you find a study about eating preferences by age. If the researchers used the broad category "younger than 21," the study won't help you understand how your target group (children 6–9 years old) responded.

How consistent is the data with that from other studies?

When you find the same general conclusions in several independent sources, you can have greater confidence in the data.

Example: If four studies conclude that children don't like fish unless it is fried, and a fifth study reached an opposite conclusion, you might be skeptical of the fifth study.

How old is the data?

Data that was true at the time it was collected may not be true today.

Example: A 1980 study of children's food preferences may not be relevant to your decision today, when more food choices are available, people are dining out more frequently, and people are more health conscious.

9-3 Collecting Data Through Questionnaires

LO3 Develop a questionnaire and cover letter.

If your research fails to find enough high-quality secondary data to help you make a decision, you will probably need to collect primary data.

A survey is a data-collection method that gathers information through questionnaires, telephone or email inquiries, or interviews. The questionnaire (a written instrument with questions to obtain information from recipients) is the most frequently used method in business research. For relatively little expense, the researcher can get a representative sampling over a large geographical area. It costs no more to send a questionnaire through the postal service or by email across the country than across the street.

Also, the anonymity of a questionnaire increases the validity of some responses. When respondents aren't identified, they may give more complete and honest personal and financial information. In addition, no interviewer is present to possibly bias the results. Finally, respondents can answer at a time convenient for them, which is not always the case with telephone or interview studies.

The big disadvantage of questionnaires is the low response rate, and those who do respond may not be representative (typical) of the population. Extensive research has shown that respondents tend to be better educated, more intelligent, and more sociable, and have higher social status and a higher need for social approval than those who choose not to respond.[11,12] Thus, questionnaires should be used only under certain conditions (Figure 9).

When to Develop Questionnaires | Figure 9

When the information can be provided easily and quickly

Questionnaires should contain mostly yes-or-no questions, check-off alternatives, or one- to two-word fill-in responses. People tend not to complete questionnaires that call for lengthy or complex responses.

When the target audience is homogeneous

To ensure a high response rate, your study must interest the respondents, and you must use language they understand. It is difficult to construct a questionnaire that would be clearly and uniformly understood by people with widely differing interests, education, and socioeconomic backgrounds.

When sufficient time is available

Three to four weeks is generally required from questionnaire mailing to final returns—including follow-ups of the nonrespondents. (Emailing questionnaires, of course, requires less total time.) A telephone survey, on the other hand, can often be completed in one day.

9-3a Constructing the Questionnaire

Because the target audience has limited time, make sure that every question you ask is necessary. Each question should be essential to your research and yield information that you can't get from other sources (such as through library or online research). Follow the guidelines in Figure 10 for constructing a questionnaire. A well-designed questionnaire about guests' restaurant experience is shown in Figure 11.[13]

To get valid and reliable data from your target audience, your language must be clear, precise, and understandable. Imagine spending time and money on a questionnaire and then making a decision based on invalid data. At best, you would have to disregard the data; at worst, you

Figure 10 | Constructing a Questionnaire

Content

- Ask only for information that is not easily available elsewhere.
- Have a purpose for each question. Make sure that all questions directly help you solve a problem or make a decision. Avoid asking for unimportant or merely "interesting" information.
- Use precise wording so that no question can possibly be misunderstood. Use clear, simple language, and define unfamiliar or confusing terms.
- Use neutrally worded questions and deal with only one topic per question. Avoid loaded, leading, or multifaceted questions.
- Ensure that the response choices are both **exhaustive** (one appropriate response for each question) and **mutually exclusive** (no overlapping categories).
- Be careful about asking sensitive questions, such as information about age, salary, or morals. Consider using broad categories for such questions (instead of narrow, more specific categories).
- Pilot-test your questionnaire on a few people to check that all questions function as intended. Revise as needed.

Organization

- Arrange the questions in some logical order. Group questions that deal with a particular topic. If your questionnaire is long, divide it into sections.
- Arrange the alternatives for each question in some logical order—such as numerical, chronological, or alphabetical.
- Give the questionnaire a descriptive title, provide whatever directions are necessary, and include instructions for returning the questionnaire.

Format

- Use an easy-to-answer format. Check-off questions draw the most responses and are easiest to answer and tabulate. Use free-response items only when necessary.
- To increase the likelihood that your target audience will cooperate and take your study seriously, ensure that your questionnaire has a professional appearance: use a simple and attractive format and proofread carefully.

might decide, for example, to offer a product that few people buy. You are responsible for the quality of the information you include in your reports and presentations—and the collection process starts with neutral (unbiased) questions.

☒ NOT   Do you think our company should open an on-site child care center as a means of ensuring the welfare of our employees' small children?

    ❑ yes

    ❑ no

This wording of the question favors the "pro" side, which biases the responses. A more neutral question will result in more valid responses.

☑ BUT   Which one of the following possible additional benefits would you most prefer?

    ❑ a dental insurance plan

    ❑ an on-site child care center

    ❑ three personal-leave days annually

    ❑ other (please specify:_____)

Questionnaire About Guests' Restaurant Experience | Figure 11

Personal space questionnaire

This restaurant and Cornell University are working together to study how to create better dining experiences. You can help by taking a moment to complete the following short survey. Please leave your completed survey in the check folder, or you may give it to the host as you depart. Thank you for your feedback!

> *Includes clear statements and defined choices.*

1. Please indicate your agreement with each of the following questions about your dining experience today.

   (1 — Strongly Disagree, 7 — Strongly Agree)

   I was pleased with my dining experience.
   1   2   3   4   5   6   7

   I had enough room at my table.
   1   2   3   4   5   6   7

   I was happy with my food.
   1   2   3   4   5   6   7

   This restaurant was a wise choice.
   1   2   3   4   5   6   7

   I felt rushed during my dining experience.
   1   2   3   4   5   6   7

   The servers did a good job for me.
   1   2   3   4   5   6   7

   I was uncomfortable in my seat.
   1   2   3   4   5   6   7

   The staff was friendly and hospitable.
   1   2   3   4   5   6   7

   My table was too close to other tables.
   1   2   3   4   5   6   7

   I was very dissatisfied by my experience.
   1   2   3   4   5   6   7

2. Is this your first visit to this restaurant?
   Yes   No
   If yes, how did you find out about this restaurant?

   _____

3. How likely are you to return to this restaurant?

   (1 — Very Unlikely, 7 — Very Likely)
   1   2   3   4   5   6   7

4. How likely are you to recommend this restaurant to others?

   (1 — Very Unlikely, 7 — Very Likely)
   1   2   3   4   5   6   7

> *Uses check-off items for sensitive information.*

5. Please tell us a little about yourself (to be completed by only one member of your party).
   You are: Male _____ Female _____
   Your age is: Under 25 _____   26-49 _____   50+ _____

6. How often do you eat out at a restaurant for dinner? (please choose one)
   More than twice a week   _____
   1–2 times a week   _____
   2–3 times a month   _____
   Once a month   _____
   Less than once a month   _____

> *Uses a free-response question for more in-depth information.*

7. If you were the manager of this restaurant, what would you change about the experience? _____

> *Expresses appreciation.*

THANK YOU FOR PARTICIPATING AND FOR DINING WITH US TODAY.

Also be certain that each question contains a single idea.

☒ NOT   Our company should spend less money on advertising and more money on research and development.

   ❏ agree

   ❏ disagree

Suppose the respondent believes that the company should spend more (or less) money on advertising *and* on research and development? How would he or she answer? The solution is to put each of the two ideas in a separate question.

Finally, ensure that your categories are mutually exclusive, with no overlap.

⊠ NOT   In your opinion, what is the major cause of high employee turnover?

☐ lack of air conditioning

☐ noncompetitive financial package

☐ poor health benefits

☐ poor working conditions

☐ weak management

The problem with this item is that the "lack of air conditioning" category overlaps with the "poor working conditions" category, and "noncompetitive financial package" overlaps with "poor health benefits." Also, all four of these probably overlap with "weak management." Intermingling categories will confuse the respondent and yield unreliable survey results.

Respondents may be hesitant to answer sensitive questions, for example, about their age or salary. Even worse, they may deliberately provide *inaccurate* responses. To improve your chances of getting sensitive information, try the following:

- Assure the respondent (in your cover letter or email) that the questionnaire is anonymous.
- Use broad categories (accurate estimates are better than incorrect data).
- Include a list of options rather than a fill-in response.

⊠ NOT   What is your annual gross salary?

$ _____

☑ BUT   Please check the category that best describes your annual salary:

☐ Less than $25,000

☐ $25,000–$50,000

☐ $50,001–$75,000

☐ $75,001–$100,000

☐ More than $100,000

In the third category, "$50,001" is necessary to avoid overlap with the figure "$50,000" in the second category. Without this distinction, the categories would not be mutually exclusive.

Even experienced researchers find it difficult to spot ambiguities or other problems in their own questionnaires. Before sending the questionnaire to a large population, run a pilot test with a small sample of respondents, or at a minimum, ask a colleague to edit your instrument with a critical eye. Then, you can make revisions before distributing the final version.

9-3b Writing the Cover Letter or Email

Unless you will distribute the questionnaires personally (in which case, you could explain the purpose and procedures in person), include a cover letter or email, such as the one shown in Figure 12, with your questionnaire. The cover letter or email should be written as a persuasive message (see Chapter 7). Your job is to convince the reader that it's worth taking the time to complete the questionnaire.

LO4 Display quantitative information

9-4 Displaying Quantitative Information

At some point in the reporting process, you'll have enough data from your secondary and primary sources to help you make a decision. (Of course, during data analysis and report writing, you may realize that you need to collect more information.)

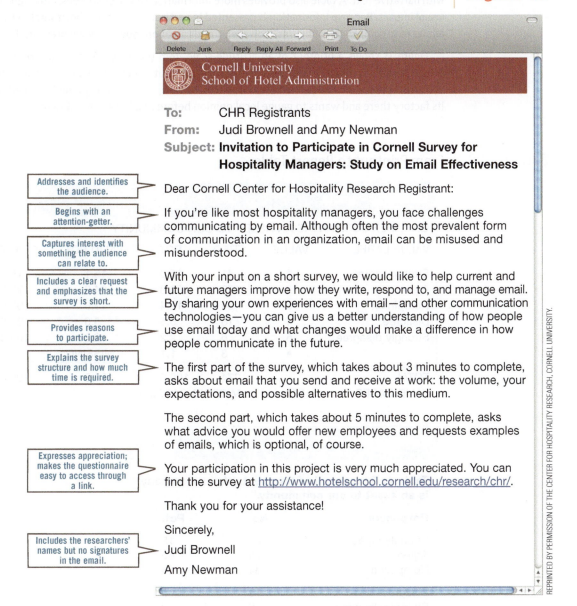

Email

Delete Junk Reply Reply All Forward Print To Do

Cornell University
School of Hotel Administration

To: CHR Registrants
From: Judi Brownell and Amy Newman
Subject: Invitation to Participate in Cornell Survey for Hospitality Managers: Study on Email Effectiveness

Addresses and identifies the audience.

Dear Cornell Center for Hospitality Research Registrant:

Begins with an attention-getter.

Captures interest with something the audience can relate to.

If you're like most hospitality managers, you face challenges communicating by email. Although often the most prevalent form of communication in an organization, email can be misused and misunderstood.

Includes a clear request and emphasizes that the survey is short.

Provides reasons to participate.

With your input on a short survey, we would like to help current and future managers improve how they write, respond to, and manage email. By sharing your own experiences with email—and other communication technologies—you can give us a better understanding of how people use email today and what changes would make a difference in how people communicate in the future.

Explains the survey structure and how much time is required.

The first part of the survey, which takes about 3 minutes to complete, asks about email that you send and receive at work: the volume, your expectations, and possible alternatives to this medium.

The second part, which takes about 5 minutes to complete, asks what advice you would offer new employees and requests examples of emails, which is optional, of course.

Expresses appreciation; makes the questionnaire easy to access through a link.

Your participation in this project is very much appreciated. You can find the survey at http://www.hotelschool.cornell.edu/research/chr/.

Thank you for your assistance!

Sincerely,

Includes the researchers' names but no signatures in the email.

Judi Brownell

Amy Newman

Next, your job is to convert your raw data (from your notes, copies of journal articles, completed questionnaires, recordings of interviews, and web links) into information—meaningful facts, statistics, and conclusions—that will help the reader of your report make a decision. In addition to interpreting your findings in narrative form, you will likely prepare visual aids—tables, charts, photographs, or other graphic materials—to improve comprehension and add interest. Some of these visuals may be used in presentation software, such as PowerPoint, to support an oral presentation.

Data analysis takes time and skill. The more familiar you become with the data and the more insight you can provide the reader about the *meaning* of the data, the more helpful your report will be.

9-4a Constructing Tables

A table is an orderly arrangement of data into columns and rows. It represents the most basic form of statistical analysis and is useful for showing a large amount of numerical data in a small space. With a table, you can show numerical data in a more efficient and interesting way than with narrative text. A table also provides more information than a chart does, although with less visual impact. Because information is presented in vertical columns and horizontal rows, a table allows easy comparison of figures. However, trends are more obvious when presented in graphs.

Figure 13 shows a printout of an attitude-scale item (Question 9) on a questionnaire and the corresponding table constructed from this printout. Apex Company, a manufacturer of consumer products headquartered in Des Moines, Iowa, is considering building an addition to its factory there and wants to gauge local opinion before making a commitment.

Figure 13 | **From Printout to Report Table**

Computer Printout

Q.9 "APEX COMPANY IS AN ASSET TO OUR COMMUNITY"

VALUE LABEL	VALUE	FREQ	PCT	VALID PCT	CUM PCT
Strongly agree	1	41	15.0	15.1	15.1
Agree	2	175	63.8	64.6	79.7
No opinion	3	34	12.4	12.6	92.3
Disagree	4	15	5.5	5.5	97.8
Strongly disagree	5	6	2.2	2.2	100.0
	•	3	1.1	MISSING	
TOTAL		274	100.0	100.0	100.0
VALID CASES	271	MISSING CASES 3			

Corresponding Report Table

Table 4. Response to Statement, "Apex Company is an asset to our community."

Response	No.	Pct.
Strongly agree	41	15
Agree	175	65
No opinion	34	13
Disagree	15	5
Strongly disagree	6	2
Total	271	100

On the printout, you see the following column headings:

- *Value Label:* Shows the five alternatives given on the questionnaire.
- *Value:* Shows the code used to identify each of these five alternatives.
- *Freq:* Shows the number of respondents who checked each alternative.
- *Pct:* Shows the percentage of each response, based on the total number of respondents ($N = 274$), including those who left this item blank.
- *Valid Pct:* Shows the percentage of each response, based on the total number of respondents who answered this particular question ($N = 271$).
- *Cum Pct:* Shows the cumulative percentage—that is, the sum of this response plus those above it (e.g., 79.7% of the respondents either agreed or strongly agreed with the statement).

The researcher must determine whether the "Pct" or "Valid Pct" column is more appropriate for the analysis. In most cases, choose "Valid Pct" column, which ignores any blank responses. These numbers were selected for the table at the bottom of Figure 13.

Your reader must be able to understand each table on its own, without having to read the surrounding text. Thus, at a minimum, each table should contain a table number, a descriptive but concise title, column headings, and body (the items under each column heading). If you need footnotes to explain individual items within the table, put them immediately below the body of the table, not at the bottom of the page. Similarly, if the table is based on secondary data, type a source note below the body, giving the appropriate citation. Common abbreviations and symbols are acceptable in tables.

Cross-Tabulation Analysis

In some cases, the simple question-by-question tabulation illustrated in the table in Figure 13 would be enough for the reader's purpose. However, in most cases, such simple tabulations would not yield all of the useful information from the data. Most data can be further analyzed through cross-tabulation, a process by which two or more pieces of data are analyzed together.

The table in Figure 14 shows not only the total responses (both the number and the percentages) but also the percentage responses for the subgroups according to marital status, sex, and age.

Cross-Tabulation Analysis | **Figure 14**

Table 4. Response to Statement, "Apex Company is an asset to our community."										
	Total		Marital Status		Sex		Age			
	Total	**Pct.**	**Married**	**Single**	**Male**	**Female**	**Under 21**	**21–35**	**36–50**	**Over 50**
Strongly agree	41	15.1%	14.0%	17.6%	15.7%	10.4%	21.7%	8.4%	12.0%	28.4%
Agree	175	64.6%	67.5%	58.8%	67.6%	46.3%	47.8%	65.1%	69.1%	61.0%
No opinion	34	12.6%	11.2%	15.4%	11.4%	20.9%	17.5%	13.0%	14.3%	9.2%
Disagree	15	5.5%	5.1%	5.5%	4.0%	13.4%	13.0%	8.4%	4.0%	0.7%
Strongly disagree	6	2.2%	2.2%	2.7%	1.3%	9.0%	0.0%	5.1%	0.6%	0.7%
Total	271	100.0%	100.0%	100.0%	100.0%	100.0%	100.0%	100.0%	100.0%	100.0%

A quick "eyeballing" of the table shows that there do not seem to be any major differences in the perceptions of married versus single respondents. However, there does seem to be a fairly sizable difference between male and female respondents: males have a much more positive view of the company than do females.

If the table in Figure 14 were one of only a few tables in your report, it would be just fine the way it's shown. However, suppose that the statement "Apex Company is an asset to our community" is one of a dozen attitude items, each of which requires a similar table. It is probably too much to expect the reader to study a dozen similar tables; in such a situation, you should consider simplifying the table.

You can use several approaches to simplify a table. You should recognize right from the start, however, that whenever you simplify a table (that is, whenever you merge rows or columns or simply delete data), your table loses some of its detail. The goal is to gain more in comprehensibility than you lose in specificity. Your knowledge of the readers and their needs will help you determine how much detail to present.

With that in mind, consider the simplified version of this table shown in Figure 15. The two positive responses ("strongly agree" and "agree") have been combined into one "agree" row, as

Figure 15 | Simplified Table

Table 4. Response to Statement, "Apex Company is an asset to our community." (N = 271; all figures in percent)								
	Total	**Marital Status**		**Sex**		**Age**		
		Married	**Single**	**Male**	**Female**	**Under 21**	**21–50**	**Over 50**
Agree	80	82	77	83	57	69	77	90
No opinion	12	11	15	12	21	18	14	9
Disagree	8	7	8	5	22	13	9	1
Total	100	100	100	100	100	100	100	100

have the two negative responses. Combining not only simplifies the table, but also prevents some possible interpretation problems.

Given the original table in Figure 14, for example, would you consider the following statement to be accurate?

Less than half of the females agree that Apex Company is an asset to their community.

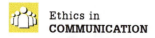

Ethics in COMMUNICATION

Technically, the statement is accurate, because the 46.3% who "agree" is *less* than half. However, the statement leaves an incorrect impression because more than half of the females (57%—those who "agree" *and* who "strongly agree") believe that Apex Company is an asset to their community. Presenting an incomplete picture could be considered unethical if used inappropriately. This conclusion is made clear in Figure 15.

Note also that the two center age groups ("21–35" and "36–50") have been combined into one age group ("21–50"). Because the company's products are geared mainly to this large age group, the company wanted to compare the responses of this important group with the responses of the less important younger and older groups.

Two other changes help simplify the table. First, only percentages are provided, which eliminates the need for the percentage sign after each number (readers can compute the raw numbers for themselves because the sample size is shown in the table subtitle). Second, each percentage is rounded to its nearest whole—a practice recommended for most business reports when presenting percentages that total 100%.

Follow these practices when rounding numbers:

- Any number with a decimal less than 0.50 gets rounded *down* to the next nearest whole number; any number with a decimal greater than 0.50 gets rounded *up*.
- To avoid bias, odd numbers with a decimal of exactly 0.50 get rounded *up*; even numbers with a decimal of exactly .50 get rounded *down*.
- If your table shows the total percentages and your rounding efforts result in totals that do not equal 100% (such as 99% or 101%), you have the option of either (1) showing the actual resulting totals or (2) readjusting one of the rounded numbers (the one that will cause the least distortion to the number) to "force" a 100% total.

Simplifying this table (reducing Figures 14 to 15) has deleted two of the ten columns and two of the five rows. Applying this process to all tables could reduce your report length substantially.

Arranging Data in Tables

As discussed earlier, the check-off alternatives in your questionnaire items should be arranged in some logical order, most often either numerical or alphabetical, to avoid possibly biasing the responses. Once you have the data in hand, however, it is often helpful to the reader if you rearrange the data from high to low.

In Figure 16, for example, the categories have been rearranged from their original *alphabetical* order in the questionnaire into *descending* order in the report table. Note also that the four smallest categories have been combined into a miscellaneous category, which always goes last, regardless of its size. Finally, note the position and format of the table footnote, which may be used to explain an entry in the table.

Arranging Data in Tables | **Figure 16**

From This Survey Response:

6. In which of the following categories of clerical workers do you expect to hire additional workers within the next three years? (Check all that apply.)

211	bookkeepers and accounting clerks
31	computer operators
30	data-entry clerks
24	file clerks
247	general office clerks
78	receptionists and information clerks
323	secretaries/administrative assistants
7	statistical clerks
107	typists and word processors

To This Report Table:

TABLE 2. COMPANIES PLANNING TO HIRE ADDITIONAL CLERICAL WORKERS, BY CATEGORY (*N* = 326)

Category	Pct.*
Secretaries/administrative assistants	99
General office clerks	76
Bookkeepers and accounting clerks	65
Typists and word processors	33
Receptionists and information clerks	24
Miscellaneous	28

*Answers total more than 100% because of multiple responses.

9-4b Preparing Charts

Well-designed charts and graphs can improve reader comprehension, emphasize certain data, create interest, and save time and space. Charts help readers understand main points from large amounts of statistical data.

Because of their visual impact, charts receive more emphasis than tables or narrative text. Use charts when the overall picture is more important than the individual numbers. Also, charts are ideal when using visual support for an oral presentation; tables with a lot of data are difficult to read when projected onto a screen.

Technically, graphs are shown on graph paper; however, the terms *graph* and *chart* are used interchangeably.

However, avoid using too many charts. In a written report, because charts have strong visual appeal, the more charts you include, the less impact each chart will have. Also, tables may be a better choice for some data. Research indicates that managers have more confidence in their decisions based on data from tables alone as opposed to data from graphs alone, but managers have the most confidence when both formats are used.[14] In another study, respondents chose more accurate answers about data displayed in tables than data in charts.[15] Charts will highlight data and add visual appeal to your reports, but be sure to use them to complement your text.

Designing Simple, Clear Charts

When creating a chart for a report or to support an oral presentation, first determine the main point you wish to convey. For a persuasive report, use your audience analysis skills to decide what is most important to the audience, and then design a chart to emphasize this information.

The chart in Figure 17 focuses on a narrow question—technology use among hotel managers.[16] The chart is easy to read and follow.

Figure 17 | Clear, Simple Chart from a Written Report

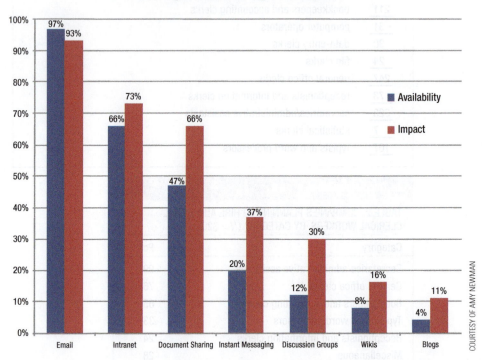

COURTESY OF AMY NEWMAN

Cramming too much information into one chart will confuse the reader and lessen the impact of the graphic. In *The Visual Display of Quantitative Information*, Edward Tufte, an expert in information design, warns against chartjunk—visual elements that call attention to themselves instead of the information on a chart.[17] Avoid using too many, too large, too garish, and too complicated charts. The chart in Figure 18 is impossible to read—and ugly.

Ethics in COMMUNICATION

An ethical manager ensures that charts don't mislead the audience. One common problem is presenting only data that supports your case. Of course, data selection is part of creating charts instead of listing full results in a table. And, if your report is persuasive rather than merely informative, you'll want to present the best possible picture—but not at the expense of ethics, which may affect your credibility.

Choosing an Appropriate Chart Type

The main types of charts used in business reports and presentations are line charts, bar charts, and pie charts. All of these present data to show comparisons. Data without context has little meaning. If you learned that a company reported a $307,000 profit in the fourth quarter, would you be impressed? It's a good sum of money, but what if this is $100,000 less than the previous three quarters? At a minimum, you would want to know how this figure compares to results from previous quarters—and possibly how this compares to competitors' profits.

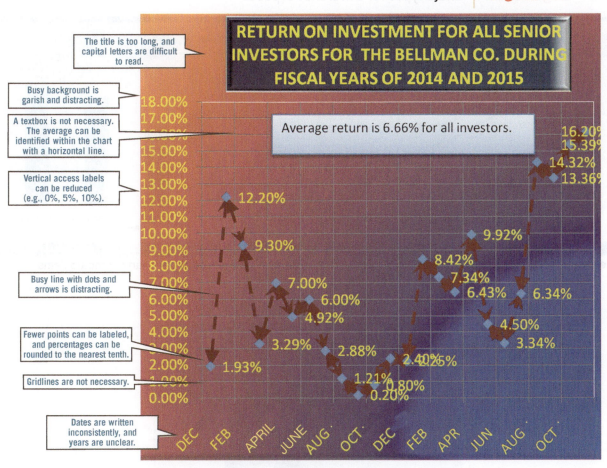

The title is too long, and capital letters are difficult to read.

Busy background is garish and distracting.

A textbox is not necessary. The average can be identified within the chart with a horizontal line.

Vertical access labels can be reduced (e.g., 0%, 5%, 10%).

Busy line with dots and arrows is distracting.

Fewer points can be labeled, and percentages can be rounded to the nearest tenth.

Gridlines are not necessary.

Dates are written inconsistently, and years are unclear.

RETURN ON INVESTMENT FOR ALL SENIOR INVESTORS FOR THE BELLMAN CO. DURING FISCAL YEARS OF 2014 AND 2015

Average return is 6.66% for all investors.

Choose a chart type—or other graphic—to meet your communication objectives. A human resources manager may use different types of charts in a presentation to senior management (Figure 19).

Regardless of their type, label all your charts in a report as *figures,* and assign them consecutive numbers, separate from table numbers. Although tables are captioned at the top, charts may be captioned at the top or bottom. Charts preceded or followed by text or containing an explanatory paragraph are typically captioned at the bottom. As with tables, you may use commonly understood abbreviations.

Line Charts. A line chart is a graph based on a grid of uniformly spaced horizontal and vertical lines. The vertical dimension represents values; the horizontal dimension represents time. Line charts show changes or trends in data over long periods of time, as illustrated in Figure 19.

Both axes should be marked off at equal intervals and clearly labeled. The vertical axis should begin with zero, even when all the amounts are quite large. In some situations, you may want to show a break in the intervals. Fluctuations of the line over time indicate variations in the trend; the distance of the line from the horizontal axis indicates quantity.

Bar Charts. A bar chart is a graph with horizontal or vertical bars representing values. Bar charts are one of the most useful, simple, and popular graphic techniques. They are particularly appropriate for comparing the magnitude or size of items, either at a specified time or over a period of time. The bars should all be the same width, with the length changing to reflect the value of each item.

Figure 19 | Chart Types for Different Purposes

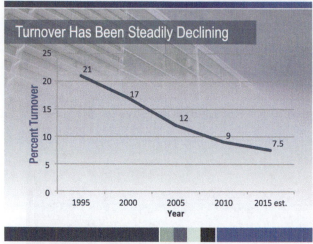

Line charts show trends over time.

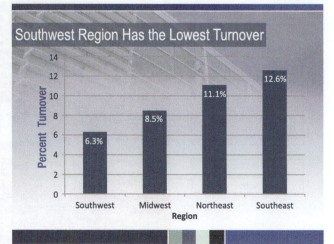

Vertical and horizontal bar charts compare items.

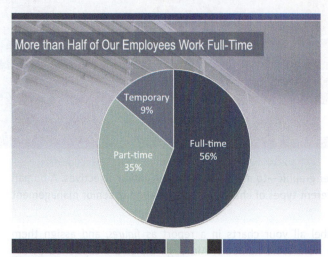

Pie charts show parts of a whole.

Bars may be grouped (as in Figure 17) to compare several variables over a period of time or may be stacked to show component parts of several variables. As with tables, the bars should be arranged in some logical order. Include the actual value of each bar for quicker comprehension.

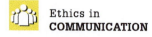
Ethics in COMMUNICATION

With bar charts, data is easily skewed to be misleading. Compare the bar charts in Figures 21 and 22. In Figure 21, on the left side, the vertical axis starts at zero, whereas in Figure 22, the vertical axis starts at $3 billion, exaggerating the increase in revenue. Of course, the arrow in Figure 22 is misleading too! It's a good idea to highlight the percentage increase for your reader, but the angle of the arrow certainly is greater than 4.5%.

Pie Charts. A pie chart is a circle graph divided into component wedges. It compares the relative parts that make up a whole. In an exploding pie, one wedge is pulled out for emphasis.

Pie charts are useful for showing how component parts add up to a total. Pie charts are popular but should be used when you have three to five or so component parts. More categories are difficult to distinguish.

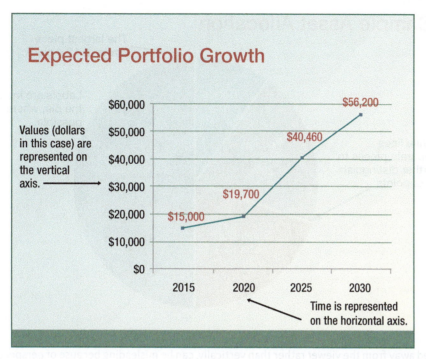

The Effects of Vertical Axis Scales | **Figures 21 & 22**

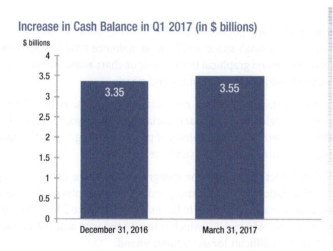

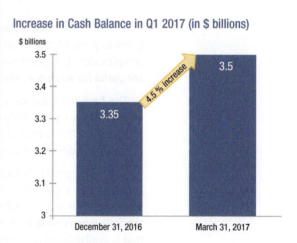

Begin "slicing" the pie at the 12 o'clock position and move clockwise in some logical order (often in order of descending size). The labels should be placed either inside each wedge or directly opposite the wedge but outside the pie. You may use a separate legend or key, but labels are easier to comprehend.

To distinguish each wedge, use shading, cross-hatched lines, different colors, or some other visual device (Figure 23).

Three-dimensional graphs contribute to chartjunk and are difficult to interpret.[18] Because graphs are often used to display only two-dimensional data (horizontal and vertical), the third dimension (depth) has no significance. Similarly, three-dimensional pie charts, which are shown

Figure 23 | Pie Chart

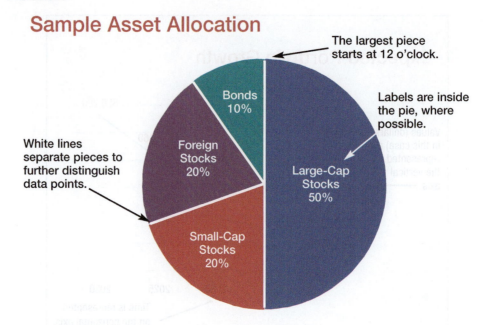

Sample Asset Allocation

The largest piece starts at 12 o'clock.

Labels are inside the pie, where possible.

White lines separate pieces to further distinguish data points.

Bonds 10%

Foreign Stocks 20%

Large-Cap Stocks 50%

Small-Cap Stocks 20%

slanted away from the viewer rather than vertically, can be misleading because of perspective—the slices farthest away appear smaller than they actually are. These charts may look good, but they aren't precise enough for a business audience.

9-4c Creating Infographics

Infographics—or information graphics—are popular ways of showing data visually. These graphics pack a lot of information into a small space and help an audience easily understand complex statistics. More comprehensive and graphical than a table or chart alone, infographics are useful for audiences who need to see information simply and clearly.

The best infographics will go social, passed along on social media sites. With relevant information, a catchy design, search engine attention, and social marketing, your infographic may go viral. "What are the odds?" garnered 1.7 million views of people wanting to see the data behind "the odds that you exist, as you are, today"—"basically zero."[19]

You'll find plenty of bad infographics, for which the designer cares more about kitschy graphics than about conveying information. But, when designed well, infographics tell a story visually, combining text, tables, charts, maps, and more. In the example in Figure 24,[20] IBM uses the following criteria to show us sources of big data, which refers to the vast amount of data that is available today—so much that it's difficult for us to comprehend:

- Clarity and accuracy: Is the graphic easily understood, and does it tell a clear story? Is the data accurate and useful? Do the layout and navigation support the main points? Does it make standalone sense, with clear explanatory text where required to turn data into information?
- Design: Are colors, fonts, point size, and emphasis used to create hierarchy, organize information, and emphasize most relevant points? Does the design complement the message?[21]

To create infographics, follow these steps:

- Storyboard the content: You started the data-collection phase of your research by factoring the problem. Now decide what story your infographic will tell. You may

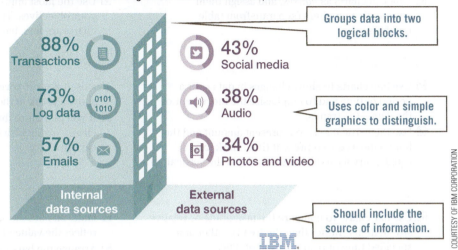

Could use a message title here, such as "Most Big Data Comes from Internal Sources."

Where does big data come from?

Most big data efforts are currently focused on analyzing internal data to extract insights. Fewer organizations are looking at data outside their firewalls, such as social media.

Groups data into two logical blocks.

88% Transactions

73% Log data

57% Emails

43% Social media

38% Audio

34% Photos and video

Uses color and simple graphics to distinguish.

Clearly labels each set of data.

Internal data sources

External data sources

Should include the source of information.

IBM

COURTESY OF IBM CORPORATION

choose to create a flowchart of information or some other way to show hierarchy and relationship of information. Place your most important point in a prominent position.

- Choose graphics and styles: Select charts, tables, illustrations, maps, and other graphics to visually display your content. Be creative, but find ways to give meaning to your data rather than distract from it. Choose eye-catching visuals and attractive colors—pastels and bright hues—but not too many of them.[22]
- Explain the data: Write clear, simple text to help the audience find meaning.

Several tools will help you generate an infographic. Piktochart (www.piktochart.com) and Visual.ly (http://create.visual.ly) are popular tools that provide some functionality for free.

The Checklist for Displaying Quantitative Information summarizes the most important points on this topic.

Checklist for Displaying Quantitative Information

TABLES

☑ Use tables to present a large amount of numerical data in a small space and to compare figures.

☑ Number tables consecutively, and use concise but descriptive table titles and column headings.

☑ Ensure that the table is understandable by itself—without reference to the accompanying narrative.

☑ Arrange the rows of the table in some logical order (most often, in descending order).

☑ Combine smaller, less important categories into a miscellaneous category, and put it last.

☑ Use cross-tabulation analysis to compare different subgroups.

☑ Use only as much detail as necessary; for example, round figures off to the nearest whole to increase comprehension.

☑ Use easily understood abbreviations and symbols as needed.

☑ Ensure that the units (e.g., dollars, percentages, or tons) are identified clearly.

CHARTS

- ☑ Use charts only when they will help the reader interpret the data better—never just to make the report look better.
- ☑ Label all charts as *figures*, and assign them consecutive numbers (separate from table numbers).
- ☑ Keep charts simple. Strive for a single, immediate, correct interpretation, and keep the reader's attention on the *data*.
- ☑ Use the most appropriate type of chart to achieve your objectives. The three most popular business charts are line, bar, and pie.

LINE CHARTS

- ☑ Use line charts to show changes in data over a period of time and to emphasize the movement of the data—the trends.
- ☑ Use the vertical axis to represent amount and the horizontal axis to represent time. Mark axes at equal intervals and label them. Begin the vertical axis at zero; if necessary, use slash marks (//) to show a break in the interval.
- ☑ If you plot more than one variable on a chart, clearly distinguish between the lines, and label each clearly.

BAR CHARTS

- ☑ Use bar charts to compare the magnitude or relative size of items (rather than the trend), either at a specified time or over a period of time.
- ☑ Make all bars the same width; vary the length to reflect the value of each item.
- ☑ Arrange the bars in a logical order and clearly label each.

PIE CHARTS

- ☑ Use pie charts to compare the relative parts that make up a whole.
- ☑ Begin slicing the pie at the 12 o'clock position, moving clockwise in a logical order.
- ☑ Label each wedge of the pie, indicate its value, and clearly differentiate the wedges.

INFOGRAPHICS

- ☑ Use infographics to help your audience understand complex data and to make your content go social.
- ☑ Produce infographics with clear, accurate information. Strive for standalone sense.
- ☑ Create an infographic by storyboarding the content, choosing graphics and styles, and explaining the data.

LO5 Interpret data for the report reader.

9-5 Interpreting Data

As the name visual *aids* implies, charts act as a *help*—not a substitute—for the narrative presentation and interpretation. When analyzing the data, first determine whether the data does, in fact, answer your question. You'll waste time preparing elaborate tables and other visual aids if your data is irrelevant, incomplete, or inaccurate. Use the process in Figure 25 to interpret your data.

9-5a Making Sense of the Data

As a report writer, you cannot simply present the raw data without interpreting it. The data in your tables and charts helps answer a question. In the report narrative, you don't have to discuss *all* the data in the tables and charts; that would be boring and insulting to the reader's intelligence. Instead, discuss the implications of your data most relevant to the reader's question.

Scenario: Imagine that you're trying to determine the exercise habits of college students. Perhaps you're considering opening a fitness center or offering individual yoga classes.

For this example, let's also assume that you gathered only three pieces of information: a paraphrase from a newspaper article, a chart you developed from a recent study published in a journal article, and primary data from a questionnaire you distributed on campus.

Step 1: Isolation

Look at each piece of data in isolation. If the newspaper article were the only piece of data you collected, what would that mean for your business idea? For example, if the article discussed students throughout the United States, what, if any, conclusions could you draw about your local campus? Follow the same process for the study and your questionnaire, examining each in isolation, without considering any other data.

Step 2: Context

Look at each piece of data in combination with the other bits. For example, the newspaper article may lead you to believe that few students exercise regularly, but 67% of students who responded to your questionnaire reported belonging to a gym. What could this combination of data mean (e.g., perhaps students belong to a gym but rarely go)? If your data sources reinforce each other, you can use stronger, more conclusive language in your analysis. If not, you may want to use less certain language or perhaps not draw any conclusions at all.

Step 3: Synthesis

Synthesize all the information you've collected. When you consider all the facts and their relationships together, what do they mean for your business idea? Do you have enough data to conclude whether the business has a good chance of success? If so, you're ready to begin the detailed analysis and presentation that will help the reader—perhaps a business investor—understand your findings. If not, you must backtrack and start the research process again.

Almost always, the most important finding is the overall response to a question (rather than the responses of the cross-tabulation subgroups). And almost always the category within the question that receives the largest response is the most important point. So discuss this question and this category first. Let's take another look at the Apex example (Figure 26).

Simplified Table | **Figure 26**

Table 4. Response to Statement, "Apex Company is an asset to our community."
(*N* = 271; all figures in percent)

	Total	Marital Status		Sex		Age		
		Married	Single	Male	Female	Under 21	21–50	Over 50
Agree	80	82	77	83	57	69	77	90
No opinion	12	11	15	12	21	18	14	9
Disagree	8	7	8	5	22	13	9	1
Total	100	100	100	100	100	100	100	100

In Figure 26, the major finding is this: four-fifths of the respondents believe that Apex Company is an asset to their community. If you give the exact figure from the table (here, 80%), you can use less precise language in the narrative—"four-fifths" in this case, or in other cases "one in four," or "a slight majority." Doing so helps you avoid presenting facts and figures too quickly. Pace your analysis because the reader may struggle to understand data presented too quickly or too densely.

Once you've discussed the overall finding, discuss the cross-tabulation data as necessary. Look for trends, unexpected findings, data that reinforces or contradicts other data, extreme values, and data that raises questions. If these features are important, discuss them. In our example, there were no major differences in the responses by marital status, so you would probably not need to discuss them. However, you would need to discuss the big difference in responses between males and females. If possible, discuss the *reasons* for these differences.

Finally, point out the trend that is evident with regard to age: the older the respondent, the more positive the response. If it's important enough, you might display this trend in a graph for more visual effect.

Sometimes you will want to include descriptive statistics (such as the mean, median, mode, range, and standard deviation). At other times, your data will require inference (significance) testing to determine whether the differences found in your sample data are also likely to exist in the general population.

After all of your data collection and analysis, you'll likely know more about the topic than your reader does. Help the reader by pointing out the important implications, findings, and relationships of your data. With your guidance, the reader will draw the same conclusions you have.

Emotional INTELLIGENCE

When have you been involved in research that has tested your ethics? How has this experience affected you and your approach to future research?

Ethics in COMMUNICATION

9-5b Considering the Ethical Dimension

In gathering, analyzing, and reporting data, everyone involved has both rights and obligations. The researcher has the right to expect that respondents will be truthful in their responses and has an obligation not to deceive respondents. The organization that is paying for the research has the right to expect that the researcher will provide valid and reliable information and has an obligation not to misuse that data. And consumers of information—readers of data analysis—have a right to expect an accurate portrayal of the research.

Unethical practices in managing data can have serious consequences. A pharmaceutical company that bribes drug trial participants to get positive results may bring an unsafe product to market. A credit card company that reveals only "teaser" interest payments—before rates increase—may force a family into bankruptcy.

Television personality Dr. Mehmet Oz has been criticized for promoting products that have little, if any, research supporting the advertised benefits. Dr. Oz's enthusiasm for garcinia extract for burning fat was challenged by Edzard Ernst, who studied the substance more than 15 years ago: "Dr. Oz's promotion of this and other unproven or disproven alternative treatments is irresponsible and borders on quackery." The so-called "Oz Effect"— people spending lots of money on products presented on his show—can be dangerous. As Ernst says, "Using bogus treatments for serious conditions may cost lives."[23]

If you want your research to solve problems and help in decision making, everyone involved must use common sense, good judgment, and an ethical mindset to make the project successful.

Creating an Infographic

››› PURPOSE

Imagine that you work for Pancreatic Cancer Action. The director has asked you to create an infographic to raise awareness about pancreatic cancer.

››› PROCESS

1. **What is the purpose of your communication?**
   To communicate how serious pancreatic cancer is and how funding is distributed among types of cancers.

2. **Who is your audience, and how will you reach them?**
   The public is my audience, and I'm hoping that my infographic will go viral.

3. **What information and data will you include?**
   I want to focus on the low survival rates of people who are diagnosed with pancreatic cancer. I'll show cancer death rates and compare those numbers to how funding is distributed. I'll also show that the U.K. survival rate is the lowest in the world.

››› PRODUCT

You create the following infographic (also at bit.ly/1DzqUlV).

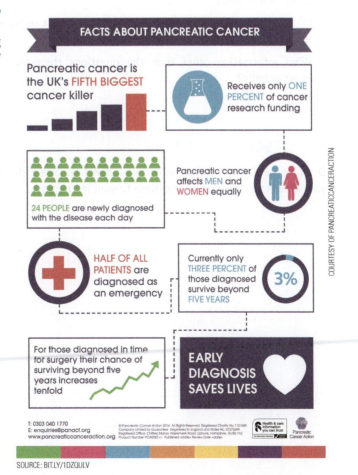

SOURCE: BIT.LY/1DZQULV

3Ps

< IN PRACTICE

Developing a Questionnaire About Cancer Awareness

>>> PURPOSE

As an intern for the American Cancer Society, you have been asked to find out what people know about cancer survival rates and funding. This will help the organization create a marketing campaign to raise awareness. Develop a questionnaire that can be circulated online.

>>> PROCESS

1. Brainstorm for 10 minutes. List every possible question you might ask about cancer survival rates and funding; don't worry at this point about the wording of the questions or their sequence.

2. Review your questions. Are all of them necessary to get information you need?

3. Edit your questions to ensure that they are clear and unbiased.

4. Arrange the questions in some logical order.

5. Where possible, format each question with check-off responses, arranging the responses in some logical order.

6. Do any of the questions ask for sensitive information, or are any of them difficult to answer? If so, how will you handle these questions?

7. What information other than the questions themselves should you include on the questionnaire?

>>> PRODUCT

Draft, revise, format, and proofread your questionnaire. Submit both your questionnaire and your answers to the process questions to your instructor.

296 | **PART 4** Report Writing

> SUMMARY

LO1   Find relevant sources for a report.
Search for data that will achieve your purpose, for example, to solve a problem or make a decision. By factoring the problem, you'll determine what primary and secondary data are needed to answer important questions. Where available, choose library databases over broad Internet searches to get the best sources.

LO2   Evaluate the quality of data.
The quality of information on the Internet varies widely. When evaluating web resources, consider authority, accuracy and reliability, purpose/objectivity, coverage, and currency. When using research studies as secondary sources, first consider the purpose of the study, how the data was collected and analyzed, how consistent the data is with other studies, and how old the data is.

LO3   Develop a questionnaire and cover letter.
Primary data is collected by various survey methods, mainly questionnaires, telephone inquiries, and interviews. Ensure that all survey questions are necessary, clearly worded, complete, and unbiased. Organize the questions and possible responses logically, provide clear directions, and choose an attractive format. The cover letter or email should be persuasive and explain why it is in the reader's interest to answer the survey.

LO4   Display quantitative information.
Data is converted into information by careful analysis and is interpreted in narrative form and by visual aids. Each table you construct from the data should be interpretable by itself, without reference to the text. Include only as much data in a table as is helpful, keeping the table as simple as possible. Use well-designed line, bar, and pie charts to increase reader comprehension, emphasize certain data, create interest, and save time and space. Avoid using too many, too large, too garish, or too complicated charts. Consider creating infographics to help readers quickly grasp large amounts of information.

LO5   Interpret data for the report reader.
Do not analyze every figure from the table in your narrative. Instead, interpret the important points from the table, pointing out the major findings, trends, and contradictions. Avoid misrepresenting your information. A competent reporter of business information is an ethical reporter of business information.

> EXERCISES

1. **Find relevant sources to support a business decision.**

   Choose one of the following small business situations—or another situation that interests you:

   - You own a clothing store and want to know whether to offer hats.
   - You own an ice cream store and want to know whether to offer products other than ice cream (e.g., other desserts or soda).
   - You own a jewelry store and want to know which precious gems are most popular (and what quantities you should order).
   - You own a stationery store and want to know how to stock greeting cards—which are most popular?

> LO1   Find relevant sources for a report.

- You own a sporting goods store and want to know the most popular bicycle brands by riders' age group.
- You own a computer repair business and want to know what services customers will want.

Conduct research and find a few articles to help you make your decision. Provide a list of the most relevant sources you found.

2. **Compare search results on Google, Google Scholar, and a library database.**

   Enter a few keywords into Google, Google Scholar, and a library database. You may use a scenario from Exercise 1 or choose a different situation. Try to get the most relevant, reliable results from each search by narrowing results a few times.

3. **Find data to decide whether to open a store.**

   You have been asked to determine the feasibility of opening a frozen yogurt store in Greenville, North Carolina. Answer the following questions, using the latest figures available. Provide a citation for each source.

   a. What were the number of stores and the total sales last year for TCBY, a frozen yogurt franchise?

   b. What is the population of Greenville? What percentage of this population is between the ages of 18 and 24?

   c. What is the per capita income of residents of Greenville?

   d. What is the name and address of the president of TCBY?

   e. What is the climate of Greenville?

   f. How many students are enrolled at East Carolina University?

   g. What is the market outlook for frozen yogurt stores nationwide?

   h. What is the most current journal or newspaper article you can find on this topic?

LO2 Evaluate the quality of data.

4. **Write an email to improve accuracy in reporting.**

   Imagine that you're the chief editor for *The Baltimore Sun*. Use the Mike Wise situation discussed in this chapter to reinforce principles for evaluating information from the Internet (see Figures 5 and 6). Write an email to all reporters. You might start by briefly summarizing the situation; then, use the questions presented in "Evaluating Web Resources" to write a few paragraphs as reminders for the reporters. Try to put the questions into your own words and make the principles relevant to experienced reporters.

5. **Evaluate the quality of Internet resources.**

   Select two Internet resources and evaluate them based on the five criteria: authority, accuracy and reliability, purpose/objectivity, coverage, and currency. You might search for news about a company that interests you. Use the questions for "Evaluating Web Resources," and submit a brief summary of your analysis to your instructor.

6. **Distinguish between high- and low-quality Internet sources.**

   Imagine that a person you admire is coming to speak on campus. You have been selected to introduce the speaker to your entire graduating class. Of course you want to ensure you have accurate information about this person. Search the Internet for information and identify at least five resources. Use the questions in "Evaluating Web Resources" (Figure 7) to determine the quality of the information. Write a brief summary of your analysis and submit it to your instructor.

7. **Evaluate studies for a report.**

Imagine that you're the corporate communications vice president for Harley-Davidson Motor Company. To promote motorcycle use in the United States, you're planning a communication campaign focused on safety. Your objective is to overcome the public's perception that motorcycles are dangerous.

You decide to include some scholarly research to support your point of view. But, of course, you want to present an ethical argument, so you'll evaluate each study carefully. Use the following questions from "Evaluating Research Studies" to ensure the studies meet your quality standards:

- What was the purpose of the study?
- How was the data collected?
- How was the data analyzed?
- How consistent is the data with that from other studies?
- How old is the data?

Write a few paragraphs that you plan to put on the Harley-Davidson website. Remember your objective: you want people to believe that motorcycles are safe (or, at least aren't as dangerous as people perceive them to be). Include references to the articles you decide to use so that your instructor can evaluate your choices.

8. **Create a questionnaire about a new restaurant.**

As the marketing vice president of Piedmont Seafood Restaurants, you are considering opening a new restaurant in Fort Collins, Colorado. You currently have 15 restaurants in surrounding states, and last year you opened a Piedmont in Denver. The Denver restaurant has been very successful, so you want to expand to other suitable areas.

To determine the suitability of a seafood restaurant in Fort Collins, you are preparing a short questionnaire to be completed by people living in the Fort Collins area. Your restaurant features a full seafood menu, with fresh seafood flown in daily. You are a full-service restaurant with a family-style atmosphere. Your prices range from $7.99 for a children's combo plate to $19.99 for your top-priced meal. The average price for a lunch or dinner would be $14.50.

Working with a partner, prepare a short questionnaire to be completed by the residents of Fort Collins. You should have a title for your questionnaire and a brief introduction. Then ask six to ten appropriate questions that are clearly worded and unbiased. Put the questions in a logical sequence, and make sure the response options are mutually exclusive and exhaustive. Submit the questionnaire to your instructor for evaluation.

9. **Write a cover letter for your questionnaire.**

Prepare a cover letter to introduce the questionnaire prepared for Exercise 8. The letter should encourage readers to complete the questionnaire and return it quickly in the stamped, addressed envelope. It should also lay some groundwork for establishing potential customers if the restaurant becomes a reality. If the demand is sufficient, a Piedmont Seafood Restaurant could be opening in Fort Collins soon.

10. **Write a questionnaire about ice cream flavors.**

You are planning to open an ice cream parlor. You want to have a wide variety of flavors for your patrons to select from, so you are going to ask potential customers to identify their favorite flavors of ice cream.

1. Write a question that presents an exhaustive list of ice cream flavors. You also want to know how much people are willing to pay for a single scoop of ice cream and a double scoop of ice cream.

LO3 Develop a questionnaire and cover letter

2. Prepare questions that list the various price ranges people would be willing to pay for a single scoop of ice cream and a double scoop of ice cream. Make sure the questions are exhaustive and mutually exclusive.

3. Finally, you want to know what other ice cream novelty items your store should offer. Write a question that gathers this information.

Make sure the options for each question are listed in an appropriate order.

11. Write a questionnaire about a new store.

Assume that you have been asked to write a report on the feasibility of opening a packaging and shipping store, such as UPS, in your town. Because students at your school would be a major source of potential customers for your store, you decide to survey the students to gather relevant data. Working in a group of four or five, develop a two-page questionnaire and a cover letter that you could mail to a sample of these students.

Ensure that the content and appearance of the questionnaire follow the guidelines given in this chapter. Pilot-test your questionnaire and cover letter on a small sample of students, and then revise it as necessary and submit it to your instructor.

12. Convert your questionnaire to an online survey.

Go to a free online survey site (such as www.surveymonkey.com), and reformat the questionnaire you developed in Exercise 11 as an online survey. Your instructor may ask you to administer this questionnaire online by emailing it to a few students.

13. Create an online survey for your classmates.

Working in small groups, imagine that you're planning a start-up business targeted to students. First, decide on your business concept. This can be anything: a service (e.g., laundry or grocery shopping) or a product (e.g., custom T-shirts or imported hats).

Next, write about ten questions to determine whether your idea will be popular. Remember to use the principles for writing effective questions described in this chapter.

When you're satisfied that your questions meet the criteria for well-designed questionnaires, create a free online survey on a site such as www.surveymonkey.com. Distribute the survey to your classmates. (See the next exercise for a related activity.)

Finally, with your group, analyze the responses and make a preliminary judgment about whether your business would be successful.

14. Evaluate your classmates' online surveys.

For Exercise 13, you worked in a group to create a questionnaire for other students in your class. Pair up with another group to evaluate each other's questionnaires. As you're completing the other group's questionnaire, take notes to evaluate each question. In class, meet with your partner group and provide each other with feedback on your questionnaires. Which questions were most effective, and why? Which questions were least effective, and why?

15. Analyze a line chart.

LO4 Display quantitative information.

When Google faced antitrust allegations from the European Union, the company responded with a blog post and several line charts. Read more about the situation at bit .ly/1yHwDXJ and analyze the line chart below. Which principles from this chapter does the author miss? Considering the audience and communication objectives of the data, how effective is the chart?

Travel sites in Germany

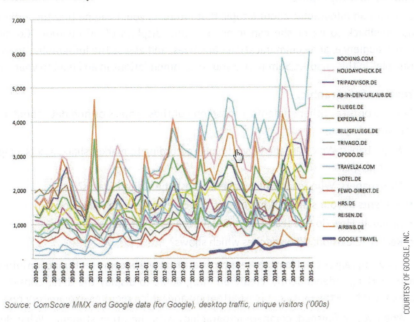

Source: ComScore MMX and Google data (for Google), desktop traffic, unique visitors ('000s)

COURTESY OF GOOGLE, INC.

16. **Determine which type of visual is best.**

For the following situations, select the most appropriate visual aid for presenting the data, and explain why it is the best option. Consider a line chart, bar chart, pie chart, table, or map.

a. To show the daily sales for your small computer business

b. To show the proportion of your budget spent on each of the four fixed costs for your company during the year

c. To show the results of six survey questions asking people's opinion regarding the economy

d. To show the comparisons of the first quarter's net sales for departments A, B, and C

e. To show the locations of your international offices

f. To show total sales by region and the percentage of increase or decrease from the previous year

g. To show the average annual rainfall in selected cities in the nation

17. **Construct a chart from data presented in a table.**

Imagine that you own an independent paint and home decorating store. To determine which product lines bring in the most revenue, you have created the following table.

Product	Revenue Contribution
Wallpaper	10%
Paint	49%
Tools and supplies	24%
Home accents	4%
Stain	13%

To communicate this information to store employees, create a chart from this data.

18. Analyze an infographic.

Search for an infographic about a topic that interests you. Imagine that the author wants your feedback so he or she can improve future displays of information. Consider the source, audience, and communication objectives, and assess the infographic according to principles in this chapter. Summarize your recommendations in an email to your client.

19. Create an infographic.

With two or three other students, choose one of these topics or find data about a subject that interests you:

- Major banks: Which are the biggest banks according to market share, assets, employees, or other measures?
- Newspapers: Who reads which papers across the United States?
- Students at your school: What majors and career paths do they choose?
- Baseball: How do two teams compare for the past five years?
- Reality television: Who watches which shows?

As a group, agree on at least three sets of data that will become sections of an infographic. Then, working independently, create an infographic to display the data. Consider which data should have the most and least attention and which requires explanatory text.

When you're finished, compare infographics with the other students. What decisions did you make in choosing text and graphics? Which work best and why?

LO5 Interpret data for the report reader.

20. Make sense of performance review data.

Imagine that you are a team leader at Anders Consulting and manage a group of junior consultants. Your manager asks you to consider whether Kyle, one of your direct reports, is ready for promotion to team leader. You have the data collected from 15 of Kyle's peers (Figure 27). Write an email to your manager with your assessment. Be sure to provide a

Figure 27 | Ratings Based on 15 Team Evaluations

Major Assessment Categories	Specific Behaviors	Kyle Houston
Ratings Key 3 = The member has performed very well in this area; 2 = The member has performed OK in this area; 1 = The member has not performed very well in this area; 0 = The member has performed poorly in this area.		
Overall Rating		**Mean (2.42)**
		Mode (2)
Contributing	Offers ideas, suggestions, etc.	Mean (2.83)
	Attends all meetings.	
	Meets all deadlines.	Range (2 to 3)
Listening	Lets other members talk.	Mean (1.96)
	Limits discussion to main point of meeting.	
	Summarizes or clarifies other members' ideas.	Range (0 to 3)
	Resists telling other members what to think.	
Facilitating Group Problem Solving	Asks questions to organize discussion.	Mean (2.18)
	Defines questions in order to stay on topic.	
	Selects criteria for evaluating suggested ideas.	Range (0 to 3)
	Encourages suggestions of alternative solutions.	
	Discards all but the best solution.	

clear picture of Kyle's strengths and areas for development. Support your opinion with specific examples of Kyle's behavior, which you may invent.

Exercise 20 refers to Write Experience, a technology that uses artificial intelligence to score student writing and provide feedback to help them improve.

21. **Determine whether statements accurately represent data.**

    The following sentences interpret the table in Figure 26. Analyze each sentence to determine whether it represents the data in the table accurately.

    1. Males and females alike believe Apex is an asset to the community.

    2. More than one-fifth of the females (22%) did not respond.

    3. Age and the generation gap bring about different beliefs.

    4. Married males over age 50 had the most positive opinions.

    5. Females disagree more than males, probably because most of the workers at Apex are male.

    6. Female respondents tend to disagree with the statement.

    7. Apex should be proud that four-fifths of the residents believe the company is an asset to the community.

    8. Thirteen percent of the younger residents have doubts about whether Apex is an asset to the community.

    9. More single than married residents didn't care or had no opinion about the topic.

    10. Overall, the residents believe that 8% of the company is not an asset to the community.

22. **Evaluate the ethics of a television promotion.**

    In this chapter, you read about Dr. Oz's questionable ethics in promoting products that have little scientific evidence of success. Evaluate one of the products he promotes—chia seeds—to determine whether enough research exists to justify using it.

    You may watch Dr. Oz's video on YouTube at bit.ly/WAn9UE to see how he presents the benefits of chia seeds. According to Dr. Oz, what specific results can people expect from taking chia seeds? Be sure to conduct thorough research through credible online sources and journal articles. What is your conclusion? Would you use the product yourself? Would you recommend it to others?

COMPANY SCENARIO

PersuadeCafé

COURTESY OF ED MARION, EDMARION.COM

Let's revisit PersuadeCafé, the coffee and pastry company. Now that you have pitched an idea and received feedback, you'll want to research and develop the idea further.

On the PersuadeCafé intranet site, you'll find information and data that will be useful for you to support your proposal: the current menu, revenue trends, stock performance, the number of stores, customer and employee survey data, and other background information. Review everything available to you.

How will you make sense of the data, research other relevant information, and present findings in ways that support your idea?

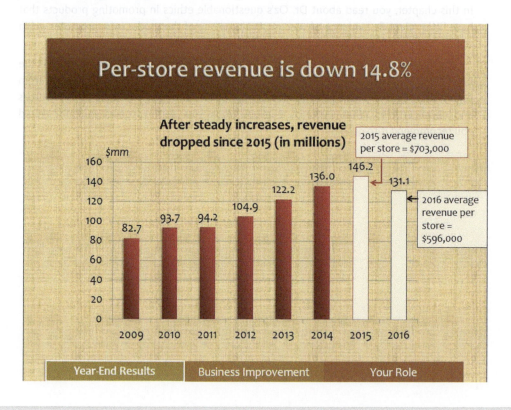

Endnotes

1. Ali Stunt, "No Cancer Advert That Saves a Single Life Can Be Accused of Going Too Far," Pancreatic Cancer Action, http://pancreaticcanceraction.org/community/blog/i-wish-i-had/, accessed April 19, 2015.

2. Mary Elizabeth Williams, "'I Wish I Had Breast Cancer': The Latest Terrible Cancer Campaign," Salon.com, February 5, 2014, www.salon.com/2014/02/05/i_wish_i_had_breast_cancer_the_latest_terrible_cancer_campaign/, accessed April 19, 2015.

3. Ali Stunt.

4. "Pancreatic Cancer Action Campaign: I Wish I Had Breast Cancer," *IHateBreastCancer* (blog), February 5, 2014, http://ihatebreastcancer.wordpress.com/2014/02/05/pancreatic-cancer-action-campaign-i-wish-i-had-breast-cancer/, accessed April 19, 2015.

5. Adapted and used with permission from the author, Grace Lee.

6. Andy Alexander, "Post Columnist Mike Wise Suspended for Fake Twitter Report," Omblog, *The Washington Post*, August 31, 2010, http://voices.washingtonpost.com/ombudsman-blog/2010/08/post_columnist_mike_wise_suspe.html, accessed April 19, 2015.

7. Michael David Smith, "Washington Post's Mike Wise Fabricates Story to Prove Point," *AOL News*, August 30, 2010, www.aolnews.com/2010/08/30/washington-posts-mike-wise-fabricates-a-story-to-prove-a-point/, accessed July 8, 2011.

8. "2014 Study Impact of Social Media on News: More Crowd-Checking, Less Fact-Checking," ING, www.ing.com/Newsroom/All-news/NW/2014-Study-impact-of-Social-Media-on-News-more-crowdchecking-less-factchecking.htm, accessed April 16, 2015.

9. Geoffrey Nunberg, "Teaching Students to Swim in the Online Sea," *New York Times*, February 13, 2005, sec. 4, p. 4; and Judy Foreman, "A Wealth of E-Health: There's a Ton of Medical Data on the Internet, But How Much Is Reliable?" *Los Angeles Times*, November 29, 2004, p. F3.

10. Adapted from "Evaluating Web Resources," Nestlé Library, School of Hotel Administration, Cornell University, April 2015.

11. Charles Seife, *Proofiness: The Dark Arts of Mathematical Deception* (New York: Viking Penguin, 2010).

12. Robert Rosenthal and Ralph L. Rosnow, *The Volunteer Subject* (New York: John Wiley, 1975), pp. 195–196.

13. Stephani K.A. Robson and Sheryl E. Kimes, "Don't Sit So Close to Me: Restaurant Table Characteristics and Guest Satisfaction," *Cornell Hospitality Reports* 9, no. 2. (January 2009).

14. "Financial Presentation Format and Managerial Decision Making: Tables Versus Graphs," *Management Communication Quarterly* 2 (November 1988): 194–216.

15. Matthias Schonlau and Ellen Peters, "Graph Comprehension," Working Paper, Rand Labor and Population, September 2008, www.rand.org/pubs/working_papers/2008/RAND_WR618.pdf, accessed April 19, 2015.

16. Judi Brownell and Amy Newman, "Hospitality Managers and Communication Technologies: Challenges and Solutions." *Cornell Hospitality Reports* 9, no. 18 (December 2009).

17. Edward Tufte, *The Visual Display of Quantitative Information* (Cheshire, CT: Graphics Press, 1983).

18. Theophilus B. A. Aldo, "The Effects of Dimensionality in Computer Graphics," *Journal of Business Communication* 31 (December 1994): 253–265.

19. Ali Binazir, "What Are the Odds?" Visual.ly, November 2011, http://visual.ly/what-are-odds, accessed April 19, 2015.

20. "Where Does Big Data Come From?" IBM, Ibmphoto24's photostream, Flickr, October 17, 2012, www.flickr.com/people/ibm_media/, accessed January 14, 2013.

21. Adapted from Alberto Cairo, *The Functional Art* (blog), www.thefunctionalart.com/2012/12/claiming-word-infographics-back.html, accessed April 19, 2015.

22. Adapted from Kasim Aslam, "How to Make an Infographic in Five Steps," *Social Media Today*, October 15, 2012, http://socialmediatoday.com/kasimaslam/893051/how-make-infographic-five-steps, accessed April 19, 2015, and Samantha Murphy, "How to Create an Awesome Infographic," Mashable, July 9, 2012, http://mashable.com/2012/07/09/how-to-create-an-infographic/, accessed April 19, 2015.

23. Julia Belluz and Steven J. Hoffman, "Dr. Oz's Miraculous Medical Advice: Pay No Attention to That Man Behind the Curtain," *Slate*, January 1, 2013, www.slate.com/articles/health_and_science/medical_examiner/2013/01/can_you_trust_dr_oz_his_medical_advice_often_conflicts_with_the_best_science.html, accessed April 16, 2015.

Writing the Report

LEARNING OBJECTIVES

After you have finished this chapter, you should be able to

LO1 Determine an appropriate report format and organization.

LO2 Draft the report body and supplementary pages.

LO3 Use an effective writing style.

LO4 Document sources accurately.

LO5 Design, format, and finalize the report.

  Ada Meloy, general counsel for the American Council on Education, which represents colleges and universities, said she was pleased the report recognized sex assault as a complex problem. [1]

—Nick Anderson and Katie Zezima, *Washington Post* article

CHAPTER INTRODUCTION

White House Report on Sexual Assault on College Campuses

In a highly publicized, 23-page report, a White House task force published its findings about sexual assault on college campuses.

The report structure follows group's goals, described in a fact sheet on the White House website:

> Today, the Task Force is announcing a series of actions to (1) identify the scope of the problem on college campuses, (2) help prevent campus sexual assault, (3) help schools respond effectively when a student is assaulted, and (4) improve, and make more transparent, the federal government's enforcement efforts. We will continue to pursue additional executive or legislative actions in the future.[2]

The report was a wake-up call for many institutions. Catherine Lhamon, from the U.S. Department of Education, said, "We know that too many universities are still discouraging survivors from filing complaints. They are still delaying investigations for months, or longer. They are still retaliating against students for speaking out about their assaults."[3]

As a result of the task force's work, a "school-by-school enforcement map" on www.notalone.gov shows resolution agreements with schools under investigation for sexual assault incidents. This could be embarrassing for institutions that mishandle complaints. The hope is to improve reporting and disciplinary action and to reduce the large numbers of incidents on campuses, estimated at one in five women in college.[4] The group's report was a clear first step.

Read the entire report at https://www.notalone.gov/assets/report.pdf.

NOT ALONE

The First Report of the White House Task Force to Protect Students From Sexual Assault

April 2014

10-1 Planning the Report

Reports are a tough sell to today's business audience. Decision makers may prefer shorter documents, but interpreting and presenting information is critical for major decisions, which may affect people's lives and cost millions—or billions—of dollars. In addition to the sexual assault report you read about in the chapter introduction, the U.S. government recently produced an 829-page, 174-MG document, *Climate Change Impacts in the United States*. The controversial report blames human activity on climate change and warns of increasing erratic weather, damage to food supplies, and more warming conditions.[5] Such reports pave the way for initiatives to improve our lives, even if the news isn't what we want to hear.

Reports may be written in response to a request or by the writer's initiative. Requests for proposals (RFPs) are formal, detailed documents issued by organizations looking for bids from a variety of sources. To address sexual assault issues on campus, a college may send an RFP to consulting firms. In response, these firms submit reports that meet the client's requirements, sometimes in a highly specific format. When writers initiate a report, they have more flexibility and may choose a less formal approach.

For all reports, you'll follow the same process we discussed for other types of business writing: planning, drafting, revising, and proofreading. Although you'll spend plenty of time planning the report (even before you collect data), presenting the results requires its own stage of planning. You need to decide what format to use, how to organize the content, and what headings to include.

10-1a Selecting a Report Format

What type of report is best for your message and audience? Text-based reports, such as *Not Alone*, are still common, but many companies are producing more graphical documents. Instead of Microsoft Word, PowerPoint software is often used for reports that combine text and graphics. When printed, these reports are sometimes called decks. Even more graphical is Facebook's online annual report, which the company referred to as a "digital magazine."[6] The online report uses infographics, which we discussed in Chapter 9. Other reports are strictly numerical, such as an expense report created in Excel. We can think of these different types of reports along a continuum (Figure 1).

In this chapter, we'll focus on text-based and PowerPoint reports (or decks). Of course, you don't have to use PowerPoint, but we discuss it here as the default program for business. Although both formats are fairly formal documents, significant differences exist. A text-based report is written in narrative (paragraph) form, with headings and subheadings separating each section. In a PowerPoint report, very little, if any, paragraph text is used. Instead, text is written in bulleted form, often incorporated into graphical elements, such as tables or shapes. Each slide is a separate page of the report: the pages function as section divisions, and the slide titles function as headings.

Comparing the reports in Figure 1, you can see why PowerPoint reports have become so popular. In many ways, these reports are easier to create and easier to read than text-based reports. With more graphics and less dense text, the format has much more visual appeal and is far more skimmable than a paragraph-based report. But don't confuse these reports with PowerPoint slides that you would project on a screen during an oral presentation; the YZ Travel example in Figure 1 is far too dense for an audience to read as slides during an oral presentation, which we'll discuss in the next chapter.

For less formal reports, such as a proposal to your manager, you may include the report within an email message. As an example, let's revisit Grace Lee's idea of adding hot food items at Jason's Deli from Chapter 7. You may remember that Grace's manager rejected her idea in Chapter 8. But let's imagine that she had taken a different approach: rather than presenting

Emotional
INTELLIGENCE

Which report type do you prefer—one that's mostly test or mostly graphics? Should your own preference factor into your decision about which to choose for an audience?

Communication
TECHNOLOGIES

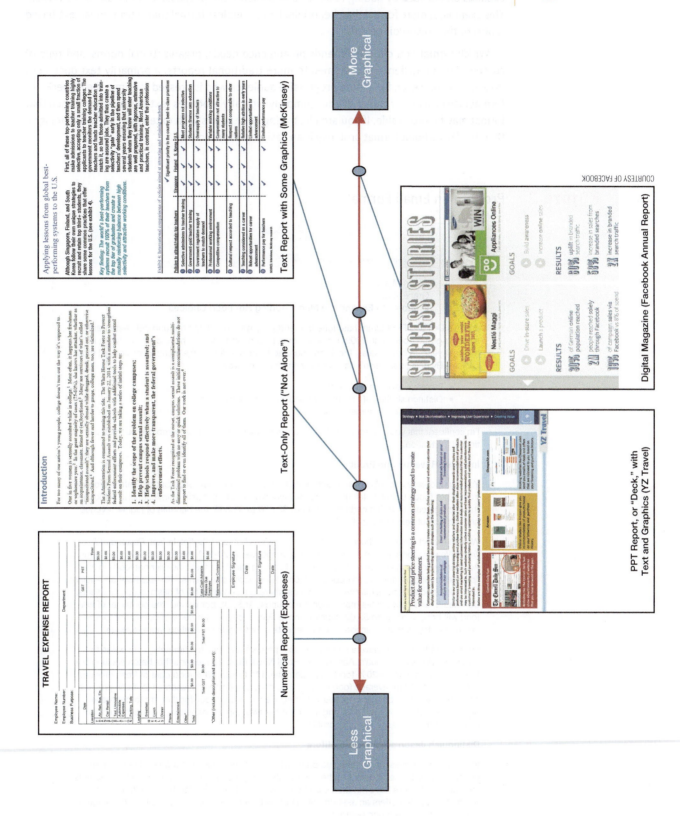

Numerical Report (Expenses)

Text-Only Report ("Not Alone")

Text Report with Some Graphics (McKinsey)

PPT Report, or "Deck," with
Text and Graphics (YZ Travel)

Digital Magazine (Facebook Annual Report)

More Graphical

Less Graphical

COURTESY OF FACEBOOK

her idea in a short email (as in Chapter 7), she writes a more formal proposal. In Figure 2, Grace expands on her idea by adding research and presents the proposal as an email to the owner.[7] This example is more formal than her original email but less formal than a traditional text-based report or the PowerPoint format.

Which format you choose depends on audience needs, organizational norms, and type of content. For an audience accustomed to more traditional reports, a primarily text document may be best; however, for a more progressive audience who is pressed for time, the PowerPoint format may be a better choice. If your company typically produces text-based reports, then that format may be preferable. If you are illustrating your points with extensive charts and images, then the PowerPoint format probably is an easier medium to use.

Figure 2 | Proposal in Email Format

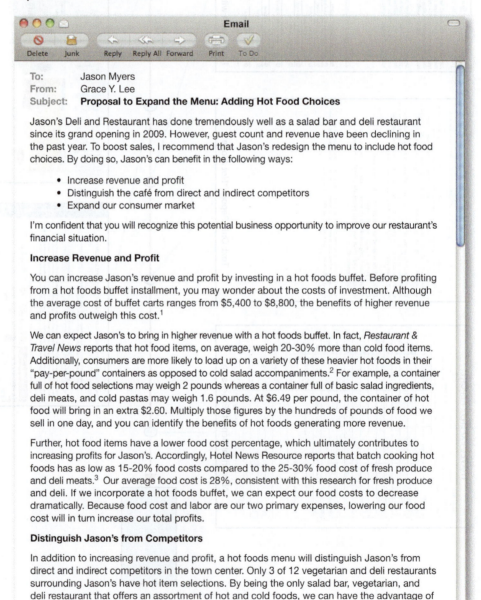

Email

Delete   Junk   Reply   Reply All   Forward   Print   To Do

To: Jason Myers
From: Grace Y. Lee
Subject: **Proposal to Expand the Menu: Adding Hot Food Choices**

Jason's Deli and Restaurant has done tremendously well as a salad bar and deli restaurant since its grand opening in 2009. However, guest count and revenue have been declining in the past year. To boost sales, I recommend that Jason's redesign the menu to include hot food choices. By doing so, Jason's can benefit in the following ways:

- Increase revenue and profit
- Distinguish the café from direct and indirect competitors
- Expand our consumer market

I'm confident that you will recognize this potential business opportunity to improve our restaurant's financial situation.

Increase Revenue and Profit

You can increase Jason's revenue and profit by investing in a hot foods buffet. Before profiting from a hot foods buffet installment, you may wonder about the costs of investment. Although the average cost of buffet carts ranges from $5,400 to $8,800, the benefits of higher revenue and profits outweigh this cost.[1]

We can expect Jason's to bring in higher revenue with a hot foods buffet. In fact, *Restaurant & Travel News* reports that hot food items, on average, weigh 20-30% more than cold food items. Additionally, consumers are more likely to load up on a variety of these heavier hot foods in their "pay-per-pound" containers as opposed to cold salad accompaniments.[2] For example, a container full of hot food selections may weigh 2 pounds whereas a container full of basic salad ingredients, deli meats, and cold pastas may weigh 1.6 pounds. At $6.49 per pound, the container of hot food will bring in an extra $2.60. Multiply those figures by the hundreds of pounds of food we sell in one day, and you can identify the benefits of hot foods generating more revenue.

Further, hot food items have a lower food cost percentage, which ultimately contributes to increasing profits for Jason's. Accordingly, Hotel News Resource reports that batch cooking hot foods has as low as 15-20% food costs compared to the 25-30% food cost of fresh produce and deli meats.[3] Our average food cost is 28%, consistent with this research for fresh produce and deli. If we incorporate a hot foods buffet, we can expect our food costs to decrease dramatically. Because food cost and labor are our two primary expenses, lowering our food cost will in turn increase our total profits.

Distinguish Jason's from Competitors

In addition to increasing revenue and profit, a hot foods menu will distinguish Jason's from direct and indirect competitors in the town center. Only 3 of 12 vegetarian and deli restaurants surrounding Jason's have hot item selections. By being the only salad bar, vegetarian, and deli restaurant that offers an assortment of hot and cold foods, we can have the advantage of menu variety over our competitors.

For example, on Yelp.com, a user review website for restaurants, Jason's is classified as a salad bar, deli, and vegetarian joint—along with 27 other restaurants in the town center; however, adding a "traditional American" tag, after installing a hot foods menu, would separate Jason's from 21 of our competitors.[4]

Expand Our Consumer Market

In addition to distinguishing Jason's from local competitors, our hot food selections can expand our consumer market by appealing to more people. According to a consumer choice study by *Restaurants & Institutions* publications, menu variety is a highly influential factor in consumer dining decisions.[5] Holding all other factors constant, the larger and more diverse the salad bar or buffet, the more the restaurant appeals to the public. More specifically, *Hotels Magazine* suggests an increase in consumer demand for savory foods and hot comfort foods—a trend expected to continue for several years.[6]

On a more local scale, I conducted a small survey this summer of business people at City Center and discovered that most men preferred a hot lunch to a cold salad or sandwich; however, they were often too busy to bother dining at restaurants or ordering take-out. Rather, businessmen usually purchased lunch from quick-service or fast-casual restaurants. Therefore, if we offer restaurant-quality hot foods in a grab-and-go buffet, we could reach out to this untapped market.

On the other hand, women make up the majority of our calorie-conscious guests who may not be initially inclined to purchase hot foods (which are perceived to be high in calories and fat). Yet a study conducted at Columbia and Harvard University revealed that people tend to indulge the occasional urge for guilt-free eating. Women who strictly maintained a low-calorie, low-fat diet would build up "wistful feelings of missing out on life's pleasures."[7] As such, our hot foods buffet will be available to women who want to indulge their occasional urges for guilt-free meals.

In summary, a hot foods menu and buffet at Jason's will make more money, distinguish the café from local competitors, and expand market reach and appeal. With further research on costs and methods to implement this idea, I am certain the addition of hot food items will contribute to a successful, long-term change.

I look forward to hearing your reaction to this idea and to talking about next steps.

[1] "Kitchen & Bars for Outdoor Living," *Vermont Islands*, www.vermontislands.com, accessed March 15, 2017.
[2] "How Do Restaurant Buffets Make Money?" *Pricing for Profit*, www.pricingforprofit.com/pricing-strategy-blog /how-do-restaurant-buffets-make-money.htm, accessed March 14, 2017.
[3] Joe Dunbar, "Food & Beverage: Hot Food Cost Topic," Hotel News Resource, *Hotel Industry News*, www.hotelnewsresource.com/article36259.html, accessed March 14, 2017.
[4] "Jason's Deli," *New York Restaurants, Dentists, Bars, Beauty Salons, Doctors*. www.yelp.com/biz, accessed March 16, 2017.
[5] "Top of the Food Chains: Consumers' Choice in Chains—Restaurants and Institutions," *Foodservice Industry News, Recipes, Research, Restaurants & Institutions*. www.rimag.com/article/CA6686573.html, accessed March 15, 2017.
[6] "Experts Offer Top Food Trends For Hotels and Restaurants," *HOTELS—The Magazine Of The Global Hotel Industry*, www.hotelsmag.com/article/ca6616400.html, accessed March 15, 2017.
[7] "Why It's Good to Indulge the Urge to Splurge," Times Online, Women | Fashion, Health, Beauty, Body & Soul, http://women.timesonline.co.uk/tol/life_and_style/women/fashion/article6091793.ece, accessed March 13, 2017.

10-1b Organizing the Report

A songwriter doesn't necessarily start at the first bar and work toward the last. He or she may find a beautiful refrain and then fill in the rest later. For report writing, you may have collected data in some order, but that's not necessarily the best sequence in which to present the data to your audience.

To organize the report, we have to understand the difference between findings, conclusions, and recommendations—and then decide how to organize the findings.

Findings, Conclusions, and Recommendations

The differences among findings, conclusions, and recommendations are illustrated in Figure 3.

Figure 3 | Examples of Findings, Conclusions, and Recommendations

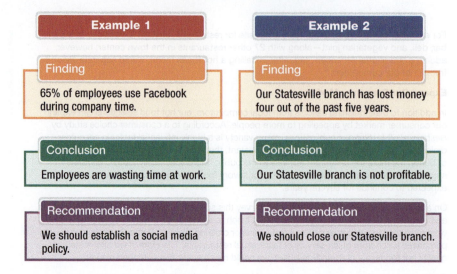

Example 1	Example 2
Finding	**Finding**
65% of employees use Facebook during company time.	Our Statesville branch has lost money four out of the past five years.
Conclusion	**Conclusion**
Employees are wasting time at work.	Our Statesville branch is not profitable.
Recommendation	**Recommendation**
We should establish a social media policy.	We should close our Statesville branch.

As discussed earlier in the book, most business reports for American audiences use the direct organization plan, with the conclusions and recommendations up front. This is the preferable structure for your manager, for audiences who will be receptive to your conclusions and recommendations, and for readers to have context before reading the details of your report. However, the indirect style may be appropriate in some situations. Consider the indirect style when your audience prefers the indirect style (e.g., some international audiences), when your audience may be resistant to your conclusions and recommendations, or when the topic is so complex that the reader needs detailed explanations to understand your conclusions.

Of course, you can use a hybrid approach. For example, instead of putting all the conclusions and recommendations either first or last, you might split them up, discussing each in the appropriate subsection of your report. Or, even though you write a report using an indirect plan, you may add an executive summary or cover letter or email to communicate the conclusions and recommendations to your audience before the report is read.

Organizational Strategies for Findings

The four most common ways to organize your findings are according to time, location, importance, and criteria. Of course, you may choose other patterns for organizing data; for example, you can move from the known to the unknown or from the simple to the complex. The purpose of the report, the type of content, and your knowledge of the audience will help you select the organizational framework that will be most useful.

Time. Chronology, or time sequence, is appropriate for agendas, meeting minutes, schedules, and status reports. For informational reports—to simply inform rather than persuade your reader—discussing events in order is an efficient way to organize and is easy to follow. The following headings use time to detail plans for a companywide event.

Eastern Region Sales Conference
- Monday, January 6: Present year-end reports and sales goals.
- Tuesday, January 7: Attend "The Collaborative Sale" training program.
- Wednesday, January 8: Participate in sales tracking system redesign.

Sequence is an easy way to organize topics but isn't appropriate in all situations. For example, just because you *record* data in sequence, it may not be the most efficient way to *present* that data to your readers. Assume, for example, that you are writing a progress report on a recruiting trip you made to four college campuses. The first passage, given in time sequence, is hard to follow and provides information about timing that isn't relevant to the reader.

⊠ NOT   On Monday morning, I interviewed one candidate for the budget analyst position and two candidates for the junior accountant position. Then, in the afternoon, I interviewed two candidates for the asset manager position and another for the budget analyst position. Finally, on Tuesday, I interviewed another candidate for budget analyst and two for junior accountant.

☑ BUT   On Monday and Tuesday, I interviewed three candidates for the budget analyst position, four for the junior accountant position, and two for the asset manager position.

Location. Like time sequence, location as the basis for organizing a report is often appropriate for simple informational reports. Discussing topics according to their geographical or physical location (e.g., describing an office layout) may be the most efficient way to present the data.

The following example, Renovation Plans for the SAS Dallas Office, uses location to organize the topics; however, the writer probably is using a second variable—for example, time (when the projects will be started or completed) or importance (how much each project will cost). In most cases, you'll use more than one variable for organizing between and within sections.

Renovation Plans for the SAS Dallas Office
- Converting the Cafeteria to Office Space
- Replacing the Roof
- Redecorating the Executive Suite
- Upgrading the Bathroom Facilities

Importance. For the busy reader, the most efficient organizational plan may be to have the most important topic discussed first, followed in order by topics of decreasing importance. The reader then gets the major idea up front and can skim the less important information as desired or needed. This organizational plan is routinely used by newspapers, where the most important points are discussed in the lead paragraph, and in proposals such as Grace Lee's about Jason's Deli.

The following example uses level of importance to organize information for a progress report about the SAS renovation.

Progress on SAS Renovation Project
- Renovation Is on Budget
- Time Schedule Has Slipped One Month
- Houston Office Was Added to Project

Criteria. For most analytical and recommendation reports, where the purpose is to analyze the data, draw conclusions, and recommend a solution, the most logical arrangement is by criteria. For these reports, you may develop a hypothesis and break down factors or causes of a problem. The following example, Selecting a Consultant for the Communication Audit, uses criteria against which the writer evaluates consultants.

By focusing attention on the criteria—in this case, cost and experience—you help lead the reader to the same conclusion you reached. This strategy is another good option if your reader might be resistant to your recommendations.

10-1c Outlining the Report

Although we introduced the concept of outlining in Chapter 4, the process is more complex for a longer, formal report. An outline is a useful step to help you plan which points are to be covered, in what order they will be covered, and how the topics relate to the rest of the report.

Consider your outline as a working draft to be revised as you compose the report. The wording doesn't matter too much at this point; you just want to have the major and minor topics identified. You may use any combination of multilevel numbers, letters, or bullets for your outline. Figure 4 shows an outline of Grace Lee's proposal for Jason's Deli.

Figure 4 | Proposal in Outline Format

Proposal to Expand the Menu: Adding Hot Food Choices

1. Introduction
   a. Background about Jason's
   b. Purpose
   c. Main Points (benefits of the proposal)
   d. Preview of Topics to Be Covered (same as the main points in this case)

2. Increase Revenue and Profit
   a. Implementation Costs
   b. Higher Revenue
   c. Lower Food Costs

3. Distinguish Jason's from Competitors
   a. Competition in the Town Center
   b. Yelp Classifications

4. Expand Our Consumer Market
   a. External Research
   b. Local Customer Data
   c. Possible Downside: Women's Preferences

5. Summary

Headings help orient your reader and give your report unity and coherence. As you refine your outline, you'll choose the actual wording for your headings and decide how many you'll need.

Generic Headings and Message Titles

Imagine reading proposals from four energy auditors about your company's property. Each wants to sell you energy-saving solutions, such as a new heating system or new windows. Sure, headings such as "Costs," "Advantages," and "Disadvantages" explain major sections of the reports, but they're hardly descriptive—and they do nothing to distinguish one report from the others. These are generic headings, which identify only the topic of a section, without giving the conclusion.

Message titles (or talking headings), unlike generic headings, help distinguish your main points for the reader on each PowerPoint page or each section of report. Also used in newspapers and magazines, descriptive headings allow the reader to simply skim the article for the most important ideas.

You might use generic headings if you didn't want to reveal your main points as in these examples about the energy audit:

- Decreasing Heat Loss
- Upgrading Exterior Features
- Improving Efficiency

Now compare the previous headings to these message titles, which convey the main points but might scare the client because of perceived costs:

- Insulating the Walls and Attic Will Decrease Heat Loss
- Replacing the Windows and Doors Will Reduce Air Leaks and Improve Appearance
- Installing an Efficient Furnace Will Reduce Fuel Costs

When you read message titles across a PowerPoint report or in a text-based report, you understand the entire argument, as in the YZ Travel report (Figure 5). These may seem long, but page titles in PowerPoint reports typically are written as full sentences, and they may span two lines. Check that each page conveys one well-supported point and that the title (like a topic sentence for a paragraph) covers the entire idea on the page but doesn't mention points that aren't supported.

Read the entire YZ Travel report—and slides for an oral presentation for comparison—in the Reference Manual.

Message Titles Convey an Argument | **Figure 5**

- YZ Travel is implementing a price steering strategy that alters the initial display of search results based on users' operating systems.

- Price steering is not price discrimination: it does not show different prices for the same product to different users.

- Price steering is one of many criteria that YZ Travel.com uses to predict user preferences and improve the user experience.

- Mac users pay a much higher price for their computers and tend to spend more on hotels than PC users.

- The price steering strategy improves the user experience for both Mac and PC users by providing a more efficient booking process.

- Product and price steering is a common strategy used to create value for customers.

- The price steering strategy is a good opportunity to help increase customer satisfaction and capture market share in the industry.

Parallelism

Although full sentences are increasingly popular as message titles, you may phrase your headings in a variety of ways. Consider using phrases (e.g., Decreasing Heat Loss) or questions (e.g., How Much Will Replacing Windows Save?).

Whichever form of heading you select, be consistent within each level of heading. If the first major heading (a first-level heading) is a noun phrase, all first-level headings should be noun phrases. If the first major heading is a descriptive heading, the others should be too. As you move from level to level, you may switch to another form of heading if this works better, but all headings within the same level and section must be parallel. See Figure 6 for an example from a report about Snapchat.

Figure 6 Parallel Headings in a Report

Improving Snapchat's Reputation: Table of Contents

Length and Number of Headings

For text-based reports, four to eight words is about the right length for most headings. Headings that are too long lose their effectiveness; the shorter the heading, the more emphasis it receives. Yet headings that are too short are ineffective because they do not convey enough meaning.

Similarly, choose an appropriate number of headings. For text-based reports, having too many headings weakens the unity of a report—they chop the report up too much, making it look more like an outline than a reasoned analysis. Having too few headings, however, overwhelms the reader with an entire page of solid text, without the chance to stop periodically and refocus on the topic. Short reports may have only first-level subheadings, and long reports may have as many as four levels of headings.

Balance

Maintain a sense of balance within and among sections. It would be unusual to give one section of a report five subsections and give the following section none. Similarly, it would be unusual to have one section five pages long and another section only half a page long. Also, ensure that the most important ideas appear in the highest levels of headings. If you are discussing four criteria for a topic, for example, all four should be in the same level of heading—presumably in first-level headings.

When you divide a section into subsections, it must have at least two subsections. You cannot logically have just one second-level heading within a section because when you divide something, it divides into more than one part.

10-2 **Drafting the Report**

You may have spent months—or years—collecting data, but your final report is the only way your audience knows how much time and effort you dedicated to the project. Even your skillful analysis of the data will be lost unless your written report explains the significance of your data and helps the reader reach a decision and solve a problem.

Everything you learned in Chapter 4 about the writing process applies directly to report writing: choosing a productive work environment, scheduling a reasonable block of time, letting ideas flow quickly during the drafting stage, and leaving time for revising. However, report writing requires several additional considerations as well.

10-2a **Drafting the Body**

The report body consists of the introduction; the findings; and the summary, conclusions, and recommendations. As stated earlier, the conclusions may go first (e.g., in an executive summary) or last in the report.

Introduction

The introduction sets the stage for understanding the findings that follow. In the *Not Alone* report, the introduction, shown in Figure 1, describes the prevalence of sexual assault, background about the task force, and a list of four steps the task force is taking, described in detail in the following pages.

The topics and amount of detail in an introduction vary according to the type and complexity of the report and the audience's needs. You might not cover related studies, but you might add a section about methodology (procedures to gather and analyze the data). PowerPoint reports omit the introduction entirely, merging this information into the executive summary or first page of the deck.

Findings

Discuss and interpret relevant primary and secondary data you gathered. Using objective language, present the information clearly, concisely, and accurately.

Most reports will display numerical information in tables and figures, which may be bar, line, or pie charts. The information in these displays should be self-explanatory; that is, readers should understand it without having to refer to the text. At the same time, you should refer to and explain all tables and figures so that the text, too, is self-explanatory.

Summarize important information from the graphics. Give enough interpretation to help the reader comprehend the table or figure, but don't repeat all the information it contains. Discuss data most relevant to your main points, pointing out important items, implications, trends, contradictions, unexpected findings, and similarities and differences.

Use emphasis, subordination, previews, summaries, and transitions to make the report read clearly and smoothly. Avoid presenting facts and figures so fast that the reader is overwhelmed with data. How much does the reader need to know? How much is too much? Be sure to make the transition from your own work on the project to what the reader needs to know.

Summary, Conclusions, and Recommendations

The length of your report summary depends on the length and complexity of the report. A one- or two-page report may need only a one-sentence or one-paragraph summary.

Longer or more complex reports, however, should include a more extensive summary. You may briefly review the issues and provide an overview of the major findings. For a McKinsey report encouraging better teacher selection in the United States, the last page suggests areas for further research and ends with a short conclusion to encourage action (Figure 7).

Figure 7 | Conclusion of the McKinsey Report

46

A top third+ strategy for the teaching
profession should be part of the debate.

Areas for further research

This work raises questions for further study:

Regional and local labor markets for top-third students. We focused on the nation as a whole, but teachers are hired primarily in local labor markets. Research might examine which elements of teaching's value proposition are most important in particular geographies. For example, the nation-wide average compensation we surveyed would almost certainly not be perfect fits for the biggest urban districts or for poorer rural areas, given disparities in the cost of living. States or districts pursuing a top-third strategy might find it useful to develop region specific "demand curves" for local talent.

Economy-wide salary structure. One strong hypothesis emerging from this research is that a higher income potential for top-third students in the U.S. has a large impact on the salaries needed to attract top third students to teaching. A more detailed comparison of U.S. and top-performing

nation wage structures could shed light on this issue.

Retention scenarios. Some experts believe that it takes around two to three years for top talent to deliver in the classroom, and that compensation boosts once effectiveness is demonstrated are essential for retention. It would be worth examining options for raising and restructuring compensation between years two and three and, say, five to seven, to retain top students who become top classroom performers. Singapore's differential pay practices and retention bonuses might offer a model, in which a top third+ recruitment strategy and rigorous performance management reinforce one another.

Teacher effectiveness "plateaus." Top-performing nations don't appear to share the view of some U.S. researchers that a teacher's gains in effectiveness stop after three years. Because this judgment can affect many aspects of a national or regional human capital strategy, this question may merit further examination, perhaps in a collaborative effort with top-performing nations.

Conclusion

With more than half of America's teacher corps turning over in the next decade, the nation should be asking, "Who should teach?" Most world-class organizations have a talent strategy: concrete ideas about the human resources they need to succeed, and how to recruit and retain this talent. American education has long followed a more haphazard approach, with its teacher corps the byproduct of broad social and economic trends rather than any conscious design. Recruiting approaches that worked 30 or 40 years ago won't

suffice today. Every country must find its own path and operate in a unique cultural setting. But the extraordinary success of the top-performing nations, who view their teachers as integral to their economic strategies, suggests that the composition of America's teacher corps deserves a national debate. Shifts in America's talent strategy for teaching would take years to fully implement, making it critical to start the conversation now. We hope this research can contribute to the discussion.

If your report only analyzes the information presented and does not make recommendations, you might label the final section of the report "Summary" or "Summary and Conclusions." If your report includes both conclusions and recommendations, ensure that the conclusions stem directly from your findings and that the recommendations stem directly from the conclusions. Either way, end your report with a clear concluding statement. Don't leave your reader wondering if more pages will follow.

For direct-style reports, such as proposals, the summary repeats conclusions or recommendations presented in the executive summary. The YZ Travel PowerPoint report ends with a summary of why the price steering strategy is justified (Figure 8).

10-2b Drafting Supplementary Sections

What additional components are included in reports? Depending on the length, formality, and complexity of the report, you may include additional sections to supplement the report body.

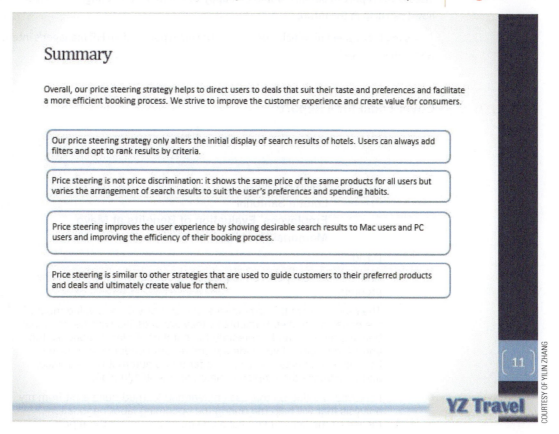

Title Page

Include a title page for text-based and PowerPoint reports, but not for reports that are typed within an email or letter format (such as the Jason's Deli email). The title page typically includes the title (and perhaps subtitle) of the report, the company name and logo, the writer's name (and perhaps the reader's name—as well as titles and departments), and the date the report was written. As the first impression of your report, the title page should look attractive and inviting to read, as is the *Not Alone* title page shown in the introduction to this chapter.

Cover Letter, Memo, or Email

Include a cover note with your report. If you're providing a printed copy, write a short letter (for people outside the company) or memo (for people inside the company). Otherwise, write an email and attach the report. Consider saving your report as a PDF file before attaching it to an email message. This way, your formatting will be preserved, and your report won't be changed without your permission.

In your cover note, provide a summary of the report. State up front that the report is attached, and provide background information, for example, that the report responds to a request. Perhaps give an overview of the conclusions and recommendations of the report (unless you want the reader to read your evidence first); this is a short, more conversational, personal version of your executive summary. Briefly discuss any other information that will help the reader understand and make use of the report (e.g., "The report covers data through March; when we receive the data for April, we'll send you an update"). Include a goodwill ending, for example, "Thank you for the opportunity to present this proposal," or "If you would like to discuss the report in detail, I would be happy to schedule a meeting," or "Please let me know how I can help in the future."

A sample cover email, which summarizes the main points of an HR manager's internal report, is shown in Figure 9.

Figure 9 | Cover Email for a Report

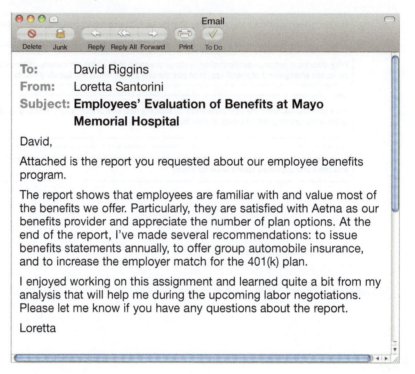

To: David Riggins
From: Loretta Santorini
Subject: Employees' Evaluation of Benefits at Mayo Memorial Hospital

David,

Attached is the report you requested about our employee benefits program.

The report shows that employees are familiar with and value most of the benefits we offer. Particularly, they are satisfied with Aetna as our benefits provider and appreciate the number of plan options. At the end of the report, I've made several recommendations: to issue benefits statements annually, to offer group automobile insurance, and to increase the employer match for the 401(k) plan.

I enjoyed working on this assignment and learned quite a bit from my analysis that will help me during the upcoming labor negotiations. Please let me know if you have any questions about the report.

Loretta

Executive Summary

An executive summary, also called an *abstract* or *synopsis*, is a condensed version of the body of the report (including introduction, findings, and any conclusions or recommendations). Although some readers may scan the entire report, most will read the executive summary carefully—and some will read *only* the executive summary. Some companies that do original research make an executive summary of a report publicly available, while charging a hefty fee (e.g., $2,500) for the detailed findings.

The executive summary is an optional part of the report, most commonly used for long and direct-plan reports. Because the executive summary saves the reader time, this part should be short—no more than 10% of the entire report. Think of the executive summary as a standalone document: assume that the reader will not read the whole report, so include as much useful information as possible.

Use the same writing style for the summary as you used in the report. Figure 10 shows the executive summary for the YZ Travel report. For comparison, the four-page executive summary from the *Not Alone* report is in the Reference Manual; however, this is a bit long. Executive summaries for text-based reports typically are about 10% of the report length.

Table of Contents

Long reports with many headings and subheadings usually benefit from a table of contents. Use the same wording in the table of contents that you use in the body of the report. Typically,

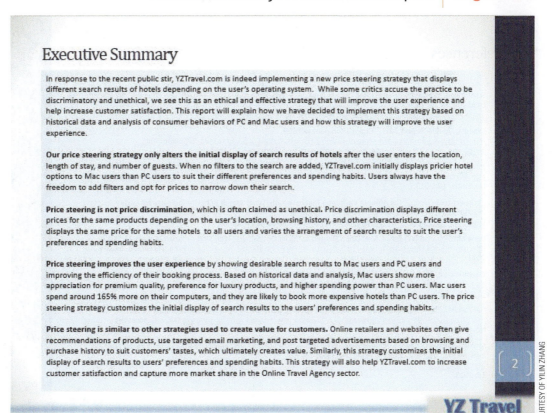

only two or three levels of headings are included in the table of contents—even if more levels are used in the body of the report. For text-based reports, include in the table of contents the reference page, appendices, and a list of tables and figures.

Page numbers in the table of contents, as you saw in Figure 6, identify where each section begins. You may find it useful to automate the pagination in a program such as Microsoft Word. This way, the page numbers in the table of contents automatically update as you edit the report.

Appendix

You may include supplementary information or documents in an appendix at the end of a report. For example, you might include a copy of the cover letter and questionnaire used to collect data or supplementary tables that might be helpful to the reader but that are not important enough to include in the body of the report. Label each appendix separately, by letter—for example, "Appendix A: Questionnaire" and "Appendix B: Cover Letter." In the body of the report, refer by letter to any items placed in an appendix.

References

The reference list contains all of your secondary sources cited in the report. The reference list for the YZ Travel report is shown in Figure 11. For a printed report, you may remove the hyperlinks to web addresses and keep the plain text.

A good indication of a report writer's scholarship is the accuracy of the reference list—in terms of both content and format—so proofread this part of your report carefully.

Figure 11 | Reference Page for the YZ Travel Report

References

- Scott Allan, "Consumer Behavior And Today's Publishers: Why Advertisers Love The Affiliate Channel," *Marketing Land*, August 10, 2012, http://marketingland.com/consumer-behavior-and-todays-publishers-why-advertisers-love-the-affiliate-channel-18048, accessed November 10, 2013.
- Expedia, "Annual Report 2011," Expedia company website, http://files.shareholder.com/downloads/EXPE/2795601475x0x563653/F74F3434-1286-49ED-9953-8016246AD6F3/EXPE_2011_Annual_Report.pdf, accessed November 10, 2013.
- Jordan Golson, "Nearly All Apple Hardware Costs More Than the Average PC," *MacRumors*, October 20, 2011, http://www.macrumors.com/2011/10/20/nearly-all-apple-hardware-costs-more-than-the-average-pc, accessed November 10, 2013.
- iProspect Luxe Group, "The Affluent Consumer Purchase Path: What Search Behavior Indicates for Luxury Success in 2011–2012," *iProspect*, June, 2010, http://www.iprospect.com/wp-content/uploads/2011/11/The-Affluent-Consumer-Purchase-Path-Whitepaper.pdf, accessed November 10, 2013.
- Dana Mattioli, "On [YZ] Travel, Mac Users Steered to Pricier Hotels," *The Wall Street Journal*, August 23, 2012, http://online.wsj.com/news/articles/SB10001424052702304458604577488822667325882, accessed January 20, 2014.
- Priceline.com, "Annual Report 2011," Priceline company website, http://files.shareholder.com/downloads/PCLN/2795602495x0x561766/CB103EAD-2799-49FD-991C-F192C5F8223A/PCLN_2011_Annual_Report.pdf, accessed November 10, 2013.
- Gary Stoller, "New J.D. Power survey ranks travel-booking websites," *USA Today*, November 30, 2012, http://www.usatoday.com/story/travel/2012/11/30/jd-power-travel-website-survey/1735579/, accessed November 10, 2013.
- Jennifer Valentino-Devries, Jeremy Singer-Vine, and Ashkan Soltani, "Websites Vary Prices, Deals Based on Users' Information," *The Wall Street Journal*, December 24, 2012, http://online.wsj.com/news/articles/SB10001424127887323777204578189391813881534, accessed November 10, 2013.

[12]

COURTESY OF YILIN ZHANG

YZ Travel

LO3 Use an effective writing style.

10-3 Developing an Effective Writing Style

An effective writing style will improve how well your report is received.

10-3a Tone

Regardless of the structure of your report, the writing style is typically more objective and less conversational than in a letter or an email. Avoid colloquial expressions, attempts at humor, subjectivity, bias, and exaggeration.

❎ **NOT**   The company *hit the jackpot* with its new MRP program.

☑ **BUT**   The new MRP program saved the company $125,000 the first year.

❎ **NOT**   He *claimed* that half of his projects involved name-brand advertising.

☑ **BUT**   He stated that half of his projects involved name-brand advertising.

10-3b Pronouns

Formal language, which focuses on the information rather than on the writer, typically is used for reports. Where you can, use third-person pronouns and avoid using *I*, *we*, and *you*. However, if your perspective is emphasized or using *you* improves the readability of the report, you may use these pronouns as well.

You can avoid the awkward substitute "the writer" by revising the sentence. Most often, it is evident that the writer is the person doing the action communicated.

Informal:	I recommend that the project be canceled.
Awkward:	The writer recommends that the project be canceled.
Formal:	The project should be canceled.

Using the passive voice is a common device for avoiding the use of *I* in formal reports, but doing so weakens the impact. Instead, revise some sentences to avoid overuse of the passive voice.

Informal:	I interviewed Jan Smith.
Passive:	Jan Smith was interviewed.
Formal:	In a personal interview, Jan Smith stated . . .

You will probably also want to avoid using *he* as a generic pronoun when referring to an unidentified person. Chapter 2 discusses several ways to use gender-neutral language.

10-3c Verb Tense

Use the verb tense (past, present, or future) that is appropriate at the time the reader *reads* the report—not necessarily at the time that you *wrote* the report. Use past tense to describe procedures and to describe the findings of other studies already completed, but use present tense for conclusions from those studies.

When possible, use the stronger present tense to present the data from your study. You can assume that your findings continue to be true—if your findings are no longer true, then you should probably not use them in the report.

☒ NOT   These findings *were based* on interviews with 62 football fans.

 ☑ BUT   These findings *are based* on interviews with 62 football fans.

☒ NOT   Three-fourths of the managers *believed* quality circles *were* effective at the plant.

 ☑ BUT   Three-fourths of the managers *believe* quality circles *are* effective at the plant.

Procedure:	Nearly 500 people *responded* to this survey.
Findings:	Only 11% of the managers *received* any specific training on the new procedure. *(The event happened in the past.)*
Conclusion:	Most managers *do not receive* any specific training on the new procedures.

10-3d Emphasis and Subordination

Wouldn't it be nice if all of your data pointed to one conclusion? That rarely happens—and if it does, you might question the accuracy of your data. More likely, you'll have a mix of data and will have to evaluate the relative merits of each point for your reader. To help your reader understand how important you view each point, use the emphasis and subordination techniques learned in Chapter 5 when discussing your findings.

Consider an excerpt from a research report and how the authors show the relative importance of their findings (Figure 12).[8]

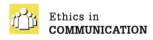

Ethics in
COMMUNICATION

Use emphasis and subordination to let the reader know what you consider most and least important—but *not* to inappropriately sway the reader. If the data honestly leads to a strong, definite conclusion, then by all means make your conclusion strong and definite. But if the data permits only a tentative conclusion, then say so.

Also avoid overstating conclusions by using weak descriptions. Words such as *plethora*, *constantly*, and *countless* are inaccurate and could make your reader question your results—or worse, distrust you personally.

Figure 12 | How Authors Use Emphasis and Subordination

> A sixth of cell phone owners have bumped into someone or something while using their handhelds.
>
> Of the 82% of American adults who own cell phones, fully 17% say they have bumped into another person or an object because they were distracted by talking or texting on their mobile phones. That amounts to 14% of all American adults who have been so engrossed in talking, texting, or otherwise using their cell phones that they bumped into something or someone.

Devote an appropriate amount of space to a topic.

This section (with two more paragraphs) takes up only one-third of a page. Data about cell phone distractions while driving fill the remaining 3.5 pages of the findings section of the report.

Position your major ideas first for the direct plan.

This section appears last in the report, after the more dangerous cell phone behaviors.

Use language that directly tells what is more and less important.

Words such as "fully" express the authors' view of the data. Without this emphasis, the reader might interpret 17% to be a smaller number.

10-3e Coherence

One of the difficulties of writing any long document—especially when the document is drafted in sections and then put together—is making the finished product read smoothly and coherently, like a unified presentation rather than a cut-and-paste job. The problem is even greater for team-written reports, discussed in Chapter 2.

One way to achieve coherence in a report is to use previews, summaries, and transitions regularly. At the beginning of each major section, preview what is discussed in that section. At the conclusion of each major section, summarize what was presented and provide a smooth transition to the next topic. For long sections, the preview, summary, and transition might each be a separate paragraph; for short sections, a sentence might suffice.

Note how preview, summary, and transition are used in the following example of a report section opening and closing.

Training System Users

The training program can be evaluated in two ways: the opinions of the users and the cost of training as a percentage of total system costs. . . . *(After this topic preview, several paragraphs follow that discuss the opinions of the users and the cost of the training program.)*

Even though a slight majority of users now feel competent in using the system, the training falls far short of the 20% of total system cost recommended by experts. This low level of training may have affected the precision of the data generated by the MRP system. *(The first sentence summarizes this section, and the second provides a transition to the next.)*

Don't depend on your heading structure for coherence. Your report should read smoothly and coherently without the headings. For variety and to reflect a sophisticated writing style, avoid repeating the exact words of the heading in the subsequent narrative, and avoid using the heading as part of the narrative.

☒ NOT **The two departments should be merged.** The reason is that there is a duplication of services.

☑ BUT **The two departments should be merged.** Merging the two departments would eliminate the duplication of services.

Always introduce a topic before dividing it into subtopics. You should never have one heading following another without some intervening text; these are called stacked headings. (The exception to this guideline is that the heading "Introduction" may be used immediately after the report title or subtitle.) Instead, use a section overview to preview for the reader how the topic will be divided before you actually make the division. For a direct-plan report, section overviews will also highlight main points to follow. Compare the stacked headings and section overview in Figure 13.

Avoiding Stacked Headings with a Section Overview | **Figure 13**

Stacked headings lack introductory text for a section.

Selecting a Consultant for the Communication Audit

Although the Most Expensive, McKinsey Offers the Most Depth
text text text text text text text text text text text text text text text text

Deloitte Has Experience with the Northeast Region
text text text text text text text text text text text text text text text text

Towers Watson Is the Least Expensive Option
text text text text text text text text text text text text text text text text

Section overviews highlight main points covered under subheadings.

Selecting a Consultant for the Communication Audit

McKinsey is the best choice for the communication audit. Competitors Deloitte and Towers Watson offer advantages, but McKinsey has the most depth in this area.

Although the Most Expensive, McKinsey Offers the Most Depth
text text text text text text text text text text text text text text text text

Deloitte Has Experience with the Northeast Region
text text text text text text text text text text text text text text text text

Towers Watson Is the Least Expensive Option
text text text text text text text text text text text text text text text text

10-4 Documenting Your Sources

When you write a report, you'll include information from other sources that must be documented. Unless you identify a source, your audience will assume all ideas are your own. Documenting your sources will save you from embarrassment and potentially worse consequences: at school, you may be violating a code of academic integrity, and at work, you may lose credibility or—in some situations—your job.

LO4 Document sources accurately.

Watch a video about how to use footnotes: bit.ly/1nWJ22Q

10-4a Why We Document Sources

A Harvard student's falsifications landed him with criminal charges including larceny for accepting $50,000 in financial aid and prizes. Adam Wheeler's "life of deception," reported by *The New York Times*, included rounding up his SAT scores by a few hundred points, faking letters of recommendation, and claiming that he wrote "numerous books."[9] This is an extreme case but offers a word of caution for smaller transgressions.

When writing for business audiences, we document sources for several reasons:

- To avoid accusations of plagiarism
- To give credit to the originator of information
- To demonstrate the validity of our work with credible sources
- To instruct readers where to find additional information

Plagiarism is using another person's words or ideas without giving proper credit. Although each country has different laws regarding the use of others' written work, in the United States, copyright and other laws guide how we treat writers' words—as legal property. Using words without permission or acknowledgement is considered theft.

Documentation is identifying sources by giving credit to another person, either in the text or in the reference list, for using his or her words or ideas. For many business reports, secondary information may be the *only* data you use. This is entirely acceptable, but you must provide appropriate documentation whenever you quote, paraphrase, or summarize someone else's work.

10-4b What Has to Be Documented

All content from secondary sources (information or ideas that aren't your own) must be documented: articles, books, website content, blogs, quotations, graphics, interviews, and so on. However, you do not need to cite information considered common knowledge, for example, "Customer satisfaction is important in the retail industry" or information that is easily verifiable, for example, "Isadore Sharp is the founder of Four Seasons." If in doubt, it's always safer to provide a reference.

Most of your references to secondary data should be in the form of paraphrases. A paraphrase is a summary or restatement of a passage in your own words. A direct quotation, on the other hand, contains the exact words of another. Use direct quotations (always enclosed in quotation marks) only for definitions or for text that is written in a unique way or is not easily paraphrased. The beginning of this section refers to Adam Wheeler's "life of deception," a quotation that is unique, precise, and not easily improved upon.

Paraphrasing involves more than just rearranging words or leaving out a word or two. Instead, try to understand the writer's idea and then restate it in your own language. When you paraphrase, change the sentence structure, and do not use any three consecutive words from the original source, unless the words represent, for example, a company name that cannot be changed.

A *New York Times* reporter, Zachery Kouwe, was accused of plagiarizing *Wall Street Journal* reporter Amir Efrati's work.[10] In the following example, you can see that Kouwe's version of the story is too close to the original.

> Mr. Efrati wrote:
> The family members agreed not to transfer or sell property or assets valued at more than $1,000 or incur debts and obligations greater than $1,000 without approval of the trustee.
>
> Mr. Kouwe wrote:
> Under the agreement, the family members cannot transfer or sell property or assets valued at more than $1,000 or incur debts and obligations greater than $1,000 without approval of Mr. Picard.

This is just one of six examples of plagiarism *The Wall Street Journal* noted within one article.

Ethics in **COMMUNICATION**

International **COMMUNICATION**

Emotional **INTELLIGENCE**

What's your view of documenting sources? Do you find it important, an inconvenience, or something else?

Why do you think laws vary by country? What cultural factors may account for these differences?

Although all secondary sources must be documented, unpublished sources (e.g., not in a journal or on a website) do not need a formal citation. Instead, provide enough text to explain the source, as in these examples.

> According to the company's "Telephone Use Policy," last updated in March 2015, the company "has the right to monitor calls not made within normal business hours."
>
> The contractor's letter of May 23, 2015, stated, "We agree to modify Blueprint 3884 by widening the southeast entrance from 10 feet to 12 feet 6 inches for a total additional charge of $273.50."

Occasionally, enough information can be given in the narrative so that a formal citation is unnecessary even for published sources. This format is most appropriate when only one or two sources are used in a report.

> In the second edition of *Economic Facts and Fallacies*, Thomas Sowell discusses the discrepancy in pay between men and women.

After you cite a source once, you may mention it again on the same or even on the next page without another citation, as long as the reference is clear.

10-4c How to Document Sources

The three major forms for documenting the ideas, information, and quotations of other people in a report are footnotes, endnotes, and author-date references. The method you select depends on organizational norms, the formality of the report, the audience—and, for school reports, your instructor's guidelines.

Footnotes and Endnotes

Footnotes and endnotes are the business standard for documenting sources. For writers, footnotes and endnotes are easy to create in programs like Microsoft Word; for readers, footnotes are easy to view because they appear on the same page as the referenced text. Endnotes follow the same format as footnotes but simply shift the reference to the end of the paper. This is useful when you have so many footnotes on one page that your text is dwarfed by the citations. In this case, endnotes may be preferable for a better design and easier reading. When you use footnotes, you do not need a separate bibliography or reference page.

Although footnotes are ideal for text-based reports, they tend to clutter slide design in PowerPoint reports. A separate reference page for graphical reports is preferable. To connect your slide content to a source, use descriptive text, for example, "According to PKF's annual lodging report . . ."

Footnotes appear as superscript text at the end of each sentence—or part of a sentence—that requires a citation. If one source is used for an entire paragraph, you do not need to add a footnote after each sentence; instead, you may use only one footnote at the end of the paragraph. Footnotes appear after all punctuation.

> SeaWorld and Southwest ended their promotional partnership, which began in 1988. The joint press release describes "shifting priorities" as the reason,[11] but news articles blame backlash from the movie *Blackfish*.[12]

To appropriately describe a source, use the guidelines in Figure 14, which are consistent with those recommended by Harvard Business School—an updated version of guidelines recommended by *The Chicago Manual of Style*. This is a simple way to identify the author, title

Figure 14 | Formatting Sources for Footnotes

TYPE OF REFERENCE MATERIAL	HOW TO FORMAT THE FOOTNOTE	NOTES/ALTERNATIVES
Article from a periodical	Fabrizio Ferri and David A. Maber, "Say on Pay Votes and CEO Compensation: Evidence from the UK," *Review of Finance*, Vol. 17, No. 2 (2013), pp. 527–563.	Although some traditional citation formats suggest including the database you used to find articles (e.g., Factiva or ProQuest), this is not necessary for footnoting in business writing.
Article from a newspaper accessed online	Steve Lohr, "IBM Shares Fall After Earnings Miss Estimates," *The New York Times*, April 18, 2013, www.nytimes.com, accessed May 1, 2015.	If you retrieved this article from the print newspaper, include the section and page number instead of the website and accessed date. If an article doesn't identify an author, simply start with the title.
Article from a website	Juliana Shallcross, "Hotel Indigo San Diego Gets iPad Happy," *HotelChatter*, April 12, 2010, www.hotelchatter.com, accessed September 4, 2015.	To keep footnotes short and save space, you may shorten most URLs to include only the main site reference (up to ".com" in this case), as long as the reader can find the original source easily.
Blog post	Jitendra Jain, "Pinterest for Hoteliers," *Hotel eMarketer* (blog), February 28, 2012, http://hotelemarketer.com, accessed June 25, 2016.	To cite comments on blogs, write the poster's username and the date and time of the post before the rest of the blog citation, for example, "Claude, February 29, 2012 (4:02 p.m.), comment on Jitendra Jain . . ."
Book	Timothy R. Hinkin, *Cases in Hospitality Management: A Critical Incident Approach,* 2nd ed. (New York: Wiley, 2005), p. 72.	For books and articles with more than three authors, include only the first author's name, followed by "et al.," to mean "and others."
Content from a website	Marriott International, Inc., "Who We Support," Marriott company website, www.marriott.com, accessed October 4, 2015.	Providing the date accessed is particularly important for content that exists only online because pages may be moved or removed. You also may include the day of the month if the site changes frequently.
Notes from a class discussion	Katherine Morley, "Services as Experiences," MGT 2490 class discussion, September 10, 2015, Drury University, Springfield, MO.	To cite PPT slides or handouts, simply replace "class discussion" with the name of the source material.
Personal conversations or interviews	Abigail Charpentier, conversation with author, Ithaca, NY, April 19, 2015.	Another variation may be, "Abigail Charpentier, phone interview by author, April 19, 2015."
Tweet	Cornell Hotel School (@TheHotelSchool), "Senior lecturer Rupert Spies teaches astronaut trainees how to cook on Mars: ithacajr.nl/LIiA9X," Twitter, June 18, 2012, https://twitter.com/TheHotelSchool/status/214715857975255040, accessed June 25, 2015.	If you include the entire tweet within your text, you can omit the quoted tweet in your footnote. To find the URL, click on "Details" at the bottom of a tweet.

of the work, publication, date, and other information to tell your reader that your source is credible and retrievable. If your source material isn't included in this chart, use a format that mirrors these, or you can find additional guidelines in the *Harvard Business School Citation Guide* (www.library.hbs.edu/guides/citationguide.pdf).

Author-Date Format

For the author-date format, the writer inserts at an appropriate point in the text the last name of the author and the year of publication in parentheses, for example, (Yuan, 2015). Complete bibliographic information is then included in the References section at the end of the report. More typically used for APA and MLA formats, these in-text citations may interrupt the flow of a paragraph.

10-4d Distortion by Omission

It would be unethical to leave an inaccurate impression, even when what you do report is true. Distortion by omission can occur when using quotations out of context, when omitting relevant background information, or when including only the most extreme or most interesting data. It would be inappropriate, for example, to include quotations from an employee's comments on a company gossip blog and imply that his or her views represent those of all or most employees.

Be especially careful to quote and paraphrase accurately from interview sources. Provide enough information to ensure that the passage reflects the interviewee's *intention*. Examples of possible distortions are in Figure 15.

Ethics in **COMMUNICATION**

Distortions of an Interview Statement | **Figure 15**

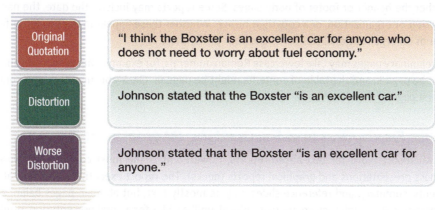

Original Quotation	"I think the Boxster is an excellent car for anyone who does not need to worry about fuel economy."
Distortion	Johnson stated that the Boxster "is an excellent car."
Worse Distortion	Johnson stated that the Boxster "is an excellent car for anyone."

10-5 Designing, Formatting, and Refining the Report

LO5 Revise, format, and proofread the report.

A well-designed and formatted report improves how easily the reader understands your information. After designing and formatting a report, the last step is refining it: revising the text and proofreading.

10-5a Designing and Formatting Text-Based Reports

When creating a text-based report, you'll incorporate graphics to complement text and increase visual appeal; choose spacing and fonts for easier reading; and use headers, footers, and page numbers for clear organization.

Graphics

Even in a primarily text-based report, you may want to include graphics. All references should be numbered (e.g., "as shown in Table 4"). Be careful with phrases such as "as shown below" because the table or figure might actually appear at the top of the following page.

The table or figure should be placed immediately *below* the first paragraph that refers to the graphic. Avoid splitting a table or figure between two pages. If not enough space is available on the page for the display, continue with the narrative to the bottom of the page and then place the display at the very top of the following page.

Spacing and Fonts

Spacing and fonts make your report easier to read. Use a two-inch top margin for the first page of each special part (e.g., the table of contents, the executive summary, the first page of the body of the report, and the first page of the reference list). Leave a one-inch top margin for all other pages and at least a one-inch bottom and side margin on all pages.

Business reports are typically single-spaced. Although you may indent at the beginning of paragraphs, this is not necessary. Instead, all paragraphs may be left justified with one line space between paragraphs.

Use a standard business font such as Times New Roman 12, Arial 10, or Calibri 11. With different fonts, colors, or enhancements (e.g., bold or italic), make sure that the reader can easily distinguish between major and minor headings.

Headers, Footers, and Page Numbers

Business reports typically have the report title (and perhaps the subtitle) and page number in either the header or footer of body pages. Some reports may include the date, the name of the writer or organization, or a copyright notice. Whether these appear in the header or footer depends on organizational standards and your preference.

Preliminary pages may take lowercase Roman numerals; for example, the executive summary might be page ii, and the table of contents might be page iii. Or, Arabic numbers may begin on the first page of the report body.

10-5b Designing and Formatting PowerPoint Reports

See the YZ Travel report as an example in the Reference Manual.

Like Microsoft Word for text-based reports, PowerPoint is the most common software for business presentations and graphical reports (decks). The report executive summary, table of contents, summary, and reference slides may be mostly text, but all main pages balance text and graphics. Although they are more graphical, unlike slides for an oral presentation, printable PowerPoint reports should make "standalone sense" just like a text-based report.

Designing decks can be tricky. Follow the guidelines below and summarized in Figure 16.

Graphics

Formatting standards tend to be more flexible for PowerPoint reports than for text-based reports, but balancing text and graphics is critical. Although the page in Figure 16 is mostly text, the author uses boxes, colors, and bullets to connect points and add visual interest. Try to visualize your information. Use parallel text boxes, diagrams, arrows, and other tools, such as SmartArt. Remember that decks reports typically are printed, so the pages should be far denser than slides you would use for an oral presentation.

Unlike a text-based report, you have don't have to label graphics in a deck, but you do need to explain them. Place explanatory text near graphics or use text boxes and arrows. All visuals should be relevant to the main point. Skip the clip art and photos that you might use in a PowerPoint slide for an oral presentation just for visual interest.

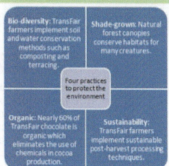

A white background improves readability; check contrast by printing in both color and black and white.

Message titles describe the main point in full sentences using sentence case. When read in sequence across the report, titles convey a cohesive argument.

Mars has already started down a socially responsible path by choosing sustainable cocoa but has the opportunity to expand.

Detailed, explanatory text allows the report to stand alone; check that you have enough evidence to prove your message title.

Business fonts, sizes 11 – 16, are used.

Bullets are preferred over paragraph text; check for parallel phrasing within lists, and check for proper alignment under bullets.

Main points are reinforced on each page.

Mars takes initiative to be a leader in sustainable practices.

A commitment to sustainability builds off an ethical commitment to the individual and the larger community. This commitment is demonstrated by these practices:
- Engagement in cocoa production research to find new and more environmentally friendly production techniques.
- Involvement in organizations such as the World Cocoa Foundation that brings education about sustainable practices to farmers.
- Development research labs to eliminate or reduce the fungal diseases that kill off many cocoa plants.
- Innovation in waste management. The technique of mixing the cocoa waste with piglet food helps pigs transition from mother's milk to solid food. Prior to this, piglets would lose significant weight during this transition.

TransFair shares this commitment to sustainability.

Bio-diversity: TransFair farmers implement soil and water conservation methods such as composting and terracing.

Shade-grown: Natural forest canopies conserve habitats for many creatures.

Four practices to protect the environment

Organic: Nearly 60% of TransFair chocolate is organic which eliminates the use of chemicals in cocoa production.

Sustainability: TransFair farmers implement sustainable post-harvest processing techniques.

Each page uses a mix of text and graphics. Only relevant graphics are included (no photos just for visual appeal).

All pages except the title page are numbered.

Sustainability limits the focus on helping the earth. Fair trade focuses both on this earth-friendly impact through sustainability and a positive impact for others who share this earth.

COURTESY OF MARS

9

Follow these guidelines when choosing colors for your report:

- Avoid dark-colored backgrounds; white is a safe choice. But dark-colored text boxes may be used for message titles and other headings.
- Avoid using too many colors. Choose a professional-looking color scheme and create a visual template for your report.
- Use colors in a meaningful way: they may signal connections between ideas belonging to the same category, progression, contrasting ideas (with contrasting colors), and so on. This color symbolism will intensify your point but will not be sufficient to elaborate or interpret it—make sure your reader still receives enough explanation.
- Avoid color combinations that may be problematic for some readers (e.g., red/green combination is difficult for colorblind people).
- Before you finalize your design and color choice, print a test page to make sure it will look as you planned.[13]

Fonts, Spacing, and Page Numbers

Follow these guidelines when choosing fonts and formatting the report:

- Use consistent fonts and font sizes for titles, subheadings, and body text on each page.
- Use the same size for all message titles (usually between 20 and 28 points).
- Use the same size for all subheadings (e.g., over text boxes), and make these smaller than the message titles.
- Use the same size for body text (usually between 11 and 16 points).
- Choose business fonts, and don't use more than two to avoid busyness.
- Use sentence case. Set message titles flush left rather than centered.
- For bulleted or numbered lists, fix the alignment to avoid hanging indentation. Check that multi-level bullets vary by level.
- Insert page numbers, but omit the number on the first page—your title page.[14]

10-5c Refining Your Report

Once you have produced a first draft of your report, put it away for a few days. This will give you a fresh perspective and will help you find new ways of communicating your ideas.

Revising

As you revise your draft, don't try to correct all problems in one review. Instead, look at this process as having three steps, as discussed in Chapter 5—revising for content, style, and correctness (Figure 17).

Figure 17 | Steps for Revising

1. Revise for content.

- Have you included sufficient information to support each point?
- Have you excluded extraneous information (regardless of how interesting it might be or how hard you worked to gather the information)?
- Is all information accurate?
- Is the information presented in an efficient and logical sequence?

2. Revise for style.

- Are words clear, simple, and concise?
- Are you using a variety of sentence types?
- Do your paragraphs have unity and coherence, and are they of reasonable length?
- Have you maintained an overall tone of confidence, sincerity, and objectivity?
- Have you used appropriate emphasis and subordination?

3. Revise for correctness.

- Do you find any errors in grammar, spelling, punctuation, and word usage?
- Does a colleague catch any errors you may have overlooked?

Proofreading

How would you react if you saw a typographical or data error in a report? Some managers and prospective clients may let this go, but others will judge the writer negatively.

After making all your revisions and formatting the pages, give each page one final proofread. Check closely for errors and appearance. Do you have blank lines, extra page breaks, or inconsistent use of fonts and colors? Although not 100% helpful, run the spelling checker a final time after making all changes.

Checking grammar online isn't 100% accurate either but is useful. Use this tool to check for passive voice, sentence length, misuse of words, unmatched punctuation (e.g., an opening parenthesis not followed by a closing parenthesis), and readability. Use every tool you have to ensure that your report reflects the highest standards of scholarship and diligence.

Let your pride of authorship show through in every facet of your report. Appearances and details count. Review your entire document to ensure that you can answer "yes" to every question in the Checklist for Reviewing Your Report Draft.

Checklist for Reviewing Your Report Draft

INTRODUCTION AND SUPPLEMENTARY PAGES

☑ Is the report title accurate and descriptive?

☑ Does the introduction convey the main points?

☑ Is the executive summary short, descriptive, and in proportion to the report itself?

☑ Is the table of contents accurate, with correct page numbers and wording that is identical to that used in the report headings?

☑ Is any appended material properly labeled and referred to in the body of the report?

FINDINGS AND ORGANIZATION

☑ Is the data analyzed completely, accurately, and appropriately?

☑ Is the analysis free of bias and misrepresentation?

☑ Is the data interpreted (its importance and implications discussed) rather than just presented?

☑ Are the sections logically divided and sequenced?

☑ Does each major section contain a preview, summary, and transition?

☑ Are the headings descriptive, parallel, and appropriate in number?

☑ Are headings and subheadings clearly distinguished?

WRITING STYLE AND FORMAT

☑ Is the report appropriately tailored to the audience?

☑ Are emphasis and subordination used effectively?

☑ Has proper verb tense been used throughout?

☑ Has an appropriate level of formality been used?

SUMMARY, CONCLUSIONS, AND RECOMMENDATIONS

☑ Is the wording used in the summary consistent with that used initially to present the data?

☑ Are the conclusions drawn supported by ample, credible evidence?

☑ Do the conclusions answer the questions or issues raised in the introduction?

☑ Are the recommendations reasonable in light of the conclusions?

☑ Does the report end with a sense of completion and convey an impression that the project is important?

DESIGN AND FORMAT

☑ Have the principles of document design been followed to enhance the report's effectiveness?

☑ Does the report include appropriate graphics, and are the graphics explained in the text?

☑ Are graphics correct, clear, appropriately sized and positioned, and correctly labeled?

☑ Is the report free from spelling, grammar, and punctuation errors?

☑ Are all sources properly documented and consistently formatted?

☑ Does the report make a positive impression overall?

Writing Message Titles for a PowerPoint Report

>>> PURPOSE

Imagine that you work for Dunkin' Donuts and want to convince the management team to offer soy milk. You have researched the question and found that the company would benefit by increasing profits and improving social responsibility. To present your ideas, you write a PowerPoint report with message titles to convey your argument.

>>> PROCESS

1. **Who is the audience for your report?**
   Senior management, who will consider customers' and franchisee owners' perspectives.

2. **What the main points of your argument that should be conveyed in message titles?**
   I want to start with corporate social responsibility and then discuss three customer groups that would benefit from soy milk. I'll give the total potential increase in profits first. Then, one page will describe each of the three groups.

3. **How will you phrase your titles?**
   I'll use full sentences with strong verbs.

>>> PRODUCT

You decide on the following message titles for your report:

- Three segments of the population are affected by Dunkin' Donuts' decision not to offer soy milk to its customers.
- The cost differential of offering soy milk is minimal, and competitors are upcharging.
- A cup of soy milk coffee is 30¢ more profitable than a cup of dairy milk coffee.
- Combined, the unserved market could increase profits by $119 million annually.
- Individuals with dietary restrictions, such as lactose intolerance, could increase annual profits by $73 million.
- Individuals with cultural restrictions, such as veganism and religious limitations, could increase annual profits by $12 million.
- Individuals with personal preferences for plant-based diets could increase annual profits by $33 million.
- Introducing soy milk at Dunkin' Donuts could increase profits significantly.

Writing an Executive Summary for a PowerPoint Report

>>> PURPOSE

Imagine that you're a member of the White House Task Force to Protect Students from Sexual Assault. You're proud of the report *Not Alone*, which received wide publicity and positive responses from universities. Now you want to create a PowerPoint report for easier reading, and you start with the executive summary page. See the full report at https://www.notalone. gov/assets/report.pdf and the current executive summary in the Reference Manual, section B.

>>> PROCESS

1. Who is your audience for the report?

2. What is most important for your audience to know? How will you summarize the 23-page report (which currently includes a four-page executive summary) into just one page? Describe your strategy for identifying main points.

3. Although the page will be mostly text, what graphical elements can you use to add visual interest and make it easier to read? Consider simple approaches, such as boxes, fonts, bullets, and colors.

>>> PRODUCT

Create your one-page executive summary using PowerPoint or another presentation software.

LO1 Determine an appropriate report format and organization.

Reports may be formatted as primarily text documents or as a combination of text and graphics, as in a report created in PowerPoint or other presentation software. The most common ways to organize the findings of a report are by time, location, importance, and criteria. Conclusions typically are presented at the beginning of the report. Report headings should be composed carefully—in terms of their type, parallelism, length, and number.

LO2 Draft the report body and supplementary pages.

The body of the report consists of the introduction; findings; and, as needed, the summary, conclusions, and recommendations. Long, formal reports might also require supplementary components: title page, cover note, executive summary, table of contents, appendix, and reference list.

LO3 Use an effective writing style.

Use an objective writing style, appropriate pronouns, and accurate verb tenses that reflect the reader's time frame (rather than yours, as the writer). Use emphasis and subordination techniques to help alert the reader to what you consider important; and use preview, summary, and transitional devices to help maintain coherence.

LO4 Document sources accurately.

Use direct quotations sparingly; most references to secondary data should be paraphrases. Provide appropriate documentation whenever you quote, paraphrase, or summarize someone else's work by using footnotes, endnotes, or the author-date method of citation. Do not omit important, relevant information from the report.

LO5 Design, format, and finalize the report.

For text-based reports, incorporate graphics to complement text and for visual appeal, choose appropriate spacing and fonts for easier reading, and use page numbers and other features to clarify the organization. For PowerPoint reports (decks), balance text and graphics and follow guidelines for fonts, spacing, and page numbers. Ensure that your deck makes standalone sense.

> EXERCISES

LO1 Determine an appropriate report format and organization.

1. **Determine which report format is best.**

   For each of the following scenarios, which report format would you choose and why? If you would use a primarily text-based report format, identify whether you would create a separate document (with a cover note) or include the report within the body of a letter, memo, or email. (Note: You will find more than one "correct" answer, but whichever you choose, be prepared to justify your response.)

Scenario	Report Format	

1. You work for a conservative university as the head of the residence halls for students. You write a report to the dean of students to provide unsolicited information about the number of false fire alarms in the 16 campus dorms. Your purpose is to request an upgraded fire alarm system for all dorms.	☐ Create a PowerPoint Report	☐ Create a Primarily Text-Based Report
		  ☐ Create a separate document
		  ☐ Include within a letter
		  ☐ Include within a memo
		  ☐ Include within an email

2. You work as a consultant, and you're trying to win new business from a prospective client, a software maker. You propose a training program to improve customer service skills for call center representatives. The estimated costs are $15,000.	☐ Create a PowerPoint Report	☐ Create a Primarily Text-Based Report
		  ☐ Create a separate document
		  ☐ Include within a letter
		  ☐ Include within a memo
		  ☐ Include within an email

3. You work for an independent clothing store and have been asked to compare the number of items made in China, South American countries, and the United States. The report will be sent to the store manager, who works on site, and the owner, who is located in another state.	☐ Create a PowerPoint Report	☐ Create a Primarily Text-Based Report
		  ☐ Create a separate document
		  ☐ Include within a letter
		  ☐ Include within a memo
		  ☐ Include within an email

4. You work for a regional bank and have been asked to research new ATMs. Your report will be sent to the chief technology officer and the head of the consumer banking division.	☐ Create a PowerPoint Report	☐ Create a Primarily Text-Based Report
		  ☐ Create a separate document
		  ☐ Include within a letter
		  ☐ Include within a memo
		  ☐ Include within an email

2. **Explain the different report formats.**

   Imagine that a colleague asks for your help in deciding what format to use for a report for a prospective client. Write an email describing the differences between a primarily text-based report and a PowerPoint report. Without knowing more about the situation, you probably can't advise which is best, but be sure to include criteria for choosing the most appropriate format. In other words, what considerations should your colleague use when making the decision?

3. **Convert an executive summary from a text-based report to a PowerPoint report.**

   Imagine that you wrote the executive summary of the *Not Alone* report (see www.notalone .gov/assets/report.pdf or the Reference Manual, section B). When you showed your draft to your manager, he or she asked you to rewrite it for a PowerPoint report. Your manager believes that your client would prefer this format.

4. **Write a report outline for a financial client.**

   As a financial advisor, you provide expert advice for your clients. A new client has asked you to evaluate a potential investment opportunity: purchasing an existing used bookstore in Norfolk, Virginia. Before you begin your research, you write a very preliminary report outline, which will help you determine what data and other information you need to gather. Working in small groups, first brainstorm what information would be valuable in helping your client make the decision. Next, create an outline of major topics, with at least two minor topics under each.

Exercises 5, 11, 12, and 18 refer to Write Experience, a technology that uses artificial intelligence to score student writing and provide feedback to help them improve.

5. Write a report outline for a restaurant group owner.

You manage Aqua, a fine-dining restaurant in Malibu, California, which is part of a restaurant group. Canoe, another restaurant in the group, is being sold because of profitability and potential compliance issues. As an experienced manager who has maintained high standards at Aqua, you have been asked to write a preliminary report to help a real estate firm value the property for sale.

In the Write Experience case, "Crisis at Canoe," read the county ordinance requirements for food handling, storage, and preparation. Also read what you observe on site at Canoe. Create an outline for your report.

6. Convert generic headings to message titles.

From a preliminary outline for a report, you have the following major and minor generic headings. Convert these to message titles that you'll include in your final report. You may add information to make each heading more descriptive. Either research each topic or, if your instructor allows, make up information just for the purpose of the exercise.

- Obesity in the United States
  - Adult Obesity
  - Childhood Obesity
- Contributors
  - Fast Food
  - School Lunches
  - Processed Food

LO2 Draft the report body and supplementary pages.

7. Write an introduction for a report.

T&C, a consumer products company, has long been known for its product development prowess. You were recently hired by the company's public affairs department to manage the development of a new and unusual product: a book about the history of T&C's product development. The company plans to use this book for new employee training. You believe that making the book available to a wider audience would enhance T&C's reputation without giving away any of its secrets. You also know that you will need professional help to research the book—based on information in your archives and on interviews with current and former employees—and to write it.

Doing a bit of research, you learn that you can choose among four companies specializing in corporate histories: Winthrop Group in Cambridge, Massachusetts; History Associates in Rockville, Maryland; History Factory in Chantilly, Virginia; and Business History Group in Columbia, Maryland. Before your boss will approve this expensive project, you need to prepare a brief report showing the services offered by each company, some clients served by each, and your recommendations for which company seems the best fit given T&C's requirements.

How will you conduct more research? What do you need to know to make a recommendation? What is the purpose of your report? Describe your audience. What data will you include in the report? Using your knowledge of report writing, draft an introduction to this report.

8. Research secondary data and write a PowerPoint report.

Your client is a community foundation, which provides funding to small, local, not-for-profit organizations. With an endowment of $1 million, the foundation is looking for sound investments to grow the possible funds available to support the community. Choose any publicly traded company that interests you, and research whether this company would be a worthy investment for some of the foundation's endowment funds. Your purpose is to identify *whether* the company is a good choice—you do not need to give a positive recommendation.[15]

To formulate your argument, you might research some of the following about your company of choice:

- Background Information: What does your client need to know about the company?
- Mission and Vision: Does the company align with the foundation's mission?
- Stock Trend and Analysts' Recommendations: Is this a sound investment likely to give positive returns?
- Growth Trends: What do you know about the company's revenue and profits? What plans (e.g., for new products and new locations) might be relevant to the foundation?
- Management: Does the company have a strong, stable management team capable of running the company well in the future?
- Current News: What news items about the company might be relevant to the decision?

Prepare a PowerPoint report to the foundation's board of directors. Include a title page, executive summary, table of contents, several pages of findings, and a summary.

9. **Write a short report within an email.**

The Federal Trade Commission, a government agency that protects consumers, has hired you to summarize the issue of rising U.S. consumer debt. Your task is to write a short report within the body of an email that the agency will send to other government constituencies. The agency wants to highlight the importance of their work by showing the seriousness of the problem.

Working in groups of three or four, complete the following:

a. Independently research current data about consumer debt. Be sure to use credible sources, primarily government and academic research.

b. As a group, discuss your research and select the most relevant data for your purpose. In your short report, you won't be able to cover all data, so be selective and focus on three or four points.

c. Create an outline for your email report.

d. Draft the first paragraph, which will include the purpose and main points (your conclusions).

e. Draft the email and share your version with the rest of the class.

f. Vote on which group's email works best. What makes this email most effective?

10. **Adjust the tone of a report section.**

You are a consultant working in the education division of a major firm. One of your group's clients is a federal government agency trying to increase how much time people spend reading. As part of the argument—and the final report—your client asks you how much time people spend on social networking sites, particularly Facebook.

You find this interesting story online. It's a good starting point, but to present this in a credible way for your client, you'll need to find updated data and, of course, present the data using a more objective tone. Write one or two paragraphs with the most recent data you can find.

> Back in July, we reported that Facebook had become the Internet's ultimate time waster, with users spending an average of 4 hours, 39 minutes on it per month, more than any other site on the web.

LO3 Use an effective writing style.

Since then, however, that number has only gone up. According to numbers from Nielsen Online, users spent an average of 5 hours, 46 minutes on Facebook in the month of August. To put that in perspective, that's triple the amount of time they spent on Google!

In fact, the next closest site in Nielsen's top 10 is Yahoo, which, despite still having huge traffic in time consuming areas like news, sports, and financial data, could only get users to stick around for 3 hours and 14 minutes on average during the month. YouTube, surprisingly, only occupied 1 hour and 17 minutes of the average user's time.[16]

11. **Adapt the tone of a report for different audiences.**

The Write Experience exercise, "Staying the Course," asks you, the chief marketing officer of a financial services firm, to decide whether the company should sponsor a golf tournament at a club that doesn't admit women. In the case, you're asked to write a recommendation report to the CEO of the company.

Regardless of what you decide, create a different version of the report—this time for the Women's Rights Organization, the activist group that has pressured your company to withdraw its sponsorship.

12. **Check the tone of a report.**

For the Write Experience exercise, "Need for More Environmentally Friendly Practices," you write a report to your supervisor to outline your plan to reduce office waste. You identified one practice (e.g., wasting paper, not recycling, not composting, or discarding reusable equipment) and described your ideas for more sustainable practices.

Exchange reports with a partner, and imagine that you're an employee instead of the writer's supervisor reading the report. How does the tone sound? Does it accuse or blame employees for poor practices? What, if any, changes should the writer make if the report were sent to employees instead of to the supervisor?

13. **Write a section overview.**

Assume that you're writing a report with the following headings within one section. Write a brief section overview after the major heading to preview topics within the section and summarize the main points. Avoid using the same wording; instead, rephrase the subheadings to form a meaningful section overview.

> The Alliam Hotel can conserve water by making a few minor changes.
> - Install Dual-Flush Toilets
> - Install Oxygen-Assisted Shower Heads
> - Capture Rainwater for Landscaping

LO4 Document sources accurately.

14. **Determine whether information has to be documented.**

Imagine that you're writing a case study report about the bookseller Barnes & Noble. Which of the following information has to be documented in a report?

a. Barnes & Noble's corporate headquarters is located at 122 Fifth Avenue, New York City, New York.

b. The company's online division uses the website www.bn.com.

c. The company's online division generates 10% of the company's revenue.

d. Michael Huseby is the CEO of Barnes & Noble.

e. Barnes & Noble closed its Lincoln Center store in New York City.

f. Most stores are between 10,000 and 60,000 square feet.

15. **Paraphrase sources for a report.**

Imagine that you're writing a report about pet overpopulation. You find these excerpts on the Humane Society website and want to incorporate the information into your report. Paraphrase the text into your own words.

- Four million cats and dogs—about one every eight seconds—are put down in U.S. shelters each year. Often these animals are the offspring of cherished family pets. Spay/neuter is a proven way to reduce pet overpopulation, ensuring that every pet has a family to love them.

- Between six and eight million dogs and cats enter U.S. shelters every year—far too many to all find homes.[17]

16. **Use footnotes to document sources.**

Assume you are writing a report and have used the following secondary sources.

a. An article written by Mary Morgan on pages 45–48 of the April 2, 2015, edition of *Bloomberg Businessweek* entitled "How Big Profits Compare."

b. A quotation by Taylor Scott in an article entitled "Holiday Profits—Boom or Bust" on page A2, column 1, of the April 17, 2015, edition of *The Atlanta Herald*.

c. Statistics from page 233 in a book entitled *Service over Profit: Who Wins?* written by Cameron Della Santi in 2015 and published by Harper Publishing in New York.

d. A quote from an interview conducted on March 30, 2016, with T. Warren Towes, a professor of economics at the University of Wisconsin.

Using these sources and the guidelines in the chapter, prepare footnotes for your report.

17. **Use secondary sources to write a report about female leaders in business.**

2020 Women on Boards is an organization dedicated to raising the percentage of women on corporate boards to at least 20% by the year 2020. As part of the organization's work, imagine that it wants to include case studies of female leaders and wants your help in writing these reports. The reports will be publicly accessible on its website.

For Exercises 17–20, follow your instructor's directions in terms of report length, format, degree of formality, and supplements.

Identify three women who are presidents or CEOs of companies listed on the New York Stock Exchange. Provide information on their backgrounds. Did they make it to the top by rising through the ranks, by starting the firm, by taking over from a family member, or by following some other path?

Analyze the effectiveness of these three individuals. How profitable are the firms they head in relation to others in the industry? Are their firms more or less profitable now than when they assumed the top job? Finally, try to uncover information regarding their management styles—how they see their role, how they relate to their employees, what problems they've experienced, and so on.

From your study of these three individuals, can you draw any valid conclusions? Write a report objectively presenting and analyzing the information you've gathered.

18. **Use secondary sources to write a report cover letter.**

In the Write Experience exercise, "Proceed with Caution," you are a junior economist working for the Miami-Dade County Economic Development Corporation. Your manager has asked you to write a cover letter to paid subscribers for the annual "Economic Forecast Report."

Find current information to address the following questions, and write the cover letter with your sources accurately documented. If you can't get precise information, find other relevant data about Miami-Dade County and the United States.

- How many new businesses were started in Miami last year?
- How many foreign-owned companies are in Miami?
- What are the leading sectors in the United States?
- By how much did the U.S. gross domestic product (GDP) grow or shrink in the past five years?
- What are the projections of the U.S. GDP for this year and next?

19. **Use primary and secondary sources to write a report about your future career.**

Explore a career position that interests you. Determine the job outlook, present level of employment, salary trends, typical responsibilities, educational or experience requirements, and so on. If possible, interview someone holding this position to gain first-hand impressions. Then write up your findings in a report to your instructor. Include at least five secondary sources and at least three tables or graphs in your report.

20. **Use primary sources to write a report about student housing.**

Darlene Anderson, a real estate developer and president of Anderson and Associates, is exploring the feasibility of building a large student apartment complex on a lot her firm owns two blocks from campus. Even though the city planning commission believes there is already enough student housing, Anderson thinks she can succeed if she addresses specific problems of present housing. She has asked you, her executive assistant, to survey students to determine their views on off-campus living.

Specifically, she wants you to develop a ranked listing of the most important attributes of student housing. How important to students are such criteria as price, location (access to campus, shopping, public transportation, and entertainment), space and layout, furnishings (furnished versus unfurnished), social activities, parking, pets policy, and so on?

In addition, the architect has drawn a plan that features the following options: private hotel-like rooms (sleeping and sitting area and private bath but no kitchen); private one-room efficiency apartments; one-bedroom, two-person apartments; and four-bedroom, four-person apartments. Which of these arrangements would students most likely rent, given their present economic situations? Would another alternative be more appealing to them?

Develop a questionnaire and administer it either in hard copy or online to a sample of students. Then analyze the data and write a report for Anderson.

21. **Analyze a report design.**

LO5 Revise, format, and proofread the report.

As part of a campaign to remove Darden's board of directors, the hedge fund Starboard Value LLP created an extensive report. (Read the report at 1.usa.gov/1OAEsWz.) The 108-page report uses dramatic message titles to convince shareholders that the restaurant group had the wrong strategy for Red Lobster.

Imagine that you're an advisor to Starboard. Write a two-page email to compliment the strengths and suggest ways to improve the weaknesses of the report. What principles discussed in this chapter are followed, and which are not?

22. Balance text and graphics on a report page.

Slide 95 of the Starboard Value report described above includes only text. Use shapes or other elements to make this page more graphical.

Darden's new Bylaw amendments are a step in the wrong direction

Despite significant criticism from leading governance firms and shareholders regarding Darden's poor governance practices, the Company has actually taken steps to further disenfranchise shareholders.

Darden's new Bylaw amendments serve to exacerbate Darden's already alarming corporate governance concerns:

- Gives Board broad discretion to unilaterally delay the Annual Meeting beyond October.

- More stringent nomination notice and business proposal requirements.

- Sets Orange County, FL as exclusive forum for shareholders to bring derivative suits and other claims.

- Removes ability of shareholders to fill existing vacancies at next Annual or Special Meeting.

Rather than look out for the best interests of shareholders, it appears that members of Darden's Board is looking to take steps to further entrench themselves.

Darden's recent Bylaw amendments underscore what we believe to be the Company's blatant disregard for shareholder interests.

STARBOARD VALUE® 95

Please see our accompanying presentation: *A Primer on Darden's Real Estate*

COURTESY OF STARBOARD VALUE

SOURCE: WWW.SEC.GOV/ARCHIVES/EDGAR/DATA/940944/000092189514000699/EX991DFAN14A06297125_033114.PDF

23. Proofread part of a report.

Assume that the following passage is part of an informational report that you have prepared. Proofread it carefully for spelling errors, misused words, and grammar errors. Rewrite the passage showing the corrections you made.

Our lawyers have reviewed the wording of the contacts you sent us. They're advise is to except provisions 1 thru 8 and 11 thorough 15. The remainder of the provisions (9 and 10) require farther negotiation.

The number of people we want to include in these talks has not yet been determined. We do expect, however, to have fewer people involved now then in our proceeding meetings.

Marcia Nash, our chief legal council, will be your principal contact during these negotiations. Please telephone her at 555-7376 to sit a mutually beneficial time for us too meet early next month. We are eager to settle this matter soon.

24. Write a complex report.

To practice researching information and writing complex reports, you may use the following prompts:

1. Imagine that your client is in the airline, retail, or hotel industry and wants advice for using social media to connect with customers. Identify five companies within the industry, and compare their use of social media. Look at each company's Facebook page, Twitter feed, and other social media sites. How are they engaging and responding to customers? Also research news stories and other reports about these companies: which are seen as models within the industry? Use this research to provide recommendations for your client company.

2. Choose a company that handled a crisis situation recently. Imagine that you're a consultant for a similar business. How would you advise the management team to avoid such a crisis in the future? According to crisis communication research, what are the best practices for handling a crisis, and how should your client adapt these practices for the company?

3. Where should graduating students start their career? Your client is the career management office at your school, wanting to know which companies to pursue for on-campus recruiting. Recommend five companies to work for within one industry that interests you, and base your recommendation on published "best company" lists, financial performance, management, growth potential, organizational culture, career opportunities, and so on. Include at least 15 different sources.

4. How have women in business fared over the past decade? Your client is the Women's Opportunity Center, a regional organization that wants to encourage women, yet give them a realistic view of their chances of success. Looking at women in various companies and industries in the past ten years, what would you conclude about their progress, particularly their ability to reach the highest levels in organizations? The Center also wants to tell women how they can improve their chances of reaching senior-level positions. Research experts' opinions and studies to provide a list of advice. Try to avoid obvious, surface advice, such as "dress for success"; rather, what should women do in terms of education, performance, communication, relationships, and so on?

5. What are the retail trends among 18- to 25-year-olds? This is a highly coveted market for retailers, and your client, a major clothing manufacturer, wants to understand what this group is buying and how they buy. Research the data, and provide your client with recommendations for types of products, quality, service, and marketing strategies to reach this target group.

6. How do companies today support religious differences? A major consumer products company is finding that an increasing number of Muslims need prayer time during work. The company wants to know how to attract more Muslim employees (the headquarters location has a high Muslim population)—and how to accommodate these employees' needs. In addition to understanding the Muslim community, management would like to know, more broadly, what are the legal requirements for accommodating religion at work, and what do other major companies do to support employees' religious differences?

7. Your client, a philanthropist, plans to start a job skills training program in your home town and wants to know which of the following skills the program should target: computer repair, food service, home painting and repair, or building maintenance. Her plan is to work with regional prisons to offer this program to people who are incarcerated. The objective is to reduce recidivism by giving prisoners marketable skills they can use when they are released. To support your recommendation, you'll need to 1) research the success of similar reentry job training programs that focus on each skill area, and 2) find data about job availability in your area.

8. Under what situations can an employer fire someone for posting negative information online? Your client, a mid-sized technology company, wants to know the prevailing thinking. Senior managers in the organization understand that the law is still evolving, but they want your advice. To provide a balanced perspective, research recent cases and provide several examples of situations where employees were terminated, whether the company was sued, and what the outcome was in each case. You should also research information from The National Labor Relations Board to understand the concept of "protecting concerted activity." Finally, look at companies' social media policies and guidelines, and recommend an approach for your client—to prevent this situation in the first place.

COMPANY SCENARIO

PersuadeCafé

COURTESY OF ED MARION, EDMARION.COM

After all of your good research for PersuadeCafé's Business Improvement Program, you're ready to begin writing a report—a business improvement proposal.

At this point, you may want to refer back to Chapter 4, the Writing Process, to make sure you apply the planning principles discussed earlier. You will certainly want to consider your audience for the proposal, and you'll find Executive Profiles, with brief bios, on the PersuadeCafé intranet site. Before you start writing, make sure you're clear about your purpose and what you hope to achieve: you want your idea to be implemented!

Also, consider what format you'll use for the report. Will this be a text-based document or a PowerPoint report? Your instructor may ask for a particular format.

How will your executive summary reflect your main points? As you draft the report, make sure you have reinforced these main points so you produce a cohesive, convincing report.

Executive Profiles		
Jacqueline Marcus CEO and President	Christopher O'Connor VP, Business Development	Mark Parsons Chief Technology Officer

In 2002, Jackie Marcus joined PersuadeCafé as CEO and president. As the company's first external hire in this position, Jackie has taken a rather conservative approach to growing the company. Although she has been adamant about continuing the strategic plan of opening one store per month, she has not historically encouraged or rewarded innovation. However, now that PersuadeCafé is facing unprecedented financial challenges, Jackie recognizes that the company must change. She is more open to new ideas but only if they are well substantiated.

With an MBA from Stanford Business School, Jackie is known for her financial rigor and commitment to disciplined business processes. Jackie's previous work experience includes twelve years as COO of Peet's Coffee & Tea.

Endnotes

1. Nick Anderson and Katie Zezima, "White House Issues Report on Steps to Prevent Sexual Assaults on College Campuses," *The Washington Post*, April 29, 2014, www.washingtonpost.com /local/education/white-house-issues-report-on-steps-to -prevent-sexual-assault-at-college-campuses/2014/04/28 /0ebf1e22-cf1f-11e3-b812-0c92213941f4_story.html, accessed May 1, 2015.

2. "FACT SHEET: Not Alone—Protecting Students from Sexual Assault," The White House Website, Office of the Press Secretary, April 29, 2014, www.whitehouse.gov/the-press -office/2014/04/29/fact-sheet-not-alone-protecting-students -sexual-assault, accessed May 1, 2015.

3. Bill Chappell, "Campus Sexual Assaults Are Targeted in New White House Report," April 29, 2014, NPR, www.npr.org/blogs /thetwo-way/2014/04/29/307958756/campus-sexual-assaults -are-targeted-in-new-white-house-report, accessed May 1, 2015.

4. Bill Chappell.

5. "Climate Change Impacts in the United States," U.S. Global Change Research Program, National Climate Assessment, May 4, 2014, http://nca2014.globalchange.gov/report, accessed May 1, 2015.

6. Facebook, *The Annual*, December 2013, http://techcrunch .com/2013/12/29/facebook-international-user-growth/, accessed May 1, 2015.

7. Used with permission from the author, Grace Lee.

8. Mary Madden and Lee Rainie, "Adults and Cell Phone Distractions," Pew Internet, June 18, 2010, www.pewinternet .org/Reports/2010/Cell-Phone-Distractions.aspx, accessed May 1, 2015.

9. Jacques Steinberg and Katie Zezima, "Campuses Ensnared by 'Life of Deception,'" *The New York Times*, May 18, 2010, www.nytimes.com/2010/05/19/education/19harvard.html, accessed May 1, 2015.

10. John Koblin, "Robert Thomson's Letter to Bill Keller About Zachery Kouwe's 'Apparent Plagiarism,'" *The New York Observer Media Mob*, February 15, 2010, http://observer.com/2010/02 /robert-thomsons-letter-to-bill-keller-about-zachery-kouwes -apparent-plagiarism/, accessed May 1, 2015.

11. "Joint Statement on Southwest and SeaWorld Partnership," Southwest Airlines, http://swamedia.com/releases/statement -on-southwest-and-seaworld-partnership, accessed May 1, 2015.

12. Lauren Raab, "Southwest, SeaWorld End Partnership a Year After *Blackfish* Backlash," *Los Angeles Times*, July 31, 2014, www .latimes.com/business/la-fi-seaworld-southwest-airlines -20140731-story.html, accessed May 1, 2015.

13. From Maria Wolfe, "Guidelines for PowerPoint Reports," Management Communication II, Cornell University, 2015.

14. From Maria Wolfe.

15. Adapted from an assignment by Prof. Daphne Jameson, Cornell University.

16. Adam Ostrow, "People Spend 33% More Time on Facebook Than Google," *Mashable*, September 17, 2009, http://mashable .com/2009/09/17/facebook-google-time-spent/, accessed May 1, 2015.

17. The Humane Society of the United States Website, "Pet Overpopulation," www.humanesociety.org/issues/pet _overpopulation/, accessed May 1, 2015.

11

Oral Presentation

LEARNING OBJECTIVES

After you have finished this chapter, you should be able to

LO1   Plan a presentation.

LO2   Organize a presentation.

LO3   Plan a team and online presentation.

LO4   Develop effective visual support.

LO5   Practice and deliver a presentation.

" *The most seasoned CEOs quake at something like this. In that light, I think she did a spectacular job.* " [1]

—Davia Temin, owner of a crisis management firm in New York.

CHAPTER INTRODUCTION

General Motors CEO Addresses Employees

After just three months into her new role as General Motors CEO, Mary Barra was propelled into the international media spotlight. Accused of failing to recall cars that caused several deaths, GM was tasked with rebuilding the company's image, and Barra was on the front line.

Mary Barra Update On Recalls

COURTESY OF GENERAL MOTORS

In a four-minute video to employees, Barra explained the investigation and what action the company was taking. The primary audience for her video seems to be the 219,000 GM employees, but the company posted the presentation to its website,[2] expecting the media to report positively on the message.

In another video three months later, Barra provides updates at a "town hall meeting"—where all employees are invited to gather in person or remotely. Barra maintains a clear, forceful tone throughout her 17-minute presentation:

> Let me be clear: this should never have happened. It is unacceptable. Our customers have to know they can count on our cars, our trucks, and our word. Because of the actions of a few people, and the willingness of others in the company to condone bureaucratic processes that avoided accountability, we let these customers down.[3]

During her many presentations about GM recalls, we never saw her waver. Her confident presence to employees was critical to changing the culture at GM, and she kept her cool with the press and during tough hearings with senators on Capitol Hill.

How do you feel about giving presentations? For what types of presentations, settings, and audiences do you feel most and least comfortable?

11-1 The Role of Business Presentations

You may have heard that one of Americans' top fears is public speaking—perhaps it's one of yours. But presentations are inescapable in business for training employees, winning new business, and getting support for an idea. Just about everyone in business will give at least one major presentation and many smaller ones each year to employees, clients, managers, and colleagues. Your presentation skills will also be useful for your personal life—for volunteer organizations and at community meetings.

Whether you're a CEO addressing thousands of shareholders or a first-line manager speaking with a small group of employees, the costs of ineffective presentations are immense. Weak presentations waste time and money and reflect poorly on the speaker. Investors lose confidence, training programs fail, sales are lost, and good ideas aren't implemented.

Making presentations involves good planning, logical organization, effective collaboration, proficient technology use, meaningful visual support, and strong delivery skills.

LO1 Plan a presentation.

11-2 Planning the Presentation

One sure way to fail at making presentations is to try to "wing it." As discussed in our coverage of writing, planning a presentation involves determining the purpose of the presentation, analyzing the audience, and selecting a delivery method.

11-2a Purpose

Keeping your purpose in mind helps you decide what information to include and what to omit, in what order to present this information, and which points to emphasize and subordinate. Most business presentations have one of four purposes: to report, explain, persuade, or motivate. In the examples in Figure 1, you can see how a sales manager might use each.

Figure 1 | Example of a Sales Manager Making Four Presentations with Different Purposes

To Report	Updating the audience on a project or event *Example:* At a senior management team meeting, the sales manager provides a monthly report of actual sales against targets.
To Explain	Detailing how to carry out a process or procedure *Example:* The sales manager shows sales associates how to accurately complete expense reports.
To Persuade	Convincing the audience to purchase something or to accept an idea *Example:* The sales manager encourages a new client to use the company's services.
To Motivate	Inspiring the audience to take some action *Example:* At a monthly sales team meeting, the sales manager gets the associates excited about a new incentive plan.

When the presentation is over, the sales manager determines whether the presentation was successful in fulfilling its purpose. Does the senior management team understand the sales report? Do the associates complete expense reports properly? Does the client change suppliers? Do associates work harder to win incentives? No matter how well or how poorly you spoke, and no matter how impressive or ineffective your visual support, the important question is whether you accomplished your purpose.

11-2b Audience Analysis

The principles you use to analyze your audience of a presentation are the same as those discussed for writing messages and reports. What you discover gives you clues about what content to present, how to organize your presentation, what tone to use, what questions to prepare for, and even how to dress. The audience's attitude affects your presentation. If, for example, you think your listeners will be hostile—either to you personally or to your message—then you'll have to oversell yourself or your proposal. Instead of giving one or two examples, you'll need to give several. In addition to establishing your own credibility, you may need extensive research to bolster your case.

The size of your audience also determines your approach. The larger your audience, the more formal your presentation will be. For large groups, you should speak more loudly and more slowly and use more emphatic gestures and larger visuals. If you're speaking to a small group, your tone and gestures will be more like those used in normal conversation. Also, when presenting to small groups, you have more options for visual support.

Delivering a presentation to an international audience presents additional challenges. If your presentation is in English, and your audience speaks English as a second or third language, you will want to prepare and practice carefully, and follow this advice:

International
COMMUNICATION

- Use simple, clear language and a slower delivery pace.
- Avoid acronyms, euphemisms, humor, and gestures that might not translate well.
- Check jargon with your host ahead of time to make sure the terms will be understood by the local audience, and define any questionable words.
- Enlist your host or an audience member who speaks English well to help translate rough parts for other listeners.
- Gauge the audience's response throughout so that you can make adjustments.
- Include several forms of visuals that the audience can follow during your presentation and take with them to read later.

If your audience is unfamiliar with your topic, you should use clear, easy-to-understand language, with extensive visuals and many examples. If the audience is more knowledgeable, you can go more quickly. If your audience is mixed, you could give two separate presentations to tailor content to each group. Although this takes more time and planning, breaking up groups is usually worth the effort.

The best approach may be to tailor your presentation to the key decision maker in the group—often the highest-ranking person. Take time especially to understand this decision maker's needs, objectives, and interests as they relate to your purpose.

The same content presented to different audiences has to be tailored to each. If you were the sales manager, your monthly sales report to the senior management team would emphasize your strong sales results against targets. But you would probably reposition the monthly sales data as a motivational presentation to the sales associates. Sample agenda slides for these two presentations are shown in Figure 2; you can see how the audience and purpose of the presentation determine the content.

Try not to go into a presentation cold. Meeting with decision makers before your presentation can help predispose the audience in your favor, or at least tell you what resistance you might encounter. For example, if you know that a prospective client is unhappy with the service provided by the current vendor, you can spend more time talking about your company's high level of personalized service.

Figure 2 | Agenda Slide Tailored to Different Audiences

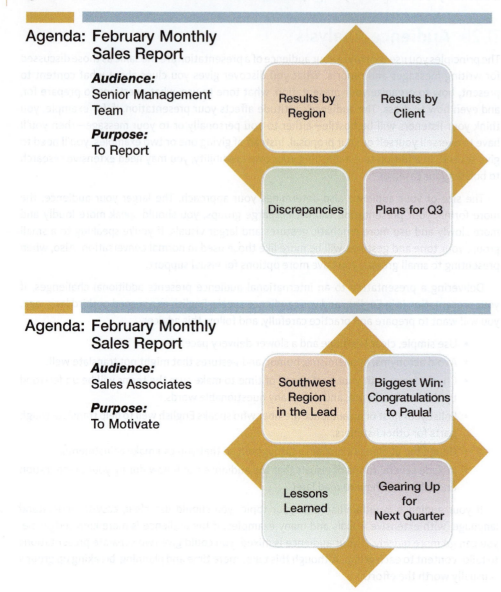

11-2c Delivery Method

At some point during your planning, you'll decide how to deliver your presentation. Plotted along a continuum in Figure 3, delivery styles span informal and formal formats.

Figure 3 | Informal and Formal Delivery Styles

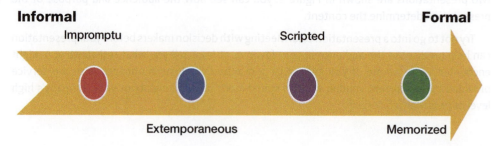

Impromptu and Extemporaneous Presentations

Most business presentations are impromptu or extemporaneous. You cannot prepare much for an impromptu presentation; for example, during a meeting, someone might ask you for your opinion on a new product. If you did your homework, you'll be able to answer the question well, but the presentation is quite informal. You probably won't have any visuals if you weren't expecting the question, and you'll speak in a conversational, unrehearsed style.

Like an impromptu presentation, an extemporaneous presentation requires an unrehearsed style—but it is an enhanced conversational style. The presentation is organized and fluid, typically delivered from an outline or with visuals. As business environments become less formal, so have presentations. Even a sales presentation, which could be considered quite formal, should be delivered using an extemporaneous style. You might miss a word here and there or use a couple of fillers, but this method is far preferable to a stilted, formal style. Trying to build a client relationship or motivate a team with a memorized speech would be off-putting.

Preparation for extemporaneous presentations requires good notes, useful visuals, or both. With presentation software, such as PowerPoint, your slides can function as your outline. The most adept business presenters do not need additional notes, unless covering highly detailed or technical information. Reading diminishes eye contact, confidence, and connection with the audience.

If you do use notes, choose a structure and format that work for you. Consider writing only key phrases rather than complete sentences. You also may include notes to yourself, such as when to pause. Write your notes as a formal outline on full sheets of paper or as notes on index cards. If you use full pages, use larger type and avoid all capital letters, which are harder to read, and staples, which require you to flip pages and can be distracting. Either way, you can make your notes less obtrusive by placing them on a desk or by holding them low on your body with one hand while you gesture with the other.

A natural, extemporaneous speaking style is ideal for building a relationship with your audience.

ISTOCKPHOTO.COM/CATHERINE YEULET

Scripted and Memorized Presentations

In a few business situations, a scripted or memorized style may be appropriate. For a scripted presentation, the presenter reads directly from notes, as you see business leaders do at news conferences. For crisis situations, for example, this is a good approach to make sure you don't say anything on camera that you'll later regret. You also may read notes for ceremonial speeches—for example, at a retirement dinner.

Very few situations call for a memorized speech. Memorizing takes time, is risky, and like a scripted presentation, usually makes the speaker sound mechanical rather than like an accessible, authentic, adaptable business professional. Unless you're giving a TED Talk, stick with the extemporaneous style.

Whichever method you choose, the key to a successful delivery is practice, practice, practice until you sound confident, fluid, and conversational, as if you barely rehearsed at all.

Emotional INTELLIGENCE

What is your experience delivering scripted and memorized presentations? What were the advantages for you, and how did they fall short?

11-3 Organizing the Presentation

For most presentations, the best way to begin is simply to brainstorm: write down every point you can think of that might be included in your presentation. Don't worry about the order or format—just get it all down.

Later, separate your notes into three categories: opening, body, and ending. As you begin to analyze and organize your material, you may find that you need additional information or research.

11-3a The Opening

The first 90 seconds of your presentation are crucial to capture the audience's attention. The audience will be observing and making judgments about your dress, posture, facial expressions, voice qualities, visuals, and of course, what you're saying. Begin immediately to build a relationship with your audience—not just for the duration of your presentation, but for the long term. Because the opening is so crucial to establish rapport, many professionals write out the entire opening and practice it until they are extremely familiar with it.

The kind of opening that will be effective depends on your topic, how well you know the audience, and how well they know you. If, for example, you're giving a weekly status report on a project, you can immediately announce your main points (e.g., that the project is on schedule). If, however, you're presenting a new proposal to a resistant audience, you may first have to introduce the topic and provide background information.

Consider capturing attention with a creative opening. You could start with an interesting fact, a question to the audience, or a story. But use your judgment. You might make a strong first impression—or you might immediately lose the audience. Pay careful attention to the organizational culture and know your audience well before taking a big risk.

Strong visuals in your presentation can serve as an alternative, engaging opening. When a presenter wanted to convince Dunkin' Donuts to offer soymilk, she captured attention with a strong opening slide (Figure 4).[4] Shown after the title slide but before the agenda, this slide uses builds (or animations) to display an "X" over each container—a visual way to explain the lack of options for soymilk drinkers.

Figure 4 | Engaging Opening Presentation Slide

Don't start your presentation with an apology or excuse (e.g., "I wish I had more time to prepare my remarks today," or "I'm not really much of a speaker"). The audience may agree with you! Also avoid apologizing for a cold or scratchy voice. Why start off by telling your audience to question your credibility or delivery skills?

For most business presentations, let the audience know up front what you expect of them. Are you simply presenting information for them to absorb, or are you asking for their endorsement, resources, or help? If you want the audience to invest in your new ice cream shop, tell them early on what you want and what they can expect, for example, "I'm going to show you how a minimum investment of $50,000 will bring you returns of 10% to 15% beginning in year two."

Your opening should lead into the body of your presentation by previewing your content: "Today, I'll cover four main points. First,…" Typically, this will be your agenda for the presentation.

11-3b The Body

The body of your presentation conveys the real content. Here you'll develop the points you introduced in the opening, giving background information, specific evidence, examples, implications, consequences, and other information.

Choose a Logical Sequence

Just as you do when writing a letter, email, or report, choose an organizational plan that suits your purpose and your audience's needs. The most commonly used organizational plans are described in Figure 5.

Whatever organizational plan you choose, make sure that your audience knows at the outset where you're going and is able to follow you throughout the presentation. In a written document, signposts such as headings tell the reader how the parts fit together. In an oral presentation,

	Sample Organizational Plans for Presentations	**Figure 5**

Criteria	Introduce each criterion in turn, and show how well each alternative meets that criterion (typically used for presenting proposals).
Direct Sequence	Give the major conclusions first, followed by the supporting details (typically used for presenting routine information).
Indirect Sequence	Present the reasons first, followed by the major conclusion (typically used for hostile or highly resistant audiences).
Chronology	Present the points in the order in which they occurred (typically used in status reports or when reporting on some event).
Cause/Effect/ Solution	Present the sources and consequences of some problem, and then pose a solution (useful for problem solving).
Order of Importance	Arrange the points in order of importance, and then pose each point as a question and answer it (an effective way of helping the audience follow your arguments).
Elimination of Alternatives	List all alternatives, and then gradually eliminate each one until only one option remains—the one you're recommending (useful to guide decision making).

frequent and clear transitions tell your listeners where you are within the presentation and how points connect to each other.

Establish Your Credibility

Convince the audience that you've done a thorough job of collecting and analyzing the data and that your points are reasonable. Support your arguments with credible evidence—statistics, experiences, examples, and support from experts. Use objective language; let the data—not exaggeration or emotion—persuade the audience. Be guided by the same principles you use when writing a persuasive letter or report.

Avoid saturating your presentation with so many facts and figures that your audience won't be able to absorb them. Regardless of their relevance, statistics will not strengthen your presentation if the audience can't digest all the data. Instead, you might prepare handouts or distribute copies of additional slides with detailed statistics.

Manage Negative Information

What should you do about negative information, which, if presented, might weaken your argument? General Motors CEO Mary Barra, discussed in the chapter introduction, would have been foolish to ignore the safety issues in her presentations. In your own presentations, if you ignore possible downsides of or contradictions to your ideas, a savvy audience may question your credibility.

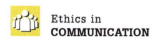

Ethics in COMMUNICATION

When faced with negative information, think about your own data analysis. Despite criticism, you still believe in your idea. The best approach is to present all the important information—pro and con—and to show through your own analysis that your recommendations are valid. Use the techniques you learned in Chapter 5 about emphasis and subordination to let your listeners know which points you consider major and which you consider minor.

Although you should discuss the important negative points, you may reasonably omit discussing minor ones. But be prepared to discuss all issues that the audience may raise during the question-and-answer session.

11-3c The Ending

The ending of your presentation is your last opportunity to achieve your objective. Don't waste it. A presentation without a strong ending is like a joke without a punch line.

Your closing should summarize the main points of your presentation, especially if it has been a long one. Let the audience know the significance of what you've said. Draw conclusions, make recommendations, or outline the next steps. Leave the audience with a clear and simple message.

To add punch to your ending, you might tell a story or show a dramatic visual. However, resist the temptation to end with a quotation. Quotations are overused, and you want your listeners to remember *your* words—not someone else's.

After you've developed some experience in giving presentations, you'll be able to judge fairly accurately how long to spend on each point so that you can finish on time. Until then, practice your presentation with a stopwatch. If necessary, insert reminders at critical points in your notes, indicating where you should be at what point. Avoid having to drop important sections or rush through the conclusion of your presentation because you misjudged your timing.

Finish on a strong, upbeat note. Avoid fading out with a weak "That's about all I have to say" or "I see that our time is running out." Your audience may most remember your last words— choose them carefully and deliver them confidently.

11-3d Humor in Business Presentations

Memory research indicates that when ideas are presented with humor, the audience can recall more details of the presentation and retain the information longer.[5] Humor also creates a connection between the speaker and the audience.

Most of us couldn't be stand-up comedians, even if we wanted to be. If you're not a good storyteller, practicing in front of an audience isn't the best choice. But if you believe that you can use humor effectively, doing so might add just the right touch to your presentation.

If you tell an amusing story, it must be in good taste and appropriate to the situation. Unless you're writing for an episode of *South Park*, never tell an off-color or sexist joke; use offensive language; single out an ethnic, racial, or religious group; or imitate a foreign accent in telling a story. Also avoid humor if your presentation topic is serious or has negative consequences for the audience.

French bank BNP Paribas made this mistake in a motivational video for employees. As it turns out, people don't like Nazi humor. The video was a parody from the movie *Downfall*, showing Hitler as a Deutsche Bank executive angry that competitor BNP is succeeding in the foreign exchange market. Although similar parodies have been used many times and are popular on YouTube, employees unfamiliar with the joke didn't find it funny.

Although this movie parody showing Hitler's reaction to the iPad is popular on YouTube, a similar video didn't go over well at BNP.

Personal, unexpected stories are often best for getting a good laugh. Self-deprecating humor shows that you're human and can laugh at yourself. But be careful not to damage your credibility. Joking about your lack of PowerPoint skills won't reflect well on your presentation. Instead, surprise the audience by telling a story about yourself that becomes funny. Don't warn the audience that a joke is coming, which could disappoint them.

Relate your story to the next part of your presentation. If the audience laughs, this transition will be smooth. If the audience doesn't laugh—it happens—then just continue on with confidence.

Even if you're an expert joke teller, use humor sparingly. You want your audience to respect your ideas—not how funny you are.

11-4 Planning Team and Online Presentations

LO3 Plan a team and online presentation.

Most of your presentations probably will be solo performances in front of live audiences, but you may present as part of a team or over the web.

11-4a Team Presentations

Team presentations are common for communicating about complex projects. For example, presenting a large company's marketing strategy to management or updating the five-year plan may require the expertise and time of several people.

Team presentations, like team writing projects, require extensive planning, close coordination, and a measure of maturity and goodwill. Just as you would for team writing assignments, discussed in Chapter 2, delegate responsibilities according to each person's strengths. Not everyone has to have equal time in front of the audience, but it's odd to have one person speak for 20 minutes and another for only 3. Most important, your presentation should come across as coherent and well coordinated.

Achieving Coherence

Because people have different speaking styles, sounding like one cohesive unit is a challenge for team presentations. Group members should decide beforehand on the presentation tone, format, organization, and visuals. They should also agree on what to wear, how to handle questions, and how to transition from one speaker to another.

Use a presentation template to maintain one "look and feel" for all slides. Have one editor review all slides for consistency throughout the presentation.

Practicing the Team Presentation

A full-scale rehearsal with visuals—in the room where the presentation will be made—is crucial for team presentations. If possible, record the rehearsal on video so that you can review it later. Schedule your final practice session early enough that you will have time to make changes—and then run through the presentation once more, if possible.

Critiquing the performance of a colleague requires tact and empathy, and accepting feedback requires grace and maturity. Revisit the guidelines for Commenting on Peer Writing in Chapter 2—similar techniques apply to oral presentations.

This team is being photographed, but during a presentation, people who aren't presenting should sit down to avoid looking like a "police line-up."

DATACRAFT CO LTD/PHOTOLIBRARY/GETTY IMAGES

Coordinate introductions, transitions, and positioning. Will the first speaker introduce all team members at the beginning, or will speakers introduce themselves as they get up to speak? How will you transition to the next speaker and pass off the slide remote, if you're using one? Where will each of you stand? When others are speaking, consider sitting down rather than creating a police line-up in which presenters nervously look at their notes and mouth the words to their upcoming section.

Also plan how you'll handle questions. Will you take questions throughout the presentation or ask the audience to wait until the end? If a question comes up during the presentation that you know a team member will answer during a subsequent segment, avoid stealing the team member's thunder. Instead, respond, for example, with, "Dylan will cover that point in a few minutes." Refrain from adding to another member's response unless what you have to contribute is truly an important point not covered in the original answer.

Finally, consider yourself on stage during the entire team presentation—no matter who is presenting. If you're waiting for your turn, pay attention to the presenter (even though you may have heard the content a dozen times), and try to read the audience for nonverbal signs of confusion, boredom, or disagreement.

11-4b Online Presentations

Communication
TECHNOLOGIES

Whether solo or with a team, you may deliver presentations over the Internet. Online presentations have many of the challenges of online meetings, discussed in Chapter 3, with a few more complications.

People may lose attention more quickly during a web presentation delivered to several locations. You might consider shorter presentations: perhaps two half-hour sessions rather than a one-hour session, or a half-hour with you as the presenter and then a half-hour for discussion in local offices.

Keep the audience engaged—even more so for an online presentation than an in-person presentation. Check in with the people at each location periodically if you don't hear from them to make sure they are still interested and are following along.

As the presenter, you will be perceived as the person in control. Having good technology support—someone who knows the system well—is a bonus, but know the system yourself so you can confidently take control if problems occur.

Always have a backup plan for the worst-case scenario. If the video goes out, how can you continue your presentation? Have another system ready if yours fails: send your slides in advance and arrange for a speakerphone.

11-5 Developing Visual Support for Business Presentations

LO4 Develop effective visual support.

Most business presentations include some visual support. Visuals complement your message, increase comprehension, and make your presentation easier to follow—for you as well as your audience. When you are asked to give a presentation for a business audience, the default is to use PowerPoint or some other presentation software, projected onto a screen or large monitor.

But slides aren't right for every presentation. A demonstration of safety procedures to line workers should use the equipment as a model. A layoff announcement might include a handout with information employees can take home. And a motivational speech might not use any visuals other than a dynamic, inspiring presenter. Every situation is different, but consider the examples in Figure 6 for which, if any, type of visuals you might use for a presentation.

Examples: When to Use Which Type of Visual | Figure 6

	NO VISUALS	TRADITIONAL PPT (WITH AN ORAL PRESENTATION)	PPT REPORT/ DECK (DURING A MEETING OR CONFERENCE CALL)	PPT REPORT/ DECK (STANDALONE)
Formal	Award Ceremony Eulogy Ribbon-Cutting Ceremony	In-Person Sales Presentation to Client Keynote Address	Sales Presentation to Client via Video or Conference Call Business Improvement Recommendation Report	Sales Proposal to Client Technical Recommendation Report
Informal	One-on-One Meeting Daily Team Meeting	In-Person Monthly Sales Meeting (Internal)	Monthly Sales Meeting via Video or Conference Call (Internal) Project Team Meetings	Monthly Sales Update (Internal) Project Updates

© AMY NEWMAN

When visuals are used, they must be done well, or they'll detract from your presentation. Presentation slides should be clear, easy to follow, attractive—and well integrated into the presentation. Handouts should provide the right amount of information at the right time.

11-5a Creating Presentation Slides

Although PowerPoint is the business standard, many tools are available for creating presentations. Some people prefer Apple's Keynote to PowerPoint. Google Docs is making some headway into the presentation market with its easy-to-use and easy-to-share program. Or, as an alternative to linear slides, Prezi, a web-based program, uses one large canvas for

Communication **TECHNOLOGIES**

transitioning and zooming in and out. In Prezi, you can incorporate a variety of text, images, videos—any object you would use in presentation slides. Newer entrants into the market are Powtoon, ClearSlide, Speaker Deck, Haiku Deck, SlideShark, SlideKlowd, Story Desk, and Zoho.[6] Here, we'll focus on PowerPoint, but most of the principles discussed in this section apply equally to other presentation tools.

Present Your Main Points Clearly

For direct-plan presentations—which most business presentations will be—you'll want your main points up front and reinforced throughout your slides. Let's use an example of an entrepreneurial venture: seeking investors for Ithaca's Ice Cream Shoppe. In Figure 7, a title slide, main point slide, and agenda slide present clear messages from the start.

Figure 7 | Clear Main Points in a Slide Presentation

Your **title slide** should convey what your presentation is about and, if relevant, what result you expect from the presentation. Notice that the presentation is also customized to the audience by mentioning the investment group's name.

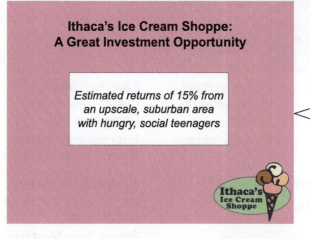

A **main point slide**, presented before the agenda slide, conveys the most important message to the audience—what they can expect from their investment. You don't always have to use a main point slide, but this extra step will make your communication objective clear. Showing a separate slide also ensures that you don't rush through your introduction but instead give your audience enough time to understand your key messages.

Next, your **agenda slide** describes main points. Rather than generic headings, such as Market, Products, Competition, and Financials, you can use message titles as we discussed in Chapter 10. Using message titles for all of your slides will reinforce your main points throughout.

Make Your Presentation Easy to Follow

Developing a well-organized presentation is only half the battle; now you have to reflect that clear organization through your visuals. Clear organization keeps your audience—and you as the presenter—focused.

In your slide presentation, you can include divider slides or a slide tracker. With divider slides, you repeat your agenda slide, highlighting each topic as you cover it. Divider slides are particularly useful for team presentations as you transition to new topics as well as different presenters.

An alternative to divider slides is a slide tracker to show where you are within the presentation. A slide tracker shows the major divisions of your presentation and is repeated on all slides after the agenda. With each section of the presentation highlighted as you get to it, a tracker is the audience's guide (see "Benefits" in Figure 8). Although trackers typically appear at the bottom of a slide (see Figure 9), they may appear at the top. The Facebook example was part of a presentation encouraging Starbucks to use Facebook as a communication tool for its employees. With the changing tabs at the top, the design fits the topic nicely.

Slide Tracker | **Figure 8**

Choose an Attractive, Appropriate Design

Design is never as important as content, but visual appeal can affect your credibility and, at times, the audience's understanding. Choose complementary colors, a cohesive design, simple photographs, and shapes as visual cues. The example in Figure 9 is fresh and appropriate for the topic.

Unless your company has a standard design that you must use, you can use one of the many templates available for presentation slides. A template is a good starting point for your slide design, but the few offered with a program such as PowerPoint get old fast. Adapt templates by, at a minimum, adjusting the colors, changing the fonts, and choosing a different background.

Figure 9 | Modern, Original Slide Design

Figure 10 shows a customized design with a simple color palette. You may use more colors, but avoid too many that conflict with each other. You might also consider a color scheme that reflects your company's colors. Because 8% of men (and .5% of women) are color blind, avoid using shades of red and green next to each other—they're too hard to distinguish.[7]

Simple backgrounds are best for slides. Choose a solid color, gradient, or very light image that travels the edges of the slide but doesn't interfere with text or other graphics. You may use either a dark background with light text or dark text on a light background.

Figure 10 | Custom Slide Design with a Simple Color Palette

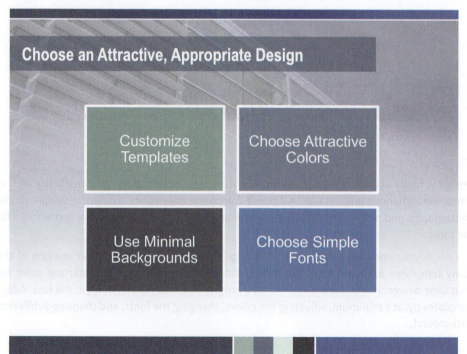

If possible, look at your slides projected in the room where you'll deliver your presentation. All projectors show colors slightly differently, which could affect, for example, your company's logo. Also, only with the appropriate room lighting can you determine whether your color contrast is sufficient.

Choose no more than two fonts for your slides. One font for a slide title and another for the body works well, but more than that may look busy. Unless you're presenting for a creative audience, choose standard business fonts. Serif fonts, such as Cambria and Times New Roman, which have small lines connecting to the letters, have a more classic look. Sans serif fonts (without serifs), such as Arial and Calibri, present a more modern look. Sometimes sans serif fonts are easier to read on a projected screen, so check the fonts when you do your presentation run-through in the room.

Replace Text with Graphics

Presentation slides with few or no words are becoming more popular. Rather than showing lots of bulleted text, the creator uses mostly graphics. For this approach, the presentation relies more on the delivery skills of the speaker. A Walmart executive presented highly visual slides at a global retailing conference (Figure 11).[8] The first slide is his agenda.

Graphical Walmart Slides | Figure 11

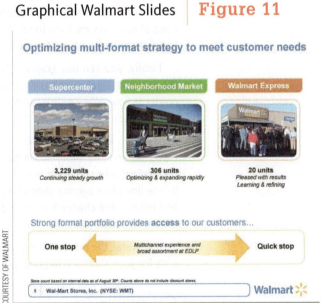

Even for more traditional presentations, avoid slide after slide of bulleted text. Some text on slides is useful for audiences—and will serve as a guide for you as the presenter. But too much text tempts you to read off the slides rather than rely on your own preparation. Text-only slides are mind-numbing for your audience and inspire jokes about "death by PowerPoint." Instead, use your creativity—and tools such as SmartArt in PowerPoint—to convert text into graphics.

Graphics make your slides more visually appealing and, more important, show your audience how concepts relate to each other, as shown in Figure 12. As a bulleted list, the text would miss the point: that these three improvements will lead to more profits.

Also consider using photos or other graphics to replace text. But avoid irrelevant photos and goofy clip art, which detract from your main points. Unless you're presenting to elementary school students, stick with more professional images.

Figure 12 | Graphics Show How Points Relate to Each Other

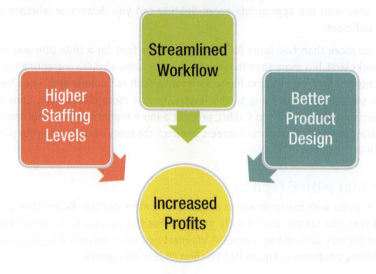

Equally mind-numbing as text-heavy slides are large tables of data projected for your audience. A table of dense numbers is fine for a printed report but not for a slide. Columns and rows of numbers are hard to see and do nothing to help your audience make sense of the data. Instead, convert tables into charts, as we discussed in Chapter 9.

Finally, you can use graphics to highlight data, and add animations to help the audience follow along. Change colors and text enhancements, such as boldface, to draw attention to key points as you review a slide. And use animations to control when the audience sees certain text and graphics.

But keep animations simple and avoid overusing them. Nobody needs to see a line of text travel around the slide, accompanied by a Lady Gaga song, before it finally lands next to a bullet. Similarly, you don't need to control every word for your audience. Presenters who bring in one line of an agenda slide at a time are keeping their audience in suspense for no reason—and missing the chance for the audience to see the big picture of the presentation and read at their own pace.

In general, the more white space and simplicity, the better. Keep your slides clean so they are easy for your audience to grasp quickly.

Write Simply and Clearly

When you do use text, keep it simple and clear. Edit relentlessly to keep just the most important points. The example in Figure 13 shows how you can convert paragraph text to bulleted text. Notice how parallel phrasing is used for each level of bullets, just as you would do for a written report. Use all of your proficient revising and editing skills to perfect the few words you include on your slides.

By further simplifying this text, you can create a graphic suitable for a presentation slide. In Figure 14, a graphic shows the three strategies for increasing profits as sequential steps—a different approach from that used in Figure 12. This slide loses the detail from the bulleted text but may work better for some situations. How much text you include on your slide depends on your audience and your delivery skills.

11-5b Using Presentation Slides

Delivering your presentation with slides requires practice and a bit of choreography. When you present to an audience, your slides are just one visual—you are the main attraction. Use your visuals as support, with the main focus on you.

Three major initiatives will ensure that profits increase over the next 12 months. First, we must increase our staffing levels. We are currently operating at 100% capacity, yet we cannot keep up with demand, which has increased over 20% in the past six months alone. Second, we need to improve our workflow. We have people duplicating work in several departments, and this is leading not only to wasted time but also inconsistent output. Finally, we need better product design. Customer feedback tells us that our design should be simpler and easier to use. With a product return rate of 14%, we're losing our reputation for quality.

How to Increase Profits over the Next 12 Months

- Increase Staffing Levels
  – Operating currently at 100% capacity
  – Failing to keep up with increasing demand

- Streamline Workflow
  – Duplicating work in several departments
  – Causing wasted time and inconsistent output

- Improve Product Design
  – Ignoring customer feedback
  – Receiving 14% product returns
  – Losing reputation for quality

Converting Text to a Graphic | **Figure 14**

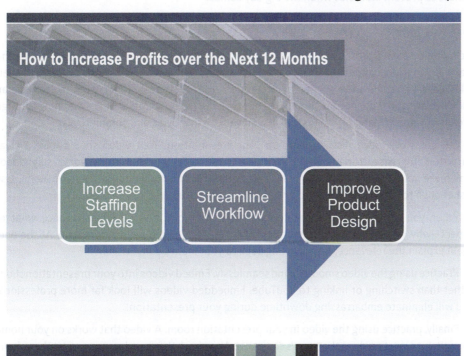

When using slides for your presentation, avoid standing or walking in front of the projection.

Depending on the room and screen or monitor, positioning yourself may be a challenge. Make sure the audience can see you and the slides easily, and always avoid walking in front of the slides and having your back to the audience. Try standing on the left side (from the audience's point of view) for English-speaking audiences, who read from left to right. With this setup, the audience looks toward the left to view you, glances slightly to the right to refer to the slides, and then moves back left to you again. Ideally, you'll find at least two places where you can stand so that you can move around during your presentation. To draw attention to slides occasionally, you can refer to the slide with your body, an arm gesture, or a laser pointer.

Consider when you'll display your slides. You may want to have your title slide up when people enter the room, or you may want to connect with the audience and introduce your topic before showing your first slide. Also, you don't need your slides up during the entire presentation. When telling a story, discussing a controversial topic, or answering questions, consider blanking the slide temporarily to engage the audience so that you can walk in front of the screen projection. During a PowerPoint slideshow on a PC or a Mac, you can hit the Shift key + B to blank the slide, and then hit these keys again when you're ready to continue. Or you can use the remote for a projector to "blank" or "mute" the light for the same effect.

Use a remote to control your slides. A remote lets you walk around freely, so you're not tied to the computer. To advance slides, you don't need to point your remote to the screen or the projector—it's not a TV. Just continue with your natural hand and arm gestures, and push the button when you're ready to go to the next slide. Give yourself time to practice using the remote to prevent stumbles when the big day comes.

11-5c Using Video

Communication
TECHNOLOGIES

Including video in a presentation is a good way to engage the audience, illustrate a point, and make an emotional appeal. If you want in-store customer service associates to improve their sales skills, you could show a video of interactions with customers. If you want to convince an audience about the dangers of climate change, you might show a polar bear swimming through oceans of water looking for ice (as you may have seen in movies and commercials).

But don't use video just to break up your presentation. Your video should have a clear purpose—otherwise, it may detract from your presentation. Irrelevant or, worse, silly videos may make your audience question why your content isn't strong enough to stand alone. Use just enough to make your point, editing content to keep only the relevant points.

When you do use video, integrate it into the presentation. Tell your audience what to expect—why you're showing it, generally what it's about, and how long it will be. At the end, again explain the relevance, transitioning back to your main point.

Practice using the video smoothly and seamlessly. Embed videos into your presentation slides rather than switching or linking to YouTube. Embedded videos will look far more professional and will eliminate embarrassing downtime during your presentation.

Finally, practice using the video in your presentation room. A video that works on your home computer may not work on the room's computer. Also check the sound so you can set the volume level in advance, to make sure your audience won't miss the first few seconds of your video.

11-5d Creating and Using Handouts

Audience handouts—printed copies of slides, notes, tables, or illustrations—help the audience follow a presentation and provide a "takeaway."

Many presenters will distribute copies of the slides (the deck). The deck can include the projected slides or a report version of the slides that has more content. To save paper, you might print two or three slides to a page, leaving space for notes, as long as the slides are still legible. Before you print 100 copies, make sure the colors print well. Colors will look different printed and, if you're printing in black and white, some content originally in color may be difficult to see.

Additional handouts to supplement the slides may be useful. You might include full tables of data, for example, that were not projected on the screen.

When is the best time to distribute your handout—before, during, or after your presentation? If the audience needs to understand complex information as context for your presentation, send handouts ahead of time. If you'll refer to material during your presentation, distribute handouts immediately before the presentation. This has an obvious disadvantage: the audience may refer to the notes rather than listen to you. Instead, you may choose to wait until the end of your presentation to distribute any handouts. This will keep the audience focused on you but may frustrate people who want to take notes throughout. Use your judgment and your knowledge of the audience to make the best decision and leave a positive impression.

11-6 Practicing and Delivering the Presentation

LO5 Practice and deliver a presentation.

Now that you have prepared your presentation, you should practice so that you can deliver it with confidence.

11-6a Practicing the Presentation

Practice enough so that you can present with no notes or only a few notes. Otherwise, it will be difficult to use an extemporaneous style and build rapport. Instead, you'll be looking down at your notes or at a slide for help. Practice the most important parts (introduction, summary of key points, conclusion) the most number of times.

Practicing your presentation will build your confidence and help you engage your audience rather than put them to sleep.

Record your rehearsal on video to help you review and modify your voice qualities, gestures, and content. Play back the video several times, paying attention to the following:

- Is your tone engaging and conversational? Vary your volume and your rate of speaking, slowing down when presenting important or complex information and speeding up when summarizing. Use periodic pauses to emphasize important points.
- Are you clear and easy to understand? Use correct diction, avoid slurring or dropping off the endings of words, and practice pronouncing difficult names.
- Are you using natural hand and arm gestures? Gestures add interest and emphasis but only if they are appropriate and appear natural. If you never "talk with your hands" in normal conversation, it is unlikely you will do so naturally while presenting. Generally, one-handed gestures are more effective and less distracting than two-handed ones.
- Are you calm and focused? Avoid distracting mannerisms and gestures, such as jingling coins or keys in your pocket; coughing or clearing your throat; waving or tightly clasping your hands; playing with your hair or jewelry; or peppering your speech with fillers, such as *um, uh, like,* or *you know.*
- Do you look professional, enthusiastic, and confident? Plan what you'll wear, erring on more conservative, less revealing clothes. As the presenter, dress just slightly better than the audience, but don't go overboard. If the office is casual, you don't have to wear a suit. Smile when appropriate, and keep your body balanced. Take steps naturally, and avoid swaying or pacing.

For important presentations, plan on a minimum of three run-throughs. The first run-through should focus on approximate timing and continuity (does everything you say make sense when you say it aloud?). If necessary, cut out a point so that you have time for a solid, well-rehearsed, and non-rushed summary and conclusion. Schedule your practice sessions far enough ahead of time to allow you to make changes. Your first run-through should probably be private, or perhaps with one close friend or colleague listening to give feedback. Then, when you're satisfied, you can include more people.

11-6b Delivering the Presentation

Now that you know your presentation well, you are ready for a live audience. Take steps to minimize speech anxiety, and prepare for audience feedback and questions.

Use natural hand and arm gestures to add interest and emphasize points in your presentation.

Managing Speech Anxiety

According to author Mark Twain, "There are two types of speakers—those who are nervous and those who are liars." For some people, giving a presentation makes them feel faint or nauseated ("butterflies in the stomach"); makes their hands or legs shake and their palms sweat; gives them a rapid, loud heart beat; makes their face or neck look red and blotchy; or makes them speak too fast and in a high-pitched voice. If you have experienced these symptoms, you're not alone.

The Oscar-winning movie *The King's Speech* portrayed England's King George VI, who suffered with a stammer. The film raised awareness of how many people—even kings—suffer from speech anxiety and other hurdles to speaking in public.

Fortunately, people can overcome their anxiety to become more confident speakers. For many people, nervousness itself is the only issue. Simply changing how we think about ourselves and our delivery skills can reduce speech anxiety.

Anxiety affects people differently. How we experience nervousness—how it manifests in our bodies—and how we combat counterproductive thoughts and feelings vary. What works for one person will not necessarily work for another.

A web-based tool, "How to Feel Confident for a Presentation . . . and Manage Speech Anxiety" describes 22 possible preparation strategies (Figure 15). Although you'll notice some overlap in how the strategies are classified, cognitive approaches involve changing what you believe or how you think about your fears, your audience, your presentations, or yourself. Behavioral (or physical) strategies focus on how you prepare, understand, and use your body. Affective strategies relate to emotions. Changing how you feel helps you focus on your success.

Emotional INTELLIGENCE

What are your fears about public speaking? What successes and negative experiences have you had, and how have they shaped how you feel about giving presentations?

How to Feel Confident for a Presentation

Site: speaking .amynewman.com

Email = user

Password = statler65

Tool for Managing Speech Anxiety | **Figure 15**

How to Feel Confident for a Presentation
....and overcome speech anxiety

INSTRUCTIONS: Click on a strategy to read a more detailed description and reference. Drag a few strategies to try before, the day of, and after a presentation. Click here for a mobile and printer-friendly list of strategies and descriptions. Read more instructions.

Before	Presentation Day	After

Write out all your fears, identify which are irrational, and write a coping statement for each one.

Exercise.

Focus on the audience instead of yourself.

Don't worry about being nervous.

Practice focusing on your words and actions.

Practice mindfulness.

Recognize that you don't look as nervous as you feel.

Find ways to relax.

Understand physical reactions as biological differences.

Practice in front of 4 or more people.

Practice in front of a mirror.

Think of your presentation as a conversation—not a performance.

Power pose.

Pause just before you start.

Distract yourself so you don't think about it.

Think and act positively.

Practice out loud, using different words each time.

Visualize success.

Breathe from your diaphragm and tighten and release muscles. Yawn.

Let yourself relax.

Watch a video of your presentation with an open mind.

Write down everything you did well.

Teal = Cognitive, **Red** = Physical/Behavioral, **Orange** = Affective

COURTESY OF AMY NEWMAN

With tactics to try before, the day of, and after a presentation, this tool generates a custom plan:

- Before the Presentation: How you prepare for and think about a presentation can help reduce anxiety. Writing coping statements, understanding one's physical reactions, and practicing in front of others are among the strategies that can reduce nervousness.
- The Day of the Presentation: On the day of the presentation, presenters can improve their delivery by, for example, practicing "power poses" described in Amy Cuddy's TED Talk (Figure 16), breathing deeply, and visualizing success.
- After the Presentation: Research shows that watching a video of yourself with an open mind, letting yourself relax, and writing down what went well can improve how a presenter feels about his or her delivery.

Figure 16 | Power Poses

High-Power Poses

Low-Power Poses

FROM AMY CUDDY'S TED TALK

Some nervousness is good, so don't fret it too much. Anxiety gets the adrenaline flowing and gives your speech an edge. If you do make a mistake, don't apologize for it. Dropped the remote? Just pick it up. Lost your place? Refer briefly to your notes. If you handle it smoothly and with grace, your audience will remember your recovery more than the mistake.

Responding to Questions and Feedback

One advantage of oral presentations over written reports is the opportunity to engage in two-way communication. Audiences can participate in your presentation by asking questions and by using the "backchannel" for online conversations. You should prepare for both.

Decide whether you'll take questions throughout your presentation or only at the end. Particularly for large, formal presentations, holding questions until the end helps you avoid being interrupted and losing your train of thought, or running out of time and not being able to complete your prepared content. Also, a question may be answered later in your presentation. However, for senior-level audiences, prospective clients, complex topics, and informal settings, you should take questions throughout your presentation. In these situations, you'll be able to adapt your presentation based on questions and can help audiences understand the content without getting too lost.

If you take questions throughout the presentation, you'll have to manage them well. For a hostile audience, at the beginning of the presentation, consider using a detailed agenda and acknowledging potential concerns up front. This tells your audience that you will address their concerns, which could prevent early interruptions. During the presentation, if a question will be answered later, decide how much time to spend. You could defer it if the answer will be addressed soon, answer it briefly, or answer it fully if, for example, it's an emotional question that could detract from the rest of the presentation. If questions get unmanageable, try saying something such as, "I know you have more questions. I want to end on time, and I think these next slides will address many of them." Asking permission to continue may put the audience at ease and help you maintain control of the presentation.

As you prepare your presentation, anticipate questions you might get from the audience. Make a list of them and think through possible answers. If your list of questions is very long, consider revising your presentation to incorporate some of the answers into your prepared presentation.

Always listen carefully to the question; repeat it, if necessary, for the benefit of the entire audience; and look at the entire audience as you answer—not just at the questioner. If necessary, make notes to refer to while answering. Treat each questioner with unfailing courtesy. If the question is antagonistic, be firm but fair and polite. If you don't know the answer to a question, say so and promise to have the answer within a specific period.

If no one asks a question, you either did a great job of explaining your topic, or no one wants to be the first to ask a question. If you suspect the latter, to break the ice, you might start the questions yourself by saying something like, "One question I'm frequently asked is . . ." Or you may ask someone ahead of time to ask the first question if no one else does.

Communication
TECHNOLOGIES

You also may respond to questions and other comments posted online. People may use the backchannel—such as Twitter—during your presentation. This may feel daunting—having your ideas shared or criticized so immediately and so publicly, and you may want to restrict the use of smartphones. But, as we discussed in Chapter 1, you should consider the conventions of your company, where multicommunicating may be the norm. Also, although the backchannel may be distracting, limiting smartphone use may not be realistic—and you may miss out on the chance to address feedback.[9]

You may decide to encourage, rather than limit, the backchannel. Setting up a Twitter hashtag, as the popular South by Southwest (SXSW) conference does every year, lets presenters and participants continue discussions, share ideas, find each other, and promote sessions. During some presentations, the speaker will project tweets during breaks. This is risky—you never know what people will write—but is a nice way to include the audience in the presentation and keep people engaged.

Adria Richards @adriarichards   5 Feb
Cut through the emotion, get to the data - @anjuan on dealing
with racism in the workplace #sxsw #techdiv

COURTESY OF TWITTER.COM

A conference presenter capitalizes on the backchannel by promoting her session.

When your presentation is over and you're back in your office, evaluate your performance. Use the Checklist for Oral Presentations to benefit from the experience. What seemed to work well and what not so well? Analyze each aspect of your presentation—from initial research through delivery. Regardless of how well the presentation went, work to improve your performance next time.

Checklist for Oral Presentations

PLANNING THE PRESENTATION

☑ Determine whether an oral presentation will be more effective than a written report.

☑ Determine your purpose. What response do you want from your audience?

☑ Analyze your audience in terms of demographic factors, level of knowledge, and psychological needs.

☑ Select an appropriate delivery method.

ORGANIZING THE PRESENTATION

☑ Brainstorm. Write down every point you think you might cover in the presentation.

☑ Separate your notes into the opening, body, and ending. Gather additional data if needed.

☑ Write an effective opening that introduces the topic, discusses the points you'll cover, and tells the audience what you hope will happen as a result of your presentation.

☑ In the body, develop the points fully, giving background data, evidence, and examples.

☑ Organize main points logically.

☑ To maintain credibility, discuss any major negative points and be prepared to discuss any minor ones.

☑ Pace the presentation of data to avoid presenting facts and figures too quickly.

☑ Finish on a strong, upbeat note by summarizing your main points, adding a personal appeal, drawing conclusions and making recommendations, discussing what needs to be done next, or using some other logical closing.

☑ Use humor only when appropriate and only if you are effective at telling amusing stories.

PLANNING TEAM AND ONLINE PRESENTATIONS

☑ Spend adequate time preparing for a team presentation to ensure coherence. Coordinate introductions, transitions, positioning—and how you'll handle questions.

☑ When delivering a presentation online, consider shorter segments, plan ways to keep the audience engaged, and practice using the technology.

DEVELOPING VISUAL SUPPORT

☑ Create visuals to complement your presentation.

☑ Present main points clearly and reinforce them throughout your presentation with divider slides or a slide tracker.

☑ Customize a slide design template to create something original and relevant to your presentation. Choose simplicity over complexity.

☑ Where possible, replace text with graphics for easier reading and to show how your points relate to each other.

☑ Supplement your presentation with video and handouts, as appropriate for your audience and objectives.

PRACTICING AND DELIVERING THE PRESENTATION

☑ Rehearse your presentation extensively, simulating the actual speaking conditions as much as possible and using your visual aids.

☑ Check your tone, clarity, gestures, movement, and so on.

☑ Manage anxiety by thinking positively about your presentation and by preparing your body.

☑ Consider incorporating the backchannel into your presentation.

☑ Plan your answers to possible questions ahead of time. Listen to each question carefully, and address your answer to the entire audience.

Giving Speech Feedback to Mary Barra, General Motors CEO

3Ps
‹ IN ACTION

⟫⟫ PURPOSE

You are the owner of a media training company, and Mary Barra, General Motors CEO, has asked for your feedback about her video to employees (see bit.ly/1o4dY1Z for the YouTube video). She wants your professional opinion about what she did well and how she can improve for future presentations. You use a feedback form to summarize your notes before meeting with her.

⟫⟫ PROCESS

1. **What was the purpose of Barra's speech?**
   To update employees on the recalls and prove to the public that GM is cooperating with the investigation and is taking serious action.

2. **Describe the audience.**
   Employees may be dismayed by the news and worried about their jobs. The media wants a good story, and the public probably is angry about what has been reported as GM's failure to recall defective cars.

3. **How was the presentation organized?**
   Barra started by providing an update on the investigation process and promising the company's cooperation. Early on, she admitted "terrible things happened." She then reminded people of what the company has already done, including communicating with customers. Next she talked about additional plans, including adding resources to call centers. She then assured employees that the company is committed to improvement and focus on the customer. Barra then discussed other actions the company is taking, including additional recalls and an "intense review" of internal processes. She ends by expressing her confidence in the company's new cars and the process going forward. She thanks people for their time.

4. **What was the best delivery style for the presentation purpose and audience?**
   Scripted. As a short, formal speech, Barra would be expected to read from a script and not show visuals.

Presentation Feedback

	Not at All	Somewhat	Yes	Definitely
1. The organization works well for the topic and is easy to follow.				
COMMENTS:				
Overall, the organization is logical, but at times, Barra sounded like she was ending the speech. Transitions could have been clearer.	1	2	(3)	4
2. The content is clear and is well supported with details and examples.				
COMMENTS:				
The content was relevant to the situation and audience—primarily employees. Focusing on the customer worked well as a theme.	1	2	3	(4)
3. The delivery style is engaging and appropriate for the audience.				
COMMENTS:				
Barra was clear and confident. Her posture, facial expressions, and hand gestures were natural and appropriate.	1	2	3	(4)

Preparing for an Industry Conference Presentation

3Ps
‹ IN PRACTICE

>>> PURPOSE

Imagine that you are Mary Barra, General Motors CEO, preparing for a presentation at an automotive industry conference. Your topic is "Lessons Learned," and you plan to discuss the company's failure to recall GM vehicles and how the company handled the communication. To include current information, research the topic and GM's most recent actions taken.

>>> PROCESS

1. What is the purpose of your presentation?

2. Describe your audience.

3. What level of knowledge is your audience likely to have about your topic?

4. How will you capture your audience's attention in the first minute of your presentation? Draft your opening section.

5. What points will you cover in the body of your presentation and in what order?

6. Write a closing section that summarizes your points and reinforces the purpose of your presentation.

7. What delivery techniques will you use to make your presentation dynamic?

8. What visuals will you use? Try to avoid traditional presentation slides with heavy text in favor of a simpler, more graphical style.

>>> PRODUCT

Using your knowledge of oral presentations, prepare an outline for this presentation, and submit it to your instructor for feedback. Then, prepare visuals and practice your presentation. When you're ready, deliver your presentation to the class. You might deliver part of your presentation in person in front of the class—and part via the Internet.

LO1   Plan a presentation.

To plan a presentation, determine the purpose, analyze the audience, and plan the delivery method. Most business presentations are impromptu and extemporaneous rather than scripted or memorized.

LO2   Organize a presentation.

Organizing the presentation requires developing an effective opening, developing each point logically in the middle, and closing on a strong, confident note. Use your opening remarks to capture the interest of your audience and build rapport. In the body, choose a logical sequence and deal effectively with any negative information. At the end, summarize your main points and outline the next steps. At any point in your presentation, you may use humor if it is appropriate to the situation.

LO3   Plan a team and online presentation.

When making a team presentation, allow enough time to prepare, assign responsibilities, and rehearse sufficiently to ensure that the overall presentation has coherence and unity.

When giving an online presentation, keep the audience engaged, be proficient with the technology, and have a backup plan in case the technology fails.

LO4   Develop effective visual support.

Visuals complement your presentation and help the audience understand your message. When creating presentation slides, present your main points clearly, make your presentation easy to follow, choose an attractive design, replace text with graphics and numbers with charts, and write simply and clearly. Practice using your visuals until you can deliver your presentation seamlessly.

Videos and handouts also can complement your presentation. Use these supplements to further enhance your oral delivery.

LO5   Practice and deliver a presentation.

Practice your presentation as much as necessary. Use an extemporaneous delivery style—an enhanced conversational tone. Use appropriate hand and arm gestures, but avoid annoying and distracting mannerisms and gestures.

When delivering your presentation, dress appropriately, speak in a clear and confident manner, and maintain eye contact with the audience. If needed, follow the recommended techniques for dealing with speech anxiety. Plan answers to possible questions, and consider incorporating the backchannel for feedback.

> EXERCISES

LO1   Plan a presentation.

1. **Adapt a presentation for different audiences.**

   Imagine that you work for a university as the head of transportation. You want to encourage people to take the bus, rather than park on campus, because spots are limited. Prepare agenda slides for two different audiences: faculty and students.

   Your presentation may include the challenges of parking on campus, the bus schedule, a cost comparison between driving and taking the bus, and any other information you believe may be relevant to persuade each of your audiences.

2. **Prepare a presentation to a Brazilian audience.**

   The manager of a Brazilian bank has approached your school about the possibility of sending 30 of its managers to your institution to pursue a three-month intensive course in written and oral business communication. The purpose of the course is to make the Brazilian managers better able to interact with their American counterparts.

As the assistant provost at your institution, you have been asked to give a six- to eight-minute presentation to the four Brazilian executives who will decide whether to fund this program at your institution. The purpose of your presentation is to convince them to select your school. Prepare a title and outline for your presentation.

3. **Prepare a presentation to a South Korean audience.**

Imagine that you invented a new product that you would like to sell to the South Korean market. The product can be anything consumers might find useful. The audience consists of wealthy individuals from South Korea.

Plan the presentation and determine the timing and method of delivery (the purpose and audience have already been determined). Prepare an outline and submit this to your instructor. In addition to the outline, write a cover memo explaining why you made certain decisions regarding cultural differences.

4. **Identify methods of delivery.**

For each of the following situations, which delivery method—impromptu, extemporaneous, scripted, or memorized—would be best?

Situation	Ideal Delivery Method
The HR director asks you to explain to a group of new employees starting next month what your department does.	
The VP of your division walks over to your desk with two clients and asks you to describe a new product you're developing.	
You're extremely nervous about an upcoming presentation and are preparing your first two sentences.	
By conference call to 150 analysts across the country, you're explaining why third-quarter profits are down.	

5. **Practice different delivery styles.**

In small groups, practice each of the four delivery styles. First, each of you chooses a topic that interests you; this can be a hobby, volunteer work, or an aspect of business. Second, prepare to deliver two or three sentences of a presentation about the topic, using the three delivery styles for which you can prepare: extemporaneous, scripted, and memorized. Of course, you'll have to change what you say for each method.

Taking turns, have each person present the four styles using this approach:

1. Deliver your memorized speech.
2. Deliver your scripted presentation.
3. Deliver your extemporaneous presentation.
4. Wait until a team member asks you a related question, and then deliver your response using the impromptu style.

After your presentations, discuss what you learned. Which methods were easiest and most natural for you to deliver? Which were most difficult? How can you adjust to different styles, even though you may be more comfortable with one than the others?

6. **Plan a presentation for a job interview.**

Imagine that you made it through first-round interviews with your favorite company. For the second round, they ask you to prepare a three-minute presentation on any topic. You'll deliver this to the hiring manager, three people who work on her team, and two representatives from HR. To prepare for your presentation, answer the following questions.

    a. What topic will you choose for your presentation?

    b. What is the purpose of your presentation?

    c. What do you know about your audience that might help you prepare a more effective presentation?

    d. What points will you include in your presentation?

    e. What method of delivery should you use?

LO2 Organize a presentation.

7. **Prepare an outline for a report presentation.**

Review an analytical or recommendation report you prepared in Chapter 10. Assume that you have been given 15 minutes to present the most important information from your written report to a committee of your managers who will not have an opportunity to read the report. What sequencing will you use for your presentation? Prepare an outline for your instructor's feedback.

8. **Prepare presentation notes.**

Prepare a three-minute oral presentation on a business topic of your choice. First, write out the complete presentation. Next, select several excerpts of the complete script to be used as notes for your presentation. Then, prepare an outline of notes for your presentation. Submit all three versions of the presentation to your instructor for evaluation.

9. **Develop an opening for a presentation.**

Write two different openings for the same oral presentation. First, plan your presentation by describing your purpose; second, perform an audience analysis by identifying the demographics, the knowledge level, and the psychological needs of a potential audience; third, prepare two effective openings for your presentation, and explain why you selected these types.

10. **Deliver a response to the interview question, "Tell me about yourself."**

First impressions happen particularly quickly during a job interview. Some recruiters will begin your interview with a general question: "Tell me about yourself." Sometimes called "elevator speeches," these presentations can be stressful and awkward if you're unprepared. But once you've developed and practiced a script, you can use parts of it in everyday situations, feeling more natural and confident each time.

Prepare a brief response (30–45 seconds) to the question, and deliver it to the rest of the class. To prepare your notes, you might include the following:

- Year and major or special interests in school
- Work or internship experience
- Skills and abilities
- Anything else you believe is relevant or significant about you (e.g., sports or other interests, hometown)
- What you're looking for (e.g., a summer job in a high-end restaurant)

Also consider these questions:

- What about you will be most relevant and interesting to this person?
- What do you think is this person's attitude toward you?
- What do you want him or her to remember most about you?

After your presentation, write a self-assessment memo that addresses the following questions:

- What did you do that you feel most proud of? What parts of your presentation were most powerful?
- What parts of the presentation do you feel least confident about?
- If you had the opportunity to prepare and deliver this message again, what would you do differently to improve your presentation?

11. **Deliver a speech as part of a team panel.**

LO3 Plan a team and online presentation.

Prepare a two-minute speech (using note cards) on the business topic of your choice. Then, form into groups of six or seven to make up the head table. A few minutes before starting, randomly select roles to be played: host, head table guests (with professional titles), and a guest speaker. The rest of the class will serve as the audience.

The person selected to be the host should quickly obtain the professional titles and names of the people at the head table. Then, the host should seat the members of the head table in their chairs. The host should then introduce the people at the head table—including the speaker. The speaker should then give his or her two-minute speech. After the speech is finished, the host should present the speaker with a token of appreciation.

Next, a member of the audience should be selected for an award, such as employee of the year, and the host should invite him or her to the podium to receive the award and to make a short impromptu acceptance speech.

Roles can be changed to allow others to be host, guest at the head table, speaker, or employee of the year. Have everyone submit his or her notes for the two-minute speech whether or not he or she actually spoke.

12. **Divide speaking responsibilities for a team presentation.**

In teams of three or four, plan how to divide parts of a presentation. Your topic is international copyright laws, and your audience consists of an international group of businesspeople who are concerned about using others' intellectual property. Follow these steps to plan your team presentation:

a. Brainstorm a list of topics for your presentation. Consider what would be valuable to your audience.

b. Create an outline of topics for your presentation. Plan on a logical sequence.

c. Identify how much time you would dedicate to each topic.

d. Select topics to cover in your presentation according to knowledge level and interests. Also select someone to open and close the presentation.

After you have finished your plan, discuss your team process. Is everyone happy with how responsibilities were shared and how the team worked together? Why or why not?

13. **Prepare and deliver a team presentation.**

Divide into teams of four or five students. Your instructor will assign you to either the pro or the con side of one of the following topics:

- Drug testing should be mandatory for all employees.
- All forms of smoking should be banned from all public spaces.
- Employers should provide flextime (flexible working hours) for all office employees.
- Employers should provide on-site childcare facilities for the preschool children of their employees.
- Employees who work with the public should be required to wear a company uniform.

Assume that your employee group has been asked to present its views to a management committee that will make the final decision regarding your topic. The presentations will be given as follows:

a. Each side (beginning with the pro side) will have eight minutes to present its views.

b. Each side will then have three minutes to confer.

c. Each side (beginning with the con side) will deliver a two-minute rebuttal—to refute the arguments and answer the issues raised by the other side.

d. Each side (beginning with the pro side) will give a one-minute summary.

e. The management committee (the rest of the class) will then vote by secret ballot regarding which side (pro or con) presented its case more effectively.

Gather whatever data you think will be helpful to your case, organize it, divide up the speaking roles, and prepare speaker notes. (*Hint:* It might be helpful to gather information on both the pro and the con sides of the issue in preparation for the rebuttal session, which will be given impromptu.)

14. **Prepare for an online presentation with remote offices.**

Imagine that you work as the purchasing manager who is planning a presentation about a new process for ordering equipment costing over $100,000. Your audience will be the office managers in four locations: the United States (where you are based), Toronto, Geneva, and London. To save travel expenses, you decide to deliver the presentation online through Skype, Google Hangouts, or another web program.

List the steps you will take to prepare for the presentation. Include everything you would do, up to the point of starting the presentation.

15. **Practice delivering and participating in an online presentation.**

Working in groups of three or four, have one person deliver a short presentation over the web to the rest of the team. At least two of you (one will be the presenter) will have to sign up for a free account on Skype, Google Hangouts, or another web program.

Select a presenter, who will be in a separate room from the rest of the team. The presenter can choose any topic relevant to the rest of the team, and this can be an informal presentation.

During the presentation, the rest of the team takes notes on the following. After the presentation, the audience gives feedback to the presenter.

Presentation Feedback

	Not at All	Somewhat	Yes	Definitely
1. Engaged the audience throughout. COMMENTS:	1	2	3	4
2. Demonstrated proficiency with the technology. COMMENTS:	1	2	3	4
3. Used a backup plan effectively. COMMENTS:	1	2	3	4

16. **Prepare for an online presentation to fail.**

As you did for the previous exercise, plan for one person in another room to present to two or three team members over the web. But this time, imagine that the technology fails. When you begin the presentation, you can see each other, but the audience can't hear you. (People on the receiving end have their speakers off—but you don't know that.)

Plan for this to happen, and arrange an alternative (e.g., a speakerphone or a cell phone that has a good speaker). Role-play this situation as realistically as possible. How will the presenter smoothly transition to the alternative?

After the presentation, discuss how well the speaker handled the situation. Discuss lessons you learned for the future.

17. **Convert a report to slides for an oral presentation.**

If you wrote a report using presentation software (discussed in Chapter 10), this is your chance to change it so that you can use it for an oral presentation. Convert heavy text to graphics, convert tables to charts, and edit text until it's concise and readable.

LO4 Develop effective visual support.

18. **Reduce text on a slide.**

If a colleague showed you this slide, how would you help him or her change it? In pairs, work together to reduce the text on this slide to make it easier to read, more logically organized, and more graphical.

LEONARD'S ART GALLERY

- Leonard, the art gallery's chief curator, was born into the business.
- His father and uncle founded the gallery in 1961.
- He was in charge of selecting both art and artists for each gallery show.
- Gallery shows were held six times a year, once every two months.
- Summer and winter months were tough times to sell art.
- Art sold best at the gallery's annual spring opening.
- Leonard's last major sale covered the gallery's operating costs for the coming year.
- Leonard was named after his mother's favorite painter, Leonardo da Vinci.

---

19. **Convert paragraph text to graphics.**

Imagine that you want to present the ideas for using video in presentations from this chapter to a group of people. Convert the Using Video section of this chapter to one slide. Use only a few words, and arrange them in a graphical way.

20. **Create a customized slide template.**

You are the owner of a mid-sized insurance company. You have 25 agents who travel throughout the country, making presentations to small groups of people (10 to 20) regarding retirement programs.

You want to create a template that all agents can use for their presentations. Your agents have been making their own slides or using no visuals at all, but you want consistency across all regions.

Invent a company name and logo, and then create a template that all agents can use. Choose a design, colors, and a few standard graphics. Include five or six slides in your sample deck—title slide, agenda slide, two or three examples of graphical slides (e.g., with SmartArt in PowerPoint), and a closing slide.

21. **Evaluate visuals used for a presentation.**

Attend a business meeting, a city council meeting, a student council meeting, a business conference, an executive presentation, or some other event where oral presentations will be taking place.

Evaluate the visuals that were used in the presentation. What, if any, visuals were used? Did the presenter have handouts? When were the handouts distributed? How effective were the visuals? What changes could have improved the visuals? Write a one-page email to your instructor, addressing these and other aspects of how the presentation was delivered.

22. **Embed a video into a presentation.**

If you don't have experience embedding a video into a presentation, research how to embed one into your favorite presentation program (PowerPoint, Keynote, Prezi, or another program). Search YouTube videos and other sources to find step-by-step instructions.

Select any YouTube video or other video that gives you embedding code. Practice inserting it into a new presentation. For the class, demonstrate how you embedded the video.

23. **Integrate a video into a presentation.**

Create a presentation to convince your classmates to donate to or volunteer for your favorite not-for-profit organization. Create a title slide, main point slide, agenda slide, a few content slides, and a summary slide.

Find a short (two- to three-minute) video to complement your message and provide emotional appeal. Embed the video into your presentation, and deliver the presentation, integrating the video seamlessly. For a smooth delivery, introduce your video, and then transition back to the rest of your presentation when the video ends.

24. **Analyze how a video is managed in a presentation.**

Watch Kai Tan's video segment, provided in the instructor's PowerPoint. What does Kai do well in managing the video, and what could he improve? Discuss how he introduces the video, positions himself, and transitions back to his presentation.

25. **Discuss whether to use a handout.**

Revisit a presentation you delivered recently. In small groups, discuss whether you used a handout, and your rationale. If you had to deliver the presentation again today, would you distribute a handout? Explain your response to your teammates.

26. **Create a handout.**

For your second-round job interview, a prospective employer has asked you to deliver a presentation on any topic (see Exercise 6). To make the best impression—and to leave something for the audience to remember you—create a handout. Include a summary of your main points and your contact information.

27. **Create a plan for managing speech anxiety.**

    Use the online tool to learn how to feel more confident for a presentation and to create a customized plan. Go to the following:

    > Site: speaking.amynewman.com
    >
    > Email = user
    >
    > Password = statler65

    Read the strategies and choose a few to try before, during, and after a presentation. Print your results and bring them to class to discuss.

LO5 Practice and deliver a presentation.

28. **Prepare a presentation about speech anxiety.**

    Prepare a three-minute presentation, using an outline, about one strategy for managing speech anxiety. You may include sources in the tool (speaking.amynewman.com) or through your own research. Before making the presentation, write a list of the questions you anticipate being asked and possible answers to those questions. Then, in groups of four or five, take turns delivering your presentation.

    After each presentation, the audience should ask the presenter questions about his or her topic. Did the presenter anticipate the questions the group asked? If so, did he or she have effective answers? If not, how did he or she handle the questions that were asked?

    Submit an email to your instructor. The email should include your outline, a list of the questions you anticipated, your answers to those questions, the actual questions asked (if different from the ones anticipated), and your answers to those questions. Also give your instructor a short post-presentation evaluation of what you did well and what changes you would make to improve your presentation.

29. **Practice a presentation and track your progress.**

    Practice an upcoming presentation several times—at least once in the room where you will deliver it. Each time you practice, write notes about your observations and plans for improvements. You might use a simple format such as the following:

	Location	Timing	Major Strengths	Areas to Improve
Practice Round 1				
Practice Round 2				
Practice Round 3				
Practice Round 4				
Practice Round 5				

30. **Analyze how a question is handled in a presentation.**

    Watch Michael Lieberman's video segment, provided in the Instructor's PowerPoint. What does Michael do well in addressing the question, and what suggestions do you have for him to improve?

31. **Prepare a presentation and respond to questions from prospective employees.**

    Ken Shwartz wants you, the new director of human resources, to recruit more production workers for his hat embroidery company, Ahead Headgear. Based in New Bedford,

Massachusetts, Ahead creates caps and visors for golf courses, resorts, and tournaments. Founder and CEO Shwartz has turned Ahead into one of the fastest-growing small businesses in the United States.

In just a few years, the company has gone from a start-up operation to a firm that earns more than $18 million in annual sales. However, filling open production jobs can be a struggle. "We have a very high-tech company, but younger workers don't seem to want our production jobs," he tells you. "They equate us with the old, dirty sewing factories."

You decide to make a presentation about Ahead at the next Southern Massachusetts Job Fair, which typically attracts 1,000 high school graduates. You are allotted five minutes to speak to the audience and another five minutes for a question-and-answer period. What kinds of questions do you anticipate? List at least six questions you expect to be asked. Using the Internet or other sources, research Ahead Headgear to find the answers to these questions.

32. Provide feedback.

Using this presentation feedback form, evaluate your own and a peer's presentation. In your comments for each category, be sure to focus on both strengths and areas for development.

Presentation Feedback

	Not at All	Somewhat	Yes	Definitely
1. The organization works well for the topic and is easy to follow. COMMENTS:	1	2	3	4
2. The content is clear and is well supported with details and examples. COMMENTS:	1	2	3	4
3. The delivery style is engaging and appropriate for the audience. COMMENTS:	1	2	3	4
4. Visual support is relevant and interesting. COMMENTS:	1	2	3	4

33. **Practice using the backchannel.**

In class, have one student deliver a three-minute presentation on any topic. During the presentation, five students in the audience sign onto Twitter and, using the same hashtag (e.g., #BusComm402), tweet one encouraging comment and one question. After the presentation, show the Twitter feed, and discuss the benefits and challenges of using the backchannel in this way.

Then, have the speaker continue the presentation by debriefing comments and answering questions from the Twitter feed. Try to do this within three minutes (you won't be able to address everything) to summarize the presentation.

COMPANY SCENARIO

PersuadeCafé

COURTESY OF ED MARION, EDMARION.COM

After all of your hard work proposing an idea for PersuadeCafé, researching the situation, and producing a report, imagine that you're lucky enough to present your recommendation to the executive management team.

Develop your slides to focus on your main points and reinforce your oral delivery. How will you use text and graphics to support your business improvement idea?

As you design your slides, you might consider PersuadeCafé's graphical style. You can see this from the intranet site, menu, and Jackie Marcus's slides. You don't have to use her slides as a template, but for consistency, your visuals should have the look and feel of the company.

Endnotes

1. Amy Haimerl, "Barra's Review, from Those Who've Been on Hot Seat," *Crain's Detroit Business*, April 6, 2014, www.crainsdetroit.com/article/20140406/NEWS/304069974/barras-review-from-those-whove-been-on-hot-seat,

2. "Mary Barra Update On Recalls—Message to GM Employees," March 17, 2014, GM News, http://media.gm.com/media/us/en/gm/news.detail.html/content/Pages/news/us/en/2014/mar/0317-video.html, accessed May 8, 2015.

3. "Text, Video of GM CEO Mary Barra on Switch Report," *USA Today*, June 5, 2014, www.usatoday.com/story/money/cars/2014/06/05/gm-ceo-mary-barra-speech-switch-recall-report/10012715, accessed May 8, 2015.

4. Used with permission from Grace Oplinger.

5. Madelijn Strick, Rob W. Holland, et al. "Humor in the Eye Tracker: Attention Capture and Distraction from Context Cues," *The Journal of General Psychology*, 2010, 137(1), 37–48.

6. Gavin McMahon, "Is PowerPoint's Reign Over? Meet 9 Heirs to the Throne," Make a Powerful Point, June 25, 2014, http://makeapowerfulpoint.com/2014/06/25/powerpoints-reign-meet-9-heirs-throne, accessed May 8, 2015.

7. Janet L. Heitgerd, Andrew L. Dent, et al., "Community Health Status Indicators: Adding a Geospatial Component," *Preventing Chronic Disease*, July 2008, 5(3), www.cdc.gov/pcd/issues/2008/Jul/pdf/07_0077.pdf, accessed May 8, 2015.

8. Wal-Mart Stores, Inc. Presentation by Bill Simon, Goldman Sachs 2013 Annual Global Retailing Conference, September 11, 2013, http://az204679.vo.msecnd.net/media/documents/bill-simon-goldman-sachs-2013-presentation_130233858314846907.pdf, accessed May 8, 2015.

9. Cliff Atkinson, *The Backchannel: How Audiences are Using Twitter and Social Media and Changing Presentations Forever* (Berkeley, CA: New Riders, 2009).

LEARNING OBJECTIVES

After you have finished this chapter, you should be able to

LO1 Write and format a résumé.

LO2 Manage your online image.

LO3 Write a cover letter or inquiry email.

LO4 Present yourself well during the interview and throughout the selection process.

LO5 Practice business etiquette in the workplace.

> *Human Resources is going social.* [1]

—Michael Blanding, Director, Corporate Responsibility, Asia, Middle East & Africa
and Greater China at InterContinental Hotels Group

CHAPTER INTRODUCTION

Social Recruiting at IHG

Companies are catching on to the newest way to find job candidates—online. Social recruiting is on the rise, and InterContinental Hotel Group (IHG) is taking full advantage of the trend.

Companies that search for candidates on social networks report significant benefits. With only 21% of workers actively seeking new employment,[2] social recruiting can yield 52% more applications for open positions and 48% more referrals.[3] Employers who recruit online say that the visibility improves company branding,[4] reduces the time to hire, and improves the quality of candidates.[5] These benefits are consistent with IHG's four goals for its social recruiting efforts:

COURTESY OF INTERCONTINENTAL HOTEL GROUP

- Enhance awareness of our employer brand

- Increase engagement among our colleagues

- Establish ourselves as an employer of choice

- Drive more applicants and better quality hires[6]

When Michael Blanding was managing IHG's new media recruiting for Asia, the Middle East, and Africa as well as the company's college relations, graduate, and employer branding programs, he developed a strategy to reach these goals. After analyzing his audience, identifying examples of companies succeeding at social recruiting, and determining how to measure success, Blanding set in motion a comprehensive plan to attract prospective employees. In addition to its LinkedIn profile, Facebook page, and Twitter feed, IHG has a "Careers" blog (shown here), where employees post stories about their experiences working for the company. The stories give prospective employees a firsthand look at what it could be like to develop a career at IHG.[7] With companies such as IHG looking for top candidates on social networks, it pays to develop an online presence that will get you noticed.

12-1 Putting Your Best Self Forward

Applying for a job puts all of your communication skills to the test. This is your chance to impress an employer and land your dream job. Because companies receive many résumés for each open position, how you represent yourself during the employment process will determine whether you are the selected candidate.

What is your personal brand? Your brand distinguishes you from other applicants and portrays your competencies (knowledge, skills, or abilities)—your reputation. Consulting firm PwC provides an extensive online toolkit for developing your brand, which the company calls, "what you're known for and how people experience you."[8]

The first step is to identify your strengths, gifts, and values. Consider the questions in Figure 1 as you begin to shape the story of who you are and what you will contribute to the workplace.

Figure 1 | Identifying Your Strengths, Gifts, and Values

- What am I most proud of?
- What is the most significant project I have accomplished?
- What do others consider to be my most important strengths or contributions?
- What's important to me in selecting an employer or workplace?
- What do I most enjoy doing? What do I least enjoy doing?

Typically, a company will follow a selection process such as that shown in Figure 2. Of course, this process varies by company and position, but these are the usual steps from when a company identifies a hiring need to when a new employee starts the job. Throughout this process, you are putting your best self forward and—if the process goes well—continuously communicating with your future employer.

12-2 Preparing Your Résumé

Your résumé summarizes your history and qualifications for a job. The best résumé is tailored to show how your education and work experience have prepared you for a specific job.

The purpose of the résumé is to get you an interview, and the purpose of the interview is to get you a job. You will not likely be hired based on the résumé alone, but your résumé and cover letter will set you apart from potentially thousands of job applicants.

More than 2,500 recruiters in the United States and Canada were asked for their résumé "pet peeves." Their top ten are listed in Figure 3 and offer good advice for what to avoid when preparing your résumé.[9]

In addition to these missteps, one of the worst mistakes you can make on your résumé is lying about your experience or academic background. Lying is common but has severe consequences. Hiring managers in financial services companies report finding false claims in 73% of résumés, an increase from previous years.[10] In another study, 57% of managers who caught lies said they immediately dismissed the candidate.[11]

CareerBuilder.com asked hiring managers "to share the most memorable or outrageous lies they came across on résumés." Figure 4 shows what they reported.[12]

Company

1. Posts the Job:
HR and hiring manager determine hiring needs and job requirements.

3. Screens Résumés:
HR manager, recruiter, or hiring manager reviews résumés and selects a few candidates for the first interview.

6. Narrows the Pool:
HR determines who will be called back for an in-person interview.

9. Narrows the Pool:
HR and hiring manager determine who will be interviewed again (sometimes called "second round").

12. Narrows the Pool:
HR and hiring manager make the final selection and decide who will receive a job offer.

14. Accepts the Job: Accepts the terms or negotiates salary, start date, relocation expenses, bonus, etc.

Applicant

2. Applies for the Job:
Submits an application and/or email or letter and résumé.

4. Receives the News:
Receives a request for an interview or receives a rejection email or letter.

5. Screening Interview:
HR typically conducts the first interview in person, by phone, or online.

7. Receives the News:
Invited for an interview or receives rejection email or letter.

8. First Interview:
HR and hiring manager typically will conduct one-hour interviews with applicants in person.

10. Receives the News:
Invited for more interviews or receives rejection email or letter.

11. Second Interview:
Additional managers and possibly coworkers interview applicants. This could last a half or a full day and may include team projects or group interviews.

13. Receives the News:
• Receives a job offer (usually by phone). The offer may be contingent on reference checks, or
• Receives a rejection email or letter.

Turns Down the Job: Calls or sends a thank-you email.

Sends a Thank-You Email: Sends a "goodwill" email expressing appreciation for the opportunity.

New employee starts the job and participates in orientation ("on boarding").

Figure 3 | Recruiters' Top Ten Résumé Pet Peeves

1. Spelling errors, typos, and poor grammar
2. Too duty oriented—reads like a job description, failing to explain the job seeker's relevant accomplishments
3. Missing dates or inaccurate dates
4. Missing contact information or inaccurate or unprofessional email addresses
5. Poor formatting—boxes, templates, tables, use of header and footers, etc.
6. Résumés organized by job function as opposed to chronological by employer
7. Long résumés—greater than two pages
8. Long, dense paragraphs—no bullet points
9. Unqualified candidates—candidates who apply to positions for which they are not qualified
10. Personal information not relevant to the job

Figure 4 | Memorable and Outrageous Lies

- Claimed to be a member of the Kennedy family
- Invented a school that did not exist
- Submitted a résumé with someone else's photo inserted into the document
- Claimed to be a member of Mensa
- Claimed to have worked for the hiring manager before, but never had
- Claimed to be the CEO of a company when the candidate was an hourly employee
- Listed military experience dating back to before he was born
- Included samples of work that the interviewer actually did
- Claimed to be Hispanic when he was 100% Caucasian
- Claimed to have been a professional baseball player

12-2a Résumé Length

How long should your résumé be? One consideration is how much time employers spend reviewing a résumé: about 60 seconds.[13] Only 42% of managers say they spend more than two minutes looking at a résumé.[14] This probably seems absurd, considering how much time and energy you'll devote to perfecting your résumé, but this is enough time for an experienced recruiter to quickly decide whether you meet the minimum qualifications for the job.

Most recruiters prefer one-page résumés from students and new graduates. However, two-page résumés are becoming more acceptable now.[15] If you have been working for a few years and are applying for a higher-level position, then you can continue your résumé onto a second page.

Writing a one-page résumé doesn't mean cramming two pages of information into one page by using tiny text and narrow margins. Your résumé must be attractive and easy to read, as is the sample résumé in Figure 5.

Shorten your résumé by including only what is most relevant to the particular job and by using concise language. For example, do you really need to include your high school choir experience? This may have been important to you, but perhaps you have more relevant, more recent experience. The before and after examples in Figure 6 show how to describe your experience concisely. In both of these examples, revising the text using principles from Chapter 5 saves valuable résumé space.

Uses a simple, creative design; includes clear contact information and a professional email address.

Starts with educational background, most relevant for a graduating student.

Highlights experience to differentiate his candidacy.

Uses bold type to emphasize job title, which is more important than the names of this applicant's employers.

Chooses present tense verbs to describe current responsibilities.

Chooses past tense verbs to describe previous experience.

Includes relevant skills and hobbies (optional).

Marcus C. Benini

1445 College Avenue
Palos Hills, IL 60465
708.555.4539
mbenini@555.com

Education

Moraine Valley Community College, Palos Hills, IL

- Associate in Science Degree (A.S.), 3.8 G.P.A., Expected Graduation 2016
- Dean's List All Semesters
- Coursework: International Business, Fundamentals of Accounting, Business Mathematics, Financial Accounting, Computer Applications in Accounting

The American International University in Rome Study Abroad,
High School Program, Summer 2014

- Lived with a host family for three weeks
- Studied Italian and Introduction to Business Management

Employment

Moraine Valley Community College

Teaching Assistant, Computer Applications in Accounting, 2015 – present

- Assist professor with grading 150 papers each semester
- Hold daily office hours for students
- Provide tutoring on challenging course material

Lakewatch Apartments

Property Accountant, 2013 – 2016

- Processed all accounts payable including taxes, mortgages, and monthly bills
- Maintained cash receipt journals for various properties
- Processed and deposited rental income
- Maintained general ledger and reconciled all bank statements
- Produced special reports for the partners and investors

Other

- Notary Public, State of Illinois
- Proficient in Peachtree and Microsoft Word, Excel, and Outlook
- Proficient Italian
- Hobbies include guitar, tennis, model airplanes

Using Concise Language | **Figure 6**

Before

Was put in charge of managing one of the company's retail stores, which had the most revenue, including overseeing three sales associates.

After

Managed the company's largest revenue-producing store with three sales associates.

Before

Was responsible for the design, development, and delivery of several programs to train new park employees in safety practices.

After

Designed, developed, and delivered safety training programs for new park employees.

On the other hand, don't make your résumé *too* short. A résumé that doesn't fill a page highlights your lack of experience. If you haven't worked many jobs, include more detail for the experience you do have, list your coursework, and write more about your extracurricular activities. You also may use a slightly larger font, more spacing, and more design features (within reason).

12-2b Résumé Format

Although the content of your résumé is obviously more important than the format, a recruiter will get a strong first impression from your design. The format should make your résumé easy for the recruiter to scan and quickly determine whether your background meets the job qualifications. Include lots of white space, easy-to-read fonts, and tasteful design features (e.g., columns or horizontal lines). To highlight important content, use font enhancements (bold or italics), bullets, and varied spacing.

You can start with a résumé template in Microsoft Word or another program, but customize the template for your own style. Some of these formats are too flashy for business positions.

When you go to a career fair or an interview, bring copies of your résumé. Print it onto white or off-white, 8½ × 11-inch, 20-pound, résumé paper using a high-quality laser printer. For traditional companies, skip the fancy stationery and bright colors. Unless you're applying for a creative position (such as an advertising job), err on the side of conservatism.

Finally, your résumé and cover letter must be 100% free from error—in content, spelling, grammar, and format. One survey found that one or two typos are enough for 76% of executives to decide not to interview an applicant. Figure 7 shows a few outrageous errors on real résumés.[16]

Figure 7 | Real Errors on Résumés

Hope to hear from you, shorty.

Have a keen eye for derail

Dear Sir or Madman

I'm attacking my résumé for you to review.

I am a rabid typist.

My work ethics are impeachable.

Nervous of steel

Following is a grief overview of my skills.

GPA: 34.0

Graphic designer seeking no-profit career

12-2c Résumé Content

Every résumé is different, but recruiters expect to see some standard parts included. Figure 8 shows content typically included in a college student's résumé.

Identifying Information

Figure 9 addresses questions students typically have about what to include—or not to include—in identifying themselves.

Job Objective

Job objectives on résumés have fallen out of favor.[17] Some recruiters believe an objective is obvious—you want the position. Also, you can explain your career objective in your cover letter.

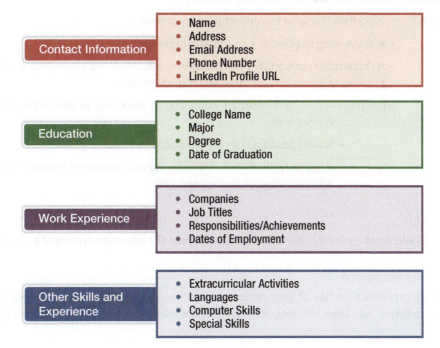

- Contact Information
  - Name
  - Address
  - Email Address
  - Phone Number
  - LinkedIn Profile URL

- Education
  - College Name
  - Major
  - Degree
  - Date of Graduation

- Work Experience
  - Companies
  - Job Titles
  - Responsibilities/Achievements
  - Dates of Employment

- Other Skills and Experience
  - Extracurricular Activities
  - Languages
  - Computer Skills
  - Special Skills

Q&A About Identifying Information | **Figure 9**

Question	Answer
Should I include my family's address?	This is optional. If you live on a college campus away from home, companies probably won't send letters to your family's house, but you may include their address if, for example, you're in the process of moving, or your campus mail is unreliable.
Should I include background information about myself, such as my age and ethnicity?	For U.S. résumés, do not include a photograph or any such personal information (e.g., age, ethnicity, religion, sex, marital status, whether you have children). Because it's illegal to hire or not hire someone on the basis of these characteristics, you should not include them.
Can I include my nickname instead of my given name? How about my middle name?	Include your given name so that employers can easily check references. You may also include a nickname if it's significantly different from your given name, for example, "Matsuko (Mike) Takahashi." Include your middle name or middle initial if you use it when signing your name.

However, you could use an objective to clarify your career goals if, for example, your experience doesn't match the job for which you're applying. Or, instead of an objective, some career professionals suggest a summary of qualifications (shown in Sample Résumé 2 in Figure 11), which identifies your key skills and experience. This is more typical for applicants who have significant full-time work experience.

If you do include an objective, write one that is clear and specific—but not so specific that you exclude yourself from positions that may interest you.

☒ NOT
- A position that offers an opportunity for growth.
- A challenging position in a progressive organization.
- A responsible position that lets me use my education and experience and that provides opportunities for increased responsibilities.

☑ BUT
- A paid, one-semester internship in marketing or advertising in the Atlanta area.
- A sales position in a medium-sized manufacturing firm.
- A public relations position requiring well-developed communication, administrative, and computer skills.

Education

Figure 10 addresses typical questions from students about the education section of a résumé.

Work Experience

The work experience section of your résumé shows how your previous jobs have prepared you for a future job. Most résumés, for example, Sample Résumé 1, use the chronological

Figure 10 | Q&A About Education

Which should come first—my education or experience?	Unless you have extensive work experience, your education is probably your strongest job qualification and therefore comes first on the résumé. After your first full-time job, you might start with your experience and move the education section to the bottom of your résumé.
What if I didn't graduate yet?	You may include language such as "Expected date of graduation." (See Sample Résumé 1 for an example.)
Should I include my grade-point average?	Include your grade-point average (GPA) if it will set you apart from the competition (generally, at least a 3.3 or 3.5 on a 4.0 scale). If you made the dean's list, write which semesters you achieved this distinction.
Should I include the name of my high school and grade-point average or rank?	After freshman year in college, you can probably omit your high school information unless it might attract attention from a recruiter (e.g., if you attended a highly selective or unique school or if you were valedictorian). By your junior or senior year, you may find that you have more worthy information (work and leadership experience) to fill your one-page résumé.
Should I include a list of classes?	Include classes when you need to fill space or when the classes will distinguish you in some way. Listing core classes that every student takes may not be a differentiator when recruiters are flipping through résumés from students at the same school.

format to list work history, starting with the most recent position. In a study, HR and other company representatives were asked, "What style of résumé does your company prefer?" An overwhelming 92% responded that they prefer a chronological résumé.[18] By far, this is the most common type of résumé—particularly for college students.

In some situations, a functional résumé—organized around skills or job functions—is a better choice. Functional résumés are most appropriate when you're changing industries, moving into an entirely different line of work, or reentering the workforce after a long period of unemployment. In these situations, functional résumés emphasize your skills rather than your employment history.

Sample Résumé 2 (Figure 11) is an example of a functional résumé.[19] For Dina Fowler, a functional résumé is a good choice because she has changed careers—and now wants to make another switch (from a nonprofit organization to a for-profit company). With a chronological format, Dina's résumé would highlight her previous jobs, which do not match her current job objective. Instead, Dina needs to emphasize the *skills* that qualify her for a future position.

Sample Résumé 2 (Functional) | **Figure 11**

Dina Fowler   dinafowler555@gmail.com
612 Madeline Road, Apt. 3B, Newark, NJ 07102   (973) 555-9648

POSITION OBJECTIVE

A fundraising or community outreach position for a progressive company

QUALIFICATIONS SUMMARY

Highly organized senior manager with professional experience in the corporate, nonprofit, and government sectors. Proven ability to successfully manage projects and develop diversified fundraising strategies. Exceptional presentation skills; adept at communicating at all organizational levels and with community partners.

SELECTED ACCOMPLISHMENTS

Nonprofit Leadership and Fundraising

- Provided leadership, management, and vision for Bailey Community Center; coordinated fundraising drives, program development, volunteer services, and daily operations; worked with community coalitions and served as the primary spokesperson.

- Created and implemented comprehensive fundraising plan to diversify revenue sources, evaluate results, and engage board members in soliciting donations.

- Instituted new major donor solicitations and direct-mail fundraising campaigns resulting in 20% increase in annual fundraising revenues.

- Researched and secured new foundation and government grants through meticulous proposal writing. Managed and improved profit margin of large-scale fundraising events.

- Implemented structured volunteer services including recruitment, communications, and appreciation events for almost 100 volunteers at Bailey.

Project Management

- Administered all aspects of scholarship program for low-income students attending college. Managed collaboration between Newark County and private scholarship foundation, applicant recruitment, selection process, and annual press event.

- Organized and expanded annual conference on issues facing homeless individuals; increased attendance 25% to almost 450 participants over three years; managed logistics and tasks for volunteer committee.

Figure 11 | *(Continued)*

Dina Fowler   page 2

- Recommended and advocated for public policy changes. Tracked developments in policy on the local, state, and national levels to advise executive director on appropriate positions.
- Coordinated coalition of over 50 nonprofit and advocacy agencies to work for passage of community housing legislation.
- Worked on corporate-wide, human resources computer system conversion for Black & Decker. Analyzed and redesigned all business processes for most effective use of new technology and alignment with corporate standards.

Training and Education

- Created and managed new computer training department for 2,800 employees at the University of Maryland; responsible for computer and furniture procurement, internal marketing, scheduling, enrollment, training delivery, and management reporting.
- Designed and delivered hands-on computer training in PeopleSoft HRMS; and Microsoft Word, Excel, PowerPoint, and Access.
- Developed, marketed, and presented training programs on hunger, food security, and homelessness for hundreds of people in law enforcement, social service agencies, schools, corporations, and religious organizations.

WORK HISTORY

2014 – present	Assistant Executive Director, Newark Coalition for the Hungry and Homeless, Newark, NJ
2011 – 2014	Executive Director, Bailey Community Services Center, Newark, NJ
2007 – 2011	Computer Instructor, University of Maryland, College Park, MD
2004 – 2007	Programmer/Analyst, Black & Decker Corporation, Baltimore, MD

EDUCATION AND SKILLS

Rutgers University, Rutgers Business School, B.S. in Management, 2006

Intermediate Spanish Language Skills

Choose the functional format sparingly. Remember that one of the top pet peeves of U.S. and Canadian employers is "résumés organized by job function as opposed to chronological by employer."[20] Functional formats cause recruiters to have to fill-in-the-blanks of your work experience. It's a clever disguise for an imperfect history but makes the screening process more difficult for recruiters.

The purpose of describing your work history is to show prospective employers what you've learned that will benefit his or her organization. From your research about the job you're seeking, highlight your skills and experience that will transfer to the new position. For example, if a position description emphasizes teamwork, be sure to describe examples of your work with others.

☒ NOT   Updated the employee directory.

☑ BUT   Worked with liaisons in all departments to update the employee directory.

Complete sentences are not necessary. Instead, start your descriptions with action verbs, using present tense for current responsibilities and past tense for previous job responsibilities or accomplishments. Use concrete words to explain your work experience.

accomplished	conceived	established	managed	reported
achieved	concluded	evaluated	modified	researched
administered	conducted	generated	negotiated	revised
analyzed	constructed	guided	operated	screened
applied	coordinated	hired	organized	secured
approved	created	implemented	oversaw	simplified
arranged	delegated	increased	planned	sold
authorized	designed	instituted	prepared	supervised
budgeted	determined	interviewed	presented	trained
built	developed	introduced	produced	transformed
changed	diagnosed	investigated	purchased	updated
communicated	directed	led	recommended	wrote
completed	edited	maintained	renovated	

Avoid weak verbs such as *attempted, hoped,* and *tried.* When possible, list specific accomplishments, giving numbers or dollar amounts. Highlight accomplishments that have direct relevance to the desired job.

☒ NOT   I was responsible for a large sales territory.

    ☑ BUT   Managed a six-county sales territory; increased sales 13% during first full year.

☒ NOT   I worked as a clerk in the cashier's office.

    ☑ BUT   Balanced the cash register daily; was the only part-time employee entrusted to make nightly cash deposits.

☒ NOT   Worked as a bouncer at a local bar.

    ☑ BUT   Maintained order at Nick's Side-Door Saloon; resolved several disputes without police intervention.

☒ NOT   Sold tickets for Art Reach.

    ☑ BUT   Sold more than $1,000 worth of tickets to annual benefit dance; introduced "Each One, Reach One" membership drive that increased membership every year during my three-year term as membership chair.

In the experience section, you may include unpaid internships and volunteer work. Include activities that helped you develop skills in managing time, working with groups, handling money, organizing tasks, and managing people. Employers will not likely care whether you were paid for jobs; they are just interested in the skills you developed. However, employers may consider it a stretch to include volunteer work under "Work Experience." Instead, consider adding a section called "Other Relevant Experience" or broadening the "Work Experience" title to "Relevant Experience."

If you started your own business, include it in the work experience section. Emphasize your entrepreneurial skills, but be careful about overstating your experience (e.g., referring to yourself as "CEO, President, and COO"). Here's one description of a start-up business.

Cathy Lin Bracelets, New York, NY

Founder and Owner

- Managed business to produce over $15,000 annual revenue last fiscal year
- Designed and sold custom bracelets for over 250 customers since inception
- Marketed through flyers, word-of-mouth, and social media
- Maintained all records in Microsoft Excel
- Managed large inventory of handmade beads

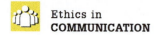

Ethics in COMMUNICATION

Your résumé represents you in the best possible light. Of course, you'll highlight your strengths and minimize your weaknesses. However, be careful about taking credit for accomplishments that weren't yours (or yours alone) and, as discussed earlier, about exaggerating responsibilities. A simple telephone call can verify any statement on your résumé. During an interview, the employer will push for details about your past responsibilities. It will be obvious if you didn't do what you claim on your résumé. This may be embarrassing for you—and for your school.

Other Relevant Information

Figure 12 addresses questions students typically have about other information to include on a résumé.

Figure 12 | Q&A About Other Relevant Information

What should I call the last section on my résumé where I have additional skills?	Here are a few options: "Leadership and Other Experience," "Other Relevant Experience," "Extracurricular Activities," or "Other Skills and Qualifications." Choose a heading that summarizes your additional qualifications for the job.
What type of information should I include?	Include anything relevant to the job or interesting to an employer: professional, athletic, or social clubs and organizations; volunteer experience; language skills; honors and awards; and computer skills, particularly programs important for an industry. If you held a leadership position in a club or organization, include the title and perhaps some of your responsibilities.
Should I include high school information here? I was on the varsity football team for three years (or I was the president of the chess club for two years).	After your college freshman year, you may want to omit all high school information. Unless the activity is very relevant to the job (e.g., you started a culinary club, and you're applying for a job as a prep chef), you will probably have more recent and relevant information from college to emphasize.
How do I represent my language skills?	Consider these categories to describe your language skills: basic, conversational, intermediate, proficient, fluent. If you're unsure, ask your language instructor for an assessment. Also, imagine yourself in front of an interviewer who is fluent in this language. How would you do?
Where do I include my study abroad experience?	You may include your study abroad experience in the last section or within the education section at the beginning of your résumé. Consider including the university name, location, dates, and possibly your coursework.
Should I include names of references or "References on Request" on my résumé?	You should omit both. Including information about references on your résumé is considered a waste of valuable résumé space. Just prepare a list of people who can vouch for you so you're ready when an employer asks.

Applications for international jobs often require a curriculum vitae (CV), a longer version of a résumé. Although personal information, such as height, weight, marital status, and children, is more common on CVs than on résumés, this information is not required and is best omitted.

Because your résumé is about you, it is perhaps the most personal business document you'll ever write. Use everything you know about effective communication to tell your story in the best way possible.

Keywords

Keywords on your résumé may make the difference between getting an interview and landing in the reject pile. If you post your résumé on a site such as Monster.com or create a profile on LinkedIn (which we'll discuss later), employers may use keywords to search for qualified candidates. Also, most large companies—and some small—have an applicant tracking system that will search your résumé for keywords. Only 3% of companies surveyed recently prefer scannable résumés (a text-only format),[21] but if this format is requested, you'll certainly want to use good keywords that will be automatically selected by a database. Here are a few tips when considering keywords for your résumé:

- Think of nouns instead of verbs (users rarely search for verbs). Browse other online résumés, job postings, and industry publications to find industry-specific terms.
- Put keywords in proper context, weaving them throughout your résumé. This is a more sophisticated approach than listing them in a block at the beginning of the résumé.
- Use a variety of words to describe your skills, and don't overuse important words. In most searches, each word counts once, no matter how many times it is used.

As a starting point, look at a few job postings. From a job posting, you can determine which words may be most important to employers (see highlighted words in Figure 13). Then, you can incorporate these words into bulleted descriptions on a résumé (Figure 14). Weaving these keywords into your cover letter may also increase your chances of being selected and will ensure a cohesive approach to your application.

Emotional **INTELLIGENCE**

What are you most proud of about yourself and your experience? How will you make this clear on your résumé?

International **COMMUNICATION**

Keywords in an Ad | **Figure 13**

HUMAN RESOURCES RECRUITER

Core Job Responsibilities:
- Write job descriptions and identify job requirements
- Screen résumés
- Conduct screening interviews in person and online
- Conduct in-person behavioral interviews
- Organize candidates' interview schedules with managers
- Make selection decisions working with managers
- Manage high school and college intern programs
- Work with an assistant for administrative support

Qualifications and Skills:
- Bachelor's degree required
- Strong interpersonal skills
- Ability to work with all levels of management
- Proficient use of Microsoft Office software
- Strong writing and editing skills
- Experience working with a recruitment management system a plus
- Meticulous organization and follow-up skills
- Professional in Human Resources (PHR) certification preferred

Figure 14 | Keywords on a Résumé

> KEYWORDS: job descriptions, selection decisions
> * Worked with managers to write job descriptions and make final selection decisions.
>
> KEYWORDS: résumés, intern
> * Screened résumés of interns and full-time applicants to determine qualifications.
>
> KEYWORDS: interviews, online, intern
> * Conducted interviews in person, by phone, and online for full-time and intern hires.
>
> KEYWORDS: Microsoft Office, recruitment management system
> * Used Microsoft Office products (Word, Excel, and PowerPoint) and Earrow Recruitment Management System (RMS).
>
> KEYWORDS: bachelor's degree, PHR
> * Earned a bachelor's degree from the University of North Carolina, 2012, and earned a PHR (Professional in Human Resources) certification in 2013.
>
> KEYWORDS: interpersonal, writing, organization
> * Impeccable organizational skills, strong business writing skills, and excellent interpersonal communication skills.

LO2 Manage your online image.

12-3 Managing Your Online Image

When recruiters search for you online, what do they find? Like a company, you should build your online image or brand. Having a LinkedIn profile is essential to your online presence, and we'll discuss other ways to improve your chances of getting hired via social networking.

Communication
TECHNOLOGIES

12-3a Your Online Reputation

Does your online presence reflect how you want to be perceived? Your professional image will be judged partly by your online reputation—how you are represented on the Internet.

How you present yourself online can make or break a hiring decision. Almost all employers (94%) search for or plan to search for candidates on the web, and 78% have successfully hired someone they discovered online: 94% through LinkedIn, 65% through Facebook, and 55% through Twitter.[22] Employers who screen candidates online are as likely to hire candidates as they are to reject candidates based on what they discover—about 70%.[23,24]

Employers report hiring candidates because their profile showed a likely fit with the organization, creativity, and good communication skills.[25] Imagine your first-choice employer Googling you and finding articles you wrote on LinkedIn or your Twitter profile with comments about industry articles. Or maybe a recruiter finds your blog about food, fashion, sports, or whatever interests you.

Set yourself apart by creating your own content, as Cameron Pritchett did. When employers search for Cameron online, they'll find his YouTube channel with videos about his run for student assembly, fraternities at his school, and his stand against sexual assault (Figure 15). *The Guardian* hosts "blogging students" (Figure 16), but you can create your own blog in WordPress or another program.

Positive content should drown out anything negative about you. The biggest culprits for negative reactions to online content are references to illegal drugs, posts of a sexual

Emotional
INTELLIGENCE

Do any online posts by or about you cause you concern? How can you remove the information, drown it out, or make peace with it?

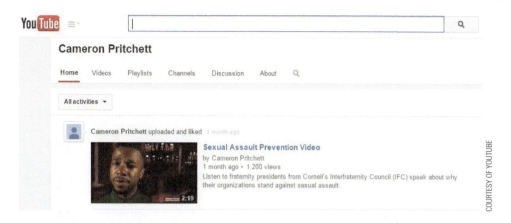

COURTESY OF YOUTUBE

Student Blogs Published at *The Guardian* | **Figure 16**

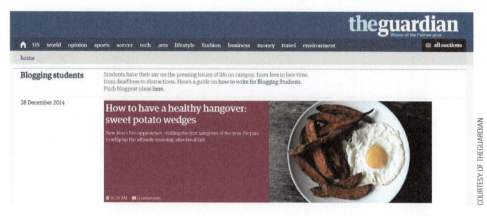

COURTESY OF THEGUARDIAN

nature, and use of profanity (Figure 17).[26] You can protect yourself by managing your online content:

- Avoid posting questionable content about yourself or your employer, coworkers, or customers. As discussed in Chapter 1, follow your employer's social media policy. If you can't remove negative content, be prepared to discuss it honestly during an interview.
- Search for your name in Google and Bing. Remove content and un-tag photos that don't represent you well. If you find negative information about someone else with your name, find a "clean version" of your name (e.g., with your middle name) and use it consistently in your email signature, résumé, cover letter, and so on.[27]
- Write well: use proper grammar, spelling, and capitalization.
- Manage your privacy settings on Facebook and other social networking sites.

Once you're hired, you'll still want to be careful about what you post online. Companies have been criticized and, in some cases, sued for their reaction to online posts, but why spoil your professional image and put your job in jeopardy?

12-3b LinkedIn

Employers use LinkedIn to post jobs and to search for, screen, contact, and keep track of candidates. Having an updated profile, endorsements, and connections shows employers more of who you are. Also, when a recruiter searches on LinkedIn, the site uses an algorithm to order the results based on your profile, activity, and connections.[28] Follow the suggestions in Figure 18 for a profile that gets you noticed.

Figure 17 | Employers' Reactions to Social Profiles

Q. How would you react to these possible items discovered by reviewing a candidate's social network profile?

	POSITIVE	NEUTRAL	NEGATIVE
References to doing illegal drugs	1%	7%	**83%**
Posts/tweets of a sexual nature	1%	16%	**71%**
Profanity in posts/tweets	4%	20%	**65%**
Spelling/grammar errors in posts/tweets	3%	29%	**61%**
References to guns	1%	31%	**51%**
Pictures of consumption of alcohol	1%	39%	**47%**
Volunteering/donations to charity	**65%**	26%	1%
Poltical posts/tweets	2%	**65%**	18%
Overtly religious posts/tweets	2%	**55%**	28%

COURTESY OF JOBVITE

12-3c Creative Résumés

Another way to stand out from the crowd of qualified candidates is to have a more creative type of résumé. As we discussed in Chapter 9, infographics are a great way to show a lot of information graphically. Infographic résumés are becoming increasingly popular and can supplement your traditional résumé. The example in Figure 19 shows the candidate's qualifications as a London Underground map. This is just one of many, many options for displaying your education and work history in a graphical way. For more ideas, search Google Images (images.google.com) for "infographic résumé."

For creative jobs, candidates take creative approaches. One applicant printed his résumé as a wrapper on a chocolate bar and received almost a million views on Reddit within an hour.[29] Clearly, this type of résumé is a risk: some employers will love it, while others may see it as pandering or hokey. Consider the type of company and job before you make any bold moves.

Communication TECHNOLOGIES

While creative résumés can go social, social résumés are designed for interactivity and allow employers to find you online. A social résumé can be as simple as a LinkedIn profile or as rich as one created on dedicated websites. VisualCV (www.visualcv.com), ResumeSocial (www.resumesocial.com), and CareerCloud (www.careercloud.com) offer interactive functionality, such as allowing for comments, posting a video, or connecting to social networks. By including links and incorporating examples of your work, you'll tell a prospective employer much more information about you than you can on a traditional résumé.

Philippe Dubost created a social résumé on his own website (Figure 20). Cleverly designed to resemble an Amazon product page, Dubost's résumé received 1.5 million views within two months.

What to include:
- A professional-looking headshot with you smiling.
- A summary. This is a good distinction from your résumé, and you can use a less formal writing style.
- Hobbies. An employer might connect with your interests, and hobbies can be a conversation starter.
- Volunteer experience. Employers react favorably to volunteer work on LinkedIn profiles.
- Links to examples of your work: a PowerPoint presentation, report, video, blog, and so on.
- Status updates. Keep your profile in front of your connections by posting comments, sharing articles, and so on.

How to create a professional profile:
- Emphasize your strengths in your profile; use keywords.
- Check for 100% accuracy. Employers will check your résumé against your profile.
- Proofread carefully. Just like your résumé, your LinkedIn profile reflects on writing ability, professionalism, and attention to detail.

How to connect with people:
- Build your network. Send connection requests to friends, classmates, instructors, and former employers. Write personalized invitations for people you admire but don't know.
- Accept invitations from people you know. Consider accepting invitations from people you don't know if they convince you it would be beneficial to connect.
- Accept endorsements, but you can be selective. Stick to the skills for which you want to be known.
- Seek recommendations from employers, professors, and others who know you well.
- Join groups. Show your interest by asking questions and engaging in discussions.

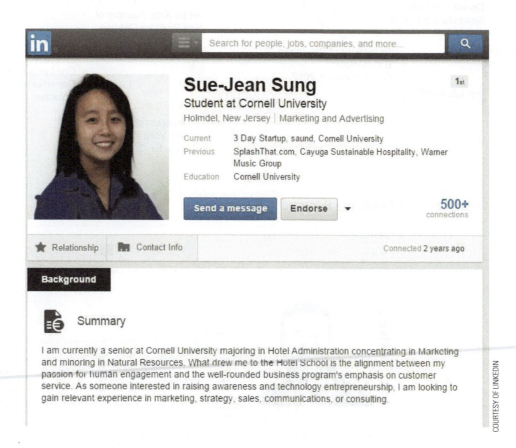

Figure 19 | Infographic Résumé

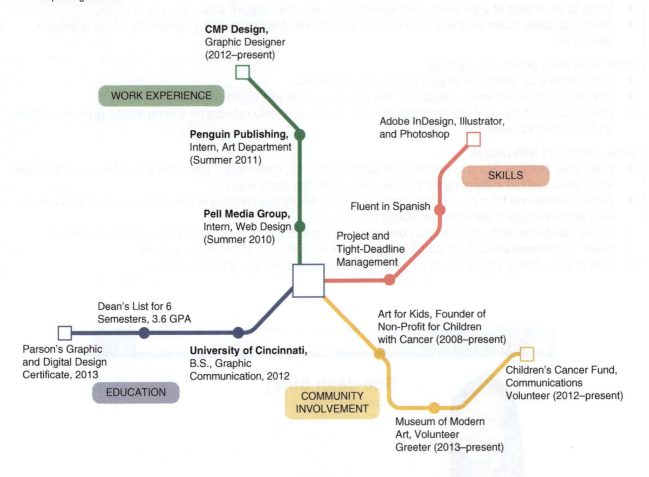

Lucinda J. Lopez

711B Marigold Road
Santa Barbara, CA 93101
(805) 565-7189
Llopez@gmail.com

CMP Design,
Graphic Designer
(2012–present)

WORK EXPERIENCE

Adobe InDesign, Illustrator,
and Photoshop

Penguin Publishing,
Intern, Art Department
(Summer 2011)

SKILLS

Fluent in Spanish

Pell Media Group,
Intern, Web Design
(Summer 2010)

Project and
Tight-Deadline
Management

Dean's List for 6
Semesters, 3.6 GPA

Art for Kids, Founder of
Non-Profit for Children
with Cancer (2008–present)

Parson's Graphic
and Digital Design
Certificate, 2013

University of Cincinnati,
B.S., Graphic
Communication, 2012

Children's Cancer Fund,
Communications
Volunteer (2012–present)

EDUCATION

COMMUNITY
INVOLVEMENT

Museum of Modern
Art, Volunteer
Greeter (2013–present)

Figure 20 | An Amaz-ing Résumé

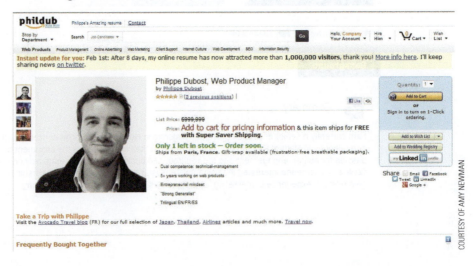

Video résumés are becoming more popular and are a great way to demonstrate your communication skills and personality. You could try your hand at producing your own video and uploading it to YouTube, or you might choose a more sophisticated approach through a dedicated video résumé website. Graeme Anthony's interactive video permits users to click links for more videos (Figure 21).

Interactive Video Résumé | **Figure 21**

12-4 Writing Cover Letters and Inquiry Emails

LO3 Write a cover letter or inquiry email.

When you send your résumé to a potential employer, you will typically include a cover letter. This may be sent as an email with the résumé attached, which is the most preferable way for employers to receive your résumé.[30] Or you may be asked by on-campus recruiters to submit a cover letter with your résumé so they can see a writing sample and how you present yourself. Also, to expand your job search, you will likely contact people who don't have advertised jobs. We'll look at formal cover letters and these inquiry emails next.

12-4a Cover Letters

A cover letter tells a prospective employer that you are interested in and qualified for a position within the organization. An effective cover letter will achieve the following:

- Express your interest in the company and the position
- Highlight how your background specifically matches job qualifications
- Reveal some of your personality
- Demonstrate your business writing skills
- Provide the employer with logistical information: how you can be reached and when you're available to work

Your cover letter is a sales letter—you're selling your qualifications to the prospective employer. This is your chance to differentiate yourself and pique the employer's interest in you as a candidate. Ideally, a recruiter reads your cover letter and thinks, "I'd like to meet this person." You want to sound confident and professional, without being too boastful or presumptuous.

Typically, cover letters for entry-level jobs are one page long, as in the Sample Cover Letter (Figure 22). This should be enough space to achieve your goals.

Although it's often still referred to as a "letter," a cover letter may be sent as an email message. Forty-one percent of employers prefer receiving a résumé by email.[31] In this case, it's best to attach your résumé as a PDF file so that all formatting will be retained. You also should shorten your traditional cover letter and place the body text (without the letter formatting) within the email, rather than attaching it as a file. This avoids the receiver having to open two attachments. Compare the Sample Cover Letter (Figure 22) with the Sample Email (Figure 23) to see the difference.

Address and Salutation

Your letter should be addressed to an individual rather than to an organization or department. Ideally, your letter should be addressed to the person who will interview you and who will likely be your manager if you get the job. Make sure you have the right name—and the correct

Figure 22 | Sample Cover Letter

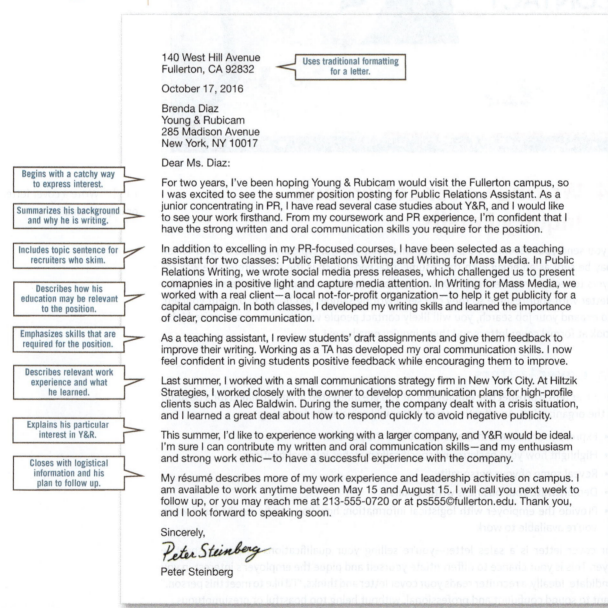

140 West Hill Avenue
Fullerton, CA 92832

Uses traditional formatting for a letter.

October 17, 2016

Brenda Diaz
Young & Rubicam
285 Madison Avenue
New York, NY 10017

Dear Ms. Diaz:

Begins with a catchy way to express interest.

For two years, I've been hoping Young & Rubicam would visit the Fullerton campus, so I was excited to see the summer position posting for Public Relations Assistant. As a junior concentrating in PR, I have read several case studies about Y&R, and I would like to see your work firsthand. From my coursework and PR experience, I'm confident that I have the strong written and oral communication skills you require for the position.

Summarizes his background and why he is writing.

Includes topic sentence for recruiters who skim.

In addition to excelling in my PR-focused courses, I have been selected as a teaching assistant for two classes: Public Relations Writing and Writing for Mass Media. In Public Relations Writing, we wrote social media press releases, which challenged us to present comapnies in a positive light and capture media attention. In Writing for Mass Media, we worked with a real client—a local not-for-profit organization—to help it get publicity for a capital campaign. In both classes, I developed my writing skills and learned the importance of clear, concise communication.

Describes how his education may be relevant to the position.

Emphasizes skills that are required for the position.

As a teaching assistant, I review students' draft assignments and give them feedback to improve their writing. Working as a TA has developed my oral communication skills. I now feel confident in giving students positive feedback while encouraging them to improve.

Describes relevant work experience and what he learned.

Last summer, I worked with a small communications strategy firm in New York City. At Hiltzik Strategies, I worked closely with the owner to develop communication plans for high-profile clients such as Alec Baldwin. During the sumer, the company dealt with a crisis situation, and I learned a great deal about how to respond quickly to avoid negative publicity.

Explains his particular interest in Y&R.

This summer, I'd like to experience working with a larger company, and Y&R would be ideal. I'm sure I can contribute my written and oral communication skills—and my enthusiasm and strong work ethic—to have a successful experience with the company.

Closes with logistical information and his plan to follow up.

My résumé describes more of my work experience and leadership activities on campus. I am available to work anytime between May 15 and August 15. I will call you next week to follow up, or you may reach me at 213-555-0720 or at ps555©fullerton.edu. Thank you, and I look forward to speaking soon.

Sincerely,

Peter Steinberg

Peter Steinberg

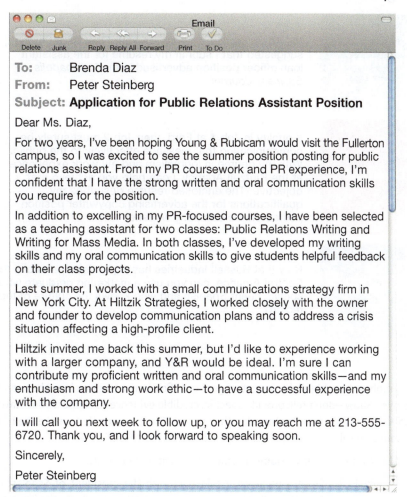

To: Brenda Diaz
From: Peter Steinberg
Subject: **Application for Public Relations Assistant Position**

Dear Ms. Diaz,

For two years, I've been hoping Young & Rubicam would visit the Fullerton campus, so I was excited to see the summer position posting for public relations assistant. From my PR coursework and PR experience, I'm confident that I have the strong written and oral communication skills you require for the position.

In addition to excelling in my PR-focused courses, I have been selected as a teaching assistant for two classes: Public Relations Writing and Writing for Mass Media. In both classes, I've developed my writing skills and my oral communication skills to give students helpful feedback on their class projects.

Last summer, I worked with a small communications strategy firm in New York City. At Hiltzik Strategies, I worked closely with the owner and founder to develop communication plans and to address a crisis situation affecting a high-profile client.

Hiltzik invited me back this summer, but I'd like to experience working with a larger company, and Y&R would be ideal. I'm sure I can contribute my proficient written and oral communication skills—and my enthusiasm and strong work ethic—to have a successful experience with the company.

I will call you next week to follow up, or you may reach me at 213-555-6720. Thank you, and I look forward to speaking soon.

Sincerely,

Peter Steinberg

spelling—and position title. In your salutation, use a courtesy title (such as *Mr.* or *Ms.*) along with the person's last name. If you're unsure whether the person is male or female, spell out the full name: "Dear Chris Warren." If you don't have someone's name, use a generic title: "Dear Human Resources Manager" or "Dear Hiring Manager."

Opening

The opening paragraph of a solicited cover letter is fairly straightforward. Because the organization has advertised the position, recruiters want to receive quality applications, so use a direct organization: state (or imply) the reason for your letter, identify the position for which you're applying, and indicate how you learned about the opening.

Tailor your opening to the job and to the specific organization. For conservative companies (e.g., financial services firms), use a restrained opening. For more creative work (e.g., sales, advertising, and public relations), you might start out on a more imaginative note. Finally, for unsolicited cover letters, which you initiate rather than responding to a job posting, you must first get the reader's attention. Try talking about the company—a recent project or a new product launch—and then show how you can contribute to the corporate effort (Figure 24).

Your opening should be short, interesting, and reader oriented. Avoid tired openings such as "Please consider this letter my application for . . ." Maintain an air of formality and avoid being too cute. Attention-grabbing gimmicks send a nonverbal message to the reader that the applicant may be trying to deflect attention from a weak résumé.

Figure 24 Openings for Cover Letters

Conservative

Mr. Adam Storkel, manager of your Fleet Street branch, suggested that I submit my résumé for the assistant loan officer position advertised in the *Indianapolis Business Journal*.

Creative

If quality is Job 1 at Ford, then Job 2 must surely be communicating that message effectively to the public. With my degree in journalism and my work experience at the Kintzell Agency, I can help you achieve that objective. The enclosed résumé describes my qualifications for the advertising copywriter position posted on the company website.

Unsolicited

Now that Russell Industries has expanded operations to Central America, can you use a marketing graduate who speaks fluent Spanish and who knows the culture of the region?

Body

In a paragraph or two, highlight your strongest qualifications and show how they can benefit the employer. Show—don't tell; provide specific, credible evidence to support your statements, using different wording from that used in the résumé. Give an example to make the bullets on your résumé come alive and help the recruiter visualize your experience.

☒ NOT   As stated on my résumé, I sometimes went on sales calls.

☑ BUT   Once, I went on a sales call with the president of Scholastic, Inc.'s Education division, and we closed a $150,000 deal—the largest for the Ugo software product. From observing the sales manager, I learned . . . .

Your letter also should reflect modest confidence rather than a hard-sell approach. Avoid starting too many sentences with *I*.

☒ NOT   I am an effective supervisor.

☑ BUT   Supervising a staff of five bank tellers taught me . . .

☒ NOT   I am an accurate person.

☑ BUT   In my two years of experience as a student research assistant, none of the spreadsheets I maintained ever came back with corrections.

☒ NOT   I took a class in business communication.

☑ BUT   The communication strategies I learned in my business communication class will help me resolve customer issues as a customer service representative at Allegheny Industries.

Refer the reader to the enclosed résumé. Subordinate the reference to the résumé and emphasize instead what the résumé contains.

☒ NOT   I am enclosing a copy of my résumé for your review.

☑ BUT   As detailed in the enclosed résumé, my extensive work experience in records management has prepared me to help you "take charge of this paperwork jungle," as mentioned in your classified ad.

Closing

Close your letter by asking for a personal interview. Indicate flexibility regarding scheduling and location. Provide your phone number and email address, either in the last paragraph or immediately below your name and address in the closing lines.

> After you have reviewed my qualifications, I would appreciate your letting me know when we can meet to discuss my employment with Connecticut Power and Light. I will be in the Hartford area from December 16 through January 4 and could come to your office at any time that is convenient for you.

Or you might try a more proactive approach. Because companies receive so many résumés, one way to distinguish yourself is to follow up with a phone call.

> I will call your office next week to see whether we can arrange a meeting to discuss my qualifications for the financial analyst position.

Use a standard closing, such as "Sincerely." For letters you send through the mail, leave enough space to sign the letter, and then type your name. For a version you send by email, just skip a line, and type your name below "Sincerely."

12-4b Inquiry Emails

When you don't know of a specific position available but want to express interest in a company, you can send an email—sometimes called a networking email or a request for an informational interview. Typically, an inquiry email is shorter than a cover letter (Figure 25). This is a good way to find job openings that may not be advertised or simply to learn more about a company

Sample Inquiry Email | **Figure 25**

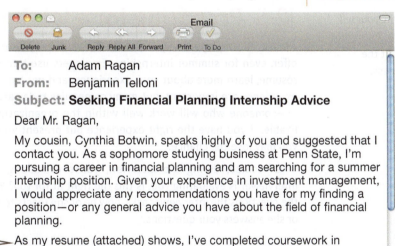

In an email, spell resume without the accents to avoid problems with character recognition. It's acceptable to use this spelling in your cover letters too.

To: Adam Ragan
From: Benjamin Telloni
Subject: Seeking Financial Planning Internship Advice

Dear Mr. Ragan,

My cousin, Cynthia Botwin, speaks highly of you and suggested that I contact you. As a sophomore studying business at Penn State, I'm pursuing a career in financial planning and am searching for a summer internship position. Given your experience in investment management, I would appreciate any recommendations you have for my finding a position—or any general advice you have about the field of financial planning.

As my resume (attached) shows, I've completed coursework in Financial & Managerial Accounting, Intro to Micro Economics, and Intro to Macro Economics, and I spent last summer working as a customer service representative at the Bank of America branch at 33 North Dearborn.

I'll be in Chicago during our spring break, March 15-19. Would it be possible for us to meet briefly during that time? I'd appreciate hearing from you by email or by phone at 555-555-1212.

Thank you for your consideration.

Regards,

Benjamin Telloni

and professionals in your area of interest. You might find an appropriate contact through your school's alumni database, friends and family, the company's website, or articles about the company.

You may not hear back from everyone who receives your inquiry email, but it's worth a shot. Making these connections is a good way to practice your networking skills.

The Checklist for Writing Cover Letters summarizes guidelines presented in this section.

Checklist for Writing Cover Letters

☑ Use your cover letter to show how the qualifications listed in your résumé have prepared you for the specific job for which you're applying.

☑ If possible, address your letter to the individual in the organization who will interview you.

☑ When applying for an advertised opening, begin by stating (or implying) the reason for the letter, identify the position for which you're applying, and tell how you learned about the opening.

☑ When writing an unsolicited cover letter, gain the reader's attention by showing that you are familiar with the company and can make a unique contribution to the business.

☑ In one or two paragraphs, highlight your strongest qualifications and relate them directly to the needs of the specific position. Refer the reader to the enclosed résumé.

☑ Treat your letter as a persuasive sales letter: provide specific evidence, stress reader benefits, avoid exaggeration, and show confidence in the quality of your product.

☑ Close by tactfully asking for an interview.

☑ Maintain an air of formality throughout the letter.

☑ Make sure the finished document presents a professional, attractive, and conservative appearance and that it is 100% error free.

LO4 Present yourself well during the interview and throughout the selection process.

12-5 Preparing for a Job Interview

Almost all employers require at least one employment interview before extending a job offer, even for summer internships. Employers use interviews to verify information on the résumé, learn more about your experience, and get to know you personally. Your skills and experience are important, but many companies today are also looking for an organizational fit—someone who will work well within the organizational culture.[32] Be yourself—and be likable. If you have the right experience but present yourself as too arrogant or too timid, you may lose the chance.

Of course, during the interview, you're evaluating the organization as much as the interviewer is evaluating you. Is this the right fit for *you*? You'll learn about the company from the questions the interviewer asks, how he or she reacts to you and your responses, and how he or she answers your questions.

12-5a Researching the Organization

You wouldn't walk into a potential customer's office without knowing about the company. The same is true for your interview. Learn everything you possibly can about the organization. Research the specific organization in depth, using the research techniques you developed from Chapter 9. Learn about the company's products and services, history, financial health, corporate structure, locations, and recent news.

You might find interesting information about the company through social media. Look at career websites, such as Glassdoor, Vault, and Indeed, where employees post comments. Many of these are petty and griping, but repeated comments may tell you about the inner workings of the company. Also explore analysts' ratings and customers' reviews and comments.

Think about the context of the company's competitors and the industry. By relating what you've learned about the company into the broader perspective of the industry, you can discuss issues affecting the company more intelligently. No one is impressed by the interviewee who, out of the blue, spouts, "I see your stock went up $5 last week." However, in response to the interviewer's comment about the company's recent announcement of a new product line, it would be appropriate to say, "I saw that the stock spiked last week." If you raise former employees' snarky comments, the interviewer may feel defensive. But if an interviewer from Time Warner Cable admits to a lot of change recently, you can simply say, "Yes, I saw some employee comments online about layoffs. I saw that Verizon also had layoffs this year." Bring up information that flows naturally into the conversation. If you don't get a chance to talk about what you learned, at least you'll know a lot about the company, which will help you make an informed decision about whether to accept a job.

12-5b Practicing Interview Questions

Recruiters and hiring managers use different techniques to interview candidates. In addition to standard interviews, many companies use behavioral interviews, case-based interviews, and unfortunately, stress interviews.

Standard Interviews

Some interviews are fairly straightforward. The interviewer may review your résumé with you, asking questions about your experience (e.g., "What did you like about working for Walgreens?"). With standard and all interview questions, the employer is interested not only in the content of your responses but also in *how* you react to the questions themselves and *how* you communicate your thoughts and ideas.

Before your interview, practice answering each of the questions in Figure 26. You may want to set up a video camera so you can watch yourself and assess how you look and sound.

Standard Interview Questions | **Figure 26**

- Tell me about yourself.
- Tell me something about yourself that I won't find on your résumé.
- What are you most proud of?
- Why did you leave your job at _____?
- Why would you like to work for our organization?
- Why should we hire you?
- What are your long-range career objectives?
- What type of work do you enjoy doing most? Least?
- What accomplishment has given you the greatest satisfaction?
- What would you like to change in your past?
- What courses did you like best and least in college?
- Specifically, how does your education or experience relate to this job?

Behavioral Interviews

Behavioral (or structured) interviews are based on the theory that past behavior predicts future performance. More than 80% of companies use this reliable technique.[33] Behavioral interview questions are highly specific questions related to competencies identified for a job. When interviewers ask these questions, they are looking for a specific example that demonstrates your ability to fulfill key job requirements—they want to hear a story. The best response follows a "STAR" format:

- **S**ituation or **T**ask: What brief context is important for the interviewer to understand?
- **A**ction: How did you handle the situation? What did you do?
- **R**esult: How did the situation turn out? How can you prove that your action was appropriate in the situation?

Two typical job competencies, behavioral interview questions, and sample responses are shown in Figure 27. Additional questions and associated competencies are in Figure 28. You can prepare for a behavioral interview by doing the following:

- Determine possible competencies for the job: look at the job description, which may list requirements.
- Plan between 10 and 15 examples: think about your work and school experience. What specific examples could you provide that might fit behavioral interview questions?
- Practice in front of a video camera: rehearse your examples and see how you come across.

Case Interviews

Some companies—particularly management consulting firms—use case interviews that present you with a problem to be solved. These companies are testing your analytical skills, creativity, problem-solving skills, ability to think on your feet, logic and reasoning, quantitative skills, and of course, your communication skills. For these types of interviews, your approach to solving the problem may be as important as the solution you offer.

Case questions may be quite complex and typically last between 20 and 40 minutes. Questions may be short, such as, "How many pieces of luggage go through JFK on an average day?" or long, such as "One of our clients, a retailer in the jewelry and luxury watch market, has experienced declining profits in the past 12 months. How would you go about assessing this problem?"

It's best to prepare for this type of interview. McKinsey & Company, the management consulting firm, offers practice cases online and tips and common mistakes for case interviews (Figure 29).[34]

Stress Interviews

Some companies simulate a stressful environment to see how well you work under pressure. In these situations, your interviewer may ask you pointed or inappropriate questions, interrupt you, or be sarcastic and just generally rude.

Try to maintain your composure if this happens. Keep telling yourself that you're qualified for the job and can handle the interview. You're under no obligation to answer inappropriate questions, and you have every right to defend your performance and experience. If an interviewer rolls his eyes and says, "You really don't have the background to work here," be clear and confident: "Yes, I do. I have strong analytical skills from my experience at . . . ."

Of course, you may decide that a company that chooses to use stress interviews isn't the place for you. If you are offered the job, you have no obligation to take it.

12-5c Managing a Video or Phone Interview

Video interviews using Skype, Google Hangout, FaceTime, and other programs are becoming increasingly popular, particularly to save time and travel expenses. According to a survey by Right Management, 19% of hiring managers and recruiters have used video interviews, and more than two-thirds expect the use to increase in the next three years.[35]

COMPETENCY AREA: INITIATIVE

Sample Behavioral Interview Question:
"Tell me about a time when you saw a problem and took initiative to solve it."

Sample Response:
"[**Situation**] Sure, when I was working for Tasty Treats Bakery last summer, we had a lot of very busy times when 15 to 20 customers were waiting. It was chaotic in the store because we didn't have enough space for a line, and people argued about who was first. [**Action**] I suggested to the owner that we implement a 'Take-a-Number' system so customers could be served in order of when they arrive. She was concerned about the cost and how it would work, so I researched three systems and explained the process in more detail. [**Result**] By the end of the summer, she had called two of the manufacturers in for quotes. When I visited the bakery over winter break, I saw she had installed a system! I felt very proud that I could contribute to the business in this way."

Notes:
With some variations, this situation could apply to different behavioral interview questions. For example, if you were asked for a time when you persuaded someone to make a change, you could focus more on the steps you took to convince the owner. Or if you were asked for an example of a problem you solved, you could focus more on the result for the owner, for example, that the business was running more smoothly and fewer customers left without ordering.

COMPETENCY AREA: TEAMWORK

Sample Behavioral Interview Question:
"Tell me about a time you worked as part of a team that didn't function too well. What did you do about it?" (Note that behavioral questions may ask for negative examples. In these situations, you should be honest and focus on how you learned from the experience.)

Sample Response:
"[**Situation**] For my marketing class in school, I worked with three other students to create a marketing plan. We started off well by assigning responsibilities and deadlines, but one student didn't submit her work on time. This was a problem for all of us because she was supposed to do the initial research, and this held up the rest of our work. [**Action**] I jumped in and did her work because I was worried about the project and wanted to move it along. [**Result**] We finished the marketing plan on time and got a 'B+,' but looking back, I'm not sure this was the best solution—everyone should participate equally, and this student got the same grade as the rest of us but didn't pull her weight. We didn't think this was fair."

Notes:
At this point during the interview, you may present another example to demonstrate what you learned from the experience and how you improved your teamwork skills. You may ask the interviewer for permission to give another example, and then describe the situation:

"[**Situation**] I had a similar situation for a finance project just last semester, but this time I did two things differently. [**Action**] First, I set up a wiki for the team so we could track everyone's progress throughout the project. This made accountability easier because when someone didn't complete a part of the assignment, it was public, and this put more pressure on each team member. Second, when one person didn't do his part on time, instead of jumping in, I took the initiative to talk to the student to see what was going on. He was having trouble finding data we needed, so I helped him but didn't complete the work for him. [**Result**] He was a couple of days late, but I'm glad he contributed his assigned part to the project. The team received an 'A,' and I think it's partly because everyone contributed fairly equally."

Figure 28 | Behavioral Interview Questions and Competencies

Relationship Building: Describe the best working relationship you've had. What did you do to make it successful? | Tell me about a time when you had to work with someone you didn't like. | Describe a time when it was particularly difficult for you to gain credibility with someone. What did you do?

Problem Solving: Tell me about a time when you were assigned work that you didn't know how to do or had difficulty completing on your own. How did you handle it? | Please give me an example of when you had to solve a particularly challenging problem.

Teamwork: Tell me about a time when you had to step in to help a group or team complete a task/project/assignment. What did you do? | Give an example of a conflict with a coworker. How did you handle it? | Think of a time when you had a major role in developing a team that became very successful. Tell me one or two things you did that contributed to the team's success.

Time Management or Planning and Organizing: Tell me about a time when you faced a strict deadline and how you handled it. | We all miss deadlines sometimes. Can you think of when this happened to you? How did it happen, and what was the result? | Tell me about a time when you had too many things to do, and you had to prioritize your tasks.

Work Ethic: Tell me about a time when you had to cut corners in order to finish a project or meet a manager's expectations. | Describe a task you truly disliked and how you handled it. | Tell me about a time when you had to go above and beyond in order to get a job done.

Ethics: Please give me an example of when you felt that your personal ethics didn't align with a company's. | Tell me about a time when your manager or client asked you to do something that you didn't think was appropriate. How did you respond? | Can you think of a time when your ethics and those of a coworker or teammate caused a conflict between you? What happened?

Decision-Making: Give me an example of a time when you had to make a split-second decision. | Tell me about a policy you didn't agree with but had to comply with anyway. What did you do? | Tell me about a difficult decision you've made in the last year.

Persuasion or Influence: Tell me about a time when you convinced someone to see your point of view. | Can you give me an example of how you successfully dealt with another person even when he or she didn't personally like you (or vice versa)? | Please describe how you persuaded someone to implement an idea you proposed.

Customer Service: Tell me about a recent situation in which you had to deal with a very upset customer or coworker. | I'd like to hear an example of when you exceeded a customer's expectations. | Tell me about a time when you had to bend a policy to accommodate a customer. What happened?

Communication TECHNOLOGIES

With a webcam, you can connect with a recruiter just as you would in person, and you should prepare for the interview the same way. Follow the tips in Figure 30 for a successful video interview.

Instead of a video interview, companies may request a phone interview, particularly for initial screening. Typically, these interviews are shorter than in-person interviews and may include general or behavioral questions. Avoid distractions and background noise just as you would for a video interview. But the real challenge is not having nonverbal cues from your interviewer, such as nodding and smiling—or trying to jump in. You might keep your answers shorter to allow the interviewer to interrupt; otherwise, you could be way off track and not know it.

The Case Interview (from McKinsey & Company)

TIPS	COMMON MISTAKES
• Listen to the problem. • Begin by setting a structure. • Stay organized. • Communicate your train of thought clearly. • Step back periodically. • Ask for additional information when you need it. • Watch for cues from the interviewer. • Be comfortable with numbers. • Don't fixate on "cracking the case." • Use business judgment and common sense. • Relax and enjoy the process.	• Misunderstanding the question or answering the wrong question. • Proceeding in a haphazard fashion. • Asking a barrage of questions. • Force-fitting familiar business frameworks to every case question. • Failing to synthesize a point of view. • Not asking for help.

TECHNIQUES AND TRICKS," MCKINSEY & COMPANY, WWW.MCKINSEY.COM. ACCESSED APRIL 7, 2013

Tips for a Successful Video Interview | **Figure 30**

CARLOSSELLER/SHUTTERSTOCK.COM

- Get comfortable with the technology: practice with someone ahead of time.
- Arrange for a quiet, uninterrupted place.
- Make sure that your background looks professional—not like a messy room.
- Dress as you would for an in-person interview, but avoid loud plaid or striped clothing, which can look distorted on video.
- Check your posture and positioning—not too far or too close.
- Close other programs on your computer to avoid alerts and other sounds.
- Log on a minute or two before the call starts.
- Look at the camera rather than at the screen to make direct eye contact.
- Speak and act naturally—no need to talk loudly or exaggerate your gestures.
- Keep the window of your image open during the interview so you can check yourself occasionally.

12-5d Preparing Your Own Questions

During the interview, many of your questions about the organization or the job will probably be answered. However, some of the best interviews are more like conversations—you may ask questions throughout.

During one 45-minute interview at Google, the candidate was asked questions for only 15 minutes. For the remaining 30 minutes, the interviewer expected him to lead with questions. As this candidate said, "It was important that I had many questions prepared that were relevant to my position and Google on a macro and micro level."[36] Asking questions such as those in Figure 31 shows the recruiter that you're engaged in the interview and interested in the job and company.

Figure 31	Possible Questions to Ask During an Interview

- How would you describe a typical day on the job?
- What opportunities exist for ongoing training and development?
- What are your expectations of new employees?
- How would my performance in this position be measured?
- What makes someone successful in this position?
- What are the organization's plans for the future?
- What do you see as the biggest opportunities and challenges for this division/company?
- To whom would I report? Would anyone report to me?
- What are the advancement opportunities for this position?

Finally, know when the interview is over. If the recruiter seems to be wrapping up, you may have to end your questions.

12-6 Conducting Yourself During and After the Interview

Making a good first impression during the interview is critical. In one study, executives said they form a positive or negative impression of a candidate within the first ten minutes of a job interview.[37] Pay attention to your dress, project a professional image, prepare for multiple interviewers, and finally, assess yourself and the company.

12-6a Dressing for Success

To make a good first impression, dress appropriately. Deciding what to wear can be tricky: every industry and company is different. Show that you understand the corporate culture by dressing just a bit more formally than what people typically wear. For example, for a manufacturing job where people dress in khakis, you might wear a button-down shirt and blazer or a skirt and blouse. For a financial services job where men dress in suits but no tie, you might wear a tie. If women wear dress pants and a blazer, you might wear a matching suit. For an advertising job where people dress casually,

Business attire usually means a suit—a suit and tie for men and either a pant suit or skirt suit for women.

you might wear jeans with a blazer—just a notch above to show your seriousness about the interview.

In general, when recruiters ask you to wear "business casual," you can skip the jacket and tie. A tailored shirt or conservative sweater with a skirt or dress pants will probably work well.

Business casual attire varies widely by organization. Err on the side of more conservative dress for job interviews, as shown here.

12-6b Acting Professionally

Your first impression starts before the interview does. Turn off your phone to avoid embarrassment, and observe the environment so you can act appropriately. Treat everyone you meet, including the receptionist and the interviewer's assistant, with respect. Be natural but professional.

When shown into the interview room, greet the interviewer by name with a firm handshake, direct eye contact, and a smile. Address the interviewer as "Mr." or "Ms.," switching to a first name if the interviewer gives you permission ("Call me Terry"). If you're not asked to be seated immediately, wait until the interviewer is seated and then take your seat. Lean forward a bit in your seat, and maintain comfortable eye contact with the interviewer. Avoid taking notes, except perhaps for a specific name, date, or telephone number.

Once the interview starts, do your best to relax, while maintaining a professional image. With enough practice—during mock interviews on campus or with a friend—you should be well prepared for even the toughest questions. Listen carefully to each question rather than focusing on what you'll say next.

Imagine that you're talking with a trusted friend of the family. One recruiter put it well when she said, "After a day of back-to-back interviews, I may not remember what everyone said, but I'll remember how I felt about each of them." People want to work with people they like.

12-6c Demonstrating Confidence and Focusing on Your Qualifications

Be confident but avoid an attitude that suggests, "You're lucky to have me here." The interviewer might not agree. Follow the interviewer's lead, letting him or her determine which questions to ask, when to move to a new area of discussion, and when to end the interview. But you needn't fawn or grovel either. You're *applying*—not begging—for a job.

Show how you're qualified for the job, but don't try to oversell yourself, or you may end up in a job for which you're unprepared. If the interviewer doesn't address one of your skills, try to work it into the discussion. At the end of an interview, many recruiters will ask you, "Is there anything else we didn't cover that you'd like to tell me?" That's your chance to talk about the business fraternity you joined or the speaker series you started.

If asked about your salary expectations, try to avoid giving a number. Instead, say that you would expect to be paid in line with other employees at your level of expertise and experience. If pressed, however, be prepared to reveal your salary expectations, preferably using a broad range. Try to find salary ranges ahead of time: ask your college career office staff, and check sites such as Salary.com for approximations. Also, when discussing salary, talk in terms of what you think the position and responsibilities are worth rather than what you think *you* are worth. Salary, vacation time, and benefits are rarely discussed during the first interview, so you may need to be patient during the process.

 Emotional INTELLIGENCE

Do you have some social anxiety, or do you get nervous when meeting new people? Try to approach the interview as a meeting with someone interesting. Your goals are simply to let that person know you and for you to know him or her and the company a little better.

12-6d Preparing for Multiple Interviewers

You might participate in a group interview, with several people asking you questions. If possible, find out about this practice ahead of time so that you can prepare yourself mentally. Address your responses to everyone, not just to the person who asked the question or to the most senior person present.

As shown in the typical selection process in Figure 2, it's also likely that you'll be interviewed more than once—with either multiple interviews the same day or, if you survive the initial interview, a "second [or third] round" of more intense, longer interviews. When you apply for a full-time job, most companies that interview on campus will invite you to the corporate office or local property for more interviews. Multiple interviewers will talk to each other about you, so be sure to give consistent responses.

12-6e Assessing Yourself and the Company

After the interview, assess your performance and the company so you can improve for future interviews and make a decision about the company (Figure 32). Asking these questions—about yourself and the company—puts you back in control and helps you develop your interview skills.

Figure 32 | Questions to Ask Yourself After an Interview

ASSESS YOURSELF	ASSESS THE COMPANY
How was your appearance and attire? Did you dress appropriately for the interview and company? How would you dress differently in the future?	How do you feel about the company? Is this a place you could see yourself working?
What qualifications are most important in this job? How can you change your cover letter, résumé, or responses to address these more directly?	How was your relationship with the interviewer and people on the team? Did you connect with them?
Which questions did you answer best? How can you present these descriptions or examples in future interviews?	What are the job responsibilities? Could you see yourself doing this job for the next two to three years?
Which questions did you have trouble answering? How can you address these differently?	How does this company compare to others you're considering? What are the advantages and disadvantages?
What questions did the recruiter ask about your résumé? What should you clarify or delete as a result?	Do you think you'll get a job offer? What would you do?

12-6f Following Up Throughout the Process

Communication throughout the selection process can be challenging. You're dealing with busy HR people and companies who—let's face it—don't always do the best job of keeping you informed.

Without being overly aggressive, you can take some initiative throughout the selection process. As you saw in the Sample Cover Letter, calling a week or so after you send a résumé is perfectly appropriate and may differentiate you from other applicants. You might leave a voice mail such as the following:

"Hello, Ms. Catona. This is Catherine Lin. I recently sent a résumé for the Finance Management Trainee position, and I'm excited about the opportunity to work for Bank on Me. I'd like to talk about my qualifications, particularly my relevant experience at Ernst & Young, and possibly set up an interview. You can reach me at 555-555-1212. Thank you, and I look forward to hearing from you."

You may not hear back from Ms. Catona, but she will likely remember your name as she reads through the stack of résumés—and perhaps she'll give yours a second look.

During the process of setting up interviews, be sure to express your appreciation and enthusiasm for the job, and try to be as flexible as possible.

After each interview, send a thank-you email within 24 hours. Decisions may be made quickly, so you want the chance to influence them. In one study, 15% of hiring managers said they wouldn't hire an applicant who didn't send a thank-you note; 32% said they would still consider the applicant but would think less of him or her.[38] In another study, 88% of executives said a thank-you note influences their decision, but only half of candidates send them.[39] Clearly, sending an email is an easy way for you to differentiate yourself.

Send a customized thank-you email that expresses genuine appreciation for the interview, reiterates your interest in the job, and reinforces your qualifications. If the interview coordinator doesn't give you email addresses for your interviewers, ask for a business card at the end of each interview. A sample email is shown in Figure 33.

Sending a printed letter as well is a nice touch but should not substitute for an email, which will arrive much more quickly. You also may send a handwritten note in special circumstances, for example, when you make a personal connection with the interviewer.

Sample Thank-You Email | Figure 33

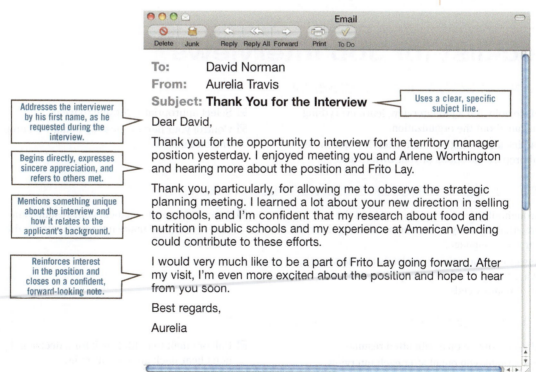

If you don't hear back from the interviewer by the deadline he or she gave you for making a decision, call or send an email for an update. If no decision has been made, your inquiry will keep your name and your interest in the interviewer's mind. If someone else has been selected, you need to know so that you can continue your job search. You might send an email such as the example in Figure 34, which is polite, yet pushes for a decision.

Figure 34 | Follow-Up Email

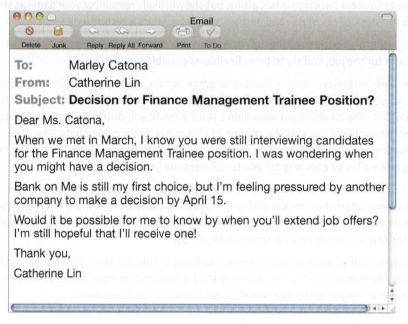

The Checklist for Job Interviews summarizes key points from this section.

Checklist for Job Interviews

PREPARING FOR A JOB INTERVIEW

- ☑ Before going on a job interview, learn everything you can about the organization.
- ☑ Practice answering common interview questions, and prepare questions of your own to ask.

- ☑ Select appropriate clothing to wear.
- ☑ Control your nervousness by being well prepared and on time.

CONDUCTING YOURSELF DURING THE INTERVIEW

- ☑ Throughout the interview, be aware of the nonverbal signals you are communicating through your body language.
- ☑ Answer each question completely and accurately, always trying to relate your qualifications to what the company needs.

- ☑ Assess your performance, your résumé, and your cover letter, and make improvements for the next interview.

FOLLOWING UP THROUGHOUT THE PROCESS

- ☑ Call to follow up on a submitted résumé.
- ☑ Send a thank-you email after each interview.

- ☑ Call or email to politely ask for a decision if you don't hear back after an interview.

12-7 Practicing Business Etiquette

LO5 Practice business etiquette in the workplace.

Business etiquette refers to appropriate behavior in a business setting. By following good etiquette, we present a professional image and interact properly with others at work. As a business professional, you want to represent yourself as a serious employee who can be trusted—and promoted.

Each organization has its own rules about what is considered appropriate in terms of dress, interactions with senior-level managers, punctuality, and other subtle forms of communication in the workplace. In addition, every country and every culture has its own rules, and these may vary even within an organization. What's considered acceptable in the IT department (e.g., casual dress and abbreviations in instant messages) may be perceived negatively in the sales department. Generally, these rules are not written down but are learned informally or through observation. Executives typically set the bar for business etiquette, so following their lead will help you determine appropriate behavior.

Business etiquette differs from social etiquette. Flirting, drinking too much, and telling questionable jokes may be acceptable at a party with your friends but not at a business function. When in doubt, use a high standard of acceptability—err on the side of being too proper rather than risk offending someone or embarrassing yourself.

12-7a Meeting and Greeting

When you meet people for the first time, take the initiative to introduce yourself. If someone is hosting you, then he or she should make the introduction—as you should for others—but if you're new to a job, at a conference, meeting with a new client, or attending a training program, introduce yourself to people around you. This initiative shows confidence and will help you meet more people at your company or in your industry.

When introducing others, the basic rule is to present the lower-ranking person to the higher-ranking person: "[CEO], this is my new assistant." You might say, "Helen, I'd like you to meet Carl Byrum. Carl just began working here as a junior account manager. Carl, this is Helen Smith, our CEO." Or in a social situation, you might just say, "Rosa, this is Gene Stauffer. Gene, Rosa Bennett." The appropriate response to an introduction is, "Hello, Gene," "I'm glad to meet you, Gene," or, more formally, "It's a pleasure to meet you, Gene." Typically, in the United States, the two people will then shake hands.

To help remember someone's name, repeat it when you shake hands. If you cannot remember someone's name, when the person approaches you, simply extend your hand and say your name. The other person will typically respond by shaking your hand and also giving his or her name. In the potentially awkward situation when you introduce two people but remember only one person's name, simply say, "Have you met Carly from Accounting?"

Whenever you see someone who may not remember you, you can help avoid embarrassment by introducing yourself and jogging the person's memory: "Hello, Mr. Wise, I'm Eileen Wagoner. We met at Chloe's party last month."

Today, most American businesspeople have business cards, although the protocol for exchanging them isn't as strict here as it is in some other countries. In business settings, present your card at the end of the encounter to communicate your interest in continuing the relationship. Never present your card during a meal (wait until it is over), and never offer your card at any time during a social function.

12-7b Dining

Whether in the employee cafeteria or at a fine restaurant, these guidelines will help you enjoy your business meal.

Before the Meal

- If you host a meal, choose a restaurant appropriate for the person and within your company's policy to be sure you'll get reimbursed. Also ask your guest whether he or she has dietary restrictions that may affect your choice.
- Be sure to make reservations. You don't want to be embarrassed by showing up at a restaurant that cannot accommodate you and your guests.
- If a *maître d'* (headwaiter) seats you and your guest, your guest should precede you to the table. If you're seating yourselves, take the lead in locating an appropriate table. Give your guest the preferred seat, facing the window with an attractive view or facing the dining room if you're seated next to the wall.
- If you're the host, to signal the waiter that you're ready to order, close your menu and lay it on the table. The host's order is generally taken last.
- Go light on the liquor. You may order wine for the table if others would like to indulge, but keep your own drinking to a minimum.
- When the food arrives, guests should not begin eating until the host begins. Never begin eating until everyone has been served. If yours is the only dish not yet served because of a delay, it's polite to invite others to begin rather than wait. They may or may not do so.

During the Meal

- A business meal is about the conversation—not the food. Stay engaged throughout the meal.
- Your mother was right: never talk with your mouth full. Take small bites so you can participate in the conversation.
- Take your host's lead for topics. Sometimes, business meals are more social, and discussing too much business is considered inappropriate.
- Your glass is at your right; your bread plate is on the left. When using silverware, start from the outside in (the smaller fork is for your salad). When passing food or condiments, pass to the right, offering items to someone else before you serve yourself. If you *must* use salt (only after tasting the food), ask someone to please pass it to you, rather than reach across the table for it. And when asked to pass the salt or pepper, pass both together.

At a formal place setting, the glass or cup on the right side and the bread plate on the left side are yours.

- To get the server's attention, say "Excuse me" when he or she is nearby, catch the server's eye and quietly signal for him or her to come to the table, or ask a nearby server to ask yours to come to your table.
- Don't put your elbows on the table while eating, although you may do so between courses.
- If you leave the table during the meal, leave your napkin on your chair. At the end of the meal, place the napkin, unfolded, on the table.
- Place the knife across the top edge of the plate, with the cutting edge toward you when it is not being used; don't keep silverware leveraged on the table and plate like oars. To signal to the server that you have finished, place your knife and fork together on the plate.

After the Meal

- For business meals, it's typically inappropriate to take leftovers home. If the server asks, politely decline.
- The person who extended the invitation is expected to pay the bill. When the server comes with the check, indicate that you will accept it. If it's placed on the table, just pick it up. If it's unclear who will pay, you should always offer. If your host declines your offer, say a polite, "Thank you."
- If someone else paid, be sure to say "Thank you" before you get up from the table.
- Tip between 15% and 20% of the bill before tax. If you can't calculate this in your head, subtly check your smartphone. If you checked coats, leave $1 per coat, and if you used valet parking, tip the attendant $2.
- If you were the guest, send a thank-you note immediately after the meal. Be sure to write more than a token note, mentioning something special about the décor, food, service, and company.

To signal to the server that you are finished, place the knife and fork together on your plate.

PAVEL IGNATOV/SHUTTERSTOCK.COM

12-7c Giving Gifts

Giving gifts to suppliers, customers, or workers is typical at many firms, especially in December during the holiday period. Although gifts are often appreciated, check your company's policy. Many companies restrict both giving and receiving gifts to avoid improprieties.

Most people would consider a gift appropriate if it meets the four criteria in Figure 35. A manager is more likely to give his or her employee a gift than the other way around. For special occasions, coworkers may contribute to a gift for the boss and present it from the entire group.

Criteria for an Appropriate Business Gift | **Figure 35**

✓ **It is an impersonal gift.** Gifts that can be used in the office or in connection with work are nearly always appropriate. For example, a notepad is appropriate; lingerie is not!

✓ **It is for past favors.** Gifts should be used to thank someone for past favors, business, or performance—*not* to create obligations for the future. Giving a fruit basket to a prospective customer who has never ordered from you before might be interpreted as a bribe.

✓ **It is given to everyone in similar circumstances.** Singling out one person for a gift and ignoring others in similar positions could be embarrassing or cause bad feelings.

✓ **It is not extravagant.** A very expensive gift might make the recipient uneasy, create a sense of obligation, and call into question your motives for giving. Inviting a customer and his family on a cruise is not appropriate and is likely against both companies' policies.

12-7d Working in an Office

How you behave around the office will determine how people feel about you as a coworker and as a business professional. Although you want to be friendly—and be yourself—you also want to be perceived as someone who is respectful of others.

Office space is a precious commodity today, and people value their own work area, which, for millions of people, is a cubicle. Because cubicles offer little privacy, courtesy is especially important. Follow these guidelines:

Tight quarters—and some strange personalities—cause people to annoy their coworkers in the movie *Office Space*.

EVERETT COLLECTION

- Always knock or ask permission before entering someone's cubicle, and never wander into someone's unoccupied cubicle without permission.
- Never shout a comment to someone in the next cubicle. If it's inconvenient to walk over, email, send an IM, or call instead.
- Do not leave valuables in your cubicle unattended.
- Avoid talking on the phone or to visitors too loudly, and avoid strong perfumes or colognes.
- Finally, honor the occupant's privacy by not staring at his or her computer screen or listening to private conversations.

Always be aware of how others behave in the workplace. Whether you're waiting for an elevator or to get a second cup of coffee, pay attention to social cues. How much small talk do people engage in? What are their conversations about? What's common practice when people come into work and when they leave for the day? The best way to fit in socially is to observe others and, as long as the behavior is professional and acceptable to you personally, adapt to the environment.

By practicing effective business communication and respecting others at work, you'll be a successful business professional—and may be next in line for that big promotion.

Sending a Thank-You Note

3Ps
‹ IN ACTION

>>> PURPOSE

Imagine that you just interviewed for your dream job—recruiting manager for a major hotel company. The interview went well, and you want to send an inspired thank-you note to seal the deal.

>>> PROCESS

1. **In what format will you send the thank-you note?**
   Email—this is how all of my communication with the company has taken place so far, and I want the hiring manager to receive it quickly.

2. **Write an opening paragraph for your email to capture attention and convey the purpose up front.**
   "Thank you for such an informative interview today. It was interesting to hear about your success recruiting through your Facebook page and other social media sites. The recruiting manager position would be the perfect place for me to start my career—and I believe I can contribute a great deal to your social recruiting efforts."

3. **How will you reinforce your relevant skills and other qualifications for the job?**
   I'll mention the work I did on Marriott's and other companies' social media sites.

4. **How will you reinforce your education as a differentiator from other applicants?**
   I'll mention my HR major and other business coursework.

5. **Write the closing paragraph.**
   "Again, thank you for the opportunity to meet with you about the position. I'm excited about the chance to be a part of such a dynamic team and look forward to hearing from you soon."

>>> PRODUCT

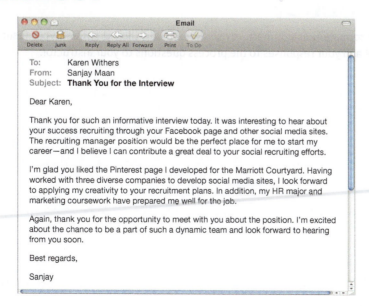

Writing a Résumé

>>> PURPOSE

Assume that you are beginning your last semester of college before graduating. Using information about your education, work experience, and so on, prepare a résumé in an effective format.

>>> PROCESS

1. How will you word your name at the top of your résumé—for example, with or without any initials?

2. What is the title of your degree? The name of your college? The location of the college? Your major and minor? Your expected date of graduation (month and year)?

3. What is your grade-point average overall and in your major? Is either one high enough to be considered a selling point?

4. Have you received any academic honors, such as scholarships or being named to the dean's list?

5. Did you take any elective courses that are relevant to the job and that might differentiate you from other applicants?

6. List in reverse chronological order (most recent job first) the following information for each job you've held during college: company name, job title, location (city and state), and dates of employment. Describe your specific responsibilities in each position. Use short phrases, beginning each responsibility with an action verb, and showing, where possible, specific evidence of the results you achieved.

7. What additional information might you include, such as special skills, extracurricular activities, volunteer work, languages spoken, and so on?

>>> PRODUCT

Using the information listed, draft, revise, format, and then proofread your résumé. Submit your résumé and your responses to the process questions to your instructor.

> SUMMARY

LO1 Write and format a résumé.

The purpose of your résumé is to get you a job interview. Strive for a one-page document with a simple, readable format. Include your name, address, phone number, email address, information about your education and work experience, and special skills. Include other information only if it will help distinguish you favorably from the other applicants. Prefer the chronological organization for your work experience, and stress the skills and experiences that can be transferred to the job you want.

LO2 Manage your online image.

Most employers search for candidates online before making a final hiring decision. Make sure that your online reputation shows you in the best possible light. Create content, participate on LinkedIn, and consider creating an infographic or social version of your résumé to supplement your employment materials. This may set you apart and make it easier for employers to find you online—where they are increasingly searching for candidates.

LO3 Write a cover letter or inquiry email.

Compose a cover letter that discusses how your education and work experience qualify you specifically for the job. If possible, address your letter to the person who will interview you for the job. Because most employers prefer résumés by email, you may write your cover note within the body of an email message.

Adjust your letter or email opening to the situation and type of job. Then highlight your strongest qualifications, relating them to the needs of the position for which you're applying. Close by politely asking for an interview.

LO4 Present yourself well during the interview and throughout the selection process.

If your cover letter is successful, you will be invited for an interview. For a successful interview, prepare by researching the company, and practice answering and asking questions. Prepare for all types of interviews: standard, behavioral, case, and stress. For behavioral interviews, which are most common, practice giving specific examples from your experience in this format: situation/task, action, and result. After the interview, evaluate your performance, résumé, and cover letter so you can do better the next time. Write a personalized thank-you note, and consider following up if you do not hear from the employer within the time frame promised.

LO5 Practice business etiquette in the workplace.

Business etiquette is a guide to help people behave appropriately in business situations. To be effective in business, learn how to make introductions, conduct business lunches, give suitable gifts, and maintain good working relationships around the office.

> EXERCISES

1. **Assess your strengths.**

   Answer the questions in Figure 1, and then discuss them with two or three family members or friends who know you well. What are their views of your assessment? How do their opinions differ, and how, if at all, do their opinions of you influence how you feel about your strengths?

LO1 Write and format a résumé.

2. Improve your résumé.

Exchange résumés with a partner. Using the principles in this chapter, analyze your partner's résumé. Imagine that you're a human resources manager who reviews hundreds of résumés every day. Use this checklist to provide feedback to your partner and suggest improvements:

Résumé Feedback

Criteria	Comments
• Formatting is attractive and easy to read.	
• Identifying information is clear.	
• Education section is accurate and emphasizes key points.	
• Work experience section is well organized.	
• Work experience section includes companies, job titles, and dates.	
• Bulleted job responsibilities start with action verbs and are phrased clearly.	
• Job responsibility descriptions highlight accomplishments.	
• Other activities are relevant and clearly explained.	
• Résumé is 100% accurate.	

3. Customize your résumé for a job.

One way to land a job is to apply for opportunities posted through your school's career center. But you can supplement your search by reaching out to other companies that interest you. Using your school's career center, the Internet, and library research tools, brainstorm a list of companies where you would like to work. On Hoovers (www.hoovers.com), for example, you can search for companies by industry or location. After you identify companies that interest you, take a look at their career websites. What positions are available? How do they describe the organizational culture?

If a company and position seem like a fit for you, then prepare a customized résumé. You might change, for example, which past jobs you include on your résumé, how you describe your responsibilities, and which extracurricular activities or skills you include. Imagine yourself receiving the résumé. Does it seem like a fit for the organization and culture?

LO2 Manage your online image.

4. Evaluate your own online reputation.

Congratulations! You just got a final interview with your favorite company. Imagine that the recruiter searches for you online to see what additional information she can find about you. First, Google yourself using a few combinations of your name, nickname, school, and town. What positive and potentially negative information do you find? Next, look at your Facebook page and review posts for the past three months. Do you see any red flags? Finally, look at your LinkedIn profile, and compare it to your résumé. Do you see any inconsistencies?

You don't need to give your instructor details about what you found, but write an email summarizing whether your favorite employer would find reasons to reject you as a candidate or hire you. Also include what, if any, changes you will make to ensure that you're represented online in the best possibly way.

5. **Ask two friends to search for you online.**

Ask two trusted friends to search for you on Google and Bing. Have them assess what they find. Do the results for your name relate to you or someone else? Does any negative information need to be removed? Do they find enough positive content? Consider their advice and suggestions in this chapter to manage your online image.

6. **Participate in LinkedIn groups.**

Join a LinkedIn professional group that interests you. Spend a couple of weeks observing the online discussions, and then post a couple of questions and see what responses you get.

7. **Create an infographic résumé.**

Using principles from Chapter 9, create a graphical representation of your education and work history. What format and colors would work best for your skills, experience, and personality? For ideas, you might search Google Images (images.google.com). You'll see hundreds of creative approaches.

8. **Customize a cover letter.**

After you identify a company and position that interests you and for which you're qualified, write a customized cover letter. How will you express interest in this specific company? Which experiences will you highlight?

LO3 Write a cover letter or inquiry email.

9. **Change your cover letter to an email message.**

Change a cover letter you wrote previously (or the one you wrote for Exercise 8) to a version you'll send as an email. What changes will you make in the salutation and formatting? How can you reduce the length? How will you change the tone to make it more appropriate for an email message?

10. **Applying for an internal position.**

A position has just opened in another department at the company where you work. While you have a lot of experience in your current job, the new position would require you to learn about new products and procedures. Write a cover letter in the form of an email to the hiring manager to express your interest in the new position, describe your accomplishments in your current position, and explain how your skills will help you succeed.

Exercise 10 refers to Write Experience, a technology that uses artificial intelligence to score student writing and provide feedback to help them improve.

11. **Rewrite a networking email.**

Imagine that your friend Ron asks you to review a draft networking email before he sends it. His goal is to get a summer internship in the marketing department of the company. What advice would you give to your friend? If you were Ron, how would you revise the email?

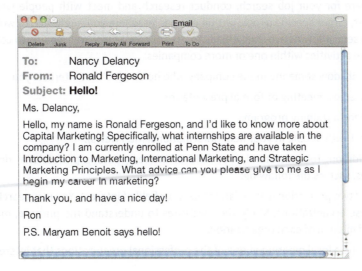

To: Nancy Delancy
From: Ronald Fergeson
Subject: Hello!

Ms. Delancy,

Hello, my name is Ronald Fergeson, and I'd like to know more about Capital Marketing! Specifically, what internships are available in the company? I am currently enrolled at Penn State and have taken Introduction to Marketing, International Marketing, and Strategic Marketing Principles. What advice can you please give to me as I begin my career in marketing?

Thank you, and have a nice day!

Ron

P.S. Maryam Benoit says hello!

12. Expand your network by meeting new people.

To expand your job search, push yourself to join groups that may be uncomfortable for you. Most of us have some social anxiety when meeting people for the first time, but the more you meet new people, the easier it will be. Look for professional associations near you and register to attend a meeting. When you're there, look for one or two friendly looking people and introduce yourself. Spend some time observing how people behave and interact with each other, and see whether this is a place where you could feel comfortable returning. If you do, try to make one or two new connections each time.

13. Write networking emails.

Find a few executives with whom you would like to network. For this exercise, you can decide—based on your own career goals—what you would like to get out of the experience: a visit to the company's headquarters, a chance to meet with an executive to see what it's like to work for your dream company, more information about a field that interests you, or a summer internship. Just be realistic and avoid placing a burden on someone you don't know.

To find people to contact, you might search your college's alumni database, ask friends or family for recommendations, look at companies' websites, or search online for people's names and titles. The more people you include, the more likely you will get responses.

Prepare a draft generic email. Then, tailor the email to each executive on your list. Think about ways to connect with each person to encourage a positive response.

LO4 Present yourself well during the interview and throughout the selection process.

14. Research a potential employer.

Assume that your favorite company has invited you to interview. To prepare for the interview, research the company by reviewing its website, reading news stories, and exploring websites such as Hoovers, Vault, Glassdoor, and Indeed. Concentrate on information most likely to help you during the interview.

Now assume that another student, who is also interested in the company, asks you what you have learned. You're such a nice person that you're willing to tell him or her everything! Write an email to this student summarizing your research.

15. Prepare a list of questions for a potential employer.

For an upcoming interview (or from your research completed in Exercise 14), prepare a list of questions you might ask during the interview. You may not have the time to ask everything, but prepare a long list, just in case.

16. Prepare a career preparation portfolio.

To prepare for your job search, conduct research and meet with people who can help you. First, target specific people within companies where you might like to work. You will need to send a few networking emails to ask for assistance. Your goal is to complete the following activities within one or more companies:

- Job shadow someone in the company who holds a job that interests you.
- Observe a meeting or formal presentation.
- Attend a training program.
- Meet with people in your field (informational interviews).

In addition, to understand your field of interest, pursue professional development activities, such as the following:

- Find two professional associations for your field of interest. You may search online for these organizations. Study their websites to understand the purpose, membership, and mission of each organization.
- Attend a local meeting of one of the professional organizations that interests you.

- Find two professional journals within your field of interest, and study one article from each.
- Search for news stories or credible blogs about your field. Study what these sources say about important trends or developments within your field.

Prepare a portfolio of your work, and submit it to your instructor. You might be instructed to include the following:

- A cover memo summarizing what you learned from these activities
- Observations from your job shadowing experience
- Copies of handouts or presentation decks you received during meetings or training programs
- Notes from your informational interviews
- Observations about professional associations in your field
- Notes from the professional association meeting you attended
- Summaries of journal articles you read
- An analysis of trends and developments that might affect your career choice in the future

Organize your portfolio in a way that makes sense to you—not necessarily in the order presented here. Include a table of contents for your materials and a title page.

17. **Practice a behavioral interview.**

To prepare for this exercise, identify between 10 and 15 examples of stories from your experience, as described in this chapter. Then, in class, work in groups of three to practice answering a behavioral interview question from Figure 28. Take turns, with one of you asking the question, another responding, and the third person observing and taking notes, using the checklist below to evaluate the candidate's response:

Content & Organization	❑ Did you get a complete story (STAR)?
	❑ Did it demonstrate the competency you were looking for?
	❑ Was it well organized?
	❑ Did you get the right amount of detail (enough, not too much)?
	❑ COMMENTS:

Delivery	❑ Easy to understand
	❑ Good eye contact
	❑ Appropriate pace
	❑ Good volume
	❑ Effective hand gestures
	❑ Few fillers (*uh, um*)
	❑ Appropriate pauses
	❑ COMMENTS:

18. **Practice dressing up for an interview.**

    With your classmates, agree on a date when everyone will come to class dressed for a job interview. If you're shy, you can meet in small groups to give each other feedback. If you're bold, have a fashion show. One person at a time can walk in front of the class for feedback. Be kind, of course. Give each other tips on professional attire and grooming.

19. **Write a thank-you email.**

    Imagine that you had a great interview for your ideal job. Write a thank-you email to your interviewer to reinforce your interest in the position and your qualifications. Send the email to your instructor for feedback.

20. **Follow up after an interview.**

    Have you had an interview in the past, and the interviewer never got back to you? Or have you sent a résumé and not received a response? Think about one of these situations, and write an email to follow up. Exchange drafts with a partner to make sure your request is clear and your tone is appropriate.

21. **Practice introducing people at work.**

    Assume the role of Pat Gibson, catering director for Writeaway Hotels. You're expecting Carly Singleton, an event manager and important potential client from Atlanta, for a business meeting at 10 a.m. Carly will be accompanied by Eunji Shun, who reports to her. You've met both of them once before. Working with other students who will play these roles, make the following introductions:

    a. Carly Singleton and Ian Mendoza (Pat's manager)

    b. Carly Singleton and Margaret Bryant (Ian's assistant)

    c. Eunji Shun and Ian Mendoza (Pat's manager)

    d. Eunji Shun and Jay Chan (summer intern)

22. **Practice eating a business meal.**

    Imagine that you're taking two or three clients out for lunch. With your classmates, arrange a meeting time at a local restaurant or a dining hall on campus. Assign roles: one of you will be the host, and the others will play various levels within the client organization—director, assistant director, and manager.

    If you go to a dining hall, imagine that you have to explain to your guests what is available and the process for getting food and returning trays and silverware. Invite your guests to go ahead of you and direct them where to sit, being sensitive to their preferences.

    If you go to a restaurant, follow guidelines from this chapter for ordering food. Perhaps the host can pay (but then get reimbursed by the guests).

LO5   Practice business etiquette in the workplace.

COMPANY SCENARIO

Bank on Me

Bank on Me, a financial services company, is hiring for its Finance Management Training Program. In this company scenario, you'll see employment communication from the other side of the table—the employer's perspective—and will learn to do the following:

- Evaluate employment communication against given job requirements.
- Practice interviewing skills as a company recruiter or as a job applicant.
- Participate in a decision-making meeting.
- Communicate positive and negative hiring decisions.

This is a good opportunity for you to apply what you learn to your own communication during a hiring process. At www.cengagebrain.com, you'll find these materials:

- Job description for finance management trainee
- Résumés and cover letters for five candidates
- Three voice mail messages (two from candidates who said they would call and one from a candidate's mother!)
- Interviewer's Guide
- Hiring Decision Matrix

BANK on ME 🏛

Bank on Me
Hiring Decision Matrix

Instructions: Please rate each candidate's qualifications against the criteria defined in the "Finance Management Trainee" job description. For each criterion, click on "Choose an item" to select a rating from the drop-down list. Write a few comments to explain and support your rating (the box will expand).

	Finance Coursework	Finance Experience	Leadership Experience	Degree and GPA	Communication Skills	Attention to Detail (assessed from the cover letter and résumé)	Proficiency in Excel	Spanish Language	Candidate Ranking (1 = highest, 5 = lowest)
Marcus Benini	Choose an item. Comments:	Choose an item. Comments:	Choose an item. Comments:	Choose an item. Comments:	Choose an item. Comments:	Choose an item. Comments:	Choose an item. Comments:	Choose an item. Comments:	Choose an item.
Laurie Carpenter	Choose an item. Comments:	Choose an item. Comments:	Choose an item. Comments:	Choose an item. Comments:	Choose an item. Comments:	Choose an item. Comments:	Choose an item. Comments:	Choose an item. Comments:	Choose an item.
Catherine Lin	Choose an item. Comments:	Choose an item. Comments:	Choose an item. Comments:	Choose an item. Comments:	Choose an item. Comments:	Choose an item. Comments:	Choose an item. Comments:	Choose an item. Comments:	Choose an item.
Landon Lowry	Choose an item. Comments:	Choose an item. Comments:	Choose an item. Comments:	Choose an item. Comments:	Choose an item. Comments:	Choose an item. Comments:	Choose an item. Comments:	Choose an item. Comments:	Choose an item.
Ana Santos	Choose an item. Comments:	Choose an item. Comments:	Choose an item. Comments:	Choose an item. Comments:	Choose an item. Comments:	Choose an item. Comments:	Choose an item. Comments:	Choose an item. Comments:	Choose an item.

COURTESY OF AMY NEWMAN

Your instructor may assign these activities for you to engage in this scenario:

- Analyze the employment information from the five candidates and complete the hiring matrix.
- Interview one of the candidates (or play the role of a candidate being interviewed).
- Make a hiring decision as part of a team of interviewers.
- Communicate a positive or negative hiring decision with a phone call, email, or both.

Endnotes

1. Michael Blanding, "Even Human Resources Is Going Social," IHG WebEx Presentation for Cornell School of Hotel Administration, HADM 3640, Corporate Communication, April 10, 2013.

2. Lisa Jones, "6 Thoughts About Recruitment Strategy for 2013," *Within Reach Blog*, Bullhorn Reach, http://blog.bullhornreach .com /post/35212752173/6-thoughts-about-recruitment -strategy-for-2013, accessed April 10, 2013.

3. Coleman, "Is Social Recruiting Real?" Social Recruiting Survey, TweetMyJobs.com, 2012, January 31, 2012, www.tweetmyjobs .com/blog/2012/01/is-social-recruiting-real-video/, accessed December 30, 2014.

4. Coleman.

5. Jobvite, "2013 Social Recruiting Survey Results," http:// web.jobvite.com/rs/jobvite/images/Jobvite_2013 _SocialRecruitingSurveyResults.pdf, accessed August 5, 2014.

6. Michael Blanding.

7. Michael Blanding.

8. "Your Personal Brand," PwC, www.pwc.com/us/en/careers /campus/programs-events/personal-brand/index.jhtml, accessed August 6, 2014.

9. "Recruiter 'Pet Peeve' Survey," Resume Doctor, www .resumedoctor.com, accessed March 30, 2013.

10. Anne Fisher, "Resume Lies Are on the Rise," *Fortune*, September 10, 2014, http://fortune.com/2014/09/10 /resume-lies-are-on-the-rise/, accessed December 31, 2014.

11. "Nearly Half of Employers Have Caught a Lie on a Resume, CareerBuilder Survey Shows," Career Builder, July 30, 2008, www.careerbuilder.com, accessed April 6, 2013.

12. CareerBuilder.com.

13. Jason Ferrara, "Are Employers Looking at Your Résumé?" Career Builder, March 27, 2009, www.careerbuilder.com, accessed December 30, 2014.

14. Anne Fisher.

15. "Resumes Inching Up," Accountemps, News Release, http:// accountemps.com, accessed April 6, 2013.

16. "Have a Keen Eye for Derail," Accountemps, News Release, http:// accountemps.com, accessed December 30, 2014.

17. Barbara Safani, "Your Resume Is Ready for the Attic," The Ladders, June 7, 2010, www.theladders.com, accessed December 30, 2014.

18. Nancy M. Schullery, Linda Ickes, and Stephen E. Schullery, "Employer Preferences for Résumés and Cover Letters," *Business Communication Quarterly*, vol. 72, no. 2 (June 2009), 163–176.

19. Adapted and used with permission from the author.

20. Resume Doctor.

21. Nancy M. Schullery, Linda Ickes, and Stephen E. Schullery, "Employer Preferences for Résumés and Cover Letters," *Business Communication Quarterly*, vol. 72, no. 2 (June 2009), 163–176.

22. Jobvite.

23. "Job Screening with Social Networks," *Reppler*, October 2011, http://reppler.files.wordpress.com/2011/09/reppler -infographic-job-screening-with-social-networks2.jpg, accessed December 28, 2014.

24. Susan P. Joyce, "Smart Job Search Strategy: Defensive Googling," February 18, 2014, *Huffington Post*, www.huffingtonpost.com /susan-p-joyce/smart-job-search-strategy_b_4777881.html, accessed August 5, 2014.

25. *Reppler*.

26. Jobvite.

27. Susan P. Joyce.

28. Read more at "LinkedIn Search Relevance – People Search," https://help.linkedin.com/app/answers/detail/a_id/4447 /~/linkedin-search-relevance-people-search, accessed January 4, 2015.

29. Eli Langer, "Chocolate Bar Resume Takes Internet by Storm," CNBC, February 21, 2013, www.cnbc.com/id/100482311, accessed December 30, 2014.

30. Schullery et al.

31. Schullery et al.

32. "Targeted Selection: Meeting Today's Selection Challenges," Development Dimensions International, White Paper, www .ddiworld.com, accessed April 6, 2013.

33. "Survey Signals Sharp Rise in Behavioral Interviewing," Novations, January 18, 2008, www.novations.com, accessed April 9, 2013.

34. "Techniques and Tricks," McKinsey & Company, www.mckinsey .com, accessed April 7, 2013.

35. Right Management, "Survey Tracks Technology's Growing Role in Job Hunt," August 7, 2013, www.right.com/news-and-events /press-releases/2013-press-releases/item25383.aspx, accessed December 21, 2014.

36. Email interview with Google applicant, June 13, 2010.

37. Debbie L. Sklar, "Survey: Employers Form Opinions of Interviewees Within 10 Minutes," Patch, November 1, 2012, http://patch.com/california/lagunaniguel-danapoint/survey -most-employers-form-opinions-of-interviewees-wf099c39895, accessed December 30, 2014.

38. Rosemary Haefner, "No Thank You Could Mean No Job," CareerBuilder.com, September 29, 2009, www.careerbuilder .com, accessed December 30, 2014.

39. "Thanks, But No Thanks," Accountemps, August 9, 2007, www .accountemps.com, accessed December 30, 2014.

Reference Manual

A | Language Arts Basics

Lab 1: Parts of Speech

We use words, of course, to communicate. Of the hundreds of thousands of words in an unabridged dictionary, each can be classified as one of just eight parts of speech: noun, pronoun, verb, adjective, adverb, preposition, conjunction, or interjection. These eight parts of speech are illustrated in the sentence below:

Interjection	Pronoun	Adverb	Verb	Preposition	Adjective	Noun	Conjunction	Noun

Oh, I eagerly waited for new computers and printers.

Many words can act as different parts of speech, depending on how they are used in a sentence. (A *sentence* is a group of words that contains a subject and predicate and that expresses a complete thought.)

Consider, for example, the different parts of speech played by the word *following*:

We agree to do the *following*. *(noun)*

I was only *following* orders. *(verb)*

We met the *following* day. *(adjective)*

Following his remarks, he sat down. *(preposition)*

All words do not serve more than one function, but many do. Following is a brief introduction to the eight parts of speech.

1.1 Nouns A *noun* is a word that names something—for example, a person, place, thing, or idea:

Person:	employee, Mr. Watkins
Place:	office, Chicago
Thing:	animal, computer
Idea:	concentration, impatience, week, typing

The words in italics in the following sentences are all nouns.

Olaf promoted his *idea* to the *vice president* on *Wednesday*.

Problem solving is just one of the *skills* you'll need as an *intern*.

How much does one *quart* of *water* weigh on our bathroom *scales?*

The animal *doctor* treated my *animal* well in *Houston*.

If you were asked to give an example of a noun, you would probably think of a *concrete noun*—that is, a *physical* object that you can see, hear, feel, taste, or smell. An *abstract noun*, on the other hand, names a quality or concept and not something physical.

Concrete Noun	Abstract Noun
book	success
stapler	patience
computer	skills
dictionary	loyalty

A *common noun,* as its name suggests, is the name of a *general* person, place, thing, or idea. If you want to give the name of a *specific* person, place, thing, or idea, you would use a *proper noun.* Proper nouns are always capitalized.

Common Noun	Proper Noun
man	Rodolfo Escobar
city	Los Angeles
car	Corvette
religion	Judaism

A *singular noun* names one person, place, thing, or idea. A *plural noun* names more than one.

Singular Noun	Plural Noun
Smith	Smiths
watch	watches
computer	computers
victory	victories

1.2 Pronouns A *pronoun* is a word used in place of a noun. Consider the following sentence:

Anna went to *Anna's* kitchen and made *Anna's* favorite dessert because *Anna* was going to a party with *Anna's* friends.

The noun *Anna* is used five times in this awkward sentence. A smoother, less monotonous version of the sentence substitutes pronouns for all but the first *Anna:*

Anna went to *her* kitchen and made *her* favorite dessert because *she* was going to a party with *her* friends.

The words in italics in the following sentences are pronouns. The nouns to which they refer are underlined:

<u>Angélica</u> thought *she* might get the promotion.

None of the <u>speakers</u> were interesting.

<u>Juan</u> forgot to bring *his* slides.

1.3 Verbs A *verb* is a word (or group of words) that expresses either action or a state of being. The first kind of verb is called an *action verb;* the second kind is known as a *linking verb.* Without a verb, you have no sentence because the verb makes a statement about the subject.

Most verbs express action of some sort—either physical or mental—as indicated by the words in italics in the following sentences:

Iram *planted* his garden while Lian *pulled* weeds.

I *solved* my problems as I *baked* bread.

Jeremy *decided* he should *call* a meeting.

A small (but important) group of verbs do not express action. Instead, they simply link the subject with words that describe it. The most common linking verbs are forms of the verb *to be*, such as *is, am, are, was, were*, and *will*. Other forms of linking verbs involve the senses, such as *feels, looks, smells, sounds*, and *tastes*. The following words in italics are verbs (note that verbs can comprise one or more words):

Rosemary *was* angry because Ivanov *looked* impatient.

If Franz *is having* a party, I *should have been* invited.

Jason *had* already *seen* the report.

1.4 Adjectives You can make sentences consisting of only nouns or pronouns and verbs (such as "Dogs bark."), but most of the time you'll need to add other parts of speech to make the meaning of the sentence clearer or more complete. An *adjective* is a word that modifies a noun or pronoun. Adjectives answer questions about the nouns or pronouns they describe, such as *how many?*, *what kind?*, and *which one?* (*Articles* are a special group of adjectives that include the words *a, an*, and *the*.)

As shown by the words in italics in the following sentences, adjectives may come before or after the nouns or pronouns they modify:

Seventeen applicants took the *typing* test.

The interview was *short*, but *comprehensive*.

She took the *last* plane and landed at a *small Mexican* airport.

1.5 Adverbs An *adverb* is a word that modifies a verb (usually), an adjective, or another adverb. Adverbs often answer the questions *when?*, *where?*, *how?*, or *to what extent?* The words in italics in the following sentences are adverbs:

Please perform the procedure *now*. (When?)

Put the papers *here*. (Where?)

Alice performed *brilliantly*. (How?)

I am *almost* finished. (To what extent?)

The *exceedingly* expensive car was *very carefully* protected.

In the last sentence, the adverb *exceedingly* modifies the adjective *expensive* (how expensive?) and the adverb *very* modifies the adverb *carefully* (how carefully?).

Many (but by no means all) adverbs end in *–ly*, such as *loudly, quickly, really*, and *carefully*. However, not all words that end in *–ly* are adverbs; for example, *friendly, stately*, and *ugly* are all adjectives.

1.6 Prepositions A *preposition* is a word (such as *to, for, from, of*, and *with*) that shows the relationship between a noun or pronoun and some other word in the sentence. The noun or pronoun following the preposition is called the *object* of the preposition, and the entire group of words is called a *prepositional phrase*. In the following sentences, the preposition is shown in italics; the entire prepositional phrase is underlined:

The ceremony occurred *on* the covered bridge.

The ceremony occurred *under* the covered bridge.

Lucia talked *with* Mr. Hines.

Lucia talked *about* Mr. Hines.

1.7 Conjunctions A *conjunction* is a word (such as *and, or,* or *but*) that joins words or groups of words. For example, in the sentence "Ari and Alice are brokers," the conjunction *and* connects the two nouns *Ari* and *Alice*. In the following sentences, the conjunction is shown in italics; the words it joins are underlined:

Francesca *or* Teresa will attend the conference. (*joins two nouns*)

Chang spoke quietly *and* deliberately. (*joins two adverbs*)

Harriet tripped *but* caught her balance. (*joins two verbs*)

1.8 Interjections An *interjection* is a word that expresses strong emotions. Interjections are used more often in oral communication than in written communication. If an interjection stands alone, it is followed by an exclamation point. If it is a part of the sentence, it is followed by a comma. You should not be surprised to learn that some words can serve as interjections in some sentences and as other parts of speech in other sentences. In the following sentences, the interjection is shown in italics:

Good! I'm glad to learn that the new employee does good work.

Oh! I didn't mean to startle you.

My, I wouldn't do that.

Gosh, that was an exhausting exercise. *Whew!*

Application

Note: For all LAB application exercises, first photocopy the exercise and then complete the exercise on the photocopied pages.

Directions Label each part of speech in Sentences 1–8 with the abbreviation shown below.

adjective	*adj.*
adverb	*adv.*
conjunction	*conj.*
interjection	*interj.*
noun	*n.*
preposition	*prep.*
pronoun	*pron.*
verb	*v.*

1. Oh, don't tell me I missed my flight.
2. My, your new chair is comfortable.
3. When I received your package, I was relieved. Whew!
4. Gosh! I could not believe the depth of the raging water in the river.
5. When the quail and her chicks came into the yard, the hen carefully checked the area for predators.
6. Alas! By the time he received her report, the decision had been made.
7. I was disappointed we missed your input to the decision-making process.
8. Valerie Renoir, the major conference speaker, was delayed at O'Hare and did not arrive at the hall until 2 p.m.

Lab 2: Punctuation—Commas

Punctuation serves as a roadmap to help guide the reader through the twists and turns of your message—pointing out what is important (italics or underscores), subordinate (commas), copied from another source (quotation marks), explained further (colon), considered as a unit (hyphens), and so on. Sometimes correct punctuation is absolutely essential for comprehension. Consider, for example, the different meanings of the following sentences, depending on the punctuation:

What's the latest, Dope?
What's the latest dope?

The social secretary called the guests names as they arrived.
The social secretary called the guests' names as they arrived.

Our new model comes in red, green and brown, and white.
Our new model comes in red, green, and brown and white.

The play ended, happily.
The play ended happily.

A clever dog knows it's master.
A clever dog knows its master.

We must still play Michigan, which tied Ohio State, and Minnesota.
We must still play Michigan, which tied Ohio State and Minnesota.

"Medics Help Dog Bite Victim"
"Medics Help Dog-Bite Victim"

The comma rules presented in LAB 2 and the other punctuation rules presented in LAB 3 do not cover every possible situation; comprehensive style manuals, for example, routinely present more than 100 rules just for using the comma rather than just the 11 rules presented here. These rules cover the most frequent uses of punctuation in business writing. Learn them—because you will be using them frequently.

Commas are used to connect ideas and to set off elements within a sentence. When typing, leave one space after a comma. Many writers use commas inappropriately. No matter how long the sentence, make sure you have a legitimate reason before inserting a comma.

Commas Used *Between* Expressions

Three types of expressions (an expression is words or groups of words) typically require commas between them: independent clauses, adjacent adjectives, and items in a series.

2.1 Independent Clauses Use a comma between two independent clauses joined by a coordinate conjunction (unless both clauses are short and closely related). *, ind*

> Mr. Karas discussed last month's performance, and Ms. Daniels presented the sales projections.

> The meeting was running late, but Mr. Chande was in no hurry to adjourn.

> *But:* The firm hadn't paid and John was angry.

The major coordinate conjunctions are *and, but, or,* and *nor.* An independent clause is a subject-predicate combination that can stand alone as a complete sentence.

Do not confuse two independent clauses joined by a coordinate conjunction and a comma with a compound predicate, whose verbs are not separated by a comma. *Hint:* Cover up the conjunction with your pencil. If what's on both sides of your pencil could stand alone as complete sentences, a comma is needed.

No comma:	Mrs. Ames had read the report_but had not discussed it with her colleagues. (*"Had not discussed it with her colleagues" is not an independent clause; it lacks a subject.*)
Comma:	Mrs. Blanco had read the report, but she had not discussed it with her colleagues.

2.2 Adjacent Adjectives Use a comma between two adjacent adjectives that modify the same noun. *, adj*

> He was an aggressive, unpleasant manager.

> *But:* He was an aggressive_and unpleasant manager. (*The two adjectives are not adjacent; they are separated by the conjunction "and."*)

Do not use a comma if the first adjective modifies the combined idea of the second adjective plus the noun. *Hint:* Mentally insert the word "and" between the two consecutive adjectives. If it does not make sense, do not use a comma.

> Please order a new bulletin board for the executive_conference room.

Do not use a comma between the last adjective and the noun.

> Wednesday was a long, hot, humid_day.

2.3 Items in a Series Use a comma between each item in a series of three or more. Do not use a comma after the last item in the series. *, ser*

> The committee may meet on Wednesday, Thursday, or Friday_of next week.

> Carl wrote the questionnaire, Anna distributed the forms, and Jacinto tabulated the results_for our survey on employee satisfaction.

Some style manuals indicate that the last comma before the conjunction is optional. However, to avoid ambiguity in business writing, you should insert this comma.

> *Not:* We were served salads, macaroni and cheese and crackers.

> *But:* We were served salads, macaroni and cheese, and crackers.

> *Or:* We were served salads, macaroni, and cheese and crackers.

Commas Used *After* Expressions

Two types of expressions typically require commas after them: introductory expressions and complimentary closings in letters.

, intro

2.4 Introductory Expressions Use a comma after an introductory expression. An *introductory expression* is a word, phrase, or clause that comes before the subject and verb of the independent clause. When the same expression occurs at the end of the sentence, no comma is used.

> No, the status report is not ready. *(introductory word)*
>
> Of course, you are not required to sign the petition. *(introductory phrase)*
>
> When the status report is ready, I will call you. *(introductory clause)*
>
> *But:* I will call you when the status report is ready.

Do not use a comma between the subject and verb—no matter how long or complex the subject is.

> To finish that boring and time consuming task in time for the monthly sales meeting_was a major challenge.
>
> The effort to bring all of our products into compliance with ISO standards and to be eligible for sales in Common Market countries_required a full year of detailed planning.

, clos

2.5 Complimentary Closing Use a comma after the complimentary closing of a business letter formatted in the standard punctuation style.

> Sincerely,   Cordially yours,
>
> Yours truly,   With warm regards,

With standard punctuation, a colon follows the salutation (such as "Dear Ms. Jones:") and a comma follows the complimentary closing. With open punctuation, no punctuation follows either the salutation or complimentary closing.

Commas Used *Before* and *After* Expressions

Numerous types of expressions typically require commas before *and* after them. Of course, if the expression comes at the beginning of a sentence, use a comma only after the expression; if it comes at the end of a sentence, use a comma only before it.

, nonr

2.6 Nonrestrictive Expressions Use commas before and after a nonrestrictive expression. A *restrictive expression* is one that limits (restricts) the meaning of the noun or pronoun that it follows and is, therefore, essential to complete the basic meaning of the sentence. A *nonrestrictive expression*, on the other hand, may be omitted without changing the basic meaning of the sentence.

> **Restrictive:**   Anyone *with some experience* should apply for the position. ("With some experience" restricts which "anyone" should apply.)
>
> **Nonrestrictive:**   Anne Suárez, *a clerk with extensive experience*, should apply for the position. (Because Anne Suárez can be only one person, the phrase "a clerk with extensive experience" does not serve to further restrict the noun and is, therefore, not essential to the meaning of the sentence.)

Restrictive:	Only the papers *left on the conference table* are missing. (identifies which papers are missing)
Nonrestrictive:	Lever Brothers, *one of our best customers*, is expanding in Europe. ("One of our best customers" could be omitted without changing the basic meaning of the sentence.)
Restrictive:	The manager *using a great deal of tact* was Ellis.
Nonrestrictive:	Ellis, *using a great deal of tact*, disagreed with her.

An *appositive* is a noun or noun phrase that identifies another noun or pronoun that comes immediately before it. If the appositive is nonrestrictive, insert commas before and after the appositive.

Restrictive:	The word *plagiarism* strikes fear into the heart of many. ("Plagiarism" is an appositive that identifies which word.)
Nonrestrictive:	Mr. Bayrami, *president of the corporation*, is planning to resign. ("President of the corporation" is an appositive that provides additional, but nonessential, information about Mr. Bayrami.)

2.7 Interrupting Expressions Use commas before and after an interrupting expression. An *interrupting expression* breaks the normal flow of a sentence. Common examples are *in addition, as a result, therefore, in summary, on the other hand, however, unfortunately,* and *as a matter of fact*—when these expressions come in the middle of the sentence.   *, inter*

You may, of course, cancel your subscription at any time.

One suggestion, for example, was to undertake a leveraged buyout.

I believe it was John, not Nicolette, who raised the question.

It is still not too late to make the change, is it?

Aida's present salary, you must admit, is not in line with those of other network managers.

But: You must admit_Aida's present salary is not in line with those of other network managers.

If the expression does not interrupt the normal flow of the sentence, do not use a comma.

There is no doubt that you are qualified for the position.

But: There is, no doubt, a good explanation for his actions.

2.8 Dates Use commas before and after the year when it follows the month and day. Do not use a comma after a partial date or when the date is formatted in day month year order. If the name of the day precedes the date, also use a comma *after* the name of the day.   *, date*

The note is due on May 31, 2007, at 5 p.m.

But: The note is due on May 31 at 5 p.m.

But: The note is due in May 2007.

But: The note is due on 31 May 2007 at 5 p.m.

Let's plan to meet on Wednesday, December 15, 2007, for our year-end review.

2.9 Places Use commas before and after a state or country that follows a city and between elements of an address in narrative writing.   *, place*

The sales conference will be held in Phoenix, Arizona, in May.

Our business agent is located in Brussels, Belgium, in the P.O.M. Building.

You may contact her at 500 Beaufort Drive, LaCrosse, VA 23950. *(Note that there is no comma between the state abbreviation and the ZIP code.)*

, dir ad   **2.10 Direct Address** Use commas before and after a name used in direct address. A name is used in *direct address* when the writer speaks directly to (that is, directly addresses) another person.

Thank you, Ms. Zhao, for bringing the matter to our attention.

Ladies and gentlemen, we appreciate your attending our session today.

, quote   **2.11 Direct Quotation** Use commas before and after a direct quotation in a sentence.

The president said, "You have nothing to fear," and then changed the subject.

"I assure you," the human resources director said, "that no positions will be terminated."

If the quotation is a question, use a question mark instead of a comma.

"How many have applied?" she asked.

Application

Directions Insert any needed commas in the following sentences. Above each comma, indicate the reason for the comma. If the sentence needs no commas, leave it blank.

Example: As a matter of fact, you may tell her yourself. [intro]

1. A comma comes between two adjacent adjectives that modify the same noun but do not use a comma if the first adjective modifies the combined idea of the second adjective and the noun.
2. Stephen generated questions and I supplied responses.
3. At the request of your accountant we are summarizing all charitable deductions in a new format.
4. By asking the right questions we gained all the pertinent information we needed.
5. Everyone please use the door in the rear of the hall.
6. His bid for the congressional seat was successful this time.
7. I disagree with Gabriela but do feel some change in policy is needed.
8. I feel as a matter of fact that the proposed legislation will fall short of the required votes.
9. Ethan will prepare the presentation graphics and let you know when they are ready.
10. Determining purpose analyzing the audience and making content and organization decisions are critical planning steps.
11. It is appropriate I believe to make a preliminary announcement about the new position.
12. A goodwill message is prompt direct sincere specific and brief.
13. Look this decision affects me as much as it does you.
14. The teacher using one of her favorite techniques prompted the student into action.
15. Subordinate bad news by using the direct plan by avoiding negative terms and by presenting the news after the reasons are given.
16. My favorite destination is Atlanta Georgia.

17. The team presented a well-planned logical scenario to explain the company's status.

18. Evan plans to conclude his investigation and explain the results by Friday but would not promise a written report until Tuesday.

19. We appreciate your business.

Sincerely

Medea Haddad

20. Those instructors who were from southern schools were anxious to see the results of the study completed in Birmingham.

21. A group of teachers from Michigan attended the conference this year.

22. Our next training session will be located in Madison Wisconsin sometime in the spring.

23. The next meeting of our professional organization will be held in the winter not in the spring.

24. The brochure states "Satisfaction is guaranteed or your money will be freely refunded."

25. The department meeting you will note will be held every other Monday.

26. This assignment is due on April 20 which is one week before the end of the semester.

27. I need the cabinets installed by the week before my family arrives.

28. To qualify for promotion will require recommendations and long hours of preparation.

29. To qualify for promotion you will need recommendations from previous managers.

30. To earn an award for outstanding sales is an achievable goal for Mary.

31. To earn an award for outstanding sales Mary must set intermittent goals that are attainable.

32. Dave was promoted in his job by working hard.

33. Shayna's sister was born on June 6 1957, in Munster Indiana.

34. Ted could paint the house himself or he could hire a professional to do the job.

35. I am telling you Esther that your report has been misplaced.

Lab 3: Punctuation—Other Marks

Hyphens

Hyphens are used to form some compound adjectives, to link some prefixes to root words (such as *quasi-public*), and to divide words at the ends of lines. When typing, do not leave a space before or after a regular hyphen. Likewise, do not use a hyphen with a space before and after to substitute for a dash. Make a dash by typing two hyphens with no space before, between, or after. Most word processing programs automatically reformat two hyphens into a printed dash.

3.1 Compound Adjective Hyphenate a compound adjective that comes *before* a noun (unless the adjective is a proper noun or unless the first word is an adverb ending in *-ly*).   *– adj*

We hired a first-class management team.

But: Our new management team is first_class.

The long term outlook for our investments is excellent.

But: We intend to hold our investments for the long_term.

But: The General_Motors warranty received high ratings.

But: Huang presented a poorly_conceived proposal.

Note: Don't confuse compound adjectives (which are generally temporary combinations) with compound nouns (which are generally well-established concepts). Compound nouns (such as

Social Security, life insurance, word processing, and *high school*) are not hyphenated when used as adjectives that come before a noun; thus, use *income_tax form, real_estate agent, public_relations firm,* and *data_processing center.*

– num   **3.2 Numbers** Hyphenate fractions and compound numbers 21 through 99 when they are spelled out.

> Nearly three-fourths of our new applicants were unqualified.
>
> Seventy-two orders were processed incorrectly last week.

Semicolons

Semicolons are used to show where elements in a sentence are separated. The separation is stronger than a comma but not as strong as a period. When typing, leave one space after a semicolon and begin the following word with a lowercase letter.

; comma   **3.3 Independent Clauses with Commas** If a misreading might otherwise occur, use a semicolon (instead of a comma) to separate independent clauses that contain internal commas. Make sure that the semicolon is inserted *between* the independent clauses—not *within* one of the clauses.

> *Confusing:* I ordered juice, toast, and bacon, and eggs, toast, and sausage were sent instead.
>
> *Clear:* I ordered juice, toast, and bacon; and eggs, toast, and sausage were sent instead.
>
> *But:* Although high-quality paper was used, the photocopy machine still jammed, and neither of us knew how to repair it. *(no misreading likely to occur)*

; no conj   **3.4 Independent Clauses Without a Conjunction** Use a semicolon between independent clauses that are not connected by a coordinate conjunction (such as *and, but, or,* or *nor*). You have already learned to use a comma before coordinate conjunctions when they connect independent clauses. This rule applies to independent clauses *not* connected by a conjunction.

> The president was eager to proceed with the plans; the board still had some reservations.
>
> *But:* The president was eager to proceed with the plans, but the board still had some reservations. *(Use a comma instead of a semicolon if the clauses are joined by a coordinate conjunction.)*
>
> Bannon Corporation exceeded its sales goal this quarter; furthermore, it rang up its highest net profit ever.
>
> *But:* Bannon Corporation exceeded its sales goal this quarter, and, furthermore, it rang up its highest net profit ever. *(Use a comma instead of a semicolon if the clauses are joined by a coordinate conjunction.)*

; ser   **3.5 Series with Internal Commas** Use a semicolon after each item in a series if any of the items already contain a comma. Normally, we separate items in a series with commas. However, if any of those items already contain a comma, we need a stronger mark (semicolon) between the items.

> The human resources department will be interviewing in Dallas, Texas; Still-water, Oklahoma; and Little Rock, Arkansas, for the new position.
>
> Among the guests were Henry Halston, our attorney; Phaedra Hart Wilder; and Isabella Grimes, our new controller.

Colons

A colon is used after an independent clause that introduces explanatory material and after the salutation of a business letter that uses the standard punctuation style. When typing, leave one space after a colon; do not begin the following word with a capital letter unless it begins a quoted sentence.

3.6 Explanatory Material Use a colon to introduce explanatory material that is preceded by an independent clause.

: exp

> His directions were as follows: turn right and proceed to the third house on the left.
>
> I now have openings on the following dates: January 18, 19, and 20.
>
> Just remember this: you may need a reference from her in the future.
>
> The fall trade show offers the following advantages: inexpensive show space, abundant traffic, and free press publicity.

Expressions commonly used to introduce explanatory material are *the following, as follows, this,* and *these.* Make sure the clause preceding the explanatory material can stand alone as a complete sentence. Do not place a colon after a verb or a preposition that introduces a list.

> ☒ NOT   My responsibilities were: opening the mail, sorting it, and delivering it to each department.
>
>   ☑ BUT   My responsibilities were opening the mail, sorting it, and delivering it to each department.

3.7 Salutations Use a colon after the salutation of a business letter that uses the standard punctuation style.

: salut

> Dear Ms. Havelchek: Dear Human Resources Manager: Dear Rubén:

Never use a comma after the salutation in a business letter. (A comma is appropriate only in a personal letter.) With standard punctuation, a colon follows the salutation and a comma follows the complimentary closing. With *open* punctuation, no punctuation follows the salutation or complimentary closing.

Apostrophes

Apostrophes are used to show that letters have been omitted (as in contractions) and to show possession. When typing, do not space before or after an apostrophe (unless a space after is needed before another word).

Remember this helpful hint: whenever a noun ending in *s* is followed by another noun, the first noun is probably a possessive, requiring an apostrophe. However, if the first noun *describes* rather than establishes ownership, no apostrophe is used.

> Bernie's department *(shows ownership; therefore, an apostrophe)*
>
> the sales department *(describes; therefore, no apostrophe)*

3.8 Singular Nouns To form the possessive of a singular noun, add an apostrophe plus *s.*

' sing

> my accountant's fee   a child's toy
>
> the company's stock   Eva's choice
>
> Alzheimer's disease   Mr. and Mrs. Yuan's home

a year's time	the boss's contract
Ms. Morris's office	Liz's promotion
Gil Hodges's record	Carl Bissett Jr.'s birthday

'plur + s **3.9 Plural Nouns Ending in S** To form the possessive of a plural noun that ends in *s* (that is, most plural nouns), add an apostrophe only.

our accountants' fees	both companies' stock
the Dyes' home	two years' time

'plur − s **3.10 Plural Nouns Not Ending in S** To form the possessive of a plural noun that does not end in *s*, add an apostrophe plus *s* (just as you would for singular nouns).

the children's hour	the men's room
the alumni's contribution	

Hint: To avoid confusion in forming the possessive of plural nouns, first form the plural; then apply the appropriate rule.

Singular	Plural	Plural Possessive
employee	employees	employees' bonuses
hero	heroes	heroes' welcome
Mr. and Mrs. Lake	the Lakes	the Lakes' home
woman	women	women's clothing

'pro **3.11 Pronouns** To form the possessive of an indefinite pronoun, add an apostrophe plus *s*. Do not use an apostrophe to form the possessive of personal pronouns.

It is *someone's* responsibility.

But: The responsibility is *theirs*.

I will review *everybody's* figures.

But: The bank will review *its* figures.

Note: Examples of indefinite possessive pronouns are *anybody's, everyone's, no one's, nobody's, one's,* and *somebody's.* Examples of personal possessive pronouns are *hers, his, its, ours, theirs,* and *yours.* Do not confuse the possessive pronouns *its, theirs,* and *whose* with the contractions *it's, there's,* and *who's.*

It's time to put litter in *its* place.

There's no reason to take *theirs*.

Who's determining *whose* jobs will be eliminated?

'ger **3.12 Gerunds** Use the possessive form for a noun or pronoun that comes before a gerund. (A gerund is the *–ing* form of a verb used as a noun.)

Garth questioned *Karen's* leaving so soon.

Stockholders' raising so many questions delayed the adjournment.

Mr. Matsumoto knew Karl and objected to *his* going to the meeting.

Periods

Periods are used at the ends of declarative sentences and polite requests and in abbreviations. When typing, leave one space after a period (or any other punctuation mark).

3.13 Polite Requests Use a period after a polite request. Consider a statement a polite request if you expect the reader to respond by *acting* rather than by giving a yes-or-no answer.

. req

> Would you please sign the form on page 2.
>
> May I please have the report by Friday.
>
> *But:* Would you be willing to take on this assignment? *(This sentence is a real question, requiring a question mark. You expect the reader to respond by saying "yes" or "no.")*

Quotation Marks

Quotation marks are used around direct quotations, titles of some publications and conferences, and special terms. Type the closing quotation mark after a period or comma but before a colon or semicolon. Type the closing quotation mark after a question mark or exclamation point if the quoted material itself is a question or an exclamation; otherwise, type it before the question mark or exclamation. Capitalize the first word of a quotation that begins a sentence.

3.14 Direct Quotation Use quotation marks around a direct quotation—that is, around the exact words of a person.

"quote

> "When we return on Thursday," Luis said, "we need to meet with you."
>
> *But:* Luis said that when we return on Thursday, we need to meet with you. *(no quotation marks needed in an indirect quotation)*
>
> Did Helen say, "He will represent us"?
>
> Helen asked, "Will he represent us?"

3.15 Term Use quotation marks around a term to clarify its meaning or to show that it is being used in a special way.

"term

> Net income after taxes is known as "the bottom line"; that's what's important around here.
>
> The job title changed from "chairman" to "chief executive officer."
>
> The president misused the word "effect" in last night's press conference.

3.16 Title Use quotation marks around the title of a newspaper or magazine article, chapter in a book, report, conference, and similar items.

"title

> Read the article entitled "Wall Street Recovery."
>
> Chapter 4, "Market Segmentation," of *Industrial Marketing* is of special interest.
>
> The theme of this year's sales conference is "Quality Sells."
>
> The report "Common Carriers" shows the extent of the transportation problems.

> *Note:* The titles of *complete* published works are shown in italics (see below). The titles of *parts* of published works and most other titles are enclosed in quotation marks.

Italics (or Underlining)

Before the advent of word pro cessing software, underlining was used to emphasize words or indicate certain titles. Today, the use of italics is preferred for these functions.

Title

3.17 Titles Italicize the title of a book, magazine, newspaper, and other *complete* published works.

> Liang's newest book, *All That Glitters*, was reviewed in *The New York Times* and in *The Los Angeles Times*.

> The cover story in last week's *Time* magazine was "Is the Economic Expansion Over?"

Ellipses

An ellipsis signals an omission. Three periods, with one space before and after each, are used to show that something has been left out of a quotation. Four periods (the sentence period plus the three ellipsis periods) indicate the omission of the last part of a quoted sentence, the first part of the next sentence, or a whole sentence or paragraph. Here is an example of a quotation from Bank of America CEO Brian Moynihan:[1]

Complete Quotation:

Our quarterly results show that we are making progress on our strategy to align around our three core customer groups—consumers, businesses, and institutional investors—and create the financial institution that customers tell us they want, built on a broad relationship of clarity, transparency, and helping them manage through challenging times. We improved our capital foundation through retained earnings, and credit quality improved even faster than expected. We have the most complete financial franchise in the world, and we are focused on executing our strategy and delivering outstanding long term value to our customers and shareholders.

Shortened Quotation:

Our quarterly results show that we are making progress on our strategy to align around our three core customer groups . . . and create the financial institution that customers tell us they want, built on a broad relationship of clarity, transparency, and helping them manage through challenging times. . . . We have the most complete financial franchise in the world, and we are focused on executing our strategy and delivering outstanding long term value to our customers and shareholders.

Note: The typing sequence for the first ellipsis is *space period space period space period space*. The sequence for the second ellipsis is *period space period space period space period space*.

3.18 Omission Use ellipsis periods to indicate that one or more words have been omitted from quoted material.

> According to *Business Week*, "A continuing protest could shut down . . . Pemex, which brought in 34% of Mexico's dollar income last year."

---

[1]Dawn Kawamoto, "Bank of America Earnings Beat Wall Street Estimates," Daily Finance, July 16, 2010, http://www.dailyfinance.com/2010/07/16/bank-of-america-earnings-beats-wall-street-estimates/, accessed July 26, 2011.

Application

Directions Insert any needed punctuation (including commas) in the following sentences. Underline any expression that should be italicized. Above each mark of punctuation, indicate the reason for the punctuation. If the sentence needs no punctuation, leave it blank.

Example: We received our money's worth.

1. Bernice tried to use the new software but she had trouble with the computer.

2. Juanita Johnsons raising the expectations for promotion was hotly debated.

3. The short term goal of the department was improvement in software utilization.

4. It was a poorly designed office.

5. Approximately one half of the orders came from Spokane Washington.

6. Bertram preferred soda hamburgers and fries but iced tea, hot dogs and onion rings were served instead.

7. The classes started on time the school was entirely on schedule.

8. Did you meet Sally Henley our manager Paul Krause and Ana Chávez our attorney?

9. Remember this the best recommendation is a job well done.

10. Dear Mr. Weatherby

11. Did you get the total from the sales department?

12. Jasons boss will distribute the new guidelines for his department.

13. Within two years time the neighbourhood will double in size.

14. Locking the door to the department was someones responsibility.

15. Fabians guiding the discussion was a departure from the usual procedure.

16. Would you please sort these responses for me

17. The teacher said The samples you submitted were excellent.

18. Would you believe he misspelled the word their in his report?

19. The articles entitled Technology for Fitness should be required reading

20. Time magazine features a person of the year each December.

21. I want her to know she is a highly respected employee.

22. The meetings date was rescheduled.

23. If the tickets sell we will tell Mrs. Zimmer she will take it from there.

24. The hotels guests thought the conference rooms temperatures were too cold.

25. They were watching the demonstration nevertheless they didn't understand.

26. Can we keep this off the record?

27. You will receive the materials tomorrow but stop by today to see Alberto our corporate trainer for a quick preview.

28. I can do this for you either on December 5 2014 or January 13 2015.

29. This is a once in a lifetime opportunity for our employees families.

30. Mr. Henry will see you after the meeting Mr. Perez will not be available.

Lab 4: Grammar

Suppose the vice president of your organization asked you, a systems analyst, to try to locate a troublesome problem in a computer spreadsheet. After some sharp detective work, you finally resolved the problem and wrote a memo to the vice president saying, "John and myself discovered that one of the formulas were incorrect, so I asked he to revise it."

Instantly, you've turned what should have been a "good-news" opportunity for you into, at best, a "mixed news" situation. The vice president will be pleased that you've uncovered the bug in the program but will probably focus entirely too much attention on your poor grammar skills.

Grammar refers to the rules for combining words into sentences. The most frequent grammar problems faced by business writers are discussed below. Learn these common rules well so that your use of grammar will not present a communication barrier in the message you're trying to convey.

Complete Sentences

4.1 Fragment Avoid sentence fragments.

☒ NOT He had always wanted to be a marketing representative. Because he liked to interact with people.

☑ BUT He had always wanted to be a marketing representative because he liked to interact with people.

Note: A fragment is a part of a sentence that is incorrectly punctuated as a complete sentence. Each sentence must contain a complete thought.

4.2 Run-on Sentences Avoid run-on sentences.

☒ NOT Fidélia Padilla is a hard worker she even frequently works through lunch.

☒ NOT Fidélia Padilla is a hard worker, she even frequently works through lunch.

☑ BUT Fidélia Padilla is a hard worker; she even frequently works through lunch.

☑ BUT Fidélia Padilla is a hard worker. She even frequently works through lunch.

Note: A run-on sentence is two independent clauses run together without any punctuation between them or with only a comma between them (the latter error is called a *comma splice*).

Modifiers (Adjectives and Adverbs)

An adjective modifies a noun or pronoun; an adverb modifies a verb, an adjective, or another adverb.

4.3 Modifiers Use a comparative adjective or adverb (*-er, more,* or *less*) to refer to two persons, places, or things and a superlative adjective or adverb (*-est, most,* or *least*) to refer to more than two.

The Datascan is the fast**er** of the two machines.

The XR 75 is the slow**est** of all the machines.

Rose Marie is the **less** qualified of the two applicants.

Rose Marie is the **least** qualified of the three applicants.

Note: Do not use double comparisons, such as "more faster."

Agreement (Subject/Verb/Pronoun)

Agreement refers to correspondence in number between related subjects, verbs, and pronouns. All must be singular if they refer to one, plural if they refer to more than one.

4.4 Agreement Use a singular verb or pronoun with a singular subject and a plural verb or pronoun with a plural subject.

> The four **workers have** copies of **their** assignments.
>
> Roger's **wife was** quite late for **her** appointment.
>
> **Mr. Kucera and Ms. Downs plan** to forgo **their** bonuses.
>
> Included in this envelope **are a contract and an affidavit**.

Note: This is the general rule; variations are discussed below. In the first sentence, the plural subject (*workers*) requires a plural verb (*have*) and a plural pronoun (*their*). In the second sentence, the singular subject (*wife*) requires a singular verb (*was*) and a singular pronoun (*her*). In the third sentence, the plural subject (*Mr. Kucera and Ms. Downs*) requires a plural verb (*plan*) and a plural pronoun (*their*). In the last sentence, the subject is *a contract and an affidavit*—not *envelope*.

4.5 Company Names Treat company names as singular.

> ☒ NOT   Bickley and Bates **has** paid for **its** last order. **They** are ready to reorder.
>
> ☑ BUT   Bickley and Bates **has** paid for **its** last order. **It** is now ready to reorder.

4.6 Expletives In sentences that begin with an expletive, the true subject follows the verb. Use *is* or *are*, as appropriate.

> There **is** no **reason** for his behavior.
>
> There **are** many **reasons** for his behavior.

Note: An expletive is an expression such as *there is, there are, here is,* and *here are* that comes at the beginning of a clause or sentence. Because the topic of a sentence that begins with an expletive is not immediately apparent, such sentences should be used sparingly in business writing.

4.7 Intervening Words Disregard any words that come between the subject and verb when establishing agreement. See, however, Rule 4.8 regarding special treatment of certain pronouns.

> Only **one** of the mechanics **guarantees his** work. (not *their work*)
>
> The **appearance** of the workers, not their competence, **was** being questioned.
>
> The **administrative assistant**, as well as the clerks, **was** late filing **her** form. (not *their forms*)

Note: First, determine the subject; then make the verb agree. Other intervening words that do not affect the number of the verb are *together with, rather than, accompanied by, in addition to,* and *except*.

4.8 Pronouns Some pronouns (*anybody, each, either, everybody, everyone, much, neither, no one, nobody,* and *one*) are always singular. Other pronouns (*all, any, more, most, none,* and *some*) may be singular or plural, depending on the noun to which they refer.

Each of the laborers **has** a different view of **his or her** job.

Neither of the models **is** doing **her** job well.

Everybody is required to take **his or her** turn at the booth. (not *their turn*)

All the **pie has** been eaten.	**None** of the **work is** finished.
All the **cookies have** been eaten.	**None** of the **workers are** finished.

4.9 Subject Nearer to Verb If two subjects are joined by correlative conjunctions (*or, either/or, nor, neither/nor,* or *not only/but also*), the verb and any pronoun should agree with the subject that is nearer to the verb.

Either Pablo or **Harold is** at **his** desk.

Neither the receptionist nor the **operators were** able to finish **their** tasks.

Not only the actress but also the **dancer has** to practice **her** routine.

The tellers or the **clerks have** to balance **their** cash drawers before leaving.

Note: The first noun in this type of construction may be disregarded when determining whether the verb should be singular or plural. Pay special attention to using the correct pronoun; do not use the plural pronoun *their* unless the subject and verb are plural. Note that subjects joined by *and* or *both/and* are always plural: *Both* **the actress and the dancer have** to practice **their** routines.

4.10 Subjunctive Mood Verbs in the subjunctive mood require the plural form, even when the subject is singular.

I wish the situation **were** reversed.

If I **were** you, I would not mention the matter.

Note: Verbs in the subjunctive mood refer to conditions that are impossible or improbable.

Case

Case refers to the form of a pronoun and indicates its use in a sentence. There are three cases: nominative, objective, and possessive. (Possessive case pronouns are covered under "Apostrophes" in the section on punctuation in LAB 3.) Reflexive pronouns, which end in *self* or *selves,* refer to nouns or other pronouns.

4.11 Nominative Case Use nominative pronouns (*I, he, she, we, they, who, whoever*) as subjects of a sentence or clause and with the verb to be.

The customer representative and **he** are furnishing the figures. (***he** is furnishing*)

Mrs. Quigley asked if Oscar and **I** were ready to begin. (***I** was ready to begin*)

We old-timers can provide some background. (***we** can provide*)

It was **she** who agreed to the proposal. (***she** agreed*)

Who is chairing the meeting? (***he** is chairing*)

Mr. Lentzner wanted to know **who** was responsible. (***she** was responsible*)

Guadalupe is the type of person **who** can be depended upon. (***she** can be depended upon*)

Note: If you have trouble determining which pronoun to use, ignore the plural subject or substitute another pronoun. See the reworded clauses in parentheses.

4.12 Objective Case Use objective pronouns (*me, him, her, us, them, whom, whomever*) as objects in a sentence, clause, or phrase.

Thomas sent a fax to Mr. Baird and **me**. (*sent a fax to **me***)

This policy applies to Eric and **her**. (*applies to **her***)

Habib asked **us** old timers to provide some background. (*Habib asked **us** to provide*)

The work was assigned to **her** and **me**. (*the work was assigned to **me***)

To **whom** shall we mail the specifications? (*mail them to **him***)

Guadalupe is the type of person **whom** we can depend upon. (*we can depend upon **her***)

Note: For *who/whom* constructions, if *he* or *she* can be substituted, *who* is the correct choice; if *him* or *her* can be substituted, *whom* is the correct choice. Remember: *who he, whom him.* The difference is apparent in the final examples shown here and under "Nominative Case," Rule 4.11: **who** *can be depended upon* versus **whom** *we can depend upon.*

4.13 Reflexive Pronouns Use reflexive pronouns (*myself, yourself, himself, herself, itself, ourselves, yourselves,* or *themselves*) to refer to or emphasize a noun or pronoun *that has already been named.* Do not use reflexive pronouns to *substitute for* nominative or objective pronouns.

I **myself** have some doubts about the proposal.

You should see the exhibit **yourself**.

☒ NOT   Virginia and **myself** will take care of the details.

☑ BUT   Virginia and **I** will take care of the details.

☒ NOT   Maya Louise administered the test to Thomas and **myself**.

☑ BUT   Maya Louise administered the test to Thomas and **me**.

Application

Directions Select the correct words or words in parentheses.

1. (Who/Whom) is your favorite new chef? Laura Buraston, who along with Frederico Fox, (are/is) a new chef in Tucson. Some of my friends (has/have) eaten at their restaurants. Laura, they say, is the (better/best) of the two.

2. Merchant Associates is presenting (its/it's/their/there) seminar in Kansas City. The associates will work with seven or eight participants in developing (their/there) portfolios. Not only Dr. Merchant but also his associates (is/are) willing to mentor faculty members. Dr. Merchant asked all participants to acknowledge the invitation with written responses to (he/him).

3. If I (was/ were) you, I would be (more/most) helpful with organizing the conference. You can work directly with Sandra and (me/myself). After all, Sandra knows that it was (I/me) (who/whom) made key contacts. This opportunity is open to the type of person (who/whom) we can depend on.

4. The report on sales volume (is/are) finally on my desk. (Us/We) managers may be somewhat apprehensive about these reports, but sales results tend to predict (who/whom) can be depended upon.

5. Not only the lawyer but also the manager (was/ were) able to attend the conference on ethics. Everybody in the firm (is/are) trying to participate as a way to improve (their/his or her) performance. Each of the employees (is/are) eager to attend the next session.

6. There (was/were) several students in the class (who/whom) challenged whether each of the assignments (was/were) comparable in complexity. The professor asked (us/we) group leaders to evaluate the students' concerns.

7. Neither the professors nor the dean (was/were) able to meet Dr. Phyllis Hart, the conference speaker, at the airport. In fact, neither of the professors (was/were) able to pick her up at the hotel either. However, Dean Dye, as well as two other professors, (is/are) escorting her to the banquet.

8. Martin's and Ricardo's groups are the (more quicker/most quicker/quicker/quickest) in the class. Ricardo's group is the (more slow/most slow/slower/slowest) of these two groups. In any case, all of the jobs (has/have) been submitted for both groups.

9. (Who/Whom) will you ask to participate in the evaluation pro cess? If I (was/were) you, I'd consider Hillary. While Jane is the (more/most) competent software expert we have available, Hillary is the type of team player (who/whom) can provide the leadership we need.

10. I wish it (was/ were) possible for Machiko and (I/me/myself) to see both Marty and Alex in (his/their) last performance this season. Machiko and (I/me/myself) have always had a gathering in our home after they finished. Watching their reactions to the reviewers' comments as they were given (is/are) exciting, but as we are leaving too, it remains to be seen (who/whom) will assume that function next year.

Directions Revise the following paragraph to eliminate any fragments and run on sentences.

FunTimes by Travel Log is a prepaid vacation program designed with families in mind. Club owners have permanent usage rights in a continually growing system of outstanding resorts. Unlike the traditional time-share plans. Members may select any of the club resorts as a destination with optional access to other resorts through exchange programs, the owners may select additional vacation sites, both in the United States and internationally. The membership fee entitles an owner to a fixed number of points each year, up to three years' worth can be accumulated so a selected vacation can be upgraded or lengthened. Future points can be "borrowed" for use on a current vacation. Reservations may be made up to 13 months in advance these features make this plan an economical and flexible way to create family vacation memories.

Lab 5: Mechanics

Writing mechanics refer to those elements in communication that are evident only in written form: abbreviations, capitalization, number expression, spelling, and word division. (Punctuation, also a form of writing mechanics, was covered in LABs 2 and 3.) While creating a first draft, you need not be too concerned about the mechanics of your writing. However, you should be especially alert during the editing and proofreading stages to follow these common rules.

Abbreviations

Use abbreviations according to organizational norms for business writing. Be sure that your audience will understand your abbreviation, or follow the rule "When in doubt, write it out." When typing, do not space within abbreviations except to separate each initial of a person's name. Leave one space after an abbreviation unless another mark of punctuation follows immediately.

5.1 Not Abbreviated In narrative writing, do not abbreviate common nouns (such as *acct.*, *assoc.*, *bldg.*, *co.*, *dept.*, *misc.*, and *pkg.*) or the names of cities, states (except in addresses), months, and days of the week.

5.2 With Periods Use periods to indicate many abbreviations.

No.	8:00 a.m.	4 ft.
Dr. M. L. Peterson	P.O. Box 45	e.g.

5.3 Without Periods Write some abbreviations in all capitals, with no periods—including all two-letter state abbreviations used in addresses with ZIP codes.

CPA	IRS	CT
TWA	MBA	OK

Note: Use two-letter state abbreviations in bibliographic citations.

Capitalization

The function of capitalization is to emphasize words or to show their importance. For example, the first word of a sentence is capitalized to emphasize that a new sentence has begun.

5.4 Compass Point Capitalize a compass point that designates a definite region or that is part of an official name. (Do not capitalize compass points used as directions.)

Margot lives in the **S**outh.

Our display window faces **w**est.

Is **E**ast Orange in **W**est Virginia?

5.5 Letter Part Capitalize the first word and any proper nouns in the salutation and complimentary closing of a business letter.

Dear **M**r. **F**edorov:	**S**incerely **y**ours,
Dear **M**r. and **M**rs. **A**mes:	**Y**ours **t**ruly,

5.6 Noun Plus Number Capitalize a noun followed by a number or letter (except for page and size numbers).

Table 3	**p**age 79
Flight 1062	**s**ize 8D

5.7 Position Title Capitalize an official position title that comes before a personal name, unless the personal name is an appositive set off by commas. Do not capitalize a position title used alone.

Vice **P**resident Alfredo Tenegco	Shirley Wilhite, **d**ean,
our **p**resident, Joanne Rathburn,	The **c**hief **e**xecutive **o**fficer retired.

5.8 Proper Noun Capitalize proper nouns and adjectives derived from proper nouns. Do not capitalize articles, conjunctions, and prepositions typically of four or fewer letters (for example, *a, an, the, and, of,* and *from*). The names of the seasons and the names of generic school courses are not proper nouns and are not capitalized.

Xerox copier	Amherst College (*but:* the college)
New York City (*but:* the city)	the Mexican border
the Fourth of July	Friday, March 3,
Chrysler Building	Bank of America
First Class Storage Company	Margaret Adams White
business communication	the winter holidays

5.9 Quotation Capitalize the first word of a quoted sentence. (Do not capitalize the first word of an indirect quotation.)

According to Hall, "The goal of quality control is specified uniform quality."

Hall thinks we should work toward "specified uniform quality."

Hall said that uniform quality is the goal.

5.10 Title In a published title, capitalize the first and last words, the first word after a colon or dash, and all other words except articles, conjunctions, and prepositions of four or fewer letters.

"A Word to the Wise"

Pricing Strategies: The Link with Reality

Numbers

Authorities do not agree on a single style for expressing numbers—whether to spell out a number in words or to write it in figures. The following guidelines apply to typical business writing. (The alternative is to use a *formal* style, in which all numbers that can be expressed in one or two words are spelled out.) When typing numbers in figures, separate thousands, millions, and billions with commas; and leave a space between a whole number figure and its fraction unless the fraction is a character on the keyboard or is created automatically by your word processing software.

5.11 General Spell out numbers for zero through ten and use figures for 11 and higher.

the first three pages	ten complaints
18 photocopies	5,376 stockholders

Note: Follow this rule only when none of the following special rules apply.

5.12 Figures Use figures for

- dates. (Use the endings -*st, -d, -rd,* or -*th* only when the day precedes the month.)
- all numbers if two or more *related* numbers both above and below ten are used in the same sentence.
- measurements—such as time, money, distance, weight, and percentage. Be consistent in using either the word *percent* or the symbol %.
- mixed numbers.

May 9 (or the 9th of May)	10 miles
4 men and 18 women	*But:* The **18** women had **four** cars.
$6	5 p.m. (or 5 o'clock)
5 percent (or 5%)	6½
	But: 6 3/18

5.13 Words Spell out

- a number used as the first word of a sentence.
- the smaller number when two numbers come together.
- fractions.
- the words *million* and *billion* in even numbers.

Thirty-two people attended.	nearly two-thirds of them
three 41-cent stamps	150 two-page brochures
37 million	$4.8 billion

Note: When fractions and the numbers 21 through 99 are spelled out, they should be hyphenated.

Spelling

Correct spelling is essential to effective communication. A misspelled word can distract the reader, cause misunderstanding, and send a negative message about the writer's competence. Because of the many variations in the spelling of English words, no spelling guidelines are foolproof; there are exceptions to every spelling rule. The five rules that follow, however, may be safely applied to most business writing situations. Learning them will save you the time of looking up many words in a dictionary.

5.14 Doubling a Final Consonant If the last syllable of a root word is stressed, double the final consonant when adding a suffix.

Last Syllable Stressed		Last Syllable Not Stressed	
prefer	preferring	happen	happening
control	controlling	total	totaling
occur	occurrence	differ	differed

5.15 One-Syllable Words If a one-syllable word ends in a consonant preceded by a single vowel, double the final consonant before a suffix starting with a vowel.

Suffix Starting with Vowel		Suffix Starting with Consonant	
ship	shipper	ship	shipment
drop	dropped	glad	gladness
bag	baggage	bad	badly

5.16 Final E If a final *e* is preceded by a consonant, drop the *e* before a suffix starting with a vowel.

Suffix Starting with Vowel		Suffix Starting with Consonant	
come	coming	hope	hopeful
use	usable	manage	management
sincere	sincerity	sincere	sincerely

Note: Words ending in *ce* or *ge* usually retain the *e* before a suffix starting with a vowel: *noticeable, advantageous.*

5.17 Final Y If a final *y* is preceded by a consonant, change *y* to *i* before any suffix except one starting with *i.*

Most Suffixes		Suffix Starting with i	
company	companies	try	trying
ordinary	ordinarily	forty	fortyish
hurry	hurried		

5.18 EI and IE Words Remember the rhyme:

Use *i* before *e*	believe	yield
Except after *c*	receive	deceit
Or when sounded like *a*	freight	their
As in *neighbor* and *weigh.*		

Word and Paragraph Division

When possible, avoid dividing words at the end of a line, because word divisions tend to slow down or even confuse a reader (for example, *rear range* for *rearrange* or *read just* for *readjust*). However, when necessary to avoid grossly uneven right margins, use the following rules. Most word processing software programs have a hyphenation feature that automatically divides words to make a more even right margin; you can change these word divisions manually if necessary. When you are typing, do not space before a hyphen.

5.19 Compound Word Divide a compound word either after the hyphen or where the two words join to make a solid compound.

  self- service   free- way   battle- field

5.20 Division Point Leave at least two letters on the upper line and carry at least three letters to the next line.

  ex- treme   typ- ing

5.21 Not Divided Do not divide a one syllable word, contraction, or abbreviation.

  straight   shouldn't
  UNESCO   approx.

5.22 Syllables Divide words only between syllables.

  re- sources   knowl- edge

Note: When in doubt about where a syllable ends, consult a dictionary.

5.23 Web Addresses Avoid breaking a URL (web address) or email address to a second line. If you must, break it before a period. Never add a hyphen, which the reader may misunderstand to be part of the address.

5.24 Paragraphs If it is necessary to divide a paragraph between two pages, leave at least two lines of the paragraph at the bottom of the first page and carry forward at least two lines to the top of the next page. Do not divide a three-line paragraph.

Application

Directions Rewrite the following paragraphs so that all words and numbers are expressed correctly. Do not change the wording in any sentences.

1. 100 of our elementary students will receive passes to Holly's Heartland Amusement Park today. Mrs. freda t. albertson, principal, indicated students from every grade were randomly selected to receive the free passes. The students represent about a 1/5 of the school's population.

2. As of Sept. 1st, nearly $\frac{3}{4}$ of our parents have attended at least one learning style orientation seminar. The School Psychologist, John Sibilsky, summarized the response of the participants and reported a favorable evaluation by ninety-six parents.

3. The Athletes for Freedom participants sponsored 12 2-hour presentations in a 3-week period. The last stop was east St. Louis, before the long ride home.

4. As reported on Page 2 of today's newspaper, the price of a barrel of oil has continued to climb. According to president Victoria payton, the price is 1 1/2 times higher than last year.

5. This month's issue of Time magazine reports an interview with justin lake who said, "Service to our country is measured by many things, but a gift of time is one of the more significant." Our employees gave a total of two-hundred-ninety-five hours.

Directions Correct the one misspelling in each line.

1. preferring	controlling	occurence
2. shipper	droped	baggage
3. totalling	badly	shipment
4. differred	happening	gladness
5. sincerity	sincerly	noticeable
6. trying	fortyish	ordinarly
7. deceit	yeild	believe
8. advantagous	hopeful	companies
9. changeable	boundary	arguement
10. catagory	apparent	criticize
11. recommend	accomodate	weird
12. plausable	indispensable	allotted
13. camouflage	innocence	seperately
14. nickle	miniature	embarrassing
15. liaison	exhilarated	inadvertent

Directions Write the following words, inserting a hyphen or blank space at the first correct division point. If a word cannot be divided, write it without a hyphen.

Examples: mis-spelled
thought

1. freeway   chairperson   lien
2. express   exploitation   right
3. MADD   soared   solitary
4. wouldn't   mayor-elect   reliance
5. agree   re course   Ohio
6. www.homemadesimple.com
7. Saddlebrooke_tripticket@yahoo.com

Lab 6: Word Usage

The following words and phrases are often used incorrectly in everyday speech and in business writing. Learn to use them correctly to help achieve your communication goals.

In some cases in the following list, one word is often confused with another similar word; in other cases, the structure of our language requires that certain words be used only in certain ways. Because of space, only brief and incomplete definitions are given here. Consult a dictionary for more complete or additional meanings.

6.1 Accept/Except *Accept* means "to agree to"; *except* means "with the exclusion of."

I will **accept** all the recommendations **except** the last one.

6.2 Advice/Advise *Advice* is a noun meaning "counsel"; *advise* is a verb meaning "to recommend."

If I ask for her **advice,** she may **advise** me to quit.

6.3 Affect/Effect *Affect* is most often used as a verb meaning "to influence" or "to change"; *effect* is most often used as a noun meaning "result" or "impression."

The legislation may **affect** sales but should have no **effect** on gross margin.

6.4 All Right/Alright Use *all right*. (*Alright* is considered substandard.)

The arrangement is **all right** (not *alright*) with me.

6.5 A Lot/Alot Use *a lot*. (*Alot* is considered substandard.)

We used **a lot** (not *alot*) of overtime on the project.

6.6 Among/Between Use *among* when referring to three or more; use *between* when referring to two.

Among the three candidates was one manager who divided his time **between** London and New York.

6.7 Amount/Number Use *amount* to refer to money or to things that cannot be counted; use *number* to refer to things that can be counted.

The **amount** of consumer interest was measured by the **number** of coupons returned.

6.8 Anxious/Eager Use *anxious* only if great concern or worry is involved.

Andrés was **eager** to get the new car although he was **anxious** about making such high payments.

6.9 Any One/Anyone Spell as two words when followed by *of*; spell as one word when the accent is on *any*.

Anyone is allowed to attend **any one** of the sessions.

Between See *Among/Between*.

6.10 Can/May *Can* indicates ability; *may* indicates permission.

I **can** finish the project on time if I **may** hire an additional secretary.

6.11 Cite/Sight/Site *Cite* means "to quote" or "to mention"; *sight* is either a verb meaning "to look at" or a noun meaning "something seen"; *site* is most often a noun meaning "location."

The **sight** of the high rise building on the **site** of the old battlefield reminded Monica to **cite** several other examples to the commission members.

6.12 Complement/Compliment *Complement* means "to complete" or "something that completes"; *compliment* means "to praise" or "words of praise."

I must **compliment** you on the new model, which will **complement** our line.

6.13 Could of/Could've Use *could've* (or *could have*). (*Could of* is incorrect.)

We **could've** (not *could of*) prevented that loss had we been more alert.

6.14 Different from/Different than Use *different from*. (*Different than* is considered substandard.)

Your computer is **different from** (not *different than*) mine.

6.15 Each Other/One Another Use *each other* when referring to two; use *one another* when referring to three or more.

The two workers helped **each other**, but their three visitors would not even look at **one another**.

Eager See *Anxious/Eager*.

Effect See *Affect/Effect*.

6.16 e.g./i.e. The abbreviation *e.g.* means "for example"; *i.e.* means "that is." Use *i.e.* to introduce a restatement or explanation of a preceding expression. Both abbreviations, like the expressions for which they stand, are followed by commas. (Many writers prefer the full English terms to the abbreviations because they are clearer.)

The proposal has merit; **e.g.,** it is economical, forward looking, and timely.

Or: The proposal has merit; for example, it is economical, forward looking, and timely.

Unfortunately, it is also a hot potato; **i.e.,** it will generate unfavorable publicity.

Or: Unfortunately, it is also a hot potato; that is, it will generate unfavorable publicity.

6.17 Eminent/Imminent *Eminent* means "well known"; *imminent* means "about to happen."

The arrival of the **eminent** scientist from Russia is **imminent**.

6.18 Enthused/Enthusiastic Use *enthusiastic*. (*Enthused* is considered sub standard.)

I have become quite **enthusiastic** (not *enthused*) about the possibilities.

   Except See *Accept/Except*.

6.19 Farther/Further *Farther* refers to distance; *further* refers to extent or degree.

We drove 10 miles **farther** while we discussed the matter **further.**

6.20 Fewer/Less Use *fewer* to refer to things that can be counted; use *less* to refer to money or to things that cannot be counted.

Alvin worked **fewer** hours at the exhibit and therefore generated **less** interest.

   Further See *Farther/Further*.

6.21 Good/Well *Good* is an adjective; *well* is an adverb or (with reference to health) an adjective.

Joe does a **good** job and performs **well** on tests, even when he does not feel **well.**

   i.e. See *e.g./i.e.*

   Imminent See *Eminent/Imminent*.

6.22 Imply/Infer Imply means "to hint" or "to suggest"; *infer* means "to draw a conclusion." Speakers and writers *imply;* readers and listeners *infer*.

The president **implied** that changes will be forthcoming; I **inferred** from his tone of voice that these changes will not be pleasant.

6.23 Irregardless/Regardless Use *regardless*. (*Irregardless* is considered substandard.)

He wants to proceed, **regardless** (not *irregardless*) of the costs.

6.24 Its/It's *Its* is a possessive pronoun; *it's* is a contraction for "it is."

It's time to let the department increase **its** budget.

6.25 Lay/Lie *Lay* (principal forms: *lay, laid, laid, laying*) means "to put" and requires an object to complete its meaning; *lie* (principal forms: *lie, lay, lain, lying*) means "to rest."

Please **lay** the supplies on the shelf.	I **lie** on the couch after lunch each day.
I **laid** the folders in the drawer.	The report **lay** on his desk yesterday.
She had **laid** the notes on her desk.	The job has **lain** untouched for a week.

Less See *Fewer/Less.*

Lie See *Lay/Lie.*

6.26 Loose/Lose *Loose* means "not fastened"; *lose* means "to be unable to find."

Do not **lose** the **loose** change in your po cket.

May See *Can/May.*

Number See *Amount/Number.*

One Another See *Each Other/One Another.*

6.27 Passed/Past Passed is a verb (the past tense or past participle of *pass*, meaning "to move on or by"); *past* is an adjective, adverb, or preposition meaning "earlier."

The committee **passed** the no-confidence motion at a **past** meeting.

6.28 Percent/Percentage With figures, use *percent;* without figures, use *percentage.*

We took a commission of 6 **percent** (or 6%), which was a lower **percentage** than last year.

6.29 Personal/Personnel *Personal* means "private" or "belonging to one individual"; *personnel* means "employees."

I used my **personal** time to draft a memo to all **personnel.**

6.30 Principal/Principle *Principal* means "primary" (adjective) or "sum of money" (noun); *principle* means "rule" or "law."

The guiding **principle** is fair play, and the **principal** means of achieving it is a code of ethics.

6.31 Real/Really *Real* is an adjective; *really* is an adverb. Do not use *real* to modify another adjective.

She was **really** (not *real*) proud that her necklace contained **real** pearls.

6.32 Reason Is Because/Reason Is That Use *reason is that.* (*Reason is because* is considered substandard.)

The **reason** for such low attendance **is that** (not *is because*) the weather was stormy.

Regardless See *Irregardless/Regardless.*

6.33 Same Do not use *same* to refer to a previously mentioned item. Use *it* or some other wording instead.

We have received your order and will ship **it** (not *same*) in three days.

6.34 Set/Sit *Set* (principal forms: *set, set, set, setting*) means "to place"; *sit* (principal forms: *sit, sat, sat, sitting*) means "to be seated."

Please **set** your papers on the table.	Please **sit** in the chair.
She **set** the computer on the desk.	She **sat** in the first class section.
I have **set** the computer there before.	I had not **sat** there before.

6.35 Should of/Should've Use *should've* (or *should have*). (*Should of* is incorrect.)

We **should've** (not *should of*) been more careful.

Sight See *Cite/Sight/Site*.

Sit See *Set/Sit*.

Site See *Cite/Sight/Site*.

6.36 Stationary/Stationery *Stationary* means "remaining in one place"; *stationery* is writing paper.

I used my personal **stationery** to write a letter about the **stationary** bike.

6.37 Sure/Surely *Sure* is an adjective; *surely* is an adverb. Do not use *sure* to modify another adjective.

I'm **surely** (not *sure*) glad that she is running and feel **sure** that she will be nominated.

6.38 Sure and/Sure to Use *sure to*. (*Sure and* is considered substandard.)

Be **sure to** (not *sure and*) attend the meeting.

6.39 Their/There/They're *Their* means "belonging to them"; *there* means "in that place"; and *they're* is a contraction for "they are."

They're too busy with **their** reports to be **there** for the hearing.

6.40 Theirs/There's *Theirs* is a possessive pronoun; *there's* is a contraction for "there is."

We finished our meal, but **there's** no time for them to finish **theirs**.

They're See *Their/There/They're*.

6.41 Try and/Try to Use *try to*. (*Try and* is considered substandard.)

Please **try to** (not *try and*) attend the meeting.

Well See *Good/Well*.

6.42 Whose/Who's *Whose* is a possessive pronoun; *who's* is a contraction for "who is."

Who's going to let us know **whose** turn it is to make coffee?

6.43 Your/You're *Your* means "belonging to you"; *you're* is a contraction for "you are."

You're going to present **your** report first.

Application

Directions Select the correct words in parentheses.

1. I will (accept/except) your (advice/advise), but the (affect/effect) of doing so may bring (alot/a lot) of change.

2. The seminar was (all right/alright), but (among/between) Ludwig and me, most participants were (anxious/eager) to complete the training.

3. The (amount/number) of political activity generated (fewer/less) interest than anticipated.

4. (Any one/Anyone) of the students (may/can) apply that (principal/principle) if (theirs/there's) time.

5. The first (sight/cite/site) for the new office (could of/could've) (complimented/complemented) the surrounding community, mainly because it is (different from/different than) the typical building.

6. The program will succeed; (e.g./i.e.), it is positive, forward looking, and cost effective.

7. The group members supported (each other/one another) and were (enthused/enthusiastic) about their presentation.

8. The CEO (implied/inferred) that arrangements with an (eminent/imminent) scientist have been finalized, and (irregardless/regardless) of the number who are invited, we will be included.

9. How much (farther/further) can we pursue this if (its/it's) not (passed/past) on through regular channels?

10. Please (lay/lie) your (loose/lose) change on the dresser, and I'll be (real/really) pleased.

11. You (should of/should've) taken advantage of the opportunity to refinance your home under the lower (percent/percentage) rates.

12. The new investment program is open to all (personal/personnel) and will (sure/surely) build security for (their/there) future.

13. The reason for the increase in deli foods in grocery stores is (that/because) more people are buying food prepared outside the home.

14. I use my personal (stationery/stationary), and please (try to/try and) use yours.

15. Tell Henri to be (sure and/sure to) lock up before he leaves and (sit/set) the late afternoon mail on my desk.

16. We have the document and will forward (it/same) to the actuary so that (you're/your) department is included in the transaction.

17. (Who's/Whose) turn is it to clean the refrigerator because it (sure/surely) needs it?

18. I'll follow the guidelines you (advise/advice), (except/accept) the one involving the (eminent/imminent) staff change in sales.

19. There was wide disparity (between/among) the five candidates, but they supported (each other/one another).

20. Dr. Zhoa was excited about the new job but (eager/anxious) about the research required.

21. Be sure the (cites/sights/sites) are interesting because we want to do a (good/well) job.

22. What did you (imply/infer) from her (compliment/complement)?

23. The (principle/principal) reason for (their/there/they're) success is the lawyer, (whose/who's) a specialist in international law.

24. A (stationery/stationary) pump for the well was (complemented/complimented) by a mobile emergency back up.

25. They wanted us to work (less/fewer) hours so the (number/amount) of savings could be increased.

B Formatting Business Documents

Formatting Letters and Memos

The most common features of business letters and memos are discussed in the following sections and illustrated in Figure 1.

Letter and Punctuation Styles

The *block style* is the simplest letter style to type because all lines begin at the left margin. In the *modified block style,* the date and closing lines begin at the center point. Offsetting these parts from the left margin enables the reader to locate them quickly.

The *standard punctuation style*—the most common format—uses a colon after the salutation and a comma after the complimentary closing. The *open punctuation style,* on the other hand, uses no punctuation after these two lines.

Stationery and Margins

Most letters and memos are printed on standard-sized stationery, 8½ × 11 inches. The first page is printed on letterhead stationery, which shows the company logo at the top and the company address either at the top or at the bottom. Subsequent pages are printed on high-quality plain paper.

Side, top, and bottom margins should be 1 to 1¼ inches (the typical default in programs such as Microsoft Word). Vertically center one-page letters and memos. Set a tab at the center point if you're formatting a modified block style letter.

Required Letter Parts

The required letter parts are as follows:

Date Line Type the current month (spelled out), day, and year on the first line. Begin either at the center point for modified block style or at the left margin for the block style.

Inside Address The inside address gives the name and location of the person to whom you're writing. Include a personal title (e.g., *Mr., Mrs., Miss,* or *Ms.*). If you use the addressee's job title, type it either on the same line as the name (separated from the name by a comma) or on the following line by itself. In the address, use the two-letter U.S. Postal Service abbreviation, typed in all capitals with no period, and leave one space between the state and the ZIP code. Type the inside address at the left margin; skip between one and four lines below the date, depending on the size of the letter. For international letters, type the name of the country in all-capital letters on the last line by itself.

Figure 1 | Written Message Format

May 18, 2017

Ms. Amy Newman
Cornell University
331 Statler Hall
Ithaca, NY 14853

Dear Ms. Newman:

Please accept my deepest gratitude for your generous in-kind gift of food. Your gift will help feed our Southern Tier neighbors in need. The Food Bank's network of hunger-relief agencies is currently serving more households than in previous years. Within the last year, existing clients needed assistance more frequently than before, and our network experienced an increase in first-time users, many of them employed but unable to make ends meet, as well as seniors who struggle to live on fixed incomes.

Without people like you, we would not be able to keep up with the increasing demand for emergency food assistance. I am very thankful that we have such wonderful, caring donors who want to alleviate the stress that some families face.

Thank you for your generosity and support for the Food Bank's hunger-relief efforts.

Sincerely,

Natasha R. Thompson
President & CEO

NRT/lce

Block style letter

May 18, 2017

Ms. Amy Newman
Cornell University
331 Statler Hall
Ithaca, NY 14853

Dear Ms. Newman:

Please accept my deepest gratitude for your generous in-kind gift of food. Your gift will help feed our Southern Tier neighbors in need. The Food Bank's network of hunger-relief agencies is currently serving more households than in previous years. Within the last year, existing clients needed assistance more frequently than before, and our network experienced an increase in first-time users, many of them employed but unable to make ends meet, as well as seniors who struggle to live on fixed incomes.

Without people like you, we would not be able to keep up with the increasing demand for emergency food assistance. I am very thankful that we have such wonderful, caring donors who want to alleviate the stress that some families face.

Thank you for your generosity and support for the Food Bank's hunger-relief efforts.

Sincerely,

Natasha R. Thompson
President & CEO

NRT/lce

Modified block style letter

Calaway Movers

To: All Calaway Staff
From: Bill Calaway, CEO
Subject: Reorganizing Our Sales Teams
Date: September 9, 2017

As we discussed on the web conference last week, we are reorganizing the corporate office to focus more closely on customer needs. Instead of sales functions serving regional customers, we will organize around types of customers: consumer, small business, and corporate. This will allow Calaway to tailor our products and services to specific customer groups and leverage services within customer segments. The former regional model worked well for a long time, but we have outgrown this structure and must adapt, particularly to our growing base of corporate clients, who demand more customized services from Calaway.

Our goal is to make this transition as smooth as possible. Over the next 90 days, we will implement the transition plan:

- **Transfer sales representatives to new divisions (by October 15)**

  Each sales representative will be moved from our current regional teams to a new team: consumer, small business, or corporate. Managers will work closely with representatives to determine strengths, experiences, and preferences.

- **Identify account type (by October 31)**

  All sales representatives will categorize current accounts for the new divisions: consumer, small business, and corporate.

- **Transition accounts to new teams (by November 30)**

  Where accounts are changing sales representatives, we will follow this process:

  ○ For small business accounts, the former and new sales representative will send an email to the account contact, followed by a phone call and visit (if possible) by the new sales representative.

  ○ For corporate accounts, the former sales representative will send an email and schedule a conference call or visit by the account contact and new sales representative.

Seamless communication with our clients during this transition is essential. Each segment is working on email templates to ensure that our communication is clear and consistent across all divisions.

Interoffice memo (page 1)

Sales Reorganization   Page 2   September 9, 2017

I am pleased to announce the following leaders in the newly formed sales organization:

- **Melissa Chowdhury, Vice President, Sales**

  Formerly the vice president of the Northeast region, Melissa will oversee all sales functions. Melissa will report directly to me, and the following sales directors will report to Melissa.

- **Bruce Gorman, Director, Consumer Accounts**

  Bruce will move from the Midwest region to oversee the new Consumer Accounts division.

- **Ryan Korman, Director, Small Business Accounts**

  Ryan will move from the Southern region to oversee the Small Business Accounts division.

- **Manny Fernandez, Director, Corporate Accounts**

  Formerly director, customer service, Manny will oversee the Corporate Accounts division.

Please join me in congratulating these folks in their new roles.

I am very excited about the future of Calaway. With our new organizational structure, we will continue to grow—and move people safely to new homes and offices across the country. I look forward to taking this journey with all of you.

Interoffice memo (page 2)

Salutation Use the same name in both the inside address and the salutation. If the letter is addressed to a job position rather than to a person, use a generic greeting, such as "Dear Human Resources Manager." If you typically address the reader in person by first name, use the first name in the salutation (for example, "Dear Cara:"); otherwise, use a personal title and the surname only (for example, "Dear Ms. Currigan:"). Leave one blank line before and after the salutation.

Body Single-space the lines of each paragraph and leave one blank line between paragraphs.

Page 2 Insert the page number in the header or footer, centered or on the right side. Omit the page number on page 1. You should carry forward to a second page at least two lines of the body of the message.

Complimentary Closing Begin the complimentary closing at the same margin point as the date line. Capitalize the first word only, and leave one blank line before and approximately three blank lines after, to allow room for your signature before your full typed name.

Signature Sign your name legibly in blue or black ink.

Writer's Identification The writer's identification (name or job title or both) begins approximately on the fourth line immediately below the complimentary closing. Do not use a personal title. The job title may go either on the same line as the typed name, separated from the name by a comma, or on the following line by itself.

Reference Initials When used, reference initials (the initials of the typist) are typed at the left margin in lowercase letters without periods, with one blank line before. Do not include reference initials if you type your own letter.

Envelopes Business envelopes have a printed return address. You may print your name above this address, if you wish. Use plain envelopes for personal business letters; you should print the return address (your home address) at the upper left corner, or use an address label. On large (No. 10) envelopes, print the mailing address 2 inches from the top edge and 4 inches from the left edge. On small (No. 6¾) envelopes, print the mailing address 2 inches from the top edge and 2½ inches from the left edge. Fold 8½ × 11 letters in thirds and small notepaper in half to fit the envelope.

Optional Letter Parts

Optional letter parts are as follows:

Subject Line You may include a subject line in letters (identified by the words *Subject* or *Re* followed by a colon) to identify the topic of the letter. Type it below the salutation, with one blank line before and one after.

Numbered or Bulleted Lists in the Body You may include a numbered list (if the sequence of the items is important) or a bulleted list (when the sequence is not important). Single-space each item, and double-space or use 6-point spacing between items. Leave one blank line before and after the list.

Enclosure Notation You may use an enclosure notation if items are included in the envelope and are not obvious. Type "Enclosure" (or "Attachment" if the items are physically attached) on the line immediately below the reference initials, and as an option, add the description of what is enclosed.

Copy Notation If someone other than the addressee is to receive a copy of the letter, type a copy notation ("c:") immediately below the enclosure notation or reference initials, whichever comes last. Then follow the copy notation with the names of the people who will receive copies.

Postscript If you add a postscript to a letter, type it as the last item, preceded by one blank line. The heading "P.S." is optional. Postscripts are used most often in sales letters.

Memo Header Format

Internal memos may be printed, attached to email messages, or uploaded onto company intranet sites. Double-space the memo header and include the following:

To: Type the first and last name of the receiver or a group name, for example, "All Employees." You may include a job title after a receiver's name and a comma, for example, "Jason Matthews, CFO."

From: Type your first and last name. If you wrote a title after the receiver's name, include yours here. For printed memos, you may sign your initials after your name if this is standard in your organization.

Date: Type the full date: month, day, and year.

Subject: Include a descriptive subject line as you would for an email message.

Formatting Reports

In Chapter 10, you read suggestions for designing and formatting text-based reports and reports created in presentation software. The executive summary of the *Not Alone* report, with traditional text formatting, is shown in Figure 2.

Reports created in presentation software are intended as stand-alone documents without a presenter to explain the detail. Therefore, compared to slides used to complement an oral presentation, a report will be far denser with text and graphics and may use standard business font sizes. For comparison, the full YZ Travel report (Figure 3) and oral presentation slides (Figure 4) are shown. Both were created in PowerPoint, but the content and formatting are quite different.

Figure 2 | Executive Summary from the *Not Alone* Report

Executive Summary

Why We Need to Act

This report uses an older style of spacing: two spaces between sentences instead of one, which is standard today.

One in five women is sexually assaulted in college. Most often, it's by someone she knows – and also most often, she does not report what happened. Many survivors are left feeling isolated, ashamed or to blame. Although it happens less often, men, too, are victims of these crimes.

The President created the Task Force to Protect Students From Sexual Assault to turn this tide. As the name of our new website – NotAlone.gov – indicates, we are here to tell sexual assault survivors that they are not alone. And we're also here to help schools live up to their obligation to protect students from sexual violence.

Over the last three months, we have had a national conversation with thousands of people who care about this issue. Today, we offer our first set of action steps and recommendations.

1. Identifying the Problem: Campus Climate Surveys

The first step in solving a problem is to name it and know the extent of it – and a campus climate survey is the best way to do that. We are providing schools with a toolkit to conduct a survey – and we urge schools to show they're serious about the problem by conducting the survey next year. The Justice Department, too, will partner with Rutgers University's Center on Violence Against Women and Children to pilot, evaluate and further refine the survey – and at the end of this trial period, we will explore legislative or administrative options to require schools to conduct a survey in 2016.

2. Preventing Sexual Assault – and Engaging Men

Prevention programs can change attitudes, behavior – and the culture. In addition to identifying a number of promising prevention strategies that schools can undertake now, we are also researching new ideas and solutions. But one thing we know for sure: we need to engage men as allies in this cause. Most men are not perpetrators – and when we empower men to step in when someone's in trouble, they become an important part of the solution.

As the President and Vice President's new Public Service Announcement puts it: if she doesn't consent – or can't consent – it's a crime. And if you see it happening, help her, don't blame her, speak up. We are also providing schools with links and information about how they can implement their own bystander intervention programs on campus.

3. Effectively Responding When a Student Is Sexually Assaulted

When one of its students is sexually assaulted, a school needs to have all the pieces of a plan in place. And that should include:

Someone a survivor can talk to in confidence

While many victims of sexual assault are ready to file a formal (or even public) complaint against an alleged offender right away – many others want time and privacy to sort through their next steps. For some, having a confidential place to go can mean the difference between getting help and staying silent.

SOURCE: NOT ALONE THE FIRST REPORT OF THE WHITE HOUSE TASK FORCE TO PROTECT STUDENTS FROM SEXUAL ASSAULT APRIL 2014 PAGE 2–5.

Today, we are providing schools with a model reporting and confidentiality protocol – which, at its heart, aims to give survivors more control over the process. Victims who want their school to fully investigate an incident must be taken seriously – and know where to report. But for those who aren't quite ready, they need to have – and know about – places to go for confidential advice and support.

That means a school should make it clear, up front, who on campus can maintain a victim's confidence and who can't – so a victim can make an informed decision about where best to turn. A school's policy should also explain when it may need to override a confidentiality request (and pursue an alleged perpetrator) in order to help provide a safe campus for everyone. Our sample policy provides recommendations for how a school can strike that often difficult balance, while also being ever mindful of a survivor's well-being.

New guidance from the Department of Education also makes clear that on-campus counselors and advocates – like those who work or volunteer in sexual assault centers, victim advocacy offices, women's and health centers, as well as licensed and pastoral counselors – can talk to a survivor in confidence. In recent years, some schools have indicated that some of these counselors and advocates cannot maintain confidentiality. This new guidance clarifies that they can.

A comprehensive sexual misconduct policy

We are also providing a checklist for schools to use in drafting (or reevaluating) their own sexual misconduct policies. Although every school will need to tailor a policy to its own needs and circumstances, all schools should be sure to bring the key stakeholders – including students – to the table. Among other things, this checklist includes ideas a school could consider in deciding what is – or is not – consent to sexual activity. As we heard from many students, this can often be the essence of the matter – and a school community should work together to come up with a careful and considered understanding.

Trauma-informed training for school officials

Sexual assault is a unique crime: unlike other crimes, victims often blame themselves; the associated trauma can leave their memories fragmented; and insensitive or judgmental questions can compound a victim's distress. Starting this year, the Justice Department, through both its Center for Campus Public Safety and its Office on Violence Against Women, will develop trauma-informed training programs for school officials and campus and local law enforcement. The Department of Education's National Center on Safe and Supportive Learning Environments will do the same for campus health centers. This kind of training has multiple benefits: when survivors are treated with care and wisdom, they start trusting the system, and the strength of their accounts can better hold offenders accountable.

Better school disciplinary systems

Many sexual assault survivors are wary of their school's adjudication process – which can sometimes subject them to harsh and hurtful questioning (like about their prior sexual history) by students or staff unschooled in the dynamics of these crimes. Some schools are experimenting with new models – like having a single, trained investigator do the lion's share of the fact-finding – with very positive results. We need to learn more about these promising new ideas. And so starting this year, the Justice Department will begin assessing different models for

Figure 2 | *(continued)*

investigating and adjudicating campus sexual assault cases with an eye toward identifying best practices.

The Department of Education's new guidance also urges some important improvements to many schools' current disciplinary processes: questions about the survivor's sexual history with anyone other than the alleged perpetrator should not be permitted; adjudicators should know that the mere fact of a previous consensual sexual relationship does not itself imply consent or preclude a finding of sexual violence; and the parties should not be allowed to personally cross-examine each other.

Partnerships with the community

Because students can be sexually assaulted at all hours of the day or night, emergency services should be available 24 hours a day, too. Other types of support can also be crucial – like longer-term therapies and advocates who can accompany survivors to medical and legal appointments. Many schools cannot themselves provide all these services, but in partnership with a local rape crisis center, they can. So, too, when both the college and the local police are simultaneously investigating a case (a criminal investigation does not relieve a school of its duty to itself investigate and respond), coordination can be crucial. So we are providing schools with a sample agreement they can use to partner with their local rape crisis center – and by June, we will provide a similar sample for forging a partnership with local law enforcement.

4. Increasing Transparency and Improving Enforcement

A section overview before the subheading would improve organization in the report.

More transparency and information

The government is committed to making our enforcement efforts more transparent – and getting students and schools more resources to help bring an end to this violence. As part of this effort, we will post enforcement data on our new website – NotAlone.gov – and give students a roadmap for filing a complaint if they think their school has not lived up to its obligations.

Among many other things on the website, sexual assault survivors can also locate an array of services by typing in their zip codes, learn about their legal rights, see which colleges have had enforcement actions taken against them, get "plain English" definitions of some complicated legal terms and concepts; and find their states' privacy laws. Schools and advocates can access federal guidance, learn about relevant legislation, and review the best available evidence and research. We invite everyone to take a look.

Improved Enforcement

Today, the Department of Education's Office for Civil Rights (OCR) is releasing a 52-point guidance document that answers many frequently asked questions about a student's rights, and a school's obligations, under Title IX. Among many other topics, the new guidance clarifies that Title IX protects all students, regardless of their sexual orientation or gender identity, immigration status, or whether they have a disability. It also makes clear that students who report sexual violence have a right to expect their school to take steps to protect and support them, including while a school investigation is pending. The guidance also clarifies that recent amendments to the Clery Act do not alter a school's responsibility under Title IX to respond to and prevent sexual violence.

OCR is also strengthening its enforcement procedures in a number of ways – by, for example, instituting time limits on negotiating voluntary resolution agreements and making clear that schools should provide survivors with interim relief (like changing housing or class schedules) pending the outcome of an OCR investigation. And OCR will be more visible on campus during its investigations, so students can help give OCR a fuller picture about what's happening and how a school is responding.

The Departments of Education and Justice, which both enforce Title IX, have entered into an agreement to better coordinate their efforts – as have the two offices within the Department of Education charged with enforcing Title IX and the Clery Act.

Next Steps

This report is the first step in the Task Force's work. We will continue to work toward solutions, clarity, and better coordination. We will also review the various laws and regulations that address sexual violence for possible regulatory or statutory improvements, and seek new resources to enhance enforcement. Also, campus law enforcement officials have special expertise to offer – and they should be tapped to play a more central role. We will also consider how our recommendations apply to public elementary and secondary schools – and what more we can do to help there.

* * *

The Task Force thanks everyone who has offered their wisdom, stories, expertise, and experiences over the past 90 days. Although the problem is daunting and much of what we heard was heartbreaking, we are more committed than ever to helping bring an end to this violence.

Figure 3 | YZ Travel Report

YZ Travel's new price steering strategy is an ethical and effective way to improve the user experience.

Report to Shareholders
Yilin Zhang

YZ Travel

Executive Summary

In response to the recent public stir, YZTravel.com is indeed implementing a new price steering strategy that displays different search results of hotels depending on the user's operating system. While some critics accuse the practice to be discriminatory and unethical, we see this as an ethical and effective strategy that will improve the user experience and help increase customer satisfaction. This report will explain how we have decided to implement this strategy based on historical data and analysis of consumer behaviors of PC and Mac users and how this strategy will improve the user experience.

Our price steering strategy only alters the initial display of search results of hotels after the user enters the location, length of stay, and number of guests. When no filters to the search are added, YZTravel.com initially displays pricier hotel options to Mac users than PC users to suit their different preferences and spending habits. Users always have the freedom to add filters and opt for prices to narrow down their search.

Price steering is not price discrimination, which is often claimed as unethical. Price discrimination displays different prices for the same products depending on the user's location, browsing history, and other characteristics. Price steering displays the same price for the same hotels to all users and varies the arrangement of search results to suit the user's preferences and spending habits.

Price steering improves the user experience by showing desirable search results to Mac users and PC users and improving the efficiency of their booking process. Based on historical data and analysis, Mac users show more appreciation for premium quality, preference for luxury products, and higher spending power than PC users. Mac users spend around 165% more on their computers, and they are likely to book more expensive hotels than PC users. The price steering strategy customizes the initial display of search results to the users' preferences and spending habits.

Price steering is similar to other strategies used to create value for customers. Online retailers and websites often give recommendations of products, use targeted email marketing, and post targeted advertisements based on browsing and purchase history to suit customers' tastes, which ultimately creates value. Similarly, this strategy customizes the initial display of search results to users' preferences and spending habits. This strategy will also help YZTravel.com to increase customer satisfaction and capture more market share in the Online Travel Agency sector.

YZ Travel

Table of Contents

YZ Travel

YZTravel.com is implementing a price steering strategy that alters the initial display of search results based on users' operating systems.

In July, the *Wall Street Journal* and CNN reported an experiment which showed that YZTravel.com showed pricier and more high-end hotels to Mac users than PC users for Miami. Critics have claimed the practice as unethical and discriminatory.

YZTravel.com is indeed implementing a new price steering strategy that alters the initial display of hotel search results depending on the user's operating system. YZTravel.com tends to show pricier hotel options to Mac users than PC users to suit their tastes and preferences. The user has the freedom to add filters and opt for prices.

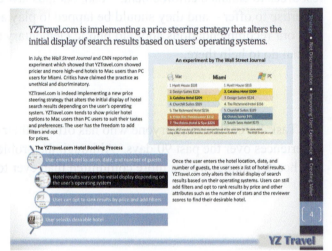

An experiment by The Wall Street Journal

The YZTravel.com Hotel Booking Process

- User enters hotel location, date, and number of guests
- Hotel results vary on the initial display depending on the user's operating system
- User can opt to rank results by price and add filters
- User selects desirable hotel

Once the user enters the hotel location, date, and number of guests, the user sees a list of hotel results. YZTravel.com only alters the initial display of search results based on their operating systems. Users can still add filters and opt to rank results by price and other attributes such as the number of stars and the reviewer scores to find their desirable hotel.

YZ Travel

Price steering is not price discrimination: it does not show different prices for the same product to different users.

Price Discrimination

Price discrimination shows different prices for the same product to different customers. Companies vary prices based on customers' location, browsing history, past purchases, and other criteria. Many view price discrimination as an unethical practice since it offers unfair price advantage towards certain consumers.

For example, John sees a Deluxe Room at the NY Hilton Midtown for $429. John's friend sees the same room at the same time for $399 due to his location, browsing and purchasing history, and/or other factors.

Price Steering

Price steering shows the same price for the same products to different customers but alters the product display to tailor to the customer's preferences. Companies may show higher priced products to users who are likely to purchase luxury products.

For example, John sees a Deluxe Room at the NY Hilton Midtown for $429 on top of your search results. John's friend sees the same hotel for the same price at the bottom of the page with different hotels.

Below are three examples of online retailers practicing price discrimination based the location of the customer:

According to the Wall Street Journal, Staples Inc. website displays different prices to people after estimating their locations. If rival stores were within 20 miles or so, Staples.com usually showed a discounted price.

Lowe's said that online shoppers receive the lower of the online store price or the price at their local Lowe's store as indicated by their ZIP Code. For example, a refrigerator costs $449 in Chicago and Los Angeles but $499 in seven other test cities.

Rosetta Stone offers discounts of as much as 20% for people who bought multiple levels of its German lessons from certain locations in the U.S. or Canada, but not others from the U.K. or Argentina.

YZ Travel

Price steering is one of many criteria that YZTravel.com uses to predict user preferences and improve the user experience.

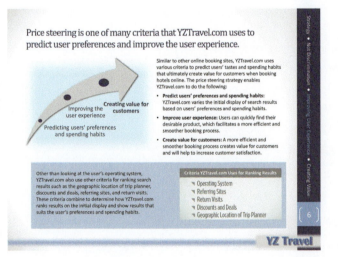

Improving the user experience

Creating value for customers

Predicting users' preferences and spending habits

Similar to other online booking sites, YZTravel.com uses various criteria to predict users' tastes and spending habits that ultimately create value for customers when booking hotels online. The price steering strategy enables YZTravel.com to do the following:

- **Predict users' preferences and spending habits:** YZTravel.com varies the initial display of search results based on users' preferences and spending habits.
- **Improve user experience:** Users can quickly find their desirable product, which facilitates a more efficient and smoother booking process.
- **Create value for customers:** A more efficient and smoother booking process creates value for customers and will help to increase customer satisfaction.

Other than looking at the user's operating system, YZTravel.com also use other criteria for ranking search results such as the geographic location of trip planner, discounts and deals, referring sites, and return visits. These criteria combine to determine how YZTravel.com ranks results on the initial display and show results that suits the user's preferences and spending habits.

Criteria YZTravel.com Uses for Ranking Results
- Operating System
- Referring Sites
- Return Visits
- Discounts and Deals
- Geographic Location of Trip Planner

YZ Travel

SOURCE: REPORT TO SHAREHOLDERS YILIN ZHANG

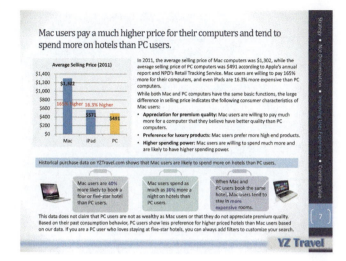

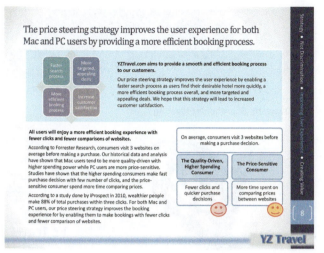

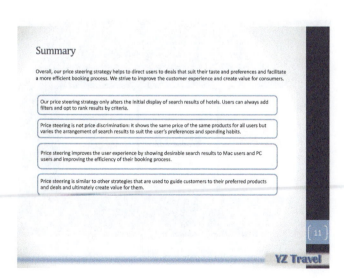

Figure 4 | YZ Travel Slides for a Presentation

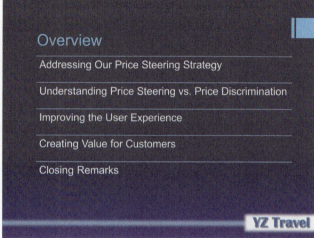

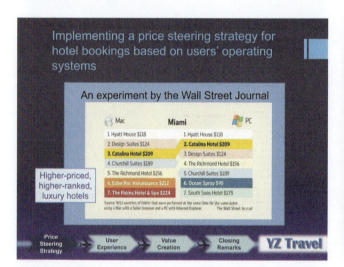

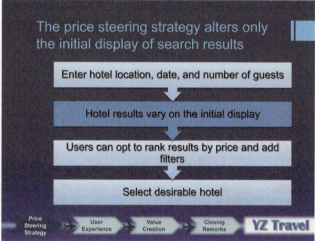

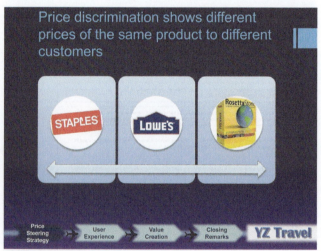

SOURCE: YZTRAVEL.COM PRICE STEERING STRATEGY

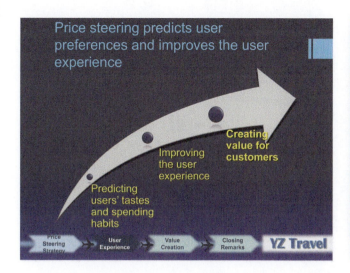

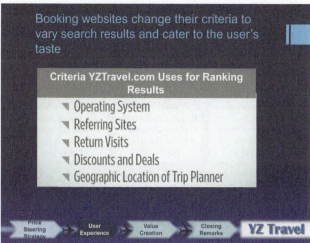

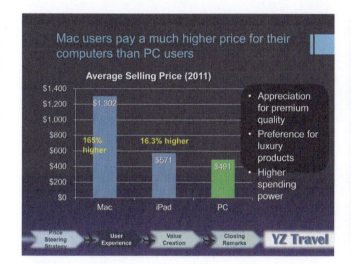

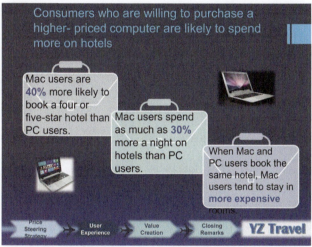

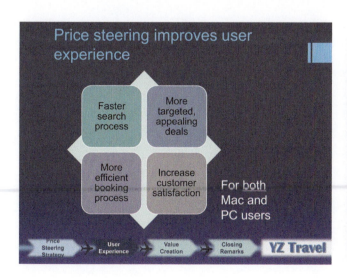

Figure 4 | *(continued)*

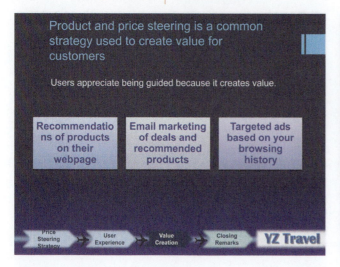

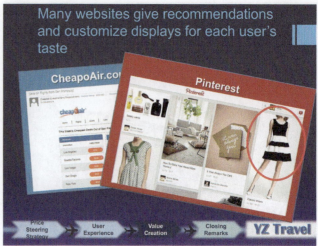

C Common Types of Reports

Management needs comprehensive, up-to-date, accurate, and understandable information to meet business objectives. Much of this information is communicated through reports. The most common types of business reports are periodic reports, proposals, policies and procedures, and situational reports.

Periodic Reports

Three common types of periodic reports are routine management reports, compliance reports, and progress reports.

Routine Management Reports

Every organization has its own set of recurring reports to provide information for decision making and problem solving. Some of these routine management reports are statistical and may be just a spreadsheet; other management reports are primarily narrative. Examples of routine management reports are quarterly earnings, annual headcount, and monthly revenue.

Compliance Reports

Many state and federal government agencies require companies to file reports showing that they are complying with affirmative action, labor relations, occupational safety, financial, and environmental regulations. Completing these compliance reports is often mostly a matter of gathering the data and reporting the information honestly and completely. Typically, very little analysis of the data is required.

Progress Reports

Interim progress reports are often used to communicate the status of long-term projects. They are submitted periodically to management for internal projects, to the customer for external projects, and to the investor for an accounting of venture capital expenditures. Typically, these reports (1) tell what has been accomplished since the last progress report, (2) document how well the project is adhering to the schedule and budget, (3) describe any problems encountered and how they were solved, and (4) outline future plans. Often these reports will be produced using project management software and will include at-a-glance or "dashboard" charts.

Proposals

A proposal is a written report with the purpose of persuading the reader to accept a suggested plan of action. Two types of business proposals are project proposals and, less common, research proposals.

Project Proposals

A manager may write a project proposal, for example, to persuade a potential customer to purchase products or services, to persuade the federal government to locate a new research facility in a particular city, or to persuade a foundation to fund a project. Proposals may be solicited or unsolicited.

Government agencies and many large companies routinely solicit proposals from potential suppliers. For example, the government might publish a request for proposal (RFP) stating its intention to purchase 5,000 computers, giving detailed specifications about the features it needs and inviting prospective suppliers to bid on the project. Similarly, the computer manufacturer that submits the successful bid might itself publish an RFP to invite parts manufacturers to bid on supplying some component the manufacturer needs for these computers.

Unlike solicited proposals, unsolicited proposals typically require more background information and more persuasion. Because the reader may not be familiar with the project, the writer must present more evidence to convince the reader of the proposal's merits.

When writing a proposal, keep in mind that the proposal may become legally binding. In spelling out exactly what the writer's organization will provide, when, under what circumstances, and at what price, the proposal report writer creates the *offer* part of a contract that, if accepted, may become binding on the organization.

As discussed in Chapter 10, proposals vary in length, organization, complexity, and format. Longer, more formal proposals include the following sections:

1. Background: Introduce the problem you're addressing and discuss why it merits the reader's consideration.

2. Objectives: Provide specific information about what the outcomes of the project will be.

3. Process or Plan: Discuss in detail how you will achieve these objectives. Include a step-by-step discussion of what will be done, when, and exactly how much each component or phase will cost. (Alternatively, you may include costs in an appendix.)

4. Qualifications: Show how you, your organization, and any others who would be involved in conducting this project are qualified to do so.

5. Request for approval: Directly ask for approval of your proposal. Depending on the reader's needs, this request could come either at the beginning or at the end of the proposal.

6. Supporting data: Include additional information that might bolster your arguments.

Research Proposals

Because research is a cost to the organization in terms of labor and expenses, senior management may want to know what they will gain in return for expending these resources. A research proposal is a structured presentation of what you plan to do in research, why you plan to conduct the research, and how you plan to accomplish it. Although formats vary, Figure 5 shows an example of a simple research proposal.

Policies and Procedures

Policies are broad operating guidelines that govern the general direction and activities of an organization; procedures are the recommended methods or sequential steps to follow when performing a specific activity. An organization's attitude toward promoting from within a company would constitute a policy, and the steps to be taken to apply for a promotion would constitute a procedure. Policy statements are typically written by top management, while procedures may be written by the managers and supervisors who are involved in the day-to-day operation of the organization.

Policies

Begin a policy statement by setting the stage—that is, justify the need for a policy. Your justification should be general enough that the policy covers a broad range of situations but not so general that it has no real "teeth." Ensure that the reader knows exactly who is covered by the policy, what is required, and any other needed information. Finally, show how the reader, the organization, or *someone* benefits from this policy. You will find sample policies online or through professional associations. These are good starting points, but always have legal counsel review a policy before publishing it to employees or clients.

**STAFF EMPLOYEES' EVALUATION OF THE BENEFITS
PROGRAM AT MAYO MEMORIAL HOSPITAL**

A Research Proposal by Lyn Santos
January 23, 2017

Employee benefits are a rapidly growing and an increasingly important form of employee compensation for both profit and nonprofit organizations. According to a recent U.S. Chamber of Commerce survey, benefits now constitute 37% of all payroll costs, costing an average of $10,857 a year for each full-time employee.[1] As has been noted by one management consultant, "The success of employee benefits programs depends directly on whether employees need and understand the value of the benefits provided."[2] Thus, an organization's employee benefits program must be monitored and evaluated if it is to remain an effective recruitment and retention tool.

Mayo Memorial employs 2,500 staff personnel who have not received a cost-of-living increase in two years. Thus, staff salaries may not have kept pace with industry, and the hospital's benefits program may become more important in attracting and retaining good workers. In addition, the contracts of three staff unions expire next year, and the benefits program is typically a major area of bargaining.

PROBLEM

To help ensure that the benefits program is operating as effectively as possible, the following problem will be addressed in this study: What are the opinions of staff employees at Mayo Memorial Hospital regarding their employee benefits? To answer this question, the following subproblems will be addressed:

1. How knowledgeable are the employees about the benefits program?
2. What are the employees' opinions of the benefits presently available to them?
3. What benefits would the employees like to have added to the program?

---

[1] Enar Ignatio, "Can Flexible Benefits Promote Your Company?" *Personnel Quarterly*, Vol. 20, September 2008, p. 812.
[2] Ransom Adams and Seymour Stevens, *Personnel Administration*, All-State, Cambridge, MA, 2004, p. 483.

Procedures

Write procedures using the active voice and a natural tone. Imagine that you are explaining the procedure orally to someone. Go step by step through the process, explaining, when necessary, what should *not* be done as well as what should be done. Use visuals and supplemental videos as much as possible.

Try to put yourself in the role of the reader. How much background information is needed; how much jargon can safely be used; what reading level is appropriate? Anticipate questions and problems, but recognize that it's impossible to answer every conceivable question; therefore, concentrate on the high-risk components—those tasks that are difficult to perform or that have serious safety or financial implications if performed incorrectly.

Figure 5 | (*continued*)

2

SCOPE

Although staff employees at all state-supported hospitals receive the same benefits, no attempt will be made to generalize the findings beyond Mayo Memorial. In addition, this study will attempt to determine employee preferences only. The question of whether these preferences are economically feasible is not within the scope of this study.

PROCEDURES

A random sample of 200 staff employees at Mayo Memorial Hospital will be surveyed to answer the three subproblems. In addition, personal interviews will be held with a compensation specialist at Mayo and with the chair of the Staff Personnel Committee. Secondary data will be used to (a) provide background information for developing the questionnaire items and the interview questions, (b) provide a basis for comparing the Mayo benefit program with that of other organizations, and (c) provide a basis for comparing the employees' opinions of the Mayo benefit program with employee opinions of programs at other organizations.

CONCLUSION

The information will be analyzed, and appropriate tables and charts will be developed. Conclusions will be drawn and recommendations made as appropriate to explain the staff employees' opinions about the benefit program at Mayo Memorial Hospital.

Minimize the amount of conceptual information included, concentrating instead on the practical information. (Someone can learn to drive a car safely without needing to learn how the engine propels the car forward.) Usually, numbered steps are appropriate, but use a narrative approach if it seems more effective.

After you have written a draft, have several employees follow the steps to see if they work. Could you easily follow the procedure in Figure 6?

Situational Reports

Unique problems and opportunities often require reports that will be written only once. These *situational reports* are perhaps the most challenging for the report writer. Because they involve a unique issue or question, the writer has no previous reports to use as a guide; he or she must decide what types of information and how much research is needed and how best to organize and present the findings. A sample situational report is shown in Chapter 9, Figure 1.

PROCEDURE FOR HIRING A TEMPORARY EMPLOYEE

Employee	Action
Requester	1. Requests a temporary employee with specialized skills by filling out Form 722, "Request for a Temporary Employee." 2. Secures manager's approval. 3. Sends four copies of Form 722 to labor analyst in Human Resources.
Labor Analyst	4. Checks overtime figures of regular employees in the department. 5. If satisfied that the specific people are necessary, checks budget. 6. If funds are available, approves Form 722, sends three copies to buyer of special services in Human Resources, and files the fourth copy.
Buyer of Special Services	7. Notifies outside temporary help contractor by phone and follows up the same day with a confirming letter or email. 8. Negotiates a mutually agreeable effective date. 9. Contacts Human Resources by phone, telling it of the number of people and the effective dates.
Human Resources	10. Notifies Security, Badges, and Gate Guards. 11. Returns one copy of Form 722 to the requester. 12. Provides a temporary ID.
Temporary Help Contractor	13. Furnishes assigned employee or employees with information on the job description, the effective date, and the individual to whom to report.
Temporary Employee	14. Reports to receptionist one half-hour early on the effective date.

D Glossary

A

Abstract word A word that identifies an idea or feeling instead of a concrete object. (1)

Active voice The sentence form in which the subject performs the action expressed by the verb. (5)

Agenda A list of topics to be covered at a meeting, often including the name of the person responsible for covering each topic and the timing for each topic. (3)

Agenda slide A slide that presents the topics or main points of a presentation. (11)

Aggregator A program that collects on-line information from multiple sources and distributes it through one site. (6)

AIDA plan The process of gaining the reader's attention, creating interest in and desire for the benefits of your product, and motivating action. (7)

Apology When the organization takes full responsibility for a crisis and asks for forgiveness. (7)

Applicant tracking system A system that companies use to track job applicants and résumés. (12)

Audience The receiver of a message. (1)

Audience analysis A critical step in communication for the writer to understand what the audience needs and how they may react to a message. (4)

B

Backchannel A forum such as Twitter for have real-time, online interactions during a presentation. (11)

Bar chart A graph with horizontal or vertical bars representing values. (9)

Behavioral interviews Interviews based on the theory that past behavior predicts future performance (also called *structured interviews*). (12)

Benefits Advantages a potential customer receives from a product or service. (7)

Big data The vast amount of data available today—so much that it is nearly impossible to fully comprehend. (9)

Blog A website that includes chronological posts and may allow for comments. (1)

Brainstorming Jotting down ideas, facts, and anything else—without evaluating the output—that might be helpful in constructing a message. (4)

Buffer A neutral opening statement designed to lessen the impact of negative news. (8)

Business etiquette A guide to appropriate behavior in a business setting. (12)

Business report An organized presentation of information used to make decisions and solve problems. (9)

C

Cascading communication When information starts at the top of the organization and flows down to each level in sequence. (1)

Central selling theme The major reader benefit that is introduced early and emphasized throughout a sales letter. (7)

Chartjunk Visual elements that call attention to themselves instead of information on a chart. (9)

Cliché An expression that has become monotonous through overuse. (5)

Cloud A reference to the Internet, where files are stored on networked servers rather than on individual computers. (1)

Coercion Force or intimidation used to get someone to comply. (4)

Coherence When each sentence of a paragraph links smoothly to the sentences before and after it. (5)

Communication The process of sending and receiving messages. (1)

Competencies The knowledge, skills, and abilities identified for a specific job. (12)

Complex sentence A sentence that has one independent clause and at least one dependent clause. (5)

Communication need The reason for communicating in organizations—what starts the process. (1)

Compound sentence A sentence that has two or more independent clauses. (5)

Concrete word A word that identifies something the senses can perceive. (1)

Conference call A meeting held using a speakerphone for people in two or more locations (also called a *teleconference*). (3)

Conflict Disagreements or arguments that may occur within a team. (2)

Conformity Agreement to ideas, rules, or principles. (2)

Connotation The subjective or emotional feeling associated with a word. (1)

Consensus Reaching a decision that best reflects the thinking of all team members. (2)

Consumer-generated media (CGM) Any media (e.g., video, images, blogs) about a company posted by consumers for public viewing (also called *user-generated content*). (1)

Corporate social responsibility (CSR) A form of self-regulation whereby a company considers the public's interest (people, planet, as well as profit) in their business practices. (1)

Cover letter Communication that tells a prospective employer that an applicant is interested in and qualified for a position within the organization. (12)

Crisis A significant threat to the organization. (7)

Crisis communication Attempts to protect and defend the company's reputation. (7)

Cross-cultural communication Communication between cultures—when a message is created by someone from one culture to be understood by someone from another culture (also called *intercultural communication*). (2)

Cross-tabulation A process by which two or more items of data are analyzed together. (9)

Culture The customary traits, attitudes, and behaviors of a group of people. (2)

Curriculum vitae (CV) A longer version of a résumé that is more typical for international (and academic) jobs. (12)

D

Dangling expression Any part of a sentence that does not logically connect to the rest of the sentence. (5)

Deck A printed report or slides created in PowerPoint, Keynote, or other presentation tools. (10)

Denotation The literal, dictionary meaning of a word. (1)

Derived benefits Similar to benefits—how marketers refer to benefits customers receive from a product or service. (7)

Direct organizational plan A plan in which the major purpose of the message is communicated first, followed by the explanation and the details. (4)

Direct quotation The exact words of another person. (10)

Diversity A variety of unique people; respecting differences we bring to work. (2)

Divider slide A slide repeated throughout a presentation, highlighting each topic as it is covered. (11)

Documentation Identifying sources (to give credit) to another's words or ideas. (10)

Downward communication The flow of information from managers to their employees. (1)

Drafting Composing a preliminary version of a message. (4)

E

Editing The stage of revision that ensures that writing conforms to standard English. (4)

Emotional intelligence Recognizing and managing our own and others' feelings. (1)

Empathy The ability to project oneself into another person's position and to understand that person's situation and feelings. (3)

Employee engagement Creating a culture in which employees feel passionate about their company and are enthusiastic about their jobs. (3)

Ethics A system of moral principles that go beyond legal rules to tell us how to act. (1)

Ethnocentrism The belief that one's own cultural group is superior. (2)

Ethos A persuasive appeal based on credibility. (7)

Euphemism An expression used in place of words that may be offensive or inappropriate. (1)

Executive summary A condensed version of the report body (also called an *abstract* or *synopsis*). (10)

Exhaustive Ensuring that items, for example, in a questionnaire, include all possible options for a response. (9)

Expletive An expression such as *there is* or *it has been* that begins a clause and for which the pronoun has no antecedent. (5)

Exploding pie chart A pie chart with one wedge pulled out for emphasis. (9)

Extemporaneous presentation A presentation delivered using an unrehearsed, enhanced, conversational style. (11)

Extranet A private computer network for a select group of people outside of the company (e.g., for customers or franchisees). (1)

F

Factoring Breaking a problem down to determine what data needs to be collected. (9)

Feature An aspect of how a product or service works. (7)

Filter Perception based on one's knowledge, experience, and viewpoints. (1)

Formal communication network The transmission of information through downward, upward, and lateral paths within an organization. (1)

G

Gender identity Someone's internal, personal sense of being a man or a woman (or someone outside of that gender binary). (2)

Generic heading A report heading that identifies only the topic of a section without giving the conclusion. (10)

Geolocation Identifying where objects are physically located. (1)

Goodwill message A message that is sent out of a sense of kindness. (6)

Google Alert An email update provided by Google when online content matches the user's predefined search terms. (6)

Grapevine The flow of information through nonofficial channels within the organization (also called the *informal communication network*). (1)

Groupthink A hindrance to team performance that happens when individuals think too similarly. (2)

H

Horizontal communication The flow of information among peers within an organization (also called *lateral communication*). (1)

I

Impromptu presentation A presentation delivered without preparation. (11)

Inclusion Creating an environment where all people are valued and can contribute to their fullest potential. (2)

Indirect organizational plan A plan in which the reasons or rationale are presented first, followed by the major idea. (4)

Individual ethics Ethics defined by a person, which are based on family values, heritage, personal experience, and other factors. (1)

Infographic résumé A graphical version of a résumé. (12)

Infographics Also known as information graphics, a popular way of showing data visually. (9)

Informal communication network The flow of information through nonofficial channels within the organization (also called the *grapevine*). (1)

Information Meaningful facts, statistics, and conclusions. (9)

Intercultural communication Communication between cultures—when a message is created by someone from one culture to be understood by someone from another culture (also called *cross-cultural communication*). (2)

Intranet A private computer network within a company or organization for employee access. (1)

J

Jargon Technical terminology used within specialized groups. (1)

L

Lateral communication The flow of information among peers within an organization (also called *horizontal communication*). (1)

Letter A written message mailed to someone outside (or external to) an organization. (4)

Line chart A graph based on a grid, with the vertical axis representing values and the horizontal axis representing time. (9)

Logos A persuasive appeal based on logic. (7)

M

Main point slide An optional slide in a presentation shown before an agenda slide to convey the most important message to the audience. (11)

Main points The major conclusions of a message. (4)

Mashups Web applications or pages that combine content from different sources. (1)

Mechanics Elements in communication that show up only in writing (e.g., spelling, punctuation, abbreviations, capitalization, number expression, and word division). (5)

Medium How a message is transmitted— for example, an email or phone call. (1)

Memo A written message sent to someone within (or internal to) an organization. (4)

Memorized presentation A presentation delivered from memory. (11)

Message The information (either verbal or nonverbal) that is communicated. (1)

Message title A report heading or slide title that identifies the major conclusion of a section or slide (also called *talking heading*). (10)

Microblogs A type of blog used for short messages with timely information. (1)

Mind mapping Generating ideas for a message by connecting them in a graphical way. (4)

Minutes An official record of a meeting that summarizes what was discussed, what decisions were made, and what actions participants will take. (3)

Mobile technologies Technologies that are portable, such as handheld devices. (1)

Multicommunicating Overlapping conversations using various forms of communication. (1)

Multiculturalism A philosophy of appreciating diversity among people, typically beyond differences in countries of origin. (2)

Multimedia The integration of several forms of media (e.g., text, video, and graphics). (1)

Mutually Exclusive Ensuring that items, for example, in a questionnaire, do not overlap. (9)

N

Networking email An email sent to a person at a company or in a field of interest for the purpose of obtaining career information or job leads. (12)

Noise Environmental or competing elements that distract one's attention during communication. (1)

Nonverbal message What is communicated without words (for example, body language). (1)

O

Online meeting A meeting held using a web-based service, such as WebEx. (3)

Online reputation How a company or an individual is represented on the Internet. (12)

Organization The sequence in which topics are presented in a message. (4)

Organizational fit A match between a prospective employee and a particular organizational culture. (12)

P

Parallelism Using similar grammatical structure to express similar ideas. (5)

Paraphrase A summary or restatement of a passage in one's own words. (10)

Passive voice The sentence form in which the subject receives the action expressed by the verb. (5)

Pathos A persuasive appeal based on emotion. (7)

Personal brand What you're known for and how people experience you. (12)

Persuasion Using communication to change another person's beliefs, feelings, or behaviors. (4)

Pie chart A circle graph divided into component wedges. (9)

Plagiarism Using another person's words or ideas without giving proper credit. (10)

Platitude A trite, obvious statement. (5)

Podcast Portable audio or video content for individuals to download and listen to at their computer or on a mobile device. (1)

Preview An overview of what the audience can expect in a message. (4)

Primary audience The most important receiver of a message (e.g., the decision maker). (4)

Primary data Data collected by the researcher to solve a specific problem. (9)

Professional ethics Ethics defined by an organization. (1)

Proposal A written sales document typically for discussion by a group of people. (7)

Purpose The reason for which a message is created. (4)

Q

Questionnaire A written document containing questions to obtain information from recipients. (9)

R

Receiver benefits The advantages a reader would derive from granting the writer's request or from accepting the writer's decision. (5)

Redundancy The unnecessary repetition of an idea that has already been expressed or intimated. (5)

Résumé A representation of an applicant's education, work history, and other qualifications. (12)

Revising Modifying the content and style of a draft to increase its effectiveness. (4)

Request for proposal (RFP) A formal, detailed document issued by organizations looking for bids from a variety of sources. (10)

Rhetorical question A question asked to get the reader thinking about the topic; a literal answer is not expected. (7)

Really Simple Syndication (RSS) A set of web-based formats used to publish frequent updates. (1)

S

Scripted presentation A presentation delivered by reading from notes. (11)

Secondary audience Receivers of a message who are not the *primary audience* but who will also read and be affected by a message. (4)

Secondary data Data (published or unpublished) collected by someone else for another purpose. (9)

Section overview Text that previews for the reader how a section will be divided and—for direct-plan reports—what main points will follow. (10)

Sender Individual responsible for creating a communication. (1)

Service recovery Responding to a service failure in a way that turns an upset customer into a satisfied customer. (7)

Simple sentence A sentence that has one independent clause. (5)

Situational ethics Ethics that are based on particular circumstances. (1)

Situational report A report that is produced only once to address unique problems and opportunities. (9)

Slang An expression, often short-lived, that is identified with a specific group of people. (1)

Slide tracker An image on the slide that repeats on every slide after the agenda to show the major divisions of a presentation, highlighting each topic as it is presented. (11)

Social ethics Ethics defined by society. (1)

Social loafing The psychological term for avoiding individual responsibility in a group setting. (2)

Social media A blending of technology and social interaction. (1)

Social networking sites Websites where communities of people who share common interests or activities can form relationships (a subset of social media). (1)

Social recruiting Using social media to recruit new talent. (12)

Social résumé A résumé designed for interactivity and to allow employers to find the candidate online. (12)

Solicited cover letter A cover letter that responds to a position advertised by a company. (12)

Solicited sales letter A company's reply to a request for product or service information from a potential customer. (7)

Stacked headings Two consecutive headings without intervening text. (10)

Style How an idea is expressed (rather than the substance of the idea). (5)

Survey A data-collection method that gathers information through questionnaires, telephone inquiries, or interviews. (9)

Sympathy Understanding and providing comfort to another person. (3)

Synchronous Simultaneous or at the same time (antonym: asynchronous). (1)

T

Table An orderly arrangement of data into columns and rows. (9)

Talking heading A report heading or slide title that identifies the major conclusion of a section or slide (also called *message title*). (10)

Team A group of individuals who depend on one another to accomplish a common objective. (2)

Teleconference A meeting held using a speakerphone for people in two or more locations (also called *a conference call*). (3)

Title slide The first slide of a presentation, which usually includes the title, date, name of presenter, company, and audience. (11)

Tone How the writer's attitude toward the reader and the subject of the message is reflected. (5)

Topic sentence The main idea of a paragraph, usually introduced at the beginning of a passage. (5)

Transgender Someone whose gender identity differs from what is typically associated with the sex they were assigned at birth. (2)

U

Unity When all parts of a paragraph work together to develop a single idea consistently and logically. (5)

Unsolicited cover letter A cover letter that is initiated by an individual searching for a job. (12)

Unsolicited sales letter A way to promote a company's products or services to potential customers who have not expressed any interest. (7)

Upward communication The flow of information from lower-level employees to upper-level employees or managers. (1)

User-generated content (UGC) Any media (e.g., video, images, blogs) about a company posted by consumers for public viewing (also called *consumer-generated media*). (1)

V

Verbal message The part of a communication that uses words to convey meaning. (1)

Videoconference A video-based meeting using videophones, smartphones, desktop programs, or dedicated services such as telepresence suites. (3)

Visual aids Tables, charts, photographs, or other graphic materials. (9)

W

Wiki A website where anyone with access can edit content directly. (1)

Writer's block The inability to focus one's attention on the writing process and to draft a message. (4)

Y

Yammer A social network like Facebook but restricted to employees within an organization. (3)

"You" attitude Emphasizing what the reader wants to know and how the reader will be affected by the message. (5)

Index

Note: Page numbers followed by "f" indicate figures.

E

EBSCO, 272–273f
effective sentences, 145–146
 active *vs.* passive voice, 146–147
 parallel structure, 148
 use of variety, 147f
Ekman, Paul, 70
ellipses, 454
email, 14
 cover letters, 408, 409f
 inquiry, 411–412
 interview follow-up, 421–422
 potential legal consequences of, 18–19
 subject lines for, 115f
 turning down a job candidate, 249
 use of for bad-news messages, 237–238, 252–253
 use of for polite requests, 176–177f
 use of persuasion in scams, 203–204
 use of to decline a job offer, 247–248
 use of with questionnaires, 280–281f
 use of with reports, 319–320f
 writing process for business communication, 112–113, 114f
emotional intelligence, 5
emotions, inappropriate, 12
empathy, 73
 levels of responding, 76f
 value of, 73
emphasis
 choice of in reporting findings, 323–324f
 use of in written communication, 154, 155f
employee engagement, 73
 listening to concerns, 91
 use of online services for, 79
employers, communication skills of candidates, 4–5
enclosures, referring to in sales letters, 213
endnotes, 327
ethical behavior, 21
ethical decision making, framework for, 22–23, 22f
ethical language, use of in sales letters, 212
ethical persuasion, 203
ethics
 communication and, 20–21
 data interpretation and, 294
 team communication, 41
 value of, 21
ethnicity, 52–53
ethnocentrism, 44
ethos, use of in persuasive messages, 201–202
etiquette
 dining, 423–425
 gift giving, 425
 meeting and greeting, 423
 working in an office, 426
euphemisms, 11

evidence
 use of in persuasive messages, 206–207
 use of in sales letters, 213f
executive summary, 320, 321f, 476–479
expletives, avoiding use of, 144
expressions, inappropriate use of, 10–11
extemporaneous presentations, 353
eye contact, 70
 cultural appropriateness of, 47

F

face-to-face meetings, 81–82
Facebook, 16
 online annual report of, 308
fact checking, 274–276
Fallon, Jimmy, 173
features *vs.* benefits, 211
feedback
 acknowledging the need for, 39
 addressing negative reviews, 218
 constructive, 252–255
 positive and negative, 39, 40f
 responding to, 215–216
 use of 3Ps model for presentations, 373–374
 using "I" statements, 40f
female communication patterns, 53f
findings, 311–312
 discussion of in reports, 317
 emphasis and subordination, 323–324f
 organizational structure for, 312–314
 use of verb tense when describing, 323
footnotes, 327, 329
 formatting sources for, 328f
Fordham University, 103
 use of 3Ps model to address mistakes at, 121–123
formal communication network, 7–9
formal language, 322–323
formal presentation styles, 352–353
formality, maintaining in cross-cultural communication, 48–49
Forman, Justin, 69
formatting errors, 119
Foursquare, 18
framework for ethical decision making, 22f
functional résumés, 397–398

G

Gap
 diversity statement for, 57
 response to racist comments, 37
gender identity, 53
gender-neutral language, 54f
General Mills, 3
 use of 3Ps model at, 24